ACCOUNTING FOR MANAGEMENT

Empire
College
London

Forest House, 16-20 Clements Road
Ilford Essex IG1 1BA UK
Tel: +44 (0)20 8553 2683
Fax: +44 (0)20 8553 2684
e-mail: info@empirecollegelondon.co.uk
www.empirecollegelondon.co.uk

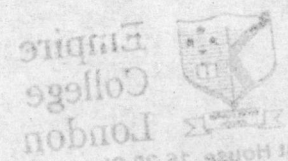

ACCOUNTING FOR MANAGEMENT

[For B.Com., B.Com(CA)., BBA., BBM., M.Com., M.Com.(CA)., M.B.A., M.C.A., of all Indian Universities and M.B.A., M.C.A., courses of Anna University]

V.R. PALANIVELU
M.Com., M.B.A., M.Phil.

Professor
Post Graduate Department of Management Studies,
Vivekanandha College of Engineering for Women,
Tiruchengode,
Tamil Nadu

LAXMI PUBLICATIONS (P) LTD

BANGALORE • CHENNAI • COCHIN • GUWAHATI • HYDERABAD
JALANDHAR • KOLKATA • LUCKNOW • MUMBAI • RANCHI
NEW DELHI • BOSTON, USA

Published by :

LAXMI PUBLICATIONS (P) LTD
113, Golden House, Daryaganj,
New Delhi-110002

Phone : 011-43 53 25 00
Fax : 011-43 53 25 28

www.laxmipublications.com
info@laxmipublications.com

© *All rights reserved with the Publisher.*

No part of this publication may be reproduced, stored in a retrieval system, or transmitted in any form or by any means, electronic, mechanical, photocopying, recording or otherwise without the prior written permission of the publisher.

Price : Rs. 195.00 Only.   First Edition : 2007

OFFICES

India		**USA**
✆ **Bangalore**	080-26 61 15 61	**Boston**
✆ **Chennai**	044-24 34 47 26	11, Leavitt Street, Hingham,
✆ **Cochin**	0484-239 70 04	MA 02043, USA
✆ **Guwahati**	0361-254 36 69, 251 38 81	✆ 781-740-4487
✆ **Hyderabad**	040-24 75 02 47	
✆ **Jalandhar**	0181-222 12 72	
✆ **Kolkata**	033-22 27 37 73, 22 27 52 47	
✆ **Lucknow**	0522-220 95 78	
✆ **Mumbai**	022-24 91 54 15, 24 92 78 69	
✆ **Ranchi**	0651-230 77 64	

EAM–0723–195–ACCOUNTING FOR MANAGEMENT   C—13255/06/11
Typeset at : ABRO Enterprises, Delhi.   *Printed at* : Mehra Offset Press, Delhi.

CONTENTS

Chapters	Pages
Foreword	*(vii)*
Preface	*(ix)*
Acknowledgement	*(x)*
Syllabus	*(xiii)*
1. Introduction to Accounting	1
2. Basic Records Maintained by a Business Concern	8
3. Revenue Recognition and Measurement	10
4. Preparation of Final Accounts	12
5. Fund Flow Statement	65
6. Cash Flow Statement	102
7. Ratio Analysis	129
8. Fixed Assets and Depreciation	174
9. Cost Accounting: Cost Sheet Accounting for Manufacturing Cost	195
10. Job Costing	216
11. Process Costing	221
12. Activity Based Costing	237
13. Inventory Pricing and Valuation	240
14. Standard Costing	252
15. Management Accounting	288
16. Marginal Costing	294
17. Relevant Cost for Decision Making	331
18. Budget and Budgetary Control	343
19. Inflation Accounting	386
20. Human Resources Accounting	399
21. Responsibility Accounting	404
22. Financial Management	410
23. Dividend	413
24. Cost of Capital	418
25. Capital Structure	430
26. Working Capital	441
27. Capital Budgeting	462
APPENDIX	501

Alagappa University
(Accredited with A grade by NAAC)
KARAIKUDI - 630 004
Department of Corporate Secretaryship

Phone : (04565) 230202
Fax : 225202
Mobile : 94431 24433
e - mail:drvmalucorp@yahoo.com

Dr. V. MANICKAVASAGAM
Professor & Head

FOREWORD

I am immensely impressed by this meticulous work, "Accounting for Management". It has been written with a view to help the students of MBA and MCA I Year programmes of Anna University to have a clear idea of the subject. The book contains 27 chapters and illustrations with 250 problems and solutions. As great attention has been paid to the details, the book is complete in every respect. The language is simple and the book will prove to be very useful to the students of MBA and MCA. The book covers all the areas of the syllabus stipulated by Anna University. I appreciate Mr. V.R. Palanivelu for his painstaking efforts in bringing out a book on Accounting. As he possesses rich experience in teaching accountancy to the students of MBA and MCA, the book will be a useful addition to the existing set of Accountancy books. The students will, no doubt, welcome this book in all earnestness.

(V. MANICKAVASAGAM)
PROFESSOR & HEAD
DEPARTMENT OF CORPORATE SECRETARYSHIP
ALAGAPPA UNIVERSITY
KARAIKUDI-630 004.

Alagappa University

Karaikudi - 630 003

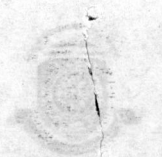

KARAIKUDI-630 003

PREFACE

Accounting is very much essential for successful operations of all business concerns. Accounting information provides valuable guidance to the management specifically for the decision making activities. Anna University has introduced MBA and MCA courses. It has rightly incorporated one paper on Financial and Management Accounting in the first semester of this course. This book has been specifically designed for the students of MBA and MCA courses according to the revised syllabus. And it is also helpful to the beginners of accounting.

Everywhere the principles of Accountancy are the same in all walks of life. But there are differences of opinion as to the suitable methods of incorporating these principles. This book is also helpful for non-accounting students as it provides simplified methods for the preparation of accounts in a lucid manner which will enable them to acquire sufficient theoretical and practical knowledge.

The foremost aim of introducing this book is to facilitate understanding of the matter at one reading without any strain in grasping the theories and illustrations. The book consists of four parts *viz.*, financial accounting, cost accounting, management accounting and financial management.

For the benefit of the students, nearly 250 problems have been collected from various university question papers. All the problems are worked out in a very simple method. For example, in the fund flow analysis, the increase or decrease in working capital is found out only on net result and not from item-wise comparison. In this way, problems in all the chapters are worked out in a short cut and easy method. For the simplification of all the chapters, procedures and/or formulas have been incorporated at appropriate places.

Generally MBA, MCA students feel accounting is a difficult subject but the readers of this book will realize that it is not so. At the same time, I do not claim any originality, but I have taken much pains to present the subject in simple and systematic manner. It is the outcome of my teaching experience in this subject for several years.

This book is useful not only for the management and commerce students but also more helpful to the students of BE courses of various branches of Anna University.

I have made serious efforts to remove the printing mistakes of the book. Apart from my serious efforts if the reader finds any error he is requested to convey the same to me. I believe that both the students and teachers will find the book very useful. I will be very happy in receiving constructive criticism and appropriate suggestions for improving the quality of presentation and standard of the book in the next edition.

I feel it is a great opportunity to construct the new edition of "Accounting for Management" book for the commerce and non-commerce students of MBA, MCA courses.

—AUTHOR

ACKNOWLEDGEMENT

I would like to place on record the valuable academic and infrastructure support given by my parent institution : *Vivekanandha College of Engineering for Women, Tiruchengode.* I would like to express my thanks to the Chairman and Secretary of *Vivekanandha Group of Educational Institutions, M. Karunanithi* without whose approval and encouragement I could not have completed this work. I am thankful to *S. Meganathan Chief Executive, M. Chokkaligam Administrative Officer* of the *Vivekanandha Group of Institutions.*

I am indebted to my colleagues, both academic and professional, and to countless students—it would be very difficult to list them all. For evincing personal interest in undertaking a project of this magnitude and making invaluable suggestions from time to time, I would like to thank professor *Dr. A. Manikavasagam, Alagappa University, Karikudi*, Principal *Dr. R. Vadivel VCEW Tiruchengodu*, my research supervisor—*Professor Dr. A. Jayakumar, Periyar University, Salem, Professor Dr. L. Manivannan Erode Arts College Erode, Prof. G. Arumugham VCEW Tiruchengodu.*

I would like to thank for my wife Sasikala, children Kavina, Kowranth for continuously providing moral support and understanding in all my creative works. Above all I feel this work is the outcome of the blessings of so many well wishers particularly my Mentors/Teachers.

I would like to extend a special thanks to my publisher Laxmi Publications (P) Ltd., its Managing Director Saurabh Gupta and his team of Editors, Production Personnels, Designers, Marketing Specialists and Sales Representatives who ensured that this book got into the hands of students and faculty in record time.

—**AUTHOR**

ACCOUNTING FOR MANAGEMENT
THEORY, TECHNIQUES, PROBLEMS & SOLUTIONS

S. No.	CONTENTS OF THE BOOK	Sub. Code	Sub. Code
1.	Introduction about the Accounting	BA1606	MC1605
2.	Basic records maintained by a business concern	BA1606	MC1605
3.	Revenue Recognition and measurement	BA1606	—
4.	Preparation of final accounts	BA1606	MC1605
5.	Fund Flow statement	BA1606	MC1605
6.	Cash flow statement	BA1606	MC1605
7.	Ratio analysis	BA1606	MC1605
8.	Fixed assets and depreciation	BA1606	—
9.	Cost accounting: Cost sheet accounting for manufacturing cost	BA1606	MC1605
10.	Job costing	BA1606	
11.	Process costing	BA1606	
12.	Activity Based costing	BA1606	—
13.	Inventory pricing and valuation	BA1606	
14.	Standard costing	BA1606	MC1605
15.	Management accounting	BA1606	MC1605
16.	Marginal costing	BA1606	MC1605
17.	Relevant cost for Decision making	BA1606	—
18.	Budget and Budgetary control	BA1606	MC1605
19.	Inflation Accounting	BA1606	—
20.	Human Resources Accounting	BA1606	—
21.	Responsibility Accounting	BA1606	—
22.	Financial Management	—	MC1605
23.	Dividend	—	MC1605
24.	Cost of capital	—	MC1605
25.	Capital structure	—	MC1605
26.	Working capital	—	MC1605
27.	Capital budgeting	—	MC 1605

S. No.	Subject code	Name of the paper	Course covered
1.	BA 1606	Accounting for management	MBA I Semester
2.	MC 1605	Accounting and financial management	MCA I Semester

SYLLABUS

ANNA UNIVERSITY (REVISED SYLLABUS 2005–2006)
MBA DEGREE EXAMINATION
BA1606 ACCOUNTING FOR MANAGEMENT

1. FINANCIAL ACCOUNTING

1.1 Introduction to Financial, Cost and Management Accounting, generally accepted Accounting Principles, Conventions and Concepts. The Balance Sheet and Related Concepts, the Profit and Loss Account and Related Concepts / Introduction to Inflation Accounting, Introduction to Human Resources Accounting.

1.2 Accounting Mechanics

Basic records, preparation of Financial Statements, Revenue Recognition and Measurement, Matching Revenues and Expenses, Inventory Pricing and Valuation, Fixed Assets and Depreciation Accounting, Intangible Assets.

1.3 Analysis of Financial Statements

Financial Ratio Analysis, Cash Flow and Funds Flow Statement Analysis

2. COST ACCOUNTING AND MANAGEMENT ACCOUNTING

2.1 Cost Accounts

Accounting for manufacturing operations, classification of manufacturing costs, accounting for manufacturing costs.

Cost Accounting system: Job Order Costing, Process Costing, Activity Based Costing, Costing and the Value Chain, Target Costing, Cost-Volume-Profit Analysis, Standard Cost System.

2.2 Management Accounting

Relevant Cost For Decision Making, Increment Analysis, Special Order Decision, Production Constraint Decisions, make or buy decisions, Sell, Scrap or Rebuild Decisions, Joint Product Budget: As a Planning and Control Tool.

ANNA UNIVERSITY (REVISED SYLLABUS 2005–2006)
MCA DEGREE EXAMINATION

MC1605 ACCOUNTING AND FINANCIAL MANAGEMENT

UNIT—I : FINANCIAL ACCOUNTING

Meaning and Scope of Accounting – Principles – Concepts Conventions – Accounting Standards – Final Accounts – Trial Balance – Trading Account – Profit and Loss Account – Balance Sheet – Accounting Ratio Analysis – Funds Flow Analysis – Cash Flow Analysis.

UNIT—II : ACCOUNTING

Meaning – Objectives – Elements of Cost – Cost Sheet – Marginal Costing and Cost Volume Profit Analysis – Break Even Analysis – Applications – Limitations – Standard Costing and Variance Analysis – Material – Labour – Overhead – Sales – Profit Variances.

UNIT—III : BUDGETS AND BUDGETING CONTROL

Budgets and Budgetary Control – Meaning, Types – Sales Budget – Production, Budget- Cost of Production, Budget – Flexible. Budgeting – Cash Budget – Master Budget – Zero Base Budgeting – Computerized Accounting.

UNIT—IV : INVESTMENT DECISION AND COST OF CAPITAL

Objectives and Functions of Financial Management – Risk – Return Relationship – Time Value of Money Concepts – Capital Budgeting – Methods of Appraisal Cost of Capital Factors Affecting Cost of Capital – Computation for each Source of Finance and Weighted Average Cost of Capital.

UNIT—V : FINANCING DECISION AND WORKING CAPITAL MANAGEMENT

Capital Structure – Factors Affecting Capital Structure – Dividend Policy – Types of Dividend Policy – Concepts of Working Capital – Working Capital Policies – Factors Affecting Working Capital – Estimation of Working Capital Requirements.

1
Introduction to Accounting

NEED FOR ACCOUNTING

The ultimate aim of any business is to earn a profit. Profit earning is not an easy task. For earning a profit the businessman will purchase the goods in one place at certain price and sell it at another place at higher price than the purchase price or convert the raw material into finished products and sell them to various customers at a certain price which will give some percentage of margin on cost of production. But, this may not be true in all cases, because the goods produced or purchased may go out of fashion or competitors may enter the market. Due to this reason, sales will decline automatically. The business runs at a loss or at a very small margin. However, the businessman wants to know the profit or loss for the consolidated transaction at the end of the financial year. So, he needs more information for planning control, evaluation of performance and decision making. This information can be provided only when business transactions are recorded, classified and summarised properly. In order to achieve the above purpose, it would be necessary to record the business transaction according to well defined Accounting system.

MEANING OF ACCOUNTING

Accounting is the art of recording, classifying, summarizing, analysing, and reporting of business transactions and interpreting their effect on the affairs of the business concerns.

As Accounting is commonly referred to as the language of business, accounting information has to be suitably recorded, classified, summarised and presented.

DEFINITION OF ACCOUNTING

In 1941, The American Institute of Certified Public Accountants defined accounting as follows. "Accounting is the art of recording, classifying and summarising in a significant manner the terms of money transaction and events which are, in part at least, of a financial character and interpreting the results thereof."

FUNCTIONS OF ACCOUNTING

A well designed Accounting System helps :
 (i) To keep the proper records of financial transaction which enables to prepare final accounts.
 (ii) To meet the legal requirements such as sales tax and income tax disputes as and when necessary.

(iii) To protect the properties of the business concerns.
(iv) To provide data to interested parties like owners, creditors, debtors, investors, employees, government authorities and researchers.

ACCOUNTING CONCEPTS

Accountants adopt the following concepts in recording the business transactions :

(i) *Separate Entity Concept.* According to this concept, the firm is separated from the owner of the business whenever the firm is born. Then, it is necessary to record the business transactions separately to distinguish it from the owner's personal transactions.

(ii) *Going Concern Concept.* In this concept, it is assumed that transactions are recorded hoping that the business concern is to exist even in the future. A firm is said to be a going concern when there is neither the intention nor the necessity to wind up its operations.

(iii) *Money Measurement Concept.* Measurement of business event in terms of money helps in understanding the state of affairs of the business in a better way.

In accounting, all transactions are expressed and interpreted in terms of money. Accounting records only those transactions which are being expressed in monetary terms though quantitative records are also kept.

(iv) *Cost Concept.* According to this concept (a) an asset is ordinarily entered in the accounting records as the price paid to acquire it and (b) this cost is the basis for all subsequent accounting for the asset.

(v) *Dual Aspect Concept.* This is the basic concept of accounting. According to this concept every business transaction has two aspects. (a) Debit, (b) Credit. If a firm has acquired an asset, it must have resulted in one of the following :

(a) The owner of the firm has contributed money for the acquisition of the asset.

(b) For the consideration of asset acquired, some other asset has been given up.

The reverse is also true. For example, A starts business with capital of Rs. 20,000/-. There are two aspects of transaction. On the one hand, business has an asset of Rs. 20,000 while on the other hand, the business has to pay to the proprietor a sum of Rs. 20,000/- which is taken as proprietory capital.

$$\text{Capital (equities)} = \text{Cash (Asset)}$$
$$20,000 = 20,000$$

The term 'Assets' denotes the resources owned by a business while the term 'Equities' denotes the claims of various parties against the assets. Equities are of two types :

- Owners' equity (or capital) is the claim of the owners against the assets of the business.
- Outsiders' equity (or liabilities) is the claim of outside parties such as creditors, debenture holders against the assets of the business. Since either owners or outsiders claim all the assets of the business, the total assets will be equal to total liabilities. Thus,

$$\text{Equities} = \text{Assets, Liabilities} + \text{Capital} = \text{Assets}$$

INTRODUCTION TO ACCOUNTING

The term "Accounting Equation" is also used to denote the relationship of equities to assets. The equation can be technically stated as, "for every debit there is an equivalent credit". Entire system of double entry book keeping is based on this concept.

(vi) *Accounting Period Concept.* A Business life is assumed to continue indefinitely. According to this concept, the life of the business is divided into appropriate intervals for studying results shown by the business and the financial position after each interval. Suppose it would not happen within the stipulated time means, necessary corrective steps cannot be initiated. In accounting such a segment or time interval is called "accounting period". It is usually of one year and at the end of this period, income statement and balance sheet are prepared.

(vii) *Realisation Concept.* Accounting is a historical record of transactions. According to this concept, revenue is recognised at the point when property in goods passes to the buyer and he becomes legally liable to pay.

(viii) *Periodic Matching of Costs and Revenue Concept.* According to this concept income made by the business during a period can be measured only when the revenue earned during a period is compared with the expenditure incurred for earning that revenue. It is based on the accounting period concept.

SOME IMPORTANT TERMS USED IN ACCOUNTANCY

Following are the Important Terms used in Accountancy :

Transaction

Day-to-day business activities are called transaction. It may involve transfer of money due to exchange of goods or services between two parties or two persons. Transaction may be cash transaction and/or credit transaction.

For Example :
(a) Purchase of machinery worth   Rs. 50,000/-
(b) Cheque Received from Ramu   Rs. 15,000/-

Capital

In order to start and run the business, the owner has to contribute some initial amount to the firm for the purpose of producing and selling the goods. The amount invested in order to earn an income is known as capital. Capital may be classified as fixed capital and working capital.

Capital is the Liability of the business to its proprietor, because as and when the owner claims, firm is liable to repay the money to its owner.

Liability

It refers to any amount which a business firm has to pay legally to outsiders. All dues to others including proprietor's capital are said to be liabilities.

Asset

Anything possessed by the firm which is of certain monetary value is called Asset. In other words, assets refer to tangible object and an intangible right of an enterprise, which carries probable future benefits. It may be classified as current assets and fixed assets.

Income

Income is a flow of benefit to the enterprise arising out of resources controlled by it. The definition of income consists of both revenue and gain. Revenue arises in the course of ordinary activities of an enterprise. In manufacturing or trading enterprises revenues arise mainly from the sale of goods.

Example : Sales, dividend received, interest received, etc.

Expenses

It means an amount spent on any item by the proprietor to acquire benefit out of it. The expenses are classified into Capital Expenditure and Revenue Expenditure.

Capital expenditure refers to any amount spent to increase the earning capacity of the business or acquisition of asset.

Revenue expenditure refers to the amount spent for the purpose of acquiring benefit for the particular year alone.

Example : Payment of salaries, rent, etc.

Purchase

Buying of goods by the trader for selling them to his customers is known as purchases. Purchases may be cash purchases and credit purchases.

For example : Ramu purchases goods of Rs. 85,000/-.

Purchase Returns

Purchase returns means a firm or buyer returns to the vendor the goods purchased due to defective parts or product.

Sales

Exchange of goods for money is called sales. Simply sales means goods sent out from the organisation to its customers. Sales can be cash sales and credit sales.

For Example : Sale of finished goods to Murali Rs. 60,000/-.

Sales Returns

When a customer returns some of the purchased goods (due to some reasons) to the firm it is called sales returns.

For Example : Murali returns goods worth Rs. 5,000/-.

Creditor

Creditor is a person who supplies finance or goods to others *i.e.*, he has to get money from others. Suppose more than one person are supplying finance or goods to others. It means the consolidated names of suppliers is called creditor. The creditors are shown as liability in the balance sheet.

INTRODUCTION TO ACCOUNTING

Debtor

Debtor is a person who owes money to others because he has purchased the goods or has got finance from others. Simply debtor is one who has to pay money to others. The Debtors are shown on the Asset side of the Balance sheet.

Goods

The things which a trader sells or purchases are called goods.

Drawings

It refers to the withdrawals of money or money's worth (goods) by the proprietor from his business for his personal use.

Journal Entry

Journal Entry means particular transactions are to be split into two parts *i.e.*, debit and credit based upon the accounting rules.

Ledger

A ledger refers to a summary statement of all the transactions relating to a person, asset, expense or income which have taken place during a given period of time and show their net effect.

Invoice

While making a sale, the seller prepares a statement giving the particulars such as quantity, price per unit, the total amount payable, any deductions made and shows the net amount payable by the buyer. This type of statement is called an invoice.

BRANCHES OF ACCOUNTING

In order to satisfy the needs of different people interested in the accounting information, different branches of accounting have developed. Accounting can be broadly classified into three types.

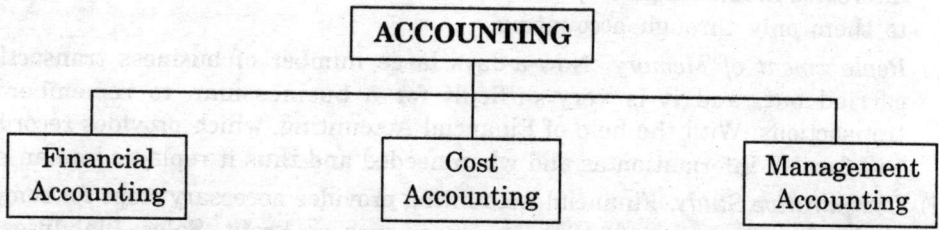

1. *Financial Accounting.* It is the original form of accounting. Financial Accounting records business transactions taking place during the accounting period with a view to prepare financial statements.

   American Institute of Certified Public Accountants has defined 'Financial Accounting' as "The art of recording, classifying and summarising in a significant manner and in terms of money transactions and events which are in part at least of financial character and interpreting the result thereof".

Ultimate object of accounting is to measure the Profit or Loss of the concern and to ascertain the financial position of the business. Thus Profit and Loss Account is prepared for a particular period to determine the profitability of the concern and Balance sheet is prepared on a particular date to determine the financial position of the concern.

2. *Cost Accounting.* Cost Accounting is the process of ascertaining cost from the point at which expenditure is incurred or committed to the establishment of its ultimate relationship with the cost centres and cost units.

3. *Management Accounting.* The term Management Accounting refers to accounting for the management. Accounting which provides necessary information to the management for taking and implementing important decisions.

Management accounting covers various areas such as cost accounting, budgetory control, inventory control, etc. This has been discussed in detail in the subsequent pages.

FUNCTIONS OF FINANCIAL ACCOUNTING

The main objectives of Financial Accounting are :

(i) *Recording Business Transaction.* The first and foremost objective of Financial Accounting is to record business transactions which are maintained systematically with the help of journal and ledger and also to prepare Final Account. With the help of these facilities it is easy to know the operating results and financial position of the organisation.

(ii) *Managerial Functions.* Decision making is an important process of the management. Financial Accounting provides necessary information to the managerial functions and decision making programmers. Without accounting proper decision making is not possible.

(iii) *Legal Requirement Function.* Business disputes are unavoidable. If there is any dispute properly maintained accounts are often treated as a good evidence in the court to settle a dispute. Auditing is compulsory in case of registered firms.

(iv) *Language of Business.* Investors, Employees, Creditors, Government etc. are interested in knowing the operational results of the firm and it can be communicated to them only through accounting.

(v) *Replacement of Memory.* Now-a-days large number of business transactions are carried out, and it is very difficult for a businessman to remember all the transactions. With the help of Financial Accounting, which provides records which will furnish information as and when needed and thus it replaces human memory.

(vi) *Comparative Study.* Financial Accounting provides necessary steps for comparative study of various aspects of the business such as Profit, Sales, Liabilities, Loans, Fixed assets etc. with that of previous year and helps the businessman to make changes if any.

(vii) *Sale of Business.* The circumstance arises when the businessman wants to sell his business means, he wants to determine the total value of his business with the help of systematic recording of financial data.

LIMITATIONS OF FINANCIAL ACCOUNTING

Financial Accounting suffers the following limitations :

(i) *Records of Monetary Transactions.* Accounting records are maintained only when transactions are expressed in monetary terms. At the same time, those transactions which cannot be measured in monetary terms are not to be recorded. It excludes qualitative elements like management reputation, employee morale, labour strike, etc.

(ii) *Recording Actual Cost.* Cost concept is found in financial accounting. If the effect of price level changes is not brought into the books, comparison of various years becomes difficult. Financial accounting records are based only on Actual Cost. This type of accounting techniques actually reduces the utilities and usefulness.

(iii) *Personal Bias of Accountant affects the Accounting Statements.* Normally Accounting policies are framed by the Accountants. They differ on the use of accounting principles. And at the same time a number of conventions, concepts and postulates have been propounded in accountancy. Their use is greatly affected by the personal judgement of Accountants. Sometime different financial results are obtained from the same concern's financial statements. Because these statements are prepared by two different accountants with varying personal judgement in using or applying particular conventions.

(iv) *Incomplete Information.* Financial Accounting discloses only the net result of the consolidated business transactions. It does not disclose profit or loss of each department's job, process, etc. The product-wise or job-wise cost of production cannot be found out.

(v) *Permits Alternative Treatments.* Financial Accounting permits alternative treatments within generally accepted accounting concepts. For example, closing stock may be valued by FIFO or LIFO or average method or market price method. Applications of different methods may give different results and at the same time results may not be comparable.

(vi) *Only Quantitative Information.* Financial Accounting will be taken into account only on those factors which are being quantitatively expressed. But quantifiable information could not be considered. Because the management has to follow the government policies which relate to the Economic development of the country.

(vii) *Technological Revolution.* Due to the development of Science and Technology, all types of business information and data are needed for effective functioning of the organisation. But financial accounting provides only elementary information. So, this is not enough to meet out the current level of competition.

□□□

2
Basic Records Maintained by a Business Concern

Small organisations have only limited transactions and they maintain very few basic accounting records such as journal book, ledger and a cash book. But in the case of large scale business organisation, they have a wider number of transaction. In this respect they maintain not only the journal book, ledger and cash book but also some other separate books which are maintained for recording credit purchases, credit sales, bills transactions etc. These books are day book, sales day book, Returns inward and outward books, Bills receivable and bills payable books, petty cash book, etc.

SUBSIDIARY BOOKS

All the business transactions are first entered in the journal and then posted to the respective accounts in the ledger, to make sub divisions of journals into various books. Recording transactions of similar nature are called subsidiary books. These subsidiary books are also known as books of prime entry. The following are the important subsidiary books which are maintained by the large business organisation.

(i) Cash Book
(ii) Purchases day Book or purchases Book
(iii) Sales day Book
(iv) Purchase return Book
(v) Sales return Book
(vi) Bills receivable Book
(vii) Bills payable Book
(viii) Journal proper.

(i) *Cash Book.* It deals with the transaction relating to the receipts and payments of cash.

(ii) *Purchases Book.* Purchase books are those books which record credit purchases of goods only. Any cash purchases or assets purchased on credit basis are not entered in this book.

(iii) *Sales Day Book.* This book is maintained in recording all credit sales made during a particular period. But any asset sold or cash sales are not recorded in this book.

(iv) *Purchase Returns (or returns outward) Book.* This book is maintained for recording the goods returned to the suppliers which had been already purchased on credit basis. And it will show the total purchase returns during the particular period.

(v) *Sales Returns Book.* This book records the goods returned by the customers which had already been sold to customers on credit basis. And it will show the total return inwards during the particular period.

(vi) *Bills Receivable Book.* It is the book for recording the bills received from customers for credit sales.

(vii) *Bills Payable Book.* It is the book for recording the acceptances (bills payable) given to the suppliers for the credit purchases.

(viii) *Journal Proper.* Those transactions which could not be recorded in any of the above books will be recorded in this book.

PREPARATION OF FINAL ACCOUNT

Final Account consists of three parts :
(i) Trading Account
(ii) Profit and loss A/c
(iii) Balance sheet

It should be prepared in the following way :
(i) Journalisation of transactions
(ii) Postings of journal entry to ledger A/c
(iii) Balancing of ledger (Find the debit or credit.)
(iv) Prepare Trial Balance with the help of balances which are found out from various ledgers.
(v) From the Trial Balance, now, we have to prepare the Final Account.
(vi) At the time of preparing Final Account, all the adjustments are taken care of at the appropriate places.

3
Revenue Recognition and Measurement

For the purpose of preparing fair and true financial statement of the company, it has to take the correct decision about the revenue for the period. Suppose the revenue is overstated or understated it should affect the reality of the financial statement. Before we proceed to consider the problem of revenue recognition and measurement, it is useful to know the meaning of revenue for an accounting period.

According to the Financial Accounting Standards Board of USA. "Revenues are inflows or other enhancements of assets of an enterprise or settlements of its liabilities (or a combination of both) during a period from the delivering or producing goods, rendering services, or other activities that constitute the enterprises ongoing major or central operations".

The problems of revenue recognition could arise due to the following reasons :
  (*i*) The seller agrees to sell his product at a particular point of time but the buyer takes delivery at a different point of time.
  (*ii*) The seller receives the money from the buyer at a time different from the time of delivery of goods sold.
  (*iii*) The buyer may pay money for the purpose of goods purchased at a point of time later than the date of billing.
  (*iv*) Receipt of the sales price prior to the delivery of goods or billing.

Following are the methods exist as to when revenue could be recognised.
  (*i*) Recognition at the time of sale
  (*ii*) Recognition at the time when the sales price is collected
  (*iii*) Recognition at the time when the product is completed
  (*iv*) Recognition proportionately over the period of performance of the contract.

METHODS FOR REVENUE RECOGNITION

(*i*) Percentage of completion method (*ii*) Completed contract method.

The above two methods are commonly followed by the contractors for the revenue recognition.

  (*i*) *Percentage of Completion Method.* The percentage of completion method refers to the income earned by the contractor determined on the basis of progress of the contract. Under this method, current assets may include costs and recognized income not yet billed with respect to certain contracts.

(ii) *Completed Contract Method.* Under this method, incomes are recognized only when the contract is completed or substantially so.

MATCHING OF REVENUES AND EXPENSES

One of the most important concepts of the accounting is the matching concept. This concept provides the guidelines as to how the expenses be matched with revenues. Expenses incurred in an accounting year should be matched with the revenues recognised in that year. But at the same time only such expenses as incurred in creating revenues during the period should be deducted from those revenues for earning the income or profit during the period. The ultimate aim of the accounting is to construct the accounting record in such a manner so as to compare the cost with revenue.

Either the comparison of costs is not possible or it is likely to be difficult. Suppose these types of situations arise when the accounting system will be considered as unsatisfactory. In order to make a satisfactory accounting system a current matching of revenue as against the expenses will be followed *i.e.,* incurred expenses will be followed and matched against the realised income.

American Institute of Certified Public Accountants Committee on accounting procedure states that "it is plainly desirable to provide by charging in the current income statement, properly classified for all foreseeable costs and losses applicable against current revenues, to the extent that they can be measured and allocated to fiscal periods with reasonable approximation". Only current year expenses/incomes are taken into account. Suppose either previous year or subsequent year's expenses or incomes, paid or received should be adjusted properly *i.e.,* if any of the current year expenses are due, it should be added to the respective expenses or deducted if paid in advance.

And if any income of the current year is due but not received, it is added to the respective incomes. Suppose it should be received for the subsequent years, it means it is deducted from the respective income.

Based upon this principle only current year expenses are matched with the current year realised revenue. By application of this matching concept, proprietor can easily determine their firm's profit or loss and he can take additional effort to increase the earning capacity of the concern if necessary.

☐☐☐

4
Preparation of Final Accounts

The scope and importance of accounting is to provide variable information about a business enterprise to those persons who are directly or indirectly interested in the progress, performance and financial position of the concern.

Information is the basis for decision making in an organization. The efficiency and soundness of the management depends upon the availability of regular and correct information to those who exercise the managerial functions. Such persons may include owners, creditors, investors, employees, government, public, research scholars and the managers.

1. *Owners.* The owners of a business could contribute capital to be used for the purpose of starting and running the business. The ultimate aim of accounting is to provide necessary information to the owners relating to their business. They want to evaluate the past financial performance and also assess the future prospects through the accounting reports.

2. *Creditors.* Creditors, debenture holders, bankers and other financial institutions are interested in knowing about the short term as well as long term financial position of the company. Because, they want to find out the ability of the firm to pay interest and principal as and when it becomes due for payment.

3. *Potential Investors.* Any investor, before making investment in any particular company shares, wants to know not only the earning capacity of the organisation but also its solvency position. For this purpose, investors take information from accounting reports to a great extent in order to determine the relative merits of the available investment opportunities.

4. *Employees.* Employees are the backbone of the organisation. They are interested in the earning capacity of a concern because their salaries, bonus, and pension schemes are dependent on the size of the profit earned.

5. *Government.* Government is the sole authority for the country's economic development. For the purpose of finding out overall economic growth point of view, the government is very much interested in accounting statements and reports in order to see the financial position of a particular unit. With the help of the accounting information, government is not only to prepare national account but also to impose tax and excise duty.

6. *Public.* The public as consumers is interested in accounting information in order to testify whether the control is properly exercised on production, selling and distribution for the purpose of reducing the prices of the goods they buy. And also they are interested to know, whether all the available economic resources of the concern are being properly utilised for the benefit of the common man or not. And at the same time, they want to examine any of the aspects of the business which can be detrimental to the public interest.

7. *Research Scholars.* Financial statements are very helpful to the research scholars. Enormous information are available from the accounting reports. Depending upon their research area, the researcher could get the data for providing their thesis on which they are working and hence to complete their research projects.
8. *Regulatory Agencies.* In order to protect the public from the fraudulent activities of the business, various governments, voluntary service institutions, and other agencies use accounting information not only for the tax assessment purpose but also in evaluating how well various business concerns are operating under legal framework.
9. *Managers.* The foremost responsibility of the managers of the organisation is to obtain maximum return over the capital invested without causing any harm to the interest of the share holders. The manager would like to have a data regarding sales, expenses, assets, liabilities etc. relating to next year and also the flow of fund for the purpose of the activities of a business. He also takes a decision and alters the decision in best way. In all these aspects, relevant accounting information is needed.

RECORDING OF BUSINESS TRANSACTION - BASIS OF ACCOUNTING

There are three different Basis systems of accounting for recording of business transaction. They are (*i*) cash basis accounting, (*ii*) mercantile basis or Accrual basis of accounting, and (*iii*) mixed-basis of accounting.

(*i*) Cash Basis of Accounting

Under this system of accounting, actual cash received and actual cash payments are recorded. Credit transactions are not recorded at all until the cash is actually received or paid. Non trading concerns such as charitable institution, a club, a college etc and a professional man like a lawyer, a doctor, a chartered accountant etc maintains accounts under this system only. This basis of accounting is not a complete record of financial transactions of a trading period, because all outstanding transactions are not recorded.

(*ii*) Mercantile Basis of Accounting or Accrual Basis of Accounting

According to mercantile system of accounting, entries are made not only for actual receipt or payment of cash but also for the amount having been due for payment or receipt. Simply, both cash transactions and credit transactions are recorded and even non-trading concerns follow this type of accounting. Financial transaction discloses correct profit or loss for a particular period and also exhibits true financial position of the business on a particular day.

Normally, trading orgainsations, to prepare final account for the purpose of finding out profit or loss during a particular period, use the mercantile system of accounting.

(*iii*) Mixed System of Accounting

Under this basis of accounting, both cash system and mercantile system are followed. Simply, combination of cash system and mercantile system is called mixed system. Some of the records are maintained under the cash system and remaining others are maintained under mercantile system.

Apart from the basis of accounting, following are the methods of accounting to be followed in a normal practice. They are (i) Single entry method and (ii) Double entry method.

SINGLE ENTRY SYSTEM OF BOOK KEEPING

Under the single entry system, the principles of Double entry book keeping are not followed. Normally, every transaction has a two fold aspect. But in the single entry system of accounting only one aspect is recorded. So it is called incomplete method of Book keeping. Trial Balance, Trading Account, Profit and Loss account, and Balance Sheet cannot be prepared with the help of the single entry system. This system is mainly followed by those organisations that have only limited number of transactions.

DOUBLE ENTRY SYSTEM OF BOOK KEEPING

Double entry system of book keeping refers to particular transactions which are entered in two aspects. It is based on the dual aspect concept. Posting of each transaction in two different accounts on opposite sides for equal value is known as the double entry system of book keeping. [Normally it is the most accurate, complete and scientific method of accounting].

Simply, every debit must have a corresponding credit and vice versa. Most of the trading organisations follow the double entry system of accounting.

Advantages of Double Entry System

(i) It provides a complete record of the financial transactions which is maintained.
(ii) It supplies complete information about the business.
(iii) It provides a check on the arithmetical accuracy of books of accounts by preparing a trial balance by taking balances of all ledger accounts.
(iv) It is helpful in ascertaining profit or loss of a particular period by preparing the trading and profit and loss account.
(v) It helps the businessman to evaluate the progress of his business through meaningful comparison of operating and financial performance over a period of time.
(vi) It helps in preventing frauds and errors.
(vii) It helps income tax and sales tax authorities.
(viii) It is helpful in preparing accurate claim for loss of stock as a result of fire to the insurance company.

Disadvantages of Double Entry System

(i) This system requires to maintain wider number of books of accounts, which is not convenient to small concerns.
(ii) There is no guarantee of absolute accuracy of the books of account which are maintained.
(iii) It requires more clerical labour, so the system is costly.

SOME IMPORTANT TERMS USED IN ACCOUNTANCY

Book Keeping

Book keeping is the systematic recording, classifying and summarizing the business transactions in the book of accounts in accordance with the principles of accounting. In the words of Carter "Book keeping is the art of correctly recording in book of accounts all those transactions that result in the transfer of money or money's worth".

Account

It is a consolidated statement of various transactions occurred between a customer and the firm. It should be clearly expressed and it is a concise record of the transactions relating to a person or a firm or a property or a liability or an income or expenditure. The abbreviation for account is A/c.

CLASSIFICATION OF ACCOUNTS

Normally, Accounts are classified into mainly two classes *viz.* (1) Personal accounts and (2) Impersonal accounts. These impersonal accounts are further subdivided into (*i*) Real account and (*ii*) Nominal account. But usually three types of accounts namely Personal Accounts, Real or Property Accounts and Nominal or Fictitious Accounts are opened to keep a complete record of business transactions.

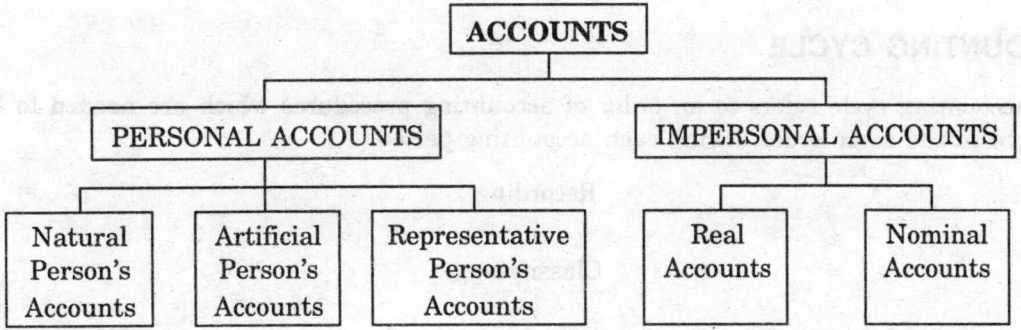

1. Personal Accounts

Personal Accounts are those which are related to persons. A separate account is prepared for each person, because the firm deals its transactions with a number of persons. Such accounts can take the following forms :

  (*i*) Natural person's accounts *e.g.,* Kumar's account
  (*ii*) Artificial persons' or body of persons' accounts *e.g.,* Bank account, any company's account
  (*iii*) Representative person's accounts *e.g.,* salaries outstanding account, prepaid expenses account.

2. Impersonal Accounts

  (*i*) *Real Accounts or Property Accounts.* Real Accounts are those accounts which can be related to a property, an asset or possession *e.g.,* plant account, machinery account, cash account etc. Separate account is prepared for each class of assets of the organisation.

(ii) *Nominal Accounts.* Nominal accounts are those which are related to the business expenses or losses and incomes or gains.

For example : Wages account, discount account, commission account.

RULES OF DOUBLE ENTRY (OR) ACCOUNTING RULES

Normally, most of the organisations follow the double entry system of accounting. The rules of double entry are as follows.

(i) **Personal Accounts**
   Rules : Debit the Receiver
   Credit the giver
(ii) **Real or property Accounts**
   Rules : Debit what comes in
   Credit what goes out.
(iii) **Nominal Accounts**
   Rules : Debit all expenses and losses
   Credit all incomes and gains.

ACCOUNTING CYCLE

Accounting cycle refers to an order of accounting procedures which are needed to be repeated in the same order during each accounting period.

Recording
↓
Classifying
↓
Summarising

(i) *Recording.* First and foremost activity of accounting is recording of business transactions in the journal.
(ii) *Classifying.* Classifying the transactions in the journal by posting them to the appropriate ledger accounts to find out at a glance the total effect of such transactions in a particular account.
(iii) *Summarising.* Summarising simply refers to consolidation of one year transactions with the help of ledger Balances. Based upon these Balances, Trial Balance, and final accounts are to be prepared with a view to ascertaining profit or loss made during the particular financial year or trading period.

BOOKS OF ACCOUNTS : RECORDING, POSTING AND PREPARATION OF TRIAL BALANCE

Journal

Journal is derived from the French word "Jour" which means a day. Journal therefore means day to day transactions which are recorded in the books. It is in the form of debit and credit and is maintained with the help of accounting rules. The process of recording the transactions in a journal is called journalising.

A journal may be defined as the book of original or prime entry containing a chronological record of the business transactions.

Journal Format

1 Date		2 Particulars	3 L.F.	4 Debit (Dr.) Rs.	5 Credit (Cr.) Rs.
Year Month	Date	Name of the Account to be debited Name of the Account to be credited To Narration		xx	xx

Explanation

1. *Date.* The date on which the transaction takes place is entered in the journal.
2. *Particulars.* Under the particulars column, the names of the account to be debited is written in the first line, and in the second line, the account to be credited is written preceded by the word To Narration which also explains briefly about the transaction.
3. *L.F.* It stands for ledger folio. It means the page number in the ledger in which the entry is posted.
4. *Debit.* Name of the account to be debited against the 'Dr' account is entered.
5. *Credit.* Name of the account to be credited against the 'Cr' account is entered.

Procedure for Journalising

In any particular transaction first of all we have to identify the receiving aspect and giving aspect of the transaction. All the transactions affect at least two of the basic accounting.

The rule for journalizing should be selected as follows.

Nature of Account	Rule for debiting an account	Rule for Crediting an account
1. Personal Account	Debit the Receiver	Credit the giver
2. Real Account	Debit what comes in	Credit what goes out
3. Nominal Account	Debit all expenses and losses.	Credit all incomes and gains

Problem 1. *Journalise the following transaction in the journal of Mr.T.R.Ramu.*

2003, Jan 1 Ramu commenced business with a capital of Rs. 50,000
    ↓   ↓
 Personal A/c   Real A/c

The above transaction has to affect the two accounts *i.e.*, (*i*) Real A/c and (*ii*) Personal A/c. After finding out the affected accounts, we have to apply the accounting rules as against the particular transaction. Here cash is coming to the business and Ramu is the giver.

Date	Particulars	L.F.	Dr. Rs.	Cr. Rs.
2003, Jan 1	Cash A/c Dr. To Ramu's Capital A/c (Being the amount invested in business)		50,000	50,000

2. Amount Deposited in Canara Bank Rs. 20,000
                      ↓   ↓
               Personal A/c   Real A/c

Affected Accounts in the above transaction :

(*i*) Personal Account

(*ii*) Real Account.

In the above transaction, the Canara Bank is the artificial person to receive the money. It relates to Personal Accounts. As per the Personal Accounts rules, Debit the Receiver. Here Canara Bank Account is debited and amount relates to real account. Amount goes out according to real account credit what goes out. Here cash goes out. So the Cash A/c is credited.

Date	Particulars	L.F.	Dr. Rs.	Cr. Rs.
2003, Jan 2	Canara Bank A/c Dr. To Cash A/c (Being Cash paid to Canara Bank)		20,000	20,000

3. Goods Purchased for cash Rs. 10,000
         ↓   ↓
      Real A/c   Real A/c

This is the cash transaction. The two aspects to be recorded are goods or purchase account and cash account. Both are related to Real Account. Now we apply Real Account rules.

Date	Particulars		Amount Dr.	Amount Cr.
2003, Jan 3	Purchase or goods A/c Dr. To Cash		10,000	10,000

PREPARATION OF FINAL ACCOUNTS

4. Purchase of goods worth Rs. 5,000 from Murali
   ↓ ↓ ↓
   Real A/c   Real A/c   Personal A/c

This is the credit transaction. But the above transaction affects three accounts.
Namely, (i) Good → Real Account
(ii) Amount → Real Account
(iii) Murali → Personal Account

Here, there is no need to give the effect on one Real Account [i.e., Amount – Real Account]. Because, at the time of purchase, there is no settlement of money.

Goods Account relates to the Real Account. As per the Real Account rules, Goods Account is to be debited.

Murali is the Personal Account. As per the Personal Account rules Murali is the giver. So his account is to be credited.

Date	Particulars		Amount Dr.	Amount Cr.
2003, Jan. 4	Goods or Purchase A/c To Murali Account	Dr.	5,000	5,000

Credit Transaction and Cash Transaction

If purchase and Sales Transaction bears a name means it is treated as credit transaction. And at the same time, even though there is a name, specifically mentioned cash means, it is treated as cash transaction.

5. Sold goods to Rajan Brothers for Rs. 10,000
   ↓ ↓ ↓
   Real A/c   Personal A/c   Real A/c

This is a credit transaction for two reasons :
   (i) Purchaser's name is given.
   (ii) There is no mention that it is cash transaction.

The above transaction affects the three Accounts. i.e.,
   (i) Real Account (goods)
   (ii) Personal Account (Rajan Brothers)
   (iii) Real Account (Amount).

In the three accounts, we have to give the effect on only two accounts
i.e., Goods account and Personal account.

Here, Rajan Brothers receives the goods, and goods go out from the business. So the journal entry will be

Date	Particulars		Amount Dr.	Amount Cr.
2003, Jan. 4	Rajan Brothers A/c To Goods or Sales A/c	Dr.	10,000	10,000

6. Sold goods worth Rs. 2,500
         ↓   ↓
     Real A/c   Real A/c

This is the cash transaction. The above transaction affects two accounts. *i.e.,*

(i) Real Account → goods
(ii) Real Account → Amount.

Amount of Rs. 2,500 is coming to the business. As per the Real Account rules, Debit when comes in. Here cash comes in. So cash account is debited and goods go out from the business. It is also a real account. As per the Real Account rules, Credit what goes out. Here goods go out from the business, so cash account is credited.

Date	Particulars		Amount Dr.	Amount Cr.
2003, Jan. 6	Cash A/c To Goods A/c	Dr.	2,500	2,500

7. Amount of Rs. 9,000 Received from Rajan Brothers as full settlement
                      ↓   ↓
                 Real A/c   Personal A/c

This transaction directly affects two accounts.

(i) Real Account (Amount)
(ii) (Personal Account) Rajan Brothers

    Indirectly, it affects one account *i.e.,* Nominal Account (Discount Account).

Actual sale of goods worth to Rajan Brothers	Rs. 10,000
Amount Received from Rajan Brothers	Rs. 9,000
The Amount treated as Discount A/c	Rs. 1,000

Here, we allow the discount to Rajan Brothers.

For receiving cash Rs. 9,000, Cash Account is to be debited. Discount is the Nominal Account. As per the Nominal Account rules Debit all expenses and losses. Here Discount is the Expenses. So Discount Account is to be debited in the value of Rs.1,000. Rajan brother is the giver, so his account is to be credited.

The journal entry will be

Date	Particulars		Amount Dr.	Amount Cr.
2003, Jan. 7	Cash A/c Discount A/c To Rajan Brothers A/c	Dr. Dr.	9,000 1,000	10,000

8. Paid Salaries Rs. 25,000
         ↓   ↓
   Nominal A/c Real A/c

PREPARATION OF FINAL ACCOUNTS

The transaction has to affect the two accounts. *i.e.,* (*i*) Salaries account relates to Nominal Account. Its rule is debit all expenses and losses and accordingly it is to be debited. (*ii*) Cash account relates to real account. Its rule is credit what goes out. Accordingly it is to be credited. Therefore the journal entry will be.

Date	Particulars		Amount Dr.	Amount Cr.
2003, Jan. 8	Salaries A/c To Cash A/c	Dr.	25,000	25,000

9. <u>Commission</u> Received Rs. <u>3,500</u>
    ↓   ↓
 Nominal A/c   Real A/c

The transaction is obviously by cash and is an income. So the two important aspects are commission and cash. (*i*) Commission account relates to Nominal Account. As per the Nominal account rules credit all incomes and gains, accordingly it is to be credited. (*ii*) Cash account relates to Real Account. As per the Real account rules Debit what comes in. Accordingly cash account is to be debited. The journal entry will be

Date	Particulars		Amount Dr.	Amount Cr.
2003, Jan. 9	Cash A/c To Commission A/c	Dr.	3,500	3,500

10. <u>Entertainment</u> expenses Rs. <u>1,000</u> paid
     ↓   ↓
   Nominal A/c   Real A/c

This is a cash transaction. Cash is going out and the entertainment is the expenditure. Cash relates to Real Account. As per Real Account Rules credit what goes out and accordingly it is to be credited. Entertainment relates to Nominal Account. Its rule is Debit all expenses and Losses. Accordingly, it is to be Debited. So the journal entry will be.

Date	Particulars		Amount Dr.	Amount Cr.
2003, Jan. 10	Entertainment Expn. A/c To Cash A/c	Dr.	1,000	1,000

Ledger

Ledger is a register having a number of pages which are numbered consecutively. Simply, ledger means consolidation of similar types of transactions under one head. In other words, a ledger may be defined as a summary statement of all the transactions relating to a person, asset, expenses or income which have taken place during a given period of time and show their net effect.

The process of preparation of accounts from the journal into ledger is called posting in the ledger. Examples of ledger accounts include sales account, purchase account, sales returns account, cash account, and so on.

Format of Ledger

Ledger can be divided into two parts (i) left hand side called debit side (Dr) and (ii) right hand side called credit side (Cr). Debit side starts with 'To' and credit side starts with 'By'. Most of the authors follow these practices.

Debit (Dr.)				Ledger			Credit (Cr.)
Date	Particulars	Folio	Amount	Date	Particulars	Folio	Amount

Posting of Journal Entry into Ledger

Problem 2. *Given the following journal entry, how do you post in into relevant ledger accounts.*

Date	Particulars	L.F.	Dr. Rs.	Cr. Rs.
2004, Jan 1	Cash A/c Dr. To Raju's Capital A/c [Being the business started]		75,000	75,000

Solution :

Cash Account

Dr.   Cr.

Date	Particulars	Folio	Amount	Date	Particulars	Folio	Amount
1.1.04	To Raju Capital A/c		75,000				

Capital Account

Dr.   Cr.

Date	Particular	Folio	Amount	Date	Particular	Folio	Amount
				1.1.04	By Cash A/c		75,000

How to Balance an account

First we have to compute the total on each side separately. Next the side which has the highest value, should be put on both side. Then, we have to find the difference from the lower value side. This value is called Balance c/d. This is the closing balance for the end of the given period. This is called Balance Brought down.

Problem 3. *Journalise the following transaction in the books of Kumar and prepare necessary ledger accounts :*

2004 Jan   1. Kumar started a Business with the capital of Rs.60,000.
           3. Amount Received from Bank Rs.10,000

PREPARATION OF FINAL ACCOUNTS

4. Purchased goods from Ravi for Rs.5,000
5. Returned goods to Ravi for Rs.1,000
6. Sold goods for cash Rs.5,000
9. Sold goods to Lakshman for Rs.3,500
10. Amount of Rs. 3,750 paid to Ravi as full settlement.
12. Lakshman returned the goods worth Rs.500. Complaint about damages
20. Paid Salaries Rs.2,500
21. Dividend Received Rs.1,000
22. Amount paid to Mohan through a bank at Rs.1,500
24. Withdraw money from business for private use Rs.1,000
30. Withdraw money from Bank for Business use Rs.3,000

Solution : **Journalisation** *(In the books of Kumar)*

Date	Particulars		L.F.	Dr. Rs.	Cr. Rs.
2003, Jan 1	Cash A/c To Kumar Capital A/c [Being the business started]	Dr.		60,000	60,000
3	Cash A/c To Bank A/c [Being the cash received from Bank]	Dr.		10,000	10,000
4	Goods A/c To Ravi A/c [Being Goods purchased from Ravi on credit basis]	Dr.		5,000	5,000
5	Ravi A/c To Purchase Return A/c [Being the goods returned to Ravi on account of damages]	Dr.		1,000	1,000
6	Cash A/c To Goods A/c [Being the goods sold for cash]	Dr.		5,000	5,000
9	Lakshman A/c To Goods A/c [Being the goods sold to Lakshman on the credit Basis]	Dr.		3,500	3,500

10	Ravi A/c
	    To Cash A/c
	    To Discount A/c
	[Being the payment of full Settlement]
		Dr.		4,000	3,750
					250

12	Sales Return A/c or Goods A/c To Lakshman A/c [Being the goods returned to Lakshman]	Dr.		500	500
20	Salaries A/c To Cash A/c [Being Salaries Paid]	Dr.		2,500	2,500
21	Cash A/c To Dividend A/c [Being Dividend Received]	Dr.		1,000	1,000
22	Mohan A/c To Bank A/c [Being amount paid to Mohan through bank]	Dr.		1,500	1,500
24	Drawing A/c To Cash A/c [Being withdrawn money from Business for private use]	Dr.		1,000	1,000
30	Cash A/c To Bank A/c [Being withdrawn money from bank for business use]	Dr.		3,000	3,000

Preparation of ledger Accounts

Cash Account

Dr.   Cr.

Date	Particulars	Folio	Amount	Date	Particulars	Folio	Amount
1.1.04	To Capital A/c		60,000	20.1.04	By Salaries		2,500
3.1.04	To Bank A/c		10,000	24.1.04	By Drawings		1,000
6.1.04	To Goods A/c		5,000	31.1.04	By Balance c/d		79,250
10.1.04	To Ravi A/c		3,750				
21.1.04	To Dividend A/c		1,000				
30.1.04	To Bank A/c		3,000				
			82,750				82,750
1.2.04	To Balance b/d		79,250				

Kumar Capital Account

Date	Particulars	Folio	Amount	Date	Particulars	Folio	Amount
31.1.04	To Balance c/d		60,000	1.1.04	By Cash A/c		60,000
			60,000				60,000
				1.1.04	By Balance b/d		60,000

PREPARATION OF FINAL ACCOUNTS

Bank Account

Date	Particulars	Folio	Amount	Date	Particulars	Folio	Amount
31.1.04	To Balance c/d		14,500	3.1.04	By Cash A/c		10,000
				22.1.04	By Mohan A/c		1,500
				30.1.04	By Cash A/c		3,000
			14,500				14,500
				1.2.04	By Balance b/d		14,500

Goods Account

Date	Particulars	Folio	Amount	Date	Particulars	Folio	Amount
4.1.04	To Ravi A/c		5,000	6.1.04	By Cash A/c		5,000
31.1.04	To Balance c/d		3,500	9.1.04	By Lakshman A/c		3,500
			8,500				8,500
				1.2.04	By Balance b/d		3,500

Ravi Account

Date	Particulars	Folio	Amount	Date	Particulars	Folio	Amount
5.1.04	To Purchase Return A/c		1,000	4.1.04	By Goods A/c		5,000
10.1.04	To Cash A/c		3,750				
	To Discount		250				
			5,000				5,000

Lakshman Account

Date	Particulars	Folio	Amount	Date	Particulars	Folio	Amount
9.1.04	To Goods A/c		3,500	12.1.04	By Sales Return A/c		500
				31.1.04	By Balance c/d		3,000
			3,500				3,500
1.2.04	By Balance b/d		3,000				

Discount Account

Date	Particulars	Folio	Amount	Date	Particulars	Folio	Amount
1.1.04	To Balance c/d		250	10.1.04	By Ravi		250
			250				250
				1.2.04	By Balance b/d		250

Sales Return Account

Date	Particulars	Folio	Amount	Date	Particulars	Folio	Amount
12.1.04	To Lakshman A/c		500	31.1.04	By Balance c/d		500
			500				500
1.2.04	To Balance b/d		500				

Salaries Account

Date	Particulars	Folio	Amount	Date	Particulars	Folio	Amount
20.1.04	To Cash A/c		2,500	31.1.04	By Balance c/d		2,500
			2,500				2,500
1.2.04	To Balance b/d		2,500				

Mohan Account

Date	Particulars	Folio	Amount	Date	Particulars	Folio	Amount
22.1.04	To Bank A/c		1,500	31.1.04	By Balance c/d		1,500
			1,500				1,500
1.2.04	To Balance b/d		1,500				

Drawing Account

Date	Particulars	Folio	Amount	Date	Particulars	Folio	Amount
24.1.04	To Cash A/c		1,000	31.1.04	By Balance c/d		1,000
			1,000				1,000
1.2.04	To Balance b/d		1,000				

Dividend Account

Date	Particular	Folio	Amount	Date	Particular	Folio	Amount
31.1.04	To Balance c/d		1,000	21.1.04	By Cash		1,000
			1,000				1,000
				1.2.04	By Balance b/d		1,000

From the above ledger accounts it can be noticed that
   (i) Ravi Account is settled.
   (ii) Some Accounts showing debit balances
   (iii) Some Accounts showing credit balance

PREPARATION OF FINAL ACCOUNTS

TRIAL BALANCE

Every transaction is recorded under double entry system. The fundamental Principle of Double entry system is that for every debit there must be a corresponding credit. All the ledger accounts are balanced. After arriving at the figures, total of all debit balances must be equaled to the total of credit balances if the accounts are arithmetically accurate.

At the end of the financial year, or at any time the balances of all the ledger accounts are extracted and written up, a statement is prepared which is known as Trial Balance.

Simply, Trial Balance is a settlement which is prepared in order to testify the arithmetical accuracy of entire financial transaction. Agreement of the Trial Balance exposes both the aspects of each transaction which have been recorded and that the books are arithmetically accurate. Suppose Trial Balance does not agree, it means there are errors which must be detected and rectified before preparing the final account. Trial Balance creates a link between ledger accounts and final accounts.

Aim of Trial Balance

1. To avoid unnecessary verification of all the pages of ledger.
2. It is a suitable and easy method of verifying the arithmetical accuracy of the entire transaction.
3. Trial Balance agrees only when the Debit side total is equal to credit side total. Otherwise, there are some errors.
4. It helps in the preparation of final Account. *i.e.,* Trading Accounts, Profit and Loss Account and Balance sheet.

Methods of preparing Trial Balance

There are two methods available for preparing Trial Balance.

1. Total Method   2. Balances Method

Under the total method, without balancing the ledgers, Debit and credit totals of each account are shown in the two columns *i.e.,* debit side total in the debit column of Trial balance and credit side total is put in the credit column of Trial Balance.

Under the Balances method, the balances are extracted from various ledgers. Simply Debit side of the ledger balance is transferred to Debit side of trial balance, credit side of the ledger balance is transferred to credit side of Trial Balance. The nil balance accounts are not taken into account in this method. So, this method is more convenient to adopt and to be followed at regular practice.

Rules

Debit side = Either Asset Account balances or Expenses Account balances
Credit side = Either Liability Account balances or Income Account balances

Format of Trial Balance

Trial Balance of …………………… as on ……………………

S.No.	Particulars	Debit Balance Amount (Rs.)	Credit Balance Amount (Rs.)

> **NOTE :** Generally whenever we prepare the Trial Balance, if it tallies, it is an indication that all the transactions recorded in the books are correct. Suppose if the trial balance disagrees, beyond our attention the difference amount is placed as in the suspense Account. Do attempt suspense account only in few cases.

Problem 4. *Prepare Trial Balance as on 31.03.2002 from the following balances of Mr. Ravi.*

Capital	1,00,000
Sales	1,50,000
Plant & Machinery	60,000
Purchases	50,000
Sales Returns	5,000
Wages	10,000
Sundry creditors	60,000
Bad debts	7,000
Bad debts provision	3,000
Land & Buildings	1,00,000
Debenture	45,000
Drawings	10,000
Commission Received	7,500
Auditor's fees	6,500
Purchase Return	10,000
Bills Payable	9,000
Carriage inwards	2,000
Goodwill	10,000
Reserve Fund	25,000
Wages & Salary	5,500
Carriage outwards	1,500
Stock on 01.04.2001	25,000
Debtors	49,000
Creditors	83,000
Interest Received	4,000
Travelling Expenses	5,000
Bank overdraft	3,000
Trade expenses	3,400
Motor vehicle	8,000
Rent received	2,000
Lease hold Property	60,600

Solution :
Trial Balance of Mr. Ravi as on 31st March 2002

Particulars	Debit (Rs.)	Credit (Rs.)
Capital	-	1,00,000
Sales	-	1,50,000
Plants & Machinery	60,000	-
Purchases	50,000	-
Sales Returns	5,000	-
Wages	10,000	-
Sundry Creditors	-	60,000
Bad Debts	7,000	-
Bad Debts Provision	-	3,000
Land & Buildings	1,00,000	-
Debentures	-	45,000
Drawings	10,000	-
Commission Received	-	7,500
Auditor's Fees	6,500	-
Purchase Return	-	10,000
Bills Payable	-	9,000
Carriage Inwards	2,000	-
Goodwill	10,000	-
Reserve Fund	-	25,000
Wages & Salary	5,500	-
Carriage Outwards	1,500	-
Stock 1.4.2001	25,000	-
Debtors	49,000	-
Interest Received	-	4,000
Travelling Expenses	5,000	-
Bank Overdraft	-	3,000
Trade Expenses	3,400	-
Motor Vehicle	8,000	-
Rent Received	-	2,000
Lease hold property	60,600	-
	4,18,500	4,18,500

Problem 5. *Prepare Trial Balance as on 31.03.2002 from the balances of Mr. Raju.*

Cash in hand 1,70,000
Building 1,60,000
Stock on 01.04.2001 70,000
Purchases 3,20,000
Sales Return 5,000

Commission Received 7,000
Interest on Drawings 5,000
Director's fees 2,000
Carriage inwards 4,000
Carriage outwards 3,000
Wages 2,000
Salaries wages 3,000
Investments 75,000
Sales 7,30,000
Preliminary expenses 5,000
Sundry Creditors 60,000
Bills Payable 30,000
Insurance 2,500
Income from Investment 3,500
Printing & Advertisement 15,000
Bank Loan 40,000
Freight on Purchase 5,000
Furniture & Fittings 18,000
Drawings Accounts 5,500
Deposits 86,000
Sundry Debtors 90,000
Bills receivables 35,000
Office Expenses 3,000
Motor Van 63,000
Loan on Mortgage 1,02,000
Interest on loan 4,500
General Expenses 6,500
Dividend Received 2,500
Interest (Cr) 1,000

Solution :   Trial Balance of Mr. Raju as on 31.03.2002

Particulars	Debit (Rs.)	Credit (Rs.)
Cash in Hand	1,70,000	-
Building	1,60,000	-
Stock 1.4.2001	70,000	-
Purchase	3,20,000	-
Sales Return	5,000	-
Commission Received	-	7,000
Interest on Drawings	-	5,000
Director's Fees	2,000	

PREPARATION OF FINAL ACCOUNTS

Carriage Inwards	4,000	-
Carriage Outwards	3,000	-
Wages	2,000	-
Salaries Wages	3,000	-
Investments	75,000	-
Sales	-	7,30,000
Preliminary Expenses	5,000	-
Sundry Creditors	-	60,000
Bills Payable	-	30,000
Insurance	2,500	-
Income from Investment	-	3,500
Printings and Advertisement	15,000	-
Bank Loan	-	40,000
Freight on Purchase	5,000	-
Furniture & Fittings	18,000	-
Deposits	-	86,000
Drawings Account	5,500	-
Sundry Debtors	90,000	-
Bills Receivables	35,000	-
Office Expenses	3,000	-
Motor Van	63,000	-
Loan on mortgage	-	1,02,000
Interest on loan	4,500	-
General Expenses	6,500	-
Dividend Received	-	2,500
Interest (Cr.)	-	1,000
	10,67,000	10,67,000

> **NOTE :** Before the preparation of the Final Account, we have to know the following concepts and their specifications. Because these four concepts are the fundamentals to all the proceedings of Accounting, either for Trial Balance or for Final Account.

I. Income

Money earned by the concern due to rendering of services or sale of goods.

Example/Specifications :

Commission Received	Interest on Investment Received
Rent Received	Apprentice Premium Received
Dividend Received	Rent Received on sub letting
Interest on Drawings	Rent from Tenants
Sales	Income from any other sources
Bad Debts Recovered	Miscellaneous Revenue Receipt
Interest Received	Salary Received

II. Expenses

Expenses are those which can be incurred *i.e.,* amount paid for the purpose of purchasing of goods or those who render services in our organisation.

Wages paid	Carriage inwards
Salaries Paid	Carriage outwards
Commission Paid	Freight on purchases
Rent Paid	Customs Duty
Interest Paid	Advertisement Expenses paid
Oil, Water	Interest on Bank loan
Gas, Electricity Charges Paid	Interest on Capital.

Drawings	Discount on Bills
Office Salaries	Loss of Fire not covered by the
Telephone Charges	Insurance company.
Legal Charges	Manager's remuneration
Audit Fees	Insurance
General Expenses	Bad Debts
Discount allowed	Agents Commission
Selling and Distribution Expenses	

III. Assets

Anything which possesses certain monetary value is called Assets.

Example :

Current Assets	Fixed Assets	Others
Cash in hand and at Bank	Land & Buildings	Preliminary Expenses
Sundry Debtors	Machinery	Goodwill
Bills Receivable	Furniture & Fittings	Patents and Trade Mark
Stock in Trade	Loose tools and spares	Prepaid Expenses
Short Term Investments	Investments	
Marketable Securities	Motor van	
Accrued Incomes		
Prepaid Expenses		

IV. Liabilities

A Business organisation which is liable to pay a certain sum of money to the outsiders is called liabilities.

Example :

Capital	Bank overdraft
Reserve Fund	Outstanding expenses
Debenture	Deposits
Bank loan	Incomes received in advance
Mortgage loan	Expenses due but not paid
Sundry Creditors	Proposed Dividend
Bills Payable	Provision for Taxation

PREPARATION OF FINAL ACCOUNTS

FINAL ACCOUNTS

Final Accounts are otherwise called Annual accounts. Normally Final Accounts are prepared at the end of the financial year or Accounting year. The purpose of preparing Final Accounts is to enable one to know the progress of the business, profit or loss and financial position of the firm at the right time.

The preparation of Final Account is not the first step of the Accounting process but it is the final product of the accounting process. It will give valuable information to the management and outsiders at the end of the Accounting period. Only after the preparation of Trial Balance it is possible to prepare Final Account. Final Account consists of the following parts.

1. Trading Account, 2. Profit and Loss Account, 3. Balance Sheet.

1. Trading Account

Trading Account is prepared to know the trading results or gross profit on trading of the business. Simply, it is to find out the gross profit from business due to buying and selling of goods or services during a particular period. In other words, Gross profit is the difference between the sales and the cost of goods sold.

In business, the expenditure and incomes are classified into Direct and Indirect. All the direct expenditure are debited into the debit side of the Trading Account and all the indirect incomes are credited into the credit side of the Trading Account. After transferring all the above details, we have to balance the Trading Account. If the balance is in the debit side it means the business is getting profit and named as Gross profit. Suppose the balance is in the credit side, it shows Loss and it is called Gross Loss. The Gross Profit or Gross Loss is transferred to the profit and Loss Account either on the Credit side or Debit side.

2. Profit and Loss Account

Profit and Loss Account is prepared to find out the net profit or net loss of the business. All the indirect incomes and expenditure are transferred to the Profit and Loss Account on the credit side and debit side respectively. After transferring all details to the Profit and Loss Account, we balance this account. If the balance is in debit side it is called Net profit. Suppose, the balance is in the credit side it is called as Net Loss. Net profit is transferred to the balance sheet Liabilities side and added to the capital. If it is Net Loss it will be deducted from the capital.

3. Balance Sheet

A Balance Sheet is a statement which is prepared for the purpose of finding out the Assets and liability position of the concern for the particular period. A Balance Sheet is also described as "Statement showing the sources and application of funds." It is a statement and not an account and prepared from real and personal Accounts. It has two sides. The left side of the balance sheet describes the Liabilities and Capital position. The right hand side of the balance sheet describes all the assets and investments.

Trading, Profit & Loss Account disclose the financial results of the concern at the end of the year. But the Balance Sheet discloses the Assets and Liability Position of the Concern as on the date.

Specimen form of Final Account Trading Account for the year ended ......31.3.

Dr.   Cr.

Particulars	Amount Rs.	Amount Rs.	Particulars	Amount Rs.	Amount Rs.
To Opening Stock		xx	By Sales	xx	
To Purchase	xx		Less : Sales Return	xx	xx
Less : Purchase Return	xx	xx	By Closing Stock		xx
			By Goods destroyed		
To Wages		xx	by fire		xx
To Carriage inward		xx	By Gross Loss		xx
To Manufacturing			[Transferred to P&L		
Expenses		xx	A/c debit side)		
To Fuel and Power		xx			
To Motive Power		xx			
To Coal, Water, Gas					
& Electricity		xx			
To Clearing Charges		xx			
To Import Duty		xx			
To Customs Duty		xx			
To Freight on Purchase		xx			
To Factory Rent					
and Insurance		xx			
To Works Managers					
Salary		xx			
To Gross Profit (B/f)		xx			
(Transferred to P&L A/c					
Credit Side)		xx			xx

Profit and Loss Account for the year ended 31.3

Dr.   Cr.

Particulars	Amount Rs.	Amount Rs.	Particulars	Amount Rs.	Amount Rs.
To Gross Loss			By Gross Profit		
(Transferred from			(Transferred from		
Trading A/c)		xx	Trading A/c)		xx
To Advertisement			By Rent received		xx
Expenses		xx			
To Carriage outwards		xx	By Commission received		xx
To Bank Charges		xx	By Income from		
			Investments		xx
To Salaries		xx	By Interest received		xx
To Rent and Taxes		xx	By Discount received		xx
To Stationeries		xx	By Income from		
			another source		xx
To Insurance		xx	By Discount on creditors		xx
To Trade Expenses		xx	By Interest on Drawings		xx
To Interest on Capital		xx	By All Business income		
To Interest on Loan		xx	Other than that		

PREPARATION OF FINAL ACCOUNTS

	Amount Rs.		Amount Rs.
To Establishment Expenses	xx	appeared in Trading Account credit side	xx
To Selling & Distribution Expn.	xx	By Net Loss	xx
To Sundry Expenses	xx	(Transferred to Balance sheet assets side)	
To Audit Fees	xx		
To Telephone Charges	xx		
To Depreciation	xx		
To Repair and Maintenance	xx		
To Bad Debts	xx		
To Bad Debts provision	xx		
To Loss on sale of fixed Assets	xx		
To Loss on stock by fire	xx		
To Agents Commission	xx		
To Discount on Debtors	xx		
To All Business Expenses (Other than that appeared in Trading Account debit side)			
By Net Profit	xx		
(Transferred to Balance sheet Liability side)	xx		xx

Balance Sheet as on 31.3

Dr.   Cr.

Liabilities	Amount Rs.	Amount Rs.	Assets	Amount Rs.	Amount Rs.
Capital		xx	Cash in Hand		xx
Add : Net Profit		xx	Cash at Bank		xx
		xx	Sundry Debtors		xx
(−) Less : Drawings	xx				
+ Interest on Drawings	xx	xx	Investments		xx
		xx	Marketable Securities		xx
Add : Interest on Capital		xx	Bills Receivable		xx
Less : Income Tax		xx	Prepaid Expenses		xx
		xx	Machinery		xx
Sundry Creditors		xx	Building		xx
Bills Payable		xx	Furniture and Fittings		xx
Bank Overdraft		xx	Loose tools		xx
Outstanding expenses		xx	Motor Car		xx
Loan from Banks		xx	House & Carts		xx
Mortgage		xx	Goodwill Patents & Trade Mark		xx
Debenture		xx	Preliminary Expenses		xx
Reserve fund		xx	Profit & Loss A/c		
Income Received in advance		xx	(Net Loss)		xx
			Closing Stock		xx

ADJUSTMENT

The ultimate aim of the Trading and Profit and Loss Account is to know the real Profit or Loss of the concern during a given period. The purpose of the Balance sheet is to know the financial position at a given period. True profit can be arrived at after adjusting all pending bills and outstanding expenses and incomes through entries. These entries which are passed at the end of the accounting period are called adjustment entries. The following important adjustments which are to be made at the end of the year are as follows.

Important Adjustments

1. Closing stock
2. Outstanding expenses
3. Prepaid or unexpired expenses
4. Income earned but not received or Accrued income
5. Income received in advance
6. Depreciation
7. Interest on capital
8. Interest on drawings
9. Interest on loan
10. Bad debts
11. Provision for bad and doubtful debts
12. Provision for discount on debtors
13. Provision for discount on creditors
14. Goods distributed as free of sample
15. Loss of stock by fire

In the actual sense all the above adjustments are given outside the Trial Balance. While preparing the Final accounts all the adjustments are to be considered. Normally all the adjustments will appear at two places in the final accounts *i.e.,* either

(*i*) Trading Account and Balance Sheet or

(*ii*) Profit & Loss Account and Balance Sheet

Adjustment and their Treatment

1. *Closing Stock*

   Trading Account — Credit side

   Balance Sheet — Asset side.

2. *Outstanding Expenses*

   Trading or Profit & Loss A/c — Debit side

   Balance Sheet — Liability side

3. *Prepaid Expenses*

   Profit & Loss Account — Credit side

   (subtract from respective expenses)

   Balance Sheet — Asset side

PREPARATION OF FINAL ACCOUNTS

4. *Income Due but not Received*
    Profit & Loss Account   -   Credit side
    (Add with respective incomes)
    Balance Sheet   -   Asset side
5. *Income Received in Advance*
    Profit and Loss Account   -   Credit side
    (Subtract from respective incomes)
    Balance sheet   -   Liability side
6. *Depreciation*
    Profit and Loss Account   -   Debit side
    Balance Sheet   -   Liability side
    (Subtract from respective Assets)
7. *Interest on Capital*
    Profit and Loss Account   -   Debit side
    Balance Sheet   -   Liability side (Add the capital)
8. *Interest on Drawings*
    Profit and Loss Account   -   Credit side
    Balance Sheet   -   Liability side (Subtract from the capital)
9. *Interest on Loan*
    Profit and Loss Account   -   Debit side
    Balance Sheet   -   Liability side
                                          (Add with the respective loan)
10. *Bad Debts*
    Profit and Loss Account   -   Debit side
    Balance Sheet   -   Asset side
    (Subtract from the sundry debtors)
11. *Provision for Bad and Doubtful Debts*
    Regarding the Bad debts and provision for Bad and doubtful debts we have to apply the following formula.

BD + NR − OR

BD : It refers to the bad debts. It should be given either Trial Balance or Adjustments or both. The value of bad debts is transferred to formula for calculation. The calculated value should be transferred either to debit side or credit side of the P.L & A/c.

Bad Debts (Adjustment)
Treatment :
(*i*) B/S Asset side [Subtract from Debtors], (*ii*) Transfer to formula [P.L & A/c]

NR : It refers to New Reserve. Normally it should be give in the adjustment, in the name of provision for doubtful debts or reserves on debtors and so on.

Treatment :
(*i*) Transfer to formula, (*ii*) Balance Sheet : Asset side (Subtract from the Debtors)

OR : It represents old reserve. Normally, bad debts provision *i.e.,* old reserve is given in the Trial Balance. The treatment is that it should be transferred to the formula for calculating new bad debts provision.

After finding the value, to apply the formula it should be transferred to P.L & A/c either debit side or credit side.

12. *Provision for Discount on Debtors*
    - Profit & Loss Accounts Debit Side
    - Balance Sheet Asset side [Deduct from sundry debtors]

13. *Provision for Discount on Creditors*
    - Profit & Loss Accounts Credit Side
    - Balance Sheet Liability side [Deduct from sundry creditors]

14. *Goods Distributed as free of samples*
    - Trading Accounts Debit Side [Deduct Purchases]
    - Profit & Loss Accounts Debit Side (treated as advertisement expenditure).

15. *Loss of Stock by fire*
    (a) **If Insurance Company admitted the full claim**
        Trading Account credit side (Total stock value destroyed by fire)
        Balance Sheet Asset side (Insurance Company Accounts)
    (b) **If Insurance Company admitted the part of the claim :** (for example 60%)
        Trading Account credit side (Total stock value Destroyed by fire) (100%)
        Profit and Loss Account Debit side (Loss by fire) (40%)
        Balance Sheet Asset side (Insurance Company Account) (60%)

Problem 6. *The following figures are available relating to the business of Shri Vel for the year 2002.*

	Rs.
Opening stock	25,000
Purchases	92,000
Direct expenses	4,000
Closing stock	29,600
Sales	1,38,000

Calculate (i) Cost of goods sold and (ii) Gross Profit.

Solution :
(i) Cost of goods sold = Opening stock + Purchases + Direct Expen – Closing Stock
   = Rs. 25,000 + 92,000 + 4,000 – 29,600
   = **Rs. 91,400**
(ii) Gross Profit = Sales – Cost of goods sold
   = 1,38,000 – 91,400
   = **Rs. 46,600**

Problem 7. *Prepare Trading Account from the following Balances :*

	Rs.
Opening stock	80,000
Purchases	3,00,000
Sales	4,50,000
Purchase Returns	10,000
Sales Returns	20,000

Wages 5,000
Carriage & Freight 15,000
Freight on purchases 12,000

Solution :

Trading Account

Dr.   Cr.

Particulars	Amount Rs.	Amount Rs.	Particulars	Amount Rs.	Amount Rs.
To Opening Stock		80,000	By Sales	4,50,000	
To Purchases	3,00,000		Less : Sales Returns	20,000	4,30,000
Less : Purchase Returns	10,000	2,90,000			
To Wages		5,000			
To Carriage & Freight		15,000			
To Freight on Purchase		12,000			
To Gross Profit		28,000			
		4,30,000			4,30,000

Problem 8. *From the following balances extracted at the close of trading period ended on 31.3.2003, prepare profit and Loss Account as on that date.*

	Rs.		Rs.
Gross profit	90,000	Discount Dr	1,000
Carriage outward	5,000	Apprentice Premium (cr)	3,000
Salaries	11,000	Advertisement	1,000
Rent & Taxes	4,000	Travelling expenses	750
Fire insurance premium	3,000	Sundry Trade expenses	500
Bad debts	2,500		

Solution :

Profit and Loss Account

Dr.   Cr.

Particulars	Amount Rs.	Amount Rs.	Particulars	Amount Rs.	Amount Rs.
To Carriage outwards		5,000	By Gross Profit		90,000
To Salaries		11,000	By Apprentice		
To Rent & Taxes		4,000	Premium		3,000
To Fire Insurance Premium		3,000			
To Bad Debts		2,500			
To Discount		1,000			
To Travelling Expenses		750			
To Sundry Trade Expenses		500			
To Advertisement		1,000			
To Net Profit		64,250			
		93,000			93,000

Problem 9. *From the following Trial balances of Mr. Ragunath for the year ending on 31.12.2003, prepare Final Accounts with the closing stock of Rs. 15,000.*

Particulars	Debit Rs.	Credit Rs.
Stock (1.1.2003)	46,800	-
Returns inwards	10,000	-
Purchases	2,40,000	-
Rents & Rates	4,000	-
Sales	-	3,21,900
Debenture	-	25,000
Reserve fund	-	45,000
Sundry Debtors	60,000	-
Salaries	3,000	-
Commission Received	-	4,900
Bad debts	2,000	-
Bad debts provision	-	6,000
Wages	6,000	-
Return outwards	-	2,000
Bills receivable	25,000	-
Investments	60,000	-
Sundry Creditors	-	20,000
Bank overdraft	-	5,000
Cash in hand	11,000	-
Goodwill	26,000	-
Capital	-	63,000
Furniture	15,000	-
General expenses	2,000	-
Discount (cr)	-	18,000
	5,10,800	5,10,800

Solution : Trading Account for the year ended 31.12.2003

Particulars	Rs.	Rs.	Particulars	Rs.	Rs.
To Opening Stock		46,800	By Sales	3,21,900	
To Purchases	2,40,000		Less : Sales Returns	10,000	
Less : Return Outwards	2,000	2,38,000			3,11,900
To Wages		6,000	By Closing Stock		15,000
To Gross Profit		36,100			
		3,26,900			3,26,900

PREPARATION OF FINAL ACCOUNTS

Profit and Loss Account for the year ended 31.12.2003

	Rs.	Rs.		Rs.	Rs.
To Rent & Rates		4,000	By Gross Profit		36,100
To Salaries		3,000	By Commission		
To Bad Debts		2,000	Received		4,900
To General Expenses		2,000	By Discount (Cr.)		18,000
To Net Profit		48,000			
		59,000			59,000

Balance Sheet as on 31.12.2003

Liabilities	Amount Rs.	Amount Rs.	Assets	Amount Rs.	Amount Rs.
Capital		63,000	Sundry Debtors		60,000
Debenture		25,000	Bills Receivable		25,000
Reserve Fund		45,000	Investments		60,000
Bad Debts Provision		6,000	Cash in Hand		11,000
Sundry Creditors		20,000	Goodwill		26,000
Bank Overdraft		5,000	Furniture		15,000
Profit Loss A/c		48,000	Closing Stock		15,000
		2,12,000			2,12,000

Problems 10. *From the following Trial Balance of Mr.X, prepare the final accounts for the year ended on 31.12.1996.*

Debit Balance	Rs.	Credit Balance	Rs.
Land and Building	50,000	Returns	2,500
Purchases	1,10,000	Discounts	1,200
Stock	40,000	Sales	2,05,000
Returns	1,500	Capital	1,15,000
Wages	10,000	Loan	15,000
Salaries	9,000	Commission	1,500
Office Expenses	2,400	Creditors	25,000
Carriage	3,200	Bills Payable	2,350
Discounts	750		
Bad Debts	1,200		
Insurance	1,500		
Machinery	50,000		
Furniture	10,000		
Bills Receivable	20,000		
Sundry Debtors	40,000		
Cash	6,000		
Office Equipment	12,000		
	3,67,550		3,67,550

The following adjustments are to be made :
(a) Closing stock Rs. 60,000
(b) Outstanding wages Rs. 2,000 and Rent Rs. 3,000
(c) Depreciate land and buildings at 5%, Machinery at 10%, office equipment and furniture by 10%
(d) Provide Reserve at 2 1/2% on debtors.
(e) Insurance prepaid Rs. 200
(f) Calculate interest on capital at 5%.   [MBA Nov. 1997, Madras]

Solution :

Trading Account of Mr. X for the year ended 31.12.1996

Particulars	Rs.	Rs.	Particulars	Rs.	Rs.
To Opening Stock		40,000	By Sales	2,05,000	
To Purchases	1,10,000		Less : Sales Returns	1,500	2,03,500
(−) Returns	2,500	1,07,500	By Closing Stock		60,000
To Wages	10,000				
(+) Outstanding	2,000	12,000			
To Carriage		3,200			
To Gross Profit		1,00,800			
		2,63,500			2,63,500

Profit and Loss Account of Mr. X for the year ended 31.12.1996

Particulars	Rs.	Rs.	Particulars	Rs.	Rs.
To Salaries		9,000	By Gross Profit		1,00,800
To Office Expenses		2,400	By Commission		1,500
To Discounts		750	By Discounts		1,200
To Bad Debts Provision		2,200			
To Rent Outstanding		3,000			
To Insurance	1,500				
(−) Prepaid	200	1,300			
To Depreciation :					
5% on Land & Building	2,500				
10% on Machinery	5,000				
10% on Office Equipment	1,200				
10% on Furniture	1,000	9,700			
To Interest on capital		5,750			
To Net Profit		69,400			
(Transfer to Balance Sheet)					
		1,03,500			1,03,500

Balance Sheet of Mr. X as on 31.12.1996

Liabilities	Amount Rs.	Amount Rs.	Assets	Amount Rs.	Amount Rs.
Capital	1,15,000		Cash		6,000
+ Interest on Capital	5,750	1,20,750	Land & Building	50,000	
Loan		15,000	(−) Depreciation	2,500	47,500
Creditors		25,000	Machinery	50,000	
Bills Payable		2,350	(−) Depreciation	5,000	45,000
Outstanding Wages		2,000	Furniture	10,000	
Outstanding Rent		3,000	(−) Depreciation	1,000	9,000
Net Profit (P&L) A/c		69,400	Bills Receivable		20,000
			Sundry Debtors	40,000	
			(−) New Reserve	1,000	39,000
			Office Equipment	12,000	
			(−) Depreciation	1,200	10,800
			Closing Stock		60,000
			Prepaid Insurance		200
		2,37,500			2,37,500

NOTE: Bad Debts

BD + NR − OR
↓   ↓   ↓
1200 1000   0   = 2200

Problem 11. *The following balances are drawn from the books of M/s Arvind Mills as on 31.12.1997.*

Account	Amount Rs.
Land	1,00,000
Building	2,00,000
Sales	3,00,000
Purchases	1,75,000
Sales returns	10,000
Purchase returns	5,000
Stock (1.1.97)	25,000
Debtors	50,000
Bank overdraft	15,200
Cash on hand	5,000
Creditors	20,000
Salaries	10,000
Wages	12,000
Goodwill	15,000
General Expenses	5,000

Selling expenses 12,000
Bad debts 1,000
Insurance 1,200
Capital 2,81,000

The following adjustments are to be made :
(a) Closing stock is Rs. 30,000.
(b) Provide depreciation at the rate of 10% on buildings.
(c) Write off further bad debts Rs. 1,000.
(d) Salaries yet to be paid Rs. 3,000.
(e) Insurance prepaid Rs. 300

You are required to prepare a Trading and Profit and loss account and balance sheet of M/s Arvind Mills. [MBA April 1998, Madras]

Solution :

Trading Account of M/s. Arvind Mills for the year ended 31.12.1997

Particulars	Rs.	Rs.	Particulars	Rs.	Rs.
To Opening Stock		25,000	By Sales		3,00,000
To Purchase	1,75,000		(–) Sales Returns		10,000
(–) Purchase Returns	5,000	1,70,000			2,90,000
To Wages		12,000	By Closing Stock		30,000
To Gross Profit		1,13,000			
		3,20,000			3,20,000

Profit and Loss Account of M/s. Arvind Mills for the year ended 31.12.1997

Particulars	Rs.	Rs.	Particulars	Rs.	Rs.
To Salaries	10,000		By Gross Profit		1,13,000
(+) Outstanding	3,000	13,000			
To General Expenses		5,000			
To Selling Expenses		12,000			
To Bad Debts					
(1000 + 1000)		2,000			
To Insurance	1,200				
(–) Prepaid	300	900			
To Depreciation on					
Building 10%		20,000			
To Net Profit		60,100			
		1,13,000			1,13,000

Balance Sheet of M/s. Arvind Mills as on 31.12.1997

Liabilities	Amount Rs.	Amount Rs.	Assets	Amount Rs.	Amount Rs.
Capital	2,81,000		Cash on Hand		5,000
(+) Net Profit	60,100	3,41,100	Land		1,00,000
Bank Overdraft		15,200	Building	2,00,000	
Creditors		20,000	(–) Depreciation	20,000	1,80,000
Outstanding Salary		3,000	Debtors	50,000	
			(–) Further Bad debts	1,000	49,000
			Goodwill		15,000
			Closing Stock		30,000
			Prepaid Insurance		300
		3,79,300			3,79,300

Problem 12. *From the following Trial Balance, prepare the Trading and Profit and Loss Account of Mr. Kumaran for the year ended December 31, 1993 and the Balance Sheet as on that date.*

Particulars	Debit Rs.	Credit Rs.
Kumaran's Capital	—	4,000
Plant and Machinery	5,000	—
Office Furniture and fittings	260	—
Stocks on January 1, 1993	4,800	—
Motor van	1,200	—
Sundry Debtors	4,470	—
Cash in hand	40	—
Cash at Bank	650	—
Wages	15,000	—
Salaries	1,400	—
Purchases	21,350	—
Sales	—	48,000
Bills Receivable	720	—
Bills Payable	—	560
Sundry Creditors	—	5,200
Returns Inwards	930	—
Provision for doubtful debts	—	250
Drawings	700	—
Returns outwards	—	550
Rent	600	—
Factory Lighting and heating	80	—
Insurance	680	—
General Expenses	250	—
Bad Debts	200	—
Discount	650	420
	58,980	58,980

The following adjustments are to be made :
(i) Stock on December 31, 1993 Rs. 5,200
(ii) 3 months factory lighting and heating is due but not paid Rs. 30/-
(iii) 5% depreciation to be written off on furniture
(iv) Write off further bad debts Rs. 70.
(v) The provision for doubts is to be increased to Rs.300 and provision for discount on debtors be provided at 2%. [MBA Nov 1995, Madras]

Solution :

Trading Account of Mr. Kumaran for the year ended 31.12.1993

Particulars	Rs.	Rs.	Particulars	Rs.	Rs.
To Opening Stock		4,800	By Sales	48,000	
To Purchases	21,350		Less : Sales Returns	930	47,070
Less : Return Outwards	550	20,800	By Closing Stock		5,200
To Wages		15,000			
To Factory lighting and heating	80				
Add : Outstanding	30	110			
To Gross Profit		11,560			
		52,270			52,270

Profit and Loss Account of Mr. Kumaran for the year ended 31.12.1993

Particulars	Rs.	Rs.	Particulars	Rs.	Rs.
To Salaries		1,400	By Gross Profit		11,560
To Rent		600	By Discount		420
To Insurance		680			
To General Expenses		250			
To Discount		650			
To Bad Debts & Provisions		320			
To Depreciation on Furniture		13			
To Discount on Debtors		82			
To Net Profit		7,985			
		11,980			11,980

PREPARATION OF FINAL ACCOUNTS

Balance Sheet of Mr. Kumaran as on 31.12.1993

Liabilities	Amount Rs.	Amount Rs.	Assets	Amount Rs.	Amount Rs.
Capital	4,000		Cash in hand		40
(−) Drawings	700		Cash at Bank		650
	3,300		Plant & Machinery		5,000
(+) Net Profit	7,985	11,285	Office Furniture & Fittings	260	
			(−) Depreciation	13	247
Bills Payable		560	Motor Van		1,200
Sundry Creditors		5,200	Bills Receivable		720
Outstanding Factory Lighting and Heating		30	Closing Stock		5,200
			Sundry Debtors	4,470	
			(−) Bad Debts	70	
				4,400	
			(−) Provision for Doubtful Debts	300	
				4,100	
			(−) Discount on Debtors	82	4,018
		17,075			17,075

Note for bad debts : BD + NR − OR = $\frac{200}{70}$ + 300 − 250 = 320.

Problem 13. *From the following Trial Balance and given information, you are requested to prepare Final Account for the year ended on 31.12.1997.*

Dr.	Rs.	Cr.	Rs.
Purchases	11,870	Capital	8,000
Debtors	7,580	Bad Debts recovered	250
Return inwards	450	Creditors	1,250
Bank Deposit	2,750	Return outwards	350
Rent	360	Bank Overdraft	1,570
Salaries	850	Sales	14,690
Travelling Expenses	300	Bills Payable	1,350
Cash	210		
Stock	2,450		
Discount allowed	40		
Drawings	600		
	27,460		27,460

The following adjustments are to be made :
(a) The closing stock on 31.12.1997 was Rs. 4,200.
(b) Write off Rs. 80 as bad debts and create a reserve for bad debts at 5% on sundry debtors.

(c) Three months rent is outstanding.
(d) Interest on Bank deposit Rs. 135 credited by the bankers and interest on overdraft Rs. 157 debited by them in the pass book have not been entered in the books.

[MCA 1999 Dec.]

Solution : **Trading Account for the year ended 31.12.1997**

Particulars	Rs.	Rs.	Particulars	Rs.	Rs.
To Opening Stock		2,450	By Sales	14,690	
To Purchases	11870		Less : Sales Returns	450	14,240
Less : Return Outwards	350	11,520			
			By Closing Stock		4,200
To Gross Profit		4,470			
		18,440			18,440

Profit and Loss Account for the year ended 31.12.1997

Particulars	Rs.	Rs.	Particulars	Rs.	Rs.
To Rent	360		By Gross Profit		4,470
(+) Outstanding (3×30)	90	450	By Bad Debts Recovered		250
To Salaries		850	By Interest on Bank Deposit		135
To Travelling Expenses		300			
To Discount Allowed		40			
To Bad Debts & Provisions (80+375)		455			
To Interest on Overdraft		157			
To Net Profit		2,603			
		4,855			4,855

Balance Sheet as on 31.12.1997

Liabilities	Amount Rs.	Amount Rs.	Assets	Amount Rs.	Amount Rs.
Capital	8,000		Cash		210
(−) Drawings	600		Debtors	7,580	
	7,400		(−) Bad Debts	80	
(+) Net Profit	2,603	10,003		7,500	
			(−) New Reserve	375	7,125
Creditors		1,250			
Bank Overdraft	1,570		Bank Deposit	2,750	
+ Interest Outstanding	157	1,727	+ Outstanding Interest	135	2,885
Bills Payable		1,350	Closing Stock		4,200
Rent Outstanding		90			
		14,420			14,420

PREPARATION OF FINAL ACCOUNTS 49

Note for bad debts : Drs : 7,580
                     (−) Bad Debts 80

BD + NR − OR   7,500
                     (−) NR (7500 × 5/100) 375
                                   -----
80 + 375 − 0 = 455   7,125

Problem 14. *From the following Trial Balance of Krishna Bros as on 31st December 1998, prepare Trading and Profit and Loss Account and a Balance sheet :*

                                                                Rs.
Credit Balance
    Capital 36,000
    Creditors 8,720
    Bills payable 2,528
    Sales 78,182
    Loan 12,000
Debit Balance
    Debtors 3,885
    Salaries 4,000
    Discount 1,000
    Postage 273
    Bad debts 287
    Interest 1,295
    Insurance 417
    Machinery 10,000
    Stock on 1st January 9,945
    Purchases 62,092
    Wages 4,300
    Buildings 23,780
    Fixtures and fittings 16,156
    Closing stock on 31st December 1998 was 14,300

[M.Sc ISM May 2000]

Solution :

Trading Account of Krishna Brothers for the year ended 31.12.1998

Particulars	Rs.	Rs.	Particulars	Rs.	Rs.
To Opening Stock		9,945	By Sales		78,182
To Purchases		62,092	By Closing Stock		14,300
To Wages		4,300			
To Gross Profit		16,145			
		92,482			92,482

Profit and Loss Account of Krishna Brothers for the year ended 31.12.1998

Particulars	Rs.	Rs.	Particulars	Rs.	Rs.
To Salaries		4,000	By Gross Profit		16,145
To Discount		1,000			
To Postage		273			
To Bad Debts		287			
To Interest		1,295			
To Insurance		417			
To Net Profit		8,873			
		16,145			16,145

Balance Sheet of Krishna Brothers as on 31.12.1998

Liabilities	Amount Rs.	Amount Rs.	Assets	Amount Rs.	Amount Rs.
Capital		36,000	Debtors		3,885
Creditors		8,720	Machinery		10,000
Bills Payable		2,528	Buildings		23,780
Loan		12,000	Fixtures & Fittings		16,156
Profit & Loss A/c		8,873	Closing Stock		14,300
		68,121			68,121

Problem 15. *Following are the balances extracted from the books of Mohammad as on 31st December 1998. Prepare Final Account as on the date.*

	Rs.		Rs.
Capital	20,000	Drawings	5,000
Cash on Hand	5,000	Cash at Bank	8,000
Buildings	20,000	Machinery	6,000
Stock on 01.01.1998	3,000	Sundry Debtors	8,000
Sundry Creditors	6,000	Repairs	400
Commission paid	700	Wages	1,700
Rent and Rates	300	Insurance Premium	300
Purchases	60,000	Sales	96,000
Purchases Returns	750	Sales Returns	400
Furniture & Fixtures	1,600	Carriage	200
Loan to Ram	1,000	Telephone Charges	250
Discount allowed	50	Salaries	600
Bad Debts	350	Discount earned	100

[M.Sc.ITM Dec.1999]

PREPARATION OF FINAL ACCOUNTS

Solution :

Trading Account of Mr. Mohammad for the year ended 31.12.1998

Particulars	Rs.	Rs.	Particulars	Rs.	Rs.
To Opening Stock		3,000	By Sales	96,000	
To Purchase	60,000		(–) Sales Returns	400	95,600
(–) Purchase Returns	750	59,250			
To Wages		1,700			
To Carriage		200			
To Gross Profit		31,450			
		95,600			95,600

Profit and Loss Account of Mr. Mohammad for the year ended 31.12.1998

Particulars	Rs.	Rs.	Particulars	Rs.	Rs.
To Repairs		400	By Gross Profit		31,450
To Commission Paid		700	By Discount earned		100
To Rent & Rates		300			
To Discount allowed		50			
To Bad Debts		350			
To Insurance Premium		300			
To Telephone Charges		250			
To Salaries		600			
To Net Profit		28,600			
		31,550			31,550

Balance Sheet of Mr. Mohammad as on 31.12.1998

Liabilities	Amount Rs.	Amount Rs.	Assets	Amount Rs.	Amount Rs.
Capital	20,000		Cash in Hand		5,000
(–) Drawings	5,000	15,000	Cash at Bank		8,000
			Buildings		20,000
Sundry Creditors		6,000	Machinery		6,000
Net Profit		28,600	Sundry Debtors		8,000
(Profit & Loss A/c)			Furniture Fixtures		1,600
			Loan to Ram		1,000
		49,600			49,600

Problem 16. *The following balance has been extracted from the books of Mr. Ganesh on 31.12.1997.*

	Rs.		Rs.
Capital	15,000	Loans Borrowed	20,000
Drawings	4,800	Stock (1.1.97)	7,500
Machinery	20,000	Purchases	60,000
Furniture	1,500	Sales	90,000

Sundry Debtors	20,000	Office Rent	1,000
Sundry Creditors	13,000	Insurance	240
Interest (Dr.)	1,250	Discount allowed	1,000
Wages	10,000	Discount earned	500
Salaries	7,500	General Expenses	1,200
Carriage Inwards	500	Cash on Hand	150
Purchase Returns	1,000	Bank balance	1,260
Sales Returns	1,500		

The following adjustments are to be made :

(a) Closing stock Rs. 10,000.
(b) Outstanding rent Rs. 100. Salaries Rs. 900.
(c) Insurance prepaid Rs. 40 and interest on loans outstanding Rs. 250.
(d) Provide Depreciation 10% on machinery and 6% of furniture.
(e) Prepare Trading account, profit and loss account and Balance Sheet for the year ending 31st December 1997.   [M.Sc Dec 1999]

Solution :

Trading Account of Mr. Ganesh for the year ended 31.12.1997

Particulars	Rs.	Rs.	Particulars	Rs.	Rs.
To Opening Stock		7,500	By Sales	90,000	
To Purchase	60,000		(−) Sales Returns	1,500	88,500
(−) Purchase Returns	1,000	59,000			
To Wages		10,000	By Closing Stock		10,000
To Carriage inwards		500			
To Gross Profit		21,500			
		98,500			98,500

Profit and Loss Account of Mr. Ganesh for the year ended 31.12.1997

Particulars	Rs.	Rs.	Particulars	Rs.	Rs.
To Interest (Dr.)		1,250	By Gross Profit		21,500
To Salaries	7,500		By Discount earned		500
(+) Outstanding	900	8,400			
To Office Rent	1,000				
(+) Outstanding	100	1,100			
To Insurance	240				
(−) Prepaid	40	200			
To Discount allowed		1,000			
To General Expenses		1,200			
To Interest on Loan Outstanding		250			
To Depreciation on Machinery		2,000			
To Depreciation on Furniture		90			
To Net Profit		6,510			
		22,000			22,000

PREPARATION OF FINAL ACCOUNTS

Balance Sheet of Mr. Ganesh as on 31.12.1997

Liabilities	Amount Rs.	Amount Rs.	Assets	Amount Rs.	Amount Rs.
Capital	15,000		Machinery	20,000	
(–) Drawings	4,800		(–) Depreciation	2,000	18,000
	10,200		Furniture	1,500	
(+) Net Profit	6,510	16,710	(–) Depreciation	90	1,410
			Sundry Debtors		20,000
Sundry Creditors		12,900	Cash on Hand		150
Outstanding Rent		100	Bank Balance		1,260
Outstanding Salaries		900	Closing Stock		10,000
Loans borrowed	20,000		Insurance Prepaid		40
(+) Interest on Loan Outstanding	250	20,250			
		50,860			50,860

Problem 17. *From the following trial balance extracted from the books of a merchant on 31.12.1998.*

	Rs.		Rs.
Furniture and Fittings	640	Purchases	5,475
Motor vehicles	6,250	Sales	15,450
Buildings	7,500	Bank Overdraft	2,850
Capital Account	12,500	Sales Returns	200
Provision for Bad Debts	20	Purchase Returns	125
Bad debts	125	Advertising	450
Sundry debtors	3,800	Interest A/c (Dr.)	118
Sundry creditors	2,680	Commission (Cr.)	375
Stock on 1.1.1998	3,460	Cash	650
General Insurance	782	Taxes & Insurance	1,250
Salaries	3,300		

The following adjustments are to be made :
(a) Closing stock was valued at Rs. 3250.
(b) Depreciate building @ 5%, furniture and fitting @ 10% and motor vehicle @ 20%.
(c) Rs. 85 is due for interest on Bank overdraft.
(d) Salaries Rs. 300 and Taxes Rs. 120 are outstanding.
(e) Insurance amounting to Rs. 100 is prepaid.
(f) One third of the commission received is in respect of work to be done next year.
(g) Write off further Rs. 100 as Bad debt and provision for bad debts is to be made equal to 5% on sundry Debtors.

Prepare Final Account for the year ended 31.12.1998.

Solution : Trading Account for the year ended 31.12.1998

Particulars	Rs.	Rs.	Particulars	Rs.	Rs.
To Opening Stock		3,460	By Sales	15,450	
To Purchase	5,475		(−) Sales Returns	200	15,250
(−) Purchase Returns	125	5,350			
To Gross Profit		9,690	By Closing Stock		3,250
		18,500			18,500

Profit and Loss Account for the year ended 31.12.1998

Particulars	Rs.	Rs.	Particulars	Rs.	Rs.
To Salaries	3,300		By Gross Profit		9,690
(+) Outstanding	300	3,600	By Commission	375	
To Insurance	782		(−) Received in Advance	125	250
(−) Prepaid	100	682			
To Advertising		450			
To Bad Debts provisions		390			
To Interest	118				
(+) Outstanding	85	203			
To Taxes & Insurance	1,250				
(+) Outstanding	120	1,370			
To Depreciation :					
Building		375			
Furniture & Fittings		64			
Motor Vehicle		1,250			
Net Profit		1,556			
		9,940			9,940

Balance Sheet as on 31.12.1998

Liabilities	Amount Rs.	Amount Rs.	Assets	Amount Rs.	Amount Rs.
Capital	12,500		Cash		650
(+) Net Profit	1,556	14,056	Furniture & Fittings	640	
Sundry Creditors		2,680	(−) Depreciation	64	576
Bank Overdraft	2,850		Motor Vehicles	6,250	
(+) Interest Due	85	2,935	(−) Depreciation	1,250	5,000
			Buildings	7,500	
Outstanding Salary		300	(−) Depreciation	375	7,125
Outstanding Taxes			Sundry Debtors	3,800	
Insurance		120	(−) Bad Debts	100	
Commission received				3,700	
In advance		125	(−) Provision	185	3,515
			Closing Stock		3,250
			Prepaid Insurance		100
		20,216			20,216

NOTE : BD + NR − OR = 225 + 185 − 20 = 390.

PREPARATION OF FINAL ACCOUNTS

Problem 18. *From the following Balance of Mr. Raju for the year ended on 31.3.2003, prepare Final Account.*

	Rs.
Capital	1,00,000
Drawings	18,000
Buildings	15,000
Furniture & fittings	7,500
Motor Van	25,000
Loan from Hari @ 12% interest	15,000
Interest paid on above	900
Sales	1,00,000
Purchases	75,000
Opening stock	25,000
Establishment expenses	15,000
Wages	2,000
Insurance	1,000
Commission Received	4,500
Sundry Debtors	28,100
Bank Balance	20,000
Sundry Creditors	10,000
Interest (Cr)	3,000

The following adjustments are to be made :
(a) The value of closing stock on 31.03.2003 was Rs. 32,000.
(b) Outstanding wages Rs. 500.
(c) Prepaid Insurance Rs. 300.
(d) Commission Received on advance Rs. 300.
(e) Allow interest on capital @ 10%.
(f) Depreciate Building 2½ %, Furniture's fittings 10%, Motor van 10%.
(g) Charge interest on Drawings Rs. 500.
(h) Accrued Interest Rs. 500/-.

Solution :

Trading Account of Mr. Raju for the year ended 31.12.2003

Particulars	Rs.	Rs.	Particulars	Rs.	Rs.
To Opening Stock		25,000	By Sales		1,00,000
To Purchases		75,000	By Closing Stock		32,000
To Wages	2,000				
(+) Outstanding	500	2,500			
To Gross Profit		29,500			
		1,32,000			1,32,000

Profit and Loss Account of Mr. Raju for the year ended 31.12.2003

Particulars	Rs.	Rs.	Particulars	Rs.	Rs.
To Interest Paid	900		By Gross Profit		29,500
(+) Due	900	1,800	By Interest on		
To Establishment Expn.		15,000	Drawings		500
To Insurance	1,000		By Interest	3,000	
(−) Prepaid	300	700	(+) Accrued Interest	500	3,500
To Interest on Capital		10,000			
To Depreciation :			By Commission		
Building		375	received	4,500	
Furniture & Fittings		750	(−) Commission		
Motor Van		2,500	received in advance	300	4,200
To Net Profit		6,575			
		37,700			37,700

Balance Sheet of Mr. Raju as on 31.12.2003

Liabilities	Amount Rs.	Amount Rs.	Assets	Amount Rs.	Amount Rs.
Capital		98,075	Bank Balance		20,000
Loan from Hari	15,000		Buildings	15,000	
(+) Interest outstanding	900	15,900	(−) Depreciation	375	14,625
Sundry Creditors		10,000	Furniture & Fittings	7,500	
Outstanding Wages		500	(−) Depreciation	750	6,750
Commission received			Motor Van	25,000	
In advance		300	(−) Depreciation	2,500	22,500
			Sundry Debtors		28,100
			Closing Stock		32,000
			Prepaid Insurance		300
			Accrued Interest		500
		1,24,775			1,24,775

NOTE :

Capital		1,00,000
(+) Interest on Capital		10,000
		1,10,000
(−) Drawings	18,000	
(+) Interest on Drawings	500	
		18,500
		91,500
(+) Net Profit		6,575
		98,075

PREPARATION OF FINAL ACCOUNTS

Problem 19. *From the following balance, prepare Final Account of Mr. Kumar for the year ended on 31.12.1997.*

	Rs.	Rs.
Capital Account		60,000
Plant & Machinery	18,000	
Depreciation on Plant & Machinery	2,000	
Repair to Plant	1,600	
Wages	28,000	
Salaries	4,000	
Income Tax	500	
Cash in hand	2,000	
Furniture	24,500	
Depreciation on Motor car	2,500	
Purchase Less returns (Adjusted)	93,500	
Sales		2,49,000
Bank Overdraft		13,800
Accrued Income	1,500	
Salaries outstanding		2,000
Bills Receivable	30,000	
Bills Payable		3,000
Provisions for Bad debts		6,000
Bad debts	1,000	
Discount on Purchases		4,000
Sundry Debtors	35,000	
Sundry Creditors		23,300
Stock on Hand 01.01.1997	37,000	
Motor Car	50,000	
Stock on 31.12.1997	30,000	
	3,61,100	3,61,100

Write off Rs. 3,000 as bad debts and maintain a provision for bad debts at 5% Sundry Debtors. [MCA 1999 Nov.]

Solution :

Trading Account of Mr. Kumar for the year ended 31.12.1997

Particulars	Rs.	Rs.	Particulars	Rs.	Rs.
To Opening Stock		37,000	By Sales		2,49,000
To Purchases (Adjusted)	93,500				
(−) Discount on Purchases	4,000	89,500			
To Wages		28,000			
To Gross Profit		94,500			
		2,49,000			2,49,000

Profit and Loss Account of Mr. Kumar for the year ended 31.12.1997

Particulars	Rs.	Rs.	Particulars	Rs.	Rs.
To Depreciation on Plant & Machinery		2,000	By Gross Profit		94,500
To Repairs		1,600	By Bad Debts & Provisions		400
To Salaries		4,000			
To Depreciation on Motor Car		2,500			
To Net Profit		84,800			
		94,900			94,900

Balance Sheet as on 31.12.2003

Liabilities	Amount Rs.	Amount Rs.	Assets	Amount Rs.	Amount Rs.
Capital Account	60,000		Plant & Machinery		18,000
(−) Income Tax	500	59,500	Cash in Hand		2,000
Bank overdraft		13,800	Furniture		24,500
			Accrued Income		1,500
Salaries outstanding		2,000	Bills receivable		30,000
Bills Payable		3,000	Sundry Debtors	35,000	
Sundry Creditors		23,300	(−) Bad debts	3,000	
Profit & Loss Account		84,800		32,000	
			(−) New Reserve	1,600	30,400
			Motor Car		50,000
			Closing Stock		30,000
		1,86,400			1,86,400

NOTE :

BD + NR − OR

$\left.\begin{array}{r}1,000 \\ + \\ 3,000\end{array}\right\} + 1,600 - 6,000 = -400$

Debtors	35,000
(−) Bad Debts	3,000
	32,000

= 5,600 − 6,000 = − 400

New Reserve = $32,000 \times \dfrac{5}{100}$ = **1,600.**

Problem 20. *From the following data, prepare Trading, Profit and Loss Account and a balance sheet as on 31.3.96*

	Rs.		Rs.
Drawings	10,000	Capital	30,000
Purchases	30,000	Purchase returns	1,000
Sales returns	5,000	Sales	60,000
Carriage in	2,000	Wages outstanding	2,000
Carriage out	3,000	Rent received	1,000
Depreciation on plant	4,000	Reserve for doubtful debts	1,000

PREPARATION OF FINAL ACCOUNTS 59

Plant Account	20,000	Interest (cr)	5,000
Wages and Salaries	3,000	Sundry creditors	6,000
Bad debts	2,000	Loans	38,000
Premises	20,000		
Stock 1.4.95	25,000		
Interest	5,000		
Sundry Debtors	15,000		
	1,44,000		1,44,000

The following adjustments are to be made :

(a) Stock on 31.3.96 was Rs 40,000. A fire broke out in the godown and destroyed stock worth Rs 5,000 Insurance company had accepted and paid the claim in full.
(b) Provide for bad debts at the rate of 10 percent and provide for discount on debtors at the rate of 5 percent and on creditors at the rate of 10 percent.
(c) Depreciate buildings at the rate of 15 percent per annum.
(d) Rent outstanding amounted to Rs. 1,000.
(e) Closing stock includes samples worth Rs 2,000.
(f) Provide interest on drawings at the rate of 10% and on capital @ 5%.

[MBA Madras Nov.1996]

Solution : Trading Account for the year ended 31.3.1996

Particulars	Rs.	Rs.	Particulars	Rs.	Rs.
To Opening Stock		25,000	By Sales	60,000	
To Purchase	30,000		(−) Returns	5,000	55,000
(−) Purchase Returns	1,000	29,000	By Loss of Stock		5,000
To Carriage inwards		2,000	By Closing Stock	40,000	
To Wages and Salaries		3,000	(−) Samples	2,000	38,000
To Gross Profit		39,000			
		98,000			98,000

Profit and Loss Account for the year ended 31.3.1996

Particulars	Rs.	Rs.	Particulars	Rs.	Rs.
To Goods sent as samples		2,000	By Gross Profit b/d		39,000
To Carriage outwards		3,000	By Rent Received	1,000	
To Depreciation on Buildings		3,000	(+) Rent outstanding	1,000	2,000
To Interest		5,000	By Interest on Drawings		1,000
To Bad debts & Provisions		2,500	By Interest		5,000
To Discount on debtors		675	By Discount on Creditors		600
To Interest on capital		1,500			
To Depreciation on plant		4,000			
To Net Profit		25,925			
		47,600			47,600

Balance Sheet as on 31.3.1996

Liabilities	Amount Rs.	Amount Rs.	Assets	Amount Rs.	Amount Rs.
Capital	30,000		Plant		20,000
(+) Interest on Capital	1,500		Debtors	15,000	
(+) Net Profit	25,925		(–) New Provision	1,500	
		57,425		13,500	
			(–) Discount	675	12,825
(–) Drawings	10,000				
(+) Interest on Drawings	1,000	11,000	Premises	20,000	
			(–) Depreciation	3,000	17,000
		46,425			
Wages outstanding		2,000	Insurance Co. Account		5,000
Creditors	6,000		Closing Stock		38,000
(–) Discount on Creditors	600	5,400			
Loan		38,000			
Rent outstanding		1,000			
		92,825			92,825

NOTE : For Bad debts and provisions, BD + NR – OR = 2,000 + 1,500 – 1,000 = 2,500

Problem 21. *From the following balance extracted from the books of Shri Madhavan, prepare Final accounts for the year ended on 30th Sep. 1998 and a Balance Sheet as on that date.*

	Rs.		Rs.
Drawings	6,480	Cash on Hand	850
Land & Building	24,000	Cash at bank	13,000
Investments	30,000	Capital Account	1,20,000
Sundry Debtors	37,800	Bad Debts provision	2,470
Plant & Machinery	14,270	Sales	91,230
Furniture & Fixtures	1,250	Discount Account	120
Carriage Inwards	4,370	Purchase Returns	8,460
Wages	21,470	Sundry Creditors	12,170
Salaries	4,670	Apprentice premium	500
Bank Charges	140		
Coal Gas & Water	720		
Rates and Taxes	840		
Purchases	42,160		
Bills Receivable	1,270		
Trade Expenses	1,990		
Stock (01.10.97)	26,420		
Fire Insurance	490		

PREPARATION OF FINAL ACCOUNTS

The following adjustments are to be made :
(a) Charge Depreciation on land & building Account at 2½%, plant and machinery at 10%, Furniture and fixtures at 10%.
(b) Make provision of 5% on Sundry Debtors for Doubtful Debts.
(c) Carry forward the unexpired amounts for fire insurance of Rs. 125, Rates and Taxes Rs. 240 and Apprentice premium Rs. 400.
(d) Charge 5% interest on capital and interest on Drawings is Rs. 300/-.
(e) The value of stock as on 30.09.1998 was Rs. 29,390/-.
(f) Outstanding wages are Rs. 530.
(g) Interest on investment Rs. 3,000 is accrued.

Solution :

Trading Account of Mr. Madhavan for the year ended 31.09.1998

Particulars	Rs.	Rs.	Particulars	Rs.	Rs.
To Opening Stock		26,420	By Sales	91,230	
To Purchases	42,160		(−) Sales Returns	1,760	89,470
(−) Purchase Returns	8,460	33,700	By Closing Stock		29,390
To Carriage inwards		4,370			
To Wages	21,470				
(+) Outstanding	530	22,000			
To Coal, Gas and Water		720			
To Gross Profit		31,650			
		1,18,860			1,18,860

Profit and Loss Account of Mr. Madhavan for the year ended 31.09.1998

Particulars	Rs.	Rs.	Particulars	Rs.	Rs.
To Salaries		4,670	By Gross Profit		31,650
To Bank Charges		140	By Discount		120
To Rate and Taxes	840		By Apprentice		
(−) Prepaid	240	600	Premium	500	
To Trade Expenses		1,990	(−) Received in		
To Fire Insurance	490		Advance	400	100
(−) Prepaid	125	365			
To Depreciation :			By Bad Debts		
Land & Building 2½%		625	Provision	2,470	
Plant & Machinery 10%		1,427	(−) New Provision	1,890	580
Furniture & Fixtures 10%		125			
To Interest on Capital		6,000	By Interest on		
To Net Profit			Drawings		300
(Transferred to Capital			By Accrued interest		
A/c)		19,808	Investments		3,000
		35,750			35,750

Balance Sheet of Mr. Madhavan as on 31.09.1998

Liabilities	Amount Rs.	Amount Rs.	Assets	Amount Rs.	Amount Rs.
Capital		1,20,000	Cash in hand		850
(+) Net Profit		19,808	Cash at bank		13,000
Interest on Capital		6,000	Bills Receivables		1,270
		1,45,808	Sundry Debtors	37,800	
(−) Drawings	6,480		(−) Provision for		
(+) Interest on			Bad Debts	1,890	35,910
Drawings	300	6,780	Investments		30,000
		1,39,028			
Sundry Creditors		12,170	Accrued Interest		3,000
Apprentice premium			Prepaid Insurance		125
Received in Advance		400	Prepaid Rates & Taxes		240
Outstanding Wages		530	Land & Building	25,000	
			(−) Depreciation	625	24,375
			Plant & Machinery	14,270	
			(−) Depreciation	1,427	12,843
			Furniture & Fixtures	1,250	
			(−) Depreciation	125	1,125
			Closing stock		29,390
		1,52,128			1,52,128

NOTE : BD + NR − OR = 0 + 1890 − 2470 = − 580.

Problem 22. *From the following Trial balance, prepare the Trading Account and Profit and Loss Account of Mr. Mugunthan for the year ended on 31.12.2000 and the Balance Sheet as on the date.*

Trial Balance

Particulars	Debit	Credit
Debtors and Creditors	6,800	4,500
Purchases and sales	6,200	19,500
Bills	450	300
Investment	3,000	-
Bad Debts & Reserve	200	400
Returns	200	100
Loose tools	1,000	
Machinery	9,600	-
Furniture	400	
Carriage inwards	300	
Opening stock	3,400	
Establishment charges	250	
Wages	2,500	-

PREPARATION OF FINAL ACCOUNTS

Coal and power	1,300	–
General Expenses	2,300	–
Rates and taxes	2,500	–
Drawings	600	–
Depreciation	1,200	–
Cash in hand	100	–
Discount	100	100
Bank overdraft		2,500
Capital		15,000
	42,400	42,400

The following adjustments are to be considered :
(a) Closing stock was valued at Rs 3500.
(b) Coal unconsumed Rs 200.
(c) Maintain 5% reserve for Bad debts.
(d) Liability for wages Rs 300.

Solution : Trading Account for the year ended 31.12.2000

Particulars	Rs.	Rs.	Particulars	Rs.	Rs.
To Opening Stock		3,400	By Sales	19,500	
To Purchases	6,200		(–) Returns	200	19,300
(–) Returns	100	6,100	By Closing Stock		3,500
Carriage inwards		300			
To Coal and power	1,300				
(–) Unconsumed	200	1,100			
Wages	2,500				
(+) Liability	300	2,800			
Gross Profit		9,100			
		22,800			22,800

Profit and Loss Account for the year ended 31.12.2000

Particulars	Rs.	Rs.	Particulars	Rs.	Rs.
To Establishment			By Gross Profit		9,100
Charges		250	By Discount		200
To General Expenses		2,300			
To Rates and Tax		2,500			
To Depreciation		1,200			
To Bad Debts &					
Provision		140			
To Net Profit		2,910			
		9,300			9,300

Balance Sheet as on 31.12.2000

Liabilities	Amount Rs.	Amount Rs.	Assets	Amount Rs.	Amount Rs.
Capital	15,000		Furniture		400
(+) Net Profit	2,910		Machinery		9,600
	17,910		Loose Costs		1,000
(–) Drawings	600	17,310	Investments		3,000
			Sundry Debtors	6,800	
Sundry Creditors		4,000	(–) New Reserve	340	6,460
Bills Payable		500	Bills Receivable		450
Outstanding wages		300	Coal stock		200
Bank overdraft		2,500	Closing Stock		3,500
		24,610			24,610

NOTE : BD + NR − OR = 200 + 340 − 400 = 140.

5
Fund Flow Statement

INTRODUCTION

The traditional concept of profit and loss account and balance sheet has a limited role to play in financial analysis. The profit and loss account reflects the results of the business operations for a specified period of time. It takes into account only the expenses incurred and income received during the accounting period. The balance sheet gives a summary of the assets and liabilities at a particular period of time. And at the same time, balance sheet does not explain the details about the movement of funds. In actual practice, a business concern receives funds from various sources and invested in various ways of investment. It is a continuous process. The ultimate aim of the financial management is to study and control these funds in order to maintain the solvency and financial soundness of the firm. For the purpose of complete study of sources and applications of funds over the accounting period, a separate statement is essential to find the periodical increase or decrease of such funds of an enterprise. This statement is called fund flow statement.

MEANING OF FUND FLOW STATEMENT

The fund flow statement is a statement which reveals the methods by which the business has been financed and how it has used its funds between two balance sheet dates.

In the words of Foulke : "A statement of sources and application of funds is a technical device, designed to analyse the changes in the financial conditions of a business enterprise between two balance sheet dates."

DIFFERENT NAMES OF FUND FLOW STATEMENT

A statement of sources and application of funds
A statement of sources and uses of funds
Where Got and where Gone statement
Inflow-outflow of fund statement
Statement of funds supplied and applied; funds received and disbursed statement

MANAGERIAL USES OF FUND FLOW STATEMENT

Fund flow statement is an invaluable analytical tool for a financial manager for the purpose of evaluating the employment of funds by a firm and also to assess sources of such funds. Following are the important managerial uses of fund flow statement.

1. The foremost use of the fund flow statement is to explain the reasons for changes in the assets and liabilities between two balance sheet dates.
2. Fund flow statement gives details about the funds obtained and used in past. Based upon this detail, manager can take correct actions at appropriate times.
3. Fund flow statement acts as a control device when compared with budgeted figures. It also gives guidance to the finance manager for taking remedial action if there is any deviation.
4. It helps the management to formulate various financial policies—viz dividend, bonus etc.
5. It gives guidance to the management with regard to working capital. Through fund flow statement, management can take proper steps for effective utilisation of surplus working capital or in case of inadequacy, suitable arrangement can be made for improving the working capital position.
6. It identifies the strong and weak financial areas of the firm.
7. It gives the answers for various financial intricate questions :
   – How much funds were generated ?
   – How were the funds used ?
8. Effective utilisation of available resources and scarce resources should be allocated according to the preferential needs.
9. With the help of the fund flow statement, financial and lending institutions can easily evaluate the credit worthiness and repaying capacity of the borrowing company.
10. It enables the management to reformulate the firm's financial activity on the basis of the statement.

LIMITATIONS OF FUND FLOW STATEMENT

1. In the real sense, the fund flow statement lacks originality because it is only a rearrangement of data given in financial statements.
2. It indicates only the past year's performance and is not for the future. Even to prepare projected fund flow statement, it cannot show much accuracy.
3. It cannot reveal continuous changes. Because only any particular two years are taken into account for analysis purpose.
4. Fund flow statement is not a substitute for a financial statement. It gives only some information about changes in working capital alone.

STEPS IN PREPARATION OF FUND FLOW STATEMENT

(i) Preparation of fund flow statement
(ii) Preparation of statement of changes in working capital.
(iii) Preparation of adjusted profits and loss account (to find out fund from operation or fund lost in operation)
(iv) Adjustment and their treatment

FUND FLOW STATEMENT

(v) Preparation of separate ledger
(vi) Treatment about the provision for taxation and proposed divider

> **NOTE :** Fund flow statement alone is a major part of the solution; remaining other things *i.e.*, working capital statement, P.L. A /c, preparation of ledger, treatment of provision for taxation and proposed dividend, adjustment etc were supported to work the fund flow statement.

I. Preparation Fund Flow Statement

Here we have to prepare the fund flow statement in the T shape.

I. Fund Flow Statement : (Specimen form)

Sources of Funds	Amount Rs.	Applications of Funds	Amount Rs.
Issue of shares	xx	Redemption of redeemable	xx
Issue of debentures	xx	Preference shares	xx
Loan borrowed	xx	Redemption of debentures	xx
(Long term, medium term)		Repayment of loans	xx
Acceptance of deposits	xx	Repayment of deposits	xx
Sale of fixed assets	xx	Purchase of fixed assets	xx
Sale of investments (Long term)	xx	Purchase of long term	
Decrease in working capital	xx	investments	xx
(Transfer from working		Payment of dividend	xx
capital statements)		Income tax paid	xx
Fund from operation	xx	Increase in working capital	xx
(Transfer from P&L A/c		Fund loss in operation	xx
Working capital statement)		(Transfer from P&L A/c)	

II. Working Capital Statement

For the purpose of finding out increase or decrease in working capital, we have to prepare statement of changes in working capital. [TCA − TCL = WC]

Particulars	Year I	Year II
Current Assets		
Cash in hand	xx	xx
Cash at bank	xx	xx
Sundry debtors	xx	xx
Bills receivable	xx	xx
Marketable securities	xx	xx
Inventory	xx	xx
Prepaid expenses	xx	xx
Short term investment	xx	xx
Accrued incomes	xx	xx
Total Current Assets (TCA) (A)	xx	xx

Current Liabilities

Sundry Creditors	xx	xx
Bills payable	xx	xx
Outstanding expenses	xx	xx
Bank overdraft	xx	xx
Income received in advance	xx	xx
Short term loans	xx	xx
Cash credit from bank	xx	xx
Provision for taxation	xx	xx
Proposed dividend	xx	xx
Provision against current assets	xx	xx
Provision for doubtful debts	xx	xx
Total Current Liabilities (TCL) (B)	xx	xx
Working Capital (A-B)	xx	xx
Increase or Decrease	xx	
[TAC – TCL = WC]		

After the computation of working capital, we have to find out the increase or decrease in working.

III. Fund from Operation : Fund from operation is found out by two methods

(i) Statement method

(ii) Accounting method.

Normally, accounting method is easy and convenient. So, we have to adopt accounting method *i.e.,* profit and loss account is used to find out the fund from operation. Here profit and loss account is prepared in a usual procedure.

Profits and Loss account for the year ended

Particulars	Amount Rs.	Particulars	Amount Rs.
To Goodwill written off	xx	By Balance b/d	xx
To Preliminary expenses written off	xx	By Profit on sale of fixed assets	xx
To Patents written off	xx		
To Depreciation	xx	By Interest sale of investment	xx
To Dividend paid	xx	By Any other non-operating incomes	xx
To Provision for taxation	xx		
To Loss on sale of fixed assets	xx	By Fund from operation	xx
To Discount on issue of shares	xx		
To Interim dividend paid	xx		
To Balance c/d	xx		
To Fund operation	xx		
	xx		xx

FUND FLOW STATEMENT

IV. Important adjustments and their treatment

All the adjustments appear in two places :

Adjustment	Treatment
1. Depreciation	- P.L. A/c debit side Respective asset A/c credit side
2. Dividend paid	- P.L. A/c debit side Fund flow statement—Application side
3. Income tax paid	- Income tax A/c debit side fund flow statement—Application side
4. Income tax provision	- P.L. A/c debit side Income tax A/c credit side
5. Loss on sale of fixed Assets	- P.L. A/c debit Respective asset A/c credit side.
6. Interim dividend paid	- P.L . A/c debit side. Fund flow statement Application side

V. Preparation of separate ledger A/c,

if necessary *i.e.,* about the non-current (either Assets or Liability) items related information given in the adjustment means we have to prepare separate ledger. Balances from this ledger can be transferred to fund flow statement means we have to prepare a separate ledger. Balances from this ledger can be transferred to fund flow statement.

VI. Treatment about the provision for taxation and proposed dividend

Provision for taxation and proposed dividend taken as current liability means it should appear under working capital statement.

Some times, regarding the provision for taxation, information is given in the adjustment. So, it should be treated as non current liability. Provision for taxation taken as non-current liability means proposed dividend is also taken as a non-current liability.

(a) Treatment of provision for taxation

(i) Income Tax provided given in the adjustment, we have to find the tax paid-
P.L. A/c debit side
Income Tax A/c credit
(Balancing figure of taxation A/c is called tax paid and then it is transferred to Applications side)

(ii) Income tax paid given in the adjustment, we have to find the income tax provision.
Fund flow statement – application side
Income tax A/c – debit side
(Balancing figure of taxation A/c is called tax provided and then it is transferred to P.L. A/c debit side)

(b) Treatment of proposed dividend

Whenever provision for taxation is treated as non-current liability, proposed dividend is also taken as non-current liability. At that time, the following rules will be applicable.

Last year amount – application side
Current year amount : profit & loss A/c debit side.

Problem 1. *The following are the summarised balance sheets of M/s.Krishna Ltd. as on 31.12.1999 and 2000.*

Liabilities	1999 Rs.	2000 Rs.
10% preference shares	1,00,000	1,10,000
Equity Shares	2,20,000	2,50,000
Share premium	20,000	26,000
Profit & Loss A/c	1,04,000	1,34,000
12% debentures	70,000	64,000
Creditors	38,000	46,000
Bills Payable	5,000	4,000
Provision for tax	10,000	12,000
Dividend Payable	7,000	8,000
	5,74,000	6,54,000

Assets	1999 Rs.	2000 Rs.
Machinery	2,00,000	2,30,000
Buildings	1,50,000	1,76,000
Land	18,000	18,000
Cash	42,000	32,000
Debtors	38,000	38,000
Bills receivable	42,000	62,000
Stock	84,000	98,000
	5,74,000	6,54,000

You are required to prepare a statement of sources and application of funds.

[BBM PU 2005]

Solution :

Fund Flow Statement

Particulars	Amount Rs.	Particulars	Amount Rs.
Issue of preference shares	10,000	Purchase of machinery	30,000
Issue of Equity shares	30,000	Purchase of Building	26,000
Share premium received	6,000	Increase in working capital	14,000
Fund from operation	30,000	Redemption of debenture	6,000
	76,000		76,000

FUND FLOW STATEMENT

Workings : **(i) Statement of changes in working capital**

	1999 Rs	2000 Rs
Current Assets :		
Cash	42,000	32,000
Debtors	38,000	38,000
Bills receivables	42,000	62,000
Stock	84,000	98,000
Total current assets	2,06,000	2,30,000
Current Liabilities :		
Creditors	38,000	46,000
Bills payable	5,000	4,000
Provision for Tax	10,000	12,000
Dividend payable	7,000	8,000
Total current liabilities	60,000	70,000
Working capital	1,46,000	1,60,000

Increase in working capital : Rs 14000 (1,46,000 – 1,60,000)
[Transfer to Fund Flow Statement]

(ii) Profit and Loss Account

To Balance b/d (Closing)	1,34,000	By Balance c/d (Opening)	1,04,000
		By Fund from operation	30,000
	1,34,000		1,34,000

Problem 2. *From the following balance sheets, prepare schedule of changes in working capital.*

Liabilities	Dec 1980 Rs.	Dec 1981 Rs.	Assets	Dec 1980 Rs.	Dec 1981 Rs.
Share capital	2,00,000	2,50,000	Cash	30,000	47,000
Creditors	70,000	45,000	Debtors	1,20,000	1,15,000
Retained } Earnings }	10,000	23,000	Land	50,000	66,000
			Stock	80,000	90,000
	2,80,000	3,18,000		2,80,000	3,18,000

[MBA April 2002 Madras University]

Solution : **Fund Flow Statement**

Source of funds	Rs.	Application of funds	Rs.
Issue of shares	50,000	Purchase of Land	16,000
Fund from operation	13,000	Increase in working capital	47,000
	63,000		63,000

Workings : **(i) Statement of changes in working capital**

	Dec. 1980 Rs.	Dec. 1981 Rs.
Current Assets :		
Cash	30,000	47,000
Debtors	1,20,000	1,15,000
Stock	80,000	90,000
Total current assets	2,30,000	2,52,000
Current liabilities :		
Creditors	70,000	45,000
Total current Liabilities	70,000	45,000
Working capital	1,60,000	2,07,000
Increase in working capital	(1,60,000 – 2,07,000)	47,000

(ii) Profit and Loss Accounts

To Balance b/d	23,000	By Balance c/d	10,000
		By Fund from operation (B/f)	13,000
	23,000		23,000

Problem 3. *The following are the summarised balance sheets of X Ltd., as on 31 December 1999 and 2000.*

Liabilities	31st Dec. 1999 Rs.	31st Dec. 2000 Rs.	Assets	31st Dec. 1999 Rs.	31st Dec. 2000 Rs.
Redeemable preference Shares	-	10,000	Fixed Assets	41,000	40,000
Equity shares	40,000	40,000	Less : Depreciation	11,000	15,000
General Reserve	2,000	2,000		30,000	25,000
Profit & loss A/c	1,000	1,200			
Debentures	6,000	7,000	Debtors	20,000	24,000
Creditors	12,000	11,000	Stock	30,000	35,000
Provision for Tax	3,000	4,200	Prepaid exp.	300	500
Proposed dividend	5,000	5,800	Cash	1,200	3,500
Bank overdraft	12,500	6,800			
	81,500	88,000		81,500	88,000

You are required to prepare :
1. A statement showing changes in the working capital
2. A statement of sources and application of funds.

[B.Com Madras, Delhi, MBA Madras]

FUND FLOW STATEMENT

Solution :

Fund Flow Statement

Source of funds	Rs.	Application of funds	Rs.
Issue of preference shares	10,000	Increase in working capital	16,200
Issue of Debentures	1,000		
Sale of fixed assets	1,000		
Fund from operation	4,200		
	16,200		16,200

Workings : *(i) Statement of changes in working capital*

	1999 Rs.	2000 Rs.
Current assets :		
Debtors	20,000	24,000
Stock	30,000	35,000
Prepaid expenses	300	500
	1,200	3,500
Total current assets	51,500	63,000
Current liabilities :		
Creditors	12,000	11,000
Provision for tax	3,000	4,200
Proposed dividend	5,000	5,800
Bank overdraft	12,500	6,800
Total Current liabilities	32,500	27,800
Working capital	11,900	35,200
Increase in working capital	16,200	(11,900 − 35,200)

Hint : Provision for taxation and proposed dividend taken as current liabilities.

(ii) Profit and Loss Account

To Balance b/d	1,200	By Balance c/d	1,000
To Depreciation	4,000	By Fund from operation	4,200
	5,200		5,200

Problem 4. *From the following balance sheets, prepare a statement showing changes in working capital during 1995.*

Balance sheet of Pioneer Ltd as on 31st December.

Liabilities	1994 Rs.	1995 Rs.
Share capital	5,00,000	6,00,000
Reserves	1,50,000	1,80,000

	1994	1995
P.L. A/c	40,000	65,000
Debentures	3,00,000	2,50,000
Creditors for goods	1,70,000	1,60,000
Provision for income tax	60,000	80,000
	12,20,000	13,35,000

Assets	1994 Rs.	1995 Rs.
Fixed assets	10,00,000	11,20,000
Less : Depreciation	3,70,000	4,60,000
	6,30,000	6,60,000
Stock	2,40,000	3,70,000
Book debts	2,50,000	2,30,000
Cash in hand and at Bank Balance	80,000	60,000
Preliminary Expenses	20,000	15,000
	12,20,000	13,35,000

[B.Com Bharathidasan Nov 1986]

Solution :

Fund Flow Statement

Source of funds	Rs.	Application of funds	Rs.
Issue of shares	1,00,000	Redemption of debentures	50,000
Fund from operation	1,50,000	Purchase of fixed assets	1,20,000
		Increase in working capital	80,000
	2,50,000		2,50,000

Workings : *(i)* **Statement of changes in working capital**

	1994 Rs.	1995 Rs.
Current Assets :		
Stock	2,40,000	3,70,000
Book Debts	2,50,000	2,30,000
Cash in hand & Bank Balance	80,000	60,000
Total Current assets	5,70,000	6,60,000
Current liabilities :		
Creditors for goods	1,70,000	1,60,000
Provision for income tax	60,000	80,000
Total current liabilities	2,30,000	2,40,000
Working capital	3,40,000	4,20,000
Increase in working capital	80,000	(3,40,000 − 4,20,000)

(ii) Profit and Loss Account

	Rs.		Rs.
To Balance b/d	65,000	By Balance c/d	40,000
To Reserves	30,000	By Fund from operation	1,50,000
To Preliminary expenses written off	5,000		
To Depreciation	90,000		
	1,90,000		1,90,000

Problem 5. *Calculate fund from operation from the information given below as on 31.3.2000.*

1. Net profit for the year ended 31.3.2000 Rs. 6,50,000.
2. Gain on sale of buildings Rs. 35,500.
3. Goodwill appears in the books at Rs. 1,80,000 out of that 10% has been written off during the year.
4. Old machinery worth Rs. 8,000 has been sold for Rs. 6,500 during the year.
5. Rs. 1,25,000 have been transferred to reserve fund.
6. Depreciation has been provided during the year on machinery and furniture at 20% whose value is Rs. 6,50,000. [B.Com Madras]

Solution : **Calculation of Fund from operation**

	Rs.	Rs.
Net profit for the year ended 31.3.2000		6,50,000
Add : Non fund items : [P.L. A/c Debit side items]		
Goodwill written off	18,000	
(1,80,000 × 10/100)		
Loss on sale of machinery		
(8000 – 6500)	1,500	
Transferred to Reserve fund	1,25,000	
Depreciation		
(6,50,000 × 20/100)	1,30,000	
		2,74,500
		9,24,500
Less : Non fund items [P.L A/c credit side items]		
Gain on sale of Buildings		35,500
Fund from operation		8,89,000

Problem 6. *From the following balance sheets of a sole trader, prepare a fund flow statement.*

Liabilities	1999 Rs.	2000 Rs.	Assets	1999 Rs.	2000 Rs.
Capital	63,000	1,00,000	Cash	15,000	20,000
Long term loans	50,000	60,000	Debtors	30,000	28,000

Trade creditors	42,000	39,000	Stock	55,000	72,000
Bank overdraft	35,000	25,000	Land & Building	80,000	1,00,000
Outstanding expenses	5,000	6,000	Furniture	15,000	10,000
	1,95,000	2,30,000		1,95,000	2,30,000

[B.Com Madras]

Solution :   **Fund Flow Statement**

Source of funds	Rs.	Application of funds	Rs.
Loan borrowed	10,000	Purchase of Land & Buildings	20,000
Sale of Furniture	5,000	Increase in working capital	32,000
Fund from operation	37,000		
	52,000		52,000

Workings :   *(i)* **Statement of changes in working capital**

	1999 Rs.	2000 Rs.
Current Assets :		
Cash	15,000	20,000
Debtors	30,000	28,000
Stock	55,000	72,000
Total current assets	1,00,000	1,20,000
Current Liabilities :		
Trade creditors	42,000	39,000
Bank overdraft	35,000	25,000
Outstanding expenses	5,000	6,000
Total current liabilities	82,000	70,000
Working capital	18,000	50,000
Increase in working capital	32,000	(18,000 − 50,000)

(ii) **Capital Account**

To Balance c/d	1,00,000	By Balance b/d	63,000
		By P.L.A/c	37,000
	1,00,000		1,00,000

(iii) **Profit and Loss Account**

To Capital Account	37,000	By Fund from operation	37,000
	37,000		37,000

FUND FLOW STATEMENT

Problem 7. *Following are the comparative balance sheets of a HAL company for the year 1989 and 1990.*

Balance Sheet

Liabilities	1989 Rs.	1990 Rs.	Assets	1989 Rs.	1990 Rs.
Share capital	70,000	74,000	Cash	9,000	7,800
Debentures	12,000	6,000	Debtors	14,900	17,700
Creditors	10,360	11,840	Stock	49,200	42,700
Profit & loss A/c	10,740	11,360	Goodwill	10,000	5,000
			Land	20,000	30,000
	1,03,100	1,03,200		1,03,100	1,03,200

The following additional information is also available :
(i) Dividends were paid totalling Rs.4,000.
(ii) Land was purchased for Rs 15,000. You are required to prepare fund flow statement.

[B.Com Madras 1993]

Solution :

Fund Flow Statement

Source of funds	Rs.	Application of funds	Rs.
Issue of shares	4,000	Redemption of Debenture	6,000
Fund from operation	9,620	Dividend paid	4,000
Decrease in working capital	6,380	Purchase of Land	10,000
	20,000		20,000

Workings : *(i)* **Statement of changes in working capital**

	1989 Rs.	1990 Rs.
Current Assets :		
Cash	9,000	7,800
Debtors	14,900	17,700
Stock	49,200	42,700
Total current assists	73,100	68,200
Current Liabilities :		
Creditors	10,360	11,840
Total current liabilities	10,360	11,840
Working capital	62,740	56,360
Decrease in working capital	(62,740 − 56,360)	6,380

(ii) Profit and Loss Account

To Balance c/d	11,360	By Balance b/d	10,740
To Goodwill written of	5,000	By Fund from operation	9,620
To Dividend Paid	4,000		
	20,360		20,360

(iii) Land Account

To Balance b/d	20,000	By Balance b/d	30,000
To Cash	10,000		
	30,000		30,000

Problem 8. *From the following balance sheets of AMB Ltd as on 31.12.98 and 1999, prepare a schedule of changes in working capital and fund flow statement.*

Balance Sheet

Liabilities	1998 Rs.	1999 Rs.
Share capital	1,00,000	1,00,000
General reserve	14,000	18,000
P.L. A/c	16,000	13,000
Sundry creditors	8,000	5,400
Bills payable	1,200	800
Provision for Tax	16,000	18,000
Provision for doubtful debts	400	600
	1,55,600	1,55,800

Assets	1998 Rs.	1999 Rs.
Goodwill	12,000	12,000
Buildings	40,000	36,000
Plant	37,000	36,000
Investments	10,000	11,000
Stock	30,000	23,400
Bills receivable	2,000	3,200
Debtors	18,000	19,000
Cash at bank	6,600	15,200
	1,55,600	1,55,800

The following additional information is also available :

1. Depreciation charges on Plant & Buildings at Rs.4,000 each.
2. Provision for taxation of Rs.19,000 was made during the year 1999.
3. Interim dividend of Rs.8,000 was paid during the year 1999.

[MCA Bharathidasan, M.Com Madras] [M.Sc PU 2000]

FUND FLOW STATEMENT

Solution :

Fund Flow Statement

Source of funds	Rs.	Application of funds	Rs.
Fund from operation	36,000	Increase in working capital	7,000
		Interim dividend paid	8,000
		Tax paid	17,000
		Purchase of Plant	3,000
		Investments	1,000
	36,000		36,000

Workings : *(i)* **Statement of changes in working capital**

Current Assets :	1998	1999
Stock	30,000	23,400
Bills receivable	2,000	3,200
Debtors	18,000	19,000
Cash at Bank	6,600	15,200
Total current assets	56,600	60,800
Current Liabilities :		
Sundry creditors	8,000	5,400
Bills payable	1,200	800
Provision for Doubtful debts	400	600
Total current liabilities	9,600	6,800
Working capital	47,000	54,000
Increase in working capital	(47,000 – 54,000)	7,000

(ii) **Profit and Loss Account**

To Balance c/d	13,000	By Balance b/d	16,000
To Depreciation on Buildings	4,000	By Fund from operation	36,000
To Depreciation on Plant	4,000		
To Income tax provided	19,000		
To Interim dividend paid	8,000		
To General reserve	4,000		
	52,000		52,000

(iii) **Provision for Taxation Account**

To Balance b/d	18,000	By Balance b/d	16,000
To Cash (Tax Paid)	17,000	By PL A/c (Income Tax Provided)	19,000
	35,000		35,000

(iv) Building Account

To Balance b/d	40,000	By Balance b/d	36,000
		By Depreciation	4,000
	40,000		40,000

(v) Plant Account

To Balance b/d	37,000	By Balance b/d	36,000
To Cash (Purchase)	3,000	By Depreciation	4,000
	40,000		40,000

Problem 9. *From the following balance sheets of Exe Ltd. prepare*
(a) A statement of changes in working capital
(b) A fund flow statement

Liabilities	1999 Rs.	2000 Rs.	Assets	1999 Rs.	2000 Rs.
Equity share capital	3,00,000	4,00,000	Good will	1,15,000	90,000
Redeemable preference share capital	1,50,000	1,00,000	Land & Building	2,00,000	1,70,000
			Plant	80,000	2,00,000
General reserve	40,000	70,000	Debtors	1,60,000	2,00,000
Profit & Loss A/c	30,000	48,000	Stock	77,000	1,09,000
Proposed dividend	42,000	50,000	Bills receivable	20,000	30,000
Creditors	55,000	83,000	Cash in hand	15,000	10,000
Bills payable	20,000	16,000	Cash at bank	10,000	8,000
Provision for taxation	40,000	50,000			
	6,77,000	8,17,000		6,77,000	8,17,000

The following additional information is also available :
(a) Depreciation of Rs.10,000 and Rs.20,000 have been charged on plant and land buildings respectively in 2000.
(b) A dividend of Rs.20,000 has been paid in 2000.
(c) Income tax of Rs.35,000 has been paid during 2000.

[M.Com Osmania B.Com (Hons) Delhi], [B.Com PU 2004]

Solution : **Fund Flow Statement**

Source of funds	Rs.	Application of funds	Rs.
Issue of Equity shares	1,00,000	Redemption of Redeemable	50,000
Sale of Land & Buildings	10,000	Dividend paid	20,000
Fund from operation	2,18,000	Income tax paid	35,000
		Purchase of Plant	1,30,000
		Proposed dividend paid	42,000
		Increase in working capital	51,000
	3,28,000		3,28,000

FUND FLOW STATEMENT

Workings : **(i) Statement of changes in working capital**

Current Assets :	1999 Rs	2000 Rs
Debtors	1,60,000	2,00,000
Stock	77,000	1,09,000
Bills receivable	20,000	30,000
Cash in hand	15,000	10,000
Cash at Bank	10,000	8,000
Total current assets	2,82,000	3,57,000
Current Liabilities :		
Creditors	55,000	83,000
Bills payable	20,000	16,000
Total current liabilities	75,000	99,000
Working capital	2,07,000	2,58,000
Increase in working capital	51,000	(2,58,000 – 2,07,000)

(ii) Profit and Loss Account

To General Reserve	30,000	By Balance c/d	30,000
To Goodwill written off	25,000	By Fund from operation	2,18,000
To Depreciation on Plant	10,000		
To Depreciation on Building	20,000		
To Dividend paid	20,000		
To Balance c/d	48,000		
To Income Tax provided	45,000		
To Proposed dividend	50,000		
	2,48,000		2,48,000

(iii) Provision for Taxation Account

To Cash (Tax paid)	35,000	By Balance b/d	40,000
To Balance c/d	50,000	By P.L. A/c	45,000
	85,000		85,000

(iv) Land & Building Account

To Balance b/d	2,00,000	By Depreciation	20,000
		By Balance c/d	1,70,000
		By Cash (Sale)	10,000
	2,00,000		2,00,000

(v) Plant Account

To Balance b/d	80,000	By Depreciation	10,000
To Cash	1,30,000	By Balance c/d	2,00,000
	2,10,000		2,10,000

Problem 10. The following are the summarised Balance Sheets of Lucky Ltd. as on 31.12.96 and 1997.

Liabilities	1996 Rs.	1997 Rs.	Assets	1996 Rs.	1997 Rs.
Share capital	2,00,000	2,50,000	Land & Buildings	2,00,000	1,90,000
General reserve	50,000	60,000	Machinery	1,50,000	1,69,000
P.L. A/c	30,500	30,600	Stock	1,00,000	74,000
Bank loan (Long term)	70,000	-	Sundry debtors	80,000	64,200
Sundry creditors	1,50,000	1,35,200	Cash	500	600
Provision for taxation	30,000	35,000	Bank	-	8,000
			Goodwill	-	5,000
	5,30,500	5,10,800		5,30,500	5,10,800

Additional information supplied during the year ended 31.12.97 :
(a) Dividend of Rs.23,000 was paid.
(b) Assets of another company were purchased for a consideration of Rs.50,000 payable in shares.
The following assets were purchased :
Machinery Rs.25,000 : stock Rs.20,000.
(c) Machinery was further purchased for Rs.8,000.
(d) Depreciation written off against machinery Rs.12,000.
(e) Income tax paid during the year Rs.33,000.
(f) Loss on sale of machinery Rs.200 was written off to general reserve.
(g) Depreciation charged against land & buildings was Rs.10,000.
You are required to prepare fund flow statement. [M.Com Madras adopted]

Solution :   **Fund Flow Statement**

Source of funds	Rs.	Application of funds	Rs.
Sale of Machinery	1,800	Repayment of Bank loan	70,000
Fund from operation	93,300	Dividend paid	23,000
Decrease in working capital	18,900	Purchase of Machinery	8,000
Issue of shares (For stock)	20,000	Income Tax paid	33,000
	1,34,000		1,34,000

Workings :   *(i)* **Statement of changes in working capital**

Current Assets :	1996 Rs.	1997 Rs.
Stock	1,00,000	74,000
Sundry Debtors	80,000	64,200
Cash	500	600
Bank	—	8,000
Total current assets	1,80,500	1,46,800

FUND FLOW STATEMENT

Current Liabilities :

	Rs.	Rs.
Sundry creditors	1,50,000	1,35,200
Total current liabilities	1,50,000	1,35,200
Working capital	30,500	11,600
Decrease in working capital	18,900	(30,500 – 11,600)

(ii) Profit and Loss Account

	Rs.		Rs.
To Dividend paid	23,000	By Balance b/d	30,500
To Depreciation on Machinery	12,000	By Fund from operation	93,300
To Depreciation on			
Land & Building	10,000		
To General Reserve	10,200		
To Income Tax provided	38,000		
To Balance c/d	30,600		
	1,23,800		1,23,800

(iii) Provision for Taxation Account

	Rs.		Rs.
To Cash	33,000	By Balance b/d	30,000
To Balance c/d	35,000	By Income Tax provided	38,000
	68,000		68,000

(iv) Machinery Account

	Rs.		Rs.
To Balance b/d	1,50,000	By Depreciation	12,000
To Shares	25,000	By General Reserve	200
To Cash (Purchase)	8,000	By Balance c/d	1,69,000
		By Cash	1,800
	1,83,000		1,83,000

(v) Goodwill Account

	Rs.		Rs.
To Balance b/d	Nil	By Balance c/d	5,000
To Shares	5,000		
	5,000		5,000

(vi) General Reserve Account

	Rs.		Rs.
To Balance c/d	60,000	By Balance b/d	50,000
To Loss on sale of Machinery	200	By Profit & Loss A/c	10,200
	60,200		60,200

(vii) Land & Buildings Account

	Rs.		Rs.
To Balance b/d	2,00,000	By Depreciation	10,000
		By Balance c/d	1,90,000
	2,00,000		2,00,000

(viii) Share Capital Account

	Rs.		Rs.
To Balance c/d	2,50,000	By Balance b/d	2,00,000
		By Machinery	25,000
		By Stock	20,000
		By Goodwill	5,000
	2,50,000		2,50,000

> **NOTE :** Total shares issued to Rs.50,000. Among this Rs.25,000 as against machinery and Rs. 5,000 as against goodwill. Both are non current items. It should not affect the working capital. So only Rs. 20,000 issued as against the stock. It should be treated as a source of funds. Because it is a current asset.

Problem 11. *From the following summarised financial statement of Anxious Ltd as on 30.04.1998, prepare*

(a) Statement of changes in working capital for the year ended 30.04.1998 and

(b) A statement showing sources and applications of funds during the same period.

Liabilities	1997 Rs.	1998 Rs.	Assets	1997 Rs.	1998 Rs.
Share capital	10,00,000	13,50,000	Fixed assets (Net)	18,00,000	20,50,000
General reserve	5,00,000	6,00,000	Investments	2,00,000	2,50,000
Profit & loss A/c	1,00,000	1,50,000	Inventories	5,00,000	7,00,000
Debentures	6,00,000	5,00,000	Debtors	5,85,000	6,40,000
Sundry creditors	9,00,000	10,50,000	Cash	15,000	10,000
	31,00,000	36,50,000		31,00,000	36,50,000

FUND FLOW STATEMENT

During the year ended on 30.04.98 depreciation charged on fixed assets amounted to Rs.2,50,000. The final dividend for the year ended 30.04.1997 amounted to Rs.1,00,000 was paid on 08.01.98.

[MCA Madras]

Solution :

Fund Flow Statement

Source of funds	Rs.	Application of funds	Rs.
Issue of Shares	3,50,000	Purchase of fixed assets	5,00,000
Fund from operation	5,00,000	Purchase of Investments	50,000
		Dividend paid	1,00,000
		Increase in working capital	1,00,000
		Redemption of debenture	1,00,000
	8,50,000		8,50,000

Working : *(i)* **Statement of changes in working capital**

	1997 Rs.	1998 Rs.
Current Assets :		
Inventors	5,00,000	7,00,000
Debtors	5,85,000	6,40,000
Cash	15,000	10,000
Total current assets	11,00,000	13,50,000
Current Liabilities :		
Sundry creditors	9,00,000	10,50,000
Total current liabilities	9,00,000	10,50,000
Working capital	2,00,000	3,00,000
Increase in working capital	1,00,000	(2,00,000 – 3,00,000)

(ii) Profit and Loss Account

	Rs.		Rs.
To General Reserve	1,00,000	By Balance b/d	1,00,000
To Dividend paid	1,00,000	By Fund from operation	5,00,000
To Depreciation	1,50,000		
To Balance c/d	2,50,000		
	6,00,000		6,00,000

(iii) Fixed Assets Account

	Rs.		Rs.
To Balance b/d	18,00,000	By Depreciation	2,50,000
To Cash	5,00,000	By Balance c/d	20,50,000
	23,00,000		23,00,000

Problem 12. *From the following balance sheet you are required to prepare schedule of changes in working capital and fund flow statement.*

Balance Sheet

Liabilities	31.3.1998 Rs.	31.3.1999 Rs.	Assets	31.3.1998 Rs.	31.3.1999 Rs.
Share capital	50,000	50,000	Cash	20,000	10,000
P.L. A/c	80,000	1,10,000	Marketable securities	10,000	-
12% debentures	-	30,000	Inventories	60,000	1,00,000
Sundry creditors	20,000	25,000	Debtors	30,000	40,000
Bills payable	20,000	5,000	Gross block	1,00,000	1,40,000
Other current liabilities	10,000	15,000	(−) accumulated depreciation	(40,000)	(55,000)
	1,80,000	2,35,000		1,80,000	2,35,000

[MBA Madras 1997]

Solution :

Fund Flow Statement

Source of funds	Rs.	Application of funds	Rs.
Issue of Debentures	30,000	Purchase of Gross block	40,000
Fund from operation	45,000	Increase in working capital	35,000
	75,000		75,000

Workings : (i) **Statement of changes in working capital**

Current Assets :	31.3.98 Rs.	31.3.99 Rs.
Cash	20,000	10,000
Marketable securities	10,000	-
Inventories	60,000	1,00,000
Debtors	30,000	40,000
Total current assets	1,20,000	1,50,000
Current Liabilities :		
Sundry creditors	20,000	25,000
Bills payable	20,000	5,000
Other Current Liabilities	10,000	15,000
Total current Liabilities	50,000	45,000
Working capital	70,000	1,05,000
Increase in working capital	35,000	(70,000 − 1,05,000)

(ii) Profit and Loss Account

	Rs.		Rs.
To Depreciation	15,000	By Balance b/d	80,000
To Balance c/d	1,10,000	By Fund from operation	45,000
	1,25,000		1,25,000

> **NOTE :** Gross Block means total fixed assets.

Problem 13. *The following are the summarized balance sheets of KNP Ltd on 31st December 2002 and 2003.*

Liabilities	2002 Rs.	2003 Rs.	Assets	2002 Rs.	2003 Rs.
Share capital	12,00,000	16,00,000	Plant & Machinery	8,00,000	12,90,000
Debentures	4,00,000	6,00,000	Land & building	6,00,000	8,00,000
Profit and loss A/c	2,50,000	5,00,000	Stock	6,00,000	7,00,000
Creditors	2,30,000	1,80,000	Bank	40,000	80,000
Provision for Bad & doubtful debts	12,000	6,000	Preliminary expenses	14,000	12,000
Depreciation on land & buildings	40,000	48,000	Debtors	1,38,000	1,22,000
Depreciation on plant & machinery	60,000	70,000			
	21,92,000	30,04,000		21,92,000	30,04,000

The following adjustments are to be made :
1. During the year a part of machinery costing Rs. 1,40,000 (accumulated depreciation there on Rs. 4,000) was sold for Rs. 12,000.
2. Dividend of Rs. 1,00,000 was paid during the year.

Prepare : (a) Statement of changes in working capital, (b) Fund flow statement

Solution :

Fund Flow Statement

Source of funds	Rs.	Application of funds	Rs.
Issue of shares	4,00,000	Dividend paid	1,00,000
Issue of Debentures	2,00,000	Purchase of	
Sale of Machinery	12,000	Plant & Machinery	6,30,000
Fund from operation	4,98,000	Purchase of Land & Building	2,00,000
		Increase in working capital	1,80,000
	11,10,000		11,10,000

Workings:

(i) Statement of changes in working capital

	2002 Rs	2003 Rs
Current Assets :		
Stock	6,00,000	7,00,000
Bank	40,000	80,000
Debtors	1,38,000	1,22,000
Total current assets	7,78,000	9,02,000
Current Liabilities :		
Creditors	2,30,000	1,80,000
Provision for doubtful debts	12,000	6,000
Total current liabilities	2,42,000	1,86,000
Working capital	5,36,000	7,16,000
Increase in working capital	1,80,000	(5,36,000 – 7,16,000)

(ii) Profit and Loss Account

	Rs		Rs
To Depreciation :		By Balance b/d	2,50,000
Plant & Machinery	14,000	By Fund from operation	4,98,000
Land & Buildings	8,000		
To Preliminary Expenses Written off	2,000		
To Dividend paid	1,00,000		
To Loss on sale of Machinery	1,24,000		
To Balance c/d	5,00,000		
	7,48,000		7,48,000

(iii) Plant and Machinery Account

	Rs		Rs
To Balance b/d	8,00,000	By Cash	12,000
To Cash (Purchase)	6,30,000	By Accumulated Depreciation	4,000
		By Profit and Loss A/c	1,24,000
		By Balance c/d	12,90,000
	14,30,000		14,30,000

(iv) Accumulated Depreciation Account on Plant & Machinery

	Rs		Rs
To Balance c/d	70,000	By Balance b/d	60,000
To Machinery A/c	4,000	By Profit & Loss A/c (Current year Depreciation)	14,000
	74,000		74,000

(v) Land & Buildings A/c

	Rs		Rs
To Balance b/d	6,00,000	By Balance c/d	8,00,000
To Cash	2,00,000		
	8,00,000		8,00,000

(vi) Accumulated Depreciation Account on Land & Building

To Balance c/d	48,000	By Balance c/d	40,000
		By Profit & Loss A/c	8,000
	48,000		48,000

> **NOTE :** Journal Entry for 1st Adjustment
>
> | | | | | |
> |---|---|---|---|---|
> | Cash A/c | Dr. | 12,000 | | [Sale of machinery] |
> | Accumulated depreciation A/c | Dr. | 4,000 | | [Depreciation] |
> | Profit & Loss A/c | Dr. | 1,24,000 | | [Loss on sale of machinery] |
> | To machinery A/c | | | 1,40,000 | [Cost of machinery] |

Problem 14. *From the following balance sheets of a Indian company Ltd. you are required to prepare fund flow statement.*

Balance Sheet

Liabilities	Jan. 2002 Rs.	Dec. 2002 Rs.	Assets	Jan. 2002 Rs.	Dec. 2002 Rs.
Current Liabilities	30,000	32,000	Cash	40,000	44,400
Bonds payable	22,000	22,000	Accounts receivable	10,000	20,700
Bonds payable discount	(2,000)	(1,800)	Inventories	15,000	15,000
Capital stock	35,000	43,500	Land	4,000	4,000
Retained earnings	15,000	19,500	Buildings	20,000	16,000
			Equipment	15,000	17,000
			Accumulated Depreciation	(5,000)	(2,800)
			Patents	1,000	900
	1,00,000	1,15,200		1,00,000	1,15,200

The following additional information is also available :

(a) Income for the period Rs. 10,000

(b) A building that costs Rs. 4,000 and which had a book value of Rs. 1,000 was sold for Rs. 1,400.

(c) The depreciation charged for the period was Rs. 800.

(d) There was an issue of common stock Rs. 5,000.

(e) Cash dividend of Rs. 2,000 and Rs. 3,500 stock dividend were declared.

[M.Com Madras]

Solution :

Fund Flow Statement

Source of funds	Rs.	Application of funds	Rs.
Sale of Building	1,400	Purchase of equipment	2,000
Issue of common stock	5,000	Cash dividend paid	2,000
Fund from operation	10,700	Increase in working capital	13,100
	17,100		17,100

Workings : **(i) Statement of changes in working capital**

Current Assets :	Jan. 2002 Rs.	Dec. 2002 Rs.
Cash	40,000	44,400
Account receivable	10,000	20,700
Inventories	15,000	15,000
Total current assets	65,000	80,100
Current Liabilities :		
Current Liabilities	30,000	32,000
Total current liabilities	30,000	32,000
Working capital	35,000	48,100
Increase in working capital [48,100 – 35,000]	—	13,100

(ii) Profit and Loss Account

Particulars	Rs.	Particulars	Rs.
To Loss on Bonds Payable discount	200	By Balance b/d	15,000
To Patent written off	100	By Profit on sale of Building	400
To Cash dividend paid	2,000	By Fund from operation	10,700
To Depreciation	800		
To Stock dividend	3,500		
To Balance c/d	19,500		
	26,100		26,100

(iii) Capital Stock Account

Particulars	Rs.	Particulars	Rs.
To Balance c/d	43,500	By Balance c/d	35,000
		By Cash	5,000
		By Stock Dividend	3,500
	43,500		43,500

(iv) Accumulated Depreciation Account

Particulars	Rs.	Particulars	Rs.
To Balance c/d	2,800	By Balance b/d	5,000
To Buildings A/c	3,000	By Profit & Loss A/c	800
	5,800		5,800

(v) Building Account

Particulars	Rs.	Particulars	Rs.
To Balance b/d	20,000	By Cash	1,400
To Profit & Loss A/c (Profit on sale)	400	By Accumulated Depreciation	3,000
		By Balance c/d	16,000
	20,400		20,400

FUND FLOW STATEMENT

> **NOTE :** Journal for IInd Adjustment
>
> | | | | | |
> |---|---|---|---|---|
> | Cash A/c | Dr. | 1400 | | [Sale of Building] |
> | Accumulated Depreciation A/c | Dr. | 3000 | | [Depreciation] |
> | To Building A/c | | | 4000 | [Book value] |
> | To Profit & Loss A/c | | | 400 | [Profit] |

Problem 15. *From the following balance sheets of Kavin Ltd., prepare a statement of changes in working capital and fund flow statement for the year ended 31.3.2002.*

Liabilities	2001 Rs.	2002 Rs.	Assets	2001 Rs.	2002 Rs.
Share capital	3,00,000	3,50,000	Goodwill	1,00,000	80,000
Debentures	1,50,000	2,50,000	Machinery	4,10,000	5,40,000
General reserve	1,00,000	1,50,000	Investment	30,000	80,000
Profit & loss A/c	60,000	70,000	Discount on issue of Debentures	5,000	—
Provision for depreciation on machinery	90,000	1,30,000	Cash at bank	1,20,000	1,30,000
Sundry creditors	75,000	1,10,000	Sundry debtors	80,000	1,90,000
Bills payable	10,000	15,000	Stock	40,000	55,000
	7,85,000	10,75,000		7,85,000	10,75,000

During the year investments costing Rs. 30,000 were sold for Rs. 28,000 and a new machine was purchased for Rs. 45,000. The payment was made in fully paid shares.

[M.Com adapted]

Solution :   **Fund Flow Statement**

Source of funds	Rs.	Application of funds	Rs.
Issue of shares	5,000	Purchase of Machinery (4)	85,000
Issue of Debentures	1,00,000	Increase in Working Capital (1)	95,000
Sale of investments	28,000	Purchase of Investment (6)	80,000
Fund from operation	1,27,000		
	2,60,000		2,60,000

Workings : *(i) Statement of changes in working capital*

Current Assets :	1999 Rs.	2000 Rs.
Cash at bank	1,20,000	1,30,000
Sundry Debtors	80,000	1,90,000
Stock	40,000	55,000
Total current assets	2,40,000	3,75,000

Current Liabilities :

Sundry creditors	75,000	1,10,000
Bills payable	10,000	15,000
Total current liabilities	85,000	1,25,000
Working capital	1,55,000	2,50,000
Increase in working capital	95,000	(1,55,000 – 2,50,000)

(ii) Profit and Loss Account

To Goodwill written off	20,000	By Balance b/d	60,000
To General Reserve	50,000	By Fund from operation	1,27,000
To Discount issue of Debentures	5,000		
To Depreciation	40,000		
To Loss on Sale of Investments	2,000		
To Balance c/d	70,000		
	1,87,000		1,87,000

(iii) Share Capital Account

To Balance c/d	3,50,000	By Balance b/d	3,00,000
		By Machinery	45,000
		By Cash	5,000
	3,50,000		3,50,000

(iv) Machinery Account

To Balance b/d	4,10,000	By Balance c/d	5,40,000
To Shares	45,000		
To Cash (b/f)	85,000		
	5,40,000		5,40,000

(v) Provision for Depreciation on Machinery Account

To Balance c/d	1,30,000	By Balance b/d	90,000
		By Profit & Loss Account	40,000
	1,30,000		1,30,000

(vi) Investment Account

To Balance b/d	30,000	By Bank	28,000
To Purchase of Investment (b/f)	80,000	By Loss Sale of Investment	2,000
		By Balance c/d	80,000
	1,10,000		1,10,000

FUND FLOW STATEMENT

> **NOTE :** Sale of Investment
>
> | | | | | |
> |---|---|---|---|---|
> | Cash A/c | Dr. | 28,000 | | [Actual sale] |
> | Profit & Loss A/c | Dr. | 2,000 | | [Loss on sale] |
> | To Investments | | | 30,000 | [Value of investment] |

Problem 16. *From the following summarised balance sheets of Balaji & Co as on 31.12.2003 and other information furnished, prepare fund flow statement.*

Balance sheet

Liabilities	2003 Rs.	2002 Rs.	Assets	2003 Rs.	2002 Rs.
Share capital	2,00,000	50,000	Fixed assets	4,20,000	2,40,000
Redeemable per shares	-	1,00,000	Investments	15,000	18,000
Profit & loss A/c	3,50,000	1,20,000	Stock	1,60,000	58,500
Debentures	-	1,25,000	Bills receivable	92,000	1,37,000
Sundry creditors	1,90,000	2,25,000	Cash at bank	1,20,000	1,85,000
Provision for Tax	75,000	25,000	Prepaid expenses	8,000	6,500
	8,15,000	6,45,000		8,15,000	6,45,000

The following additional information is also available :

(a) On 31.12.2003 accumulated depreciation on fixed assets amounted to Rs. 1,20,000 and on 31st December 2002 Rs. 1,10,000

(b) Machinery costing Rs. 10,000 (accumulated depreciation thereon being Rs. 5,000) was discarded and written off during 2003.

(c) Depreciation written off during 2003 amounted to Rs. 15,000.

(d) During the year 2003 investments costing Rs. 6,000 were sold for Rs. 7,000.

(e) Dividend paid during the year was Rs. 45,000

(f) Redeemable preference shares were redeemed out of profits during the year at a premium of 5%.

Solution :

Fund Flow Statement

Source of funds	Rs.	Application of funds	Rs.
Issue of shares	1,50,000	Repayment of Secured Loan	1,25,000
Sale of investments	7,000	Dividend paid	45,000
Decrease in working capital	22,000	Redemption of preference	
Fund from operation	2,99,000	Shares	1,05,000
		Purchase of Investments	3,000
		Purchase of Fixed assets	2,00,000
	4,78,000		4,78,000

Workings : **(i) Statement of changes in working capital**

	2002 Rs	2003 Rs
Current Assets :		
Stock	58,500	1,60,000
Sundry Debtors	1,37,000	92,000
Cash at Bank	1,85,000	1,20,000
Prepaid expenses	6,500	8,000
Total current assets	3,87,000	3,80,000
Current Liabilities :		
Sundry creditors	2,25,000	1,90,000
Provision for tax	25,000	75,000
Total current liabilities	2,50,000	2,65,000
Working capital	1,37,000	1,15,000
Decrease in working capital	22,000	(1,37,000 − 1,15,000)

(ii) Profit and Loss Account

	Rs.		Rs.
To Loss on sale of Machinery	5,000	By Balance b/d	1,20,000
To Dividend paid	45,000	By Profit on sale of Investments	1,000
To Premium on Redemption of Preference shares	5,000	By Fund from operation	2,99,000
To Depreciation	15,000		
To Balance c/d	3,50,000		
	4,20,000		4,20,000

(iii) Redeemable Preference Share Capital Account

To Cash	1,05,000	By Balance b/d	1,00,000
		By P&L A/c (premium)	5,000
	1,05,000		1,05,000

(iv) Fixed Assets Account

To Balance b/d (2,40,000 + 1,10,000)	3,50,000	By P&L A/c	5,000
		By Accumulated Depreciation	5,000
To Cash	2,00,000	By Balance c/d (4,20,000 + 1,20,000)	5,40,000
	5,50,000		5,50,000

(v) Accumulated Depreciation Account

To Fixed Assets	5,000	By Balance b/d	1,10,000
To Balance c/d	1,20,000	By P&L A/c (Current year Depreciation)	15,000
	1,25,000		1,25,000

(vi) Investment Account

To Balance b/d	18,000	By Cash	6,000
To Case	3,000	By Balance c/d	15,000
	21,000		21,000

NOTE :
(i) Journal Entry for IInd Adjustment
    Profit & Loss A/c   Dr.   5,000   [Loss]
    Accumulated depreciation A/c   Dr.   5,000   [Depreciation]
        To machinery A/c   10,000   [Value of machinery]
(ii) Journal Entry for IV transaction
    Cash A/c   Dr   7,000
        To Profit and Loss A/c   1,000
        To Investment A/c   6,000
(iii) Here provisional for Taxation assumed to a current liability.

Problem 17. *From the following data of National Auto Ltd. for the year 2000 and 2001.*

Particulars	2000 Rs,	2001 Rs.
Cash	2,000	2,500
Account receivable	2,400	2,700
Inventories	3,100	3,200
Other current assets	800	700
Fixed assets	5,000	5,800
Accumulated depreciation	2,100	2,500
Accounts payable	2,000	2,100
Long term debt	1,400	1,300
Equity capital	5,000	5,300
Retained earnings	2,800	3,700

The following additional information is also available :
(a) Fixed assets costing Rs.1,200 were purchased for cash.
(b) Fixed assets [Original cost of Rs.400 accumulated depreciation Rs.150] were sold for Rs.200.
(c) Depreciation for the year 2001 amounted to Rs.550 and duly debited to profit & loss account.
(d) Dividend paid amounted to Rs.300 in 2001.
(e) Reported income for 2001 was Rs.2,400.   [M.Com adapted]

Solution:

Fund Flow Statement

Source of funds	Rs.	Application of funds	Rs.
Issue of Equity Shares	300	Dividend paid	300
Sale of Fixed Assets	200	Purchase of Fixed Assets	1,200
Fund from operation	1,800	Repayment of Long term Debt	100
		Increase in working capital	700
	2,300		2,300

Workings : (*i*) Statement of changes in working capital

	2000 Rs	2001 Rs
Current Assets :		
Cash	2,000	2,500
Accounts receivable	2,400	2,700
Inventories	3,100	3,200
Other current assets	800	700
Total current assets	8,300	9,100
Current Liabilities :		
Account payable	2,000	2,100
Total current liabilities	2,000	2,100
Working capital	6,300	7,000
Increase in working capital	700	(6300 – 7000)

(*ii*) Fixed Assets Account

	Rs.		Rs.
To Balance b/d	5,000	By Cash	200
To Cash	1,200	By Accumulated Depreciation	150
		By Profit & Loss A/c	50
		By Balance c/d	5,800
	6,200		6,200

(*iii*) Profit and Loss Account

	Rs.		Rs.
To Fixed Assets	50	By Balance c/d	2,800
To Depreciation	550	By Fund from operation	1,800
To Dividend paid	300		
To Balance c/d	3,700		
	4,600		4,600

(*iv*) Accumulated Depreciation Account

	Rs.		Rs.
To Fixed Assets	150	By Balance b/d	2,100
To Balance c/d	2,500	By Profit & Loss A/c	550
	2,650		2,650

FUND FLOW STATEMENT

> **NOTE :**
> (i) *Journal Entry for IInd Adjustment*
>
> | | | | | |
> |---|---|---|---|---|
> | Cash A/c | Dr. | 200 | | [Sale of fixed assets] |
> | Accumulated depreciation A/c | Dr. | 150 | | [Depreciation] |
> | Profit and Loss A/c | Dr. | 50 | | [Loss on sale] |
> | To Fixed assets | | | 400 | |
>
> (ii) *Reported income*
> It is included in the Retained Earnings. So there is no need to give the effect of this Adjustment.

Problem 18. *From the following information, calculate funds from operations.*

Profit and Loss Account

	Rs.		Rs.
To expenses			
To Operating expenses	1,00,000	By Gross profit	2,00,000
To Depreciation	40,000	By Gain on sale of building	20,000
To loss on sale of machinery	10,000		
To advertisement expenses A/c	5,000		
To discount of debtors	500		
To discount on issue a shares	500		
To goodwill written off	12,000		
To preliminary expenses written off	2,000		
To Net profit	50,000		
	2,20,000		2,20,000

Solution :
Computation of fund from operation Profit and Loss Account

Expenses	Rs.	Incomes	Rs.
To Depreciation	40,000	By Balance b/d	Nil
To Loss on sale of Machinery	10,000	By Gain on sale of Buildings	20,000
To Goodwill written off	12,000	By Fund from operation	99,500
To Advertisement Expenses	5,000		
To Discount allowed	500		
To Preliminary Expenses Written off	2,000		
To Balance c/d	50,000		
	1,19,500		1,19,500

Problem 19. Balance sheets of M/s Black and White as on Ist Jan 2000 and 31st Dec 2000 were as follows :

Liabilities	Jan. 2000 Rs.	Dec. 2000 Rs.	Assets	Jan. 2000 Rs.	Dec. 2000 Rs.
Creditors	40,000	44,000	Cash	10,000	7,000
White's loan	25,000	—	Debtors	30,000	50,000
Loan from bank	40,000	50,000	Stock	35,000	25,000
Capital	1,25,000	1,53,000	Land	40,000	50,000
			Building	35,000	60,000
			Machinery	80,000	55,000
	2,30,000	2,47,000		2,30,000	2,47,000

During the year machine costing Rs. 10,000 [accumulated depreciation Rs. 3,000] was sold for Rs. 5,000. The provision for depreciation against machinery as on Ist Jan 2000 was Rs. 25,000 and on 31st Dec 2000 Rs. 40,000. Net profit for the year 2000 amounted to Rs. 54,000. Prepare fund flow statement.

[M.Com Madurai, MCA Bharathiar], [BBM PU 95]

Solution :   **Fund Flow Statement**

Source of funds	Rs.	Application of funds	Rs.
Loan from PN Bank	10,000	Repayment of Mr.White's Loan	25,000
Sale of Machinery	5,000	Purchase of Land	10,000
Fund from operation	65,000	Purchase of Building	25,000
		Increase in working capital	3,000
		Drawings (Capital A/c)	17,000
	80,000		80,000

Working :   *(i)* **Statement of changes in working capital**

	1.1.2000 Rs.	31.12.2000 Rs.
Current Assets :		
Cash	10,000	7,000
Debtors	30,000	50,000
Stock	35,000	25,000
Total current assets	75,000	82,000
Current Liabilities :		
Creditors	40,000	44,000
Total current liabilities	40,000	44,000
Working capital	35,000	38,000
Increase in working capital	3000	(35,000 – 38,000)

FUND FLOW STATEMENT

(ii) Profit and Loss Account

To Loss on sale of Machinery	2,000	By Fund from operation	65,000
To Depreciation	18,000		
To Balance c/d	45,000		
	65,000		65,000

(iii) Capital Account

To Balance c/d	1,53,000	By Balance b/d	1,25,000
To Cash (b/f)	17,000	By Profit & Loss A/c	45,000
	1,70,000		1,70,000

(iv) Machinery Account

To Balance c/d	1,05,000	By Cash	5,000
(80,000+25,000)		By P&L A/c	2,000
		By Accumulated Depreciation	3,000
		By Balance c/d	95,000
	1,05,000		1,05,000

(v) Accumulated Depreciation Account

To Machinery A/c	3,000	By Balance b/d	25,000
To Balance c/d	40,000	By P&L A/c (b/f)	18,000
	43,000		43,000

Journal Entry For 1st Adjustment :

Cash A/c Dr		5,000
Accumulated depreciation A/c Dr		3,000
Profit and Loss A/c Dr		2,000
To Machinery A/c		10,000

Problem 20. *The Balance sheets of Dharan Ltd as on 31.12.1999 and 31.12.2000 are as follows.*

Liabilities	1999 Rs.	2000 Rs.	Assets	1999 Rs.	2000 Rs.
Share capital	2,00,000	2,50,000	Fixed assets	3,50,000	4,75,000
Retained earnings	1,60,000	3,00,000	Inventory	1,00,000	95,000
Premium on share	—	5,000	Accounts receivable	43,000	50,000
Accumulated depreciation	80,000	60,000	Prepaid expenses	4,000	5,000
Debentures	60,000	—	Cash	15,800	10,200
Bank overdraft	37,800	40,200	Commission on shares	25,000	20,000
	5,37,800	6,55,200		5,37,800	6,55,200

The following additional information is also available :
(i) Net profit for the year Rs. 1,40,000
(ii) Income tax was paid Rs. 40,000
(iii) Interim dividend paid during the year was Rs. 20,000.
(iv) An addition to the fixed asset was made during the year at a cost of Rs. 1,65,000 and fully depreciated machinery costing Rs. 40,000 was discarded, no salvage being realised.
(v) Depreciation for the year Rs. 20,000 [BBM, 2000]

Solution : **Fund Flow Statement**

Source of funds	Rs.	Application of funds	Rs.
Issue of shares	50,000	Redemption of debentures	60,000
Premium on shares received	5,000	Purchase of fixed assets	1,65,000
Fund from operation	2,25,000	Income Tax paid	40,000
Decreasing in working capital	5,000	Interim dividend paid	20,000
	2,85,000		2,85,000

Workings : (i) **Statement of changes in working capital**

Current assets :	1999 Rs.	2000 Rs.
Inventories	1,00,000	95,000
Accounts receivable	43,000	50,000
Prepaid expenses	4,000	5,000
Cash	15,800	10,200
	1,62,800	1,60,200
Current Liabilities :		
Bank overdraft	37,800	40,200
Total current liabilities	37,800	40,200
Working capital	1,25,000	1,20,000
Decrease in working capital	5000	[1,25,000 – 1,20,000]

(ii) **Profit and Loss Account**

	Rs.		Rs.
To Commission on shares Written off	5,000	By Balance b/d	1,60,000
To Depreciation	20,000	By Fund from operation (b/f)	2,25,000
To Income Tax paid	40,000		
To Interim dividend paid	20,000		
To Balance c/d	3,00,000		
	3,85,000		3,85,000

(iii) Fixed Assets Account

	Rs.		Rs.
To Balance c/d	3,50,000	By accumulated depreciation	40,000
To Cash (b/f)	1,65,000	By Balance c/d	4,75,000
	5,15,000		5,15,000

(iv) Accumulated Depreciation Account

	Rs.		Rs.
To Machinery A/c	40,000	By Balance b/d	80,000
(Fully Depreciated Machinery)		By Profit & Loss A/c (b/f)	20,000
To Balance c/d	60,000		
	1,00,000		1,00,000

❑❑❑

6
Cash Flow Statement

INTRODUCTION

Cash contributes significant role in the entire economic activities of the business world. And at the same time, cash is not only essential for business, but is also essential for each and every activity of human life. What blood is to human body, cash is to a business firm. The firm receives cash from various sources like issue of shares, sale of assets etc. It needs cash to make payments for various purposes like payment to suppliers and to meet out the day to day expenses. The foremost responsibility of the financial manager is to determine cash planning activities and to maintain adequate cash balances. At this juncture cash flow statement is an important tool of cash planning and control. The term cash is used to refer to cash in hand and bank balance.

MEANING

Cash flow statement is a statement which is prepared from the historical data showing the inflow and outflow of cash. It shows the sources and uses of cash between the two balance sheet dates. It clearly explains the causes for changes in cash position between two periods. Simply, it is a receipts and payments account in a summary form.

USES OF CASH FLOW STATEMENT

Cash flow statement is an important tool of financial analysis. It is vital to financial management. Its main uses are as follows :

(i) It gives guidance to the management in taking and implementing short-term financial policies.

(ii) It helps to strengthen the borrowing capacities of the firms. The financial institutions can easily assess the repaying capacities of the firms through the cash flow analysis.

(iii) It contributes significant role for the capital budgeting decisions.

(iv) It helps in short term financial decisions relating to liquidity.

(v) In order to find out the variation and take necessary remedial measures with the help of the comparison of actual cash flow statements with the projected cash flow statements.

(vi) To overcome the problem of meeting deficit cash or investment of surplus cash with the help of the projected cash flow statement. Thus, projected cash flow statement is usually prepared on the basis of past year's experience.

CASH FLOW STATEMENT

(vii) It explains the causes for poor cash position in spite of huge profits or surplus cash balance in spite of low profits.

(viii) It explains the major sources and uses of cash for the business concern during a particular period of time.

LIMITATIONS OF CASH FLOW ANALYSIS

Cash flow statement is a systematic tool of financial analysis. However, it suffers from some limitations which are as follows :

1. A cash flow statement cannot be equated with the income statement. An income statement considers both cash and non-cash items. So cash does not mean net income of business.
2. The cash flow statement may not represent the real liquid position of the concern. Due to this aspect, postponing of purchases and payments could be developed.
3. Cash flow statement cannot replace the income statement or fund flow statement. Each and every statement has a separate function to perform.
4. Due to inflation, economic depression and other external factors, projected cash flow statement may not achieve its results.

DIFFERENCE BETWEEN CASH FLOW ANALYSIS AND FUND FLOW ANALYSIS

1. Cash flow statement starts with the opening cash balance and ends with the closing cash balance by processing through various sources and uses. But there are no opening and closing balances in fund flow statement.
2. Cash from operation can be found out under the cash flow statement. But fund from operation can be found out under the fund flow statement.
3. Separate statements are prepared for the purpose of finding out increase or decrease in working capital under the fund flow statement. But no separate statements for increase or decrease in working capital are prepared in cash flow analysis.
4. A cash flow statement explains the causes for the changes in cash and bank balances *i.e.*, cash receipts and cash payments alone. But fund flow statement indicates the causes for the changes in net working capital.
5. Cash flow statement is suitable for short term financial planning and decision, while fund flow statement is appropriate for long term financial planning and decisions.
6. Cash flow analysis deals with the movement of actual or notional cash. But fund flow statement deals with not only cash but also the items constituting working capital. Cash is one of the components of working capital.
7. Whenever, wherever there is inflow of cash there will definitely be inflow of funds. But sound fund position need not be a sound cash position.

STEPS IN PREPARATION OF CASH FLOW STATEMENT

Cash flow statement can be prepared on the same pattern on which fund flow statement is prepared. But here statement of changes in working capital does not need to be prepared. Remaining all other procedures were same in fund flow statement.

Cash flow statement is prepared on any one of the following assumptions :
— When all transactions are taken as cash transactions.
— When all transactions are not cash transactions.

Here we have to proceed with all the problems by treating all the transactions as cash transactions.

Steps

1. No need to prepare working capital statement
2. Preparation of cash flow statement
3. Preparation of profit & loss account-computation of cash from operation
4. Preparation of separate ledger if necessary
5. Treatment of adjustments

1. *No need to prepare the working capital statement*

   Changes in current assets and current liabilities are adjusted in the cash flow statement itself. So separate statement is not necessary for the changes in working capital.

2. **Cash Flow Statement (Proforma)**

Inflow of cash	Amount Rs.	Outflow of cash	Amount Rs.
Opening Cash Balance (including bank balance)	xx	Redemption of preference shares	xx
Issue of Shares	xx	Repayment debenture holders	xx
Issue of Debentures	xx	Repayment of Loans	xx
Raising of loans	xx	Purchase of fixed assets	xx
Sale of fixed assets	xx	Dividend paid	xx
Dividends received	xx	Income Tax paid	xx
Share premium received	xx	Cash from Operation (Lost in operation) Transfer from P&L A/c	xx
Cash from operation (Transfer from P&L A/c)	xx	Closing balance (including bank balance)	
	xx		xx

3. *Preparation of Profit & Loss Account - Computation of cash from operation*

   Cash from operations can be found out in two methods. One is statement form another one is preparation of profit and loss account. Normally, cash from operation can be found out with the help of the preparation of profit and loss account because it is an easy and convenient method. Here profit and loss account is prepared in usual procedure.

CASH FLOW STATEMENT

Profit and Loss A/c

Dr.   Cr.

	Amount Rs.		Amount Rs.
To Goodwill written off	xx	By Opening Balance b/d	xx
To General reserve	xx	By Dividends received	xx
To Preliminary expenses written off	xx	By Interest on investments	xx
		By Profit on sale of assets	xx
To Depreciation	xx	By Cash from operation	xx
To Loss on sale of fixed assets	xx	*(Balancing figure)*	
To Loss on sale of Investments	xx		
To Patents & Trade mark written off	xx		
To Income tax provided	xx		
To Interim dividend paid	xx		
To Closing balance c/d	xx		
To Cash from operation *(Balancing figure)*	xx		
	xx		xx

4. *Preparation of Separate Ledger*

   If information of any particular assets or liabilities are given in the adjustment, we have to prepare separate asset or liabilities account. Balances from this ledger can be transferred to cash flow statement.

5. *Treatment of adjustments*

   The additional information which are given apart from the balance sheet are, simply called as adjustment. All the adjustments will appear in two places. The following are the important adjustments and their treatment.

   (a) Dividend paid   - Cash flow statement - outflow side
                                     - Profit & loss A/c - Debit side

   (b) Depreciation   - P.L.A/c - Debit side
                                        Respective asset A/c - credit side

   (c) Loss on sale of - P.L.A/c - Debit side
        assets   Respective asset A/c - credit side

   (d) Income Tax   - P.L.A/c - Debit side
        provision   - Income Tax - Credit side.

> **NOTE :** The adjustments applicable for fund flow statements will also be applicable for cash flow statements.

Problem 1. *From the following profit and loss account, compute the case from operations.*

Profit and Loss account for the year ended 31.3.2001

	Amount Rs.		Amount Rs.
To Salaries	25,000	By Gross Profit	1,25,000
To Rent	3,000	By Profit on sale of land	15,000
To Depreciation	10,000	By Income tax refund	13,000
To Loss on Sale of plant	4,000		
To Goodwill written off	10,000		
To Proposed dividend	15,000		
To Provision for Tax	12,000		
To Net Profit	74,000		
	1,53,000		1,53,000

Solution :

Computation of case from operation

Net profit earned during the year		74,000
Add : Non-cash and Non-operating expenses		
Depreciation	10,000	
Loss on sale of plant	4,000	
Goodwill written off	10,000	
Proposed dividend	15,000	
Provision for taxation	5,000	
		44,000
		1,18,000
Less : Non-cash and Non-operating income		
Profit on sale of land	15,000	
Income tax refund	13,000	
		28,000
Cash from operation		90,000

Problem 2. *Statement of financial position of Mr.Arun is given below.*

Liabilities	01.1.2000 Rs.	31.12.2000 Rs.	Assets	01.1.2000 Rs.	31.12.2000 Rs.
Account Payable	29,000	25,000	Cash	40,000	30,000
Capital	7,39,000	6,15,000	Debtors	20,000	17,000
			Stock	8,000	13,000
			Building	1,00,000	80,000
			Other fixed Assets	6,00,000	5,00,000
	7,68,000	6,40,000		7,68,000	6,40,000

CASH FLOW STATEMENT

The following additional information is also available :
(a) There were no drawings.
(b) There were no purchases or sale of either building or other fixed assets. Prepare a statement of case flow. [BBM, MBA Anna]

Solution :

Cash Flow Statement

Inflow of cash	Amount Rs.	Outflow of cash	Amount Rs.
Opening Cash Balance	40,000	Decrease in accounts payable	4,000
Decrease in Debtors	3,000	Increase in stock	5,000
		Cash from operation (1)	4,000
		Closing cash balance	30,000
	43,000		43,000

Workings :

1. Profit and Loss Account

	Amount Rs.		Amount Rs.
To Depreciation on Building	20,000	By Capital Account (Loss)	1,24,000
To Depreciation on Plant	1,00,000		
To Cash from operation (Loss on operation)	4,000		
	1,24,000		1,24,000

2. Capital Account of Mr.Arun

To Profit & Loss A/c (Loss)	1,24,000	By Balance b/d	7,39,000
To Balance c/d	6,15,000		
	7,39,000		7,39,000

3. Building Account

To Balance b/d	1,00,000	By Depreciation (P&L A/c)	20,000
		By Balance c/d	80,000
	1,00,000		1,00,000

4. Other Fixed Assets Account

To balance b/d	6,00,000	By Depreciation (P&L A/c)	1,00,000
		By Balance c/d	5,00,000
	6,00,000		6,00,000

Problem 3. *From the following particulars of Mrs.Ragu, prepare cash flow statements.*

Liabilities :	1.1.99 Rs.	31.12.95 Rs.
Creditors	36,000	41,000
Mrs.A's Loan	—	20,000
Capital	1,48,000	1,49,000
Bank Loan	30,000	25,000
	2,14,000	2,35,000
Assets :		
Cash	4,000	3,600
Debtors	35,000	38,400
Stock	25,000	22,000
Land	20,000	30,000
Buildings	50,000	55,000
Machinery	80,000	86,000
	2,14,000	2,35,000

During the year Mrs.Ragu had drawn Rs. 26,000 for personal use. The provision for depreciation against machinery as on 1.1.99 was Rs. 27,000 and as on 31.12.99 Rs. 36,000.

Solution :   **Cash Flow Statement**

Inflow of cash	Amount Rs.	Outflow of cash	Amount Rs.
Opening cash balance	4,000	Repayment of Bank loan	5,000
Loan borrowed from Mrs. A	20,000	Increase in Debtors	3,400
Decrease in stock	3,000	Purchase of Land	10,000
Cash from operation (1)	36,000	Purchase of Buildings	5,000
Increase in creditors	5,000	Capital Account (Drawings)	26,000
		Purchase of machinery (3)	15,000
		Closing Cash Balance	3,600
	68,000		68,000

Workings :   **1. Profit and Loss Account**

	Amount Rs.		Amount Rs.
To Depreciation (4)	9,000	By Cash from operation	36,000
To Capital Account	27,000		
	36,000		36,000

2. Capital Account

To Cash (Drawings)	26,000	By Balance b/d	1,48,000
To Balance c/d	1,49,000	By Profit & Loss A/c (Transfer to P&L A/c)	27,000
	1,75,000		1,75,000

3. Machinery Account

To Balance b/d (80,000+27,000)	1,07,000	By Balance c/d (86,000+36,000)	1,22,000
To Cash (b/f)	15,000		
	1,22,000		1,22,000

4. Accumulated Depreciation Account

To Balance c/d	36,000	By Balance b/d	27,000
		By P&L A/c (b/f)	9,000
	36,000		36,000

Problem 4. *The Balance sheet of Super Computers Ltd. as on 31.12.1992 and 31.12.1993 respectively are given below.*

Liabilities	1992 Rs.	1993 Rs.	Assets	1992 Rs.	1993 Rs.
Share capital	1,00,000	1,60,000	Fixed assets at		
Retained earnings	70,250	85,300	cost	1,52,000	2,00,000
Accumulated Depreciation	60,000	40,000	Inventory	93,400	89,200
			Sundry Debtors	30,800	21,100
6% Debentures	50,000	—	Prepaid expenses	3,950	3,000
Sundry creditors	28,000	48,000	Bank	28,100	20,000
	3,08,250	3,33,300		3,08,250	3,33,300

The following additional information for the year 1993 is also available.
 (i) Net profit Rs. 27,050
 (ii) Depreciation charged Rs. 10,000
 (iii) Cash dividend declared during the period Rs. 12,000
 (iv) An addition to the building was made during the year at a cost of Rs. 78,000 and fully depreciated equipment costing Rs. 30,000 was discarded, no salvage value being realised. Prepare a cash flow statement. [BE Anna 2004]

Solution :

Cash Flow Statement

Inflow of cash	Amount Rs.	Outflow of cash	Amount Rs.
Opening cash balance	28,100	Redemption of debentures	50,000
Decrease in inventory	4,200	Cash dividend paid	12,000
Decrease in debtors	9,700	Purchase of building	78,000
Decrease in prepaid expenses	950	Closing cash balance	20,000
Issue of shares	60,000		
Cash from operation	37,050		
Increase in creditors	20,000		
	1,60,000		1,60,000

Workings :

1. Profit and Loss Account

	Amount Rs.		Amount Rs.
To Cash dividend paid	12,000	By balance b/d	70,250
To Depreciation (Current Year)	10,000	By Cash from Operation (b/f)	37,050
To Balance c/d	85,300		
	1,07,300		1,07,300

2. Accumulated Depreciation Account

To Fixed Assets (Discarded Equipment)	30,000	By Balance b/d	60,000
		By P&L A/c	10,000
To Balance c/d	40,000		
	70,000		70,000

3. Fixed Assets Account

To Balance b/d	1,52,000	By Depreciation	30,000
To Cash (Purchase)	78,000	By Balance c/d	2,00,000
	2,30,000		2,30,000

Problem 5. *The following are the summarised balance sheets of South Computers Ltd. as on 31.12.2000 and 31.12.2001.*

Liabilities	2000 Rs.	2001 Rs.	Assets	2000 Rs.	2001 Rs.
Share Capital	2,00,000	2,50,000	Land & Buildings	2,00,000	1,90,000
General Reserve	50,000	60,000	Machinery	1,50,000	1,69,000
P&L A/c	30,500	30,600	Stock	1,00,000	74,000
Bank loan	70,000	—	Sundry Debtors	80,000	64,200
Sundry Creditors	1,50,000	1,35,200	Cash	500	600
Provision for Taxation	30,000	35,000	Bank	—	8,000
			Goodwill	—	5,000
	5,30,500	5,10,800		5,30,500	5,10,800

CASH FLOW STATEMENT

The following additional information for the the year 2001 is also available :
(i) Dividend of Rs. 23,000 was paid.
(ii) The following assets of another company were purchased for a consideration of Rs. 50,000 paid in shares.
   (a) Stock Rs. 20,000 and (b) Machinery Rs. 25,000
(iii) Machinery was further purchased for Rs. 8,000
(iv) Depreciation written off machinery Rs. 12,000
(v) Income Tax provided during the year Rs. 33,000
(vi) Loss on sale of machinery Rs. 200 was written off to general reserve.
(vii) Prepare cash flow statement.

[M.Com Madurai]

Solution :

Cash Flow Statement

Inflow of cash	Amount Rs.	Outflow of cash	Amount Rs.
Opening cash balance	500	Repayment of Bank Loan	70,000
Sale of Land & Building	10,000	Decrease in Sundry Creditors	14,800
Decrease in Sundry Debtors	15,800	Dividend paid	23,000
Sale of Machinery	1,800	Purchase of Machinery	8,000
Sale of Stock	46,000	Income Tax paid	28,000
Cash from operation	78,300	Closing cash balance (8,000 + 600)	8,600
	1,52,400		1,52,400

Workings :

1. Share Capital Account

	Amount Rs.		Amount Rs.
To Balance c/d	2,50,000	By Balance b/d	2,00,000
		By Stock	20,000
		By Machinery	25,000
		By Goodwill	5,000
	2,50,000		2,50,000

2. General Reserve Account

	Amount Rs.		Amount Rs.
To Loss on sale of Machinery	200	By Balance b/d	50,000
To Balance c/d	60,000	By Profit & Loss A/c	10,200
	60,200		60,200

3. Provision for Taxation Account

	Amount Rs.		Amount Rs.
To Cash (Tax paid)	28,000	By Balance b/d	30,000
To Balance c/d	35,000	By P & L A/c	33,000
	63,000		63,000

4. Profit and Loss Account

To Dividend Paid	23,000	By Balance b/d	30,500
To Depreciation on Machinery	12,000	By Cash from operation	78,300
To Income tax provided	33,000		
To Transfer to General Reserve	10,200		
To Balance c/d	30,600		
	1,08,800		1,08,800

5. Machinery Account

To Balance b/d	1,50,000	By Depreciation	12,000
To Shares	25,000	By Loss on sale of Machinery	200
To Cash	8,000	By Cash (b/f)	1,800
		By Balance c/d	1,69,000
	1,83,000		1,83,000

6. Stock Account

To Balance b/d	1,00,000	By Cash (b/f)	46,000
To Shares	20,000	By Balance c/d	74,000
	1,20,000		1,20,000

7. Goodwill Account

To Balance b/d	Nil	By Balance c/d	5,000
To Shares	5,000		
	5,000		5,000

> **NOTE :** In the absence of direction, the differences in the Land & Building value (*i.e.*, 2,00,000 − 1,90,000 = 10,000) are treated as sale of Land & Building and not as depreciation. If any specific direction is given in the problem, we proceed with the problem according to the direction.

Problem 6. *Balance Sheets of M/s.Black and White as on 1st Jan.2000 and 31st Dec. 2000 were as follows.*

Liabilities	Jan.2000 Rs.	Dec.2000 Rs.	Assets	Jan.2000 Rs.	Dec.2000 Rs.
Creditors	40,000	44,000	Cash	10,000	7,000
White loan	25,000	—	Debtors	30,000	50,000
Loan from bank	40,000	50,000	Stock	35,000	25,000
Capital	1,25,000	1,53,000	Land	40,000	50,000
			Building	35,000	60,000
			Machinery	80,000	55,000
	2,30,000	2,47,000		2,30,000	2,47,000

CASH FLOW STATEMENT

During the year machine costing Rs. 10,000 (accumulated depreciation Rs. 3,000) was sold for Rs. 5,000. The provision for depreciation against machinery as on 1st Jan.2000 was Rs. 25,000 and on 31st Dec.2000 Rs. 40,000. Net profit for the year 2000 amounted to Rs. 54,000. Prepare cash flow statement.   [M.Com Madurai, MCA Bharathiar, BBM PU95]

Solution :

Cash Flow Statement

Inflow of cash	Amount Rs.	Outflow of cash	Amount Rs.
Opening cash balance	10,000	Increase in Debtors	20,000
Decrease in stock	10,000	Purchase of Land	10,000
Increase in Creditors	4,000	Purchase of Buildings	25,000
Loan from Bank	10,000	Repayment of Mr.White's	
Sale of Machinery	5,000	Loan	25,000
Cash from Operation (1)	65,000	Capital Account (3)(Drawings)	17,000
		Closing Cash Balance	7,000
	1,04,000		1,04,000

Workings :

1. Profit and Loss Account

	Amount Rs.		Amount Rs.
To Loss on sale of Machinery	2,000	By Balance b/d	Nil
To Depreciation (4)	18,000	By Cash from operation	65,000
To Balance c/d	45,000		
	65,000		65,000

2. Machinery Account

	Amount Rs.		Amount Rs.
To Balance b/d (80,000 + 25,000)	1,05,000	By Cash	5,000
		By P&L A/c	2,000
		By Accumulated Depreciation	3,000
		By Balance c/d (55,000 + 40,000)	95,000
	1,05,000		1,05,000

3. Capital Account

	Amount Rs.		Amount Rs.
To Cash	17,000	By Balance b/d	1,25,000
To Balance c/d	1,53,000	By P&L A/c	45,000
	1,70,000		1,70,000

4. Accumulated Depreciation Account

	Amount Rs.		Amount Rs.
To Machinery A/c	3,000	By Balance b/d	25,000
To Balance c/d	40,000	By P&L A/c	18,000
	43,000		43,000

Journal for Ist Adjustment :

Cash A/c	Dr.	5000	(Sale of Machinery)
Accumulated Depreciation A/c	Dr.	3000	(Depreciation)
P.L A/c	Dr.	2000	(Loss on Sale of Machinery)
To Machinery A/c		10,000	

Problem 7. *From the following balance sheet of Exe Ltd., prepare cash flow statement*

Liabilities	1999 Rs.	2000 Rs.
Equity share capital	3,00,000	4,00,000
Redeemable preference		
Share capital	1,50,000	1,00,000
General Reserve	40,000	70,000
Profit & Loss A/c	30,000	48,000
Proposed dividend	42,000	50,000
Creditors	55,000	83,000
Bills Payable	20,000	16,000
Provision for taxation	40,000	50,000
	6,77,000	8,17,000

Assets	1999 Rs.	2000 Rs.
Goodwill	1,15,000	90,000
Land & Buildings	2,00,000	1,70,000
Plant	80,000	2,00,000
Debtors	1,60,000	2,00,000
Stock	77,000	1,09,000
Bills Receivable	20,000	30,000
Cash in hand	15,000	10,000
Cash at bank	10,000	8,000
	6,77,000	8,17,000

The following additional information is also available :

(a) Depreciation of Rs. 10,000 and Rs. 20,000 have been charged on Plant and Land and Buildings in 2000.

(b) A dividend of Rs. 20,000 has been paid in 2000.

(c) Income tax of Rs. 35,000 has been paid during 2000. [B.Com PU 2004]

CASH FLOW STATEMENT

Solution :

Cash Flow Statement

Inflow of cash	Amount Rs.	Outflow of cash	Amount Rs.
Opening Cash Balance	25,000	Redemption of preference	
Issue of Shares	1,00,000	Shares	50,000
Increase in Sundry Creditors	28,000	Dividend paid	42,000
Sale of Land & building	10,000	Decrease in Bills Payable	4,000
Cash from operation	2,18,000	Increase in Debtors	40,000
		Increase in Stock	32,000
		Increase in bills receivable	10,000
		Purchase of Plant	1,30,000
		Interim dividend paid	20,000
		Income Tax paid	35,000
		Closing Cash balance	18,000
		(10,000 + 8,000)	
	3,81,000		3,81,000

Workings :

1. Profit and Loss Account

	Amount Rs.		Amount Rs.
To General Reserve	30,000	By Balance c/d	30,000
To Proposed dividend	50,000	By Cash from operation	2,18,000
To Goodwill written off	25,000		
To Depreciation of Plant	10,000		
To Depreciation of			
Land & Buildings	20,000		
To Interim dividend paid	20,000		
To Income Tax provided (2)	45,000		
To Balance c/d	48,000		
	2,48,000		2,48,000

2. Provision for Taxation Account

To Cash (Tax paid)	35,000	By Balance b/d	40,000
To Balance c/d	50,000	By P&L A/c	45,000
		(Tax Provisions)	
	85,000		85,000

3. Land & Buildings Account

To Balance b/d	2,00,000	By Depreciation A/c	20,000
		By Balance c/d	1,70,000
		By Cash (b/f)	10,000
	2,00,000		2,00,000

4. Plant Account

	Rs.		Rs.
To Balance b/d	80,000	By Depreciation	10,000
To Cash (b/f)	1,30,000	By Balance c/d	2,00,000
	2,10,000		2,10,000

Problem 8. *From the following comparative Balance Sheet of ABC Ltd. as on 31.12.2002 and 2002.*

Liabilities	2001 Rs.	2002 Rs.	Assets	2001 Rs.	2002 Rs.
Share Capital	70,000	74,000	Cash	9,000	7,800
Debentures	12,000	6,000	Trade Debtors	14,900	17,700
Creditors	10,360	11,840	Marketable Securities	49,200	42,700
Provision for Doubtful debts	700	800	Land	20,000	30,000
Profit & Loss A/c	10,040	10,560	Goodwill	10,000	5,000
	1,03,100	1,03,200		1,03,100	1,03,200

The following additional information is also available :
  (i) Dividend of Rs. 3,500 was paid during the year 2002.
  (ii) Land was purchased for Rs. 10,000 and amount provided for the amortization of goodwill of Rs. 5,000.
  (iii) Debentures was repaid Rs. 6,000.
     Prepare cash flow statement.

[B.Com Madurai]

Solution :

Cash Flow Statement

Inflow of cash	Amount Rs.	Outflow of cash	Amount Rs.
Opening cash balance	9,000	Increase in debtors	2,800
Issue of Shares	4,000	Dividend paid	3,500
Increase in Creditors	1,480	Purchase of land	10,000
Decrease in Marketable Securities	6,500	Redemption of debentures	6,000
Cash from operation	9,120	Closing cash balance	7,800
	30,100		30,100

Workings :

1. Profit and Loss Account

	Amount Rs.		Amount Rs.
To Provision for Doubtful debts	100	By Balance b/d	10,040
To Dividend Paid	3,500	By Cash from operation	9,120
To Goodwill written off	5,000		
To Balance c/d	10,560		
	19,160		19,160

2. Debentures Account

To Cash (b/f)	6,000	By Balance b/d	12,000
To Balance c/d	6,000		
	12,000		12,000

3. Land Account

To Balance b/d	20,000	By Balance c/d	30,000
To Cash	10,000		
	30,000		30,000

4. Goodwill Account

To Balance b/d	10,000	By P&L A/c	5,000
		By Balance c/d	5,000
	10,000		10,000

Problem 9. *From the following Balance Sheet of Gristol Ltd., make out the statement of sources and uses of case.*

Liabilities	1998 Rs.	1999 Rs.	Assets	1998 Rs.	1999 Rs.
Capital	1,15,000	1,15,000	Cash & Bank		
Sundry Creditors	51,500	48,000	Balance	45,000	45,000
Outstanding Expn.	6,500	6,000	Sundry Debtors	33,500	21,500
8% Debentures	45,000	35,000	Temporary		
Depreciation Fund	20,000	22,000	Investment	55,000	37,000
Reserve for			Prepaid Expenses	500	1,000
Contingencies	30,000	30,000	Stock in Trade	41,000	53,000
Profit & Loss A/c	8,000	11,500	Land & Buildings	75,000	75,000
			Machinery	26,000	35,000
	2,76,000	2,67,500		2,76,000	2,67,500

The following additional information is also available :
 (i) *10% dividend was paid in cash.*
 (ii) *New machinery for Rs. 15,000 was purchased but old machinery costing Rs. 6,000 was sold for Rs. 2,000; accumulated depreciation was Rs. 3,000.*
 (iii) *Rs. 10,000 8% debentures were redeemed by purchase from open market @ Rs. 96 for a debenture of Rs. 100.*
 (iv) *Rs. 18,000 investments were sold at book value.* [M.Com. Bombay]

Solution :

Cash Flow Statement

Inflow of cash	Amount Rs.	Outflow of cash	Amount Rs.
Opening Cash balance	45,000	Decrease in Sundry Creditors	3,500
Decrease in Sundry debtors	12,000	Decrease in Outstanding	
Sale of Machinery	2,000	Expenses	500
Sale of Investments	18,000	Increase in prepaid expenses	500
Cash from operation	20,600	Redemption of debentures	9,600
		Increase in Stock in Trade	12,000
		Payment of dividend	11,500
		Purchase of Machinery	15,000
		Closing Stock balance	45,000
	97,600		97,600

Workings :

1. Profit and Loss Account

	Amount Rs.		Amount Rs.
To Payment of dividend	11,500	By Balance b/d	8,000
To Loss on sale of Machinery	1,000	By Profit on Redemption of	
To Depreciation	5,000	Debentures	
To Balance c/d	11,500	(10,000−9,600)	400
		By Cash from operation	20,600
	29,000		29,000

2. Accumulated Depreciation Account

	Amount Rs.		Amount Rs.
To Machinery	22,000	By Balance b/d	20,000
To Balance c/d	3,000	By P&L A/c (b/f)	5,000
	25,000		25,000

3. Machinery Account

	Amount Rs.		Amount Rs.
To Balance b/d	26,000	By Cash	2,000
To Cash (b/f)	15,000	By P&L A/c	1,000
		By Accumulated Depreciation	3,000
		By Balance c/d	35,000
	41,000		41,000

4. Debenture Account

	Amount Rs.		Amount Rs.
To Cash	9,600	By Balance b/d	45,000
To Profit on Redemption	400		
To Balance c/d	35,000		
	45,000		45,000

5. Investment Account

To Balance b/d	55,000	By Cash	18,000
		By Balance c/d	37,000
	55,000		55,000

NOTE : Redemption of debenture $\frac{96}{100} \times 10,000 = 9,600$

Actual value of debenture = 10,000
Amount paid = 9,600
Profit on Redemption of debenture = 400

Problem 10. *The Comparative Balance Sheets of Mr. Hitler for the two years are as follows.*

Liabilities	2002 Rs.	2003 Rs.	Assets	2002 Rs.	2003 Rs.
Loan from wife	—	20,000	Cash	11,000	15,000
Bills Payable	12,000	8,000	Debtors	40,000	35,000
Creditors	25,000	52,000	Stock	25,000	30,000
Loan from Bank	43,000	60,000	Machinery	20,000	14,000
Capital	66,000	34,000	Land & Buildings	50,000	80,000
	1,46,000	1,74,000		1,46,000	1,74,000

The following additional information is also available :
   (i) Net Loss for the year 2003 amounted to Rs. 13,000.
   (ii) During the year machine costing Rs. 5,000 (accumulated depreciation Rs. 2,000) was sold for Rs. 2,500. The provision for depreciation against machinery as on 31.12.2002 was Rs. 6,000 and on 31.12.2003 was Rs. 7,000. [MBA Anna 2005]

Solution :   **Cash Flow Statement**

Inflow of cash	Amount Rs.	Outflow of cash	Amount Rs.
Opening Cash Balance	11,000	Decrease in bills payable	4,000
Loan borrowed from wife	20,000	Increase in Stock	5,000
Increase in Creditors	27,000	Purchase of Land & Buildings	30,000
Loan borrowed from bank	17,000	Drawings (2) (Capital A/c)	19,000
Decrease in Debtors	5,000	Cash from operation	9,500
Sale of Machinery	2,500	Closing cash balance	15,000
	82,500		82,500

Workings :

1. Profit and Loss Account

	Amount Rs.		Amount Rs.
To Loss on sale of Machinery	500	By Balance b/d	13,000
To Depreciation A/c	3,000		
To Cash from operation	9,500		
	13,000		13,000

2. Capital Account

	Amount Rs.		Amount Rs.
To Profit & Loss A/c (Net Loss)	13,000	By Balance b/d	66,000
To Balance c/d	34,000		
To Cash (b/f)	19,000		
	66,000		66,000

3. Machinery Account

	Amount Rs.		Amount Rs.
To Balance b/d	26,000	By Cash	2,500
(20,000 + 6,000)		By Profit & Loss A/c	500
		By Accumulated Depreciation	2,000
		By Balance c/d	21,000
		(14,000 + 7,000)	
	26,000		26,000

4. Accumulated Depreciation Account

	Amount Rs.		Amount Rs.
To Machinery A/c	2,000	By Balance b/d	6,000
To Balance c/d	7,000	By P&L A/c	3,000
	9,000		9,000

NOTE :
Journal Entry for IInd Adjustment

Cash A/c	Dr.	2,500		(Sale price)
Accumulated Depreciation	Dr.	2,500		(Depreciation)
Profit & Loss A/c	Dr.	500		(Loss)
To Machinery			5,000	(Value of machinery)

Problem 11. *From the comparative balance sheets of Serial Engineering Ltd. As at 31.12.1998 and other information furnished, prepare a cash flow statement for the year ended on 31.12.1998.*

CASH FLOW STATEMENT

Liabilities	1997 Rs.	1998 Rs.	Assets	1997 Rs.	1998 Rs.
Equity Share Capital	50,000	2,00,000	Fixed Assets	2,40,000	4,20,000
Redeemable Pref. Share Capital	1,00,000	—	Investments	18,000	15,000
			Stock	58,500	1,60,000
			Sundry Debtors	1,37,000	92,000
Retained Earning	1,20,000	3,50,000	Cash at Bank	1,85,000	1,20,000
Unsecured Loan	1,25,000	—	Prepaid expenses	6,500	8,000
Bills payable	2,25,000	1,90,000			
Provision for Tax	25,000	75,000			
	6,45,000	8,15,000		6,45,000	8,15,000

The following additional information is also available :

(i) On 31.12.1998 accumulated depreciation on fixed assets amounted to Rs. 1,20,000 and on 31st December 1997 to Rs. 1,10,000.

(ii) Machinery costing Rs. 10,000 (Accumulated depreciation thereon being Rs. 5,000) was discarded and written off during 1998.

(iii) Depreciation written off during 1998 amounted to Rs. 15,000.

(iv) During the year 1998 investments costing Rs. 6,000 were sold for Rs. 7,000.

(v) Dividend paid during the year was Rs. 45,000.

(vi) Redeemable preference shares were redeemed out of profile during the year at a premium of 5%.

Solution :

Cash Flow Statement

Inflow of cash	Amount Rs.	Outflow of cash	Amount Rs.
Opening Cash Balance	1,85,000	Repayment unsecured loan	1,25,000
Issue of Shares	1,50,000	Decrease in bills payable	35,000
Increase in provision for taxation	50,000	Increase in stock	1,01,500
Decrease in Sundry Debtors	45,000	Increase in prepaid expenses	1,500
		Dividend paid	45,000
Sale of Investments	7,000	Purchase of fixed assets (3)	2,00,000
Cash from operation	2,99,000	Redemption of preference Shares	1,05,000
		Purchase of investment (4)	3,000
		Closing Cash balance	1,20,000
	7,36,000		7,36,000

Workings :

1. Profit and Loss Account

	Amount Rs.		Amount Rs.
To Loss on Machinery (Discarded)	5,000	By Balance b/d	1,20,000
To Dividend paid	45,000	By Profit on sale of Investment	1,000
To Premium on Redemption of Preference shares	5,000	By Cash from Operation	2,99,000
To Depreciation	15,000		
To Balance c/d	3,50,000		
	4,20,000		4,20,000

2. Redeemable Preference Share Capital Account

	Rs.		Rs.
To Cash	1,05,000	By Balance b/d	1,00,000
		By Premium	5,000
	1,05,000		1,05,000

3. Fixed Assets Account (Machinery)

	Rs.		Rs.
To Balance b/d	3,50,000	By Profit & Loss A/c	5,000
To Cash	2,00,000	By Accumulated Depreciation	5,000
		By Balance c/d (4,20,000 + 1,20,000)	5,40,000
	5,50,000		5,50,000

4. Investment Account

	Rs.		Rs.
To Balance b/d	18,000	By Cash	6,000
To Cash	3,000	By Balance c/d	15,000
	21,000		21,000

5. Accumulated Depreciation Account

	Rs.		Rs.
To Balance c/d	1,20,000	By Balance b/d	1,10,000
To Machinery	5,000	By P&L A/c	15,000
	1,25,000		1,25,000

NOTE : Journal Entry for Adjustment (ii & iv)

(ii) Profit & Loss A/c Dr. 5,000
    Accumulated Depreciation A/c Dr. 5,000
        To Machinery A/c 10,000

(iv) Cash A/c Dr. 7,000
        To Profit & Loss A/c 1,000
        To Investment A/c 6000

CASH FLOW STATEMENT

Problem 12. *Prepare a cash flow statement from the balance sheets of TTD & Co. as on 31.3.2000 and 31.3.2001. (Rs. In thousands)*

Liabilities	2000 Rs.	2001 Rs.	Assets	2000 Rs.	2001 Rs.
Capital	140	140	Fixed Assets (Net)	90	87
Reserves	74	105	Cash	75	97
Creditors	32	35	Debtors	43	40
Outstanding Wages	3	4	Inventory	49	58
Expenses Outstanding	11	3	Prepaid Expenses	3	5
	260	287		260	287

Accumulated depreciation was Rs. 16,000 and Rs. 19,000 respectively at the beginning and end of the year 2001.

Other information Sales Rs. 3,00,000, Wages Rs. 23,000, Operating Expenses Rs. 47,000, Cost of goods Rs.1,90,000, Rent Rs. 6,000 and Depreciation Rs. 3,000. [MBA Madras]

Solution :

Cash Flow Statement

Inflow of cash	Amount Rs.	Outflow of cash	Amount Rs.
Opening cash balance	75,000	Increase in inventory	9,000
Increase in creditors	3,000	Decrease in Miscellaneous Expenses outstanding	8,000
Increase in wages outstanding	1,000		
Decrease on debtors	3,000	Increase in prepaid expenses	2,000
Cash from operation (1)	34,000	Closing cash balance	97,000
	1,16,000		1,16,000

Workings :

1. Profit and Loss Account

	Amount Rs.		Amount Rs.
To Depreciation	3,000	By Balance b/d	74,000
To Balance c/d	1,05,000	By Cash operation	34,000
	1,08,000		1,08,000

2. Fixed Assets Account

To Balance b/d (90,000 + 16,000)	1,06,000	By Balance c/d (87,000 + 19,000)	1,06,000
	1,06,000		1,06,000

3. Accumulated Depreciation Account

To Balance c/d	19,000	By Balance b/d	16,000
		By P&L A/c	3,000
		(Current year Depreciation)	
	19,000		19,000

Problem 13. *Kapin Ltd. furnishes you the following balance sheet for the year ending on 31.12.2002 and 2003. You are required to prepare cash flow statement of the year ended on 31.12.2003.*

Liabilities	2002 Rs.	2003 Rs.	Assets	2002 Rs.	2003 Rs.
Equity Share Capital	10,000	10,000	Goodwill	1,200	1,200
General Reserve	1,400	1,800	Land	4,000	3,600
Profit & Loss A/c	1,600	1,300	Building	3,700	3,600
Sundry Creditors	800	540	Equipment	1,000	1,100
Bills payable	120	80	Stock	3,000	2,340
Provision for Taxation	1,600	1,800	Accounts Receivable	2,000	2,220
Provision for Bad Debts	40	60	Bank Balance	660	1,520
	15,560	15,580		15,560	15,580

The following additional information is also available :
(i) A piece of land has also been sold for Rs. 800.
(ii) Depreciation amounting to Rs. 600 has been charged on building.
(iii) Provision for taxation has been made for Rs. 1,700 during the year.

[B.Com adapted]

Solution :   **Cash Flow Statement**

Inflow of cash	Amount Rs.	Outflow of cash	Amount Rs.
Opening Cash balance	660	Decrease in Sundry Creditors	260
Decrease in stock	660	Decrease in Bills payable	40
Sale of land	800	Purchase of equipment	100
Cash from operation	2,420	Increase in account receivables	220
		Tax paid	1,500
		Purchase of building	500
		Land purchased	400
		Closing Cash balance	1,520
	4,540		4,540

CASH FLOW STATEMENT

Workings :

1. Profit and Loss Account

	Amount Rs.		Amount Rs.
To General Reserve	400	By Balance b/d	1,600
To Provision for Doubtful debts	20	By Cash from Operation	2,420
To Depreciation on Building	600		
To Income Tax Provision	1,700		
To Balance c/d	1,300		
	4,020		4,020

2. Provision for Taxation Account

	Amount Rs.		Amount Rs.
To Cash (Tax paid)	1,500	By Balance b/d	1,600
To Balance c/d	1,800	By Profit & Loss A/c (Income Tax provision)	1,700
	3,300		3,300

3. Land Account

	Amount Rs.		Amount Rs.
To Balance b/d	4,000	By Cash	800
To Cash	400	By Balance c/d	3,600
	4,400		4,400

4. Building Account

	Amount Rs.		Amount Rs.
To Balance b/d	3,700	By Depreciation (P&L A/c)	600
To Cash	500	By Balance c/d	3,600
	4,200		4,200

Cash Flow (AS 3) Revised Format

Under the revised format, cash flow statement should be prepared in such a way as to report the cash flows during the periods separately for operating, investing and financing activities.

I Cash Flows from Operating Activities

Net profit earned during the year	xx
Add : Depreciation	xx
Loss on sale of machinery	xx
Preliminary expenses written off	xx
Goodwill written off	xx
Patents and copy right written off	xx
Operating profit before working capital changes	xx

Adjustment of working capital
(Add cash flow, less cash out flows)

Decrease in current assets	xx
Decrease in current liabilities	xx
Increase in current assets	xx
Increase in current liabilities	xx
Cash flows from operating activities	xx

II Cash Flows from Investing Activities

Purchase of machinery	xx
Purchase of land & building	xx
Purchase of goodwill	xx
Purchase of furniture	xx
Sale of machinery	xx
Sale of land & building	xx
Sale of furniture	xx
Interest on investment received	xx
Cash flows from investing activities	xx

III Cash Flows from Financing Activities

Issue shares	xx
Issue debentures	xx
Loan borrowed	xx
Redemption of shares	xx
Redemption of debentures	xx
Loan repaid	xx
Dividend paid	xx
Interim dividend paid	xx
Drawings	xx
Net cash flows from financing activities	xx
Net increase or decrease in cash and cash equivalent	xx
Add : Opening cash balance	
(Adjust BOD if any given the problem)	xx
Closing cash Balance	xx
(Adjust BOD if any given the problem)	

NOTE : In the question will specifically mention for the applying revised methods only, we follow the revised format otherwise better to follow Existing format.

CASH FLOW STATEMENT

Problem 14. Prepare cash flow statement under Revised format from the following balance sheets of Tiruchengodu Traders Ltd.

Liabilities	2000 Rs.	2001 Rs.	Assets	2000 Rs.	2001 Rs.
Share Capital	17,00,000	18,35,000	Buildings	8,00,000	10,00,000
Reserves	40,000	83,700	Plant and Machinery	2,50,000	3,70,000
P & LAPP. A/c	1,00,000	1,30,000	Furniture	5,000	6,000
Provision for dividends	70,000	50,000	Cash	2,000	2,200
Creditors	1,00,000	95,000	Debtors	1,00,000	45,000
Bank overdraft	8,000	18,000	Bills receivable	8,000	9,000
Bills payable	14,000	13,000	Stock	4,00,000	3,43,700
Mortgage Loan	10,000	70,000	Prepaid expenses	3,000	3,100
			Investments	1,64,000	1,70,000
			Goodwill	3,00,000	3,43,700
			Preliminary Expenses	10,000	2,000
	20,42,000	22,94,700		20,42,000	22,94,700

The following additional information is also available :

(a) Depreciation is charged on buildings at 3% of cost of Rs. 9,00,000 on plant and machinery at 8% of cost of Rs. 4,00,000; Furniture at 5% of cost Rs. 8,000.

(b) Investments were purchased and interest was received Rs. 3,000 which was used in writing down the book value of investment.

(c) The declared dividends for 70,000 were paid and interim dividend for Rs. 20,000 was paid out of P & L App. A/c.

Solution :   **Cash Flow Statement (Revised Method)**

			Rs.	Rs.
I	Cash flow from operating activities			
	Net profit before tax and extraordinary item		1,43,700	
	Adjustment for depreciation for furniture		400	
	Adjustment for depreciation for plant and machinery		32,000	
	Adjustment for depreciation on buildings		27,000	
	Preliminary expenses written off		8,000	
	Operating profit before working capital changes		2,11,100	
	Decrease in debtors		55,000	
	Decrease in stock		56,300	
	Decrease in creditors		(5,000)	
	Increase in bills receivable		(1,000)	
	Decrease in bills payable		(1,000)	
	Increase in prepaid expenses		(100)	
	Net cash flow from investing activities			3,15,300
II	Cash flow from investing activities :			
	Interest on investments		3,000	
	Purchase of investment		(9,000)	
	Purchase of buildings		(2,27,000)	
	Purchase of machinery		(1,52,000)	
	Purchase of furniture		(1,400)	
	Purchase of goodwill		(43,700)	
	Net cash flow from investing activities :			4,30,100

III	Cash flow from financing activities			
	Issue of shares		1,35,000	
	Mortgage loan		60,000	
	Dividend paid for 2000		(70,000)	
	Interim dividend paid		(20,000)	
	Net cash flows from financing activities			1,05,000
	Net increase (decrease) in cash and cash equivalents			(9,800)
	Cash and cash equivalents opening balance (Bank O/D-cash)			(6,000)
	Cash and cash equivalents closing balance (Bank O/D -cash)			(15,800)

Workings :

1. Profit and Loss A/c

To Balance c/d	1,30,000	By Balance b/d	1,00,000
To Transfer reserves	43,700		
To Provision for dividend	50,000	By	1,43,700
To Interim dividend paid	20,000		
	2,43,700		2,43,700

2. Buildings A/c

To Balance b/d	8,00,000	By Balance c/d	10,00,000
To Purchase (Bf)	2,27,000	By Depreciation (9,00,000 × 3/100)	27,000
	10,27,000		10,27,000

3. Plant and Machinery A/c

To Balance b/d	2,50,000	By Balance /d	3,70,000
To Purchase (Bf)	1,52,000	By Depreciation (4,00,000 × 8/100)	32,000
	4,02,000		4,02,000

4. Furniture A/c

To Balance b/d	5,000	By Balance c/d	6,000
To Purchase (Bf)	1,400	By Depreciation (8,000 × 5/100)	400
	6,400		6,400

5. Investment A/c

To Balance b/d	1,64,000	By Balance c/d	1,70,000
To Purchase Investment (Bf)	9,000	By Bank (Interest)	3,000
	1,73,000		1,73,000

❏❏❏

7
Ratio Analysis

MEANING

Ratio is simply a number expressed in terms of another. It refers to the numerical or quantitative relationship between two variables that are comparable. It is a comparison of the numerator with the denominator.

In other words, the ratio means relationship between two figures expressed mathematically. It can be expressed in terms of percentage proportions and quotient too.

SIGNIFICANCE OF RATIO ANALYSIS

Ratio analysis is an effective and suitable tool of financial analysis. Analysis of financial statement with the support of ratios would guide the management in important decision making, implementation and control. Ratio analysis is an instrument for diagnosing the financial health of an enterprise. The usefulness of the ratio analysis is not only for the financial manager, but also to various parties who are interested to know different purposes of financial information. In the real sense, ratio analysis is based on the accounting data contained in the financial statements. Various classifications of ratios are used for different purposes.

ADVANTAGES OF RATIO ANALYSIS

1. *Simplifies financial statement.* Financial Statement contains the summary of one year's financial activities that is, application of Ratio as against the financial statements. The interested people can know the information without any difficulty because the entire financial statement is simplified in an easy manner.
2. *Facilitates intra-firm comparison.* Analysis and interpretation of a particular firm over a period of year can be made. And also comparison among different divisions of the organisation is made easy with the help of various ratios.
3. *Planning and Forecasting.* Actually ratios are derived from the past financial statements. Ratios give suitable guidance to management for formulating various budgets and construct relevant policies and also to prepare the future plan of action etc.
4. *Aid to inter firm comparison.* Comparison between two or more firms is more essential. In this regard, absolute figures are not sufficient to determine the correct comparison of firms. With the help of the ratios, one firm is able to compare with another firm and also find out their position.

5. *Facilitates decision making.* Ratios throw light on the degree of efficiency of the management and utilisation of the assets. That is why it is called surveyor of efficiency. They help the management in the aspect of decision making.
6. *Helps in corrective action.* Ratio analysis facilitates the inter-firm comparison. It exposes the successful and unsuccessful firms. At the time of comparison, if any of the unfavourable variations are identified, immediately the corrective actions should be taken.
7. *Aid to co-ordination.* The management wants to establish harmonious and cordial relationship among all the departments in the organisation. Meanwhile, the strength and weakness of the organisation should be communicated in an easily understandable manner. This type of quick and clear communication can achieve better co-ordination.

LIMITATIONS OF RATIO ANALYSIS

1. *Limitations of financial statements.* Ratios are usually calculated on the past year's financial data contained in the financial statement. In the real sense, financial statements suffer a number of limitations. When ratios are derived from the financial statements, they also suffer from the same limitations.
2. *Differences in Definition.* There is no clear cut formula for computing ratios. Each and every company follows a separate formula for computing different ratios. Due to these different types of formulas, comparison of different industries becomes difficult.
3. *Ratios alone are not adequate.* Various tools are available for evaluating the financial performance of a company. Under this aspect, ratios are tools of quantitative analysis only. Normally qualitative factors which may generally influence the arrival of conclusion are ignored while computing ratios.
4. *Problems of price level changes.* Even though there are certain limitations, inflation is utmost important for industrial and economic development of the country. Due to this aspect, price fluctuation could not be eliminated. Ratios fail to reflect the price level changes as they are based on Historical data. Hence, they may give misleading results when inflationary conditions are ignored.
5. *It is not substitute for personal judgement.* It is only a beginning and gives limited information for decision making. It is just an aid and cannot replace thinking and personal judgement employed in the decision making aspect.
6. *Ratios can be manipulated.* There will be a great demand for goods during the festival season when compared to previous periods. Suppose this inventory turnover ratio is considered for decision making, the results get distorted. It is necessary to take the average inventories to present a fair view of the business activity.

Despite certain limitations, ratio analysis continues to be a powerful tool for analysis and interpretation of financial statements.

CLASSIFICATION OF RATIOS

For the purpose of financial performance analysis, ratios are classified into the following categories.

RATIO ANALYSIS

A. Liquidity (Short-term Solvency) Ratios

Formula

1. $\text{Current Ratio} = \dfrac{\text{Current Assets}}{\text{Current Liabilities}}$

   Current Assets

   Cash in hand and Bank, Stock, sundry Debtors, bills receivable, short term investments, marketable securities, accrued incomes, prepaid expenses.

   Current Liabilities

   Sundry creditors, bills payable, Bank overdraft, outstanding expenses, income received in advance, income tax provisions, bad debts provisions, dividend payable, any other account which is payable in short period.

2. Quick Ratio or Liquid Ratio or Acid test ratio

   $\text{Acid Test Ratio} = \dfrac{\text{Quick Assets}}{\text{Quick Liabilities}}$ (or) $\dfrac{\text{Liquid Assets}}{\text{Liquid Liabilities}}$ (or) $\dfrac{LA}{CL}$

   Quick assets or liquid assets = All current assets except stock

   Quick Liabilities or liquid liabilities = All current liabilities except bank overdraft

3. $\text{Cash Position Ratio} = \dfrac{\text{Cash + Marketable Securities}}{\text{Current Liabilities}}$

4. $\text{Net working Capital Ratio} = \dfrac{\text{Net working Capital}}{\text{Net Assets}}$

   Net working capital = Current assets − Current liabilities

5. $\text{Solvency Ratio} = \dfrac{\text{Outside Liabilities}}{\text{Total Assets}}$

B. Long-term Solvency Ratios

1. $\text{Debt-Equity Ratio} = \dfrac{\text{Debt}}{\text{Equity}}$ (or) $\dfrac{\text{External Equities}}{\text{Internal Equities}}$ (or) $\dfrac{\text{Outsider's Fund}}{\text{Shareholder's Fund}}$

   External Equities refer to the total outside liabilities. The term internal equities refers to all claims of preference shareholders and equity share holders such as share capital reserves and surplus. Outsider's fund refers to all short term debts like mortgage, bills etc.

   Computation of long term financial ratios, the term debt, like debentures are to be considered.

   Acceptable norm for this ratio is considered to be 2:1.

2. $\text{Proprietary Ratio} = \dfrac{\text{Shareholder's Fund}}{\text{Total Assets}}$ (or) $\dfrac{\text{Shareholder's Fund}}{\text{Total Tangible Assets}}$

   Shareholder's fund includes preference share capital, Equity share capital, Reserves surplus, Profit & Loss Account Balance if any.

Total Assets

Total assets represent all assets including goodwill. But total tangible assets means total assets minus goodwill, Profit & Loss A/c (Debit) Balance, Preliminary Expenses.

3. Ratio of fixed assets to proprietor's fund = $\dfrac{\text{Fixed Assets}}{\text{Proprietor's Fund}}$

[Fixed assets are valued at original cost of the assets less depreciation].

4. Current assets to proprietor's fund Ratio = $\dfrac{\text{Current Assets}}{\text{Proprietor's Fund}}$

C. Profitability Ratios

1. Gross Profit Ratio = $\dfrac{\text{Gross Profit}}{\text{Sales}} \times 100$

2. Net Profit Ratio = $\dfrac{\text{Net Profit}}{\text{Sales}} \times 100$

3. Operating Ratio = $\dfrac{\text{Cost of Goods Sold + Operating Expenses}}{\text{Sales}} \times 100$

   Cost of Goods Sold = Sales – Gross Profit
   Operating Expenses = All the expenses debited in the profit & Loss A/c except financial expenses i.e., Administrative Expenses, Selling & Distribution Expenses, Financial Expenses.

   Financial expenses may or may not include the operating expenses.

4. Return on Capital Employed = $\dfrac{\text{Return}}{\text{Capital Employed}} \times 100$

   Return : Net profit
   Capital employed : Share holders fund + long term liabilities
   (or)
   Fixed assets + Current Assets – Current Liabilities

   $\dfrac{\text{Profit Before Tax and Interest}}{\text{Capital Employed}}$

5. Operating Profit Ratio = $\dfrac{\text{Operating Profit}}{\text{Net Sales}} \times 100$

   Operating Profit = Net Profit + Non-Operating Expenses – Non-Operating Income

6. Return on Total Assets = $\dfrac{\text{Return}}{\text{Total Assets}} \times 100$

   [Return = PAT]

7. Return on Shareholder Return = $\dfrac{\text{Return}}{\text{Shareholder's Fund}} \times 100$

8. Dividend Payout Ratio = $\dfrac{\text{Dividend Per Share}}{\text{Earning Per Share}}$

RATIO ANALYSIS

9. $\text{Dividend Per Share} = \dfrac{\text{Dividend paid to Equity Shareholders}}{\text{No. of Equity Shares}}$

10. $\text{Earning Per Equity Share} = \dfrac{\text{Profit Available to Equity Shares}}{\text{No. of Equity Shares}}$

11. $\text{Dividend Yield} = \dfrac{\text{Dividend Per Share}}{\text{Market Price Per Share}}$

12. $\text{Price Earning Ratio} = \dfrac{\text{Market Price of a Share}}{\text{Earning Per Share}}$

13. $\text{Fixed Interest Coverage} = \dfrac{\text{Operating Income}}{\text{Annual Interest Expenses}}$

14. $\text{Interest Coverage Ratio} = \dfrac{\text{EBIT}}{\text{Fixed Interest Expenses}}$

D. Activity or Turnover Ratios

1. $\text{Stock Turnover Ratio} = \dfrac{\text{Cost of Goods Sold}}{\text{Average Stock}}$

2. *Debtors Turnover Ratio or Debtors Velocity*

$\qquad = \dfrac{\text{Debtors + Bills Receivable}}{\text{Credit Sales}} \times \text{No. of Working Days}$

3. $\text{Creditors Turnover Ratio} = \dfrac{\text{Creditors + Bills Payable}}{\text{Credit Purchase}} \times 365$

4. $\text{Average Payment Period} = \dfrac{\text{Account Payable}}{\text{Net Credit Purchase}} \times 365$

5. $\text{Working Capital Turnover Ratio} = \dfrac{\text{Cost of Sales}}{\text{Net Working Capital}}$

6. $\text{Fixed Assets Turnover Ratio} = \dfrac{\text{Cost of Sales}}{\text{Net Fixed Assets}}$

7. $\text{Total Capital Turnover Ratio} = \dfrac{\text{Cost of Sales}}{\text{Total Capital Employed}}$

8. $\text{Capital Turnover Ratio} = \dfrac{\text{Cost of Sales}}{\text{Net Working Capital}}$

9. $\text{Current Assets Turnover Ratio} = \dfrac{\text{Cost of Sales}}{\text{Current Assets}}$

10. $\text{Sales to Net worth Ratio} = \dfrac{\text{Cost of Sales}}{\text{Net worth}}$

11. $\text{Expenses Ratio} = \dfrac{\text{Individual Expenses}}{\text{Sales}}$

E. Leverage or Capital Structure Ratios

1. $\text{Debt - Equity Ratio} = \dfrac{\text{Debt}}{\text{Equity}}$

2. $\text{Proprietary Ratio} = \dfrac{\text{Shareholder's Fund}}{\text{Total Assets}}$

3. $\text{Capital Gearing Ratio} = \dfrac{\text{Fixed Interest Bearing Securities}}{\text{Equity Share Capital}}$

   (or)

   $= \dfrac{\text{Pre Share Capital + Debentures + Other Borrowed Funds}}{\text{Equity}}$

4. $\text{Reserves to Equity Capital Ratio} = \dfrac{\text{Revenue Reserve}}{\text{Equity Capital}}$

5. $\text{Fixed Assets to Net worth Ratio} = \dfrac{\text{Fixed Assets}}{\text{Net worth}}$

6. $\text{Current Assets to Net worth Ratio} = \dfrac{\text{Current Assets}}{\text{Net worth}}$

7. $\text{Current Liabilities to Net worth Ratio} = \dfrac{\text{Current Liabilities}}{\text{Net worth}}$

8. $\text{Fixed Assets to Current Assets Ratio} = \dfrac{\text{Fixed Assets}}{\text{Current Assets}}$

9. $\text{Fixed Assets Ratio} = \dfrac{\text{Fixed Assets}}{\text{Long - Term Funds}}$

Type I : Final Account to Ratio

Problem 1. *From the data calculate :*

(i) Gross Profit Ratio (ii) Net Profit Ratio (iii) Return on Total Assets
(iv) Inventory Turnover (v) Working Capital Turnover (vi) Net worth to Debt

Sales	25,20,000	Other Current Assets	7,60,000
Cost of sale	19,20,000	Fixed Assets	14,40,000
Net profit	3,60,000	Net worth	15,00,000
Inventory	8,00,000	Debt.	9,00,000
		Current Liabilities	6,00,000

[B.Com Madurai] [BBM PU May 2005]

Solution :

(i) Gross Profit Ratio $= \dfrac{\text{GP}}{\text{Sales}} \times 100 = \dfrac{6,00,000}{25,20,000} \times 100 = 23.81\%$

Sales - Cost of Sales = Gross Profit
25,20,000 - 19,20,000 = 6,00,000

RATIO ANALYSIS

(ii) $\quad$ Net Profit Ratio $= \dfrac{NP}{Sales} \times 100 = \dfrac{3,60,000}{25,20,000} = 14.28\%$

(iii) $\quad$ Inventory Turnover Ratio $= \dfrac{Turnover}{Inventory} \times 100 = \dfrac{19,20,000}{8,00,000} = 2.4$ times

Turnover Refers Cost of Sales

(iv) $\quad$ Return on Total Assets $= \dfrac{NP}{Total\ Assets} = \dfrac{3,60,000}{30,00,000} \times 100 = 12\%$

FA + CA + inventory [14,40,000 + 7,60,000 + 8,00,000] = 30,00,000

(v) $\quad$ Net worth to Debt $= \dfrac{Net\ worth}{Debt} = \dfrac{15,00,000}{9,00,000} \times 100 = 1.66$ times

(vi) $\quad$ Working Capital Turnover $= \dfrac{Turnover}{Working\ Capital}$

$\quad\quad$ Working Capital = Current Assets − Current Liabilities
$\quad\quad\quad\quad\quad\quad\quad\quad\quad$ = 8,00,000 + 7,60,000 − 6,00,000
$\quad\quad\quad\quad$ 15,60,000 − 6,00,000 = 9,60,000

Working Capital Turnover Ratio $= \dfrac{19,20,000}{9,60,000} = 2$ times.

Problem 2. *Perfect Ltd. gives the following Balance sheet. You are required to compute the following ratios.*

(a) Liquid Ratio $\quad\quad$ (b) Debt–Equity Ratio
(b) Solvency Ratio $\quad$ (d) Stock of Working Capital Ratio

Balance Sheet

	Rs.		Rs.
Equity share capital	15,00,000	Fixed Assets	14,00,000
Reserve fund	1,00,000	Stock	5,00,000
6% Debentures	3,00,000	Debtors	2,00,000
Overdraft	1,00,000	Cash	1,00,000
Creditors	2,00,000		
	22,00,000		22,00,000

Solution :

(a) $\quad$ Liquid Ratio $= \dfrac{Liquid\ Assets}{Liquid\ Liabilities}$ (or) $\dfrac{Liquid\ Assets}{Current\ Liabilities}$

$\quad\quad$ LA Debtors = 2,00,000 $\quad$ i.e., $\quad \dfrac{3,00,000}{2,00,000} = 1.5$
$\quad\quad\quad\quad$ Cash = 1,00,000
$\quad\quad\quad\quad\quad\quad$ = 3,00,000

$\quad$ Liquid Liabilities : Creditors = 2,00,000

(b) Debt – Equity Ratio = $\dfrac{\text{External Equities}}{\text{Internal Equities}}$

External Equities :
All outsiders loan Including current liabilities
3,00,000 + 1,00,000 + 2,00,000 = 6,00,000

Internal Equities :
It Includes share holders fund + Reserves
15,00,000 + 1,00,000 = 16,00,000

Debt – Equity Ratio = $\dfrac{6,00,000}{16,00,000}$ = 0.375

(c) Solvency Ratio = $\dfrac{\text{Outside Liabilities}}{\text{Total Assets}}$

Outside Liabilities = Debenture + Overdraft + Creditors
= 3,00,000 + 1,00,000 + 2,00,000 = 6,00,000

∴ Solvency Ratio = $\dfrac{6,00,000}{22,00,000} \times 100$ = 27.27%

(d) Stock of Working Capital Ratio = $\dfrac{\text{Stock}}{\text{Working Capital}}$

Working Capital = Current Assets – Current Liabilities
= 8,00,000 – 3,00,000 = 5,00,000

Stock of Working Capital Ratio = $\dfrac{5,00,000}{5,00,000} \times 100$ = 100%

Problem 3. *Calculate the following ratios from the balance sheet given below :*
(i) Debt – Equity Ratio
(ii) Liquidity Ratio
(iii) Fixed Assets to Current Assets
(iv) Fixed Assets Turnover

Balance Sheet

Liabilities	Rs.	Assets	Rs.
Equity shares of Rs. 10 each	1,00,000	Goodwill	60,000
Reserves	20,000	Fixed Assets	1,40,000
P.L. A/c	30,000	Stock	30,000
Secured loan	80,000	Sundry Debtors	30,000
Sundry creditors	50,000	Advances	10,000
Provision for taxation	20,000	Cash Balance	30,000
	3,00,000		3,00,000

The sales for the year were Rs. 5,60,000. [MBA adapted]

RATIO ANALYSIS

Solution :

(i) Debt – Equity Ratio = $\dfrac{\text{Long – Term Debt}}{\text{Shareholders Fund}}$

Long-term Debt = Secured loan Rs. 80,000

Shareholder's Fund = Equity Share Capital + Reserves + P.L.A/c
= 1,00,000 + 20,000 + 30,000 = 1,50,000

Debt-Equity Ratio = $\dfrac{80,000}{1,50,000}$ = .53

(ii) Liquidity Ratio = $\dfrac{\text{Liquid Assets}}{\text{Liquid Liabilities}}$

Liquid Assets = Sundry Debtors + Advances + Cash Balance
= 30,000 + 10,000 + 30,000 = 70,000

Liquid Liabilities = Provision for Taxation + sundry creditors
= 20,000 + 50,000 = 70,000

Liquid Ratio = $\dfrac{70,000}{70,000}$ = 1

(iii) Fixed Assets to Current Assets

= $\dfrac{\text{Fixed Assets}}{\text{Current Assets}}$ = $\dfrac{1,40,000}{1,00,000}$ = 1.4

(iv) Fixed Assets Turnover = $\dfrac{\text{Turnover}}{\text{Fixed Assets}}$ = $\dfrac{5,60,000}{1,40,000}$ = 4

Problem 4. *The Balance sheet of Naronath & Co. as on 31.12.2000 shows as follows :*

Liabilities	Rs.	Assets	Rs.
Equity capital	1,00,000	Fixed Assets	1,80,000
15% Preference shares	50,000	Stores	25,000
12% Debentures	50,000	Debtors	55,000
Retained Earnings	20,000	Bills Receivable	3,000
Creditors	45,000	Bank	2,000
	2,65,000		2,65,000

Comment on the Financial position of the Company i.e., Debt - Equity Ratio, Fixed Assets Ratio, Current Ratio, Liquidity. [M.Com, Bhopal]

Solution :

(i) Debt – Equity Ratio = $\dfrac{\text{Debt – Equity Ratio}}{\text{Long – Term Debt}}$

Long-term Debt = Debentures
= 50,000

Shareholder's Fund = Equity + Preference + Retained Earnings
= 1,00,000 + 50,000 + 20,000
= $\dfrac{50,000}{1,70,000}$ = .29

(ii) Fixed Assets Ratio = $\dfrac{\text{Fixed Assets}}{\text{Proprietor's Fund}}$ = 1,80,000

Proprietor's Fund = Equity Share Capital + Preference Share Capital + Retained Earnings

= 1,00,000 + 50,000 + 20,000 = 1,70,000

Fixed Assets Ratio = $\dfrac{1,80,000}{1,70,000}$ = 1.05

(iii) Current Ratio = $\dfrac{\text{Current Assets}}{\text{Current Liabilities}}$

Current Assets = Stores + Debtors + BR + Bank

= 25,000 + 55,000 + 3,000 + 2,000 = 85,000

Current Liabilities = 45,000

Current Ratio = $\dfrac{85,000}{45,000}$ = 1.88

(iv) Liquid Ratio = $\dfrac{\text{Liquid Assets}}{\text{Liquid Liabilities}}$

Liquid Assets = Debtors + Bill Receivable + Cash

= 55,000 + 3,000 + 2,000 = 60,000

Liquid Liabilities = 45,000

Liquid Ratio = $\dfrac{60,000}{45,000}$ = 1.33

Problem 5. *From the following particulars pertaining to Assets and Liabilities of a company calculate :*

(a) *Current Ratio* (b) *Liquidity Ratio* (c) *Proprietary Ratio*
(d) *Debt-equity Ratio* (e) *Capital Gearing Ratio*

Liabilities	Rs.	Assets	Rs.
5000 equity shares Rs. 10 each	5,00,000	Land & Building	6,00,000
8% 2000 pre shares Rs. 100 each	2,00,000	Plant & Machinery	5,00,000
9% 4000 Debentures of Rs. 100 each	4,00,000	Debtors	2,00,000
		Stock	2,40,000
Reserves	3,00,000	Cash and Bank	55,000
Creditors	1,50,000	Prepaid expenses	5,000
Bank overdraft	50,000		
	16,00,000		16,00,000

[MSC ITM Dec. 1999]

Solution :

(i) Current Ratio = $\dfrac{\text{Current Assets}}{\text{Current Liabilities}}$

Current Assets = Stock + Cash + Prepaid Expenses + Debtors

= 2,40,000 + 55,000 + 5,000 + 2,00,000 = 5,00,000

RATIO ANALYSIS

$$\text{Current Liabilities} = \text{Creditors} + \text{Bank Overdraft}$$
$$= 1{,}50{,}000 + 50{,}000 = 2{,}00{,}000$$
$$= \frac{5{,}00{,}000}{2{,}00{,}000} = 2.5 : 1$$

(ii) $\quad$ Liquid Ratio $= \dfrac{\text{Liquid Assets}}{\text{Liquid Liabilities}}$

$$\text{Liquid Assets} = \text{Cash and Bank} + \text{Debtors}$$
$$= 55{,}000 + 2{,}00{,}000 = 2{,}55{,}000$$

Liquid Liabilities : Creditors $= 1{,}50{,}000$

$$\text{Liquid Ratio} = \frac{2{,}55{,}000}{1{,}50{,}000} = 1.7 : 1$$

(iii) $\quad$ Proprietary Ratio $= \dfrac{\text{Proprietor's Fund}}{\text{Total Tangible Assets}}$

Proprietor's Funds = Equity Share Capital + Preference Share Capital + Reserves and Surplus
$$= 5{,}00{,}000 + 2{,}00{,}000 + 3{,}00{,}000$$

$$\text{Proprietary Ratio} = \frac{10{,}00{,}000}{16{,}00{,}000} = 0.625 : 1$$

(iv) $\quad$ Debt – Equity Ratio $= \dfrac{\text{External Equities}}{\text{Internal Equities}}$

External Equities = Long-term Liabilities + Short-term Liabilities
$$= 4{,}00{,}000 + 2{,}00{,}000 = 6{,}00{,}000$$

Internal Equities = Proprietor's funds

$$= \frac{6{,}00{,}000}{10{,}00{,}000} = 0.6 : 1$$

(v) $\quad$ Capital Gearing Ratio $= \dfrac{\text{Fixed Interest Bearing Securities}}{\text{Equity Share Capital} + \text{Reserves}}$

Fixed Interest Bearing Securities = Preference Shares $\quad$ 2,00,000
$\hspace{7.3cm}$ Debentures $\hspace{1.5cm}$ 4,00,000
$\hspace{10.5cm}$ —————
$\hspace{10.7cm}$ 6,00,000
$\hspace{10.5cm}$ ═════

$$= \frac{6{,}00{,}000}{8{,}00{,}000} = 0.75 : 1$$

Problem 6. *From the following details of a trader you are required to calculate :*
 (i) *Purchase for the year.*
 (ii) *Rate of stock turnover*
 (iii) *Percentage of Gross profit to turnover*

Sales Rs.	33,984	Stock at the close at cost price	1,814
Sales Returns	380	G.P. for the year	8,068
Stock at the beginning at cost price	1,378		

Solution :

Trading Account

To Opening stock	1,378	By Sales	33,984
To Purchase (Bf)	25,972	(–) Sales Returns	380
To gross profit	8,068		33,604
		By Closing stock	1,814
	35,418		35,418

(i) Purchase for the year Rs. 25,972

(ii) $\text{Stock Turnover} = \dfrac{\text{Cost of Goods Sold}}{\text{Average Stock}}$

Cost of Goods Sold = Sales – GP = 33,984 – 8,068 = 25,916

$\text{Average Stock} = \dfrac{\text{Opening Stock} + \text{Closing Stock}}{2}$

$= \dfrac{1,372 + 1,814}{2} = 1,596$

$= \dfrac{25,916}{1,596} = 16.23 \text{ times}$

(iii) Percentage of Gross Profit to Turnover

$= \dfrac{\text{Gross Profit}}{\text{Sales}} \times 100 = \dfrac{8,068}{33,984} \times 100 = 23.74\%.$

Problem 7. *Calculate stock turnover ratio from the following information :*

Opening stock	58,000
Purchases	4,84,000
Sales	6,40,000
Gross Profit Rate - 25% on Sales.	

[M.Sc, Dec.1999]

Solution :

$\text{Stock Turnover Ratio} = \dfrac{\text{Cost of Goods Sold}}{\text{Average Stock}}$

Cost of Goods Sold = Sales – G.P

= 6,40,000 – 1,60,000 = 4,80,000

$\text{Stock Turnover Ratio} = \dfrac{4,80,000}{58,000} = 8.27 \text{ times}$ **Ans.**

Here, there is no closing stock. So there is no need to calculate the average stock.

Problem 8. *Calculate the operating Ratio from the following figures.*

Items	(Rs. in Lakhs)
Sales	17,874
Sales Returns	4
Other Incomes	53
Cost of Sales	15,440

RATIO ANALYSIS

Administration and Selling Exp.   1,843
Depreciation   63
Interest Expenses (Non-operating) 456

Solution :

$$\text{Operating Ratio} = \frac{\text{Cost of Goods Sold} + \text{Operating Expenses}}{\text{Sales}} \times 100$$

$$= \frac{15{,}440 + 1{,}843}{17{,}870} \times 100 = 97\%$$

Problem 9. *The following is the Trading and Profit and loss account of Mathan Bros Private Limited for the year ended June 30, 2001.*

	Rs.		Rs.
To Stock in hand	76,250	By Sales	5,00,000
To Purchases	3,15,250	By Stock in hand	98,500
To Carriage and Freight	2,000		
To Wages	5,000		
To Gross Profit	2,00,000		
	5,98,500		5,98,500
To Administration Expenses	1,01,000	By Gross profit	2,00,000
To Finance Expenses :		By Non-operating Incomes	
Interest 1,200		Interest on Securities 1,500	
Discount 2,400		Dividend on Shares 3,750	
Bad Debts 3,400		Profit on Sale of Shares 750	
	7,000		6,000
To Selling Distribution Expenses	12,000		
To Non-operating expenses			
Loss on sale of securities 350			
Provision for legal suit 1,650	2,000		
To Net profit	84,000		
	2,06,000		2,06,000

You are required to calculate :
 (i) Gross profit Ratio   (ii) Expenses Ratio (individual)
 (iii) Net profit Ratio   (iv) Operating profit Ratio
 (v) Operating Ratio   (vi) Stock turnover Ratio

Solution :

(i) $\quad \text{Gross Profit Ratio} = \dfrac{\text{Gross Profit}}{\text{Sales}} \times 100 = \dfrac{2{,}00{,}000}{5{,}00{,}000} \times 100$

(ii) $\quad \text{Expenses Ratio} = \dfrac{\text{Individual Expenses}}{\text{Sales}}$

(a) $\dfrac{\text{Administration Expenses}}{\text{Sales}} \times 100 = \dfrac{1,01,000}{5,00,000} \times 100 = 2.02\%$

(b) $\dfrac{\text{Finance Expenses}}{\text{Sales}} \times 100 = \dfrac{7,000}{5,00,000} \times 100 = 1.40\%$

(c) $\dfrac{\text{Selling and Distribution Expenses}}{\text{Sales}} \times 100 = \dfrac{12,000}{5,00,000} \times 100 = 2.40\%$

(d) $\dfrac{\text{Non - Operating Expenses}}{\text{Sales}} \times 100 = \dfrac{2,000}{5,00,000} \times 100 = 0.4\%$

(iii) *Net Profit Ratio :*

$\dfrac{\text{Net Profit}}{\text{Sales}} \times 100 = \dfrac{84,000}{5,00,000} \times 100 = 16.8\%$

(iv) Operating Profit Ratio $= \dfrac{\text{Operating Profit}}{\text{Sales}} \times 100$

Operating Profit = Net Profit + Non-Operating Expenses − Non Operating Incomes

$= 84,000 + 2,000 - 6,000 = 80,000$

$= \dfrac{80,000}{50,00,000} \times 100 = 16\%$

(v) Operating Ratio $= \dfrac{\text{Cost of Goods Sold + Operating Expenses}}{\text{Sales}} \times 100$

Cost of Goods Sold = Sales − Gross profit

i.e., $5,00,000 - 2,00,000 = 3,00,000$

Operating Expenses

All Expenses Debited in the Profit & Loss A/c Except Non-Operating Expenses [including Finance expense]

$1,01,000 + 7,000 + 12,000 = 1,20,000$

Operating Ratio $= \dfrac{3,00,000 + 1,20,000}{5,00,000} \times 84\%$

(vi) Stock Turnover Ratio $= \dfrac{\text{Cost of Goods Sold}}{\text{Average Stock}}$

Costs of Goods Sold $= 3,00,000$

Average Stock $= \dfrac{\text{Opening Stock + Closing Stock}}{2}$

$= \dfrac{76,250 + 95,500}{2} = 85,875$

$\therefore \quad = \dfrac{3,00,000}{85,875} = 3.49 \text{ times}$

Problem 10. *Suraj & Co sells goods on cash as well as credit (though not on deferred instalment terms). The following particulars are extracted from their books of account for the calendar year 2004.*

RATIO ANALYSIS

Total Gross sales	= 1,00,000
Cash sales (included in above)	= 20,000
Sales Returns	= 7,000
Total Debtors for Sales on 31.12.2004	= 9,000
Bills Receivable on 31.12.2004	= 1,000
Provision for Doubtful Debts on 31.12.2004	= 1,000
Total Creditors 31.12.2004	= 10,000

Calculate the Average Collection Period. [MCA, Madras]

Solution :

Average Collection Period

$$= \frac{\text{Debtors + Bills Receivable + Provision for Doubtful Debts}}{\text{Net Credit Sales}} \times 365$$

$$= \frac{9,000 + 1,000 + 1,000}{73,000} \times 365 = 55 \text{ days}$$

Workings :

Net Credit Sales = Total Gross Sales − Cash Sales − Sales Returns
 = 1,00,000 − 20,000 − 7,000 = 73,000

Problem 11. *The following is the Trading account of M/s SKC Ltd. You are required to calculate the stock turnover Ratio.*

To Opening Stock	7,960	By Sales	39,000
To Purchases	19,500	By closing stock	7,200
To Carriage inwards	500		
To gross profit	18,240		
	46,200		46,200

Solution :

$$\text{Stock Turnover Ratio} = \frac{\text{Cost of Goods Sold}}{\text{Average Stock}}$$

$$\text{Cost of Goods Sold} = \text{Sales} - \text{Gross Profit}$$
$$= 39,000 - 18,240 = 20,760$$

$$\text{Average Stock} = \frac{\text{Opening Stock + Closing Stock}}{2}$$

$$= \frac{7,960 + 7,200}{2}$$

$$= 7,580$$

$$= \frac{20,760}{7,580} = 2.73 \text{ times}$$

Problem 12. *The Balance Sheet of Lal and Co. on 31.12.2000 shows the following details :*

	Rs.
Cash	9,500
Marketable Securities	15,000
Inventories	1,00,000
Debtors	85,000
Prepaid Expenses	5,000
Long-term Loans	1,06,000
Trade Creditors	64,000
Income Tax Payable	9,000
Accrued Expenses	12,000

You are required to compute
(i) Current Ratio (ii) Acid-Test Ratio. [MCA Madras]

Solution :

(i) $$\text{Current Ratio} = \frac{\text{Current Assets}}{\text{Current Liabilities}}$$

Current Assets = Cash + Marketable Securities + Inventories + Debtors + Prepaid Expenses
= 9,500 + 15,000 + 1,00,000 + 85,000 + 5,000 = 2,14,500

Current Liabilities = Trade Creditors + Income Tax Payable + Accrued Expenses
= 64,000 + 9,000 + 12,000 = 85,000

$$\text{Current Ratio} = \frac{\text{Current Assets}}{\text{Current Liabilities}}$$

$$\therefore \quad \frac{2,14,500}{85,000} = 2.52 : 1$$

(ii) $$\text{Acid Test Ratio} = \frac{\text{Liquid Assets}}{\text{Liquid Liabilities}}$$

Liquid Assets = Cash + Marketable Securities + Debtors + Prepaid Expenses
= 9,500 + 15,000 + 85,000 + 5,000 = 1,14,500

Liquid Liabilities = Trade Creditors + Income Tax Payable + Accrued Expenses
= 64,000 + 9,000 + 12,000 = 85,000

$$\therefore \quad \frac{1,14,500}{85,000} = 1.34 : 1$$

RATIO ANALYSIS

Problem 13. *From the following figures calculate the creditors turnover ratio and the average age of accounts payable.*

	Rs.
Credit Purchases During the Year 1998	1,00,000
Creditors on 01.01.1998	20,000
Creditors on 31.12.1998	10,000
Bills Payable on 01.01.1998	4,000
Bills Payable on 31.12.1998	6,000

[B.Com Dec 2003 Periyar]

Solution :

$$\text{Creditor's Turnover Ratio} = \frac{\text{Net Credit Purchase}}{\text{Average Account Payable}} = \frac{1,00,000}{20,000} = 5 \text{ times}$$

$$\text{Average Payment Period} = \frac{\text{Months}}{\text{Creditors Turnover}} = \frac{12}{5} = 2.4 \text{ months}$$

Problem 14. *From the data given below compute :*
(a) Working Capital   (b) Net Capital Employed   (c) Current Ratio
(d) Acid Test Ratio   (e) Debt-Equity Ratio   (f) Fixed Assets Ratio

Balance Sheet of Butterfly Ltd. as on 31st December

Liabilities	Rs.	Assets	Rs.
Equity Share Capital	25,000	Fixed Assets	30,000
Preference Share Capital	5,000	Current Assets : Stores	2,000
Reserve and surplus	4,000	Sundry Debtors	1,000
Debentures	8,000	Cash	500
Bank loan	4,000	Bank	2,500
Sundry creditors	1,000	preliminary expenses	8,000
Proposed Dividends	1,000	Brokerage on shares	2,000
Provision for Taxation	2,000	Stock	4,000
	50,000		50,000

[B.Com Madurai]

Solution :

    Working Capital = Current Assets − Current Liabilities
    Current Assets = Stores + Sundry Debtors + Cash + Bank + Stock
                   = 2,000 + 1,000 + 2,500 + 4,000 + 500 = 10,000
    Current Liabilities = Sundry Creditors + Proposed Dividends
                      + Provision for Taxation
                      = 1,000 + 1,000 + 2,000 = 4,000

(a)   Working Capital = 10,000 − 4,000 = 6,000
(b) Net Capital Employed
    All assets excluding fictitious assets − Current liabilities *i.e.,*
    Rs. 40,000 − 4,000 = 36,000

(c) $\text{Current Ratio} = \dfrac{\text{Current Assets}}{\text{Current Liabilities}} = \dfrac{10,000}{4,000} = 2.5 : 1$

(d)   Acid Test Ratio = $\dfrac{\text{Liquid Assets}}{\text{Liquid Liabilities}}$

Liquid Assets = 2,500 + 500 + 1,000 = i.e., 4,000
Liquid Liabilities = 2,000 + 1,000 + 1,000 = i.e., 4,000

$$= \dfrac{4,000}{4,000} = 1$$

(e)   Debt − Equity Ratio = $\dfrac{\text{Outsider's Fund}}{\text{Shareholder's Fund}} = \dfrac{16,000}{34,000} = .47 : 1$

Outsider's Fund   16,000

Outsider's Fund = Debentures + Bank Loan + Sundry Creditors
+ Proposed Dividends + Provision for Taxation
= 8,000 + 4,000 + 1,000 + 1,000 + 2,000 = 16,000

Shareholder's Fund = Equity Share Capital + Preference Share Capital
+ Reserves and Surplus
= 25,000 + 5,000 + 4,000 = 34,000

Debt-Equity Ratio = 0.47 : 1

(f)   Fixed Assets Ratio = $\dfrac{\text{Fixed Assets}}{\text{Long - term Funds}} = \dfrac{30,000}{46,000} = .65 : 1$

Long-term Funds = Equity Share Capital, Preference Share Capital,
Reserves and Surplus, Debentures, Bank Loan.
= 25,000 + 5,000 + 4,000 + 8,000 + 4,000 = 46,000

Type II : Ratio to Balance Sheet

Problem 1. *From the following details find out*

(i) Current Assets   (ii) Current Liabilities   (iii) Liquid Assets   (iv) Stock

Current Ratio   2.5
Liquidity Ratio   1.5
Working Capital   Rs. 60,000   [MBA Madras]

Solution :

(1) Current Assets   −   Current Liabilities   =   Working Capital
        ↓   ↓   ↓
     2.5   −   1.0   =   1.5
     ↓   ↓   ↓
   1,00,000   −   40,000   =   60,000

(2) Liquid Ratio   :   Liquid Assets   :   Liquid Liabilities
                         ↓   ↓
                         1.5   =   1.00
                         ↓   ↓
                    60,000   =   40,000

RATIO ANALYSIS

	Rs.
Current Assets	1,00,000
Current Liabilities	40,000
Liquid Assets	60,000
Stock	40,000

> **NOTE :**
> (i) Here all Current Liabilities have been taken as Liquid Liabilities.
> (ii) Difference between Current Assets and Liquid Assets is the stock.

Problem 2. *From the following details, prepare Balance sheet of Moorthy Ltd., with as many details as possible.*

(i) Stock Velocity : 6 (ii) Capital Turnover Ratio : 2
(iii) Fixed Asset Turnover Ratio : 4 (iv) Gross Profit Turnover Ratio : 20%
(v) Debtor's Velocity : 2 months (vi) Creditors Velocity : 73 days
(vii) Gross Profit was Rs. 60,000. (viii) Reserves and Surplus Rs. 20,000
(ix) Closing Stock was Rs. 5,000 in Excess of Opening Stock. [B.Com 2003 PU]

Solution :

Workings :

(i) Cost of Goods Sold + GP = Sales
   ↓   ↓   ↓
   80% 20% 100%
   2,40,000 + 60,000 = 3,00,000

(ii) Stock turnover = $\dfrac{\text{Cost of Goods Sold}}{\text{Average Stock (X)}}$ = Stock Velocity (6)

$$X = \dfrac{2,40,000}{6}$$

Average Stock = 40,000
Total Stock value = 40,000 × 2 = 80,000
Less : Excess = 5,000
                 ─────────
                 75,000

Opening Stock = 37,500
Closing Stock = 37,500 + 5,000 = 42,500

(iii) Debtor's Velocity = 2 months

$\dfrac{\text{Debtors (X)}}{\text{Sales}} \times 12 = 2$ i.e., $X = 3,00,000 \times \dfrac{2}{12}$

Debtors = Rs. 50,000

(iv) Creditor's Velocity = 73 days.

$\dfrac{\text{Creditors (X)}}{\text{Purchase}} \times 365 = 73$

147

$$X = 2,45,000 \times \frac{73}{365} = 49,000$$

NOTE : Purchase = Cost of Sales + Increase in Stock = 2,40,000 + 5,000 = 2,45,000

(v) Fixed Assets Turnover Ratio = $\dfrac{\text{Turnover}}{\text{Fixed Assets (X)}}$

$$X = \frac{2,40,000}{4} = 60,000$$

(vi) Capital Turnover Ratio = 2

$$\frac{\text{Turnover}}{\text{Capital (X)}} = 2$$

$$X = \frac{2,40,000}{2} = 2 \qquad 1,20,000$$

(vii) Total Capital = 1,20,000
Creditors = 49,000
Total Liabilities = 1,69,000

All Assets (42,500 + 50,000 + 60,000) = 1,52,500
Cash (1,69,000 – 1,52,500) = 16,500
1,69,000

Statement of Proprietary Funds :
Fixed Assets = 60,000
Working Capital
(Current Assets – CL)
Closing Stock   42,500
Debtors   50,000
Cash   16,500
                   ─────────
                    1,09,000
Less : Creditors   49,000
                              60,000
Proprietor's Fund   1,20,000

It consists of share capital and Reserves and Surplus.
Share Capital   1,00,000
Reserves and Surplus   20,000
                         ─────────
                         1,20,000

RATIO ANALYSIS

Problem 3. *Calculate the current assets of a company from the following information:*

(i) Stock Turnover 5 times
(ii) Stock at the end is Rs. 5,000; more than the stock in the beginning
(iii) Sales (all credit) Rs. 2,00,000
(iv) Gross Profit Ratio 20%
(v) Current Liabilities Rs. 60,000
(vi) Quick Ratio 0.75

Solution :

(1) Cost of Goods Sold + G.P. = Sales
 ↓ ↓ ↓
 80% + 20% = 100
 ↓ ↓ ↓
 1,60,000 + 40,000 = 2,00,000

(2) Stock Turnover Ratio = 5 times

$$\frac{\text{Cost of Goods Sold}}{\text{Average Stock (X)}} = 5 \text{ times}$$

$$X = \frac{1,60,000}{5} = 32,000$$

Average Stock = Rs. 32,000
Full Stock Value = 32,000 × 2 = 64,000
Less : Excess Value = 5,000
 ─────────
 59,000
 ═════════

$$\frac{59,000}{2} = 29,500$$

Opening Stock = 29,500
Closing Stock = 29,500 + 5,000 = 34,500

(3) Quick Ratio

Quick Assets : Quick Liabilities
 ↓ ↓
 0.75 : 1.00
 ↓ ↓
 45,000 : 60,000

Current Assets
 Closing Stock = 34,500
 Quick Assets = 45,000
 ─────────
 79,500
 ═════════

Problem 4. *From the following information, prepare a Balance sheet as on 31.3.2003 :*

(i) Working Capital Rs. 1,20,000 (iv) Assets (Fixed) – Proprietary Ratio 0.75 : 1
(ii) Reserves and Surplus 80,000 (v) Liquid Ratio 1.5
(iii) Bank Overdraft 20,000 (vi) Current Ratio 2.5

Solution :

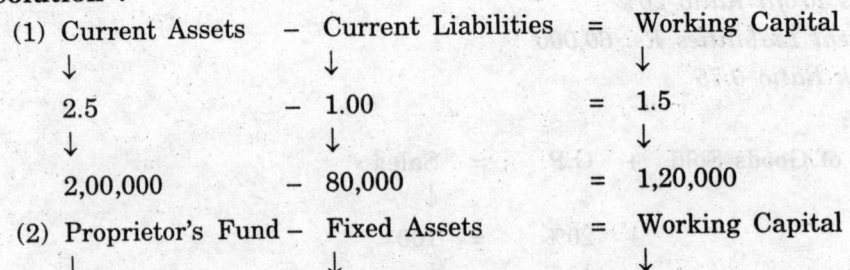

(1) Current Assets − Current Liabilities = Working Capital
    ↓   ↓   ↓
    2.5   − 1.00   = 1.5
    ↓   ↓   ↓
    2,00,000   − 80,000   = 1,20,000

(2) Proprietor's Fund − Fixed Assets = Working Capital
    ↓   ↓   ↓
    1.00   − .75   = .25
    ↓   ↓   ↓
    4,80,000   − 3,60,000   = 1,20,000

(3) Liquid Ratio

Liquid Assets	:	Liquid Liabilities
1.5	:	1.00
90,000	:	60,000

Current Liabilities	80,000	Current Assets	2,00,000
Less : BOD	20,000	Liquid Assets	90,000
Liquid Liabilities	60,000	Stock	1,10,000

Balance Sheet

Liabilities	Rs	Assets	Rs
Share Capital (4,80,000 – 80,000)	4,00,000	Fixed Assets	3,60,000
Reserves and Surplus	80,000	Stock	1,10,000
Bank Overdraft	20,000	Other Current Assets	90,000
Sundry Creditors	60,000		
	5,60,000		5,60,000

Problem 5. *From the following information prepare a Balance sheet and show the working.*

(i) Working Capital Rs. 75,000 (v) Liquid Ratio : 1.15
(ii) Reserves and Surplus Rs. 1,00,000 (vi) Long-term Liabilities Nil
(iii) Bank Overdraft Rs. 60,000 (vii) Fixed Assets to Proprietor's Fund : 0.75
(iv) Current Ratio : 1.75

[MCA, MBA, Madras]

Solution :

(1) Current Assets   –   Current Liabilities   =   Working Capital
    1.75   –   1.00   =   .75
    ↓   ↓   ↓
    1,75,000   –   1,00,000   =   75,000

(2) Proprietor's Fund   –   Fixed Assets   =   Working Capital
    ↓   ↓   ↓
    1.00   –   .75   =   .25
    ↓   ↓   ↓
    3,00,000   –   2,25,000   =   75,000

(3) Liquid Ratio

Liquid Assets   :   Liquid Liabilities
1.15   –   1.00
↓   ↓
46,000   –   40,000

Current Liabilities	1,00,000	Current Assets	1,75,000
Less : BOD	60,000	Liquid Assets	46,000
Liquid Liabilities	40,000	Stock	1,29,000

Balance Sheet

Liabilities	Rs	Assets	Rs
Share Capital		Fixed Assets	2,25,000
(3,00,000 – 1,00,000)	2,00,000	Stock	1,29,000
Reserves and Surplus	1,00,000	Other Current Assets	46,000
Bank Overdraft	60,000		
Sundry Creditors			
(1,00,000 – 60,000)	40,000		
	4,00,000		4,00,000

Problem 6. *From the following particulars prepare the balance sheet of ABC Limited.*

(i) Sales for the year Rs. 20,00,000   (ii) Gross Profit Ratio 25%
(iii) Current Ratio : 1.50   (iv) Quick (cash Drs) Ratio : 1.25
(v) Stock Turnover Ratio : 15   (vi) Debt Collection Period : 1 ½ months
(vii) Turnover to Fixed Assets : 1.5   (viii) Fixed Assets to Networth : 5/6 (.83)
(ix) Ratio of Reserves to Share Capital 1/3 (0.33) *[The term turnover refers to cost of sales and stock refers to closing stock]*

[B.Com Madras : MCA Bharathidasan MBA Madras].

Solution :

(i)

Cost of goods sold	+	Gross Profit	=	Sales
↓		↓		↓
75%	+	25%	=	100%
↓		↓		↓
1,50,000	+	5,00,000	=	20,00,000

(ii) Stock Turnover Ratio

$$\frac{\text{Cost of Goods Sold}}{\text{Average Stock (X)}} = 15 \qquad \frac{15,00,000}{X} = 15$$

$$X = \frac{15,00,000}{15}$$

Average Stock = 1,00,000

(iii)

Current Ratio	:	1.50	6,00,000
Quick Ratio	:	1.25	5,00,000
Stock		.25	1,00,000

(iv) Current Ratio

Current Assets	:	Current Liabilities
↓		↓
1.50		1.00
6,00,000		4,00,000

(v) Debt Collection Period : 1½ months

$$\frac{\text{Debtors}}{\text{Sales}} \times 12 = 1.5 \qquad \frac{X}{20,00,000} \times 12 = 1.5$$

$$X = 20,00,000 \times \frac{1.5}{12}$$

Debtors = 2,50,000

(vi) Turnover to Fixed Assets : 1.5

$$\frac{\text{Cost of Goods Sold}}{\text{Fixed Assets (X)}} = 1.5$$

$$X = \frac{15,00,000}{1.5}$$

Fixed Assets = 10,00,000

(vii) Fixed Assets to : Networth = 5/6

↓		↓
5	:	6
10,00,000	:	12,00,000

$$\left[\frac{10,00,000}{5} \times 6 = 12,00,000\right]$$

(viii) Ratio of Reserves to Share Capital = 1/3

Reserves	+	Share Capital	=	Net Worth
1	+	3	=	4
3,00,000	+	9,00,000	=	12,00,000

$$\left[\frac{12,00,000}{4} \times 3 = 9,00,000\right]$$

Balance Sheet

Liabilities	Rs.	Assets	Rs.
Share Capital	9,00,000	Fixed Assets	10,00,000
Reserves	3,00,000	Current Assets	6,00,000
Current Liabilities	4,00,000		
	16,00,000		16,00,000

Problem 7. *From the following information you are required to prepare a balance sheet :*

Current Ratio	– 1.75
Liquid Ratio	– 1.25
Stock Turnover Ratio (Cost of Sales / Closing Stock)	– 9
Gross Profit Ratio	– 25%
Debt Collection Period	– 1 ½ months
Reserves and Surplus to Capital	– 0.2
Turnover of Fixed Assets	– 1.2
Capital Gearing Ratio	– 0.6
Fixed Assets to Net worth	– 1.25
Sales for the year	– Rs. 12,00,000

[B.Com Madras]

Solution :

(i) Cost of Goods Sold + Gross Profit = Sales
   ↓   ↓   ↓
   75%   − 25%   = 100%
   9,00,000   + 3,00,000   = 12,00,000

(ii) Stock Turnover Ratio = 9

$$\frac{\text{Cost of Goods Sold}}{\text{Average Stock (X)}} = 9 \qquad \frac{9,00,000}{X} = 9$$

$$X = \frac{9,00,000}{9}$$

Stock = 1,00,000

(iii) Current Ratio   1.75   3,50,000
      Quick Ratio   1.25   2,50,000
      Stock   0.50   1,00,000

(iv) Debt Collection Period = 1 ½ months

$$\frac{\text{Debtors}}{\text{Sales}} \times 12 = 1.5$$

Debtors = 1,50,000

$$X = 12,00,000 \times \frac{1.5}{12}$$

Debtors = 1,50,000

(v) Turnover of Fixed Assets 1.2

$$\frac{\text{Turnover}}{(X) \text{ Fixed Assets}} = 1.2 = \frac{9,00,000}{X} = 1.2$$

$$X = \frac{9,00,000}{1.2}$$

Fixed Assets = 7,50,000

(vi) Fixed assets to : Networth = 1.25 : 1
↓ ↓
1.25 : 1.00
7,50,000 : 6,00,000

(vii) Reserves and Surplus to Capital : 0.2 : 1

Reserves	+	Share Capital	=	Net worth
0.2	+	1.00	=	1.2
↓		↓		↓
1,00,000	+	5,00,000	=	6,00,000

$$\left[\frac{6,00,000}{1.2} \times 1 = 5,00,000 \right]$$

(viii) Capital Gearing Ratio

$$\frac{(X) \text{ Fixed Interest Bearing}}{\text{Equity Share Capital}} = 0.6$$

X = 5,00,000 × 0.6

Long-term Debt = Rs. 3,00,000

Balance Sheet

Liabilities	Rs.	Assets	Rs.
Equity Share Capital	5,00,000	Fixed Assets	7,50,000
Long-term Debt	3,00,000	Current Assets	3,50,000
Reserves	1,00,000		
Current Liabilities	2,00,000		
	11,00,000		11,00,000

NOTE : Current Ratio
Current Assets : Current Liabilities
1.75 1.00
3,50,000 2,00,000

RATIO ANALYSIS

Problem 8. *Using the information and the form given below compute the balance sheet items for a firm having a sale of Rs. 36 lakhs.*

Sales/Total Assets	3	Sales/Debtors		15
Sales/Fixed Assets	5	Current Ratio		2
Sales/Current Assets	7.5	Total Assets/Net worth		2.5
Sales/Inventories	20	Debt Equity		1

Balance Sheet

Liabilities	Rs.	Assets	Rs.
Networth	***	Fixed Assets	***
Long-term Debt	***	Inventories	***
Current Liabilities	***	Debtors	***
		Liquid Assets	***
		Current Assets	***

Solution :

(1) Sales : Total assets = 3
   ↓   ↓
   3   :   1
   36,00,000 :   12,00,000

(2) Sales : Fixed assets = 5
   5   :   1
   36,00,000 :   7,20,000

(3) Sales : Current assets = 7.5
   7.5   :   1.00
   36,00,000 :   4,80,000

(4) Sales : Inventories
   20   :   1
   36,00,000 :   1,80,000

(5) Sales : Debtors
   15   :   1.00
   36,00,000 :   2,40,000

(6) Current Ratio : $\dfrac{\text{Current Assets}}{\text{Current Liabilities}}$
   2   :   1.00
   4,80,000 :   2,40,000

(7) Total Assets : Net worth = 2.5
   ↓   ↓
   2.5   :   1.00
   12,00,000 :   4,80,000

(8) Debt   : Equity
    1.0   : 1.0
    4,80,000   : 4,80,000

Balance Sheet

Liabilities	Rs.	Assets	Rs.
Net worth	4,80,000	Fixed Assets	7,20,000
Long-term Debt	4,80,000	Inventories	1,80,000
Current Liabilities	2,40,000	Debtors	2,40,000
		Liquid Assets	60,000
	12,00,000		12,00,000

Current Assets		4,80,000
Debtors	2,40,000	
Stock	1,80,000	
		4,20,000
Liquid Assets		60,000

Problem 9. *From the following information compute the Balance sheet*

Total Assets/Net worth = 3.5
Sales to fixed Assets = 6
Sales to current Assets = 8
Sales to inventory = 15
Sales to Debtors = 18
Current Ratio = 2.5
Annual sales = Rs. 25,00,000   [MBA Madras]

Solution :

(i)   Sales to Fixed Assets = 6 : 1
              ↓   ↓
         25,00,000   4,16,667

(ii)   Sales to Current Assets = 8

$$\frac{\text{Sales}}{(X)\ \text{Current Assets}} = 8$$

$$X = \frac{25,00,000}{8}$$

Current Assets = 3,12,500

(iii) Debtors = $\frac{\text{Sales}}{(X)\ \text{Debtors}} = 18$

$$X = \frac{25,00,000}{18} = 1,38,889$$

RATIO ANALYSIS 157

(iv) Sales   : Inventory = 15 : 1
    15   : 1
    ↓   : ↓
    25,00,000   : 1,66,667

(v) Current Ratio
    Current Assets : Current Liabilities
    2.5   : 1.0
    ↓   : ↓
    3,12,500   : 1,25,000

(vi) Total Assets : Net worth = 3.5
    3.5   : 1.00
    ↓   : ↓
    7,29,167   : 2,08,333

$$\left[\frac{7,29,167}{3.5} \times 1.00 = 2,08,333\right]$$

Total Assets   =   Fixed Assets   4,16,667
                   Current Assets   3,12,500
                                      ─────────
                                      7,29,167

Long Term Debt :
Total Assets   = [Net worth + Current liabilities)
7,29,167   = [1,78,667 + 1,25,000]
Long-term Debt = Rs. 4,25,500

Balance Sheet

Liabilities	Rs.	Assets	Rs.
Net worth	1,78,667	Fixed Assets	4,16,667
Long-term Debt	4,25,500	Current Assets	3,12,500
Current Liabilities	1,25,000		
	7,29,167		7,29,167

Current Assets :
 Inventory   1,66,667
 Debtors   1,38,889
 Liquid Assets   6,944
                 ─────────
Current Assets   3,12,500

Problem 10. *Following are the ratios to the trading activities of Indian Traders Ltd.*

Debtor's Velocity	3 months
Stock Velocity	8 months
Creditors Velocity	2 months
Gross Profit Ratio	25%

Gross Profit for the year ended 31.12.2001 amounts to Rs. 4,00,000. Closing stock of the year is Rs. 10,000 above the opening stock. Bills receivable are worth Rs. 25,000 and bills payable Rs. 10,000.

Find out (a) Sales (b) Sundry Debtors (c) Closing Stock and (d) Sundry Creditors.

[B.Com., Madras 1991]

Solution :

(1) Cost of Goods Sold + GP = Sales
   75% + 25% = 100%
   ↓   ↓   ↓
   12,00,000 + 4,00,000 = 16,00,000

(2) Debtor's Velocity : 3 months

$$\frac{\text{Debtors}}{\text{Sales}} \times 12 = 3, \text{ i.e., } \frac{X}{16,00,000} \times 12 = 3$$

$$= 4,00,000$$

Less : Bills receivable = 25,000

Sundry Debtors = 3,75,000

(3) Stock Velocity : 8 months

$$\frac{\text{Cost of Goods Sold}}{\text{Average Stock (X)}} \times 12 = 8 = \frac{12,00,000}{X} \times 12 = 8$$

$$X = 12,00,000 \times \frac{8}{12}$$

Average Stock = 8,00,000
Total Stock Value 8,00,000 × 2 = 16,00,000
Excess Stock = 10,000
                          15,90,000

Opening Stock = 7,95,000
                               7,95,000
Closing Stock = 7,95,000
Excess Value = 10,000   8,05,000
                               16,00,000

(4) Sundry Creditors

Opening Stock	+	Purchase − Closing Stock	=	Cost of Goods Sold
7,95,000	+	x − 8,05,000	=	12,00,000
x = 12,00,000	+	8,05,000 − 7,95,000	=	12,10,000

RATIO ANALYSIS

(5)   Creditor's Velocity = 2 months

$$\frac{\text{Creditors + Bills Payable}}{\text{Purchase}} \times 12 = 2, \text{ i.e., } \frac{X}{12,00,000} \times 12 = 2$$

$$\begin{aligned} \text{Account Payable} &= 2,01,667 \\ \text{Less : Bills Payable} &= 10,000 \\ \hline \text{Creditors} &= 1,91,667 \end{aligned}$$

Problem 11. *From the following information prepare a Balance Sheet with as many details as possible.*

Gross Profit	Rs. 80,000	Current Assets	Rs. 1,50,000
Gross Profit to Cost of Goods Sold Ratio	1/3	Account Payable Velocity	90 days
		Bills Receivable	Rs. 20,000
Stock Velocity	6 times	Bills Payable	Rs. 5,000
Opening Stock	Rs. 36,000	Fixed Assets Turnover Ratio	8 times
Account Receivable Velocity	72 days		

(Year 360 days)

Note : *Turnover refers to Cost of Sales.*

                      [M.Com Madras Nov 1978] [B.Com Madras Nov.1978 PU 2004]

Solution :

(1)   Cost of Goods Sold   +   GP   =   Sales
                     ↓   ↓   ↓
                   3   +   1   =   4
           2,40,000   +   80,000   =   3,20,000

(2)   Stock Velocity = 6 times

$$\frac{\text{Cost of Goods Sold}}{\text{Average Stock (X)}} = \frac{2,40,000}{X} = 6$$

      ∴   Average Stock = 40,000

(3)   Average Stock = Rs. 40,000

          Full Stock Value = 40,000 × 2 = 80,000

               Less : Opening Stock = 36,000
                                                ─────
                           Closing Stock = 44,000

(4) Debtors Velocity

$$\frac{\text{Debtors + Bill Receivable}}{\text{Sales}} \times 360 = 72$$

$$X = 3,20,000 \times \frac{72}{360} = 64,000$$

      ∴   Drs + Bills Receivable = 64,000
            Less : Bills Receivable = 20,000
                                 ─────
                           Debtors = 44,000

(5) Creditor's Velocity or Accounts Payable Velocity

$$\frac{\text{Creditors + Bills Payable}}{\text{Purchase}} \times 360 = 90, \text{ i.e., } \frac{X}{12,48,000} \times 360 = 90$$

$$X = 2,48,000 \times \frac{90}{360}$$

Bills Payable + Creditors = 62,000
Less : Bills payable = 5,000
Creditors = 57,000

Find out the Purchases

Opening Stock + Purchase − Closing Stock = Cost of Goods Sold
↓ ↓ ↓ ↓
36,000 + x − 44,000 = 2,40,000
x = 2,40,000 + 44,000 − 36,000
Purchase Rs. = 2,48,000

(6) Fixed Assets Turnover Ratio

$$\frac{\text{Turnover}}{\text{Fixed Assets (X)}} = 8, \text{ i.e., } X = \frac{2,40,000}{8}$$

Fixed Assets = 30,000

Balance Sheet

Liabilities	Rs.	Assets	Rs.
Capital (B/F)	1,18,000	Fixed Assets	30,000
Creditors	57,000	Closing Stock	44,000
Bills Payable	5,000	Debtors	44,000
		Bills Receivable	20,000
		Other Current Assets	42,000
	1,80,000		1,80,000

Total Current Assets given : 1,50,000
Stock 44,000
Debtors 44,000
B.R. 20,000   1,08,000
Other Current Assets 42,000

Problem 12. *From the following information presented by a firm for the year ended 31st December, find out :*

(i) Net worth (ii) Current Liabilities
(iii) Total Debt to Net worth (iv) Long-term Debt
(v) Current Assets (vi) Stock
(vii) Debtors and (viii) Fixed Assets

RATIO ANALYSIS

Sales to Net worth : 5 times
Current Liabilities to Net worth : 50%
Total Debts to Net worth : 60%
Current Ratio : 2
Sales to Stock : 10 times
Debtor's Velocity : 9 times
Annual Sales : Rs. 15,00,000
Cash Sales : 40% of Sales   [M.Com (CA) May 2004 PU]

Solution :

(i) Sales to Net worth : 5 times
    Sales   : Net worth
    5   : 1
    15,00,000   : 3,00,000

$$\left[\frac{15,00,000}{5} \times 1 = 3,00,000\right]$$

(ii) Current Liabilities to Net worth
     Current Liabilities = 50% of Rs. 3,00,000
                        = 1,50,000

(iii) Total Debt to Net worth = 60%
     Total Debt is 60% of 3,00,000 = 1,80,000 (or)
     Total Debt   : Net worth
     60%   : 100%
     ↓   : ↓
     1,80,000   : 3,00,000

(iv) Long-term Debt
     Long term Debt = Total Debt − Current Liabilities
                    = 1,80,000 − 1,50,000 = 30,000

(v) Current Assets
    Current Ratio
    Current Assets : Current Liabilities
    2.0   : 1.00
    3,00,000   : 1,50,000

(vi) Stock
     Sales to Stock = 10 times
     Sales   : Stock
     10.0   : 1.00
     15,00,000 : 1,50,000

(vii) Debtor's Velocity : 9 times

$$\text{Credit Sales} = 15,00,000 \times \frac{60}{100}$$
$$= 9,00,000$$

Debtor's Turnover Ratio = $\dfrac{\text{Debtors (X)}}{\text{Sales}}$ = 9, i.e., $\dfrac{X}{9,00,000}$ = 9

$$X = \dfrac{9,00,000}{9}$$

Debtors = 1,00,000

(viii) Fixed Assets

Fixed Assets to Net worth Ratio = 60%

$$\left[\dfrac{3,00,000}{100} \times 60 = 1,80,000\right]$$

i.e., Fixed Assets : Net worth
↓   ↓
60%   : 100%
1,80,000   : 3,00,000

Problem 13. *With the help of the following Ratios regarding Narmatha Tex, draw the Trading, Profit and Loss A/c and Balance Sheet of the company for the year 2004.*

(i) *Current Ratio* : 2.5
(ii) *Liquidity Ratio* : 1.5
(iii) *Net working capital* : Rs. 3,00,000
(iv) *Stock Turnover Ratio* : 6 times (Cost of Sales/Closing Stock)
(v) *Gross profit Ratio* : 20%
(vi) *Fixed Assets Turnover Ratio (on Cost of Sales)* : 2 times
(vii) *Debt Collection Period* : 2 months
(viii) *Fixed Assets to Shareholder's Net worth* : 0.80
(ix) *Reserves and Surplus to Capital* : 0.5   [M.Com Bharathiar 1991]

Solution :

(1) Current Assets − Current Liabilities = Working Capital
    ↓   ↓   ↓
    2.5   − 1.00   1.5
    ↓   ↓   ↓
    5,00,000   2,00,000   = 3,00,000

(2) Current Ratio   2.5 → 5,00,000
    Liquidity Ratio 1.5 → 3,00,000
    Stock   1.0 → 2,00,000

(3) Stock Turnover Ratio : 6 times

$$\dfrac{\text{(X) Cost of Goods Sold}}{\text{Closing Stock}} = 6, \text{ i.e., } \dfrac{X}{2,00,000} = 6$$

Cost of Goods Sold = 12,00,000

RATIO ANALYSIS

(4) Cost of Goods Sold + GP = Sales
80% + 20% = 100%
12,00,000 + 3,00,000 = 15,00,000

$$\left[\frac{12,00,000}{80} \times 20\right] = 3,00,000$$

(5) Debt Collection Period = 2 months

$$\frac{X \text{ Drs} + BR}{\text{Sales}} \times 12 = 2, \text{ i.e., } \frac{X}{15,00,000} \times 12 = 2$$

$$X = 15,00,000 \times \frac{2}{12}$$

Debtors + BR = 2,50,000

(6) Fixed Assets Turnover Ratio

$$\frac{\text{Turnover}}{\text{Fixed Assets}} = 2, \text{ i.e., } \frac{12,00,000}{X} = 2$$

$$X = \frac{12,00,000}{2} = 6,00,000$$

(7) Fixed Assets to Shareholder's Net worth = .80

$$\frac{\text{Fixed Assets } (6,00,000)}{\text{Shareholder's Net worth } (X)} = .80$$

$$X = \frac{6,00,000}{.80}$$

Shareholder's Net worth = 7,50,000

(8) Reserves and Surplus to capital : 0.5
Reserves + Share Capital = Net worth
.50 + 1.00 = 1.50
↓ ↓ ↓
2,50,000 + 5,00,000 = 7,50,000

Balance Sheet

Liabilities	Rs.	Assets	Rs.
Share Capital	5,00,000	Fixed Assets	6,00,000
Reserves and Surplus	2,50,000	Current Assets	5,00,000
Current Liabilities	2,00,000		
Long-term Loan	1,50,000		
	11,00,000		11,00,000

Total Current Assets given : 5,00,000
Stock 2,00,000
Debtors 2,50,000 4,50,000
Cash 50,000

Problem 14. *From the following figures and ratios draw out trading, profit and loss account and balance sheet.*

Share capital   = 1,80,000
Working capital   = 63,000
Bank overdraft   = 10,000

There is no fictitious asset. In current assets there is no asset other than Stock debtors and cash. Closing stock is 20% higher than the opening stock.

Current Ratio	:	2.5
Proprietary Ratio	:	0.7
Stock Velocity	:	4
Net Profit Ratio	:	10% (to average Capital employed)
Quick Ratio	:	1.5
Gross Profit Ratio	:	20% to Sales
Debtor's Velocity	:	365 days

Answer : Gross Profit Rs. 38,500, NP 23,950, B/s total 2,22,000.

Problem 15. *With the following Ratios and further information given below, prepare Trading, Profit and Loss A/c and a Balance Sheet of Shri Surjit & Co.*

  (i) Gross Profit Ratio   : 25%   (vi) Fixed Assets/Capital : 5/4
 (ii) Net Profit/Sales   : 20%   (vii) Fixed Assets/Total Current Assets : 5/7
(iii) Stock Turnover Ratio   : 10   (viii) Fixed Assets   : Rs. 10,00,000
 (iv) Net Profit Capital   : 1/5   (ix) Closing Stock   : Rs. 1,00,000
  (v) Capital to Total Liabilities : 1/2

Solution :

(i) Capital

Fixed Assets	:	Capital
5	:	4
10,00,000	:	8,00,000

$$\left[\frac{5}{10,00,000} \times 4\right] = 8,00,000$$

(ii) Net Profit Ratio

Net Profit	:	Capital
1.00	:	5.00
↓		↓
1,60,000		8,00,000

(iii) Net Profit/Sales   : 20%

$$\frac{\text{Net Profit } (1,60,000)}{\text{Sales } (X)} \times 100 = 20$$

$$X = 1,60,000 \times \frac{100}{20}$$

Sales = Rs. 8,00,000

RATIO ANALYSIS

(iv) Cost of Goods Sold + GP = Sales
75% + 25% 100%
6,00,000 + 2,00,000 8,00,000

(v) Stock Turnover Ratio

$$\frac{\text{Cost of goods sold (6,00,000)}}{\text{Average Stock (X)}} = 10$$

$$X = \frac{6,00,000}{10}$$

Average stock = 60,000
Actual/Full stock value 60,000 × 2   1,20,000
Less : Closing Stock   1,00,000
Opening Stock   20,000

(vi) Total Liabilities : Capital to total liabilities $\frac{1}{2}$

$$\frac{\text{Capital}}{\text{(X) Total Liabilities}} = \frac{1}{2}$$

$$\frac{8,00,000}{\text{Total Liabilities}}$$

X = 8,00,000 × 2 = 16,00,000

(vii) Total Current Assets

Fixed Assets to Total Current Assets : 5/7

Fixed Assets = Rs. 10,00,000

$$\frac{\text{Fixed Assets}}{\text{(X) Total Current Assets}} = 5/7$$

$$X = 10,00,000 \times \frac{7}{5}$$

= 14,00,000

Less : Closing Stock = 1,00,000

Current Assets = 13,00,000

Trading and Profit and Loss Account for the year ended

	Rs.		Rs.
To Opening Stock	20,000	By Sales	8,00,000
To Purchases	6,80,000	By Closing Stock	1,00,000
To Gross Profit	2,00,000		
	9,00,000		9,00,000
To Expenses	40,000	By Gross Profit	2,00,000
To Net Profit	1,60,000		
	2,00,000		2,00,000

Balance Sheet

Liabilities	Rs.	Assets	Rs.
Share Capital		Fixed Assets	10,00,000
(8,00,000 – 1,60,000)	6,40,000	Stock	1,00,000
Net Profit	1,60,000	Other Current Assets	13,00,000
Current Liabilities	16,00,000		
	24,00,000		24,00,000

Problem 16. *You are given the following information pertaining to the Financial Statements of Reliance Ltd as on 31.12.2004. On the basis of the information supplied, you are required to prepare Trading, Profit and Loss Account for the year ended and a Balance Sheet as on the date.*

Net Current Assets	: 2,00,000
Issued Share Capital	: 6,00,000
Current Ratio	: 1.8
Quick Ratio [Ratio of Debtors and Bank Balance to Current Liabilities]	: 1.35
Fixed Assets to Shareholder's Equity	: 80%
Ratio of Gross Profit on Turnover	: 25%
Net Profit to Issued Share Capital	: 20%
Stock Turnover Ratio	: 5 times
Average of Outstanding for the year	: 36 ½ days

On 31.12.2004, the Current Assets consisted only of Stock Debtors and Bank Balance. Liabilities consisted of Share Capital, Current Liabilities and Assets consisted of Fixed Assets and Current Assets.

Solution :

(1) Current Assets − Current Liabilities = Working Capital
    1.8   1.00   .8
    4,50,000   − 2,50,000   = 2,00,000

(2) Quick Ratio
    Quick Assets   : Current Liabilities
    1.35   1.00
    3,37,500   2,50,000

(3) Stock
    Current Assets − Quick Assets   = Stock
    4,50,000   − 3,37,500   = 1,12,500

(4) Stock Turnover

$$\frac{\text{Cost of Goods Sold (X)}}{\text{Closing Stock (1,12,500)}} = 5$$

$$X = 1,12,500 \times 5 = 5,62,500$$

RATIO ANALYSIS

(5) Ratio of Gross Profit on Turnover 25%

Cost of Goods Sold	+	GP	=	Sales
75%	+	25%		100%
5,62,500	+	1,87,500		7,50,000

(6) Debtor's Turnover Ratio (Here there are no Bills Receivable)

$$\frac{Drs}{Sales} \times 365 = 36.5, \text{ i.e., } \frac{X}{7,50,000} \times 365 = 36.5$$

$$X = 7,50,000 \times \frac{36.5}{365}$$

Debtors = Rs. 75,000

(7) Quick Assets (Debtors + Bank) = 3,37,500
    Less : Debtors = 75,000
    Cash in hand = 2,62,500

(8) Net Profit to Issued Share Capital : 20%

20%   :   100
↓   ↓
1,20,000 : 6,00,000

$\left[\frac{6,00,000}{100} \times 20\right] = 1,20,000$

(9) Fixed Assets

Fixed Assets to Shareholder's Equity, change into

Shareholder's equity	−	Fixed Assets	=	Net Current Assets
↓		↓		↓
100%	−	80%	=	20
↓		↓		↓
10,00,000	−	8,00,000	=	2,00,000

$\left[\frac{2,00,000}{20} \times 80\right] = 8,00,000$

Trading and Profit and Loss Account for the year ended

	Rs.		Rs.
To Cost of Goods Sold	5,62,500	By Sales	7,50,000
To Gross Profit	1,87,500		
	7,50,000		7,50,000
To Expenses	67,500	By Gross Profit	1,87,500
To Net Profit	1,20,000		
	1,87,500		1,87,500

Balance Sheet

Liabilities	Rs.	Assets	Rs.
Share Capital	6,00,000	Fixed Assets	8,00,000
Reserves and Surplus (B/F)	2,80,000	Current Assets :	
		Stock	1,12,500
		Debtors	75,000
		Bank	2,62,500
Profit for the year	1,20,000		
Current Liabilities	2,50,000		
	12,50,000		12,50,000

Problem 17. *The following are the Ratios and other details of Rubix Ltd :*

Debtor's velocity	:	3 months
Creditor's velocity	:	2 months
Stock turnover	:	8 times
Capital - turnover Ratio	:	2.5 times
Fixed Assets - Turnover Ratio	:	8 times
Gross profit Turnover Ratio	:	25%

Gross Profit in a year amounts to Rs. 80,000. There is no Long-term Loan or Overdraft. Reserves and Surplus amount to Rs. 28,000. Liquid Assets are Rs. 97,333. Closing Stock of the year is Rs. 2,000 more than the Opening Stock. Bills Receivable amount to Rs. 5,000 and Bills Payable to Rs. 2,000.

Find out :

    (i) Sales   *(ii) Sundry Debtors*   *(iii) Sundry Creditors*
    (iv) Closing Stock   *(v) Fixed Assets*   *(vi) Proprietor's Fund*

Construct the Balance Sheet with as many details as possible. [M.Com, 2004]

Solution :

(i) Sales

Cost of Goods Sold	+	G.P.	–	Sales
75%		25%		100%
2,40,000		80,000		3,20,000

(ii) Sundry Debtors

$$\text{Debtor's Velocity} = \frac{\text{Debtors + Bill Receivable (X)}}{\text{Sales (3,20,000)}} \times 12 = 3$$

$$X = 3,20,000 \times \frac{3}{12} = 80,000$$

Debtors + Bills Receivable = 80,000
Less : Bills Receivable = 5,000
Debtors = 75,000

RATIO ANALYSIS

(iii) Sundry Creditors

$$\frac{\text{Creditors + Bills Payable}}{\text{Purchase (Credit)}} \times 12 = 2$$

$$X = 2,42,000 \times \frac{2}{12} = 40,333$$

Less : Bills Payable = 2,000

Creditors = 38,333

Find out the Purchase

Opening Stock + Purchase − Closing Stock = Cost of Goods Sold
29,000 + X − 31,000 = 2,40,000
X = 2,40,000 + 31,000 − 29,000
X = 2,42,000 i.e, Purchase = Rs 2,42,000

(iv) Closing Stock

$$\frac{\text{Cost of Goods Sold}}{\text{Average Stock (X)}} = 8 \text{ times}$$

$$X = \frac{2,40,000}{8}$$

Average Stock = 30,000
Total Stock Value 30,000 × 2 = 60,000
Less : Excess = 2,000
                 58,000

Opening Stock = 29,000
Closing Stock 29,000 + 2,000 = 31,000

(v) Fixed Assets

$$X = \frac{3,20,000}{8} = 40,000$$

Fixed Assets Turnover Ratio = 8

(vi) Proprietor's Fund

Proprietor's Fund = Fixed Assets + Stock + Liquid Assets − Current Liability
                  = 40,000 + 31,000 + 97,333 − 40,333 = Rs. 1,28,000

Cash and Bank Balance

Quick Assets		97,333
Less : Bills Receivable	5,000	
Debtors	75,000	80,000
Cash at Bank		17,333

Balance Sheet

Liabilities	Rs.	Assets	Rs.
Share Capital	1,00,000	Fixed Assets	40,000
Reserves and Surplus	28,000	Stock	31,000
Bills Payable	2,000	Debtors	75,000
Sundry Creditors	38,333	Bills Receivable	5,000
		Cash and Bank	17,333
	1,68,333		1,68,333

Problem 18. *From the following information of a Textile Company complete the Proforma balance Sheet if Sales are worth Rs. 28,00,000.*

Sales to Net worth	=	2.3 times
Current Debt to Net worth	=	42%
Total Debt to Net worth	=	75%
Current Ratio	=	2.9 times
Net Sales to Inventory	=	4.7 times
Average Collection Period	=	64 days
Fixed Assets to Net worth	=	53.2%

Proforma Balance Sheet

Net worth	?	Fixed Assets	?
Long-term Debt	?	Cash	?
Current Debt	?	Stock	?
		Sundry Debtors	?

[M.Com. Annamalai 1982]

Solution :

(1) Sales to Net worth : 2.3 times

$$\frac{\text{Sales } (23,00,000)}{\text{Net worth } (X)} = 2.3 \text{ times}$$

$$X = \frac{23,00,000}{2.3} = 10,00,000$$

Net worth = Rs. 10,00,000

(2) Current Debt

Current Debt : Net worth
↓ ↓
42% : 100%
↓ ↓
4,20,000 10,00,000

$$\frac{10,00,000}{100} \times 42 = 4,20,000$$

RATIO ANALYSIS

(3) **Total Debt**

Total Debt to Net worth = 75%

Total Debt : Net worth
75% : 100
7,50,000 : 10,00,000

[i.e., Total debt is 75% of net worth $10,00,000 \times \dfrac{75}{100} = 7,50,000$]

(4) **Long-term Debt**

Long-term Debt = Total Debt − Current Debt
= 7,50,000 − 4,20,000
= 3,30,000

(5) **Current Assets**

Current Ratio : 2.9
Current Assets : Current Liabilities
2.9   1.0
12,18,000   4,20,000

$\dfrac{4,28,000}{10} \times 2.9 = 12,18,000$

(6) **Inventory**

Net Sales to Inventory

$\dfrac{\text{Sales } (23,00,000)}{\text{Inventory } (X)} = 4.6$ tonnes

$X = \dfrac{23,00,000}{4.6}$

Inventory = 5,00,000

(7) **Debtors**

Average Collection Period
Here there is no bill receivable. Hence the formula

$\dfrac{\text{Debtors } (X)}{\text{Sales } (23,00,000)} \times 360 = 90$

$X = 23,00,000 \times \dfrac{90}{360}$

Debtors = 5,75,000

(8) **Fixed Assets**

Fixed Assets to Net worth

$\dfrac{\text{Fixed Assets}}{\text{Net worth}} = 53.2\%$

Fixed Assets   Net worth
↓   ↓
53.2%   100%
5,32,000   10,00,000

$\dfrac{10,00,000}{100} \times 53.2$

(9) Find out the Cash

Total Current Assets		12,18,000
Less Stock	5,00,000	
Debtors	5,75,000	10,75,000
Cash		1,43,000

Balance Sheet

Liabilities	Rs.	Assets	Rs.
Net worth	10,00,000	Fixed Assets	5,32,000
Long-term Debt	3,30,000	Debtors	5,75,000
Current Debt	4,20,000	Stock	5,00,000
		Cash	1,43,000
	17,50,000		17,50,000

Problem 19. Srinivasan Cotton Company's Stock Turnover is 5 times stock at the end is Rs. 20,000 which is more than at the beginning. Sales (all Credit) are Rs. 8,00,000. Rate of Gross Profit on Cost is 1/4. Current Liabilities Rs. 1,20,000. Quick Ratio is 0.75. Calculate Current Assets. [MBA Madras]

Solution :

$$\text{Stock Turnover Ratio} = \frac{\text{Cost of Goods Sold (6,00,000)}}{\text{Average Stock (X)}} = 5$$

$$X = \frac{6,00,000}{5} = 1,20,000$$

Average Stock = 1,20,000

NOTE :

Cost of Goods Sold	= Sales	− Gross Profit	
	= 8,00,000	− 2,00,000	= 6,00,000
Total Stock Value	: 1,20,000 × 2	2,40,000	
Less : Excess Value		20,000	
		2,20,000	

Opening Stock = Rs. 1,10,000
Closing Stock = Rs. 20,000 + 1,10,000 = 1,30,000
Quick Ratio :
Quick Assets   :   Current Liabilities
↓   ↓
.75   1.00
↓   ↓
90,000   1,20,000

RATIO ANALYSIS

Current Assets :
- Quick Assets = Rs. 90,000
- Closing Stock = Rs. 1,30,000
- Current Assets = Rs. 2,20,000

Problem 20. *Calculate Stock Turnover Ratio from the following details :*
- (i) Opening Stock Rs. 29,000
- (ii) Closing Stock Rs. 31,000
- (iii) Sales Rs. 3,20,000
- (iv) Gross Profit – Ratio 25% on Sales

[B.Com 2003 PU]

Solution :

$$\text{Stock Turnover Ratio} = \frac{\text{Cost of Goods Sold}}{\text{Average Stock}}$$

$$= \frac{2,40,000}{30,000} = 8 \text{ times}$$

$$\text{Average Stock} = \frac{29,000 + 31,000}{2} = 30,000$$

Cost of Goods Sold	+	G.P.	–	Sales
75%	+	25%		100%
2,40,000		80,000		3,20,000

◻◻◻

8
Fixed Assets and Depreciation

FIXED ASSETS

At the time of commencement of business, the owner of the organisation can invest money into the concern as assets. These assets may be current asset and/or fixed asset. Current assets are those which can be converted into cash quickly. But fixed assets are those assets which cannot be converted into cash quickly. Both assets are essential for the successful running of the business. But current assets are maintained in the business in order to operate the fixed assets and carry on the business activities. It is otherwise called as working capital. In the actual sense, fixed assets can be classified into Tangible fixed assets and Intangible fixed assets. Normally fixed assets are utilised for the productive purpose of the organisation. For the purpose of utilisation of fixed assets to the production purpose, certain values of fixed assets are to be reduced. Such reduced value is called depreciation. So depreciation is treated as admissible business expenditure upto a prescribed limit. At the same time, depreciation can be Tangible fixed assets which include a physical form of asset such as plant and machinery, land and buildings, furniture and fittings, replacement of tools, vehicles etc. and Intangible fixed assets which include goodwill, patents, copyright, trademark etc.

MEANING OF DEPRECIATION

The concept of depreciation is related to fixed assets only. Current assets are never depreciated rather these are valued. Simply, Depreciation means it is a permanent and gradual shrinkage in the book value of fixed asset. Depreciation is charged on the book value only. Once Depreciation is charged, it should gradually reduce the value of fixed assets.

The Institute of Chartered Accountants of India defines depreciation as "a measure of the wearing out, consumption or other loss of value of a depreciable asset arising from use, affluxion of time or obsolescence through technology and market changes. Depreciation is allocated so as to charge a fair proportion of the depreciable amount in each accounting period during the expected useful life of the asset. Depreciation includes amortisation of assets whose useful life is predetermined".

According to the International Accounting Standard Committee "depreciation is the allocation of the depreciable amount of an asset over its estimated useful life. Depreciation for the accounting period is charged to income either directly or indirectly".

FIXED ASSETS AND DEPRECIATION

CAUSES OF DEPRECIATION

The following are the main causes of depreciation :

(i) *Physical Cause.* It is caused mainly from the wear and tear due to friction, pull, impact, fatigue, twisting etc. And also it includes lack of maintenance and repairs in time.

(ii) *Time Factors.* Some assets lose its value simply with passage of time in the practical business life. There are certain assets with a fixed period of legal life such as lease, patents and copyrights. Here, instead of depreciation, provision for the consumption of these assets is created. This is called amortisation.

(iii) *Economic Factors.* Depreciation arises due to the changes in Fashion and Technology. In the real sense, new model and new technology may make the asset become obsolete even if it is in good physical condition. Some times, due to organisational growth, usage of assets are to be stopped or inadequacy of existing equipment due to the expansion of the business.

(iv) *Abnormal Occurrences.* The value of asset may be decreased because of accidents due to some wrong operations or some loose component which may result in heavy damages to the industry. Inferior quality of materials also decreases the value of asset.

(v) *Depletion.* Certain assets are of wasting character perhaps due to the extraction of raw materials from them. In lieu of writing off depreciation to provide for the consumption or utilisation of an asset of a wasting character is called provision for depletion.

OBJECTIVES OR NEED FOR PROVIDING DEPRECIATION

(i) To ascertain correct profits of the organisation
(ii) To show the accurate financial position of the organisation
(iii) To make provision for replacement of assets
(iv) To determine the correct tax liability
(v) To provide guidance to the management for important financial matters
(vi) To keep the capital intact
(vii) To provide depreciation is a statutory need - statutory obligation.

BASIC FACTORS FOR CALCULATING DEPRECIATION

(i) The cost of the asset
(ii) The estimated number of years of its life
(iii) The estimated residual or scrap value at the end of its life.

METHODS FOR PROVIDING DEPRECIATION

(i) Fixed Instalment or Straight Line Method
(ii) Fixed Percentage on Diminishing Balance Method

(iii) Sum of the years Digits Method.
(iv) Annuity Method.
(v) Depreciation Fund Method.
(vi) Insurance Policy Method.
(vii) Revaluation Method.
(viii) Machine Hour Rate Method.
(ix) Depletion Method.
(x) Repairs Provision Method.

(i) *Fixed Instalment or Straight Line or Fixed Percentage on Original Cost.* Under this method, the Depreciation is calculated on the basis of either a fixed percentage of the original value of the asset or divide the original value of asset by the number of years of its estimated life. Every year, the same amount is written off as Depreciation so as to reduce the asset account to nil.

Depreciation =

$$\frac{\text{Cost of the Asset + Installation Charges − Scrap Value + Removal Cost}}{\text{Estimated useful Life of the Asset}}$$

(ii) *Diminishing Balance Method.* Under the diminishing Balance method, depreciation is calculated at a fixed percentage on the opening balance of each year. Each year the opening balance may be decreasing in value. This decreasing book value is commonly known as written down value of the asset. While applying the depreciation rate both salvage or scrap value and removal costs are ignored. There are no possibilities to reduce the book value to zero.

(iii) *Sum of the Years Digits Method.* It gives decreasing depreciation charge year by year. For the purpose of obtaining yearly depreciation diminishing percentages to the cost of the asset, less salvage value is applied. Under this method, the rate of depreciation is a fraction having the sum of the digits representing the useful life of the asset as its denominator and individual year as its numerator.

(iv) *Annuity Method.* Under the Annuity method, the annual depreciation charges would be ascertained with the help of Annuity table. This method gives importance to interest factor. Other methods do not take into account the interest factor while investing the assets. Fixed interest rate is charged on the opening balance of each year and then cost of asset together with interest thereon is written off equally over the life of the asset.

(v) *Depreciation Fund Method.* Depreciation fund method provides an adequate financial requirement for the replacement of the asset when the asset is replaced by a new one. Depreciation fund account is opened and the amount of depreciation is credited to that account. The asset account stands year after year at its original cost. At the end of each year, the amount of depreciation is debited and depreciation fund account is credited and the corresponding amount is invested in securities of some reputed companies, for the purpose of mobilising funds for replacement.

(vi) *Insurance Policy Method.* Under this method, an insurance policy is taken from the insurance company for the purpose of replacement of an asset. At the end of the definite period, the insurance company will pay the assured sum with the help of which asset can be repurchased.

FIXED ASSETS AND DEPRECIATION

(vii) *Revaluation Method.* This method is suitable for small and diverse items of asset such as bottles, corks, trade marks, loose tools, livestock etc. Under this method the amount of depreciation is ascertained to find the difference between the book value of the asset and the real value of the asset. At the end of the year the difference is taken as depreciation.

(viii) *Machine Hour Rate Method.* The Economic Life of the asset is estimated in terms of working hours. Hourly rate is determined by dividing total cost of the asset by total number of hours to be operated in its life time. The annual depreciation charge is calculated by applying this rate to the actual number of hours operated in the particular accounting period.

$$\text{Machine hour rate} = \frac{\text{Cost} - \text{Scrap Value}}{\text{Total hours (whole lifetime)}}$$

Depreciation for the year = Machine Hour value × Estimated Hours in a year.

(ix) *Depletion Method.* The Economic Life of the asset is determined by geographical survey methods in terms of total units of resource deposits. The depletion rate per unit is calculated by dividing the total cost of the asset by the estimated available number of units.

(x) *Repairs Provision Method.* Under this method, first the total repair and renewal costs are determined for the whole life of the asset and then it is added to the capital cost to get a total value. Then, this value is divided by its estimated life. The resultant value is treated as Repair, Renewals and depreciation. It has to be charged to the profit and loss Account each year. The corresponding Credit is given to provision for depreciation and Repairs account.

Problem 1. *On 1.1.1998 X Ltd purchased a machinery for Rs. 58,000 and spent Rs. 2,000 on its execution. On 1.7.1998 an additional Rs. 20,000 worth of machinery was purchased. On 1.7.2000 the machine was purchased and on 1.1.1998 was sold for Rs. 28,600 and on the same date a new machine was purchased at a cost of Rs. 40,000. Show the machinery account for the first four calendar years according to written down value method taking the rate of depreciation @ 10%.* [MBA Anna Dec 2003]

Solution :   **Machinery Account**

Date	Particulars	Amount Rs.	Date	Particulars	Amount Rs.
1.1.98	To Cash	60,000	31.12.98	By Depreciation	6,000
1.7.98	To Cash	20,000	31.12.98	By Depreciation	1,000
				$\left[20,000 \times \dfrac{10}{100} \times \dfrac{6}{12} \right]$	
			31.12.98	By Balance c/d	73,000
		80,000			80,000
1.1.99	To Balance b/d	73,000	31.12.99	By Depreciation	7,300
			31.12.99	By Balance c/d	65,700
		73,000			73,000

1.1.00	To Balance b/d	65,700	1.7.00	By Depreciation for 6 months	2,430
1.7.00	To Cash	40,000	1.7.00	By P&L A/c (Loss on sale)	17,570
			1.7.00	By Cash	28,600
			31.12.00	By Depreciation on Balance machinery (80,000 − 60,000 = 20,000)	1,710
			31.12.00	By Depreciation $\left[40,000 \times \dfrac{10}{100} \times \dfrac{6}{12}\right]$	2,000
			31.12.00	By Balance c/d	53,390
		1,05,700			1,05,700
1.1.01	To Balance b/d	53,390	31.12.01	By Depreciation	5,339
			31.12.01	By Balance c/d	48,051
		53,390			53,390

1. Workings :

Value of Machinery on the date of purchase 1.1.98	60,000
Less : Depreciation for 1.1.98 to 31.12.98	6,000
	54,000
Less : Depreciation for 1.1.99 to 31.12.99	5,400
	48,600
Less : Depreciation for 6 months 1.1.2000 to 1.7.2000 (48,600 × 10/100 × 6/12)	2,430
Value of Machinery as on the date of sale	46,170
Sale price of the machinery	28,600
Loss on sale of Machinery	17,570

2. Depreciation on Balance Machinery :

Total	80,000	
Sold	60,000	
Balance Machinery	20,000	
Value of Machinery on 1.7.98		20,000
Depreciation for 6 months 1.7.98 to 31.12.98		1,000
		19,000

Less : Depreciation for 1.1.99 to 31.12.99					1,900
					17,100
Less : Depreciation for 1.1.2000 to 31.12.2000					1,710
					15,390
Less : Depreciation for 1.1.2001 to 31.12.2001					1,539
					13,851

3. Total Depreciation for 2001

Depreciation for new machinery i.e., purchased on 1.7.2000
(40,000 − 2,000 = 38,000 × 10/100) 3,800
Depreciation on old machinery 1,539
                                          ———
                                          5,339

Problem 2. *X Ltd purchased a machine for Rs. 60,000 on 1.1.1998. Depreciation is provided @ 10% p.a. on diminishing Balance method. Prepare machinery account for the year 2000 in each of the following alternative cases.*

(i) If the machine is sold on 1.7.2000 for Rs. 28,600.

(ii) If a new machine costing Rs. 60,000 is purchased on 1.7.2000 after surrendering the old one and paying cash Rs. 35,000. [MBA Anna Dec. 2002]

Solution : (i) If the machine is sold on 1.7.2000 for Rs. 28,600

Machinery Account

Date	Particulars	Amount Rs.	Date	Particulars	Amount Rs.
1.1.1998	To Bank	60,000	31.12.1998 31.12.1998	By Depreciation By Balance c/d	6,000 54,000
		60,000			60,000
1.1.1999	To Balance b/d	54,000	31.12.1999 31.12.1999	By Depreciation By Balance c/d	5,400 48,600
		54,000			54,000
1.1.2000	To Balance b/d	48,600	1.7.2000	By Depreciation (48,600 × 10/100 × 6/12) By Cash By Loss on Sale of machinery	2,430 28,600 17,570
		48,600			48,600

Workings :

	Rs.
Cost of the Machinery	60,000
Less : Depreciation [6,000 + 5,400 + 2,430]	13,830
Value of Machinery as on the date of Sale	46,170
Sale Price of the machinery	28,600
Loss on Sale of machinery	17,570

(ii) If the new machine costing Rs. 60,000 is purchased on 1.7.2000 after surrendering the old one and paying cash Rs. 35,000.

Date	Particulars	Amount Rs.	Date	Particulars	Amount Rs.
1.1.1998	To Cash	60,000	31.12.1998 31.12.1998	By Depreciation By Balance c/d	6,000 54,000
		60,000			60,000
1.1.1999	To Balance b/d	54,000	31.12.1999 31.12.1999	By Depreciation By Balance	5,400 48,600
		54,000			54,000

Machinery Account

Date	Particulars	Amount Rs.	Date	Particulars	Amount Rs.
1.7.2000	To Cash (35,000 cash 25,000 adjustment from old machine)	60,000		By Depreciation on old machine (49,600 × 10/100 × 6/12) By Depreciation on new machine (60,000 × 10/100 × 6/12) By Balance c/d	2,430 3,000 54,570
		60,000			60,000

Problem 3. *Mr. Kumar purchased a machine for Rs. 1,60,000 on 1.1.2000. Its probable working life was estimated as 10 years and its probable scrap value at the end of that time is Rs. 10,000. You are required to prepare necessary accounts based on straight line method of depreciation for three years.*

FIXED ASSETS AND DEPRECIATION

Solution :

$$\text{Annual Depreciation} = \frac{\text{Cost of the Asset} - \text{Scrap Value}}{\text{Life of the Asset}}$$

$$= \frac{\text{Rs. } 1,60,000 - 10,000}{10 \text{ years}} = \frac{1,50,000}{10 \text{ years}} = \text{Rs. } 15,000.$$

Machinery Account

Date	Particulars	Amount Rs.	Date	Particulars	Amount Rs.
1.1.2000	To Cash	1,60,000	31.12.2000 31.12.2000	By Depreciation By Balance c/d	15,000 1,45,000
		1,60,000			1,60,000
1.1.2001	To Balance b/d	1,45,000	31.12.2001 31.12.2001	By Depreciation By Balance c/d	15,000 1,30,000
		1,45,000			1,45,000
1.1.2002	To Balance b/d	1,30,000	31.12.2002 31.12.2002	By Depreciation By Balance c/d	15,000 1,15,000
		1,30,000			1,30,000

Depreciation Account

Date	Particulars	Amount Rs.	Date	Particulars	Amount Rs.
31.12.2000	To Machinery A/c	15,000	31.12.2000	By P.L A/c	15,000
		15,000			15,000
31.12.2001	To Machinery A/c	15,000	31.12.2001	By P.L A/c	15,000
		15,000			15,000
31.12.2002	To Machinery A/c	15,000	31.12.2002	By P.L A/c	15,000
		15,000			15,000

Problem 4. *On 1.1.1999 machinery was purchased by Mr. X for Rs. 50,000. On 1.7.2000 additions were made to the extent of Rs. 10,000. On 1.4.2001 further additions were made to the extent of Rs. 6,400.*

On 30.6.2002 machinery, the original value of which was Rs. 8,000 on 1.1.1999 was sold for Rs. 6,000. Depreciation is charged at 10% p.a. on original cost.

Show the machinery account for the years from 1999 to 2002 in the books of Mr. X. Closes his books on 31st December every year. [ICWA Inter]

Solution :

Machinery Account

Date	Particulars	Amount Rs.	Date	Particulars	Amount Rs.
1.1.1999	To Cash	50,000	31.12.1999 31.12.1999	By Depreciation By Balance c/d	5,000 45,000
		50,000			50,000
1.1.2000 1.7.2000	To Balance b/d To Cash	45,000 10,000	31.12.2000 31.12.2000	By Depreciation (50,000 × 10/100 = 5,000) (10,000 × 10/100 × 6/12 = 500) By Balance c/d	5,500 49,500
		55,000			55,000
1.1.2001 1.4.2001	To Balance b/d To Cash	49,500 6,400	31.12.2001 31.12.2001	By Depreciation By Balance c/d	6,480 49,420
		55,900			55,900
1.1.2002 30.6.2002	To Balance b/d To Profit on Sale of Machinery	49,420 800	30.6.2002 31.12.2002 31.12.2002	By Bank By Depreciation By Balance c/d	6,000 6,240 37,980
		50,220			50,220
1.1.2003	To Balance c/d	37,980			

Workings :

(i) Depreciation for 2001

10% on Rs. 50,000 for one year 50,000 × 10/100	=	5,000
10% on Rs. 10,000 for one year 10,000 × 10/100	=	1,000
10% on Rs. 64,000 for 9 months (6,400 × 10/100 × 9/12)	=	480
		6,480

(ii) Depreciation for 2002

10% on Rs. 42,000 for one year 42,000 × 10/100 (i.e., 50,000 − 8,000)	=	4,200
10% on Rs. 10,000 for one year 10,000 × 10/100	=	1,000
10% on Rs. 6,400 for one year 6,400 × 10/100	=	640
10% on Rs. 8,000 for 6 months 8,000 × 10/100 × 6/12	=	400
		6,240

FIXED ASSETS AND DEPRECIATION

(iii) Computation of Profit on Sale of Machinery

Original value of Machinery	8,000
Less : Depreciation for 3½ years @ 10% i.e., 800 × 3.5	2,800
Written down value of machinery on 30.6.2002	5,200
Amount realised on Sale	6,000
Profit on Sale of Machinery	800

Problem 5. *On 1.1.1999 ABC Ltd purchased five machines for Rs. 20,000 each. Depreciation is charged at the rate of 10% p.a on cost. The accounting year ends on 31st December each year. On 31.3.2000 one machine was sold for Rs. 16,000 and on 30.9.2001 another machine was sold for Rs. 15,000. A new machine was purchased on 30.6.2002 for Rs. 24,000. Prepare machinery account and provision for depreciation account for four years*

Solution :

Machinery Account

Date	Particulars	Amount Rs.	Date	Particulars	Amount Rs.
1.1.1999	To Cash	1,00,000	31.12.1999	By Cash	16,000
				By Provision for Depreciation A/c	2,500
				By P & L A/c	1,500
			31.12.1999	By Balance c/d	80,000
		1,00,000			1,00,000
1.1.2000	To Balance B/d	80,000	30.9.2000	By Bank A/c	15,000
30.9.2000	To P.L A/c	500		By Provision for Depreciation A/c	5,500
			30.12.2000	By Balance c/d	60,000
		80,500			80,500
1.1.2001	To Balance B/d	60,000	31.12.2001	By Balance c/d	84,000
30.6.2001	To Bank A/c	24,000			
		84,000			84,000
1.1.2002	To Balance B/d	84,000			

Provision for Depreciation Account

Date	Particulars	Amount Rs.	Date	Particulars	Amount Rs.
31.12.1998	To Balance c/d	10,000	31.12.1998	By Depreciation	10,000
		10,000			10,000

Date	Particulars	Amount	Date	Particulars	Amount
31.3.1999	To Machinery A/c	2,500	1.1.1999	By Balance B/d	10,000
			31.3.1999	By Depreciation (on 20,000 for 3 months)	500
31.12.1999	To Balance c/d	16,000	31.12.1999	By Depreciation (on 80000 for one year)	8,000
		18,500			18,500
30.9.2000	To Machinery A/c	5,500	1.1.2000	By Balance B/d	16,000
31.12.2000	To Balance c/d	18,000	30.9.2000	By Depreciation (on 20,000 for 9 months)	1,500
			31.12.2000	By Depreciation	6,000
		23,500			23,500
31.12.2001	To Balance c/d	25,200	1.1.2001	By Balance B/d	18,000
			31.12.2001	By Depreciation (on 60,000 for one year)	6,000
				By Depreciation (on 24,000 for 6 months)	1,200
		25,200			25,200

Problem 6. *India Ltd charges depreciation on plant and machinery under Reducing Balance System @ 15% per annum. On 1.4.1998, the Balance in Ledger stood at Rs. 4,60,000. The following particulars are given relating to plant and machinery during the four years ended 31.3.2002.*

Date		Particulars
(1) 1.9.1998	:	A machine Purchased for Rs. 20,000 (Installation Expenses Rs. 1,000) on 1.5.96 was fully destroyed in an accident.
(2) 1.7.1999	:	Purchased a new machine costing Rs. 50,000 (Installation Expenses Rs. 2,500). A sum of Rs. 30,000 was paid on the same date and the Balance was paid in May 2000.
(3) 31.8.2000	:	Plant purchased on 1.4.97 for Rs. 30,000 (Installation Expenses Rs. 1,500) was disposed off for Rs. 36,000.
(4) 1.11.2001	:	Some old machineries (Book value on 1.4.98 at Rs. 10,000) were sold for Rs. 4,000.

Show the plant & machinery Account as would appear in the books of the company for the four years ended 31.3.2002 assuming depreciation is charged proportionately even if the asset is sold or destroyed.

[M.Com Madras]

FIXED ASSETS AND DEPRECIATION

Solution : **Plant and Machinery Account**

Date	Particulars	Amount Rs.	Date	Particulars	Amount Rs.
1.4.1998	To Balance B/d	4,60,000	1.1.1998	By Profit & Loss Account	14,434
			31.3.1999	By Depreciation for 5 months (1)	962
			31.3.1999	By Depreciation Account @ 15% on Rs. 4,44,604	66,691
			31.3.1999	By Balance c/d	3,77,913
		4,60,000			**4,60,000**
1.4.1999	To Balance B/d	3,77,913	31.3.2000	By Depreciation A/c (56,687 + 5,906)	62,593
1.7.1999	To Bank	32,500	31.3.2000	By Balance c/d	3,67,820
1.7.1999	To Creditors	20,000			
		4,30,413			**4,30,413**
1.4.2000	To Balance B/d	3,67,820	31.8.2000	By Bank A/c (Sale)	36,000
31.8.2000	To P & L A/c (2) (Profit on sale of machinery)	17,864	31.3.2001	By Depreciation (2)	1,209
			31.3.2001	By Depreciation A/c 15% on 3,48,475 (i.e., 3,67,820 − 19,345)	52,271
				By Balance c/d	2,96,204
		3,85,684			**3,85,684**
1.4.2001	Balance B/d	2,96,204	1.11.2001	By Bank A/c (Sale)	4,000
			1.11.2001	By Depreciation (for 7 months on Rs. 6,141)	537
			1.11.2001	By P & L A/c (3) (Loss)	1,604
			31.3.2002	By Depreciation A/c (15% 2,90,063 full year)	43,509
			31.3.2002	By Balance c/d	2,46,554
		2,96,204			**2,96,204**

Working Notes :

1. *Calculation of Loss on Accident*

	Rs.
Cost on 1.5.1996	21,000
Less : Depreciation for 11 months in 1996-97	2,887
Value on 1.4.1997	18,113
Less : Depreciation for 1997-98	2,717

		Rs.
	Value on 1.4.98	15,396
Less :	Depreciation for 5 months	962
	Loss on accident	14,434

2. *Calculation of Profit on Sale for Machinery on 31.8.2000*

		Rs.
	Cost on 1.4.1997	31,500
Less :	Depreciation for 11 months in 1997-98	4,725
	Value on 1.4.1998	26,775
Less :	Depreciation for 1998-99	4,016
	Value on 1.4.99	22,759
Less :	Depreciation for 1999-2000	3,414
	Value on 1.4.2000	19,345
Less :	Depreciation for 5 months	1,209
	Value on 31.8.2000	18,136
Less :	Amount realised on Sale	36,000
	Profit on Sale of Machinery	17,864

3. *Calculation of Loss on Sale of Machinery on 1.11.2001*

		Rs.
	Book value on 1.4.98	10,000
Less :	Depreciation for 1998-99	1,500
	Value on 1.4.99	8,500
Less :	Depreciation for 1999-2000	1,275
	Value on 1.4.2000	7,225
Less :	Depreciation for 2000-2001	1,084
	Value on 1.4.2001	6,141
Less :	Depreciation for 7 months	537
	Value on 1.11.2001	5,604
Less :	Amount realised on Sale	4,000
	Loss on Sale of Machinery	1,604

Problem 7. *A firm purchases a 5 year lease for Rs. 30,000. It is decided to write off depreciation on the annuity method, presuming the rate of interest to be 5% per annum. If annuity of Re.1 for 5 years at 5% is 0.230975. Show the lease account for the full period of 5 years*

Solution :

The amount of depreciation to be charged every year

$$= 0.230975 \times 30,000 = \text{Rs. } 6,929.25$$

Lease Account

Date	Particulars	Amount Rs.	Date	Particulars	Amount Rs.
1st year	To Bank To Interest (30,000 × 5/100)	30,000.00 1,500.00	1st year	By Depreciation By Balance c/d	6,929.25 24,570.75
		31,500.00			31,500.00
2nd year	To Balance B/d To Interest (24,570.75 × 5/100)	24,570.75 1,228.54	2nd year	By Depreciation By Balance c/d	6,929.25 18,870.04
		25,799.29			25,799.29
3rd year	To Balance B/d To Interest (18,870.04 × 5/100)	18,870.04 943.50	3rd year	By Depreciation By Balance c/d	6,929.25 12,884.29
		19,813.54			19,813.54
4th year	To Balance B/d To Interest (12,884.29 × 5/100)	12,884.29 644.21	4th year	By Depreciation By Balance c/d	6,929.25 6,599.25
		13,528.50			13,528.50
5th year	To Balance B/d To Interest (6,599.25 × 5/100)	6,599.25 330.00	5th year	By Depreciation	6,929.25
		6,929.25			6,929.25

Problem 8. *Ramu & Co., purchased a machine at a cost of Rs. 99,600. It was expected to last for 6 years with a scrap value of Rs. 3,000. Find out the depreciation for each of the six years under*

   (i) *Production units method and*
   (ii) *Machine Hour Rate method.*

Total estimated life in units of production is 87,380 units and total estimated life in machine is 20,900 hours.

Additional Data are :

Year	1	2	3	4	5	6	Total
Units produced	11,900	14,000	13,000	12,500	16,250	19,730	87,380
Working Hours	3,400	3,800	3,000	2,800	3,900	4,000	20,900

Solution :
Production Units method :

Depreciation Rate per unit = $\dfrac{\text{Cost} - \text{Salvage Value}}{\text{Estimated Life in Hours}}$ = $\dfrac{99{,}600 - 3{,}000}{87{,}380}$

$= \dfrac{96{,}600}{87{,}380}$ = Rs. 1.10

Computation of Annual Depreciation

Year	Units Produced	Rate Per Unit	Annual Depreciation (Rs.) (Units Produced × Rate Per Unit)
1	11,900	1.10	13,090
2	14,000	1.10	15,400
3	13,000	1.10	14,300
4	12,500	1.10	13,750
5	16,250	1.10	17,875
6	19,730	1.10	21,703

Machine Hours or Working Hours Method :

Depreciation Rate Per Hour = $\dfrac{\text{Cost} - \text{Scrap value}}{\text{Estimated life in hours}}$ = $\dfrac{99{,}600 - 3{,}000}{20{,}900}$

= Rs. 4.62

Computation of Annual Depreciation

Year	Working Hours	Rate Per Hour Rs.	Depreciation (Working Hour × Rate Per Hour) Rs.
1	3400	4.62	15,708
2	3800	4.62	17,556
3	3000	4.62	13,860
4	2800	4.62	12,936
5	3900	4.62	18,018
6	4000	4.62	18,480

Problem 9. *ABC Ltd purchased a car at a cost of Rs. 3,00,000 and its estimated life is 60,000 running hours. The car runs for 2000 miles in the first year. 3,000 miles for the second year, 2,500 miles for the third year. Compute per mile and yearly Depreciation.*

Solution :

Depreciation = $\dfrac{\text{Cost} - \text{Scrap}}{\text{Estimated Life in Running Miles}}$ = $\dfrac{3{,}00{,}000}{60{,}000}$ = Rs. 5

FIXED ASSETS AND DEPRECIATION

Computation of Annual Depreciation

Year	Running Miles	Depreciation (Running Miles × Rate Per Running Miles)
1	2000	10,000
2	3000	15,000
3	2500	12,500

Problem 10. *KLP Ltd leased a manganese ore mine on 30th June 2000 for a sum of Rs. 6,00,000. It is estimated that the total Quantity of ore in the mine is 60,000 tonne of which 80% may be raised. The annual output is as follows.*

Year	2000	2001	2002	2003	2004
Output (Tonnes)	2,500	7,500	5,000	9,000	10,000

Solution :

Depreciation charge per tonne = Total cost/Effective production [80% of 60,000]

$$i.e., \frac{6,00,000}{48,000} \quad [60,000 \times 80/100 = 48,000]$$

= Rs. 12.5

Mine Account

Date	Particulars	Amount Rs.	Date	Particulars	Amount Rs.
30.6.2000	To Cash	6,00,000	31.12.2000	By Depreciation (2,500 × 12.5) By Balance c/d	31,250 4,68,750
		6,00,000			6,00,000
1.1.2001	To Balance B/d	4,68,750	31.12.2001 31.12.2001	By Depreciation (7,500 × 12.5) By Balance c/d	93,750 3,75,000
		4,68,750			4,68,750
1.1.2002	To Balance B/d	3,75,000	31.12.2002 31.12.2002	By Depreciation (5,000 × 12.5) By Balance c/d	62,500 3,12,500
		3,75,000			3,75,000
1.1.2003	To Balance B/d	3,12,500	31.12.2003 31.12.2003	By Depreciation (9,000 × 12.5) By Balance c/d	1,12,500 2,00,000
		3,12,500			3,12,500

1.1.2004	To Balance B/d	2,00,000	31.12.2004	By Depreciation (10,000 × 12.5)	1,25,000
			31.12.2004	By Balance c/d	75,000
		2,00,000			2,00,000
1.1.2005	To Balance B/d	75,000			

Problem 11. *On 1.1.2002 Rahim Ltd had a stock of bottles valued at Rs. 12,000. On 1.7.2002 the company purchased additional bottles for Rs. 4,000. On 31.12.2002 the entire stock of bottles was revalued at Rs. 15,000. Calculate the amount of Depreciation.*

Solution :

Bottles Account

Date	Particulars	Amount Rs.	Date	Particulars	Amount Rs.
1.1.2002	To Balance B/d	12,000	31.12.200	By Depreciation (16,000 – 15,000)	1,000
1.7.2002	To Cash	4,000	31.12.2002	By Balance c/d	15,000
		16,000			16,000
1.1.2003	To Balance B/d	15,000			

Problem 12. *On 1.1.99 Nasma Ltd purchased a machine for Rs. 60,000 which was expected to last for 4 years. The repairs and maintenance charges were estimated to be Rs. 19,000 during the life time of the asset. Actual expenses for repair and maintenance during 1999, 2000, 2001, 2002, had been Rs. 2,000, Rs. 5,000, Rs. 6,500, Rs. 7,000 respectively. At the end of the fourth year, the machine is sold at Rs. 11,500. Prepare necessary accounts using an equitable method of charging depreciation and maintenance expenses.*

Solution :

Provision for Depreciation and Repair Account

Date	Particulars	Amount Rs.	Date	Particulars	Amount Rs.
31.12.1999	To Repair & maintenance	2,000	31.12.1999	By P.L Account	17,500
	To Balance c/d	15,500			
		17,500			17,500
31.12.2000	To Repairs & maintenance A/c	5,000	1.1.2000	By Balance B/d	15,500
	To Balance c/d	28,000	31.12.2000	By P.L A/c	17,500
		33,000			33,000

FIXED ASSETS AND DEPRECIATION

31.12.2001	To Repair & maintenance A/c	6,500	1.1.2001	By Balance B/d	28,000
	To Balance c/d	39,000	31.12.2001	By P.L A/c	17,500
		45,500			45,500
31.12.2002	To Repair & maintenance	7,000	1.1.2002	By Balance c/d	39,000
	To Balance c/d	49,500	31.12.2003	By P.L A/c	17,500
		56,500			56,500

Machinery Account

Date	Particulars	Amount Rs.	Date	Particulars	Amount Rs.
1.1.1999	To Bank	60,000	31.12.1999	By Balance c/d	60,000
1.1.2000	To Balance B/d	60,000	31.12.2000	By Balance c/d	60,000
1.1.2001	To Balance B/d	60,000	31.12.2001	By Balance c/d	60,000
1.1.2002	To Bank B/d	60,000	31.12.2002	By Cash	11,500
31.12.2002	To P.L. A/c	1,000	31.12.2002	By Provision for Depreciation & Repairs	49,500
		61,000			61,000

Workings :

Cost of the Machine	60,000
Less : Scrap Value	9,000
	51,000
Add : Estimated Repairs and Maintenance Expenses	19,000
Composite Cost	70,000

Annual Cost of Depreciation and Repairs

$$\frac{\text{Composite cost}}{\text{Number of years}} = \frac{70,000}{4} = \text{Rs. } 17,500$$

Problem 13. *KRN & Co purchased a machinery at a cost of Rs. 80,000 on 1.1.1997. On 1.1.1998 additions were made to the amount of Rs. 40,000. On 31.3.1999 machinery purchased on 1.1.1998 costing Rs. 12,000 was sold for Rs. 11,000 and on 30.6.1999 machinery purchased on 1.1.1997 costing Rs. 32,000 was sold for Rs. 26,700. On 1.10.1999 additions were made to the amount of Rs. 20,000. Depreciation was provided at 10% p.a. on Diminishing Balance method. Show the machinery account for the three years from 1997 to 1999. [Year ended on Dec 31]*

[B.Com Madras]

Solution :

Machinery Account

Date	Particulars	Amount Rs.	Date	Particulars	Amount Rs.
1.1.1997	To Bank A/c	80,000	31.12.1997	By Depreciation	8,000
			31.12.1997	Balance c/d	72,000
		80,000			80,000
1.1.1998	To Balance B/d	72,000	31.12.1998	By Depreciation	11,200
1.1.1998	To Bank A/c	40,000	31.12.1998	By Balance c/d	1,00,800
		1,12,000			1,12,000
1.1.1999	To Balance B/d	1,00,800	31.3.1998	By Depreciation	270
	To P & L A/c			By Bank A/c	11,000
	(Profit Transferred)	470		By Depreciation	1,296
	To P & L A/c			By Bank A/c	26,700
	(Profit Transferred)	2,076	31.12.1999	By Depreciation	6,908
1.10.1999	To Bank A/c	20,000		By Balance c/d	77,172
		1,23,346			1,23,346
1.1.2000	To Balance B/d	77,172			

Working Notes :

		Rs.
1.	Machinery Purchased on 1.1.1998	12,000
	Less : Depreciation for 1998 @ 10%	1,200
	Balance as on 1.1.99	10,800
	Depreciation for 3 months in 1999	270
	Book Value as on 31.3.99	10,530
	Profit (Balancing Figure)	470
	Amount realised	11,000
2.	Cost of Machinery on 1.1.1997	32,000
	Less : Depreciation for 1997	3,200
	Balance on 1.1.1998	28,800
	Less : Depreciation for 1998	2,880
	Balance on 1.1.1999	25,920
	Less : Depreciation for 6 months in 1999	1,296
	Book Value on 30.6.99	24,624
	Profit (Balancing Figure)	2,076
	Sold for	26,700

FIXED ASSETS AND DEPRECIATION

3. **Depreciation for the Remaining Machines**

Book value of machines on 1.1.99	1,00,800
Book value of machines on 1.1.99 sold in 1999	36,720
	64,080
Depreciation for 1999 on 64,080 @ 10%	6,408
Depreciation for New Machine for 3 months on Rs. 20,000	500
Total	6,908

Problem 14. *On 1.4.1995 a firm purchased a machinery worth Rs. 3,00,000. On 1.10.1997 it buys additional machinery worth Rs. 60,000/- and spends Rs. 6,000 on its erection. The accounts are closed each year on 31st March. Assuming the annual depreciation to be 10%, show the machinery account for 5 years under straight line method and written down value method.*

Solution :   **Straight Line Method : Machinery Account**

Date	Particulars	Amount Rs.	Date	Particulars	Amount Rs.
1.4.1995	To Cash	3,00,000	31.3.1996 31.3.1996	By Depreciation By Balance c/d	30,000 2,70,000
		3,00,000			3,00,000
1.4.1996	To Balance B/d	2,70,000	31.3.1997 31.3.1997	By Depreciation By Balance c/d	30,000 2,40,000
		2,70,000			2,70,000
1.4.1997 1.10.1997	To Balance B/d To cash	2,40,000 66,000	31.3.1998 31.3.1998	By Depreciation (30,000 + 3,300) By Balance c/d	 33,300 2,72,700
		3,06,000			3,06,000
1.4.1998	To Balance B/d	2,72,700	31.3.1998 31.3.1998	By Depreciation By Balance c/d	36,600 2,36,100
		2,72,700			2,72,700
1.4.1999	To Balance B/d	2,36,100	31.3.1999 31.3.1999	By Depreciation By Balance c/d	36,600 1,99,500
		2,36,100			2,36,100
1.4.2000	To Balance B/d	1,99,500			

Written Down Value Method : Machinery Account

Date	Particulars	Amount Rs.	Date	Particulars	Amount Rs.
1.4.1995	To Cash	3,00,000	31.3.1996 31.3.1996	By Depreciation By Balance c/d	30,000 2,70,000
		3,00,000			3,00,000
1.4.1996	To Balance B/d	2,70,000	31.3.1997 31.3.1997	By Depreciation By Balance c/d	27,000 2,43,000
		2,70,000			2,70,000
1.4.1997 1.10.1997	To Balance B/d To Cash	2,43,000 60,000	31.3.1998 31.3.1998	By Depreciation By Balance c/d	27,300 2,75,700
		3,03,000			3,03,000
1.4.1998	To Cash	2,75,700	31.3.1998 31.3.1999	By Depreciation By Balance c/d	27,570 2,48,130
		2,75,700			2,75,700
1.4.1999	To Balance B/d	2,48,130	31.3.2000 31.3.2000	By Depreciation By Balance c/d	24,813 2,23,317
		2,48,130			2,48,130
1.4.2000	To Balance B/d	2,23,317			

Depreciation for 1997 :
Depreciation on Rs. 2,43,000 @ 10% for one year   24,300
Depreciation on 60,000 @ 10% for 6 months   3,000
                                                          27,300

Problem 15. *From the following data find out the depreciation for period of 5 years. The cost of machine is Rs. 2,00,000. The scrap value after a period of 5 years is estimated at Rs. 40,000. Using the sum of the digits method, calculate the depreciation for every year.*

Solution :
The sum of the years digits   = 5 + 4 + 3 + 2 + 1 = 15
Cost of the machine   = 2,00,000
Scrap value   = 40,000
Therefore, cost of machine − scrape value = 2,00,000 − 40,000 = 1,60,000
Now Depreciation Charge for each Year can be Calculated as follows :
Depreciation charge for the I year   = 5/15 × 1,60,000 = 53,334
Depreciation charge for the IInd year = 4/15 × 1,60,000 = 42,667
Depreciation charge for the IIIrd year = 3/15 × 1,60,000 = 32,000
Depreciation charge for the IVth year = 2/15 × 1,60,000 = 21,334
Depreciation charge for the Vth year   = 1/15 × 1,60,000 = 10,667

❏❏❏

9
Cost Accounting : Cost Sheet, Accounting for Manufacturing Cost

INTRODUCTION

Financial Accounting concentrates in the preparation of Trading Account, Profit and Loss Account and Balance Sheet. Profit and Loss Account shows the net profit of the organisation. And Balance Sheet shows the true financial position of the organisation. But the financial accounting does not concentrate on the operational efficiency of the organisation. Financial Accounting serves several functions to the organisation such as finance, administration, production but the operational efficiency of those functions is lacking. Apart from these activities, Financial Accounting has certain limitations. In order to overcome these limitations and to obtain more efficient operations of the organisation the cost accounting system is developed.

CONCEPT OF COST ACCOUNTING

Cost

The term cost is very often used in day to day activities. The cost is the amount of resources given up in exchange for some goods or services.

American Institute of Certified Public Accountants defined cost as expanded or other property transferred, capital, stock issued, services performed or liability incurred in consideration of goods or services received or to be received.

Costing

Costing may be referred "as classifying, recording and appropriate allocation of expenditure for the determination of costs of products or services".

Cost Accounting

The Institute of Cost and Works Accountants (ICWA) (UK) defines cost accounting as "the process of accounting for cost from the point at which expenditure is incurred or committed to the establishment of its ultimate relationship with cost centres and cost units". In its widest usage, it embraces the preparation of statistical data, the application of cost control methods and the ascertainment of the profitability of activities carried out or planned.

According to Wheldon "cost accounting is the application of accounting and costing principle methods are techniques in the ascertainment of costs and the analysis of saving or excess cost incurred as compared with previous experience or with standards".

Cost Accountancy is the application of costing and cost accounting principles, methods and techniques to the science, art and practice of cost control and the ascertainment of profitability.

OBJECTIVES OF COST ACCOUNTING

1. It enables the management to ascertain the unit cost of product, service, job or department, and also to estimate the profit or loss of each operation.
2. To guide the management on future expansion programmes and proposed capital projects.
3. To provide necessary guidance to fix the accurate selling price of the product.
4. To co-ordinate cost reduction programme along with the different departmental heads.
5. To assist the management in preparing Budgets and necessary steps which are to be taken for the implementation of budgeting control.
6. To collect and supply relevant data to the management for taking important financial decisions.
7. To interpret and present data to the management for planning, evaluation of performance and control.
8. To provide specialised services of cost audit.
9. To assist the management in the future production policies.

ADVANTAGES OF COST ACCOUNTING

(i) To disclose the profitable and unprofitable activities of the organisation.
(ii) It supplies information upon which estimates and tenders are based.
(iii) To facilitate the introduction of suitable plans of wage payment to reward efficiency and to provide adequate incentive to the less efficient workers.
(iv) Helpful to the Government.
(v) Installation of Costing System will strengthen confidence in the minds of the public about the fairness of the prices charged.

LIMITATIONS OF COST ACCOUNTING

The following are the main limitations of cost accounting :

(i) *It is Expensive.* The installation of costing system in the industry requires huge amount of capital. Because, double set of account books has to be maintained. And at the same time it requires the persons who have specialised knowledge in costing. They require higher amount of salary and other benefits.

(ii) *Failure of Costing System.* Cost accounting system has failed to bring expected results in many cases. Under this background, it is treated as a defective system. However, it is not a faulty system.

(iii) *It Ignores a Uniform Procedure.* In the practical sense of cost accounting in a particular situation, two competent cost accountants may arrive at different results from the same information. Because of this, we can say, there is no uniform procedure for cost accounting.

(iv) *Matter of Routine Forms and Statements.* Sending of costing information to the management requires large number of forms and statements. Simply says, introduction of costing system involves additional and unnecessary paper work.

(v) *It is an Unnecessary Application.* Cost Accounting is only recently developed and installed in many industries. They have been progressing tremendously. And at the same time, some of the organisations can successfully run without the applications of cost accounting.

GENERAL PRINCIPLES OF COST ACCOUNTING

The following are some of the principles of costing :
(i) Cost accounting should ignore the convention of prudence.
(ii) Cause effect relationship
(iii) Past costs should not form part of future costs
(iv) Exclusion of abnormal costs from cost accounts
(v) Principle of double entry should be followed preferably.

ELEMENTS OF COST

In order to implement the effective cost control for the sound managerial decisions, the management may be provided with adequate data. For the purpose of achieving the above objectives, the total cost of the product is analysed by the elements of cost *i.e.,* nature of expenses. Actually, the product cost is divided into three elements *i.e.,* Material, Labour, and Overheads.

The elements of cost show the following graphical form.

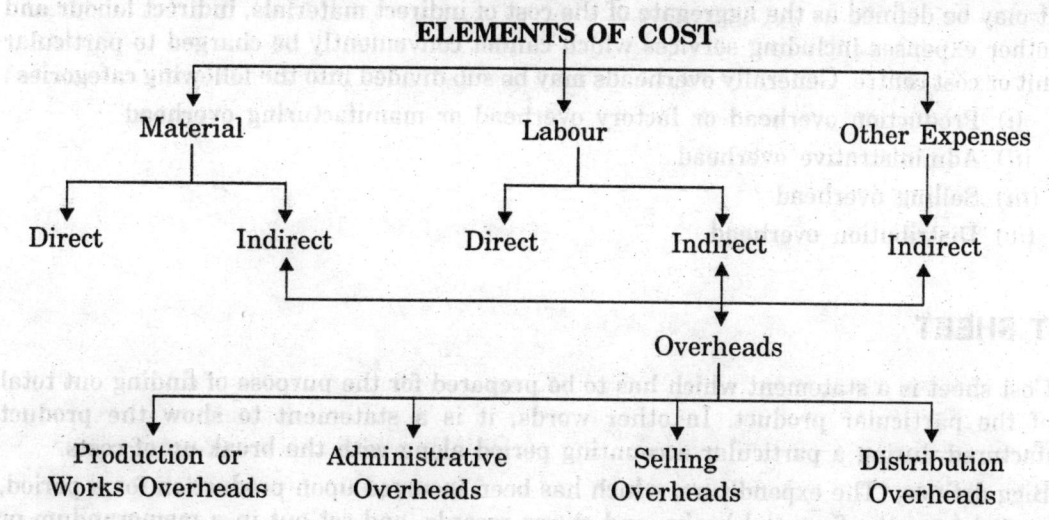

ELEMENTS OF COST

```
                    ELEMENTS OF COST
            ┌──────────────┼──────────────┐
         Material        Labour      Other Expenses
         ┌───┴───┐       ┌───┴───┐         │
      Direct  Indirect Direct Indirect  Indirect
                 └─────────┬───┴─────────┘
                        Overheads
         ┌──────────────┬──────────────┬──────────────┐
    Production or  Administrative   Selling       Distribution
    Works Overheads   Overheads    Overheads       Overheads
```

By Grouping the above elements of cost, the following divisions of costs are obtained.

(i) Direct Material + Direct Labour = Prime Cost
(ii) Prime Cost + Works or Factory Overheads = Works or Factory Cost.
(iii) Cost Production + Selling and Distribution Overhead = Total Cost (Cost of Sales)
(iv) Work cost + Administration Overhead = Cost of Production

Strictly Speaking the Elements of Cost can be classified into :
- Direct Material
- Direct Labour
- Overheads.

Direct Material

Direct materials are those materials which can be directly identified with each unit of the finished product. It directly enters the production process and forms a part of the finished product. Direct materials can be classified in the following forms :

(i) All raw materials
(ii) Raw Materials specifically purchased for specific job
(iii) Parts purchased or produced
(iv) Packing materials.

Direct Labour

Direct wages refer to all labour expenses in altering the construction, composition, confirmation of the product. Simply, it is that labour which can be conveniently identified or attributed wholly to a particular job or converting raw material into finished goods. Wages of such labour force are known as direct wages.

Overheads

It may be defined as the aggregate of the cost of indirect materials, indirect labour and some other expenses including services which cannot conveniently be charged to particular cost unit or cost centre. Generally overheads may be sub divided into the following categories :

(i) Production overhead or factory overhead or manufacturing overhead
(ii) Administrative overhead
(iii) Selling overhead
(iv) Distribution overhead.

COST SHEET

Cost sheet is a statement which has to be prepared for the purpose of finding out total cost of the particular product. In other words, it is a statement to show the product manufactured during a particular accounting period along with the break-up of costs.

Bigg defines, "The expenditure, which has been incurred upon production for a period, is extracted from the financial books, and stores records, and set out in a memorandum or a statement. If this statement is confined to the disclosure of the cost of the units produced during the period, it is termed as cost sheet".

Important Purposes of Cost Sheet

(i) It shows the total cost and cost per unit of the products manufactured during a particular period.
(ii) It facilitates the comparative study of various elements of current cost with previous results and estimated costs.
(iii) It helps to formulate a concrete production policy.
(iv) It helps in fixing selling price.
(v) It guides the businessmen to minimise the cost of production.

Specimen Form of Cost Sheet

	Opening stock of Raw material	xx	
Add :	Purchase of Raw materials	xx	
			xx
Less :	Closing stock of Raw materials		xx
	Cost of Raw materials consumed		xx
Add :	Direct wages		xx
	Prime cost		xx
Add :	Factory overhead [i]		xx
	Total factory cost incurred during the year		xx
Add :	Opening stock of work in progress		xx
Less :	Closing stock of work in progress		xx
	Works cost		xx
Add :	Administration overhead [ii]		xx
	Cost of production		xx
Add :	Opening stock of finished goods		xx
Less :	Closing stock of finished goods		xx
	Cost of goods sold		xx
Add :	Selling and Distribution overhead [iii]		xx
	Cost of sales		xx
Add :	Profit for the period		xx
	Sales		xx

Details about the various Overheads

(i) **Factory Overheads**
Wages of Foremen
Factory Lighting
Consumable Stores
Lubricants
Electric Power
Oil and Water
Factory Manager's Salary
Time Keeper's Salary
Material Transportation Expenses

Factory Rent, Factory Lighting, Employees State Insurance Contribution,
Depreciation – Factory Plant
Electric Power
Heat and Lighting
Insurance and Taxes
Miscellaneous Expenses – Factory
Plant maintenance – Stationery in Factory

(ii) **Administrative Overheads**
Office Rent
Bank Charges
Telephone Charges
Salaries of Office Staff
Repairs and Renewals – Office
Depreciation on Office Building
Manager's Salary
Director's Fees
Office Stationery
Postage and Telegrams
Insurance
Lighting of the Office
Rates and Taxes

(iii) **Selling and Distribution Overheads**
Expenses on Packing Materials
Salaries of Sales Staff
Sales Manager's Salary
Carriage Outward
Travelling Expenses
Advertising
Delivery Van Expenses
Godown Rent
Distribution Department - Salaries and Expenses
Sales Commission
Sales Promotion
Depreciation of Delivery Van.

NOTE : The following expenses are excluded from cost accounts. Even though it should be given in the problem, it should not appear anywhere in the cost sheet. Because it is purely financial nature rather than costing nature.

    (i) Transfer to Reserves   *(ii)* Income-tax Paid
    (iii) Dividend Paid   *(iv)* Discount on Shares Written Off

Simplified form of Cost Sheet

Particulars	Total Cost Rs.	Cost Per Unit Rs.
Direct Material	xx	xx
Direct Labour	xx	xx
Prime Cost	xx	xx
Add : Works Overhead or factory Overhead	xx	xx
Works Cost	xx	xx
Add : Administrative Overhead	xx	xx
Cost of Production	xx	xx
Add : Selling and Distribution Overheads	xx	xx
Total Cost or Cost of Sales	xx	xx
Add : Profit	xx	xx
Sales	xx	xx

Problem 1. *From the following details calculate prime cost, factory cost, cost of production, cost of sales and profit from the following particulars :*

	Rs.		Rs.
Direct Materials	1,20,000	Depreciation :	
Direct Wages	40,000	Factory Plant	1,000
Wages of Foremen	5,000	Office Premises	2,500
Electric Power	1,000	Consumable Stores	5,000
Lighting : Factory	3,000	Manager's Salary	10,000
Office	1,000	Director's Fees	2,500
Store Keeper's Wages	2,000	Office Stationery	1,000
Oil and Water	1,000	Telephone Charges	250
Rent: Factory	10,000	Postage and Telegrams	5,000
Office	2,500	Salesmen's Salaries	2,500
Repairs and Renewals:		Travelling Expenses	1,000
Factory Plant	3,500	Advertising	3,000
Office Premises	1,000	Warehouse Charges	1,000
Transfer to Reserve	2,000	Sales	3,80,000
Dividend Paid	1,000	Carriage Outward	800
		Income-tax	15,000

Solution :   **Statement of Cost and Profit**

Particulars	Rs.	Rs.
Direct Materials		1,20,000
Direct Wages		40,000
Prime Cost		1,60,000
Add : Factory Overheads :		
Wages of Foreman	5,000	
Electric Power	1,000	
Storekeeper's Wages	2,000	
Oil and Water	1,000	
Factory Rent	10,000	
Repairs and Renewals – Factory Plant	3,500	
Factory Lighting	3,000	
Depreciation – Factory Plant	1,000	
Consumable Stores	5,000	
		31,500
Factory Costs		1,91,500
Add : Administration Overheads :		
Office Rent	2,500	
Repairs and Renewals – Office Premises	1,000	
Office Lighting	1,000	
Depreciation : Office Premises	2,500	
Manager's Salary	10,000	
Director's Fees	2,500	
Office Stationery	1,000	
Telephone Charges	250	
Postage and Telegrams	500	
		21,250
Cost of Production		2,12,750
Add : Selling and Distribution Overheads		
Carriage Outward	800	
Salesmen's Salaries	2,500	
Travelling Expenses	1,000	
Advertising	3,000	
Warehouse Charges	1,000	
		8,300
Cost of Sales		2,21,050
Profit		1,58,950
Sales		3,80,000

Problem 2. *The following information has been obtained from the records of Narmatha Corporation Ltd for the period from January 1 to June 30, 2003.*

	1.1.2003 Rs.	30.6.2003 Rs.
Cost of Raw Materials	30,000	25,000
Cost of Work in Progress	12,000	15,000
Cost of Stock of finished Goods	60,000	55,000
Transactions during six months are :		
Purchase of Raw Materials	1,50,000	-
Wages Paid	3,30,000	-
Factory Overheads	92,000	-
Administration Overheads	60,000	-
Selling and Distribution Overhead	30,000	-
Sales	12,50,000	

Prepare Cost Sheet.

Solution :

Statement of Cost

	Rs.
Opening Stock of Raw Materials	30,000
Add : Purchase of Raw Materials	5,50,000
	5,80,000
Less : Closing Stock of Raw Materials	25,000
Cost of Materials Consumed	5,55,000
Direct Wages	3,30,000
Prime Cost	8,85,000
Add : Factory Overheads	92,000
Factory Cost Incurred	9,77,000
Add : Opening Work-in-progress	12,000
	9,89,000
Less : Closing Work-in-progress	15,000
Factory (or) Manufacturing or Works Cost	9,74,000

Income Statement

Particulars	Rs.	Rs.
Sales		12,50,000
Less : Cost of Goods Sold :		
Opening Stock of Finished Goods	60,000	
Add : Factory Cost of the year	9,74,000	
	10,34,000	
Less : Closing Stock of Finished Goods	55,000	
		9,79,000
Gross Profit		2,71,000

	Rs.	Rs.
Less : Indirect Expenses :		
Administration Expenses	60,000	
Selling and Distribution Expenses	30,000	
		90,000
Net Profit		1,81,000

Problem 3. *Suriyat & Co Ltd requires a statement showing the result of its production, operation for Sep. 2002. Cost records give the following information.*

	1.9.2002 Rs.	30.9.2002 Rs.
Raw Materials	1,00,000	1,23,500
Finished Goods	71,500	42,000
Work in Progress	31,000	34,500

Transactions during the month of Sep. 2002 :

	Rs.
Purchase of Raw Materials	88,000
Direct Wages	70,000
Works' Expenses	39,500
Administration Expenses	13,000
Sale of Factory Scrap	2,000
Selling and Distribution Expenses	15,000
Sales	2,84,000

Solution :   **Statement of Cost**

	Rs.	Rs.
Opening Stock of Raw Materials		1,00,000
Add : Purchase of Raw Materials		88,000
		1,88,000
Less : Closing Stock of Raw Materials		1,23,500
Value of Material Consumed		64,500
Add : Direct Wages		70,000
Prime Cost		1,34,500
Add : Factory Overhead :		
Works Expenses	39,500	
Less : Sale of Factory Scrap	2,000	37,500
Total Factory Cost		1,72,000
Add : Opening Stock of Work-in-progress		31,000
		2,03,000

COST ACCOUNTING : COST SHEET, ACCOUNTING FOR MANUFACTURING COST

Less : Closing Stock of Work-in-progress		34,500
Works Cost		1,68,500
Add : Administration Expenses		13,000
Cost of Production		1,81,500
Add : Opening Stock of Finished Goods		71,500
		2,53,000
Less : Closing Stock of Finished Goods		42,000
Cost of Goods to be sold		2,11,000
Add : Selling and Distribution Expenses		15,000
Cost of Sales		2,26,000
Profit		58,000
Sales		2,84,000

Problem 4. *Mr. Gopal furnishes the following data related to the manufacturing of a product during the month of April 2004.*

	Rs.
Raw Materials Consumed	15,000
Direct Labour Charges	9,000
Machine Hours Worked	900
Machine Hour Rate (Rs.)	5
Administrative Overheads	20% on works cost
Selling Overheads	Res.0.50 per unit
Units Produced	17,100
Units Sold	16,000
@ Rs. 4 per unit	

You are required to prepare a cost sheet from the above showing (i) the cost of production per unit (ii) profit per unit sold and profit for the period. [B.Com]

Solution :

Cost Sheet

Particulars	Amount Rs.	Cost per Unit Rs.
Raw Material Consumed	15,000	
Direct Labour	9,000	
Direct Expenses	Nil	
Prime Cost	24,000	
Add : Factory Overheads 900 × 5 =	4,500	
Works Cost of 17,100 units	28,500	
Add : Admn. Overhead 20% on Works Cost	5,700	
Cost of Production 17,100 units (Rs. 34,200/17,100 units = Rs. 2 per unit)	34,200	2.00

	Particulars	Rs.	Rs.
Add :	Opening Stock of Finished Goods	Nil	
Less :	Closing Stock of Finished Goods 1,100 units at Rs. 2	2,200	
Add :	Cost of Goods Sold 16,000 units	32,000	
	Selling Overheads 16,000 × 0.50 =	8,000	0.50
	Cost of Sales 16,000 units	40,000	2.50
	Sales 16,000 × 4 =	64,000	
	Profit on 16,000 units	24,000	

Problem 5. *The following extracts of costing information relate to product z for the year ending 31.3.2003.*

	Rs.
Purchase of Raw Materials	48,000
Direct Wages	40,000
Stock of Raw Materials on 1.4.2002	8,000
Stock of Finished Goods on 1.4.2002 (1,600 units)	6,400
Stock of Raw Material on 31.3.2003	8,800
Stock of Finished Goods [3200 units] at Current Cost of Production	12,840
Works Overheads	16,800
Work in Progress on 1.4.2002	1,920
Work in Progress on 31.3.2003	6,400
Office on Cost	3,200
Sales (Finished Product)	1,20,000

Selling and Distribution Cost is 40 paise per unit. During the year 25,600 units were produced. Calculate the cost of production and extend the cost sheet to show the profit also.

Solution : **Cost Sheet for the year ended 31.3.2003**

Particulars	TC Rs.	Rs.
Raw Material Used :		
Opening Stock	8,000	
Add : Purchases	48,000	
	56,000	
Less : Closing Stock	8,800	
	47,200	
Add : Direct Wages	40,000	
Prime Cost	87,200	
Add : Factory Overheads	16,800	
Factory Cost	1,04,000	
Add : Opening stock of work in progress (1.4.2002)	1,920	
	1,05,920	

Less : Closing Stock of Work in Progress (31.3.2003)	6,400	
Works Cost	99,520	3.89
Add : Office on Cost	3,200	0.12
Cost of Production (25,600 units)	1,02,720	4.01
Add : Opening Stock (1,600 units)	6,400	
(27,200 units)	1,09,120	-
Less : Closing Stock 3,200 units	12,840	-
Cost of Goods Sold	96,280	4.01
Add : Selling cost @ 40 paise per unit	9,600	0.40
(24,000 × .40)	1,05,880	4.41
Profit	14,120	0.59
Sales	1,20,000	5.00

Problem 6. *RCH Ltd is manufacturing refrigerators. The following details are furnished in respect of its factory operations for the year ended 31-12-2002.*

Work in Progress 1.1.2002	61,000	
At Prime Cost	20,000	81,000
Manufacturing Expenses		
Work in Progress 31.12.2002		
At Prime Cost	54,000	
Manufacturing Expenses	9,000	63,000
Opening Stock of Raw Materials		3,25,000
Purchase of Raw Material		5,00,000
Direct Labour		2,31,000
Manufacturing Expenses		96,000
Closing Stock of Raw Material		2,24,000

On the basis of above data, prepare a statement showing the cost of production. Also indicate separately the amount of manufacturing expenses which enter the cost of production.

Solution : **Cost Sheet**

	Rs.	Rs.
Raw Material		
Opening Stock	3,25,000	
Add : Purchases	5,00,000	
	8,25,000	
Less : Closing Stock of Raw Material	2,24,000	
Value of Raw Material Consumed		6,01,000
Add : Direct Labour		2,31,000
		8,32,000
Add : Work in Progress in the beginning		61,000
		8,93,000

		Rs.
Less : Work in Progress at the end		54,000
Prime Cost		7,17,000
Add : Manufacturing Expenses :		
Relating to Opening Work in Progress	20,000	
Add : Relating to 2002	96,000	
	1,16,000	
Less : Relating to Closing Work in Progress	9,000	1,07,000
Cost of Production		8,24,000

Problem 7. *The following details are available from the costing records of Himalaya & Co Ltd.*

Stock of Raw Materials on 1.1.2003	12,800
Stock of Finished Goods on 1.1.2003	28,000
Purchases during the year	2,92,000
Productive Wages	1,98,000
Sale of Finished Goods	5,92,000
Stock of Finished Goods on 31.12.2003	30,000
Stock of Raw Materials on 31.12.2003	13,600
Works Overheads	43,736
Office and General Expenses	35,524

The Company is about to send a tender for plant. The costing department estimates that the materials required would cost Rs. 20,000 and wages for making the plant would cost Rs. 12,000. Tender is to be made keeping a net profit of 20% on selling price. State what would be the amount of the tender if based on the percentages. [B.Com Madras]

Solution : Cost sheet for the year ended 31.12.2003

	Rs.	Rs.
Opening Stock of Raw Materials	12,800	
Add : Purchases during the year	2,92,000	
	3,04,800	
Less : Closing Stock of Materials	13,600	
Value of Material Consumed		2,91,200
Productive Wages		1,98,000
Prime Cost		4,90,000
Add : Works Overheads		43,735
Factory Cost		5,33,736
Add : Office and General Overheads		35,524
Cost of Production		5,69,260
Add : Opening Stock of Finished Goods		28,000
		5,97,260
Less : Closing Stock of Finished Goods		30,000
Cost of Goods Sold		5,67,260
Profit		24,740
Sales		5,92,000

Workings :

(i) Percentage of factory overheads to productive wages

$$\frac{43{,}736}{1{,}98{,}000} \times 100 = 22\%$$

(ii) Percentage of office on cost to factory cost

$$\frac{35{,}524}{5{,}33{,}736} \times 100 = 6.66\%$$

	Rs.
Materials	20,000
Productive wages	12,000
Prime Cost	32,000
Factory Overheads (22% on Wages)	2,640
Factory Cost	34,640
Office on Cost (6.66% on Factory Cost)	2,307
Total Cost	36,947
Profit (20% on Selling Price)	9,237
Tender price	46,184

Problem 8. *The following is the trading profit and loss A/c and other details. You are required to prepare a cost sheet showing the price at which the coolers should be marketed in order to earn a profit of 10% on selling price.*

Trading Account

	Rs.		Rs.
To Cost of Materials	80,000	By Sales	4,00,000
To Direct Wages	1,20,000	(1000 Coolers)	
To Other Manufacturing Cost	50,000		
To Gross Profit	1,50,000		
	4,00,000		4,00,000
To Office Salaries	60,000	By Gross Profit	1,50,000
To Rent and Insurance	10,000		
To Selling Expenses	30,000		
To General Expenses	20,000		
To Net Profit	30,000		
	1,50,000		1,50,000

For the year ending 31.12.2003 it is estimated that

(i) Output and sales will be 1,200 coolers.
(ii) Prices of material will rise by 20% on the 2002 level.
(iii) Wages will increase by 5%.
(iv) Manufacturing cost will rise in proportion to the prime cost.
(v) Selling expenses per unit remain unaffected.
(vi) Other expenses will remain constant.

Solution : Cost sheet for the year ending 31.12.2003

Output for 1,000

Particulars	CPU Rs.	Total Cost Rs.
Cost of Materials	80.00	80,000
Direct Wages	120.00	1,20,000
Prime Cost	200.00	2,00,000
Manufacturing Expenses	50.00	50,000
Factory Cost	250.00	2,50,000
Office Salaries	60.00	60,000
Rent and Insurance	10.00	10,000
General Expenses	20.00	20,000
Cost of Production	340.00	3,40,000
Selling Expenses	30.00	30,000
Cost of Sales or Total Cost	370.00	3,70,000
Profit	30.00	30,000
Sales	400.00	4,00,000

Estimated cost sheet for the year ending 31.12.2004

[Estimated output of 1,200 coolers]

	Particulars		CPU Rs.	Total Cost Rs.
	Materials	80.00		
Add :	20% increase	16.00	96.00	1,15,200
	Wages	120.00		
Add :	5% increase	6.00	126.00	1,51,200
	Prime Cost		222.00	2,66,400
	Manufacturing Expenses (25% on Prime Cost)		55.50	66,600
	Works Cost		277.50	3,33,000
Add :	Administration Overheads			
	Office Salaries		50.00	60,000
	Rent and Insurance		8.33	10,000
	Other Expenses (Constant)		16.67	20,000
	Cost of Production		352.50	4,23,000
	Selling Expenses (Constant per unit)		30.00	36,000
	Cost of Sales or Total Cost		382.50	4,59,000
	Profit (10% on selling Price)		42.50	51,000
	Sales		425.00	5,10,000

Workings :

Computation of Profit 10% on Selling Price

If selling price is Rs. 100 then profit is Rs. 10 and cost is Rs. 90 (100-10) if cost is Rs. 90 then profit is Rs. 10.

If Cost is Rs. 382.50, then profit is 382.50/90 × 10 = 42.50

Total Profit = Rs. 42.50 × 12,00 = **Rs. 51,000.**

Problem 9. *Compute works cost from the following where indirect wages are 50% of direct wages; indirect materials are 50% of direct materials and indirect expenses are 100% of direct expenses.*

Direct Expenses	Rs. 10,000
Direct Wages	Rs. 30,000
Direct Materials	Rs. 10,000

[B.Com, Osmania Oct. 93]

Solution : Cost Sheet

Particulars	Rs.	Rs.
Direct Materials		10,000
Direct Wages		30,000
Direct Expenses		10,000
Prime Cost		50,000
Indirect materials	5,000	
Indirect Wages	15,000	
Indirect Expenses	10,000	30,000
Works Cost		80,000

Problem 10. *From the following information calculate cost of production :*

Raw Materials Consumed	30,000
Productive Wages	18,000
Machine Hours Worked	900
Administrative Overheads :	
20% on Works Cost	
Machine Hour Rate Rs. 10	

[B.Com, Nagpur, March 1989]

Solution : Cost Sheet
Calculation of Cost of Production :

	Rs.
Raw Material Consumed	30,000
Productive Wages	18,000
Factory Overheads :	
Machine hours worked 900 at Rs. 10	9,000
Works cost	57,000
Add : Admn. overheads 20% on works cost	11,400
Cost of Production	68,400

Problem 11. *From the following data, prepare a statement showing cost and profit per unit for the month of January 1988.*

Raw Material used	Rs. 40,000
Direct Wages	Rs. 22,400
Man Hours Worked	9500 hours
Man Hour Rate	Rs. 4 per unit
Office Overhead	20% on works cost
Units Produced and Sold	20,000
Selling Price	Rs. 10 per unit

[B.Com, Calicut, Oct. 89]

Solution :

Cost Sheet

Particulars	Amount Rs.	Cost Per Unit Rs.
Raw Materials used	40,000	2.00
Direct Wages	22,000	1.10
Direct Expenses	-	-
Prime Cost	62,000	3.10
Add : Factory Overhead : Indirect Wages	16,000	0.80
Works Cost	78,000	3.90
Add : Office overhead at 20% on works cost	15,600	0.78
Cost of Production	93,600	4.68
Add : Selling Overhead at Rs. 1 per unit	20,000	1.00
Total Cost	1,13,600	5.68
Sales at Rs. 10 per unit	2,00,000	10.00
Less : Total Cost	1,13,600	5.68
Profit	86,400	4.32

Workings :

Man Hours Worked	=	9500 hours
Man Hour Rate	=	Rs. 4 per hour
Total Wages 9500x4	=	38,000
Less : Direct Wages	=	22,000
Indirect Wages		16,000 (Treated as Factory Overhead)

Problem 12. *Prepare a Cost Sheet :*

Labour Rs. 1,50,000, Prime Cost Rs. 3,50,000, Factory Expenses Rs. 98,000, Office expenses Rs. 85,000, 10% of the output is in stock and the sales total upto Rs. 5,10,000.

[B.A Madras]

Solution :

Particulars	Rs.
Materials	2,00,000
Labour	1,50,000
Prime Cost	3,50,000
Factory Expenses :	98,000
Works Cost	4,48,000
Office Expenses	85,000
Cost of Production	5,33,000
Less : Closing Stock of Finished Goods (10% of Cost of Production)	53,300
Cost of Goods Sold	4,79,700
Profit	30,300
Sales	5,10,000

Problem 13. *The Southern Traders Ltd, manufactured and sold 800 cookers in the year ending 31st March 2002. The summarised Trading and Profit and Loss Account is given below.*

	Rs.		Rs.
To Cost of Materials	64,000	By Sales	3,20,000
Direct Wages	96,000		
Manufacturing Expenses	40,000		
Gross Profit c/d	1,20,000		
	3,20,000		3,20,000
To Office Salaries	48,000	By Gross Profit B/d	1,20,000
Rent, Rates & Taxes	8,000		
Selling Expenses	16,000		
General Expenses	24,000		
Net Profit	24,000		
	1,20,000		1,20,000

For the year ending 31st March 2003 it has been estimated that
(a) Output and sales will be 1,000 cookers.
(b) Price of materials will rise by 25% on the previous year's level.
(c) Wages will rise by 12 ½%.
(d) Manufacturing cost will rise in proportion to the combined cost of materials and wages.
(e) Selling cost per unit will remain unchanged.
(f) Other expenses will remain unaffected by the rise in output.
Prepare a cost statement showing the price at which cookers would be marketed so as to show a profit of 12% on the selling price.

Solution : **Cost Sheet**

Particulars	Total Cost Rs.	Per Unit Cost Rs.
Cost of Materials	64,000	80.00
Direct Wages	96,000	120.00
Prime Cost	1,60,000	200.00
Manufacturing Expenses	40,000	50.00
Factory Cost	2,00,000	250.00
Add : Office Overheads : Office Salaries	48,000	60.00
Rent, Rates & Taxes	8,000	10.00
General Expenses	24,000	30.00
Cost Production	2,80,000	350.00
Add : Selling Expenses	16,000	20.00
Total Cost	2,96,000	370.00
Profit	24,000	30.00
Sales	3,20,000	400.00

Calculation of percentage of manufacturing expenses on combined cost of materials and wages.

$$\frac{\text{Manufacturing Expenses}}{\text{Cost of Material \& Wages}} \times 100 \quad i.e., \quad \frac{40,000}{1,60,000} \times 100 = 25\%$$

Cost Statement for 1000 Cookers

Particulars	Total Cost Rs.	Cost Per Unit Rs.
Materials 64,000/800 × 1,000	80,000	
Add : Increase 25%	20,000	
	1,00,000	100.00
Direct Wages 96,000/800 × 1,000	1,20,000	
Add : Increase 12 ½ %	15,000	
	1,35,000	135.00
Prime Cost	2,35,000	235.00
Manufacturing Wages : 25% on Prime Cost	58,750	58.75
Works Cost	2,93,750	293.75
Add Office Overheads :		
Office Salaries	48,000	48.00
Rent, Rates & Taxes	8,000	8.00
General Expenses	24,000	24.00
Cost of Production	3,73,750	373.75
Selling Expenses	20,000	20.00
Total Cost	3,93,750	393.75
Profit 12% on Selling Price	53,693	53.69
Sales	4,47,443	447.44

Problem 14. *The following data related to the manufacture of a standard product during the 4 weeks of Feb 2003.*

	Rs.
Raw Materials Consumed	20,000
Direct Wages	12,000
Machine Hours Worked	1,000
Machine Hour Rate	Rs. 2
Office Overhead	15% on works cost
Selling Overhead	37 paise per unit
Units Sold	18,000 at Rs. 2.50 each

You are required to prepare a cost sheet in respect of the above, showing (a) cost per unit (b) The profit for the 4 weekly period.

Solution :

Cost Sheet

Period 4 weeks ended 28th Feb 2003   Output : 18,000 units

Particulars	Total Cost Rs.	Per Unit Cost Rs.
Raw Materials Consumed	20,000	1.11
Direct Wages	12,000	0.67
Prime Cost	32,000	1.78
Factory Overheads @ Rs. 2 per machine hour for 1,000 hours	2,000	0.11
Factory Cost	34,000	1.89
Office Overhead @ 15% on factory cost	5,100	0.28
Cost of Production	39,100	2.17
Selling overhead @ 37 paise per unit for 18,000 unit	6,600	0.37
Total Cost	45,760	2.54
Loss	– 760	– 0.04
Sales	45,000	2.50

❏❏❏

10
Job Costing

Most industries may be broadly classified into two major heads.
  (i) Job order industries
  (ii) Mass production industries

Normally job order industries engage in production based upon the customers' orders. Each and every job has its own features and requires a special attention.

The ICMA terminology defines job costing as "that form of specific order costing which applies where the work is undertaken to customers' requirements and each order is of comparatively short duration. The work is usually carried out within a factory or workshop and moves through processes or operations as a continuously identifiable unit".

ADVANTAGES OF JOB ORDER COSTING

  (i) It enables the organisation to find which jobs are more profitable and those which are unprofitable.
  (ii) It helps the management to determine the operating efficiency of the various factors of production and some of the functional units.
  (iii) It helps in determining the cost of similar jobs taken up in future and thus helps in formulation of future production planning.
  (iv) Accurate identification of wastage, spoilage and defectives with respect to the production orders may assist the management to take effective steps in reducing these to minimum extent.
  (v) By employing predetermined overhead rates in job costing, all the advantages of budgetory control can be obtained.

LIMITATIONS

  (i) Cost comparison among different jobs becomes difficult or meaningless because there may be major economic changes.
  (ii) Job costing is a historical costing in nature, so it may not be useful for future planning and control.
  (iii) Job costing system cannot be operated effectively without having a sound production control system
  (iv) Job costing is expensive.
  (v) It requires more clerical work for cost collection of each job.

JOB COSTING

BATCH COSTING

Batch costing is forming a part of job costing. Batch costing is done when production consists of a certain specified number of articles or production involves limited repetition work. Normally, under the job costing, production is carried out on the basis of specific orders. But, in Batch costing products are manufactured and retained as stock and sold on demand.

The total of batch cost can be found out by totalling each order number. The cost of production per unit can be ascertained by dividing the total cost by total batch quantity.

Problem 1. *The details given below have been taken from the cost records of an engineering works in respect of the job No 303.*

Material Rs 4,010
Wages :   Department A : 60 hours @ Rs 3 per hour
*   Department B : 40 hours @ Rs 2 per hour*
*   Department C : 20 hours @ Rs 5 per hour*
The overhead expenses are as follows.
Variable : Department A : Rs 5,000 for 5000 hours.
*   Department B : Rs 3,000 for 1500 hours.*
*   Department C : Rs 2,000 for 500 hours.*
Fixed expenses Rs 20,000 for 10,000 working hours.

Calculate the cost of the job No 303 and the price for the job to give a profit of 25% on the selling price.

[B.Com Madurai]

Solution :

Job Cost Sheet (Job No. 303)

Particulars	Rs.	Rs.
Materials		4,010
Wages : Dept A (60 × Rs. 3)	180	
Dept B (40 × Rs. 2)	80	
Dept C (20 × Rs. 5)	100	360
Overhead Expenses :		
Variable		
Dept A = $\frac{5,000}{5,000}$ = Rs. 1 × 60 =	60	
Dept B = $\frac{3,000}{1,500}$ = Rs. 2 × 40 =	80	
Dept C = $\frac{2,000}{500}$ = Rs. 4 × 20 =	80	220
Fixed Expenses :		
$\frac{20,000}{10,000}$ = 2 × (60 + 40 + 20)		240
Cost of job		4,830
Add : Profit 25% on Selling Price		1,610
Selling Price		6,440

Problem 2. Printwell Ltd took up two jobs during the 1st week of April 1992. The following details are available.

Particulars	Job 101 Rs.	Job 102 Rs.
Material Supplied	2,000	1,400
Wages Paid	900	600
Direct Expenses	100	—
Material Transferred from 101 to 102	100	100
Material Returned to Stores	—	50
Find the Cost of each job.		

[B.Com Osmania April, 1993]

Solution :   **Job Account**

Particulars	Job 101 Rs.	Job 102 Rs.	Particulars	Job 101 Rs.	Job 102 Rs.
To Materials	2,000	1,400	By Materials transferred to job 102	100	-
To Wages	900	600	By Materials returned to Stores	-	50
To Direct Expenses	100	-	By Balance c/d	2,900	2,050
To Materials transferred from job 101		100			
	3,000	2,100		3,000	2,100

Cost of each job :
    Job 101 : Rs. 2,900
    Job 102 : Rs. 2,050

Problem 3. *A worker takes 9 hours to complete a job on daily wages and 6 hours on scheme of payment by results. His day rate is 75 paise per unit. The material cost of the product is Rs 4 and the works overheads are recovered at 15% of the total direct wages. Calculate the factory cost of the product under (a) Halsey plan and (b) Rowan plan.*

[B.Com Osmania Oct. 1995]

Solution :   **Under Halsey Plan**

Time Taken × Hourly Rate + (50% of time Saved × Hourly Rate)

    = 6 hours × 0.75 + (50% of 3 hours × 0.75)

    = 4.5 + 1.12 = Rs. 5.62

Time saved : 9−6   = 3 Hours

Under Rowan Plan

Time Taken × Hourly Rate + $\left[\dfrac{\text{Time Taken}}{\text{Standard Time}} \times \text{Time Saved} \times \text{Hourly Rate}\right]$

    = 6 hours × 0.75 + [6/5 × 3 × 0.75]

    = 4.50 + 1.50 = Rs. 6.00

Statement of Factory Cost

Particulars	(a) Rs.	(b) Rs.
Materials	4.00	4.00
Direct Wages	5.62	6.00
Prime Cost	9.62	10.00
Add : Factory overheads : (15% of wages)	0.84	0.90
Factory Cost	10.46	10.90

Problem 4. *A company has to submit a tender for the manufacture of a machine in 1988. The estimate of the costing department indicates that the materials and wages would cost Rs. 40,000 and Rs. 50,000 respectively. Percentage of factory on cost to wages and percentage of office on cost to works cost would be 20% and 10% respectively.*

[B.Com, Nagpur 1989]

Solution :

Estimate for Tender Price

	Rs.
Materials	40,000
Wages	50,000
Prime cost	90,000
Factory on cost 20% on wages	10,000
Works cost	1,00,000
Office on cost 10% on works cost	10,000
Cost of production	1,10,000
Profit 20% on selling price *i.e.*, 25% on cost	27,500
Selling price for tender	1,37,500

Problem 5. *From the following particulars of KRG Ltd. find out the value of the tender*

	Rs.
Material used	3,000
Production Wages	2,300
Direct Expenses	250

Provide 60% of productive wages for works on cost and 12½% on works cost for office on cost. Profit to be realised 15% on the tender price.

[B.Com, Nagpur 1988]

Solution : **Statement of Value of Tender**

Particulars	Rs.
Materials	3,000.00
Productive Wages	2,300.00
Direct Expenses	250.00
Prime Cost	5,550.00
Works on cost 60% of productive wages	1,380.00
Works Cost	6,930.00
Office on cost 12½% on the works cost	866.25
Cost of production	7,796.25
Profit 15% on the tender price *i.e.*, 15/85 of the cost	1,375.81
Value of the Tender	9,172.06

Problem 6. *What is the cost of a job consuming materials worth Rs. 8,000, wages for 200 Labour hours at Rs. 5 per hours in Dept. A and 100 Labour hours at Rs. 4 per hour in Dept. B. The overheads of the factory amounted to Rs 15,000 for 7,500 total working hours of all the departments.* [B.Com Osmania Oct. 93]

Solution : **Cost Sheet**

	Amount Rs.	Amount Rs.
Materials		8,000
Wages : Dept A 200 × 5	1,000	
Dept B 100 × 4	400	1,400
Overhead Expenses :		
$\left[\dfrac{15,000}{7,500} = \text{Rs. 2 per hour}\right]$		
i.e., 300 hours × Rs. 2.00		600
Total cost of a job		10,000

❏❏❏

11
Process Costing

Process costing is one of the important methods of costing. This method of costing is normally applicable to the different processes involved while converting a raw material into finished product when the raw material has passed through different stages before completion. With the help of the process costing, the manufacturer can find out the cost of each process and the cost of the product.

Simply, it refers to find out the cost at different stages of process and cost of product to industries is known as process costing.

DEFINITION

Operation costing is "the category of basic costing methods applicable where standardised goods or services result from a sequence of repetitive and more or less continuous operations or processes to which cost are charged before being averaged over the units produced during the period".

[ICMA Definition]

ICMA defines process costing as "that form of operation costing which applies where standardised goods are produced".

APPLICATION OF PROCESS COSTING

The following are some of the industries where process costing system is normally applied.

Paper mills	Paint, Ink and
Biscuit works	Varnishing etc.
Oil refining	Meat Products Factory
Chemical works	Milk Dairy
Soap making	Textile, Weaving,
Distillation process	Spinning etc.
Sugar mills	Food Products
	Coke Works
	Gas Manufacturing

In the real sense, process costing may be adopted in organisations producing a single commodity in bulk or a group of products of different types.

FEATURES OF PROCESS COSTING

(i) Production is a continuous flow and the final product is the result of sequence of processes.
(ii) Clearly defined process cost centres
(iii) Different types of products with or without by-products are simultaneously produced at one or more stages of manufacture.
(iv) Under the method of process costing normal and abnormal losses or gains are to be treated properly.
(v) The output of one process becomes the raw material of another process.
(vi) All the finished products are uniform and all units are exactly identical during one or more processes.
(vii) To calculate the effective units of production is possible under this method, even all the inputs may not be converted into finished goods.

ELEMENTS OF PRODUCTION COST

The following are the important elements of production cost under process costing:
(i) Material
(ii) Labour
(iii) Production overhead.

(i) Material

The material required for production is issued to the first process, then offer processing. Then it can be transferred to next process and so on. In some situations, material may pass from the first process to the next process where an additional material is to be added; it may continue until completion. Normally, material requisitioned in the prescribed form only may be issued. Cost incurred for this operation is treated as material cost.

(ii) Labour

Some of the Labour Forces are directly engaged in manufacturing of a product. But generally employees are utilised continuously on one process and time spent by them is debited to the process account. Amount paid for the utilisation of Labour force is treated as labour cost. Normally the cost of direct labour constitutes a very small part of the cost of production in industries. Because more number of automatic machineries are installed in the industry.

(iii) Production Overhead

Any expenses incurred for the production other than the material and labour come under the head of production overhead. Normally the overhead element of total constitutes generally a very huge portion in the process costing. So appropriate decision is required to ensure that reasonable share of production is charged to each process.

Material cost, Labour cost, and Production Overhead cost, these three elements taken together are called the cost of production of the product.

ADVANTAGES OF PROCESS COSTING

(i) To find out the cost of each process in an easy manner without any difficulty and of the final product at short intervals.
(ii) To find out the cost in simple and economical ways than job costing.
(iii) To adopt the standard costing principles effectively in process costing.
(iv) Appropriate allocation of the expenses can be made easily and the costs in each process accurately determined.
(v) Enables to determine the correct valuation of closing inventories.

LIMITATIONS OF PROCESS COSTING

(i) It is based on the historical cost system. So, the available cost information may not be useful for further important organisational decision making.
(ii) The entire process costing system is based on the average cost methods. But average costs do not always reflect the true costs.
(iii) Any of the unfinished products which are available in any process at the end of the period are expressed in equivalent production units. It develops subjective element in scientific cost determination.
(iv) Frequently it is very difficult to estimate the normal quantity loss in process.
(v) Process costing system does not evaluate the efforts of individual workers or supervisors.

DIFFERENCES BETWEEN PROCESS COSTING AND JOB COSTING

Process Costing

Process costing means finding out the cost of product at each process or stages of the production.

Job Costing

Job costing is a method of cost ascertainment in industries engaged in different jobs. Under this method, costs are collected and accumulated for each job or operation or project separately.

Process Costing	*Job Costing*
In the process costing, the production is a continuous flow and the products are being homogenous.	Under job costing, production is carried out as against the specific orders.
Each and every process is related to another process. So, products lose their individuality.	Each job is separate and independent.
Costs are calculated at the end of the specific cost period.	Costs are calculated when a particular job is completed.

Cost of one process being transferred to the next process is a usual feature.	Here, there is no transfer of costs from one job to another.
Normally, the production is continuous so there is work in progress at the beginning and at closing.	There may or may not be work in progress at opening or closing in an accounting period.
Production is standardized and stable, therefore control is easier.	Cost control is comparatively more difficult because each job needs more managerial attention.

Process Cost Accounting Procedure

(i) Prepare separate account for each process. It is called process account.//
(ii) All the direct and indirect expenses are debited to the respective processes.//
(iii) Input (Raw material) introduced are entered in the first process account.//
(iv) The total cost of one process is transferred to the next process as an initial cost till the production is completed.//
(v) If any Normal Loss, Abnormal Loss, Normal Gain and Abnormal Gain arises, it should be treated properly.

Specimen Form of Process I A/c

Particulars	Cost Per Unit Rs.	Total Cost Rs.	Particulars	Cost Per Unit Rs.	Total Cost Rs.
To input (Raw Material Introduce)	xx	xx	By Transfer to Process II A/c	xx	xx
To Direct Wages		xx			
To Direct Expenses		xx			
To Production Overheads		xx			
	xx	xx		xx	xx

Specimen Form of Process II A/c

Particulars	Cost Per Unit Rs.	Total Cost Rs.	Particulars	Cost Per Unit Rs.	Total Cost Rs.
To Transfer from process I A/c	xx	xx	By Loss of weight (Normal Loss)	xx	xx
To Direct Material		xx	By Sale of Scrap	xx	xx
To Direct Wages		xx	By Abnormal Loss	xx	xx
To Abnormal Gain		xx	By Transfer to Process III A/c	xx	xx
	xx	xx		xx	xx

Specimen Form of Process III A/c

Particulars	Cost Per Unit Rs.	Total Cost Rs.	Particulars	Cost Per Unit Rs.	Total Cost Rs.
To Transfer from process II A/c	xx	xx	By Normal Loss	xx	xx
To Material		xx	By Abnormal Loss	xx	xx
To Direct Labour		xx	By Finished Stock	xx	xx
To Manufacturing Expenses		xx			
	xx	xx		xx	xx

Process Losses

The Process Losses can be classified into (i) Normal process Loss, (ii) Abnormal process Loss.

Normal Process Loss. The amount of loss which is unavoidable on account of inherent nature of production. This loss is quite expected under normal conditions.

Normal Loss is generally calculated as a certain percentage of input. But sometimes, such a loss is due to loss of weight, say due to evaporation or other action. In this regard, such wastage is not physically present, obviously it cannot have any value. But, anyhow, normal loss is physically present in the form of scrap; it may have some value, so it should be credited to the process account.

Abnormal Process Loss. Any loss arising due to any of the unforeseen factors, which is over and above the Normal Loss is termed as Abnormal Loss. It arises due to carelessness, machine breakdown, use of defective material and so on.

Simply, Actual Loss is more than the estimated normal loss and the difference may be categorised as Abnormal Loss. Abnormal Loss account is debited with the quantity and the cost therefore process account is credited.

(i) *Formula For Abnormal Loss*

$$\frac{\text{Normal Cost of Normal Production}}{\text{Normal Output}} \times \text{Units of Abnormal Loss}$$

(ii) *Abnormal Gain*

Abnormal gain arises when the actual loss is less than the estimated normal loss and the difference may be treated as abnormal gain.

$$\frac{\text{Normal Cost of Normal Output}}{\text{Units of Normal Output}} \times \text{Units of Abnormal Gain}$$

(iii) *Value of Abnormal Wastage*

$$\frac{\text{Normal Cost of Normal Output}}{\text{Normal Output}} \times \text{Abnormal Loss}$$

Problem 1. *A product passes through two distinct processes A and B and then to finished stock. The output of A, passes direct to B and that of B passes to finished stock. From the following information you are required to prepare process account.*

Particulars		Process A	Process B
Material Consumed	(Rs)	12,000	6,000
Direct Labour	(Rs)	14,000	8,000
Manufacturing Expenses	(Rs)	4,000	4,000
Input in Process A		10,000 (units)	—
Input in Process A	(Rs)	10,000 (value)	—
Output (units)		9,400	8,300
Normal Wastage		5%	10%
Value of Normal Wastage (per 100 units)	(Rs)	8	10

No opening or closing stock is held in the process.

[MBA Anna Dec 2003] [B.Com, Madurai]

Solution :

Process A Account

Particulars	Units	Amount Rs.	Particulars	Units	Amount Rs.
To Input	10,000	10,000	By Normal Wastages	500	40
To Material Consumed		12,000	By Abnormal Wastage	100	421
To Director Labour		14,000	By Transfer to Process B A/c	9,400	39,539
To Manufacturing Expenses		4,000			
	10,000	40,000		10,000	40,000

$$\left[\text{Rs. } 40,000 - 40 = \frac{39,960}{9,500} \times 100 = \text{Rs. } 420.6 \right] \text{ i.e., Rs. } 421$$

Process B Account

Particulars	Units	Amount Rs.	Particulars	Units	Amount Rs.
To Process A A/c	9,400	39,539	By Normal Wastages	940	94
To Material Consumed		6,000	By Abnormal Wastage	160	1,087
To Director Labour		8,000	By Finished stock A/c @ Rs.6.80	8,300	56,358
To Manufacturing Expenses		4,000			
	9,400	57,539		9,400	57,539

PROCESS COSTING

Problem 2. *50 units are introduced into process at a cost of Rs. 50. The total additional expenditure incurred by the process is Rs. 30. Of the units introduced 10% are normally spoilt in the course of manufacture but these possess a scrap value of Rs. 0.25 each. Owing to an accident, only 40 units are produced. You are required to prepare process account.*

[MBA Anna Dec 2002] [B.Com Kerala May 86]

Solution :

Process Account

	Units	Amount Rs.		Units	Amount Rs.
To Material Introduced @ Re 1 per unit	50	50	By Normal Loss 50 × 10/100 = 5 × 0.25	5	1.25
To Additional Direct Expenditure		30	By Abnormal Loss (5 × 1.75)	5	8.75
			By Output Transferred to next process (40 × 1.75)	40	70.00
	50	80		50	80.00

Workings :

(i) Normal output 50 – 5 = 45
   Actual output   40
   Abnormal Loss   5 Units

(ii) Cost per unit = $\dfrac{80 - 1.25}{45}$ = Rs. 1.75

Problem 3. *In process A, 100 units of raw materials were introduced at a cost of Rs. 1,000. The other expenditure incurred by the process is Rs. 600. Of the units introduced, 10% are normally scraped in the course of manufacture and they possess a scrap value of Rs. 7 per unit. The output of process A was only 75 units. Calculate the value of abnormal loss.* [MBA Anna Jan 2005]

Solution :

Process A Account

Particulars	Units	Amount Rs.	Particulars	Units	Amount Rs.
To Materials	100	1,000	By Normal Loss	10	70
To Other Expenses		600	By Abnormal Loss	15	255
			By Process B A/c @ Rs.17	75	1,275
	100	1,600		100	1,600

Workings :

Value of Abnormal Wastage = $\dfrac{\text{Normal Cost of Normal Output}}{\text{Normal Output}}$ × Abnormal Loss

Normal Cost = Rs 1,600 – 70 = Rs. 1,530

Amount of Abnormal Units = $\dfrac{1{,}530}{90} \times 15 = 255$

Amount of Normal Units = $\dfrac{1{,}530}{90} \times 75 = 1{,}275$

Problem 4. *In process A, 100 units of raw materials were introduced at a cost of Rs. 1,000. The other expenditure incurred by the process was Rs. 602. Of the units introduced, 10% are normally lost in the course of manufacture and they possess a scrap value of Rs. 3 each. The output of process A was only 75 units. Prepare process A Account and Abnormal Loss account.*

[B.Com Madras]

Solution :

Process A Account

Particulars	Units	Amount	Particulars	Units	Amount
To Raw Materials	100	1,000	By Normal Loss 10% of 100 units @ Rs.3 each	10	30
To Other Expenses		602	By Abnormal Loss	15	262
			By Process B (output)	75	1,310
	100	1,602		100	1,602

Working Notes :

Units entered	100
Less : Normal loss	10
Normal output	90
Actual output	75
Units of Abnormal loss	15

Value of Abnormal Loss

$= \dfrac{\text{Normal Cost of Normal Output}}{\text{Normal Output}} \times \text{Units of Abnormal Loss}$

$= \dfrac{1{,}572}{90} \times 15 = 262 \quad \left[\dfrac{1{,}602 - 30}{100 - 10} \times 15\right]$

Abnormal Loss Account

Particulars	Units	Amount Rs.	Particulars	Units	Amount Rs.
To Process	15	262	By Cash (Scrap value of Loss @ Rs. 3)	15	45
			By Costing P.L A/c		217
	15	262		15	262

PROCESS COSTING

Problem 5. *The following details have been extracted from the costing records of an oil mill for the year ended 30.6.1996. The product passes through two distinct processes A and B and then to finished stock. It is known from the past experience that wastage occurs in the process as under.*

In process A 5% of the units entering and in process B, 10% of the units entering.

The scrap value of the wastage in process A is Rs 8 per 100 units and in process B is Rs 10 per 100 units.

The process figures are as follows.

	A Rs.	B Rs.
Material	25,000	10,000
Wages	30,000	20,000
Manufacturing Expenses	10,000	10,000
Factory Lighting	5,000	5,000
Sundry Expenses	5,000	-
5,000 units were introduced into process A costing	25,000	-

The output were
From process A : 4,700 units
From process B : 4,150 units
Prepare process cost – Accounts showing cost of output per unit.

[B.Com Bangalore May 1987]

Solution :

Process A Account

	Units	TC Rs.		Units	TC Rs.
To Units Introduced	5,000	25,000	By Wastage 5% of 5,000 tonnes	250	20
To Materials		25,000	By Abnormal Loss	50	1,052
To Wages		30,000	By Output Transferred to B	4,700	98,928
To Manufacturing exp.		10,000			
To Factory Lighting		5,000			
To Sundry Expenses		5,000			
	5,000	1,00,000		5,000	1,00,000

NOTE :

(i) Normal Output 5,000 – 250 units = 4,750
   Actual Output = 4,700
   Abnormal Loss = 50 units

(ii) Cost per unit

$$\frac{\text{Total Cost} - \text{Value of Normal Wastage}}{\text{Normal Output}}$$

$$\frac{1,00,000 - 20}{4,750} = \frac{99,980}{4,750} = Rs.\ 21.0484$$

$$\text{Abnormal Loss} = 50 \times 21.0484 = 1,052$$

$$\text{Output} = 4,700 \times 21.0484 = 98,928$$

Process B Account

	Units	TC Rs.		Units	TC Rs.
To Output from Process A	4,700	98,928	By Normal Wastage 10% of 4,700 tonnes	470	47
To Materials		10,000	By Abnormal Loss	80	2,721
To Wages		20,000	By Finished Stock	4,150	1,41,160
To Sundry expenses		5,000			
To Manufacturing Expenses		10,000			
	4,700	1,43,928		4,700	1,43,928

Workings :

(i) Normal output 4700 − 470 = 4,230
   But Actual output = 4,150
   Abnormal Loss = 80

(ii) Cost per unit $= \dfrac{1,43,928 - 47}{4,230} = \dfrac{1,43,881}{4,230}$
   = Rs. 34.0144 per unit
   Abnormal Loss = 80 × 34.0144
   = 2,721

(iii) Value of Finished Stock
   Output × Cost per unit = 4,150 × 34.0144
   = 1,41,160

Problem 6. *2,000 units costing Rs. 4 per unit were introduced to process I. Labour costs and other expenses were Rs. 1,080 and Rs. 120 respectively. Its output was 1,900 units. The normal scrap was 10% of the input and had a realisable value of Re. 1 per unit. Prepare process I Account, Normal Loss Account and Abnormal Gain Account.* [B.Com Delhi 1994]

Solution :

Process I Account

	Units	TC Rs.		Units	TC Rs.
To Raw Materials	2,000	8,000	By Normal Loss	200	200
To Labour		1,080	By Transfer to Process II	1,900	9,500
To Other Costs		120			
To Abnormal Gain	100	500			
	2,100	9,700		2,100	9,700

PROCESS COSTING

$$\text{Cost per unit} = \frac{9{,}200 - 200}{2{,}000 - 200} = 5.00$$

Value of Output = 1,900 × 5 = 9,500
Value of Abnormal Gain = 100 × 5 = 500

Normal Loss Account

Particulars	Units	Amount	Particulars	Units	Amount
To Process	200	200	By Sale of Scrap	100	100
			By Abnormal Gain (Short fall in Scrap Value)	100	100
	200	200		200	200

Abnormal Gain Account

Particulars	Units	Amount	Particulars	Units	Amount
To Normal Loss	100	100	By Process I	100	500
To P & L A/c	—	400			
	100	500		100	500

Problem 7. *Make out the necessary accounts from the following details :*

		Process A	Process B
Materials	(Rs.)	30,000	3,000
Labour	(Rs.)	10,000	12,000
Overheads	(Rs.)	7,000	8,600
Input (units)		20,000	17,500
Normal Loss		10%	4%
Sale of wastage per unit		Re. 1	Re. 2

There was no opening or closing stock or work in progress. Final output from process B was 17,000 units.

[B.Com Calcutta]

Solution :

Process A Account

Particulars	Units	Amount Rs.	Particulars	Units	Amount Rs.
To Material	20,000	30,000	By Normal Loss (10%)	2,000	2,000
To Labour	—	10,000	By Abnormal Loss	500	1,250
To Overheads	—	7,000	By Process B A/c @ Rs. 2.50	17,500	43,750
	20,000	47,000		20,000	47,000

Workings :

$$\text{Cost per unit} = \frac{\text{Total Process Cost} - \text{Scrap Value from Normal Loss}}{\text{Input} - \text{Normal Loss}}$$

$$= \frac{47,000 - 2,000}{20,000 - 2,000} = 2.50$$

Abnormal Wastages (in units)

Input	=	20,000
Less : Normal Wastage 10%	=	2,000
Normal Output	=	18,000
Less : Actual Output	=	17,500
Abnormal Wastage	=	500

Process B Account

Particulars	Units	Amount Rs.	Particulars	Units	Amount Rs.
To Process A A/c	17,500	43,750	By Normal Loss 4%	700	1,400
To Materials		3,000			
To Labour	-	12,000	By Finished stocks	17,000	66,735
To Overheads	-	8,600			
To Abnormal Gain	200	785			
	17,700	68,135		17,700	68,135

$$\text{Cost of Abnormal Gain} = \frac{65,950}{16,800} \times 200 = 785$$

$$\text{Cost of Finished Stocks} = \frac{65,950}{16,800} \times 17,000 = 66,735$$

Abnormal Gain = Actual Output − Normal Output
= 17,000 − (17,500 − 4% of 17,500)
= 17,000 − 16,800 = 200 units

Normal Loss Account

Particulars	Units	Amount Rs.	Particulars	Units	Amount Rs.
To Process A A/c	2,000	2,000	By Sale (Process A : 2000 × Re. 1 + Process B 500 × Rs. 2)	2,500	3,000
To Process B A/c	700	1,400	By Abnormal Gain A/c	200	400
	2,700	3,400		2,700	3,400

PROCESS COSTING

Abnormal Loss Account

Particulars	Units	Amount Rs.	Particulars	Units	Amount Rs.
To Process A A/c	500	1,250	By Sales (500 × Re. 1)	500	500
			By Costing P.L & A/c.	-	750
	500	1,250		500	1,250

Abnormal Gain Account

Particulars	Units	Amount Rs.	Particulars	Units	Amount Rs.
To Normal Loss A/c	200	400	By Process B A/c	200	785
To Costing P&L A/c	-	385			
	200	785		200	785

Costing Profit and Loss Account

Particulars	Amount. Rs.	Particulars	Amount Rs.
To Abnormal Loss A/c	750	By Abnormal Gain A/c	385

Problem 8. *Product x is obtained after it passes through distinct processes. You are required to prepare process accounts from the following information.*

	Total Rs	Process I	Process II	Process III
Materials	15,084	5,200	3,960	5,924
Direct Wages	18,000	4,000	6,000	8,000
Production Overheads	18,000	—	—	—

1,000 units @ Rs.6 per unit were introduced in process I. Production overheads are to be distributed as 100% on direct wages.

Actual Output	Unit	Normal Loss	Value of Scrap per unit Rs.
Process I	950	5%	4
Process II	840	10%	8
Process III	750	15%	10

[B.Com Delhi]

Solution :

Process I Account

Particulars	Units	Amount	Particulars	Units	Amount
To Materials Introduced @ Rs.6 per unit	1,000	6,000	By Normal Loss	50	200
To Materials	-	5,200	By Transferred to process II @ Rs. 20 per unit	950	19,000
To Direct Wages		4,000			
To Production Overheads		4,000			
	1,000	19,200		1,000	19,200

Process II Account

Particulars	Units	Amount	Particulars	Units	Amount
To Transferred from Process I A/c	950	19,000	By Normal Loss	95	760
To Materials		3,960	By Abnormal Loss	15	600
To Direct Wages		6,000	By Transferred to the next process @ 40 per unit	840	33,600
To Production Overheads		6,000			
	950	34,960		950	34,960

Workings : $\left[\text{Abnormal Loss} = \dfrac{34{,}960 - 760}{950 - 95} \times 15 = 600 \right]$

Process III Account

Particulars	Units	Amount	Particulars	Units	Amount
To Transferred from Process II	840	33,600	By Normal Loss	126	1,260
To Materials		5,924	By Transferred to finished goods @ 76 per unit	750	57,000
To Direct Wages		8,000			
To Production Overheads		8,000			
To Abnormal Gain @ Rs. 76 per units	36	2,736			
	876	58,260		876	58,260

Workings : Abnormal Gain = $\dfrac{55{,}524 - 1{,}260}{840 - 126}$ = Rs. 76 × 36 units = Rs. 2,736.

Abnormal Loss Account

Particulars	Amount	Particulars	Amount
To Process II A/c	600	By Cash (Sale of Scrap of Abnormal Loss of unit)	120
		By Costing P & L A/c	480
	600		600

PROCESS COSTING

Abnormal Gain Account

Particulars	Rs.	Particulars	Rs
To Process III	360	By Process III	2,736
To costing Profit and Loss Account	2,376		
	2,736		2,736

Workings :

Loss of units : 90. On sale of 90 units amount recovered is Rs. 900.
Therefore, 1,260 – 900 = Rs. 360 is debited.

Problem 9. *A product passes through three processes A, B and C. 10,000 units at a cost of Re.1 were issued to process A. The other direct expenses were :*

	Process A Rs.	Process B Rs.	Process C Rs.
Sundry Materials	1,000	1,500	1,480
Direct Labour	5,000	8,000	6,500
Direct Expenses	1,050	1,188	1,605

The wastage of Process A was 5% and Process B 4%. The wastage of process A was sold at Rs. 0.25 per unit and that of B at Rs. 0.50 per unit and that of C at Rs. 1.00 per unit. The overhead charges were 168% of direct labour. The final product was sold at Rs. 10 per unit, fetching a profit of 20% on sales. Find the percentage of wastage in process C.

[B.Com Andhra]

Solution :

Process A Account

Particulars	Units	Amount Rs.	Particulars	Units	Amount Rs.
To Units introduced	10,000	10,000	By Normal Wastage	500	125
To Sundry Materials		1,000	By Process B	9,500	25,325
To Direct Labour		5,000			
To Direct Expenses		1,050			
To Overheads		8,400			
	10,000	25,450		10,000	25,450

Process B Account

Particulars	Units	Amount Rs.	Particulars	Units	Amount Rs.
To Process A	9,500	25,325	By Normal Wastage	380	190
To Sundry Materials		1,500	By Process C	9,120	49,263
To Direct Labour		8,000			
To Direct Expenses		1,188			
To Overheads		13,440			
	9,500	49,453		9,500	49,453

Process C Account

Particulars	Units	Amount Rs.	Particulars	Units	Amount Rs.
To Process B	9,120	49,263	By Normal Wastage	456	456
To Sundry Materials		1,480	By Sales Rs. 10	8,664	86,640
To Direct Labour		6,500			
To Direct Expenses		1,605			
To Overheads		10,920			
	9,120	69,768		9,120	87,096

Normal Wastage is Computed as follows :

Total cost in process C = Rs. 69,768

Suppose, No.of Normal Wastage units = x

Sales Value of Waste one is = Re. 1 i.e., x units @ Re. 1 per unit

Total Cost – Sales Value of Normal Wastage

= Rs. 69,768 – Re. x i.e., Total Cost – No.of units produced × cost per unit.

When selling price is Rs. 10 per unit, the cost per unit is

Rs. 10–20% = Rs.8 per unit

Thus total cost = $(9,120 - x) \times$ Rs. 8

= 72,960 – Rs. 8x

$69,768 - x = 72,960 - 8x$

$8x - x = 72,960 - 69,768$

$7x = 3,192$

$x = 456$

Therefore percentage of Normal wastage

$$= \frac{456}{9,120} \times 100 = 5\%.$$

❑❑❑

12
Activity Based Costing

Activity Based Costing is the new approach of cost accounting. Under the Activity Based Costing costs are first found out to the activities and then to products. It focuses on activities performed to produce products.

Under the traditional costing, there is an absence of appropriate basis of allocation of cost and that should be left to the decision of the cost accountant to select appropriate basis for allocation. In accurate cost information, thus provided by the traditional costing, methods may lead to wrong decisions if used for control purposes or determination of selling price.

Professor Vipul pointed out, "Activity Based Costing had its genesis in the increasing importance of indirect Costs in the manufacturing operations. The direct processing costs which are easier to handle are being relegated to the background with each passing day due to automation. In this modern scenario, where indirect costs for outweighing the direct processing costs in many a situations, one cannot be content with rough and ready methods of yester years in dealing with the indirect costs."

The present industrial organisation follows an advanced manufacturing technology in the allocation. Because the traditional costing system will not be suitable for the present high tech manufacturing industries.

The CIMA official Terminology defines Activity Based Costing as "Cost attribution to cost units on the basis of benefit received from indirect activities *e.g.,* ordering, setting up, assuring quality".

CONCEPT OF ACTIVITY BASED COSTING

In the present globalisation era, each and every organisation will successfully compete its products in the international market only with the efficient application of Activity Based Costing. An organisation, to hold itself on the market, has to manage properly the value chain at each stage. Value added at all the stages are to be compared with the costs associated and on that basis decisions are implemented, which enables cutting of the unnecessary activities and adding the new activities. In order to improve the quality of managerial decisions, Activity Based Costing supplies exact cost information to the management.

IMPLEMENTATION OF ACTIVITY BASED COSTING

The following are the important steps involved in implementing Activity based Costing to achieve the desired results.

(*i*) Identifying the functional areas involved in the organisation.
(*ii*) To determine the key activities involved in all the functional areas.

(iii) Allocating the common indirect cost to various activities at all the functional areas.
(iv) To determine the most suitable cost driver in each activity under the functional areas of management.
(v) To prepare activity wise expenditure statement.

FUNCTIONAL AREAS OF THE ORGANISATION

(i) Production Management
(ii) Personnel Management
(iii) Sales management
(iv) Repairs maintenance
(v) Administration
(vi) Public Relation and
(vii) Quality Control Management.

Some of the cost drivers in Activity Based costing system are as follows :

(i) Number of receiving orders for the receiving department
(ii) Number of despatch orders for the despatch department
(iii) Number of units
(iv) Amount of Labour cost incurred
(v) Value of materials in a product
(vi) Number of inspections
(vii) Number of parts received per month
(viii) Number of direct Labour hours
(ix) Number of purchasing and ordering hours
(x) Number of Labour transactions
(xi) Number of Customers orders processed
(xii) Number of employees

The following factors are to be considered while selecting cost drivers :

(i) Cost of measurement and
(ii) Degree of correlation between cost drivers and the actual consumption of overhead.

CLASSIFICATION OF ACTIVITIES

Under the production process, activities are identified and classified into different categories or segments. Basically activities are classified into the following four activity categories.

(i) Unit level activities
(ii) Batch level activities
(iii) Product level activities
(iv) Facility level activities

BENEFITS OF IMPLEMENTING ACTIVITY BASED COSTING

The following are the important benefits of implementing activity based costing :

(i) Activity Based Costing provides valuable information to the management to identify the areas of cost reduction. If a company's financial position is not satisfactory, it advises the management to go for lay off measures.

(ii) Now-a-days non-manufacturing costs play a prominent role in the constituent of total cost. Activity Based Costing provides appropriate guidance for the allocation of non-manufacturing cost.

(iii) Activity Based Costing provides accurate cost information which is essential for most of the recent productivity approaches. With the help of these activities overall performance of the organisation will be improved.

(iv) It assists the management to formulate an effective pricing policy.

(v) Activity Based Costing helps the manager to take decisions whether he should get the activity done within the firm or sub contract the same to an outside agency.

(vi) With the help of the Activity Based Costing, cost of each activity is to be determined accurately. It enables the manager to evaluate the performance of transferor and transferee departments.

❏❏❏

13
Inventory Pricing and Valuation

The term inventory generally refers to stock or stock in trade. Inventory includes (i) stock of finished goods (ii) work in progress (iii) raw materials and components. In a trading organisation inventory refers to goods meant for resale or unsold stock. In case of manufacturing organisation, inventory consists of raw materials, semi-finished goods, finished goods and stores.

The Institute of Chartered Accountants of India (ICAI) defines in accounting standard number 2. Inventories as tangible properties held.

(i) Enable to make a sale in the ordinary course of the business.
(ii) In the process of production for such sale
(iii) To be consumed in the production of goods or services for sale including maintenance supplies and consumables other than machinery spares.

Inventory valuation is more essential for the organisation, in order to assess the operating performance and financial position of the company. Normally, inventory valuation is done at the end of the financial year.

OBJECTIVES OF INVENTORY VALUATION

(i) The ultimate object of the inventory valuation is the determination of the true profit earned by the organisation during a particular accounting period.
(ii) To determine the correct financial position of the concern because inventory is shown as the current asset in the Balance sheet. Suppose, it could not be properly valued means it is difficult to determine the correct financial position.

BASES OF INVENTORY VALUATION

(i) *Historical Cost.* Under the historical cost, cost accounting provides a certain rule that the inventory should be valued at cost.
(ii) *Either the Cost or Market Price : Whichever is lower.* Under this method, the inventory is valued at cost or market price whichever is lower.
(iii) *Net Realizable Method.* Net realizable value represents the estimated selling price less cost of the completion. But under this method, the stock is valued at historical cost as the selling price will be lower to a certain extent.
(iv) *Replacement Cost Method.* Under this method inventories are valued at a replacement value. It may be taken as either the market value or reproduction value.

INVENTORY PRICING AND VALUATION

TECHNIQUES OF INVENTORY CONTROL

The following are the important techniques of inventory control normally followed in practice :

    (i) Level setting
    (ii) JIT (Just in time) inventory system
    (iii) Economic ordering quantity
    (iv) ABC (Always better control) analysis
    (v) VED analysis [Vital, Essential, Desirable]
    (vi) Perpetual inventory system
    (vii) Inventory turnover ratio
    (viii) Inventory cost report
    (ix) FNSD analysis
        F : Fast moving items
        N : Normal moving items
        S : Slow moving items
        D : Dead items.

METHODS OF VALUATION OF INVENTORIES

The following methods for pricing material issues are generally followed :

    (i) First in First out method
    (ii) Last in first out method
    (iii) Average cost method
    (iv) Inflated price method
    (v) Specific price method
    (vi) Highest in first out method
    (vii) Base stock method
    (viii) Replacement price method
    (ix) Realisable value method
    (x) Current standard price method
    (xi) Market price method

Problem 1. *The stock of material in hand as on 1st September was 500 units @ Rs. 10 per unit. The following purchases and issues were subsequently made. Prepare the stores ledger account showing how the value of the issues would be recorded under FIFO method.*

Purchases :
    6th Sep   100 units   at Rs. 11
    20th Sep.   700 units   at Rs. 12
    27th Sep.   400 units   at Rs. 13
    13th Oct.   1000 units   at Rs. 14
    20th Oct.   500 units   at Rs. 15
    17th Nov   400 units at   Rs. 16

Issues :
9th Sep. 500 units
22nd Sep. 500 units
30th Sep. 500 units
15th Oct. 500 units
22nd Oct. 500 units
11th Nov. 500 units

[B.Com., Andhra, Madurai]

Solution :

Date	Particulars	Stores ledger Account						FIFO		
		Receipts			Issues			Balance		
		Qty	CPU	TC	Qty	CPU	TC	Qty	CPU	TC
Sep 1	Balance B/d	—	—	—	—	—	—	500	10.00	5000
Sep 6	Goods received	100	11	1100	—	—	—	500	10.00	5000
								100	11.00	1100
Sep 9	Requisition slip. No of Issues	—	—	—	500	10.00	5000	100	11.00	1100
Sep 20	Goods Received	700	12	8400	—	—	—	100	11.00	1100
								700	12.00	8400
Sep 22	Goods issued	—	—	—	100	11.00	1100	300	12.00	3600
					400	12.00	4800			
Sep 27	Goods Received	400	13	5200	—	—	—	300	1200	3600
								400	13.00	5200
Sep 30	Goods issued	—	—	—	300	12.00	3600	—	—	—
					200	13.00	2600	200	13.00	2600
Oct 13	Goods received	1000	14	14,000	—	—	—	200	13.00	2600
								1000	14.00	14000
Oct 15	Requisition Slip	—	—	—	200	13.00	2600	—	—	—
					300	14.00	4200	700	14.00	9800
Oct 20	Goods received	500	15	7,500	—	—	—	700	14.00	9800
								500	15.00	7500
Oct 22	Requisition Slip No	—	—	—	500	14.00	7000	200	14.00	2800
								500	15.00	7500
Nov 11	Requisition slip No	—	—	—	200	14..00	2800	—	—	—
					300	15.00	4500	200	15.00	3000
Nov 17	Goods Received	400	16	6,400	—	—	—	200	15.00	3000
								400	16.00	6400

Value of the stock in hand Rs. 9,400
i.e., 200 × 15 + 400 × 16 = Rs. 9,400

Problem 2. *Prepare stores ledger account from the following transaction under FIFO method :*

(1) Jan 1   Received   1000 units   at Rs. 20   per unit
(2) Jan 10 Received   260 units   at Rs. 21   per unit
(3) Jan 20 Issued   700 units
(4) Feb 4   Received   400 units   at Rs. 23   per unit

INVENTORY PRICING AND VALUATION

(5) Feb 21   Received   300 units   at Rs. 25   per unit
(6) Mar 16   issued   620 units
(7) Mar 18   issued   240 units
(8) Mar 21   Received   500 units   at Rs. 22   per unit
(9) Mar 29   issued   380 units

[B.Com PU May 2002]

Solution :

Stores ledger FIFO method

Date	Particulars	Receipts			Issues			Balance		
		Qty	CPU	TC	Qty	CPU	TC	Qty	CPU	TC
Jan 1	Goods received	1000	20.00	20,000	—	—	—	1000	20.00	20,000
Jan 12	Goods received	260	21.00	5,460	—	—	—	1000	20.00	20,000
								260	21.00	5,460
Jan 20	Requisition Slip No	—	—	—	700	20.00	14,000	300	20.00	6,000
								260	21.00	5,460
Feb 4	Goods received	400	3.00	1,200	—	—	—	300	20.00	6,000
								260	21.00	5,460
								400	3.00	1,200
Feb 21	Goods received	300	25.00	7,500	—	—	—	300	20.00	6,000
								260	21.00	5,460
								400	3.00	1,200
								300	25.00	7,500
Mar 16	Goods issued	—	—	—	300	20.00	6000			
					260	21.00	5460			
					60	3.00	180	340	3.00	1020
								300	25.00	7500
Mar 18	Requisition slip No.	—	—	—	240	3.00	720	100	3.00	300
								300	25.00	7500
Mar 21	Goods received	500	22.00	11,000	—	—	—	240	3.00	720
								100	3.00	300
								300	25.00	7500
								240	3.00	720
								500	22.00	11000
Mar 29	Requisition slip No.	—	—	—	100	3.00	300	20	25.0	500
					280	25.0	7000	240	3.00	720
								500	22.00	11000

Value of the stock in hand = $20 \times 25 + 240 \times 3 + 500 \times 22 = 12{,}220$

Problem 3. *From the following transaction, prepare separate stores ledger accounts using the following pricing methods.*

(i) FIFO and   (ii) LIFO

January 1   Opening balance   100 units   @ Rs. 6 each
January 5   Received   500 units   @ Rs. 6 each
January 20   Issued   300 units

February 5   Issued   200 units
February 6   Received   500 units @ Rs. 5 each
March 10   Issued   300 units
March 12   Issued   250 units

[B.A. (Corp) PU 2002]

Solution :

Stores ledger (FIFO)

Date	Particulars	Receipts			Issues			Balance		
		Qty	CPU	TC	Qty	CPU	TC	Qty	CPU	TC
Jan 1	Balance B/d	—	—	—	—	—	—	100	5	500
Jan 5	Goods received	500	6	3,000	—	—	—	100	5	500
								500	6	3,000
Jan 20	Requisition slip	—	—	—	100	5	500	—	—	—
					200	6	1,200	300	6	1,800
Feb 5	Requisition slip	—	—	—	200	6	1,200	100	6	600
Feb 6	Goods received	500	5	2,500	—	—	—	100	6	600
								500	5	2,500
Mar 10	Goods issued	—	—	—	100	6	600	300	5	1,500
					200	5	1000			
Mar 12	Goods issued				250	5	1250	50	5	250

Value of stock in hand is Rs. 250 *i.e.,* [50 × 5 = 250].

Stores ledger (LIFO)

Date	Particulars	Receipts			Issues			Balance		
		Qty	CPU	TC	Qty	CPU	TC	Qty	CPU	TC
Jan. 1	Blance B/d	—	—	—	—	—	—	100	5	500
Jan 5	Goods received	500	6	3,000	—	—	—	100	5	500
								500	6	3,000
Jan 20	Requisition slip	—	—	—	200	6	1,200	100	5	500
								300	6	1,800
Feb 5	Goods requisition	—	—	—	200	6	1,200	100	5	500
								100	6	600
Feb 6	Goods received	500	5	2,500	—	—	—	100	6	600
								100	5	600
								500	5	2,500
Mar 10	Goods requisition	—	—	—	300	5	1,500	100	5	500
								100	6	600
								200	5	1,000
Mar 12	Goods requisition	—	—	—	200	5	1,000	100	5	500
					50	6	300	50	6	300

Value of Stock in hand is Rs. 800 [100 × 5 + 50 × 6 = 800]

INVENTORY PRICING AND VALUATION

Problem 4. *The following is an extract of the record of receipts and issues of sulphur in a chemical factory during Feb 1998.*

    1998 Feb 1 Opening balance 500 tonnes @ Rs. 200
             3 Issue   : 70 tonnes
             4 Issue   : 100 tonnes
             8 Issue   : 80 tonnes
            13 Received from suppliers 200 tonnes @ Rs. 190
            14 Returned from dept 15 tonnes
            16 Issue   : 250 tonnes
            20 Received from suppliers 240 tonnes @ Rs. 190
            24 Issue   : 300 tonnes
            25 Received from suppliers 320 tonnes @ Rs. 190
            26 Issue   : 115 tonnes
            27 Returned from dept. 35 tonnes
            28 Received from supplier 100 tonnes @ Rs. 190

Issues are to be priced on the principle of FIFO. The stock *verifier* of the factory had found a shortage of 10 tonnes on the 22nd and left a note accordingly. Prepare the stores ledger account.

[M.Com, Periyar May 2003]

Solution :

Date	Particulars	Stores ledger (FIFO)								
		Receipts			Issues			Balance		
		Qty	CPU	TC	Qty	CPU	TC	Qty	CPU	TC
Feb 1	Balance B/d	—	—	—	—	—	—	500	200	1,00,000
Feb 3	Issued	—	—	—	70	200	14,000	430	200	86,000
Feb 4	Issued	—	—	—	100	200	20,000	330	200	66,000
Feb 8	Issued	—	—	—	80	200	16,000	250	200	50,000
Feb 13	Goods received	200	190	38,000	—	—	—	250	200	50,000
								200	190	38,000
Feb 14	Returns	15	10	2,850	—	—	—	250	200	50,000
								200	190	38,000
								15	190	2,850
Feb 16	Issued	—	—	—	250	200	50,000	200	190	38,000
								15	190	2,850
Feb 20	Goods Received	240	190	45,600	—	—	—	200	190	38,000
								15	190	2,850
								240	190	45,600
Feb 22	Shortage	—	—	—	10	200	2,000	190	190	36,100
								15	190	2,850
								240	190	45,600
Feb 24	Issued	—	—	—	190	190	36,100	—	—	—
					15	190	2,850			
					95	190	18,050	145	190	27,550
Feb 25	Goods Received	320	190	60,800	—	—	—	145	190	27,550
								320	190	60,800

Feb 26	Issued	—	—	—	115	190	21,850	30	190	5,700
								320	190	60,800
Feb 27	Returned	35	190	6650	—	—	—	30	190	5,700
								320	190	60,800
								35	190	6,650
Feb 28	Goods Received	100	190	19,000	—	—	—	30	190	5,700
								320	190	60,800
								35	190	6,650
								100	190	19,000

Value Stock in hand is Rs. 92,150 [5700 + 60,800 + 6650 + 19000].

Problem 5. *Balaji Industries had an opening stock of 300 units of materials valued at Rs. 600. Receipts and Issues during August 1998 were as follows.*

	Units	Value (Rs)
August 2 Received	200	440
August 4 Issued	150	—
August 6 Received	200	460
August 11 Issued	150	—
August 19 Issued	200	—
August 22 Received	200	480
August 31 Issued	250	—

Show the stores ledger account using LIFO Method. [M.Com (CA) Periyar May 2004]

Solution :

		Stores ledger (LIFO)								
		Receipts			Issues			Balance		
Date	Particulars	Qty	CPU	TC	Qty	CPU	TC	Qty	CPU	TC
Aug 1	Balance B/d	—	—	—	—	—	—	300	2.00	600
Aug 2	Goods Received	200	2.20	440	—	—	—	300	2.00	600
								200	2.20	440
Aug 4	Goods issued	—	—	—	150	2.20	330	300	2.00	600
								50	2.20	110
Aug 6	Goods Received	200	2.30	460	—	—	—	300	2.00	600
								50	2.20	110
								200	2.30	460
Aug 11	Goods issued	—	—	—	150	2.30	345	300	2.00	600
								50	2.20	110
								50	2.30	115
Aug 19	Goods issued	—	—	—	50	2.30	115	—	—	—
					50	2.20	110			
					100	2.00	200	200	2.00	400
Aug 22	Goods received	200	2.40	480	—	—	—	200	2.00	400
								200	2.40	480
Aug 31	Goods issued	—	—	—	200	2.40	480			
					50	2.00	100	150	2.00	300

Value of stock in hand Rs. 300.

INVENTORY PRICING AND VALUATION

Problem 6. *Prepare stores ledger Account from the following information*

Jan	1	Purchased	500 kg	at Rs. 20 per kg
Jan	10	Purchased	300 kg	at Rs. 21 per kg
Jan	15	Issued	600 kg	—
Jan	20	Purchased	400 kg	at Rs. 22 per kg
Jan	25	Issued	300 kg	—
Jan	27	Purchased	500 kg	at Rs. 21 per kg
Jan	31	Issued	200 kg	—

Adopt the Base stock method of issue and ascertain the value of closing stock. Assume Base stock 200 kg.

[B.Com Madurai]

Solution :

Stores ledger (FIFO) – Base stock

Date	Particulars	Receipts			Issues			Balance		
		Qty	CPU	TC	Qty	CPU	TC	Qty	CPU	TC
Jan 1	Balance B/d	500	20	10,000	—	—	—	500	20	10,000
Jan 10	Goods received	300	21	6,300	—	—	—	500	20	10,000
Jan 15	Requisition slip No.	—	—	—	300	20	6000	300	21	6,300
					300	21	6300	200	20	4,000
Jan 20	Goods received	400	22	8,800	—	—	—	200	20	4,000
								400	22	8,800
Jan 25	Requisition slip No.	—	—	—	300	22	6600	200	20	4,000
								100	22	2,200
Jan 27	Goods received	500	21	10,500	—	—	—	200	20	4,000
								100	22	2200
								500	21	10500
Jan 31	Issued	—	—	—	100	22	2200			
					100	21	2100	200	20	4000
								400	21	8400

Value of closing stock of 600 kg is Rs. 12400
[200 kg × Rs. 20 + 400 kg × Rs. 21 = 12,400]

Problem 7. *The following transaction took place in respect of an item of material.*

Date	Receipts Quantity	Rate (Rs)	Issue Quantity
2.09.2000	200	2.00	—
10.9.2000	300	2.40	—
15.9.2000	—	—	250
18.9.2000	250	2.60	—
20.9.2000	—	—	200

Record the above transaction in the stores ledger pricing issues at Simple average method.

Solution :

		Stores Ledgers Simple Average Method							
		Receipts			Issues			Balance	
Date	Particulars	Qty	CPU	TC	Qty	CPU	TC	Qty	TC
2.9.2000	Goods received	200	2.00	400	—	—	—	200	400
10.9.2000	Goods received	300	2.40	720	—	—	—	500	1120
15.9.2000	Issue of material	—	—	—	250	2.20	550	250	570
18.9.2000	Goods received	250	2.60	650	—	—	—	500	1220
20.9.2000	Issue of material	—	—	—	2000	2.50	500	300	720

Problem 8. *You have been asked to calculate the following levels for part No.96867 from the following information given there under.*

    (a) Re-ordering level   (b) Maximum level

    (c) Minimum level   (d) Danger level   (e) Average stock level

The re-ordering quantity is to be calculated from the following data :

    (i) Total cost of purchasing relating to the order = Rs. 20.

    (ii) Number of units to be purchased during the year = 5000.

    (iii) Purchase price per unit including transportation cost = Rs. 50.

    (iv) Annual cost of storage of one unit = Rs. 5.

        Lead times   : Average : 11days

        Average   : 11 days

        Maximum   : 16 days

        Minimum   : 7 days

        Max. for emergency purchases 5 days

        Rate of consumption Average : 15 units per day

        Maximum   : 20 units per day

Answer. a = 300 units, b = 440 units, c = 150 units, d = 60 units, e = 250 units
Re order quantity 200 units.

Problem 9. *A publishing house purchases 2000 units of a particular item per year at a unit cost of Rs. 20.*

The ordering cost per order is Rs. 50 and the inventory carrying cost is 25%.

Find the optimal order quantity and the minimum total cost including purchase cost.

If 3% discount is offered by the supplier for the purchase in lots of 1000 or more, should the publishing house accept the offer ?   [CS Inter]

Solution :

    Optimal order quantity on EOQ = $\sqrt{\dfrac{2CO}{I}}$

    C = Annual consumption *i.e.,* 2000 units

    O = Cost of placing an order *i.e.,* Rs. 50/-; Annual carrying cost per unit = Rs. 5
        [*i.e.,* 25% of Rs. 20]

INVENTORY PRICING AND VALUATION

$$= \left[\frac{25}{100} \times 20 = 5\right]$$

$$= \sqrt{\frac{2 \times 2000 \text{ units} \times \text{Rs. } 50}{\text{Rs. } 5}} = 200 \text{ units.}$$

(i) Computation of Total cost (without discount)

Number of orders to be placed for getting 2000 units @ 200 units per order 2000/200	=	10 orders
Average inventory $\left(\dfrac{200 \text{ units per order}}{2}\right)$	=	100 units
Purchase price of 2000 units @ Rs. 20	Rs.	40,000
Ordering cost (10 orders @ Rs. 50)	Rs.	500
Carrying cost for 100 units (100 × 5)	Rs.	500
Total cost	Rs.	41,000

(ii) Computation of total cost with 3% Discount (Purchase order quantity is of 1000 units)

Unit cost	Rs.	20.00
Less : Discount 3%	Rs.	0.60
	Rs.	19.40

Lot size 1000 units		
No. of orders for 2000 units @ 1000 units		2 orders
Average inventory $\left(\dfrac{1000 \text{ units}}{2}\right)$		500 units
Purchase cost for 2000 units × Rs. 19.40	Rs.	38,800
Ordering cost for 2 orders @ Rs. 50	Rs.	100
Carrying cost for average inventory 500 units of Rs. 19.40 $\left(500 \times 19.40 \times \dfrac{25}{100}\right)$	Rs.	2,425
Total cost	Rs.	41,325

Based on the above calculation the supplier's offer of 3% discount should not be accepted because it will increase cost by Rs. 325/- as compared to the economic order quantity of 200 units.

Problem 10. *From the following Data find out Economic ordering quantity*

Annual usage	:	8000 units
Cost of material per unit	:	Rs. 20
Cost of placing and receiving one order	:	Rs. 60
Annual carrying cost of one unit	:	10% of inventory value

Solution :

Formula for the calculation of economic ordering quantity : $EOQ = \sqrt{\dfrac{2CO}{I}}$

C = Annual usage of material *i.e.,* 8000 units
O = Cost of placing one order *i.e.,* Rs. 60/-
I = Annual carrying cost per unit $\dfrac{20 \times 10}{100} = 2$

$EOQ = \sqrt{\dfrac{2 \times 8{,}000 \times 60}{2}}$

= 692 units.

Problem 11. *Find out the economic ordering quantity from the following particulars :*
Annual usage : Rs. 2,40,000
Cost of placing and receiving one order : Rs. 120
Annual carrying cost 10% of inventory value

Solution :

Formula for the calculation of economic ordering quantity : $EOQ = \sqrt{\dfrac{2CO}{I}}$

C = Annual requirement of material in Rupees 2,40,000
O = Cost of placing one order *i.e.,* Rs. 120/-
I = 10% carrying cost

$EOQ = \sqrt{\dfrac{2 \times 2{,}40{,}000 \times 120}{10/100}}$

$= \sqrt{\dfrac{2 \times 2{,}40{,}000 \times 120 \times 100}{10}}$

= Rs. 24,000/-

Problem 12. *Following information relating to a type of material is available :*
Annual Demand : 2400 units
Unit price : Rs. 2.40
Ordering cost per order : Rs. 4.00
Carrying cost : 12% p.a
Interest rate : 10% p.a
Lead time : Half month

Calculate Economic order quantity and total annual inventory cost in respect of the particular raw material.

Solution :

$EOQ = \sqrt{\dfrac{2CO}{I}}$

C = Annual Demand *i.e.,* 2400 units
O = Ordering cost Rs. 4.00/-
I = Carrying cost 12% of unit price

INVENTORY PRICING AND VALUATION

$$EOQ = \sqrt{\frac{2 \times 2400 \times Rs.\ 4}{Rs.\ 2.40 \times 12/100}}$$

= 258 units

Calculation of total inventory cost

Purchase price of 2400 units @ Rs. 2.40 per unit	Rs. 5760.00
Add : Carrying cost $\frac{1}{2} \times 258$ units $\times 2.40 \times \frac{12}{100}$	37.15
Add : Ordering cost of 10 orders @ Rs. 4 per order	40.00
Total Inventory cost	5837.15

NOTE :

$$\text{No. of orders} = \frac{\text{Annual Demand}}{\text{EOQ}}$$

$$= \frac{2400 \text{ units}}{258 \text{ units}}$$

$$= 10 \text{ orders}$$

□□□

14
Standard Costing

The standard cost is a predetermined cost which determines what each product or service should cost under given operational conditions. Simply speaking standard cost is an expected cost of producing one unit.

The efficiency of the management depends upon the effective control of costs. If there is a difficulty to control the costs, it means the organisation automatically invites the risk. So the system of standard costing is the most appropriate way of controlling costs.

DEFINITION

Standard

According to **Prof. Eric. L. Kohler,** *"Standard is a desired attainable objective, a performance, a goal, a model".*

Standard Cost

The Institute of Cost and Management Accountants, England defines standard cost is "a predetermined cost which is calculated from management's standard of efficient operation and the relevant necessary expenditure".

Standard Costing

The Institute of Cost and Management Accountants, England defines standard costing as "The preparation and use of standard costs and the analysis of variances of their causes and the points of incidence".

Historical Costing

Historical costing is the process of accumulating costs after they are incurred in an orderly manner. Costing of actual costs in a systematic manner is known as historical costing.

The ICMA defines historical cost as "the actual cost of acquiring assets, goods and services and historical costing as a "system of accounting in which all values are based on the historical costs incurred. This is the basis prescribed in the Companies Act for published accounts".

Limitations on historical costing are :
   (*i*) It is a post-mortem examination of the actual cost.
   (*ii*) It is not suitable for cost comparison.
   (*iii*) Inaccurate cost determination

STANDARD COST VS BUDGETARY CONTROL

In an organisation the ultimate aim of both standard costing and budgetary control is to maximise the efficiency and managerial control. Both the costing techniques have the predetermined costs and this should be compared with the actual performance and to find out the variance and to take corrective actions. Without standard cost, either preparation of budget or the system of practical budgeting control cannot be achieved.

Similarity between Standard Cost and Budgetary Control

(i) The ultimate object of both techniques is the determination of cost in advance.
(ii) For both of them, certain standards are fixed.
(iii) In both the cases, comparison will be carried out.
(iv) In both the situations, variations are identified and corrective actions are taken care of.

Differences between Budgetary Control and Standard Costing

Budgetary Control	Standard Costing
(i) It is more extensive in its application because it deals with the operations of the entire business.	It is intensive as it is applied to manufacturing of a product or contributing a service.
(ii) Budgets are prepared for sales, production, cash etc.	Standard costing is determined by classifying recording and apportionment expenses to respective cost unit.
(iii) Budgetary control is related to financial accounts.	It is related to cost accounts.
(iv) It can be operated without standards.	It cannot be operated without budget.
(v) It does not require standardisation of products.	It requires standardisation of products.
(vi) Budgets are expressed in total amounts.	Standards are for unit of production.
(vii) Variances are not normally revealed through the accounts.	Variances are revealed through different accounts.

ADVANTAGES OF STANDARD COSTING

(i) It guides the management in formulating price and production policy.
(ii) It facilitates the reduction in clerical and accounting cost and management time.
(iii) It helps to generate profit at higher level, through the comparison of actual cost to the standard costs. If any of the differences are identified, the corrective actions are taken immediately.
(iv) It helps to determine the accurate profit in future.
(v) The principle of management by exception can be made applicable in the business for concentrating its attention on below or above the standards set.
(vi) It helps in effective application of delegation of authority and responsibility. As a result, executives become more responsible as it clearly shows who is responsible for the cost centres.

(vii) It helps to minimise the wastages and losses. Through this higher level productivity can be achieved.
(viii) It creates an atmosphere of cost consciousness among the executives, workers and foremen because the variance analysis fixes responsibility for favourable or unfavourable performances.
(ix) It helps in budgetary control and in decision making.
(x) It facilitates timely cost reports to management and a forward looking aspect is encouraged at all levels of management.

LIMITATIONS OF STANDARD COSTING

(i) Standard costing is an expensive technique for a small level organisation.
(ii) It is costly as the fixing of standards needs advanced professional skills.
(iii) Distinction may not be always possible between controllable and uncontrollable variances, because of responsibility to a particular person or process becomes very difficult.
(iv) The effective utilisation of variances analysis depends mostly on the basis of standards set. And at the same time, setting of correct standards is also very difficult.
(v) Standard costing is not suitable for the industries which produce non-standardized products.
(vi) In the real sense, whenever the organisation fixes the standards, it should affect the freedom of the managers. So they strongly oppose this system.

DETERMINATION OF STANDARDS COSTS

The following preliminary steps are to be taken into account before setting standards for different elements of costs :
(i) Establishment of cost centre
(ii) Classification and codification of accounts
(iii) Types of standards or period of use
(iv) Setting the standards

I. Establishment of Cost Centre

Setting of cost centres is the very first step required before setting of standards. According to The Chartered Institute of Management Accountants, London cost centre is defined as "a location, person or item of equipment (or group of these) for which cost may be ascertained and used for the purpose of cost control". When the organisation establishes the cost centre, the standards are fixed and the variances are analysed. Cost centre is necessary because fixing of responsibility and defining the lines of authority becomes easier.

II. Classification and Codification of Accounts

In a business organisation various kinds of expenses are incurred. However, the actual expenses are classified under suitable heads for the purpose of establishment of codes and

STANDARD COSTING

symbols. Coding is useful for speedy collection, analysis of cost information and mechanical devices.

III. Period of Use

After the classifying and coding of accounts, the next step for the establishment of standard cost is the length of the operating period for which standards are to be used. The different types of standards are normally taken into account while determining the standards.

(a) *Basic Standards.* ICMA, London defines basic standard as "an underlying standard from which a current standard can be developed". Basic standard is set up for some base year and is not changed as material prices and labour rate change.

(b) *Ideal Standard.* Ideal standard is set up under ideal conditions. ICMA defines it as "the standard which can be attained under the most favourable condition possible". It indicates the higher level efficiency of the manufacturing process in the organisation.

(c) *Current Standard.* ICMA, London, defines it as "a standard which is established for use over a short period of time and is related to current conditions". Current standard is a short term standard as it is modified at regular intervals.

(d) *Expected Standard.* Expected standard is otherwise termed as practical standard. ICMA defines the expected standard as "the standard which is anticipated, can be attained during a future specified budget period". Whenever the organisation is setting this type of standards, due weightage is given for all the expected conditions.

(e) *Activity Level.* The quantum of output or the level of activity to be obtained in forthcoming period must be divided clearly before establishing any standards. In this regard the sales potential and production capacity decide the quantum of output to be manufactured within a specified future period. Any of the idle capacity, unutilised capacity, and other key factors should be considered before determining the attainable level of output.

(f) *Organisation for Standard Costing.* For the purpose of achieving successful standard costing system, the organisation should appoint a separate committee. The committee consists of marketing manager, production manager, purchase manager, human resource manager, chief engineer and cost accountant. The committee may supply all information to different departments. They may revise the standards if necessary and finally approve the standards according to the current price level of the economy.

IV. Setting of Standards

After approval of the standards from the committee, the standard cost is determined for each and every element of cost such as direct material, direct labour and overheads. Cost accountant act as a coordinator of these activities and also he ensures that the setting of standards is accurate.

VARIANCE ANALYSIS

Variance means difference. The term variance has been derived from the verb 'to vary' meaning to differ. The real picture of the standard costing to the management is the presentation of variances. In the practical sense, some times standard costing is meaningless because without the predetermination and analysing the variances of cost. In standard costing, variance analysis means investigating the differences between the standard cost and the actual cost. ICWA, London defines variance as "difference between a standard cost and the comparable actual cost incurred during a period".

Simply variance analysis is the process of examining the variances by sub dividing the total variance. Through this way, the organisation can fix responsibility for off-standard performance.

Favourable and Unfavourable Variances

When the actual cost incurred is less than the standard cost, the differences is known as favourable variance. It is also known as positive variance.

When the actual cost incurred is more than the standard cost, the difference is known as unfavourable or adverse variance. It is also known as negative or debit variance.

Controllable and Uncontrollable Variances

Variances are classified into controllable and uncontrollable variances.

Controllable variances are those which arise due to inefficiency of a cost centre *i.e.* individual or department. For example, excess usage of materials, excess time taken by worker etc is the relevant examples of controllable variance.

Uncontrollable variances are those variances which arise due to factors beyond the control of the management or concerned person or department of the organisation. Uncontrollable variances normally arise due to the external factors only. For example, government restrictions, change in the market price etc. Whenever uncontrollable variance arises, no particular individual can be held responsible for it.

The ultimate aim of the standard costing is the effective cost control.

COMPUTATION OF VARIANCES

Normally, the following are the common variances which are computed by the management.
   (*a*) Material variances
   (*b*) Labour variances
   (*c*) Overhead variances
   (*d*) Sales variances.

Computation of the above variances with the help of the following formula.

(a) Material Variances

(*i*) MCV = (SQ × SP) – (AQ × AP)
(*ii*) MPV = (SP – AP) × AQ
(*iii*) MUV or MQV = (SQ – AQ) × SP
(*iv*) MMV = (RSQ – AQ) × SP
(*v*) MYV or MSUV = (SQ – RSQ) × SP

$$RSQ = \frac{\text{Individual of SQ}}{\text{Total of SQ}} \times \text{Total of AQ}$$

STANDARD COSTING

Abbreviations used :

MCV	:	Material Cost Variance
MPV	:	Material Price Variance
MUV OR MQV	:	Material Usage Variance or Material Quantity Variance
MMV	:	Material Mix Variances or
MYV	:	Material Yield Variance
MSUV	:	Material Sub Usage Variance

(b) Labour Variances

(i) Labour cost variance = $(SH \times SR) - (AH \times AR)$

(ii) Labour rate variance = $(SR - AR) \times AH$

(iii) Labour efficiency variance = $(SH - AH) \times SR$

(iv) Labour mix variance = $(RSH - AH) \times SR$

$$RSH = \frac{\text{Individual of SH}}{\text{Total of SH}} \times \text{Total of AH}$$

(v) Labour sub efficiency variance or Labour yield variance = $(SH - RSH) \times SR$

Abbreviations used :

SH : Standard Hours   SR : Standard Rate
AH : Actual Hours   AR : Actual Rate

(c) Overhead Variances

Under the overhead variances the following variances are normally applied.

1. *Overhead Cost Variance*

   Standard cost of actual output – Actual cost.

   $$\text{Standard cost of actual output} = \frac{SC \times AO}{SO}$$

2. *Overhead Budget or Expenditure Variance*

   Standard cost – Actual cost

3. *Overhead Volume Variance*

   (Actual output – Std output) × Std rate per unit.

4. *Overhead Efficiency Variance*

   (Actual output – Std output in actual hours worked) × Std rate per unit.

   Standard output in actual hours

   $$\text{Worked} = \frac{\text{Standard output} \times \text{Actual hours}}{\text{Standard hours}}$$

5. *Overhead Capacity Variances*

   (Standard output in actual hours worked – Std output) × Std rate per unit.

6. *Overhead Calendar Variance (If number of days given in the problem only)*

   (Std output in actual days worked – Std output) × SR per unit.

   $$\text{Standard output in Actual days} = \frac{SO \times A \text{ days}}{S \text{ days}}$$

(d) Sales Variances

1. Sales value variance   : (AQ × AP) – (SQ × SP)
2. Sales price variance   : (AP – SP) × AQ
3. Sales volume variance   : (AQ – SQ) × SP
4. Sales mix variance   : (AQ – RSQ) × SP
5. Sales sub volume variance : (RSQ – SQ) × SP

Abbreviations Used :

AQ : Actual Quantity   SQ : Standard Quantity
AP : Actual Price   SP : Standard Price
RSQ : Revised Standard Quantity

$$\left[RSQ = \frac{SQ}{Total\ SQ} \times Total\ AQ \right]$$

Material Variances

Problem 1. *From the following information compute material variances :*

		Standard			Actual		
		Qty	CPU	Tot	Qty	CPU	TC
Material	A	10	2	20	5	3	15
	B	20	3	60	10	6	60
	C	20	6	120	15	5	75
		50		200	30		150

Solution :

(i) MCV : (SQ × SP) – (AQ × AP)

Material	A	(10 × 2) – (5 × 3)	=	5	(F)
	B	(20 × 3) – (10 × 6)	=	0	
	C	(20 × 6) – (15 × 5)	=	45	(F)
				50	(F)

(ii) Material Price Variance : (SP – AP) × AQ

A	(2 – 3) × 5	=	5	(A)
B	(3 – 6) × 10	=	30	(A)
C	(6 – 5) × 15	=	15	(F)
			20	(A)

(iii) Material Usage Variances : (SQ – AQ) × SP

A	(10 – 5) × 2	=	10	
B	(20 – 10) × 3	=	30	
C	(20 – 15) × 6	=	30	
			70	(F)

STANDARD COSTING   259

(iv) *Material Mix Variance*

	A	(6 – 5) × 2	=	2	(F)
	B	(12 – 10) × 3	=	6	(F)
	C	(12 – 15) × 6	=	18	(A)
				10	(A)

(v) *Material Yield Variances*
(SQ – RSQ) × SP

	A	(10 – 6) × 2	=	8	(F)
	B	(20 – 12) × 3	=	24	(F)
	C	(20 – 12) × 6	=	48	(F)
				80	(F)

NOTE : $\text{RSQ} = \dfrac{\text{Individual of SQ}}{\text{Total of SQ}} \times \text{Total of AQ}$

$A = \dfrac{10}{50} \times 30 = 6$

$B = \dfrac{20}{50} \times 30 = 12$

$C = \dfrac{20}{50} \times 30 = 12$

Problem 2. *From the following particulars compute (a) material cost variance, (b) material price variance, (c) material usage variance.*

Quantity of materials purchased	3000 units
Value of materials purchased	Rs. 9000
Standard quantity of materials required per tonne of output	30 units
Standard rate of material	Rs. 2.50 per unit
Opening stock of material	Nil
Closing stock of material	500 units
Output during the period	80 tonnes [MBA, MCA Madras]

Solution :

(i) MCV (SQ × SP) – (AQ × AP)
         (2000 × 2) – (2500 × 3)
         4000   – 7500 = 3500 (A)

(ii) MPV (SP – AP) × AQ
         (2 – 3)   × 2500 = 2500 (A)

(iii) MUC (SQ – AQ) × SP
          (2000 – 2500) × 2 = 1000 (A)
          AP = 9000/3000 = Rs. 3
          SQ = 80 × 25 = 2000 units
          SP = Rs. 2 per unit

AQ = Material purchased + O.P Stock − Closing Stock
= 3000 + 0 − 500
= 3000 − 500 = **2500 units.**

Problem 3. *The standard material cost for 100 kg of chemical D is made up of :*
Chemical A − 30 kg @ Rs. 4 per kg
Chemical B − 40 kg @ Rs. 5 per kg
Chemical C − 80 kg @ Rs. 6 per kg.
In a batch 500 kg of chemical D were produced over a mix of
Chemical A − 140 kg @ a cost of Rs. 588
Chemical B − 220 kg @ a cost of Rs. 1056
Chemical C − 440 kg @ a cost of Rs. 2860.

How do the yield mix and the price factors contribute to the variance in the actual cost per 100 kg of chemical D over the standard cost ? [B.Com Calicut]

Solution :

Chemical	Standard		Actual	
	Qty	Rate (per kg (Rs.))	Qty	Rate (per kg (Rs.))
A	30 kg	4.00 per kg	28	4.20
B	40 kg	5.00 per kg	44	4.80
C	80 kg	6.00 per kg	88	6.50
	150 kg		160	

Actual price = $\frac{588}{140} \times 1 = 4.20$

= $\frac{1056}{220} \times 1 = 4.80$

= $\frac{2860}{440} \times 1 = 6.50$

(i) MCV : (SQ × SP) − (AQ × AP)

Chemical	A	(30 × 4) − (28 × 4.20)	=	2.40	(F)
	B	(40 × 5) − (44 × 4.80)	=	11.20	(A)
	C	(80 × 6) − (88 × 6.50)	=	92.00	(A)
Total material cost variance			=	100.80	(A)

(ii) MPV : (SP − AP) × AQ

Chemical	A	(4 − 4.20) × 28	=	5.60	(A)
	B	(5 − 4.80) × 44	=	8.80	(F)
	C	(6 − 6.50) × 88	=	44.00	(A)
Total material price variance				40.80	(A)

STANDARD COSTING

(iii) MUV = (SQ − AQ) × SP

Chemical	A	(30 − 28) × 4	=	8	(F)
	B	(40 − 44) × 5	=	20	(A)
	C	(80 − 88) × 6	=	48	(A)
Total material price variance			=	60	(A)

(iv) MMV (RSQ − AQ) × SP

Chemical	A	(32.00 − 28.00) × 4	=	16	(F)
	B	(42.66 − 44.00) × 5	=	6.65	(A)
	C	(85.33 − 88.00) × 6	=	16.00	(A)
Total material mix variance			=	6.65	(A)

NOTE : Computation of RSQ = [Individual of SQ/Total of SQ] × Total of AQ

Chemical A = [30/150] × 160 = 32

B = [40/150] × 160 = 42.66

C = [80/150] × 160 = 85.33

(v) MYV (SQ − RSQ) × SP

Chemical	A	(30 − 32) × 4	=	8.00	(A)
Chemical	B	(40 − 42.66) × 5	=	13.35	(A)
Chemical	C	(80 − 85.33) × 6	=	31.98	(A)
Total material yield variance			=	53.33	(A)

Problem 4. *From the following particulars calculate*
(i) *Material cost variance*
(ii) *Material price variance*
(iii) *Material usage variance.*

Material	Standard		Actual	
	Units	Price Rs.	Units	Price Rs.
A	4040	4	4320	4.80
B	1640	6	1520	7.20
C	1400	8	1520	7.60

[B.Com Delhi]

Solution :

(i) *Material Cost Variance :* (SQ × SP) − (AQ × AP)

Material	A	(4040 × 4) − (4320 × 4.80)	=	4576	(A)
		(1640 × 6) − (1520 × 7.20)	=	1104	(A)
		(1400 × 8) − (1520 × 7.60)	=	352	(A)
Total material cost variance			=	6032	(A)

(ii) *Material Price Variance* : (SP − AP) × AQ

Material	A	(4 − 4.80) × 4320	=	3456	(A)
		(6 − 7.20) × 1520	=	1824	(A)
		(8 − 7.60) × 1520	=	608	(F)
Total material price variance			=	4672	(A)

(iii) *Material Usage Variance* : (SQ − AQ) × SP

Material	A	(4040 − 4320) × 4	=	1120	(A)
	B	(1640 − 1520) × 6	=	720	(F)
	C	(1400 − 1520) × 8	=	960	(A)
Total material usage variance			=	1360	(A)

Problem 5. *The Standard mix of product is :*

> Product x 600 units at 15 paise per unit
> Product y 800 units at 20 paise per unit
> Product z 1000 units at 25 paise per unit

The Consumption was :

> x 640 units at 20 paise per unit
> y 960 units at 15 paise per unit
> z 840 units at 30 paise per unit

Calculate the material variances. [B.Com]

Solution :

	Standard		Actual	
	Qty	Price	Qty	Price
Product X	600	.15	640	.20
Product Y	800	.20	960	.15
Product Z	1000	.25	840	.30
	2400		2440	

(i) *Material Cost Variance (MCV)* : (SQ × SP) − (AQ × AP)

Product	A	(600 × .15) − (640 × .2)	=	38	(A)
Product	B	(800 × .2) − (960 × .15)	=	16	(F)
Product	C	(1000 × .25) − (840 × .30)	=	2	(A)
Total MCV			=	24	(A)

(ii) *Material Price Variance* : (SP − AP) × AQ

Product	A	(.15 − .20) × 640	=	32	(A)
Product	B	(.20 − .15) × 960	=	48	(F)
Product	C	(.25 − .30) × 840	=	42	(A)
Total MPC			=	26	(A)

STANDARD COSTING

(iii) *Material Price Variance* : $(SP - AP) \times AQ$

Product	A	$(600 - 640) \times .5$	=	6	(A)
Product	B	$(800 - 960) \times .20$	=	32	(A)
Product	C	$(1000 - 840) \times .25$	=	40	(F)
		Total MPV		2	(F)

(iv) *MMV* : $(RSQ - AQ) \times SP$

Computation of RSQ

Individual of SQ/Total of AQ × Total of SQ

$$A = \frac{600}{2400} \times 2440 = 610$$

$$B = \frac{800}{2400} \times 2440 = 813.33$$

$$C = \frac{1000}{2400} \times 2440 = 1016.67$$

MMV :

Product A	:	$(610 - 640) \times .15$	=	4.5	(A)
Product B	:	$(813.33 - 960) \times .20$	=	29.33	(A)
Product C	:	$(1016.67 - 840) \times .25$	=	44.16	(F)
		Total MMV	=	10.33	(F)

(v) *MYV* : $(SQ - RSQ) \times SP$

Product A	:	$(600 - 610) \times .15$	=	1.5	(A)
Product B	:	$(800 - 813.33) \times .20$	=	2.67	(A)
Product C	:	$(1000 - 1016.67) \times .25$	=	4.17	(A)
		Total MYV		8.34	(A)

Problem 6. *The standard material cost to produce one tonne of chemical x is*

   300 kg of material A @ Rs. 10 per kg

   400 kg of material B @ Rs. 5 per kg

   500 kg of material C @ Rs. 6 per kg

During a period 100 tonnes of mixture X were produced from the usage of

   35 tonnes of material A at a cost of Rs. 9000 per tonne

   42 tonnes of material B at a cost of Rs. 6000 per tonne.

   53 tonnes of material C at a cost of Rs. 7000 per tonne.

Calculate material variances. [B.Com Delhi]

Solution :

	Standard		Actual	
	Qty (Tonnes)	Price (Rs.)	Qty (Tonnes)	Price per tonnes (Rs.)
Chemical A	30	10,000	35	9,000
Chemical B	40	5,000	42	6,000
Chemical C	50	6,000	53	7,000
	120		130	

NOTE : Here the standard data are converted on the basis of actual details.

(i) *Material Cost Variances :* $(SQ \times SP) - (AQ \times AP)$

Chemical	A	$(30 \times 10,000) - (35 \times 9000)$			
		$3,00,000 - 3,15,000$	=	15,000	(A)
Chemical	B	$(40 \times 5000) - (42 \times 6000)$			
		$2,00,000 - 2,52,000$	=	52,000	(A)
Chemical	C	$(50 \times 6000) - (53 \times 7000)$			
		$3,00,000 - 3,71,000$	=	71,000	(A)
Total material cost variance			=	1,38,000	(A)

(ii) *Material Price Variance :* $(SP - AP) \times AQ$

Chemical	A	$(10000 - 9000) \times 35$	=	35,000	(F)
Chemical	B	$(5000 - 6000) \times 42$	=	42,000	(A)
Chemical	C	$(6000 - 7000) \times 53$	=	53,000	(A)
Total material price variance			=	60,000	(A)

(iii) *Material Quantity Variance :* $(SQ - AQ) \times SP$

Chemical	A	$(30 - 35) \times 10000$	=	50,000	(A)
Chemical	B	$(40 - 42) \times 5000$	=	10,000	(A)
Chemical	C	$(50 - 53) \times 6000$	=	18,000	(A)
Total material Quantity variance			=	78,000	(A)

(iv) *Material Mix Variance (MMV) :* $(RSQ - AQ) \times SP$

Computation of RSQ :

[Individual of SQ/Total of SQ] × Total of AQ

A = 30/120 × 130 = 32.5
B = 40/120 × 130 = 43.33
C = 50/120 × 130 = 54.17

STANDARD COSTING

Chemical	A	(32.5 − 35) × 10,000	=	25,000	(A)
Chemical	B	(43.33 − 42) × 5,000	=	6,650	(F)
Chemical	C	(54.17 − 53) × 6,000	=	7,020	(F)
Total material mix variance			=	11,330	(A)

(v) **Material Yield Variance (MYV) : (SQ − RSQ) × SP**

Chemical	A	(30 − 32.5) × 10,000	=	25,000	(A)
Chemical	B	(40 − 43.33) × 5,000	=	16,650	(A)
Chemical	C	(50 − 54.17) × 6,000	=	25,020	(A)
Total material yield variance			=	66,670	(A)

Problem 7. *The standard cost of a certain chemical mixture*
  40% materials A at Rs. 25 per kg
  60% materials B at Rs. 36 per kg
A standard loss of 10% is expected in production. During a period there is used
  150 kgs of material A at Rs. 27 per kg
  260 kgs of material B at Rs. 34 per kg
The actual output was 360kgs. Compute all materials variances.

[M.Com Nov 2004 PU]

Solution :

	Standard		Actual	
	Qty (kg)	Price (per kg) (Rs.)	Qty (kg)	Price (per kg) (Rs.)
Material A	160	25	150	27
Material B	240	36	260	34
	400		410	
Less : Standard loss 10%	10		Actual loss 50	
	390		360	

(i) **Material Cost Variance (SQ×SP) − (AQ×AP)**

Material	A	(160 × 25) − (150 × 27)	=	50	(A)
Material	B	(240 × 36) − (260 × 34)	=	200	(A)
Total material cost variance			=	250	(A)

(ii) **Material Price Variance (SP − AP) × AQ**

Material	A	(25 − 27) × 150	=	300	(A)
Material	B	(36 − 34) × 260	=	520	(F)
Total material price variance			=	220	(F)

(iii) **Material Usage Variance : (SQ – AQ) × SP**

Material	A	(160 – 150) × 25	=	250	(F)
Material	B	(240 – 260) × 36	=	720	(A)
Total material usage variance			=	470	(A)

(iv) **Material Mix Variance : (RSQ – AQ) × SP**

RSQ = (Individual SQ/Total of SQ) × Total of AQ

RSQ for Material A : 160/400 × 410	=	164	Kg
RSQ for Material B : 240/400 × 410	=	246	Kg
MMV for A = (164 – 150) × 25	=	350	(F)
MMV for B = (246 – 260) × 36	=	504	A)
Total material mix variance	=	154	(A)

(v) **Material yield variance : (SQ – RSQ) × SP**

Material A	:	(160 – 164) × 25	=	100 (A)
Material B	:	(240 – 246) × 36	=	216 (A)
Total material yield variance			=	316 (A)

Problem 8. *From the following information calculate material mix variance.*

Material	Standard Quantity	Actual Quantity	Price per unit Rs
X	50	45	14
Y	40	35	12
Z	30	40	11

Due to shortage of X, it was decided to reduce its consumption by 10 and increase the consumption of Y and Z by 6 and 4 respectively. [MBA Madras]

Solution :

Material mix variance : (RSQ – AQ) × SP

RSQ = (Individual of SQ/Total of SQ) × Total of AQ

Material X : $\frac{50}{120} \times 120$	=	50 units	
Less : Reduction in consumption	=	10 units	
		40 units	
Material Y : $\frac{40}{120} \times 120$	=	40 units	
Add : Increase in consumption	=	6 units	
		46 units	
Material Z : $\frac{30}{120} \times 120$	=	30 units	
Add : Increase in consumption	=	4 units	
		34 units	

STANDARD COSTING

Material Mix Variance

Material X (40 − 45) × 14	=	70 (A)
Material Y (46 − 35) × 12	=	132 (F)
Material Z (34 − 40) × 11	=	66 (A)
Total material mix variance	=	4 (A)

Problem 9. *From the following information calculate the material mix variance.*

Material	Standard	Actual
A	200 units @ Rs. 12	160 units @ Rs. 13
B	100 units @ Rs. 10	140 units @ Rs. 10

Due to shortage of material A, it was decided to reduce consumption of A by 15% and increase that of material B by 30%. [M.Com (CA) 2004 PU, MBA Madras]

Solution :

Material mix variance : (RSQ − AQ) × SP

RSQ = (Individual of SQ/Total of SQ) × Total of AQ

Material A : $\frac{200}{300} \times 300$	=	200 units
Less : Reduction in consumption by 15%	=	30 units
$200 \times \frac{15}{300}$	=	170 units
Material B : $\frac{100}{300} \times 300$	=	100 units
Add : Increase in consumption by 30%	=	30 units
	=	130 units
Material mix variance for A (170 − 160) × 12	=	120 F)
B (130 − 140) × 10	=	100 (A)
Total material mix variance	=	20 (F)

Problem 10. *Rubix Ltd is engaged in producing a standard using 60 kg of chemical X and 40 kg of chemical Y. The standard loss of production is 30%. The standard price X is Rs. 5 per kg and of Y is Rs. 10 per kg.*

The actual mixture and yield were as follows :
X 80 kg @ Rs. 4.50 per kg and Y 70 kg @ Rs. 8.00 per kg.
Actual yield 115 kg.
Calculate material variances [Price, usage, yield, mix]. [CS Final]

Solution :

	Standard		Actual	
	Quantity	Price (Rs.)	Quantity	Price (Rs.)
Chemical X	60	5.00	80	4.50
Chemical Y	40	10.00	70	8.00
	100		150	
Less : Standard loss 30%	30		Actual loss 35	
	70		115	

Conversion Table :
  X = 60/70 × 115 = 98.57
  Y = 40/70 × 115 = 65.71

	Standard		Actual	
	Quantity	Price (Rs.)	Quantity	Price (Rs.)
X	98.57	5.00	80.00	4.50
Y	65.71	10.00	70.00	8.00
	164.28		150.00	

(i) *Material Cost Variance :* $(SQ \times SP) - (AQ \times AP)$

  X   (98.57 × 5.00) – (80.00 × 4.50)   =   132.85   (F)
  Y   (65.71 × 10.00) – (70.00 × 8.00)   =   97.1   (F)
  Total material cost variance   =   229.95   (F)

(ii) *Material Price Variance (MPV) :* $(SP - AP) \times AQ$

  Product X :   (5.00 – 4.50) × 80   =   40   (F)
  Product Y :   (10.00 – 8.00) × 70   =   140   (F)
  Total material price variance   =   180   (F)

(iii) *Material Quantity Variance (MQV) :* $(SQ - AQ) \times SP$

  Product X :   (98.57 – 80) × 5   =   92.85   (F)
  Product Y :   (65.71 – 70) × 10   =   42.90   (A)
  Total material quantity variance   =   49.95   (F)

(iv) *Material Mix Variance (MMV) :* $(RSQ - AQ) \times SP$

  RSQ   = (Individual of SQ/Total of SQ) × Total of AQ
  Product X = (98.57/164.28) × 150   =   90
  Product Y = (65.71/164.28) × 150   =   60

STANDARD COSTING

MMV :

Product X	=	(90 – 80) × 5	=	50	(F)
Product Y	=	(60 – 70) × 10	=	100	(A)
Total material mix variance			=	50	(A)

(v) *Material Yield Variance (MYV) : (SQ – RSQ) × SP*

Product A	:	(98.57 – 90) × 5	=	42.85	(F)
Product B	:	(65.71 – 60) × 10	=	57.10	(F)
Total material yield variance			=	99.95	(F)

Problem 11. *The standard mix of a product P is shown below :*
Raw material X 30 units @ Rs. 2 each.
Raw material Y 70 units @ Rs. 3 each.
Standard loss is 10% of input. Actual mix is 34 units of X and 66 units of Y. Rates are the same.
The actual loss is 15% of input. Calculate the material variances. [CS. Inter]

Solution :

	Standard		Actual	
	Quantity	Price (Rs.)	Quantity	Price (Rs.)
Raw material X	30	2	34	2
Raw material Y	70	3	66	3
	100		100	
Standard loss 10%	10		Actual loss 5% 15	
	90		85	

Conversion Table :
X : 30/90 × 85 = 28.33
Y : 70/90 × 85 = 66.11

	Standard		Actual	
	Quantity	Price (Rs.)	Quantity	Price (Rs.)
Raw material X	28.33	2	34	2
Raw material Y	66.11	3	66	3
	94.44		100	

(i) *Material Cost Variance* : $(SQ \times SP) - (AQ \times AP)$

    X $(28.33 \times 2.00) - (34 \times 2.00)$
          $(56.66 - 68)$ =   11.34   (A)
    Y $(66.11 \times 3.00) - (66 \times 3.00)$
          $198.33 - 198.00$ =   .33   (F)

    Total material cost variance   =   11.01   (A)

(ii) *Material Price Variance* : $(SP \times AP) \times AQ$

    X $(2 - 2) \times 34$ =   0
    Y $(3 - 3) \times 66$ =   0
    Total price variance   =   0

(iii) *Material Quantity Variance* $(SQ - AQ) \times SP$

    Material   X $(28.33 - 34.00) \times 2.00$ =   11.34   (A)
    Material   Y $(66.11 - 66.00) \times 3.00$ =   .33   (F)

    Total material quantity variance   =   11.01   (A)

(iv) *Material Mix Variance* : $(RSQ - AQ) \times SP$

RSQ = (Individual of SQ/Total of SQ) × Total of AQ.

Material X : $\dfrac{28.33}{94.44} \times 100 = 29.99$ i.e. 30

Material Y : $\dfrac{66.11}{94.44} \times 100 = 70$

MMV of material   X = $(30 - 34) \times 2.00$ =   8.00   (A)
                            Y = $(70 - 66) \times 3.00$ =   12.00   (F)

Total material mix variance   =   4.00   (F)

(v) *MYV* : $(SQ - RSQ) \times SP$

    X $(28.33 - 30) \times 2.00$ =   3.34   (A)
    Y $(66.11 - 70) \times 3.00$ =   11.66   (A)

Total material yield variance   =   15.00   (A)

NOTE : Standard loss and actual loss given in the problem means we have to prepare the conversion table for our convenience.

Problem 12. *A manufacturing concern which has adopted standard costing furnishes the following information.*

    Standard :

        Material for 70kg finished products : 100 kg

        Price of material Re.1 per kg.

STANDARD COSTING

Actual :
- output : 2,10,000 kg
- Material used : 2,80,000 kg
- Cost of materials : Rs. 2,52,000

Calculate :
(i) Material cost variance
(ii) Material price variance
(iii) Material usage variance. [B.Com Kerala]

Solution :

SQ = For 70 kg of finished product, it requires 100 kg of raw material. So for 2,10,000 kg of output, what is the raw material requirement ?

SQ = (100/70) × 2,10,000 = 3,00,000 kg

SP = Re. 1.00

Actual price per kg = cost/output, i.e., $\frac{2,52,000}{2,80,000}$ = 0.90

Actual quantity = 2,80,000 kg

SQ = 3,00,000   AQ = 2,80,000
SP = 1.00   AP = 0.90

(i) *Material Usage Variance*
(SQ − AQ) × SP
(3,00,000 − 2,80,000) × 1.00 = 20,000 (F)

(ii) *Material Price Variance*
(SP − AP) × AQ
(1.00 − .90) × 2,80,000 = 28,000 (F)

(iii) *Material Cost Variance*
(SQ × SP) − (AQ × AP)
(3,00,000 × 1.00) − (2,80,000 × .90) = 48,000 (F)

Problem 13. *From the following particulars calculate.*
(i) Material Cost Variance
(ii) Material Price Variance
(iii) Material Usage Variance

Standard output	100 units
Standard material per unit	3 kg
Standard price	Rs. 2.00
Actual output	80 units
Actual price	Rs. 2.50
Actual material used	250 kg

[MBA Madras]

Solution :

SQ = 240   SP = 2.00
AQ = 250   AP = 2.50

(i) *Material Cost Variance* : (SQ × SP) − (AQ × AP)
Standard material for actual output = 80 × 3 = 240
i.e., MCV = (SQ × SP) − (AQ × AP)
= (240 × 2.00) − (250 × 2.50)
= 480 − 625 = 145 (A)

(ii) *Material Price Variance*
(SP − AP) × AQ
(2.00 − 2.50) × 250 = 125 (A)

(iii) *Material Usage Variance*
(SQ − AQ) × SP
(240 − 250) × 2 = 20 (A)

Problem 14. *The standard material required to manufacture one unit of product X is 10 kg and the standard price per kg of material is Rs. 2.50. The cost accounts record however reveals that 11,500 kg of material costing Rs. 27,600 was used for manufacturing 1000 units of product X. Calculate :*

(i) *Material cost variance*
(ii) *Material price variance*
(iii) *Material usage variance.*

Solution :

Standard price of material per kg = Rs. 2.50
Standard material requirement to manufacture
one unit of product x is = 10 kg
Standard material for actual output = 1000 × 10 = 10,000 kg.
Actual usage of material = 11,500 kg
Actual cost of material = Rs. 27,600
Actual price of material per kg = $\dfrac{27,600}{11,500}$
= Rs. 2.40

SQ = 10,000   AQ = 11,500
SP = 2.50   AP = 2.40

(i) *Material Cost Variance*
(SQ × SP) − (AQ × AP)
(10,000 × 2.50) − (11,500 × 2.40)
25000 − 27600 = 2600 (A)

(ii) *Material Price Variance*
(SP − AP) × AQ
(2.50 − 2.40) × 11500 = 1150 (F)

(iii) *Material Usage Variance*
(SQ − AQ) × SP
(10,000 − 11500) × 2.50 = 3750 (A)

STANDARD COSTING

Problem 15. *The standard quantity and standard price of raw material used for one unit of product A are given below.*

Material	Quantity	Standard Price
X	2 kgs	Rs. 3 per kg
Y	4 kgs	Rs. 2 per kg

The actual production and relevant data are as follows. Output 500 units of product A.

Material	Total quantity for 500 units	Total cost Rs
X	1200 kgs	Rs. 3900
Y	1800 kgs	Rs. 4000

Calculate : (i) MCV   (ii) MPV   (iii) MUV.

Solution :

Standard quantity means standard quantity for actual production.
For one unit of product A, 2 kg of material X is required.
For 500 units of product A, 1000 kg of raw material X is required.
For one unit of product A, 4 kg of material Y is required.
For 500 units of product A, 4 × 500 = 2000 kg of raw material Y is required.

(i) *MCV : (SQ × SP) – (AQ × AP)*

Material	X	(1000 × 3) – (1200 × 3.25)		
		3000 – 3900	900	(A)
Material	Y	(2000 × 2) – (1800 × 2.50)	500	(A)
		Total MCV	1400	(A)

(ii) *Material Price Variance : (SP – AP) × AQ*

Material	X	(3 – 3.25) × 1200	=	300	(A)
Material	Y	(2 – 2.50) × 1800	=	900	(A)
Total material price variance			=	1200	(A)

(iii) *Material Usage Variance : (SQ – AQ) × SP*

Material	X	(1000 – 1200) × 3	=	600	(A)
Material	Y	(2000 – 1800) × 2	=	400	(F)
Total material usage variance			=	200	(A)

B. Labour Variances

Problem 1. *The standard labour component and the actual labour component engaged in a week for a job are as follows.*

Particulars	Skilled Workers	Semi Skilled Workers	Unskilled Workers
Standard number of workers in the gang	32	12	6
Standard wage rate per hour (Rs.)	3	2	1
Actual number of workers employed in the gang during the week	28	18	4
Actual wage rate per hour Rs.	4	3	2

During the 40 hour working week, the gang produced 1800 standard labour hours of work.

Calculate the different labour variances. [MBA Madras]

Solution :

Category of workers	Standard		Actual	
	Hours	Rate (Rs.)	Hours	Rate (Rs.)
Skilled	1280	3.00	1120	4.00
Semiskilled	480	2.00	720	3.00
Unskilled	240	1.00	160	2.00
	2000		2000	
Loss	Nil		200	
Total Hours	2000	Hours Produced	1800	

(i) 1280/2000 × 1800 = 1152
(ii) 480/2000 × 1800 = 432
(iii) 240/2000 × 1800 = 216

Category of workers	Standard		Actual	
	Hours	Rate (Rs.)	Hours	Rate (Rs.)
Skilled	1152	3.00	1120	4.00
Semiskilled	432	2.00	720	3.00
Unskilled	216	1.00	160	2.00
	1800		2000	
Loss	Nil		(–) 200	
	1800		1800	

STANDARD COSTING

Labour Variance

(i) *Labour Cost Variance : (SH × SR) − (AH × AR)*

Skilled	(1152 × 3.00) − (1120 × 4.00)	=	1,024	(A)
Semiskilled	(432 × 2.00) − (720 × 3.00)	=	1,296	(A)
Unskilled	(216 × 1.00) − (160 × 2.00)	=	104	(A)
Total labour cost variances		=	2,424	(A)

(ii) *Labour Rate Variance : (SR − AR) × AH*

Skilled	(3.00 − 4.00) × 1120	=	1,120	(A)
Semiskilled	(2.00 − 3.00) × 720	=	720	(A)
Unskilled	(1.00 − 2.00) × 160	=	160	(A)
Total labour rate variance		=	2,000	(A)

(iii) *Labour Efficiency Variance : (SH − AH) × SR*

Skilled	(1152 − 1120) × 3.00	=	96	(F)
Semiskilled	(432 − 720)	=	576	(A)
Unskilled	(216 − 160)	=	56	(F)
Total labour efficiency variance		=	424	(A)

(iv) *Labour Mix Variance : (RSH − AH) × SR*

Skilled	(1280 − 1120) × 3.00	=	480	(F)
Semiskilled	(432 − 720) × 2	=	576	(A)
Unskilled	(240 − 160) × 1.00	=	80	(F)
Total labour mix variance		=	16	(A)

> **NOTE :** RSH (Individual of std Hrs/Total of std Hrs × Total of Actual Hrs
> Skilled :   1152/1800 × 2000   =   1,280
> Semiskilled :   432/1800 × 2000   =   480
> Unskilled :   216/1800 × 2000   =   240

(v) *Labour Yield Variance : (SH − RSH) × SR*

Skilled	(1152 − 1280) × 3.00	=	384	(A)
Semiskilled	(432 − 480) × 2.00	=	96	(A)
Unskilled	(216 − 240) × 1	=	24	(A)
Total labour yield variance		=	504	(A)

Problem 2. *The details regarding the composition and the weekly wage rates of labour force engaged on a job scheduled to be completed in 30 weeks are as follows.*

Category of workers	Standard		Actual	
	No. of labours	Weekly wage rate per labourer (Rs.)	No. of labourer	Weekly wage rate per labourer (Rs.)
Skilled	75	60	70	70
Semiskilled	45	40	30	70
Unskilled	60	30	80	20

The work actually has been completed in 32 weeks. Calculate the various labour variances.

Solution :

Category of workers	Standard		Actual	
	Hours	Rate (Rs.)	Hours	Rate (Rs.)
Skilled	2,250	60	2,240	70
Semiskilled	1,350	40	960	50
Unskilled	1,800	30	2,560	20
	5,400		5,760	

(i) *Labour Cost Variance :* $(SH \times SR) - (AH \times AR)$ Rs.

Skilled	$(2250 \times 60) - (2240 \times 70)$	=	21,800 (A)
Semiskilled	$(1350 \times 40) - (960 \times 50)$	=	6,000 (F)
Unskilled	$(1800 \times 30) - (2560 \times 20)$	=	2,800 (F)
Total labour cost variances		=	13,000 (A)

(ii) *Labour Rate Variances :* $(SR - AR) \times AH$

Skilled	$(60 - 70) \times 2240$	=	22,400 (A)
Semiskilled	$(40 - 50) \times 960$	=	9,600 (A)
Unskilled	$(30 - 20) \times 2560$	=	25,600 (F)
Total labour rate variance		=	6,400 (A)

(iii) *Labour Efficiency Variance :* $(SH - AH) \times SR$

Skilled	$(2250 - 2240) \times 60$	=	600 (A)
Semiskilled	$(1350 - 960) \times 40$	=	15,600 (F)
Unskilled	$(1800 - 2560) \times 30$	=	22,800 (A)
Total labour efficiency variance		=	7,800 (A)

STANDARD COSTING

(iv) *Labour Mix Variances* : $(RSH - AH) \times SR$

RSH :	Skilled	$2250/5400 \times 5760$	=	2,400
	Semiskilled	$1350/5400 \times 5760$	=	1,440
	Unskilled	$1800/5400 \times 5760$	=	1,920

Skilled	$(2400 - 2240) \times 60$	=	9,600	(F)
Semiskilled	$(1440 - 960) \times 40$	=	19,200	(F)
Unskilled	$(1920 - 2560) \times 30$	=	19,200	(A)
Total labour mix variance		=	9,600	(F)

(v) *Labour Yield Variance* : $(SH - RSH) \times SR$

Skilled	$(2250 - 2400) \times 60$	=	9,000	(A)
Semiskilled	$(1350 - 1440) \times 40$	=	3,600	(A)
Unskilled	$(1800 - 1920) \times 30$	=	3,600	(A)
Total labour efficiency variance		=	16,200	(A)

Problem 3. *Calculate the labour variances from the following information.*

Standard wages
    Grade X : 90 labourers at Rs. 2 per hour
    Grade Y : 60 labourers at Rs. 3 per hour

Actual wages
    Grade X : 80 labourers at Rs. 2.50 per hour
    Grade Y : 70 labourers at Rs. 2.00 per hour

Budgeted hours 1000; Actual hours 900
Budgeted Gross production 5000 units, Standard loss 20%; Actual loss 900 units.

Solution :

Category of workers		Standard			Actual	
		Hours	Rate (Rs.)		Hours	Rate (Rs.)
Grade X	(90×1000)	90,000	2	900×80	72,000	2.50
Grade Y	(60×1000)	60,000	3	900×70	63,000	2.00
		1,50,000			1,35,000	

Production units	5,000		5,000
Loss 20%	1,000	Actual Loss	900
	4,000		4,100

In order to adjust this standard loss and actual loss we have to prepare another table called Conversion Table.

    Grade X : $90,000/4000 \times 4100 = 92,250$
    Grade Y : $60,000/4000 \times 4100 = 61,500$

Conversion Table

	Standard		Actual	
	Hours	Rate (Rs.)	Hours	Rate (Rs.)
Grade X	92,250	2.00	72,000	2.50
Grade Y	61,500	3.00	63,000	2.00
	1,53,750		1,35,000	

(i) *Labour Cost Variance* : (SH × SR) – (AH × AR)

Grade X : (92,250 × 2.00) – (72,000 × 2.50)	=	4500	(F)
Grade Y : (61,500 × 3.00) – (63,000 × 2.00)	=	58,500	(F)
Total labour cost variance	=	63,000	(F)

(ii) *Labour Rate Variance* : (SR – AR) × AH

Grade X : (2 – 2.5) × 72,000	=	36,000	(A)
Grade Y : (3 – 2) × 63,000	=	63,000	(F)
Total labour cost variance	=	27,000	(F)

(iii) *Labour Efficiency Variance* : (SH – AH) × SR

Grade X : (92,250 – 72,000) × 2	=	40,500	(F)
Grade Y : (61,500 – 63,000) × 3	=	4,500	(A)
Total labour efficiency variance	=	36,000	(F)

(iv) *Labour Mix Variance* : (RSH – AH) × SR

RSH Grade X = 92,250/1,53,750 × 1,35,000	=	81,000	
Grade Y = 61,500/1,53,750 × 1,35,000	=	54,000	
LMV Grade X = (81,000 – 72,000) × 2	=	18,000	(F)
Y = (54,000 – 63,000) × 3	=	27,000	(A)
Total mix variance	=	9,000	(A)

(v) *Labour Yield Variance* : (SH – RSH) × SR

Grade X : (92,250 – 18,000) × 2	=	22,500	(F)
Grade Y : (61,500 – 54,000) × 3	=	22,500	(F)
Total LYV	=	45,000	(F)

Problem 4. *From the data given below calculate labour variances for the two departments*

	Dept. A	Dept. B
Actual gross wages (Direct) (Rs)	2,000	1,800
Standard hours produced	8,000	6,000
Standard rate per hours	.30 paise	.35 paise
Actual hours worked	8,200	5,800

[ICWA Int]

STANDARD COSTING

Solution :

	Standard		Actual	
	Hours	Rate (Rs.)	Hours	Rate (Rs.)
Department A	8,000	.30	8,200	—
Department B	6,000	.35	5,800	—
	14,000		14,000	

> **NOTE :** Here actual rates are not given directly. It should be given in indirect way. When we need the actual rate at that place we apply the following techniques. Instead of actual rate, actual gross wages are given i.e., (AH × AR).

(i) **Labour Cost Variances :** (SH × SR) – (AH × AR)
   Department A   (8000 × .30) – (2000) = 400 (F)
   Department B   (6000 × .35) – (1800) = 300 (F)

(ii) **Labour Rate Variance :** (SR – AR) × AH
   Here actual rate is not given in the problem, so we apply the following formula :
   (SR – AR) × AH : (SR × AH) – (AR × AH)
   Department A   (.30 × 8200) – 2000 = 460 (F)
   Department B   (.35 × 5800) – 1800 = 230 (F)

(iii) **Labour Efficiency Variance :** (SH – AH) × SR
   Department A   (8000 – 8200) × .30 = 60 (A)
   Department B   (6000 – 5800) × .35 = 70 (F)

(iv) **Labour Mix Variance :** (RSH – AH) × SR
   RSH : For A :   8000/14000 × 14000 = 8000
   RSH : For B :   6000/14000 × 14000 = 6000
   Department A   (8000 – 8200) × .30 = 60 (A)
   Department B   (6000 – 5800) × .35 = 70 (F)

(v) **Labour Yield Variance :** (SH – RSH) × SR
   Department A   (8000 – 8000) × .30 = 0
   Department B   (6000 – 6000) × .35 = 0
   (No need to apply LMV, LYV)

Problem 5. ABC Ltd furnishes you the following particulars.
Product X requires 20 hours per unit.
Standard Rate per hour is Rs. 2
Units produced : 4000
Hours taken 76,000 (including 200 hours for power failure) at Rs. 2.10 per hour.

Calculate :
  (i) Direct labour cost variance
  (ii) Direct labour rate variance
  (iii) Direct labour efficiency variance
  (iv) Direct labour idle time variance. [M.Com Madras]

Solution :
  Standard hours : 80.000
  Standard rate : Rs. 2.00
  Actual hours : 76000 (– 200)
  Actual rate : 2.10

  (i) LCV : SH × SR – AH × AR
    (80.000 × 2.00) – (76000 × 2.10) = 400 (F)
  (ii) LRV : (SR – AR) × AH
    (2.00 – 2.10) × 76000 = 7600 (A)
  (iii) LEV : (SH – AH) × SR
    (80,000 – 75800) × 2 = 8400 (F)

NOTE :
  Actual hours = 76000
  Less : Idle time for power failure = 200
                                        75800

  (iv) LITV : (Labour idle time variance)
    Idle time × SR
    200 × 2 = 400 (A)

C. Overhead Variances

Problem 1. *In department A the following data is submitted for the week ended on 31st December.*

  Standard output for 40 hours per week   1400 units
  Standard fixed overhead   1400
  Actual output   1200 units
  Actual hours worked   32 hours
  Actual fixed overhead   1500
  Calculate overhead variances. [CA Inter & MBA]

NOTE : Before attempting to apply formula better we have to prepare following type of table for all the overhead problems.

STANDARD COSTING

Solution :

	Budget	Actual
Output (units)	1400	1200
Cost/Overhead (Rs.)	1400	1500
Hours	40	32

Overhead Variances

(i) *Overhead Cost Variance*
Standard cost of actual output – Actual cost
1200 – 1500 = 300 (A)
[SCAC = SC × AO/SO, i.e., 1400 × 1200/1400 = 1200]

(ii) *Overhead Budget Variance*
SC – AC
1400 – 1500 = 100 (A)

(iii) *Overhead Volume Variance*
(Actual output – Std output) × Std rate per unit
(1200 – 1400) × 1.00 = 200 (A)
Std Rate per unit = SC/So
[i.e., 1400/1400 = Re. 1.00]

(iv) *Overhead Efficiency Variance*
(Actual Output – Std output in actual hours worked) × SR per unit
(1200 – 1120) × 1 = 80 (F)
SO in A.Hrs worked = SO × A.Hrs/SHrs = 1400 × 32/40 = 1120

(v) *Overhead Capacity Variances*
(Std output in actual hrs worked – Std output) × Std rate per unit
(1120 – 1400) × 1 = 280 (A)

> **NOTE :** If number of days are given in the problem only we have to apply the calendar variance, otherwise there is no need to calculate calendar variance.

Problem 2. *Calculate overhead variances from the following data :*

Particulars	Budget	Actual
Fixed overhead for July	Rs. 5000	Rs. 6000
Production in July (Units)	1000	1050
Standard time for 1 unit	10 hours	
Actual hours worked	—	11,000 hrs.

Solution :

	Budget	Actual
Cost/Overhead (Rs.)	5000	6000
Production in units i.e., output	1000	1050
Hours (1000 × 10)	10,000	11000

Overhead Variances

(i) *Overhead Cost Variances*
   Std cost of actual output − Actual cost
   5250 − 5000 = 750 (A)
   [SC of AO = SC × AO/SO = 5000/1050/1000 = 5250]

(ii) *Overhead Budget Variance*
   = (Std cost − Actual cost)
   (5000 − 6000) = 1000 (A)

(iii) *Overhead Volume Variance*
   (Actual output − Std output) × Std rate per unit
   = (1050 − 1000) × 5 = 250 (F)
   [Std Rate per unit = SC/SO = 5000/1000 = Rs. 5]

(iv) *Overhead Efficiency Variances*
   (Act output − Std output in actual hours worked) × SR per unit
   = (1050 − 1100) × 5 = 250 (A)
   [Std output in actual hours worked : SO × AHRS/SHRS = 1000 × 11000/10,000
   = 1100]

(v) *Overhead Capacity Variance*
   (Std output in actual hrs worked − Std output) × SR per unit
   (1100 − 1000) × 5 = 500 (F)

Problem 3. *RAC Ltd has furnished you the following data :*

	Budget	Actual Sep. 1998
No. of working days	25	27
Production in units	20,000	22,000
Fixed overheads (Rs.)	30,000	31,500

Budgeted fixed overhead rate is Re.1 per hour. In Sep. 1998 the actual hours worked were 31,500. Calculate the overhead variances.

Solution :

	Budget	Actual
Number of working days	25	27
Production in units (*i.e.*, output)	20,000	22,000
Cost (Rs.)	30,000	31,000
Hours	30,000	31,500

(i) *Overhead Variance* : (Std cost of AO − AC)
   = (33,000 − 31,000) = 2000 (F)
   [SCAO = SC × AO/SO = 30,000 × 22,000/20,000 = 33000]

(ii) *Overhead Budget Variance* : (SC − AC)
   = (30,000 − 31,000) = 1000 (A)

(iii) *Overhead Volume Variance* : (AO − SO) × SR per unit
   = (22,000 − 2,000) × 1.5 = 3000 (F)
   [SR per unit = SC/SO = 30,000/20,000 = 1.5]

STANDARD COSTING

(iv) *Overhead Efficiency Variance* : (AO − SO in actual hours worked) × SR per unit
= (22,000 − 21,000) × 1.5 = 1500 F
[So in Actual worked = SO × AHrs/SHrs = 20,000 × 31,500/30,000 = 21000]

(v) *Overhead Capacity Variance* : (SO in actual hours worked − So) SR per unit
= (21,000 − 20,000) × 1.5 = 1500 F

(vi) *Overhead Calendar Variance* : [Number of days given in the problem]
(SO in actual days worked − SO) × SR per unit
= (21,600 − 20,000) × 1.5 = 2400 F
[So in actual days worked = SO × A. days/S.days = 20,000 × 27/25 = 21600]

Problem 4. *Calculate overhead variances* :

Particulars	Budget	Actual
No. of working days	20	22
Man hours per day	8000	8400
Output per man hour in unit	1.0	.90
Overhead cost	1,60,000	1,68,000

Solution :

Particulars	Budget	Actual
Number of working days	20	22
Cost	Rs. 1,60,000	Rs. 1,68,000
Hours	8,000	8,400
Output (8000 × 20 × 1)	1,60,000	1,66,320 (8400 × 22 × 0.90)

Overhead Cost Variance

(i) *Overhead Cost Variance* : (SC of AO − AC)
= (1,66,320 − 1,68,000) = 1680 (A)

> **NOTE** : [SC of AO = SC × AO/SO = 1,60,000 × 1,66,320/1,60,000 = 1,66,320]

(ii) *Overhead Budget Variance* : (SC − AC)
= (1,60,000 − 1,68,000) = 8000 (A)

(iii) *Overhead Volume Variance* : (AO − SO) × SR per unit
= (1,66,320 − 1,60,000) × 1
= 6320 (F)
SR per unit = SC/SO = 1,60,000/1,60,000 = 1.00

(iv) *Overhead Efficiency Variance* : (AO − SO in actual hours worked) × SR per unit
= (1,66,320 − 1,68,000) × 1 = 1680 (A)
SO in A.Hrs worked = SO × A.Hrs/S.Hrs = 1,60,000 × 8400/8000 = 1,68,000

(v) *Overhead Capacity Variance* : (SO in Actual Hrs worked − SO) × SR per unit
= (1,68,000 − 1,60,000) × 1
= 8000 (F)

(vi) *Overhead Calendar Variance* : (SO in actual days worked − SO) × SR per unit
= (1,76,000 − 1,60,000) = 16,000 F
[SO in A.days worked = SO × A.days/S.days = 1,60,000 × 22/20 = 1,76,000]

D. Sales Variances

Problem 1. *The budgeted sales for one month and the actual results achieved are as under.*

Product	Qty	Budget Rate (Rs)	Amount (Rs)	Qty	Actual Rate (Rs)	Amount (Rs)
A	1000	100	1,00,000	1200	125	1,50,000
B	700	200	1,40,000	800	150	1,20,000
C	500	500	1,50,000	600	300	1,80,000
D	300	500	1,50,000	400	600	2,40,000
	2500		5,40,000	3000		6,90,000

Calculate sales variances in respect of each product. [MBA 2005 Anna]

Solution :

(i) Sales Value Variance : $(AQ \times AP) - (SQ \times SP)$

Product A	: $(1200 \times 125) - (1000 \times 100)$	= 50,000	(F)
Product B	: $(800 \times 150) - (700 \times 200)$	= 20,000	(A)
Product C	: $(600 \times 300) - (500 \times 500)$	= 7,000	(A)
Product D	: $(400 \times 600) - (300 \times 500)$	= 9,000	(F)
	Total sales value variance	= 32,000	(F)

(ii) Sales Price Variance : $(AP - SP) \times AQ$

Product A	: $(125 - 100) \times 1200$	= 30,000	(F)
Product B	: $(150 - 200) \times 800$	= 40,000	(A)
Product C	: $(300 - 500) \times 600$	= 1,20,000	(A)
Product D	: $(600 - 500) \times 400$	= 40,000	(F)
	Total sales price variance	= 90,000	(A)

(iii) Sales Volume Variance : $(AQ - SQ) \times SP$

Product A	: $(1200 - 1000) \times 100$	= 20,000	(F)
Product B	: $(800 - 700) \times 200$	= 20,000	(F)
Product C	: $(600 - 500) \times 500$	= 50,000	(F)
Product D	: $(400 - 300) \times 500$	= 50,000	(F)
	Total Sales volume variance	= 1,40,000	(F)

(iv) Sales mix variance : $(SQ - RSQ) \times SP$ (RSQ : Revised std Qty)

RSQ

Product A	: $1000/2500 \times 3000$	=	1,200
Product B	: $700/2500 \times 3000$	=	840
Product C	: $500/2500 \times 3000$	=	600
Product D	: $300/2500 \times 3000$	=	360

STANDARD COSTING

Sales Mix Variance

Product A	:	(1200 – 1200) × 100	=	0000
Product B	:	(800 – 840) × 200	=	8,000 (A)
Product C	:	(600 – 600) × 500	=	0000
Product D	:	(400 – 360) × 500	=	20,000 (F)
		Total sales mix variance	=	12,000 (F)

(v) *Sales Sub Volume Variance :* $(RSQ - SQ) \times SP$

Product A	:	(1200 – 1000) × 100	=	20000 (F)
Product B	:	(840 – 700) × 200	=	28000 (F)
Product C	:	(600 – 500) × 500	=	50000 (F)
Product D	:	(360 – 300) × 500	=	30000 (F)
		Total sales sub volume variance	=	1,28,000 (F)

Problem 2. *From the following details find out the sales quantity variances.*

Product	Standard		Actual	
	Quantity	Price (Rs.)	Quantity	Price (Rs.)
R	400	12	300	10
S	400	15	500	16

[MBA Madras]

Solution :

(i) *Sales Value Variance :* $(AQ \times AP) - (SQ \times SP)$

Product A	:	(300 × 10) – (400 × 12)	=	1,800 (A)
Product S	:	(500 × 16) – (400 × 15)	=	2,000 (F)
		Total sales value variance	=	200 (F)

(ii) *Sales Price Variance :* $(AP - SP) \times AQ$

Product R	:	(10 – 12) × 300	=	600 (A)
Product S	:	(16 – 15) × 500	=	500 (F)
		Total sales price variance	=	100 (A)

(iii) *Sales Volume Variance* $(AQ - SQ) \times SP$

Product R	:	(300 – 400) × 12	=	1,200 (A)
Product S	:	(500 – 400) × 15	=	1,500 (F)
		Total sales volume variance	=	300 (F)

(iv) *Sales Mix Variance :* $(AQ - RSQ) \times SP$

RSQ for product R = 400/800 × 800 = 400

S = 400/800 × 800 = 400

Sales Mix Variance

Product R	: (300 – 400) × 12	=	1,200	(A)
Product S	: (500 – 400) × 15	=	1,500	(F)
	Total sales mix variance	=	300	(F)

(v) *Sales Sub Volume Variance : (RSQ – SQ) × SP*

Product R	: (400 – 400) × 12	=	0	
Product S	: (400 – 400) × 15	=	0	
	Total sales sub volume variance	=	0	

Problem 3. *Calculate sales variances from the following data*

Product	Budget		Actual	
	Quantity	Price per unit	Quantity	Price per unit
A	500	40	600	41
B	300	25	200	24
C	200	20	400	22
D	600	30	400	25

Solution :

(i) *Sales Value Variance : (AQ × AP) – (SQ × SP)*

Product A	: (600 × 41) – (500 × 40)	=	4600	(F)
Product B	: (200 × 24) – (300 × 25)	=	2700	(A)
Product C	: (400 × 22) – (200 × 20)	=	4800	(F)
Product D	: (400 × 25) – (600 × 30)	=	8000	(A)
	Total sales value variance	=	1300	(A)

(ii) *Sales Price Variance : (AP – SP) × SQ*

Product A	: (41 – 40) × 600	=	600	(F)
Product B	: (24 – 25) × 200	=	200	(A)
Product C	: (22 – 20) × 400	=	800	(F)
Product D	: (25 – 30) × 40	=	2000	(A)
	Total sales price variance	=	800	(A)

(iii) *Sales Volume Variance : (AQ – SQ) × SP*

Product A	= (600 – 500) × 40	=	4000	(F)
Product B	= (200 – 300) × 25	=	2500	(A)
Product C	= (400 – 200) × 20	=	4000	(F)
Product D	= (400 – 600) × 30	=	6000	(A)
	Total sales volume variance	=	500	(A)

STANDARD COSTING

Problem 4. *Harikan Ltd furnishes the following information relating to budgeted sales and actual sales for March 2002.*

Product	Budget Quantity	Budget Price per unit	Actual Quantity	Actual Price per unit
A	1200	15	880	18
B	800	20	880	20
C	2000	40	2640	38

[CA Inter] [M.Com CA]

Solution :

(i) Sales Value Variance $(AQ \times AP) - (SQ \times SP)$

Product A : $(880 \times 18) - (1200 \times 15)$ =	2,160	(A)
Product B : $(880 \times 20) - (800 \times 20)$ =	1,600	(A)
Product C : $(2640 \times 28) - (2000 \times 40)$ =	20,320	(F)
Total sales value variance =	16,560	(F)

(ii) Sales Price Variance : $(AP - SP) \times AQ$

Product A : $(18 - 15) \times 880$ =	2,640	(F)
Product B : $(20 - 20) \times 880$ =	0	
Product C : $(38 - 40) \times 2640$ =	5,280	(A)
Total sales volume variance =	2,640	(A)

(iii) Sales Volume Variance : $(AQ - SQ) \times SP$

Product A : $(880 \times 1200) \times 15$ =	4,800	(A)
Product B : $(880 \times 800) \times 20$ =	1,600	(F)
Product C : $(2640 - 2000) \times 40$ =	25,600	(F)
Total sales volume variance =	22,400	(F)

(iv) Sales Mix Variance : $(AQ - RSQ) \times SP$

RSQ for A 1200/3200 × 4400 = 1650
B 800/3200 × 4400 = 1100
C 2000/3200 × 4400 = 2750

Product A : $(880 - 1650) \times 15$ =	11,550	(A)
Product B : $(880 - 1100) \times 20$ =	4,400	(A)
Product C : $(2640 - 2750) \times 40$ =	4,400	(A)
Total sales mix variance =	20,350	(A)

(v) Sales sub volume variance : $(RSQ - SQ) \times SP$

Product A : $(1650 - 1200) \times 15$ =	6,750	(F)
Product B : $(1100 - 800) \times 20$ =	6,000	(F)
Product C : $(2750 - 2000) \times 40$ =	30,000	(F)
Total sales sub volume variance =	42,750	(F)

15
Management Accounting

INTRODUCTION

Financial accounting had started at an earlier times along with the development of trade activities. The ultimate aim of the financial accounting is to supply financial information to the outsiders and also to prepare final account. But it could not supply the valuable information to the management. The development of company type of organisation has resulted in a wider economic activity and separation of ownership and management. At present, our life style has become faster, technological changes taking place day by day, economic and social values being obsolete within a day. Under this situation, the management is not ready to wait upto the end of the one financial year regarding the problems arising from day-to-day transactions. The accurate information regarding the business transaction must be collected from week to week or month to month. In order to fulfill the above activities in an efficient manner, a separate system of accounting is developed. It is popularly known as Management Accounting.

MEANING

The term Management Accounting refers to accounting for the management *i.e.,* accounting which provides necessary information to the management for discharging its functions. In other words, any system of accounting which helps the management to carry out the operational activities of a concern more effectively is termed as Management Accounting.

The term Management Accounting is of recent origin even in the USA. Management Accounting has developed into a full fledged subject, distinct from accounting in the present commercial and financial world. It is otherwise known as management-oriented accounting or accounting for management.

DEFINITION OF MANAGEMENT ACCOUNTING

Some definitions of Management Accounting are as follows.

"Any form of accounting which enables a business to be conducted more efficiently can be regarded as Management Accounting".

—**Institute of Chartered Accountants of England**

"Such of its techniques and procedures by which accounting mainly seeks to aid the management collectively have come to be known as Management Accounting."

—**Institute of Chartered Accountants of India**

"Management Accounting is the adaptation and analysis of accounting information and its diagnosis and explanation in such a way as to assist the management."—**T.G. Rose**

"Management Accounting is concerned with accounting information that is useful to management."

—**Robert N. Anthony**

SCOPE OF MANAGEMENT ACCOUNTING

The scope of Management Accounting is very wide as to comprise an investigation of all the aspects and branches of business operations. The following are some of the areas of specialisation included within the orbit of Management Accounting.

(i) Financial Accounting
(ii) Cost Accounting
(iii) Budgeting and Forecasting
(iv) Statistical Data
(v) Cost Control Technique
(vi) Taxation
(vii) Methods and Procedure
(viii) Internal Financial Control
(ix) Office services

OBJECTIVES OF MANAGEMENT ACCOUNTING

The ultimate objective of the Management Accounting is to help the management in order to maximise profits or at least minimise expenses and control the losses. The foremost objective of management accounting is to assist the management to carry on an effective functioning of the overall managerial activities. A few objectives of the management accounting can be summarised as follows.

(i) *To assist in planning and formulating future policy.* Planning is one of the important functions of the business management. It includes proper analysis of available data and forecast on the basis of available information. It facilitates the preparation of statement in the light of past result and gives future estimation.

(ii) *To guide the interpretation of financial statements.* Management accounting provides guidance for analysing and interpreting the various financial statements. Through this way, business executives, investors, creditors, and employees of the organisation are enabled to obtain required information.

(iii) *Helps in decision making.* Management accounting assists in decision making process in an efficient manner with the help of the various alternative information which are available with regard to cost and revenue. Under this aspect, all the available data are analysed and correct decision may be taken with the help of the management accounting.

(iv) *Assists in organising.* Management accounting emphasizes on budgetary control, marginal costing, standard costing, cash flow, and fund flow analysis. All the above areas require an intensive study of the firm. It assists in rationalising the organisational structure of the business concern in an efficient manner.

(v) *To assist in controlling.* Some of the control techniques such as standard costing, budgetary control are helpful in controlling performance. Management accounting is one of the tools for managerial control.

(vi) *To help in effective communication of information.* Management accounting provides a means of communicating management plans and programmes through the organisation. It is a vital part of the organisation's management information system.

(vii) *Helps motivating employees.* Management accounting assists the management by providing a continuous motivation to their employees.

(viii) *Assistance in co-ordination.* Co-ordination refers to a Co-ordial and harmonious relationship maintained by the manager in an organisation. Management accounting is concerned with the efficiency of various phases of management. It helps in overall control and effective co-ordination of business operations.

LIMITATIONS OF MANAGEMENT ACCOUNTING

Management accounting suffers from some limitations. They can be summarised as follows :

(i) *Limitations of basic records.* Management accounting is generally concerned with the rearrangement of data. The correctness of management accounting depends upon some of the accounting records such as financial accounting records, cost accounting and other records. Normally, they have their own limitations which are also the limitations of management accounting.

(ii) *It is only a tool.* Management accounting is a mere tool for management. At any time, any of the important decisions, and corrective steps or measures are taken by the management itself and not by the management accountant.

(iii) *Personal bias.* Personal prejudices and bias affect the objectivity of decisions.

(iv) *Expensive.* The installation of management accounting systems in an organisation requires a huge amount of capital. So it is not suitable for the small scale organisation.

(v) *Supplies only data.* The important function of the management accounting is to supply only data and not to influence the decisions. It can only give the information and not the prescription.

(vi) *Evolutionary stage.* Management Accounting is only at a developmental stage. It could not reach the final stage. So the decision at the developmental stage is not a standardised one.

DIFFERENCES BETWEEN FINANCIAL ACCOUNTING AND MANAGEMENT ACCOUNTING

Some of the differences between financial accounting and management accounting are summarised as follows.

(i) *Objectives*. The main objective of the financial accounting is to make a periodical report to owners, creditors, investors, employees, and general public with regard to the financial position of a business at the end of the period. On the other hand, the objective of the management accounting is to assist internal management.

(ii) *Nature*. Financial accounting is concerned with past data whereas the Management accounting stresses on the future. And also it deals with the future plans and policies.

(iii) *Legal provisions*. As per the provisions of the law, financial accounting is compulsory for all the business concerns. But the management accounting is followed on voluntary basis to increase the operational efficiency of the business organisations.

(iv) *Accounting principle*. Financial accounting is governed by the generally accepted accounting principles and conventions. But no such set of principles are followed in management accounting.

(v) *Methodology*. In financial accounting, records are maintained in the form of revenue, income and expenditure, personal accounts, real accounts, and nominal accounts etc. But in the case of management accounting, costs and revenue are usually reported by responsibility centres or profit centres.

(vi) *Publication*. Financial statements like trading, profit and loss A/c and Balance sheet are published for the use of all concerned *i.e.*, investors, creditors, employees, and general public. These statements are duly audited by the practising chartered accountants. These provisions are not there in management accounting.

(vii) *Coverage*. Financial accounting covers entire business activity specifically for the whole financial transaction. But management accounting considers only the activity relevant to the management for decision making purpose.

(viii) *Periodicity of reporting*. In management accounting, immediate and prompt communication of data is essential. In real practice, if the data are received too late or not upto date, it would not be useful for the management decision making purpose. Under financial accounting, quick communication of information is not required unless otherwise stated.

DIFFERENCES BETWEEN FINANCIAL ACCOUNTING AND COST ACCOUNTING

The following are some of the differences between financial accounting and cost accounting.

(i) *Purpose*. Financial accounting provides information about the financial position of the company to its owners and other related parties.

But cost accounting provides information about the costing aspect of the management. And also provides information about the cost per unit of the product manufactured by the concern.

(ii) *Compulsory*. All the business organisations keep the financial accounting in order to meet the requirements of Partnership Act, Companies Act and Income Tax Act. But cost accounting is kept in the organisation according to its willingness.

(iii) *Overall analysis of profit.* Financial accounting concentrates on the whole business and overall analysis of profit is possible. It discloses the profit or loss of the business as a whole for the one year transaction through the financial statements. But the cost accounting has to disclose the profit or loss of a particular product during a particular period of time. Under the costing, overall analysis of profit is not possible.

(iv) *Reporting of costs.* In the financial accounting, costs are reported in a consolidated manner in the financial statements. But under cost accounting, costs are divided on a unit basis in cost accounts.

(v) *Mode of transaction.* Financial accounting is concerned with the external transaction. Normally it deals with the monetary transaction on the basis of payment or receipt of cash. But cost accounting is related to the internal transactions only. It could not deal with the monetary transaction.

(vi) *Price fixation.* Cost accounting provides sufficient information for price fixation of a product. With the help of the cost accounting only, the concern fixes the price of its product.

But financial accounting could not provide any assistance with regard to price fixation.

(vii) *Stock valuation.* Under financial accounting, stocks are valued at cost or market price whichever is less. But in the case of cost accounting, stocks are valued at cost.

(viii) *Nature of dealings.* Financial accounting is concerned with only actual facts and figures. But cost accounting is concerned partly with the actual facts and figures and partly with estimates.

(ix) *Science.* Financial accounting is a positive science. But cost accounting is sometimes positive science and sometimes normative science.

DIFFERENCES BETWEEN COST ACCOUNTING AND MANAGEMENT ACCOUNTING

Cost accounting and management accounting both have more or less same objectives for the management. In spite of the similarities, there are certain differences between these two accountings.

Some of the differences between cost accounting and management accounting are summarised as follows :

(i) *Base.* Cost accounting develops a strong base for management accounting. But the management accounting is developed from both financial accounting and cost accounting.

(ii) *Purpose.* Cost accounting takes necessary steps for collecting data in order to help the management. But management accounting supplies all accounting information to the management for solving all business problems.

(iii) *Nature of data used.* Under cost accounting only quantitative aspect is recorded. But in the management accounting, both quantitative and qualitative informations are to be recorded.

MANAGEMENT ACCOUNTING

(iv) *Object.* The primary objective of cost accounting is to ascertain the cost of producing a product or providing a service. But the aim of the management accounting is to provide information to the management for the overall operational activities of the business.

(v) *Tools techniques.* Standard costing, variance analysis, break even analysis etc, are the important tools and techniques of cost accounting.

But in the case of management accounting not only the standard costing, variance analysis, break even analysis but also fund flow statement, cash flow statements, ratio analysis etc are the tools and techniques of this accounting.

(vi) *Installation of the system.* Cost accounting can be installed without the support from management accounting.

When the organisation decides to install management accounting, it should obtain some basic details from the cost accounting and financial accounting.

But management accounting can be installed in the organisation to obtain some of the basic support from the financial accounting and cost accounting.

❑❑❑

16
Marginal Costing

INTRODUCTION

Marginal costing is one of the techniques of costing just like other methods of costing *viz.* job or process costing. It helps the management to take important decisions specifically for the price fixation and assessment of profitability. It reveals the inter-relationship between cost, volume of sales and profit. It classifies cost into two parts *viz* fixed and variable cost. Variable cost is considered only to find the cost of production. But fixed costs are not included. So a special technique of costing is developed to find out the cost of production known as marginal costing. Marginal Costing is also used to find out the cost per unit upto a particular level or output. Marginal Costing is otherwise called as direct costing, differential costing, incremental costing, or comparative costing.

DEFINITION OF MARGINAL COST AND MARGINAL COSTING

The Institute of Cost and Works Accountants of India defined marginal cost as "the amount at any given volume of output by which aggregate costs are changed, if the volume of output is increased or decreased by one". In order to find out the marginal cost, we need the following elements of cost.
  (*i*) Direct material.
  (*ii*) Direct labour.
  (*iii*) Other direct expenses.
  (*iv*) Total variable overheads.
     i.e., marginal cost = prime cost + total variable overheads.

Marginal costing is defined by the ICWA as *"the ascertainment by differentiating between fixed cost and variable costs of marginal costs and of the effect on profit of changes in volume of type of output".*

Batty defines marginal costing as *"a technique of cost accounting which pays special attention to the behaviour of costs with changes in the volume of output".*

MAIN FEATURES OF MARGINAL COSTING

1. All costs are classified into fixed and variable.
2. When evaluation of finished goods and work-in-progress are taken into account, they will be only variable costs.
3. Marginal costing is a method of costing which is used in other methods of costing.

MARGINAL COSTING

4. Fixed cost should be subtracted/deducted from the contribution for the purpose of finding out net profit or loss.
5. Total fixed cost remains constant irrespective of the level of production but fixed cost per unit cannot be uniform.
6. Selling price per unit and variable cost per unit remain the same.
7. To employ the cost volume profit relationship the firm has to determine its profitability at various levels of activity possible.
8. Contribution is otherwise called as income or profit.
9. Normally Fixed Costs are charged to the profit and loss account in which year it was actually incurred and they are not adjusted in the income of the subsequent years.
10. In all the stages, fixed and variable costs are to be segregated. Apart from this, semi variable costs are also segregated into fixed and variable.

ADVANTAGES

1. *Helps to fix selling price.* Fixation of selling price is an important task of the manufacturer. Because, depending upon the price level of the product, profit of the organisation is to be determined. The differentiation between fixed costs and variable costs is very helpful in fixing the selling price of the products.
2. *Budgetary Control.* Through the preparation of flexible budget, we have to find the total fixed cost and variable cost under different levels of activity. Without the flexible budget, it is difficult to find the total cost at various stages of activity.
3. *Make or buy decisions.* Sometimes the organisation has to take decision to manufacture a product itself or buy a product from outside suppliers. It would take the decision to purchase from outside if the price paid recovers some of the fixed expenses.
4. *Helps in production planning.* Through the break even chart, each and every stage of profit is to be determined clearly. So unprofitable products can be removed from product line. Profitable products should be increased according to the required level.
5. *Effective results.* The comparison of other systems of costing like process, job etc gives better results for the operations.
6. *Benefits of overheads simplification.* Fixed overheads are segregated from the production cost. With the help of this function, the problem of over absorption or under absorption is totally eliminated.
7. *Constant in nature.* Variable costs fluctuate from time to time. But, in the long run, marginal costs are stable irrespective of the level of production.
8. *Simplicity.* Marginal costing is simple to understand and easy to compute. So it does not require more time for computation, and its application.
9. *Cost control.* Marginal costing is combined with standard costing and budgetary control which makes the cost control mechanism more effective.

DISADVANTAGES

1. *Difficult to analyse overhead.* It is difficult to segregate fixed and variable costs accurately. In real sense, a major technical difficulty arises on drawing a sharp line of demarcation between fixed and variable costs.

2. *Time factor ignored.* Normally, in short run periods, both fixed and variable costs were constant. But in the long run all costs are variable including fixed costs. So comparison of performance between two periods is not possible.
3. *Inaccurate price fixation.* Price fixation and comparison between two jobs cannot be done in an accurate manner because selling price is fixed on the basis of contribution. Suppose cost plus contract means, it is very difficult to fix the price.
4. *Limited Role.* Marginal costing in no way, explains the reasons for the increase or decrease in production or sales because it is difficult to combine it with other techniques like standard costing and budgetary control.
5. *Claim for loss of stock.* In any business organisation, to follow a marginal costing technique for the stock valuation, in case of goods destroyed by fire, full loss cannot be recovered from the insurance company.
6. *Problem of variable overheads.* In most of the situations, marginal costing smoothly solves the problem of over and under absorption of fixed overheads. But there is a problem of variable overhead and semi variable overheads.
7. *Unsuitability for certain industries.* Marginal costing is found unsuitable in industries where the value of work in progress is high level as compared to its turnover. It is specifically for the ship industries and contract work. This type of industries have more work in progress. At the time of valuation of work in progress, fixed cost is ignored, so it shows manipulation in its profit.
8. *Objection by income tax authorities.* A concern or industry, which adopts marginal costing techniques for the valuation of inventories and profit estimation, is objected by the income tax authorities because it does not show an accurate profit.

Specimen form of marginal cost statement

Particulars	Products		Total
	A	B	
Net Sales	xx	xx	xx
Less : Variable Cost	xx	xx	xx
Prime Cost + All			
Variable overheads	xx	xx	xx
Contribution	xx	xx	xx
Less : Fixed Cost	xx	xx	xx
Profit	xx	xx	xx

ABSORPTION COSTING

Absorption costing, in actual practice, is charging of all the costs both fixed and variable to the production, processes and treats all costs as product costs. In real sense, in absorption costing, fixed overhead can never be absorbed exactly because of difficulty in determining costs and volume of output.

MARGINAL COSTING

The Institute of Cost and Management Accountants (U.K) defines it as "the practice of charging all costs both variable and fixed to operations, processes or products".

Absorption costing is otherwise called as total or full cost method.

Practical Applications of Marginal Costing

Marginal costing technique may be applied with various aims and purposes. The important purposes are as follow.

Profit Planning

In order to determine the profit level of the firm in future period is absolutely important. Profit planning is therefore a part of operational planning. Marginal costing assists the management in the profit planning through computation of contribution ratio. In the real sense, profits are affected by various factors such as the marginal cost per unit, total fixed cost, selling price and volume of sales. Hence, the organisation can achieve its profit by modifying one or more of the above variables.

Profit Volume Ratio

The ratio of contribution to sales is the p/v ratio or profit volume ratio. It may be expressed in percentage. It is one of the effective tools for studying the profitability of business.

Break Even Point

BEP may be defined as that level or point of sales volume at which the total revenue is equal to total costs. Simply, it is a no-profit, no loss point. This is also a minimum point of production where total costs are recovered. If sales exceeds the Break Even Point, organisation earns a profit. If sales are below the Break Even Point, the organisation incurs a loss. In other words, this is a point at which loss ceases and profit starts.

[Talk about the BEP in single word; it is the point where income is exactly equal to expenditure.]

Break   Means Divide
Even   Means Equally
Point   Means Position or place [sale/produced units]

1. *Margin of safety.* Margin of safety may be defined as the excess of actual sales or production at the selected activity over Break even sales or production. Simply, margin of sales is excess sales over the break even sales. It is abbreviated as M.O.S.

2. *Level of activity planning.* Now a days, business concerns face the problems of finding the level of activity which is optimum for a business to adopt. In this respect, the management wants to take right decision from the different levels of production or selling activities available. The marginal costing technique helps the management to determine the optimum level of activity.

3. *Fixation of selling price.* One of the important functions of the cost accountant is the ascertainment of cost for the purpose of fixation of selling price. At the time of price fixation, raw material cost, direct labour cost plus other overheads are also taken into account to find the total cost of the product. Apart from this, a certain percentage of profit is added to the total cost to arrive at the selling price. Marginal Costing of a product represents the minimum price for that product and any sales below marginal cost would entail a loss of cash.

4. *Decision to make or buy.* Some time, a firm may buy certain products or parts or tools from outside, which may be made by the firm itself. The management must decide which one is most profitable to the firm. If the marginal cost of the product is lower than the price of buying from outside sources, it is better for the firm to manufacture the product by itself.
5. *Introduction of a new product.* Existing firm may add additional products in its products line without any difficulty, with the help of its available production capacity. The new product is sold in the market at a reasonable price with large quantities. If it is a reputed company, the sales may increase. So, total cost would come down and automatically profit will be increased.
6. *Evaluation of performance.* With the help of the marginal costing, the management can measure the operational efficiency of all the departments or sales division. Those departments or divisions which have a highest p/v ratio indicate the highest performance efficiency.
7. *Decision making.* In normal practice, price must not be less than total cost. So, marginal costing acts as a price fixer and contributes profit. But this principle cannot be successful at all times. If in any situation price is equal to marginal cost, there will be a loss. Some times, the firm has to face a loss when (*i*) competitors cannot be driven out (*ii*) there is cut-throat competition and so on. Marginal costing guides the management to take correct decisions whenever faced with this type of situations.
8. *Maintaining a desired level of profit.* Some times, an industry has to reduce its price due to competition and government regulation. But the ultimate aim of the management is to maintain the same level of profit. For this purpose, marginal costing technique can assist the management to determine how many units have to be sold to maintain the same level of profit.
9. *Alternative methods of production.* Management has to select a method of production among so many alternatives. Marginal cost gives the marginal contribution under each of the proposed methods which are worked out and the method which gives the maximum contribution is normally adopted. And also with the help of the marginal costing, the management should compare the alternative method of manufacture : either machine work or hand work and one machine or more machines.
10. *Decision to accept bulk order or foreign order.* Some times, organisation has to receive both bulk order and foreign order for supplying the goods. A decision has to be taken now whether to accept both orders or reject them. In this respect, marginal costing technique gives the correct direction to the management for accepting or rejecting the order.

Cost Volume Profit Analysis

Cost volume profit analysis is one of the analytical tool used for studying the relationship between volume, cost, prices and profits. In cost volume profit analysis, an attempt is made to measure variations of costs and profits and volume. In the words of Heiser, "The most significant single factor in profit planning of the average business is the relationship between the volume of business costs and profits".

From time to time the management is very much interested to know and evaluate the profitability of the product or product mix. And also to analyse the effect of change in the volume of output, will have on the cost of production and profits.

MARGINAL COSTING

To understand the cost volume profit relationship in a detailed manner, we have to study the following :
  (i) Break even analysis
  (ii) Marginal cost formula
  (iii) Profit volume ratio
  (iv) Profit graph
  (v) Key factor
  (vi) Sales mix etc.

Break Even Analysis

It is a tool for analysing the financial aspect whereby the impact on profit, of the changes in volume, price costs and sales mix can be estimated with higher level accuracy.

Profit Volume Ratio

It is an important tool in decision making. It is used for the calculation of BEP and in problems regarding profit and sales relationship. A higher P/V ratio indicates the greater profitability and vice versa. So the organisation makes necessary effort to obtain higher P/V ratio.

Margin of Safety

Margin of safety may be defined as the excess of actual sales or production at the selected activity over Break even sales or production. Simply, margin of sales is excess sales over the break even sales. It is abbreviated as M.O.S.

Break Even Chart

Break even point should be computed with the help of the graphical representation or applying mathematical formula. Graphical representation of break-even point is known as break even chart. Dr. Vance is of the opinion that "It is a graph showing the amounts of fixed variable costs and the sales revenue at different volumes of operation. It shows at what volume the firm first covers all costs with revenue of break-even."

From the following data, draw break even chart. Fixed cost Rs. 8000, variable cost Rs. 4.00 percentage, selling price per unit Rs. 6.00. Units produced and sold 4,000, 6,000, 8,000 and 12,000.

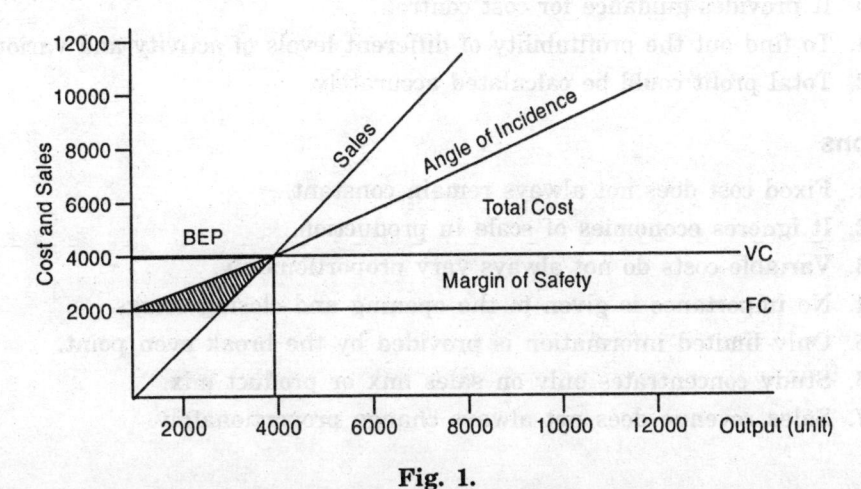

Fig. 1.

Angle of Incidence

Angle of incidence indicates the profit earning capacity. The angle is formed at the break even point where the sales line cuts the total cost line. The angle may be large or small. Large angle of incidence indicates higher profit rate and vice versa.

Assumptions of Break Even Analysis

(i) All costs are segregated into fixed and variable cost.
(ii) Total fixed costs are constant at all levels of output.
(iii) Production and sales figures are same.
(iv) Variable costs vary proportionately with the level of volume of output.
(v) Selling price per unit and operational efficiency remains unchanged.
(vi) Production and sales are same.
(vii) Volume of sales and volume of production are equal hence there is no unsold stock.
(viii) There is only one product.
(ix) If there are multiple products, sales mix remains constant.
(x) There will be no change in the general price level.
(xi) Cost and revenue depend only on volume of production or output and not on any other factor.

Advantages of Break Even Analysis and Chart

1. Enables to provide more detailed information and easily understandable than those of profit & loss account and balance sheet information.
2. To determine the total cost, fixed cost and variable cost.
3. Product planning
4. Inter-firm comparison is possible.
5. To select the best product mix.
6. Choosing the best promotion mix
7. To take the make or buy decisions.
8. Preparation of flexible budget
9. Formulation of price policy
10. It provides guidance for cost control.
11. To find out the profitability of different levels of activity and various products.
12. Total profit could be calculated accurately.

Limitations

1. Fixed cost does not always remain constant.
2. It ignores economies of scale in production.
3. Variable costs do not always vary proportionately.
4. No importance is given to the opening and closing stocks.
5. Only limited information is provided by the break even point.
6. Study concentrates only on sales mix or product mix.
7. Sales revenue does not always change proportionately.

MARGINAL COSTING

Formula : Computation of BEP

First type :

1. *Problem given in values :*

$$BEP = \frac{\text{Fixed Cost} \times \text{Sales}}{\text{Sales} - \text{Variable Cost}}$$

2. *Problem given in unit :*

$$BEP = \frac{\text{Fixed Cost}}{\text{Selling price per unit} - \text{Variable cost per unit}}$$

3. *Problem given in values :*

$$BEP = \frac{\text{Fixed Cost}}{\text{P/V Ratio}}$$

$$\text{Computation of P/V ratio} = \frac{\text{Contribution}}{\text{Sales}} \times 100$$

Contribution = Sales − Variable Cost

Second type : Only two periods' details are given in the problem, we have to find the following :

1. P/V ratio
2. BEP
3. Fixed Cost
4. Find the profit with the help of given sales.
5. Find the sales with the help of given profit.
6. MOS
7. Variable cost.

The above should be calculated with the help of the following formula

1. $$P/V \text{ Ratio} = \frac{\text{Difference of Profit}}{\text{Difference of Sales}} \times 100$$

2. $$BEP = \frac{\text{Fixed Cost}}{\text{P/V Ratio}}$$

3. *Fixed Cost*

Given Sales × P/V = Contribution	xx	[FC + Profit]
Less : Profit	xx	
Fixed Cost	xx	

4. *Find the profit with the help of given sales*

Given Sales × P/V = Contribution	xx
Less : FC	xx
Profit	xx

5. *Find the sales with the help of given profit*

$$\frac{\text{FC} + \text{Desired Profit}}{\text{P/V Ratio}}$$

6. *Margin of safety*
   (i) Margin of safety = Actual Sales − BEP Sales
   (or)
   (ii) If desired profit given in the problem = $\dfrac{\text{Desired Profit}}{\text{P/V Ratio}}$
   or
   (iii) Margin of safety in units = $\dfrac{\text{Profit}}{\text{Contribution per unit}}$

7. *Variable Cost*
Sales	xx
Less : Value of P/V ratio	xx
Variable Cost	xx

   Example :
Sales 100%	50,000
Less : Value of P/V Ratio $\left(50{,}000 \times \dfrac{40}{100}\right)$	20,000
Variable Cost	30,000

   Sales − P/V Ratio = Vc

8. *Sales in units required to maintain the present level of profit*
   $= \dfrac{\text{Total Contribution required}}{\text{New Contribution per unit}}$

   Marginal Cost Statement
Sales	xx
Less : Variable Cost	xx
Contribution	xx
Less : Fixed Cost	xx
Profit	xx

Problem 1. *From the following particulars you are required to calculate BEP.*
(a) Fixed cost Rs. 2,00,000, selling price per unit Rs. 40, variable cost per unit Rs. 1.5.
(b) Fixed cost Rs. 40,000, sales Rs. 1,00,000, variable cost Rs. 30,000.
Solution :

(a) Computation of BEP = $\dfrac{\text{Fixed Cost}}{\text{Selling price per unit − Variable cost per unit}}$

Fixed Cost = Rs. 2,00,000
Selling price per unit = Rs. 40 per unit
Variable cost per unit = Rs. 15 per unit

$= \dfrac{2{,}00{,}000}{40 - 15}$

MARGINAL COSTING

$$\text{BEP in units} = 8{,}000$$
$$\text{BEP in value} = \text{BEP units} \times \text{Selling price per unit}$$
$$= 8{,}000 \times 40$$
$$= \text{Rs. } 3{,}20{,}000$$

(b)
$$\text{BEP} = \frac{\text{Fixed Cost} \times \text{Sales}}{\text{Sales} - \text{Variable Cost}}$$
$$= \frac{40{,}000 \times 1{,}00{,}000}{1{,}00{,}000 \times 30{,}000}$$
$$= \frac{4{,}00{,}000}{7} = \text{Rs. } 57{,}142.$$

Problem 2. *From the following data calculate break even point expressed in terms of units and also the new BEP if selling price is reduced by 10%.*

	Rs.
Fixed Expenses	
Depreciation	2,00,000
Salaries	2,00,000
Variable Expenses	
Materials	Rs. 6 per unit
Labour	Rs. 4 per unit
Selling Price	Rs. 20 per unit

Solution :

$$\text{BEP} = \frac{\text{Fixed Cost}}{\text{Selling price per unit} - \text{Variable cost per unit}}$$
$$= \frac{4{,}00{,}000}{20 - 10}$$
$$\text{BEP in units} = 40{,}000 \text{ units}$$

New break even point if selling price is reduced by 10%

		Rs.
Fixed Cost	= Rs.	4,00,000
Material	= Rs.	6.00
Labour	= Rs.	4.00
	Rs.	10.00

New Selling price :

		Rs.	
Selling Price	= Rs.	20.00	
Less : 10% Reduction	= Rs.	2.00	
	Rs.	18.00	

$$\text{BEP} = \frac{\text{Fixed Cost}}{\text{Selling price per unit} - \text{Variable cost per unit}}$$
$$= \frac{4{,}00{,}000}{8}$$
$$\text{BEP in units} = 50{,}000 \text{ units}$$

Problem 3. *From the following particulars find out the BEP, what will be the selling price per unit if BEP is to be brought down to 9,000 units.*

	Rs.
Variable cost per unit	Rs. 75
Fixed expenses	Rs. 2,70,000
Selling price per unit	Rs. 100

Solution :

$$BEP = \frac{\text{Fixed Cost}}{\text{Selling price per unit} - \text{Variable cost per unit}}$$

Fixed Cost = Rs. 2,70,000
Selling price = Rs. 100
Variable cost = Rs. 75

$$= \frac{2,70,000}{100 - 75}$$

BEP in units = 10,800 units
BEP in value = 10,800 units × Selling price
= *i.e.*, 10,800 × 100
= Rs. 10,80,000

If BEP is brought down to 9,000 units

$$BEP = \frac{\text{Fixed Cost } (2,70,000)}{\text{Contribution per unit } (X)}$$

Contribution per unit is treated as X

$$X = \frac{2,70,000}{9,000} = 30$$

Therefore, New Selling price is Rs. 105 *i.e.*, (Rs. 75 + Rs. 30 = Rs. 105)

Problem 4. *The following information relating to a company is given to you :*

	Rs.
Sales	7,00,000
Fixed cost	1,80,000
Variable cost	4,00,000

Solution :

$$BEP = \frac{\text{Fixed Cost}}{\text{Contribution}} \times \text{Sales}$$

Contribution = Sales − Variable cost
= 4,00,000 − 2,50,000
= 1,50,000

$$BEP = \frac{1,80,000}{1,50,000} \times 4,00,000$$

MARGINAL COSTING

$$\begin{aligned}\text{BEP Sales} &= 4,80,000 \\ \text{Present Sales} &= 4,00,000 \\ &\overline{,80,000}\end{aligned}$$

Based upon the above calculation, sales are to be increased only by Rs. 80,000 to break even.

Problem 5. *From the following data you are required to calculate the break-even point and net sales value at this point.*

Selling price per unit	Rs. 25
Direct material cost per unit	Rs. 8
Direct labour cost per unit	Rs. 5
Fixed overhead	Rs. 24,000

Variable overheads @ 60% on Direct Labour.

Trade discount 4%

If sales are 15% and 20% above the break even volume determine the net profits.

Solution :

(i)
$$\text{BEP} = \frac{\text{Fixed Cost}}{\text{Selling price per unit} - \text{Variable cost per unit}}$$

$$= \frac{24,000}{24-16}$$

$$= \frac{24,000}{8}$$

BEP in units = 3000 units

BEP in value = BEP Units × Selling price

= 3000 units × Rs. 24

= Rs. 72,000

Workings :

(a) Selling Price :

Selling price per unit = Rs. 25.00

Less : Trade discount 4% = Rs. 1.00 $\left[25.00 \times \dfrac{4}{100}\right]$

Selling Price = Rs. 24.00

(b) Variable Cost :

Direct Material cost per unit = Rs. 8.00

Direct labour cost per unit = Rs. 5.00

Variable overhead 60% on Direct Labour = Rs. 3.00 $\left[5 \times \dfrac{60}{100}\right]$

Variable Cost = Rs. 16.00

(ii) If sales are 15% above the break even volume, find out the profit.

Formula :

$$\text{Given Sales} \times \text{P/V ratio} = xx$$
$$\text{Less : Fixed Cost} = xx$$
$$\text{Profit} = xx$$

BEP Sales is =	72,000
15% above the break even sales =	10,800
Increased sale volume =	82,800

Therefore, $82,800 \times \dfrac{33.33}{100}$ = 27,597   i.e.,   27,600

Less : Fixed cost = 24,000   24,000

Profit = 3,597   3,600

NOTE : Find the P/V ratio

$$\text{P/V ratio} = \dfrac{\text{Contribution}}{\text{Sales}}$$

Contribution = Sales – Variable cost
= 24 – 16 = Rs. 8
= $\dfrac{8}{24} \times 100$
= 33.33%

(iii) If sales are 20% above the break even, determine the profit.

Break even sales =	Rs. 72,000
20% increase =	Rs. 14,400
Increased sales volume =	Rs. 86,400

$82,800 \times \dfrac{33.33}{100}$ = 28,797   i.e.,   28,800

Less : Fixed cost =   24,000

Profit =   4,800

Problem 6 :

(i) *From the following details you are required to determine the break even point.*

Direct Labour	Rs. 100 per unit
Direct Material	Rs. 40 per unit
Variable overhead	100% of direct labour

MARGINAL COSTING

       Fixed overheads   Rs. 60,000
       Selling price   Rs. 400 per unit

(ii) In order to increase the efficiency in production, the concern installs improved machinery, which results in fixed overhead of Rs. 20,000, but the variable overhead is reduced by 40%.

Solution :

(i) Computation of Break even point

$$BEP = \frac{Fixed\ Cost}{Selling\ price\ per\ unit\ -\ Variable\ cost\ per\ unit}$$

Fixed Cost = Rs. 60,000

Variable Cost

Direct Material	= Rs.	40
Direct Labour	= Rs.	100
Variable overhead 100% on direct labour	= Rs.	100
	Rs.	240

$$BEP = \frac{60,000}{400 - 240}$$

$$= \frac{60,000}{160}$$

BEP in units = 375 units

BEP in value = BEP Unit × Selling price
                  = 375 units × Rs. 400
                  = Rs. 1,50,000

(ii) In order to increase the production : The New BEP

Fixed overhead	= Rs.	60,000
(+) Additional	= Rs.	20,000
Total fixed cost	= Rs.	80,000

Variable overhead is reduced by 40%

Variable Cost

Direct Material	= Rs.	40
Direct Labour	= Rs.	100
Variable overhead $100 \times \frac{60}{100}$	= Rs.	60
Total Variable Cost	Rs.	200

$$\text{Revised BEP} = \frac{\text{Fixed Cost}}{\text{Selling price per unit} - \text{Variable cost per unit}}$$

$$= \frac{80,000}{400-200}$$

BEP in units = 400 units
BEP in value = 400 × 400
= Rs. 1,60,000

Problem 7. *The P/V ratio of a firm dealing in Electrical equipment is 50% and the margin of safety is 40%. Find out BEP and the net profit, if sales volume is Rs. 50,00,000.* [MBA Anna, MCA 2000 PU]

Solution :

(i) Contribution

Given Sales × P/V ratio = Contribution

$$50,00,000 \times \frac{50}{100} = \text{Rs. } 25,00,000$$

(ii) Break even sales = (Actual Sales − BEP Sales = M.O.S. (or)
Actual Sales − M.O.S. = BEP Sales

Sales	= Rs. 50,00,000
Less : Margin of safety 40% on sales	= Rs. 20,00,000
Break even sales	= Rs. 30,00,000

(iii) Fixed cost

$$\text{BEP (30,000)} = \frac{\text{Fixed Cost (X)}}{\text{P/V Ratio (50\%)}}$$

$$X = 30,00,000 \times \frac{50}{100}$$

Fixed Assets = Rs. 15,00,000

(iv) **Find out profit :**

Contribution = Fixed cost + Profit or Fixed cost − Loss
Contribution = Rs. 25,00,000
Less : Fixed Cost = Rs. 15,00,000
Profit = Rs. 10,00,000

Problem 8. *Assuming that the cost structure and selling prices remain the same in both the periods.*

(a) *Profit volume Ratio*
(b) *BEP for sales*
(c) *Profit when sales are Rs. 1,00,000*
(d) *Sales required to earn a profit of Rs. 20,000*
(e) *Safety margin in both the periods*

MARGINAL COSTING

Periods	Sales Rs.	Profit Rs.
I	1,20,000	9,000
II	1,40,000	13,000

[B.Com PU 2004]

Solution :

(a) Profit Volume Ratio = $\dfrac{\text{Difference of Profit}}{\text{Difference of Sales}} \times 100$

$= \dfrac{13,000 - 9,000}{1,40,000 - 1,20,000} \times 100$

$= \dfrac{4,000}{20,000} \times 100$

P/V Ratio = 20%

(b) BEP for sales = $\dfrac{\text{Fixed Cost}}{\text{P/V Ratio}}$

$= \dfrac{15,000}{20/100}$

BEP Sales = Rs. 75,000

NOTE : Fixed Cost = Contribution − Profit

$= 1,20,000 \times \dfrac{20}{100} - 9,000$

$= 24,000 - 9,000 = 15,000$

[therefore, Contribution = Given sales × P/V Ratio]

(c) Profit when sales are Rs. 1,00,000

Profit = Contribution − Fixed cost

$= 1,00,000 \times \dfrac{20}{100} - 15,000$

$= 20,000 - 15,000 = 5,000$

(d) Sales required to earn a profit of Rs. 20,000

$= \dfrac{\text{Fixed Cost + Desired Profit}}{\text{P/V Ratio}}$

$= \dfrac{15,000 + 20,000}{20/100} =$ Rs. 1,75,000

(e) Safety margin in both the periods

    Actual Sales − BEP Sales = Margin of safety
(i) 1,20,000 − 75,000 = 45,000
(ii) 1,40,000 − 75,000 = 65,000

Problem 9. *Find out profit from the following data*

    Sales   Rs. 8,00,000
    Marginal cost   Rs. 6,00,000
    Break-even sales   Rs. 6,00,000

[SAS Commercial 1982]

Solution :

(i) $\qquad$ P/V Ratio = $\dfrac{\text{Contribution}}{\text{Sales}} \times 100$

$\qquad\qquad\qquad\quad = \dfrac{2,00,000}{8,00,000} \times 100 = 25\%$

(ii) Fixed Expenses

$\qquad$ BED (60,00,000) = $\dfrac{\text{Fixed Expenses (X)}}{\text{P/V Ratio (25\%)}}$

$\qquad\qquad\qquad\quad$ X = $6,00,000 \times \dfrac{25}{100}$ – 1,50,000

$\qquad$ Fixed Expenses = Rs. 1,50,000

(iii) Find out profit

$\qquad\qquad$ Contribution = Rs. 2,00,000

$\qquad$ Less : Fixed Expenses = Rs. 1,50,000

$\qquad\qquad\qquad$ Profit = Rs. 50,000

Problem 10. *P/V ratio is 30% and margin of safety is 40%. Find out the fixed cost and net profit if the actual sales is Rs. 5,00,000.*

Solution :

$\qquad$ Sales $\qquad\qquad\qquad\qquad$ = Rs. 5,00,000

$\qquad$ Less : Margin of safety 40% = Rs. 2,00,000

$\qquad$ BEP $\qquad\qquad\qquad\qquad$ = Rs. 3,00,000

NOTE : BEP = (Actual Sales – Margin of safety) 3,00,000

Find the Fixed cost.

$\qquad$ BEP (3,00,000) $\qquad\qquad$ = $\dfrac{\text{Fixed Cost (X)}}{\text{P/V Ratio (30\%)}}$

$\qquad\qquad\qquad$ X = $3,00,000 \times \dfrac{30}{100}$ = Rs. 90,000

$\qquad$ Profit or Loss $\qquad$ = Contribution – Fixed Cost

$\qquad\qquad\qquad\qquad\quad$ = 1,50,000 – 90,000 = Rs. 60,000

NOTE : Contribution $\qquad$ = Given sales × P/V ratio

$\qquad\qquad\qquad\qquad\qquad$ = $5,00,000 \times \dfrac{30}{100}$ = 1,50,000

MARGINAL COSTING

Problem 11. *An analysis of Digital manufacturing Co. Ltd., submits the following information :*

Cost Element	Variable Cost (% Sales)	Fixed Cost (Rs.)
Direct Material	32.8	—
Direct Labour	28.4	—
Factory overheads	12.6	1,89,900
Distribution overheads	4.1	58,400
General Administration overheads	1.1	66,700

Budgeted sales are Rs. 18,50,000. You are required to determine.
(a) The break even sales volume.
(b) Profit at the budgeted sales value
(c) The profit if actual sales
   (i) Drop by 10%
   (ii) Increase by 5% from budgeted sales. [M.Com adopted]

Solution :

(a) Break Even Sales Volume

$$\text{BEP} = \frac{\text{Fixed Cost}}{\text{P/V Ratio}}$$

$$= \frac{3,15,000}{21/100}$$

BEP = Rs. 15,00,000

Workings :

(i) Fixed Cost

$$\begin{aligned}
\text{Factory overheads} &= \text{Rs. } 1,89,900 \\
\text{Distribution overheads} &= \text{Rs. } 58,400 \\
\text{General administration overheads} &= \text{Rs. } 66,700 \\
\hline
\text{Total Fixed cost} &= \text{Rs. } 3,15,000
\end{aligned}$$

(ii) $\text{P/V Ratio} = \dfrac{\text{Contribution}}{\text{Sales}} \times 100$

Contribution = Sales − Variable cost
= 100 − 79
= 21%

(Here sales are assumed to be 100%)

(iii) Variable Cost

Direct Material = 32.8% of sales
Direct Labour = 28.4% of sales
Factory overheads = 12.6% of sales

Distribution overheads = 4.1% of sales
General administration overheads = 1.1% of sales

Total = 79.0%

(b) Profit at the budgeted sales volume of Rs. 18,50,000

Profit = Contribution − Fixed Cost

$$= 18{,}50{,}000 \times \frac{21}{100} - 3{,}15{,}000$$

$$= 3{,}88{,}500 - 3{,}15{,}000 = 73{,}500$$

> **NOTE :** Contribution = Given Sales × P/V Ratio

(c) The profit, if actual sales
  (i) Drop by 10%

Sales = Rs. 18,50,000
Less : 10% = Rs. 1,85,000
Sales (at 10% Reduction) = Rs. 16,65,000

Profit = Contribution − Fixed Cost

$$= 16{,}65{,}000 \times \frac{21}{100} - 3{,}15{,}000$$

$$= 3{,}49{,}650 - 3{,}15{,}000 = 34{,}650$$

(ii) Increase by 5% from budgeted sales

Sales = Rs. 18,50,000
+ 5% = Rs. 92,500
Sales at 5% increase = Rs. 19,42,500

Profit = Contribution − Fixed Cost

$$= 19{,}42{,}500 \times \frac{21}{100} - 3{,}15{,}000$$

$$= 4{,}07{,}925 - 3{,}15{,}000 = 92{,}925$$

Problem 12. *Raj Corporation Ltd. has prepared the following estimates for the year 1994–95.*

    Sales Units   Rs.   15,000
    Fixed Expenses   Rs.   34,000
    Sales Value   Rs.   1,50,000
    Variable Cost Rs. 6 per unit

You are required to
  (i) *Find P/V ratio, break even point, and margin of safety.*
  (ii) *Calculate the revised P/V ratio, break even point and margin of safety in each of the following cases.*

MARGINAL COSTING

(a) Decrease of 10% in selling price.
(b) Increase of 10% of variable costs.
(c) Increase of sale volume by 2000 units.
(d) Increase of Rs. 6,000 in fixed cost. [MCA 2000]

Solution :

(i)
$$\text{Selling price per unit} = \frac{1,50,000}{15,000} = \text{Rs. } 10$$

Variable cost per unit = Rs. 6

Contribution per unit = Rs. 4

$$\text{P/V Ratio} = \frac{C}{S} \times 100$$

$$= \frac{4}{10} \times 100 = 40\%$$

$$\text{BEP in units} = \frac{\text{Fixed Cost}}{\text{Selling price per unit} - \text{Variable cost per unit}}$$

$$= \frac{34,000}{4} = 8,500 \text{ units}$$

BEP in sales = 8,500 units × Rs. 10 = 85,000

Margin of safety = Actual Sales − BEP Sales
= 1,50,000 − 85,000 = 65,000

(ii)

Particulars	P/V Ratio	BEP Value	Margin of Safety
(a) Decrease in selling price $10 \times \frac{10}{100} = 1$, i.e., $10 - 1 = 9$	$\frac{9-6}{9} \times 100$ $= 33\frac{1}{3}\%$	$\frac{34,000}{33\frac{1}{3}/100}$ $= 1,02,000$	$= 9 \times 15,000$ $= 1,35,000 - 1,02,000$ $= 33,000$
(b) Increase of 10% in variable cost $6 \times \frac{10}{100} = .60$ $6 + .60 = 6.60$	$\frac{10 - 6.60}{10} \times 100$ $= 34\%$	$\frac{34,000}{34/100}$ $= 1,00,000$	$1,50,000 - 1,00,000$ $= 50,000$
(c) Increase of Sales Volume by 2000 units	No change i.e., 40%	No change i.e., 85,000	Sales 1,50,000 + 2000 × 10 20,000 1,70,000 1,70,000 − 85,000 = 85,000
(d) Increase of Rs. 6,000 in fixed cost	No change i.e., 40%	$\frac{40,000}{40/100}$ $= 1,00,000$	$1,50,000 - 1,00,000$ $= 50,000$

Problem 13. You are given the following information in respect of a company.

		Rs.
(i)	Fixed cost	13,000
(ii)	Variable cost	15,000
(iii)	Total cost	28,000
(iv)	Net profit	2,000
(v)	Net sales	30,000

(a) Find out the break-even point.
(b) Forecast the profit for sales volume Rs. 50,000.
(c) Estimate the volume of sales turnover to make a net profit of Rs. 10,000.

[ACS final]

Solution :

(a) *Break even Point*
Find the P/V ratio

NOTE : Sales − Variable Cost = Contribution
30,000 − 14,000 = 16,000

$$\text{P/V Ratio} = \frac{\text{Contribution}}{\text{Sales}} \times 100$$

$$= \frac{16,000}{30,000} \times 100 = 53\frac{1}{3}\%$$

$$\text{BEP} = \frac{F}{\text{P/V Ratio}} = \frac{13,000}{53\frac{1}{3}/100}$$

$$= \text{Rs. } 24,375$$

(b) *Find the profit when sales are Rs. 50,000*

Given sales × P/V ratio = Contribution

$$50,000 \times \frac{53\frac{1}{3}}{100} = 26,667 \text{ (FC + Profit)}$$

Less : Fixed cost = 13,000

Profit = 13,667

(c) *Sales to earn a profit of Rs. 10,000*

$$= \frac{\text{Fixed Cost + Profit}}{\text{P/V Ratio}}$$

$$= \frac{13,000 + 10,000}{53\frac{1}{3}/100}$$

$$= 13,000 + 10,000 \times \frac{100}{53} = \text{Rs. } 43,125$$

MARGINAL COSTING

Problem 14. *Sale of a product amounts to 200 units per month at Rs. 10 per unit. Fixed overheads Rs. 400 per month and variable cost is Rs. 6 per unit. There is a proposal to reduce prices by 10%. Calculate the present and future status by applying P/V ratio to find how many units must be sold to maintain total profit.* [MBA Madras]

Solution :

Profitability Statement

Number of Units	At Present	10% Reduction in selling price
	Rs.	Rs.
Number of units	200	200
Selling price	10.00	9.00
Sales value	2000	1800
Less : Variable cost (200 × 6)	1200	(200 × 6) 1200
Contribution	800	600
Less : Fixed cost	400	400
Profit	400	200

Computation of P/V ratio $= \dfrac{\text{Contribution}}{\text{Sales}} \times 100$

$= \dfrac{800}{1000} \times 100 = 40\%$

$= \dfrac{600}{1800} \times 100 = 33\dfrac{1}{3}\%$

Number of units to be sold

$\dfrac{\text{Fixed Cost + Profit}}{\text{P/V Ratio}} = \dfrac{400 + 400}{33\dfrac{1}{3}/100}$

$= 800 \times \dfrac{100}{33\dfrac{1}{3}}$

$=$ Rs. 2,402

$= \dfrac{2,402}{9} =$ Rs. 266

Result : To maintain the total profit of Rs. 800 sales of 266 units are to be achieved.

Problem 15. *The sales and turnover during two periods are given below :*

Period I : sales Rs. 20 Lakhs, profit Rs. 2.00 Lakhs

Period II : sales Rs.. 30 Lakhs, profit Rs. 4.00 Lakhs

Compute (i) P/V ratio (ii) The sales required to earn a profit of Rs. 5 Lakhs (iii) The profit when sales are Rs. 10,00 Lakhs. [MBA Madras]

Solution :

(i) $$\text{P/V ratio} = \frac{\text{Differences of Profit}}{\text{Differences of Sales}} \times 100$$

$$= \frac{2,00,000}{10,00,000} \times 100$$

$$= 20\%$$

(ii) Sales required to earn a profit of Rs. 5,00,000 lakhs.

$$\frac{\text{FC + Desired Profit}}{\text{P/V Ratio}} = \frac{2,00,000 + 5,00,000}{20/100}$$

$$= \text{Rs. } 35,00,000$$

Now we find out fixed cost

Given sales × P/V ratio = Contribution

$$20,00,000 \times \frac{20}{100} = 4,00,000 \text{ (FC + Profit)}$$

(Any one period sales assumed)

Less : Profit = 2,00,000

Fixed cost = 2,00,000

(iii) Find the profit

Given sales × P/V ratio = Contribution (FC + Profit)

$$10,00,000 \times \frac{20}{100} = 2,00,000$$

Less : Fixed cost = 2,00,000

Profit = 0

Problem 16. *From the following data calculate :*

(i) Break even point expressed in amount of sales in rupees.
(ii) Number of units that must be sold to earn a profit of Rs. 1,20,000 per year.
(iii) How many units are to be sold to earn a net income of 15% of sales ?

Selling price per unit	Rs. 40
Variable manufacturing cost per unit	Rs. 22
Variable selling cost per unit	Rs. 3
Fixed selling cost	Rs. 20,000
Fixed factory overheads	Rs. 1,60,000

Solution :

(i) $$\text{BEP} = \frac{\text{Fixed Cost}}{\text{Selling price per unit } - \text{ Variable cost per unit}}$$

$$= \frac{1,80,000}{40 - 25}$$

$$= \frac{1,80,000}{15} = 12,000 \text{ units.}$$

BEP in value 12000 units × Rs. 40 = Rs. 4,80,000

MARGINAL COSTING

> **NOTE :** *Fixed cost*
>
> Fixed factory overheads = Rs. 1,60,000
> Fixed selling costs = Rs.   20,000
>   1,80,000
>
> *Variable cost*
>
> Variable manufacturing cost per unit = Rs. 22
> Variable selling cost per unit = Rs. 3
>   25

(*ii*) Units to be sold to earn a profit of Rs. 1,20,000

$$\frac{FC + Desired\ Profit}{Contribution\ per\ unit}$$

$$\frac{1,80,000 + 1,20,000}{15} = 20,000\ units$$

(*iii*) Units are to be sold to earn a net income of 15% of sales

Number of units to be sold = N

$$N = \frac{FC + Desired\ Profit}{Contribution\ per\ unit}$$

$$N = \frac{1,80,000 + \frac{15}{100}(N \times Rs.\ 40)}{15}$$

$$15\ N = 1,80,000 + 6\ N$$
$$9\ N = 1,80,000$$
$$N = \frac{1,80,000}{9}$$
$$= 20,000\ units$$

Problem 17. *A factory engaged in manufacturing buckets is working at 40% capacity and produces 10,000 buckets per annum. The present cost break up for one bucket is as under*

	Rs.
Materials	10
Labour cost	3.00
Overheads	5 (60% fixed)

The selling price is Rs. 20 per bucket. It is decided to work the factory at 50% capacity. The selling price falls by 3%. At 90% capacity the selling price falls by 5% accompanied by a similar fall in the prices of materials.

You are required to calculate the profit at 50% and 90% capacities and also calculate the break even point for the same capacity productions.   [BBM 2000]

Solution: Profitability Statement

Capacity level Number of Units	50% 12,500		90% 22,500	
	Cost per unit (Rs.)	Total cost (Rs.)	Cost per unit (Rs.)	Total cost (Rs.)
Sales	19.40	2,42,500	19.00	4,27,500
Less : Variable Cost				
Material	10.00	1,25,000	9.50	2,13,750
Labour (Wages)	3.00	37,500	3.00	67,500
Variable Overheads	2.00	25,000	2.00	45,000
Total Variable Costs	15.00	1,87,500	14.50	3,26,500
Contribution (Sales – VC)	4.40	55,000	4.50	1,01,250
Less : FC	2.40	30,000	1.33	30,000
Profit	2.00	25,000	3.17	71,250

BEP in Units = $\dfrac{FC}{\text{Contribution per unit}}$

	50%	90%
	$\dfrac{30,000}{4.40}$	$\dfrac{30,000}{4.50}$
	6818 units	6667 units
BEP in value BEP units × Selling price	6818 units × Rs. 19.40 Rs. 1,32,270	6667 units × Rs. 19.00 Rs. 1,26,373

Workings : At 50%

(i) Selling Price Rs. 20.00
    Less : 3%   .60
    Selling price at 50% 19.40

At 90%

(ii) Selling Price Rs. 20.00
     Less : 5%   1.00
     Selling price at 90% 19.00

At 90%

(iii) Material Cost Rs. 10.00
      Less : 5%   0.50
      Material Cost at 90% 9.50

MARGINAL COSTING

Problem 18. *From the following data calculate :*
(i) P/V ratio
(ii) Profit when sales are Rs. 20,000
(iii) New break even point if selling price is reduced by 20%.
    Fixed expenses   Rs. 4,000
    Break even point   Rs. 10,000   [MBA Anna]

Solution :

(i) P/V ratio

$$\text{BEP (10,000)} = \frac{\text{Fixed Cost (4,000)}}{\text{P/V Ratio (X)}}$$

$$X = \frac{4,000}{10,000} \times 100$$

$$= 40\%$$

(ii) Profit when sales are Rs. 20,000

Given sales × P/V ratio = Contribution

$$20,000 \times \frac{40}{100} = 8,000$$

Less : Fixed cost = 4,000

Profit = 4,000

(iii) New Break even point : Selling price is reduced by 20%

Assume selling price was = Rs. 100
Less : 20% = Rs. 20
Now, new selling price is = Rs. 80

Contribution = Sales − Variable cost
= 80 − 60
= 20

Find variable cost :

Sales = 100
Less : P/V ratio = 40 (Taken only old P/V ratio)
                   60

$$\text{New P/V ratio} = \frac{\text{Contribution}}{\text{Sales}} \times 100$$

$$= \frac{20}{80} \times 100$$

$$= 25\%$$

$$\text{Break even point} = \frac{\text{Fixed Cost}}{\text{P/V Ratio}}$$

$$= \frac{4{,}000}{25/100}$$

$$= 4{,}000 \times \frac{100}{25}$$

$$= Rs.\ 16{,}000$$

Problem 19. *The particulars of two plants producing an identical product with the same selling price are as under.*

Capacity utilization	Plant A 70% (Rs. in Lakhs)	Plant B 60% (Rs. in Lakhs)
Sales	150	90
Variable cost	105	75
Fixed cost	30	20

It has been decided to merge the plant B with plant A. The additional fixed expenses involved in the merger amount to Rs. 2 lakhs.

(i) Find the Break Even point of plant A and Plant B before merger and the Break Even point of the merger plant.

(ii) Find the capacity utilisation of the integrated plant required to earn a profit of Rs. 18 lakhs. [M.Com MKU]

Solution : **Statement of Cost**

Particulars	Plant A (Rs.)	Plant B (Rs.)	Merge Plant
Sales	150	90	240
Variable cost	105	75	180
Contribution	45	15	60
Fixed cost	30	20	52
P/V Ratio = $\frac{C}{S} \times 100$	$\frac{45}{150} \times 100$ = 30%	$\frac{15}{90} \times 100$ = 16.7%	$\frac{60}{240} \times 100$ = 25%
BEP = $\frac{F}{P/V\ Ratio}$	$\frac{30}{30/100}$ 100 Lakhs	$\frac{20}{16.7/100}$ 120 Lakhs	$\frac{52}{25/100}$ 208 Lakhs

Sales of integrated plant at a profit $\frac{F + P}{P/V} = \frac{52 + 18}{25/100}$

$$= 280\ lakhs.$$

Conversion of Sales into 100% capacity at both the plants

Plant A 100% Capacity sales = $\frac{150}{70} \times 100 = 214.29$ lakhs

MARGINAL COSTING

Plant B 100% Capacity sales = $\frac{90}{60} \times 100 = 150.00$ lakhs

100% capacity of integrated plant = 214.29 + 150 = 364.29

Capacity : Sales of 280 lakhs = $\frac{280}{364.29} \times 100 = 76.86\%$

Thus, the plant operates at 76.86% capacity to earn a profit of Rs. 18.00 lakhs.

Problem 20. *S Ltd furnishes you the following information relating to the half year ended on 30th June 2000.*

Fixed expenses	Rs. 45,000
Sales value	Rs. 1,50,000
Profit	Rs. 30,000

During the second half of the year, the company has a projected loss of Rs. 10,000. Calculate :

(i) *The break even point and margin of safety for six months ending on 30th June 2000.*

(ii) *Expected sales volume for second half of the year assuming that P/V ratio and fixed expenses remain constant in the second half year also.*

(iii) *The break even point and margin of safety for the whole year 2000.*

[M.Com 2004 PU]

Solution :

(i) *Calculation of BEP*

$$BEP = \frac{\text{Fixed Expenses}}{\text{P/V Ratio}}$$

Find the P/V ratio = $\frac{\text{Contribution}}{\text{Sales}} \times 100$

Contribution = Fixed expenses + Profit
= 45,000 + 30,000 = 75,000

P/V ratio = $\frac{\text{Contribution}}{\text{Sales}} \times 100$

= $\frac{75,000}{1,50,000} \times 100$

= 50%

BEP = $\frac{45,000}{50/100}$

= $45,000 \times \frac{100}{50} = 90,000$

Margin of Safety = Actual Sales − BEP Sales
= 1,50,000 − 90,000 = 60,000

(ii) *Expected Sales for the second half of year*

$$\frac{\text{Fixed Cost + Desired Profit}}{\text{P/V Ratio}}$$

But here the company has a projected loss for second half year. So the following changes in formula

$$= \frac{\text{Fixed Cost} - \text{Loss}}{\text{P/V Ratio}}$$

$$= \frac{45{,}000 - 10{,}000}{50/100} = \frac{35{,}000}{50/100} = 35{,}000 \times \frac{100}{50}$$

Expected Sales = Rs. 70,000

(iii) BEP for the whole year

Fixed expenses for the first half year = Rs. 45,000
Fixed expenses for the whole year (45,000 × 2) = Rs. 90,000

$$\text{BEP} = \frac{\text{Fixed Expenses}}{\text{P/V Ratio}}$$

$$= \frac{90{,}000}{50/100} = 1{,}80{,}000$$

Sales for the whole year :

First half = 1,50,000
Second half = 70,000
Sales for the whole year = 2,20,000

Margin of Safety

Actual Sales − BEP Sales = MOS
2,20,000 − 1,80,000 = 40,000

Problem 21. *The R & S. Co furnishes you the following information :*

	First half	Second half
Sales (Rs.)	8,10,000	10,26,000
Profit earned (Rs.)	21,600	64,800

From the above information, you are required to compute the following, assuming that the fixed cost remains the same in both the periods.

(i) P/V ratio
(ii) Fixed cost
(iii) The amount of profit or loss where sales are Rs. 6,48,000
(iv) The amount of sales required to earn a profit of Rs. 1,08,000.

[M.Com CA, 2004 PU]

Solution :

(i) P/V ratio

$$= \frac{\text{Differences of Profit}}{\text{Differences of Sales}} \times 100$$

$$= \frac{43{,}000}{2{,}16{,}000} \times 100$$

$$= 20\%$$

MARGINAL COSTING

(ii) *Fixed cost*

$$\text{Given sales} \times \text{P/V ratio} = \text{Contribution}$$

$$8,10,000 \times \frac{20}{100} = 1,62,000$$

$$\text{Less : Profit} = 21,600$$

$$\text{Fixed cost} = 1,40,400$$

(iii) *Amount of profit or loss : Sales are Rs. 6,48,000*

$$\text{Given sales} \times \text{P/V ratio} = \text{Contribution}$$

$$6,48,000 \times \frac{20}{100} = 1,29,600$$

$$\text{Less : Fixed cost} = 1,40,400$$

$$\text{Loss} = 10,800$$

(iv) *Amount of Sales*

$$\frac{\text{FC + Given Profit}}{\text{P/V Ratio}} = \frac{1,40,400 + 1,08,000}{20/100}$$

$$= \text{Rs. } 12,42,000$$

Problem 22. *You are given the following data for the year 1998 of the company.*

    Variable cost   Rs. 6,00,000
    Fixed cost   Rs. 4,00,000
    Net profit   Rs. 2,00,000
    Sales   Rs. 12,00,000

Find (i) P/V ratio (ii) BEP (iii) Profit when sales amounted to Rs. 14,00,000 (iv) sales required to earn a profit of Rs. 6,00,000.

Solution :

Marginal Cost Statement

$$\text{Sales} = 12,00,000$$

$$\text{Less : Variable cost} = 6,00,000$$

$$\text{Contribution} = 6,00,000$$

$$\text{Less : Fixed cost} = 4,00,000$$

$$\text{Profit} = 2,00,000$$

(i)   P/V Ratio $= \dfrac{\text{Contribution}}{\text{Sales}} \times 100$

$$= \frac{6,00,000}{12,00,000} \times 100 = 50\%$$

(ii)   BEP $= \dfrac{\text{Fixed Cost}}{\text{P/V Ratio}}$

$$= \frac{4,00,000}{50/100} = 8,00,000$$

(*iii*) Profit, when sales amounted to Rs. 14,00,000

Given sales × P/V ratio = Contribution

$$= 14,00,000 \times \frac{50}{100}$$

Contribution = 7,00,000   [FC + Profit]
Less : Fixed cost = 4,00,000
Profit = 3,00,000

(*iv*) Sales, required to earn a profit of Rs. 6,00,000

$$= \frac{\text{Fixed Cost + Desired Profit}}{\text{P/V Ratio}}$$

$$= \frac{3,00,000 + 6,00,000}{50/100}$$

$$= 9,00,000 \times \frac{100}{50}$$

$$= \text{Rs. } 18,00,000$$

Problem 23. *Royal hotel has annual fixed costs applicable to rooms of Rs. 15,00,000 for a 300 room hotel with average daily room rates of Rs. 40 and average variable costs of Rs. 6 for each room rented. The hotel operates 365 days a year. Income tax rate is 30%. You are required to find the number of rooms the hotel must rent to earn a net income after tax of Rs. 10,00,000 and compute the break even point in terms of number of rooms rented.*

[MCA Madras]

Solution :   **Profitability Statement**

Desired profit after tax = Rs. 10,00,000
Less : Tax rate 30%

$$\left[10,00,000 \times \frac{30}{70}\right] = 4,28,571$$

Total expected profit = 14,28,571
Fixed cost = 15,00,000
Contribution = 29,28,571

(FC + Expected profit)

Contribution per unit = Sales – Variable cost
= 40 – 6 = 34

Number of rooms in the hotel must be rented to earn a net income

$$= \frac{\text{Total contribution}}{\text{Contribution per unit}}$$

$$= \frac{29,28,571}{34} = 86,134 \text{ room days.}$$

Break even point in units = $\dfrac{FC}{\text{Contribution per unit}}$

$= \dfrac{15,00,000}{34}$

= 44,118 room days

Problem 24. *Rams & Co manufactures and sells chairs, tables and cabinets. The cost and sales data of the company are*

Product	Selling price per unit (Rs.)	Variable cost per unit (Rs.)	% of sales value of each product to total
Chairs	90	70	20
Table	110	90	30
Cabinet	150	110	50

The annual fixed cost is Rs. 20,000. The maximum production and sales capacity is Rs. 1,50,000. At present the company is operating at 80% of its capacity.

(a) Calculate the BEP of the company.
(b) Calculate the present annual profit.
(c) What would be the effect on profit if it utilizes its full capacity.
(d) What would be the net effect on the profit if it operates only at 50% capacity assuming the product mix remains unchanged. [MBA Madras]

Solution :

Workings : *Calculation of Sales and Variable costs*

(i) Sales   Rs.

   Chairs   = 1,50,000 × 20/100 = 30,000
   Tables   = 1,50,000 × 30/100 = 45,000
   Cabinets = 1,50,000 × 50/100 = 75,000

(ii) Variable cost

   Chairs   = 30,000 × 70/100 = 23,334
   Tables   = 45,000 × 90/110 = 36,818
   Cabinets = 75,000 × 110/150 = 55,000

	Chairs	Tables	Cabinets	Total
Sales	30,000	45,000	75,000	1,50,000
Less : VC	23,334	36,818	55,000	1,15,152
Contribution	6,636	8,182	20,000	34,848
Less : Fixed cost	—	—	—	20,000
Present profit				14,848

$$\text{BEP} = \frac{\text{Fixed Cost}}{\text{Contribution}} \times \text{Total Sales}$$

$$= \frac{20,000}{34,848} \times 1,50,000 = \text{Rs. } 86,088$$

Profitability Statement of different capacity operations

	50%	100%	80%
Sales	93,750	1,87,500	1,50,000
Less : VC	57,576	1,43,940	1,15,152
Contribution	36,174	43,560	34,848
Less : Fixed cost	20,000	20,000	20,000
Profit	16,174	23,560	14,848

If the firm works at 100% capacity, the net profit will be Rs. 23,560.

If the firm works at 50% capacity the profit will be Rs. 16,174.

Problem 25. *A company produces and markets industrial containers and packing cases. Due to competition the company proposes to reduce the selling price. If the present level of profit is to be maintained, indicate the number of units to be sold if the proposed reduction in selling price is (i) 5% (ii) 10% (iii) 15%.*

The following additional information is available

Present sales (30,000 units)	3,00,000
Variable cost (30,000 units)	1,80,000
Contribution	1,20,000
Less : fixed cost	70,000
Profit	50,000

Solution :

Present sales = 3,00,000

$$\text{Selling Price} = \frac{\text{Sale Value}}{\text{Number of Units}}$$

$$= \frac{3,00,000}{30,000} = \text{Rs. } 10$$

Present selling price is Rs. 10.

(i) 5% Reduction = $10 - \left[\frac{5}{100} \times 10\right] = 9.50$

(ii) 10% Reduction = $10 - \left[\frac{10}{100} \times 10\right] = 9.00$

(iii) 15% Reduction = $10 - \left[\frac{15}{100} \times 10\right] = 8.50$

MARGINAL COSTING

Contribution at various levels of selling price :

	5%	10%	15%
Percentage of reduction at Selling price	10.00	10.00	10.00
Less : Reduction	.50	1.00	1.50
Present selling price	9.50	9.00	8.50
Less : Variable cost	6.00	6.00	6.00
Contribution	3.50	3.00	2.50

Find the total contribution in order to maintain the present level of profit :

Present sales = Rs. 3,00,000
Less : Variable cost = Rs. 1,80,000
Total Contribution = 1,20,000

Number of units to be sold to earn a total contribution of Rs. 1,20,000 to maintain the present level of profits.

(a) At 5% Reduction = Rs. $\dfrac{1,20,000}{3.50}$ = 34,286 units.

(b) At 10% Reduction = Rs. $\dfrac{1,20,000}{3}$ = 40,000 units.

(c) At 15% Reduction = Rs. $\dfrac{1,20,000}{2.50}$ = 48,000 units.

Problem 26. *The following information is given about the Kasturi Rangas & Co as on December 31 1999.*

Particulars	Rs.
Cost of goods sold	20,00,000
Sales	1,40,00,000
Advertising expenses	70,00,000
Warehousing expenses	10,00,000
Transportation expenses	10,00,000

The company has two products. Super which sells for Rs. 100 per unit and Grand, which sells for Rs. 50 per unit. During the year, sales were as follows : Super 80,000 units and Grand 1,20,000 units. Production costs (Cost of goods sold) were as follows : Super Rs. 20 per unit; and Grand Rs. 3.33 per unit. Advertising expenses were approximately 50% of the sales of each product. Warehousing expenses is a variable based on the number of units sold. Transportation costs were incurred equally for each product. You are required to

(i) *Compute the contribution to net earnings for Super.*
(ii) *Compute the contribution to net earnings for Grand.*
(iii) *Compute the total unit cost (production and marketing costs) of Super.*
(iv) *Compute the total unit cost (production and marketing costs) of Grand.*

[MBA Madras]

Solution :

Profitability Statement or Statement of Contribution to Net Earnings
(i), (ii)

Particulars	Super (Rs.)	Grand (Rs.)
Sales (i)	80,00,000	60,00,000
Less : Variable cost :		
Production cost of goods sold	16,00,000	4,00,000
Warehousing expenses	4,00,000	6,00,000
Total variable cost (ii)	20,00,000	10,00,000
Contribution (iii) [S – V.C.] (i) – (ii)	60,00,000	50,00,000
Less : Fixed cost		
Advertising Expenses	40,00,000	30,00,000
Transport Expenses	5,00,000	5,00,000
Total Fixed cost (iv)	45,00,000	35,00,000
Profit [Contribution – TFC]	15,00,000	15,00,000
Contribution to Net earnings : Formula = $\dfrac{\text{Contribution}}{\text{Net earnings}} \times 100$	400%	333.33%

Workings :

                      Super   Grand

(a) Production cost : 80,000 × 20 = 16,00,000 – 4,00,000 = [1,20,000 × 3.33]

(b) Warehousing cost :

        Total units = 2,00,000

$$\text{Super} = \frac{10,00,000}{2,00,000} \times 80,000$$

$$= \text{Rs. } 4,00,000$$

$$\text{Grand} = \frac{10,00,000}{2,00,000} \times 1,20,000 = 6,00,000$$

(c) Advertising Expenses :

    Super 50% of Sales

$$80,00,000 \times \frac{50}{100} = 40,00,000$$

    Grand 50% of Sales

$$60,00,000 \times \frac{50}{100} = 30,00,000$$

    Total Advertising expenses = 70,00,000

MARGINAL COSTING

(d) Transport Expenses : (Distributed equally to both the products)

Super = 5,00,000
Grand = 5,00,000
Total = 10,00,000

Statement of Cost per unit

Particulars	Super (Rs.)	Grand (Rs.)
Sales units	80,000	1,20,000
Sales (Rs.)	80,00,000	60,00,000
Costs		
Production cost	16,00,000	4,00,000
Advertising expenses	40,00,000	30,00,000
Warehouse expenses	4,00,000	6,00,000
Transport expenses	5,00,000	5,00,000
Total cost	65,00,000	45,00,000

(iii), (iv) Cost per unit

$$\frac{\text{Total Cost}}{\text{Number of Units}} \qquad \frac{65,00,000}{80,000 \text{ Units}} \qquad \frac{45,00,000}{1,20,000 \text{ Units}}$$

$$\text{Rs. } 81.25 \qquad \text{Rs. } 37.50$$

Problem 27. *Coimbatore Computers Ltd. decides to effect a 10% reduction in the price of its product because it is felt that such a step may lead to greater volume of sales. It is anticipated that there are no prospects of a change in total fixed costs and variable cost per unit. The directors wish to maintain net profits at the present level.*

The following information has been obtained from its books :

Sales : 10,000 units   Rs. 2,00,000
Variable cost : Rs. 15 per unit
Fixed cost :   Rs. 40,000

How does the management proceed to implement this decision ?   [MCA 1998 Madras]

Solution :   **Marginal Cost Statement**

Particulars	Per unit Rs.	Total Rs.
Sales (10,000 units)	20.00	2,00,000
Less : Variable cost	15.00	1,50,000
Contribution	5.00	50,000
Less : Fixed cost		40,000
Profit		10,000

$$\text{P/V ratio} = \frac{\text{Contribution}}{\text{Sales}} \times 100$$

$$= \frac{5}{20} \times 100 = 25\%$$

$$\text{BEP} = \frac{\text{Fixed Cost}}{\text{P/V Ratio}}$$

$$= \frac{40,000}{25/100} \times 1,60,000$$

Effect of change of 10% reduction in selling price

Selling Price =	20.00
Less : 10% =	2.00
Selling price after reduction =	18.00
Less : Variable cost =	15.00
Contribution =	3.00

$$\text{P/V ratio} = \frac{\text{Contribution}}{\text{Sales}} \times 100$$

$$= \frac{3}{18} \times 100 = 16.67\%$$

$$\text{BEP} = \frac{\text{Fixed Cost}}{\text{P/V Ratio}}$$

$$= \frac{40,000}{16.67/100} \times \text{Rs. } 3,00,000$$

Sales to earn present level of profit of Rs. 10,000

$$= \frac{\text{Fixed Cost + Desired Profit}}{\text{P/V Ratio}}$$

$$= \frac{40,000 + 10,000}{16.67/100}$$

$$= \text{Rs. } 3,00,000$$

The management decided to implement this decision because the break even sales will be increased to Rs. 2,40,000. If the company wants to maintain the present level of profit *i.e.*, Rs. 10,000, it should take steps to increase the sales amounting to Rs. 3,00,000.

❑❑❑

17
Relevant Cost for Decision Making

DECISION MAKING

Decision making is the process of choosing the best course of action among the various alternative courses since if there is no choice, there is no decision to take. Generally, a decision always focuses on the future prediction. The aim of the decision maker is therefore to select the best course of action for the future.

Relevant Costs

A cost that is relevant to a decision is called relevant cost. In an organisation the decision maker just makes use of relevant costs. In other words, costs are relevant if they guide the executive towards the decision that harmonises with top management's objectives.

Differential Cost

Differential cost means the change in costs due to change in the level of activity or pattern or method of production. Simply, differential cost is the result of an alternative course of action.

COST CONCEPTS IN DECISION MAKING

Certain concepts which are generally used in the analysis of cost for decision making are listed below.

(i) Marginal cost
(ii) Out of pocket cost
(iii) Differential costs
(iv) Sunk costs
(v) Opportunity costs
(vi) Replacement cost
(vii) Avoidable and unavoidable costs
(viii) Imputed costs
(ix) Relevant costs and irrelevant costs.

STEPS INVOLVED IN DECISION MAKING

The following steps are involved in decision making process.
(i) Problem identification
(ii) Identifying alternatives
(iii) Evaluating Quantitative factors
(iv) Examining Qualitative factors

(v) Obtaining further details if necessary
(vi) Selection of the best alternative.

AREAS OF DECISION MAKING

The executives of the organisation or the decision maker of the concern has to adopt the above steps in the following important areas of decision.

(i) Make or buy decisions
(ii) Sell or process decisions
(iii) Special order decisions
(iv) Incremental analysis
(v) Decision regarding further processing of joint/by products
(vi) Sales mix decisions
(vii) Additional shift decisions
(viii) Adding or dropping product line decisions
(ix) Plant closing down decisions

(i) *Make or Buy Decisions.* A firm may be producing some products, or tools or parts by itself. The same products or tools may be available from the outside suppliers. The management can take decision in this regard comparing the price that has to be paid and the saving that can be effected on cost.

(ii) *Sell or Process Decisions.* An organisation can sell its product when it has been partly processed or it is sent for further processing before selling it. When a product passes various stages of manufacturing operation, it may be a marketable product at a number of different points along the way. Under this type of industrial sector, the company has an option to sell the product at various stages of completion. Under the sell or process decisions, incremental analysis guides the management to take correct decisions.

(iii) *Special Order Decisions.* Large Scale purchasers may place huge orders at a price less than the customer's sale price on receiving a bulk order from the foreign companies. A decision has to be taken now whether to accept the order or to reject it. Such an order can prove beneficial to the company when it is working below full production capacity and the price offered results in incremental revenue which is higher than the differential costs.

(iv) *Incremental Analysis.* Incremental analysis refers to the changes in costs or revenue due to changes in the level of activity or pattern or method of production. Under the incremental analysis, the organisation has to get either incremental revenue and cost or decremental revenue and cost. Based upon the incremental revenue only, the management can take a decision.

(v) *Decision Regarding Further Processing of Joint or By-product.* Certain industries produce two or more products of almost more or less equal value which are simultaneously produced from the same manufacturing process and from the same raw material. They are known as joint products.

The term by-product refers to one or more products of relatively small value that are produced simultaneously with a product of greater value.

RELEVANT COST FOR DECISION MAKING

Generally, the management has to take decision regarding further processing of joint products or by-products after the split off. This type of decision is taken on the basis of comparison of differential cost and incremental revenue.

(vi) *Sales Mix Decisions.* Sales mix is the ratio in which various products are produced and sold. Generally when an industry manufactures more than one product, it has to face the problem of which product mix gives maximum profit. The best product mix is that which yields the maximum profit. Those products which give maximum contribution are to be retained and their production increased. Automatically sales is also increased. Based upon the results of p/v ratio and break even points only the organisation can take sales mix decisions.

(vii) *Additional Shift Decisions.* Any organisation, if it wants to go for the introduction of additional shift, incurs some additional cost. In this aspect, the additional cost should be compared with the additional revenue. So the management can take decision on the basis of the net effect on the profit earned by the company due to this additional shift.

(viii) *Adding or Dropping Product Line Decisions.* Some time, a manufacturing company may decide to add some new product or delete the existing product from the production line. In order to arrive at the correct decision in this regard, management has to find the profitable position of the company based upon the comparative analysis of differential cost and incremental revenue.

(ix) *Plant Closing Down Decisions.* Sometimes a manufacturing organisation should decide to close its business either on temporary basis or permanent basis. Closing down of business arises because closing is better than operating business at loss. In this situation, marginal costing assists the management to take suitable actions.

Problem 1. *HR Ltd., makes a single product which sells for Rs. 30 per unit and there is a great demand for the product. The variable cost of the product is Rs. 16 as detailed below.*

	Rs
Direct material	8
Direct Labour (2 Hrs)	4
Variable overhead	4
Total cost	16

The labour force is currently working at full capacity and no extra time can be made available. Mr. Goyal, a customer has approached the company with a request for the manufacture of a special order at Rs. 8,000. The cost of the order would be Rs. 3000 for direct material and 600 labour hours will be required and variable overhead per hour should be Rs. 2. Should the order be accepted or not. [MBA Madras]

Solution :

$$\text{Sales Price} = \text{Rs. 30}$$
$$\text{Order amount} = \text{Rs. 8000}$$
$$\text{No. of unit} \left[\frac{8{,}000}{30}\right] = 267$$

Cost details per unit

$$\text{Direct material } \frac{3{,}000}{267} = 11.23$$

Direct labour $\left(\dfrac{4}{2} \times 600 = 1{,}200\right) \dfrac{1{,}200}{267} = 4.49$

Variable Expenses $(600 \times 2 = 1{,}200) = 4.49$

Total variable cost per unit = 20.21

Total variable cost for 267 units × Rs. 20.21 = Rs. 5,396
Sales value at special order = Rs. 8,000
Less : variable cost = Rs. 5,396
Contribution = Rs. 2,604

Rs. 2,604 is treated as an Additional Contribution and it will be an income to the concern. So the order may be accepted.

Problem 2. *A Company has a capacity of producing 1,00,000 units of a certain product in a month. The sales department reports that the following schedule of sales price is possible.*

Volume of production	Selling price per unit
60%	0.90
70%	0.80
80%	0.75
90%	0.67
100%	0.61

The variable cost of manufacture between these levels is Re. 0.15 per unit. Fixed cost is Rs. 40,000.

You are required to prepare a statement showing incremental revenue and differential cost at each stage. At which volume of production, will the profit be maximum ?

If there is a bulk order at Re. 0.40 per unit for the balance capacity over the maximum profit volume for export and the price quoted will not affect the internal sale. Will you advise to accept this bid and why ?

[MBA Anna]

Solution :

(a) **Statement of incremental revenue and differential cost**

Capacity level %	Units Nos.	Variable Cost Rs.	Fixed Cost Rs.	Total Cost Rs.	Differential Cost Rs.	Sales or Revenue Rs.	Incremental Revenue Rs.
60	60,000	9,000	40,000	49,000	—	54,000	—
70	70,000	10,500	40,000	50,500	1,500	56,000	2,000
80	80,000	12,000	40,000	52,000	1,500	60,000	4,000
90	90,000	13,500	40,000	53,500	1,500	60,300	300
100	1,00,000	15,000	40,000	55,000	1,500	61,000	700

Based upon the above calculation 80% capacity level is the maximum profit.

RELEVANT COST FOR DECISION MAKING

(b) Income from the bulk order :

20,000 units @ .40 paise per unit		8,000
Less : Additional Variable cost (20,000 × .15)		3,000
Additional Net Profit		5000

It is decided to accept the bulk order. But fixed costs are not considered because fixed cost will be constant upto the production level of 1,00,000 units. This is the budgeted production.

Problem 3. *The Chennai Machinery & Co. manufactured and sold 1000 calculators last year at a price of Rs.800 each. The cost structure of a calculator is as follows.*

	Rs.
Material	200
Labour	100
Variable cost	50
Marginal cost	350
Factory overhead (Fixed)	200
Total cost	550
Profit	250
Sale price	800

Due to heavy competition, price has to be reduced to Rs. 750 for the coming year. Assuming no change in costs, state the number of calculators that would have to be sold at the new price to ensure the same amount of total profits as that of the last year.

[B.Com Madras]

Solution :

Profit for 1,000 calculators 1000 × 250 = Rs. 2,50,000

$$\text{Computation of P/V ratio} = \frac{\text{Contribution}}{\text{Sales}} \times 100$$

Contribution = Sales – V.C.
            = 750 – 350 = 400

$$\text{P/V ratio} = \frac{400}{750} \times 100 = \textbf{53.33\%}$$

Sales required to earn a profit of Rs. 2,50,000

$$= \frac{\text{Fixed Cost + Profit}}{\text{P/V Ratio}}$$

$$= \frac{2,00,000 + 2,50,000}{53.33/100}$$

= Rs.8,43,802

$$\text{Sales in units} = \frac{8,43,802}{750} = 1125 \text{ calculator.}$$

If the company is to sell 1,125 calculators only, it will earn the last year's total profit of 2,50,000 even in the reduction of selling price at Rs. 750/-.

Problem 4. *Following information has been made available from the records of KRS Ltd, manufacturing spare parts.*

	Cost per unit Rs.
Direct material	
X	8.00
Y	6.00
Direct wages	
X	24 hours @ 25 paise per hour
Y	16 hours @ 25 paise per hour.
Variable overheads	150% of wages
Fixed overheads	Rs.750
Selling price of X	Rs.25
Selling price of Y	Rs.20

The directors want to be acquainted with the desirability of adopting any one of the following alternative sales mixes in the budget for the next period.

(a) 250 units of X and 250 units of Y.
(b) 400 units of Y only.
(c) 400 units of X and 100 units of Y.
(d) 150 units of X and 350 units of Y.

State which of the alternative sales mixes you would recommend to the management.

[MBA, Anna Dec 2003] [B.Com Madurai]

Solution :   **Marginal Cost Statement**

Particulars	Product X Rs.	Product Y Rs.
Direct Material	8	6
Direct wages	6	4
Variable overheads	9	6
Total variable cost	23	16
Selling price	25	20
Less : Variable cost	23	16
Contribution	2	4

Alternative Sales Mix Decisions

(a) 250 units of X and 250 units of Y

		Rs.
Contribution : Product X, 250 × Rs. 2 =		500
Product Y, 250 × Rs. 4 =		1,000
		1,500
Less : Fixed cost =		750
Profit		750

(b) 400 units of product Y
    Contribution : Product Y : 400 × Rs.4 =   1,600
                        Less : Fixed cost =   750
                                    Profit   850

(c) 400 units of product X and 100 units of Product Y
    Contribution : Product X : 400 × Rs. 2 =   800
                   Product Y : 100 × Rs. 4 =   400
                                                1,200
                        Less : Fixed cost =   750
                                    Profit   450

(d) 150 units of Product X and 350 units of Product Y
    Contribution : Product X : 150 × Rs. 2 =   300
                   Product Y : 350 × Rs. 4 =   1,400
                                                1,700
                        Less : Fixed cost =   750
                                    Profit   950

Result and Decision :

Among the four different sales mixes, (d) is the most profitable since it gives the maximum profit of Rs. 950/-. So it should be recommended.

Problem 5. *The management of a company finds that the cost of making a component part is Rs. 10. While the same is available in the market at Rs. 9 with an assurance of continuous supply.*

Give a suggestion whether to make or buy this part. Give also your view in case the supplier reduces the price from Rs. 9 to 8.00.

The cost information is as follows

Material	Rs. 3.50
Direct Labour	Rs. 4.00
Other variable expenses	Rs. 1.00
Fixed expenses	Rs. 1.50
Total	10.00

Solution :

In order to take decision regarding the making or buying the component part, fixed cost should not be considered. Because these will be incurred even if the part is produced or not. But if the part is produced, the following additional costs should be incurred.

	Rs.
Material	3.50
Direct Labour	4.00
Other variable Expenses	1.00
Total cost	8.50

It is available in the market for Rs. 9.00. But the production cost of the part is Rs. 8.50. So the company gets contribution of .50 paise per part (9.00 – 8.50) even if it manufactures by itself.

If the same is available in the market at Rs. 8.00, the company should not manufacture the part. It is better to buy the part in the market. As per the above calculation it is better if the company manufacture the part itself.

Problem 6. *The management of a company is thinking whether it should drop one item from the product line and replace it with another. Given below are present cost and output data.*

Product	Price Rs.	Variable Costs Per unit Rs.	Percentage of sales Rs.
Book shelf	60	40	30%
Table	100	60	20%
Bed	200	120	50%

Total fixed costs per year Rs. 7.50.000
Sales Rs. 25.00.000

The change under consideration consists in dropping the line of Tables and adding the line of cabinets. If this change is made, the manufacturer forecasts the following costs and output data.

Product	Price Rs.	Variable Costs Per unit (A) Rs.	Percentage of sales Rs.
Book shelf	60	40	15%
Cabinet	160	60	10%
Bed	200	120	40%

Total fixed costs per year Rs. 7,50,000
Sales Rs. 26,00,000

Should this proposal be accepted or not ? comment. [M.Com Adapted]

Solution : **Comparative Profitability Statement**

	Book Shelves	Tables Rs.	Beds Rs.	Total Rs.	Book Shelf	Cabinets Rs.	Beds Rs.	Total Rs.
Sales	7,50,000	5,00,000	12,50,000	25,00,000	13,00,000	2,60,000	10,40,000	26,00,000
Less Variable cost	5,00,000	3,00,000	7,50,000	15,50,000	8,66,667	97,500	62,4,000	15,88,166
Contribution	2,50,000	2,00,000	5,00,000	9,50,000	4,33,333	1,62,500	4,16,000	10,11,833
Less fixed cost				7,50,000				7,50,000
Profit (Contribution - fixed cost)				2,00,000				2,16,000

Comments : Based on the above calculation, the manufacturer will stand to gain in case he drops the production of tables in preference to cabinets. But the demand for cabinets should not be a temporary period.

RELEVANT COST FOR DECISION MAKING

Workings :

Existing Situation	Sales	Variable costs
Book shelve	$25{,}00{,}000 \times \dfrac{30}{100}$	$7{,}50{,}000 \times \dfrac{40}{60}$
	= Rs. 7,50,000	= Rs. 5,00,000
Tables	$25{,}00{,}000 \times \dfrac{20}{100}$	$5{,}00{,}000 \times \dfrac{60}{100}$
	= Rs. 5,00,000	= Rs. 3,00,000
Beds :	$25{,}00{,}000 \times \dfrac{50}{100}$	$12{,}50{,}000 \times \dfrac{120}{200}$
	= Rs. 12,50,000	= Rs. 7,50,000

Proposed Situation	Sales	Variable Costs
Book shelves	$26{,}00{,}000 \times \dfrac{50}{100}$	$13{,}00{,}000 \times \dfrac{40}{60}$
	= Rs. 13,00,000	= Rs. 8,66,667
Cabinets	$26{,}00{,}000 \times \dfrac{10}{100}$	$26{,}00{,}000 \times \dfrac{60}{100}$
	= Rs. 2,60,000	= Rs. 97,500
Beds :	$26{,}00{,}000 \times \dfrac{40}{100}$	$10{,}40{,}000 \times \dfrac{120}{200}$
	= Rs. 10,40,000	= Rs. 6,24,000

Problem 7. *Modern Cutting Machines & Co manufactures hand operated cutting machines. Prepare a schedule showing the differential costs and incremental revenue at each stage from the following data. At what volume the company should set its level of production ?*

Output (No. in lakhs)	Selling price (per machine)	Total semifixed cost (Rs in lakhs)	Total variable cost (Rs in lakhs)	Total fixed cost (Rs in lakhs)
0.60	240	30	83.6	28.4
1.20	220	30	163.6	28.4
1.80	200	34	255.6	28.4
2.40	180	34	315.6	28.4
3.00	160	40	355.6	28.4
3.60	140	40	380.6	28.4

[MBA Anna]

Solution :
Schedule showing the differential costs and incremental revenues

Output (No. in lakhs)	Selling Price Per Machine (Rs.)	Sales Value Rs. (in Lakhs)	Incremental Revenue Rs. (in Lakhs)	Semi Fixed Cost Rs. (in Lakhs)	Variable Cost Rs. (in Lakhs)	Fixed Cost Rs. (in Lakhs)	Total Cost Rs. (in Lakhs)	Differential Cost Rs. (in Lakhs)
0.60	240	144	—	30.0	83.6	28.4	142.0	—
1.20	220	264	120	30.0	63.6	28.4	222.0	80.0
1.80	200	360	96	34.0	255.6	28.4	318.0	96.0
2.40	180	432	72	34.0	315.6	28.4	378.0	60.0
3.00	160	480	48	40.0	355.6	28.4	424.0	46.0
3.60	140	504	24	40.0	380.6	28.4	449.0	25.0

Comments : The company should set its level of output at 3,00,000 units. Because up to this level incremental revenue exceeds differential cost.

Problem 8. *KKS Ltd having installed capacity of 1,00,000 units of a product is currently operating at 70% utilisation. At current levels of input prices, the FOB unit costs (after taking credit for applicable export incentives) work out as follows.*

Capacity utilisation %	FOB unit costs (Rs.)
70	97
80	92
90	87
100	82

The company has received three foreign offers from different sources as under.

Source K 5000 units at Rs. 55 per unit FOB.

Source L 10,000 units at Rs. 52 per unit FOB.

Source C 10,000 units at Rs. 51 per unit FOB.

Advise the company as to whether any or all the export orders should be accepted or not. [B.Com Hons Delhi 2000]

Solution :
Statement showing differential cost of different capacity levels

Capacity %	Production units	FOB unit Cost (Rs.)	Total Cost (Rs.)	Differential Cost	Per unit Differential Cost
70	70,000	97	67,60,000	—	—
80	80,000	92	73,60,000	5,70,000	57
90	90,000	87	78,30,000	4,70,000	47
100	1,00,000	82	82,00,000	3,70,000	37

RELEVANT COST FOR DECISION MAKING

Statement showing Gain or Loss on accepting the various Export order

Export order source	Export order (units)	Capacity utilisation %	Differential cost per unit Rs.	Total (Rs.)	FOB Price per unit	Sales revenue from export	Profit or Loss
K	5,000	75%	57	2,85,000	55	2,75,000	10,000
L	10,000	85%	5000 57 } 5000 47	5,20,000	52	5,20,000	Nil
C	10,000	95%	5000 57 } 5000 37	4,20,000	51	5,10,000	90,000
Total	25,000	155%		12,25,000		13,05,000	1,00,000

Comment : The Company should accept all the three export orders.

Problem 9. *A company manufactures three products A, B and C. There are no common processes and the sale of one product does not affect prices or volume of sale of any other.*

The company's budgeted profit/Loss for 1998 has been abstracted thus.

	Total Rs	A Rs	B Rs	C Rs
Sales	3,00,000	45,000	2,25000	30,000
Production costs				
Variable :	1,80,000	24,000	1,44,000	12,000
Fixed :	60,000	3,000	48,000	9,000
Total Factory cost :	2,40,000	27,000	1,92,000	21,000
Selling admi, costs				
Variable :	24,000	8,100	8,100	7,800
Fixed :	6,000	2,100	1,800	2,100
Total cost	2,70,000	37,200	2,01,900	30,900
Profit	30,000	7,800	23,100	– 900

[Sales – Total Cost]

On the basis of the above, the board had almost decided to eliminate product C, on which a loss was budgeted. Meanwhile, they have sought your opinion. As the company's Cost Accountant, what would you advise ? Give reasons for your answer.

Solution :   **Profitability Statement**

	Rs.	A	Rs.	B	Rs.	C	Total
Sales		45,000		2,25,000		30,000	3,00,000
Less : Variable cost							
Production cost	24,000		1,44,000		12,000		
Sell Adm. Cost	8,100	32,100	8,100	1,52,100	7,800	19,800	2,04,000
		12,900		72,900		10,200	96,000

		28.67%		32.4%		34.%	
Less : Fixed cost (60,000 + 6,000)							66,000
Profit							30,000
P/V Ratio C/S × 100		28.67%		32.4%		34.%	

Based upon the above computation product C is contributing Rs. 10,200 towards the fixed expenses of the company. If the product C is discontinued the profit of the company will be reduced to Rs. 19,800 [*i.e.,* 30,000 – 10,200]. And the P/V ratio of product C is higher as compared to other products. Under this background it is advisable to continue the product C.

Problem 10. *A radio manufacturing company finds that it costs Rs. 6.25 to make each component x 6640, while the same is available in the market at Rs. 4.85 each, with an assurance of continuous supply. The break up of cost is as follows :*

Materials	Rs. 2.75 each
Labour	Rs. 1.75 each
Other variable cost	Rs. 0.50 each
Depreciation and other fixed cost	Rs. 1.25 each
	6.25

should you make or buy ? [BBA]

Solution :

Variable cost of manufacturing is Rs. 5.00.

i.e., (6.25 – 1.25)

But the market price is Rs. 4.85

If the fixed cost of Rs. 1.25 is added, it is not profitable to make the component.

Better to procure it from outside supply, because, if it purchases from outside supply it can get a profit of .15 paise.

Assignment Problem

Problem 11. *Due to industrial depression, a plant is running at present only 50% of its capacity. The following details are available.*

Particulars	Cost of production per unit (Rs.)
Direct material	2
Direct Labour	1
Variable overhead	3
Fixed overhead	2
	8
Production per month	20,000 units
Total cost of production	Rs. 1,60,000
Sales price	Rs. 1,40,000
Loss	Rs. 20,000

An exporter offer to buy 5000 units per month at the rate of Rs 6.50 per unit and the company hesitates to accept the offer for the fear of increasing its already operating losses. Advise whether the company should accept or decline this offer. [B.Com Adapted]

Answer. Loss reduced from Rs. 20,000 to Rs. 15,000. So the firm must accept the offer.

18
Budget and Budgetary Control

NEED FOR BUDGETING

Budget is not only essential for government and various business organisations but also for the individuals. So every one is very familiar with the budgeting. Without the budget or predetermined objectives no one can achieve its targets and go for performance evaluation. Whenever the organisation fixes its targets, it is necessary to evaluate its performance. *i.e.*, the actual performance can be compared to the targeted one. If any deviation arises, the organisation can take a suitable action for correcting the deviation in future with the help of budgeting.

BUDGETING AND BUDGETARY CONTROL

Introduction

Modern industrial world faces stiff competition, uncertainty and it is exposed to different types of risks. Apart from the competition, modern era is the age of technology where fast changes are taking place. Due to this fast changes, automatic competition is generated at higher level and reactions of competitors are unknown and it is difficult to determine the consumer preferences in the context of too many products are available in the market. Planning is very important function of management. It relates to what is to be done, how, when and where it is to be done. Thus planning is related to the future course of events. Ultimate aim of efficient management is that all types of operations should be predetermined in advance. So cost can be controlled at all levels. If management is effective, it accomplishes the objective with minimum effort and cost.

Budget is not a new term. Everyone is familiar with the idea of budget because it is essential in every movement of our life—individual, institution or industry, State Government or Central Government.

Definition

The word budget is derived from a French term "Bougette" which denotes a leather pouch fund allocated for meeting anticipated expenses.

According to ICMA, England, a budget is *"a financial and or quantitative statements prepared and approved prior to a defined period of time, of the policy to be pursued during the period for the purpose of attaining a given objective".*

It is also defined as *"a blue print of a projected plan of action of a business for a definite period of time".*

Budgetary Control

The Chartered Institute of Management Accountants, London, defines budgetary control "as the establishment of budgets relating to the responsibilities of executives to the requirements of a policy and the continuous comparison of actual with budgeted results either to secure by individual action the objective of that policy or to provide a basis for its revision".

Meaning of budget, budgeting and budgetary control, according to Rowland and William H. Harris, is that

"Budgets are the individual objectives of a department etc., where as budgeting may be said to be the act of building budgets. Budgetary control embraces all this and in addition includes the science of planning the budgets themselves and the utilisation of such budgets to effect on overall management tool for the business planning and control.

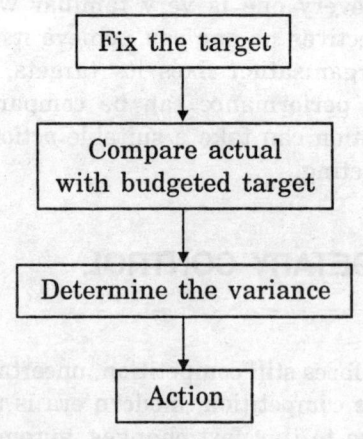

```
        Fix the target
              ↓
      Compare actual
    with budgeted target
              ↓
    Determine the variance
              ↓
           Action
```

Process of Budgetary control

Advantages of Budgetary Control

The advantages and benefits of budgetary control are summarised below.

1. It brings efficiency and economy in the work of the whole enterprise. Simply it is an impersonal policeman that generates ordered effort and brings about the efficiency in results.
2. It establishes divisional and departmental responsibilities so back passing is not possible.
3. It secures proper co-ordination among various functional activities of the organisation. And also it promotes mutual co-operation and team spirit among the persons involved.
4. Reduction in cost and elimination of inefficiency is achieved automatically. As a result, decrease in cost of production by increasing the volume of output.
5. It enables the management to decentralise responsibility without losing control of entire business operations since it pin-points inefficiency.
6. It facilitates to receive great favour from credit agencies. *i.e.*, if the organisation has a well developed budget and operates accordingly, it receives more amount of bank credit.
7. It aims at maximisation of profit through cost control and proper utilisation of resources.

8. Budget provides advance information, not only for the elimination of financial crisis but also for the efficent use of available capital.
9. It provides adequate guidance to the field of research and development in future.
10. It enables to evaluate the performance.
11. It allows to achieve the balanced capital structure *i.e.,* it avoids over capitalisation or under capitalisation.
12. Budgets fix the goals and targets without which operation lacks direction.

Disadvantages of Budgetary Control

1. Opposition against the spirit of budgeting
2. The success of the budgetary control depends upon the degree of accuracy of the estimates. Forecasting is essential for budgeting. But there are no possibilities for hundred percent accuracy in forecasts and estimates.
3. Inflation, Deflation, Economic & Government policies will affect the success of the budgetary control.
4. Effectiveness of the budgetary control depens upon the willing co-operation or team work of all concerned. If there is no co-operation the system will be ineffective.
5. Budgetary control is essentially a tool of decision making and helps the management to take various decisions. But it cannot replace the management.
6. It is not suitable for small concerns because it requires huge amount of money and professional staff for preparing budget.
7. It is a time consuming process.

Essentials of a Sound Budgetary Control

For an effective and efficient system of Budgetary control certain pre-requisites must be needed. These are :

1. The system should have full support from top management.
2. There should be a true delegation of authority and responsibility with the well planned organisational setup.
3. Staff should be strongly and properly motivated towards budgeting.
4. Budgets should actually work as a co-ordinating device rather than control device.
5. The accounting system should provide accurate and timely information.
6. Deviations from the standard targets should be reported promptly and clearly to all levels of management.
7. The budget should lay down the targets which are easily attainable.
8. Sufficient operational freedom should be given to the concerned executives within the overall framework.
9. Past experience is a very useful guide for the future. So important points revealed by past experience should be taken into account while preparing budget in future.

Objectives of Budgeting

1. To determine organisational objectives.
2. To minimise waste and control expenses.

3. To plan and control the income and expenditure of the firm.
4. To fix responsibilities in different departments or heads.
5. To ensure the availability of working capital.
6. To centralize the control system.
7. Increase profitability through elimination of waste.
8. To take remedial action in order to correct deviations from established standards.
9. To find in which area action is needed and to solve the problem without delay.
10. To provide long term and short term plans for attaining organisational goals.

Installations of Budgetary Control

The organisation which has to achieve an effective system of budgetary control, will need the following steps.

1. *Organisation Chart.* A concern must have a well defined organisation chart for budgetary control. It is essential in order to have clear determination of authority and responsibility of each individual. Determination of authorities helps to minimise conflict among the personnel.
2. *Objectives.* It requires a clearly defined objective in terms of both quantity and quality that are sought to be achieved by the system of budgetary control.
3. *Budget Centre.* A budget centre is a part of the organisation for which budget is prepared to cover entire operational activities of the organisation. It is necessary for cost control purposes. With the help of the different budget centres, performance should be evaluated in an easy manner.
4. *Budget Committee.* Budget committee should be established for the purpose of incorporation and execution of plans. In small organisations, either the Cost Accountant or Chartered Accountant prepares the budget. In case of big companies a separate committee is formed for this task. The committee consists of various section heads, the chief executive and the budget controller. The ultimate aim of budget committee is to prepare a master budget with the help of the department wise budget which has already been prepared by the departmental executives.
5. *Budget Manual.* It is a written document which sets out the authorities and responsibilities of persons engaged in regular operational activities. It clearly lays down objectives of the organisation and the procedure to be followed by the executives concerned. It is the responsibility of the budget officer to prepare and maintain this manual.
6. *Budget Period.* The length of time for which the budget is prepared and employed is called budget period. It may be different for different industries or even it may differ among the same industry or business. The budget period will depend upon the following factors.
    - The type of business
    - Length of the trade cycle
    - Nature of the product
7. *Key Factor.* Key factor is also known as limiting factor or governing factor or principal budget factor. Simply, if these factors are not available in sufficient quantity, that should be referred as limiting or key factor. It may arise due to

shortage of material, labour, hours, capital, plant capacity. It is essential for other budgets. So the concern will have to first prepare key factor related aspects and then other budgets are prepared.

Classification of Budget

Different types of budgets have been developed keeping in view the different purposes they serve. Some of the important classifications of the budgets are discussed below.

A. Classification According to Time

Based on the time factor, budgets are broadly classified in the following three types.

(i) *Long term Budgets.* The budgets are prepared to show the long term planning of the organisation. This budget is prepared normally for a period of 5 to 10 years. *Example :* Capital expenditure budget, research and development, long term finances etc.

(ii) *Short term Budgets.* Short term budgets are those which have to be prepared for a period of one or two years. *Example :* Cash Budget, Material Budget etc.

(iii) *Current Budget.* Current budget is one which has to be prepared for a very short period say a month or a quarter year and is related to the current conditions.

B. Classification According to Function

A functional budget is a budget which relates to any of the functions of an organisation. The following are the functional budgets commonly used.

(i) *Sales Budget.* Sales budget is a forecast of total sales (volume) during the budget period. It may contain the information regarding the sales, month wise, product wise, and area wise. This budget is prepared by the sales manager.

(ii) *Production Budget.* Production budget is prepared by the production manager. Its preparation depends upon the sales budget. The objective of this budget is to determine the quantity of production for a budgeted period. In other words, it is a quantity of units to be produced during a budget period.

Production units may be calculated in the following way : budgeted sales + desired closing stock − opening stock.

(iii) *Materials Budget.* Material procurement budget is an estimate of quantities of raw materials to be purchased for production during the budget period. It helps the organisation to formulate effective purpose policy of raw materials. Materials budget should be prepared normally taking into account the following factors *i.e.,* availability of finance, storage facilities, price trends in the markets.

(iv) *Labour Budget.* Labour budget is a budget which is prepared by the personnel department of the organisation. It shows the total hours required to complete the production target. And also it shows the cost incurred for the labour used for the production.

(v) *Factory Overhead Budget.* This budget indicates the estimated costs of indirect materials, indirect labour and indirect factory expenses incurred during the budget period. This budget is classified into fixed, variable and semi-variable.

(vi) *Administrative Expenses Budget.* In order to estimate the amount required to meet the administrative and operational activities of the organisation, the administrative expenses budget is prepared. This budget will provide proper guidance and estimation for the expenses incurred in the budget period.

(vii) *Selling and Distribution Overhead Budget.* This budget is prepared by the sales manager of each territory. It indicates an estimate of administrative expenses to be incurred in the budget period. Preparation of selling and distribution overhead budget depends upon the sales budget.

(viii) *Capital Expenditure Budget.* Capital expenditure budget is a long term planning for the proposed capital outlay and its financing. Capital expenditure is an expenditure which has to be incurred for the purpose of acquiring benefit not only for the particular year but also for the subsequent period of 5 to 10 years. Capital budgeting is the most important and complicated problem of managerial decisions. Capital budgeting is also known as investment decision making.

(ix) *Cash Budget.* Cash budget is prepared by the chief accountant of the organisation. It may be prepared either monthly or weekly. Cash budget is a statement to show the estimated amount of cash receipts and payment and balance during the budget period. Simply, it represents the estimated cash receipts and payments over the specific future period.

(x) *Master Budget.* Master budget is a budget which has to incorporate all functional budgets. The definition of this budget given by the Chartered Institute of Management Accountant, England is as follows. "The summary budget, incorporating its component functional budgets and which is finally approved, adopted, and employed." It is otherwise called as finalised profit plan. Normally, it has to be approved by the board of directors before it is put into operational activities.

C. Classification According to Flexibility

(i) *Fixed Budget.* A fixed budget is drawn for a fixed level of activity and a prescribed set of conditions. It has been defined as "a budget which is designed to remain unchanged irrespective of the volume of output or level of activity actually attained". In the real sense, it does not consider any change in expenditure arising out of changes in the level of activity.

(ii) *Flexible Budget.* Flexible budget is otherwise called as variable budget. The Chartered Institute of Management Accountants, England, defines a flexible budget "as a budget which by recognising the difference in behaviour between fixed and variable costs in relation to fluctuations in output, turnover or other variable factors such as number of employees is designed to change appropriately with such fluctuations".

Normally, the flexible budget is prepared in any of the following cases :

1. Where there are general changes in sales.
2. Where the business is a new one and it is difficult to forecast the demand.
3. In an industry which has to be influenced by changes in fashion.

ZERO BASE BUDGETING

The zero base budgeting, as a managerial tool, has become increasingly popular since the early 1970's. The main aim of the zero base budgeting is the cost reduction and optimum utilisation of resources. It first came into being when former president Jimmy Carter of the United States of America, then Governor of the state of Georgia, introduced it as a means of controlling state expenditure.

BUDGET AND BUDGETARY CONTROL

Definition of Zero base Budgeting

Zero base budgeting is defined as *"a planning and budgeting process which requires each manager to justify his entire budget request in detail from scratch (hence zero base) and shifts the burden of proof to each manager to justify why he should spend money at all. The approach requires that all activities be analysed in decision packages which are evaluated by systematic analysis and ranked in the order of importance".*

Steps in Zero Base Budgeting

1. Determination of objectives
2. Determination of extent of application
3. Identification of decision making units
4. Through the cost-benefit analysis
5. Preparation of budgets

PERFORMANCE BUDGETING

Any type of budgeting, in order to be successful, must provide performance appraisal as well as follow-up measures. Without performance appraisal and follow-up measures, the budget will not be successful. In this regard, responsibility centre and a programme of expected performance in physical units of that centre must be established.

According to the National Institute of Bank Management, Mumbai, performance budgeting technique is the process of analysing, identifying, simplifying and crystallising specific performance objectives of a job to be achieved over a period in the framework of the organisational objectives. The technique is characterised by its specific direction towards the business objectives of the organisation.

I. Production Budget

Problem 1. *Prepare a production budget for three months ending on March 31, 2001 for a factory producing four products on the basis of the following information.*

Type of Product	Estimated Stock on 1.1.2001 (units)	Estimated sales during Jan March 2001 (units)	Desired closing Stock on March 31, (2001 units)
A	2,000	10,000	3,000
B	3,000	15,000	5,000
C	4,000	13,000	3,000
D	3,000	12,000	2,000

[M.Com., Bharathiyar]

Solution :

Formula for production Budget : Sales + closing stock – Opening stock

Production Budget for three months from Jan to March

		Rs.
Product A :	Estimated sales	10,000
Add :	Closing stock	3,000
		13,000

Less :	Estimated opening stock	2,000	
			11,000
Product B :	Estimated sales	15,000	
Add :	Closing stock	5,000	
		20,000	
Less :	Estimated Opening stock	3,000	
			17,000
Product C :	Estimated sales	13,000	
Add :	Closing stock	3,000	
		16,000	
Less :	Estimated Opening stock	4,000	
			12,000
Product D :	Estimated sales	12,000	
Add :	Closing stock	2,000	
		14,000	
Less :	Estimated opening stock	3,000	
			11,000
	Total Production units		51,000

Problem 2. *RSP Ltd., manufactures two products A and B. A forecast of the number of units to be sold in first seven months of the year is given below. (units)*

Month	Product MP	Product ST	Product B
January	2,000	1,000	2,800
February	2,400	1,200	2,800
March	3,200	1,600	2,400
April	4,000	2,000	2,000
May	4,800	2,400	1,600
June	4,800	2,400	1,600
July	4,000	2,000	1,800

It is anticipated that (1) there will be no work in progress at the end of any month (2) finished units equal to half the sales for the next month will be in stock at the end of each month (including the previous December).

Solution :

Production Budget [for six months ending 30th June] (units)

Product – MP	Jan	Feb	March	April	May	June
Sales	1,000	1,200	1,600	2,000	2,400	2,400
Add closing stock (half the Sales for next Month)	600	800	1,000	1,200	1,200	1,000
	1,600	2,000	2,600	3,200	3,600	3,400
Less : Opening stock (half the sales for current Month)	500	600	800	1,000	1,200	1,200
Budgeted production	1,100	1,400	1,800	2,200	2,400	2,200

BUDGET AND BUDGETARY CONTROL

Total Budgeted production for Six Months
1,100 + 1,400 + 1,800 + 2,200 + 2,400 + 2,200 = 11,100 units

Product – ST (units)	Jan	Feb	March	April	May	June
Product : Sales	2,800	2,800	2,400	2,000	1,600	1,600
Add closing stock	1,400	1,200	1,000	800	800	900
	4,200	4,000	3,400	2,800	2,400	2,500
Less : Opening stock	1,400	1,400	1,200	1,000	800	800
Budgeted production	2,800	2,600	2,200	1,800	1,600	1,700

Total Budgeted production for Six Months
2,800 + 2,600 + 2,200 + 1,800 + 1,600 + 1,700 = 12,700 units

Summarised Production cost Budget

	Product MP Output 11,100 (Units)		Product ST Output 12,700 (Units)		
	Per unit	Amt (Rs.)	Per unit	Amt (Rs.)	Total
Direct material	10.00	1,11,000	15.00	1,90,000	3,01,500
Direct Labour	5.00	55,500	10.00	1,27,000	1,82,500
Prime Cost	15.00	1,66,500	25.00	3,17,500	4,84,000
Factory overheads	4.00	44,400	3.00	38,100	82,500
	19.00	2,10,900	28.00	3,55,600	5,66,500

> **NOTE :**
> Factory overheads per unit = Annual overhead/Annual output
> Product MP = 88,000/22,000 = Rs. 4.00
> ST = 72,000/24,000 = Rs. 3.00

Problem 3. *The sales director of a Narmadha Manufacturing Company reports that next year he expects to sell 50,000 units of a particular product.*

The production manager consults the storekeeper and casts his figures as follows.

Two kinds of raw materials A and B are required for manufacturing the product. Each unit of the product requires 2 units of A and 3 units of B. The estimated opening balances at the commencement of the next year are

Finished products 10,000 units

Raw materials A : 12,000 units; B 15,000 units.

The desirable closing balances at the end of the next are finished products : 14,000units; A : 13,000 units; B 16,000 units.

Draw up a quantitative chart showing materials purchase budget for the next year.

Solution :

Formula : The units to be produced
Formula = Sales + Desired closing stock – opening stock
50,000 + 14,000 – 10,000 = 54,000 units

Material Procurement Budget

	Finished Products Units	Materials A Units	Materials B Units
As per the production budget Requirement	54,000	1,08,000	1,62,000
Estimated opening Balance	+ 10,000	− 12,000	− 15,000
	64,000	96,000	1,47,000
Closing Balance	− 14,000	13,000	16,000
Estimated sales of Product	50.000	—	—
Estimated purchase of materials	—	1,09,000	1,63,000

Problem 4. *Draw a materials procurement (Quantitative) Budget from the following information. Estimated sales of a product 40,000 units. Each unit of the product requires 3 units of materials A and 5 units of B.*

Estimated opening balances at the commencement of the next year.

Finished product	5,000 units
Materials A	12,000 units
Materials B	20,000 units
Materials on order	
Materials A	7,000 units
Materials B	11,000 units

The desirable closing balances at the end of the next year.

Finished product	7,000 units
Material A	15,000 units
Material B	25,000 units
Materials on order	
Material A	8,000 units
Material B	10,000 units [B.Com Madurai]

Solution :

Production Budget (in units)

Estimated Sales	40,000
Add : Desired Closing stock	7,000
	47,000
Less : Opening Stock	5,000
Estimated production	42,000

BUDGET AND BUDGETARY CONTROL 353

Material Procurement Budget (in units)

	Material A	Material B
Estimated Consumption		
42,000 × 3	1,26,000	
Add : 42,000 × 5		2,10,000
Desired Closing Stock	15,000	25,000
Material on order (closing)	8,000	10,000
	1,49,000	2,45,000
Less : Opening Stock	12,000	20,000
Materials on order (Opening)	7,000	11,000
	19,000	31,000
Estimated Purchases	1,30,000	2,14,000
Total purchase	3,44,000 units	
Sales Budget		

Problem 5. *Ram Lal & co sells two products A and B which are manufactured in one plant. During the year 1985, it plans to sell the following quantities of each product.*

	Ist Quarter	IInd Quarter	IIIrd Quarter	IVth Quarter
Product A	90,000	2,50,000	3,00,000	80,000
Product B	80,000	75,000	60,000	90,000

Each of these two products is sold on a seasonal basis. Ram Lal plans to sell product A throughout the year at a price of Rs. 10 a unit and product B at a price of Rs. 20 a unit.

A study of the past experience reveals that Ram Lal has lost about 3% of its billed revenue each year because of returns (constituting 2% of Loss of revenue) allowances and bad debts (1% loss)

Prepare a Sales budget incorporating the above information.

Solution : **Sales Budget of Ram Lal and Co**

	First Quarter Rs.	Second Quarter Rs.	Third Quarter Rs.	Fourth Quarter Rs.	Total Rs.
Product A	9,00,000	25,00,000	30,00,000	8,00,000	72,00,000
Product B	16,00,000	15,00,000	12,00,000	18,00,000	61,00,000
Total	25,00,000	40,00,000	42,00,000	26,00,000	1,33,00,000
Less : Deductions :					
(i) Returns	50,000	80,000	84,000	52,000	2,66,000
(ii) Allowances and Bad debts	25,000	40,000	42,000	26,000	1,33,000
Total Deduction	75,000	1,20,000	1,26,000	78,000	3,99,000
Net sales (Sales − Total Deductions)	24,25,000	38,80,000	40,74,000	25,22,000	1,29,01,000

Problem 6. *Jayam & Co manufactures two products A and B and sells them through two divisions East and West. For the purpose of submission of sales budget to the budget committee, the following information has been made available.*

Budgeted sales for the current year were

Product	East	West
X	400 @ Rs. 9	600 @ Rs. 9
Y	300 @ Rs. 21	500 @ Rs. 21

Actual sales for the current year were

Product	East	West
X	500 @ Rs. 9	700 @ Rs. 9
Y	200 @ Rs. 21	400 @ Rs. 21

Adequate market studies reveal that product X is popular but under priced. It is observed that if price of X is increased by Re. 1 it will find a ready market. On the other hand, Y is overpriced to customers and market could absorb more if sales price of Y be reduced by Re. 1. The management had agreed to give effect to the above price changes.

From the information based on these, price changes and reports from salesman, the following estimates have been prepared by divisional managers.

Percentage increase in sales over current budget is

Product	East	West
X	+ 10%	+ 5%
Y	+ 20%	+ 10%

With the help of an intensive advertisement campaign the following additional sales above the estimated sales of divisional managers are possible.

Product	East	West
X	60	70
Y	40	50

You are required to prepare Budget for sales incorporating the above estimates and also show the budgeted and actual sales of the current year.

Solution :   **Sales Budget of Jayam & Co.**

Division	Product	Budget for future period			Budget for current period			Actual sales for current period		
		Qty	Price Rs.	Value Rs.	Qty	Price Rs.	Value Rs.	Qty	Price Rs.	Value Rs.
East	X	500	10	5,000	400	9	3,600	500	9	4,500
	Y	400	20	8,000	300	21	6,300	200	21	4,200
Total		900		13,000	700		9,900	700		8,700
West	X	700	10	7,000	600	9	5,400	700	9	6,300
	Y	600	20	12,000	500	21	10,500	400	21	8,400
Total		1,300		19,000	1,100		15,900	1,100		14,700
Total	X	1,200	10	12,000	1,000	9	9,000	1,200	9	10,800
	Y	1,000	20	20,000	800	21	16,800	600	21	12,600
Total		2,200		32,000	1,800		25,800	1,800		23,400

Factory Overhead Budget

Problem 7. *Rexin Ltd supplies you the following average figures of previous quarters. Prepare a manufacturing overhead budget for the quarter ending on March 31,2002. The budgeted output during this quarter is 5,000 units.*

Fixed overheads	Rs. 40,000
Variable overheads	Rs. 20,000 (varying @ Rs. 5 per unit)
Semi-variable overheads	Rs. 20,000 (40% fixed and 60% varying @ 3 per unit)

Solution : **Manufacturing Overhead Budget**

Fixed overheads		Rs. 40,000
Variable overheads		Rs. 25,000
Semi Variable overheads		
Fixed	8,000	
Variable @ Rs. 3 per unit	15,000	
		23,000
Total overhead costs		**88,000**

Selling and Distribution Overhead Budget

Problem 8. *You are requested to prepare sales overhead budget from the estimation given below.*

Advertisement	Rs. 2,500
Salaries of Sales Department	5,000
Expenses of sales Department	1,500
Counter Salesman's salaries and dearness allowance	6,000
Commission to counter salesman at 1% on their sales	

Travelling salesmen's commission at 10% on their sales and expenses at 5% on their sales. The sales during the period were estimated as follow.

Counter sales	Travelling Salesman's
Rs.	Rs.
80,000	10,000
1,20,000	15,000
1,40,000	20,000

[B.Com, BBM]

Solution : **Sales overhead Budget**
Estimated Sales

Fixed Overheads	Rs. 90,000	Rs. 1,35,000	Rs. 1,60,000
Advertisement	2,500	2,500	2,500
Expenses of Sales department	1,500	1,500	1,500
Salaries of sales department	5,000	5,000	5,000
Counter salesmen's salaries and dearness allowance	6,000	6,000	6,000
Total Fixed cost	**15,000**	**15,000**	**15,000**

Variable Cost			
Counter salesman's Commission @1% on their sales	800	1,200	1,400
Travelling salesman's Commission @ 10% on their Sales	1,000	1,500	2,000
Expenses on Travelling Salesmen's sales @ 5%	500	750	1,000
Total variable cost	2,300	3,450	4,400
Total Sales overheads (FC + VC)	17,300	18,450	19,400

Problem 9. *From the following particulars prepare a production budget of a company for the year ended on 30th June 2002.*

Product	Sales in units	Estimated stock 1.7.2001	Stock (units) 30.6.2002
X	18000	1680	1860
Y	12000	600	1740
Z	8400	960	960

[B.Com. PU 2004]

Solution :

Production Budget (Units)

	Product X	Product Y	Product Z
Sales (units)	18,000	12,000	8,400
Add : Closing stock	1,860	1,740	960
	19,860	13,740	9,360
Less : Estimated opening stock	1,860	1,740	960
Production	18,000	12,000	8,400

Total Units to be produced 18,000 + 12,000 + 8,400 = 38,400 units

Problem 10. *From the following figures prepare a raw material purchase budget for January.*

	Materials A (Units)	B (Units)
Estimated stock on 1st Jan	16,000	6,000
Estimated stock on 31st Jan	20,000	8,000
Estimated consumption	1,20,000	44,000

[BCA 2000 PU]

Solution :

	Raw material A	Raw material B
Estimated Consumption (units)	1,20,000	44,000
Add : Estimated stock on 31st Jan	20,000	8,000
	1,40,000	52,000
Less : Estimated stock on 1st Jan	16,000	6,000
Estimated Purchase (units)	1,24,000	46,000

II. Cash Budget

Problem 1. *A company expects to have Rs. 37,500 cash in hand on 1.4.1995. And requires you to prepare an estimate of cash position during the three months April to June 1995. The following information is supplied to you.*

Months	Sales Rs.	Purchases Rs.	Wages Rs.	Factory Expenses Rs.	Office Expenses Rs.	Selling Expenses Rs.
Feb.	75,000	45,000	9,000	7,500	6,000	4,500
March	84,000	48,000	9,750	8,250	6,000	4,500
April	90,000	52,500	10,500	9,000	6,000	5,250
May	1,20,000	60,000	13,500	11,250	6,000	6,570
June	1,35,000	60,000	14,250	14,000	7,000	7,000

Other Information :

1. The period of credit allowed by suppliers—2 months
2. 20% sales is for cash and period of credit allowed to customers for credit sale is one month.
3. Delay in payment of all expenses—I month.
4. Income Tax of Rs. 57,500 is due to be paid on June 15, 1995.
5. The company is to pay dividends to shareholders and bonus to workers which is Rs. 15,000 and Rs. 22,500 respectively in the month of April.
6. Plant has been ordered and is expected to be received and paid in May. It will cost Rs. 1,20,000. [B.Com Madras]

Solution :

Cash Budget

Particulars	April Rs.	May Rs.	June Rs.
Opening cash balance	37,500	11,700	(–) 91,050
Receipts :			
Amount received from cash sales (20%)	18,000	24,000	27,000
Amount received from credit Sales [80% of previous months sales]	67,200	72,000	96,000
Total Receipts	1,22,700	1,07,700	31950
Payments :			
Amount paid to creditors [2 months previous month purchase]	45,000	48,000	52,500
Wages [previous month]	9,750	10,500	13,500
Factory expenses [previous month]	8,250	9,000	11,250
Office expenses [previous month]	6,000	6,000	6,000
Selling expenses [previous month]	4,500	5,250	6,570
Income Tax paid	-	-	57,500
Dividend to shareholders	15,000	-	-
Bonus to workers	22,500	-	-
Amount paid for purchase of plant	-	1,20,000	-
Total Payment	1,11,000	1,98,750	1,47,320
Closing balance [TR – TP]	11,700	– 91,050	–1,15,370

> **NOTE :** In order to meet the cash deficiency of Rs. 91,050 and 1,15,370 in the month of May and June the company will arrange the overdraft facilities over and above the cash deficiency.
>
> If direction is given in the problem only, we arrange the overdraft facilities, otherwise no need to arrange the overdraft facilities.

Problem 2. *Prepare cash Budget for 3 months ended on 30th Sep. 1999 :*

Cash at Bank on 1.7.1999 Rs. 25,000

Salaries and wages monthly Rs. 10,000

Interest payable Rs. 5,000 (August)

Particulars	June Rs.	July Rs.	Aug. Rs.	Sep. Rs.
Cash sales	-	1,40,000	1,52,000	1,21,000
Credit sales	1,00,000	80,000	1,40,000	1,20,000
Purchases (Rs.)	1,60,000	1,70,000	2,40,000	1,80,000
Other expenses	-	20,000	22,000	21,000

Credit sales are collected 50% in the month in which sales are made, and 50% in the month following. Collection from credit sales are subject to 5% discount if payment is received during the month of sales and 2 ½% if payment is received in the month following.

Creditors are paid either on a prompt category or 30 days basis. It is estimated that 10% of creditors are in the prompt category.

Solution : **Cash Budget for three months ended 30.9.1994**

Particulars	July Rs.	August Rs.	September Rs.
Opening Cash	25,000	60,750	1,04,250
Receipts			
Cash Sales	1,40,000	1,52,000	1,21,000
Amount received from credit sales	86,750	1,05,500	1,25,250
Total Receipts	2,51,750	3,18,250	3,50,500
Payments			
Amount paid to creditors (10% prompt category)	17,000	24,000	18,000
Amount paid to creditor (90% on 30 day basis)	1,44,000	1,53,000	2,16,000
Other expenses	20,000	22,000	21,000
Salaries and wages	10,000	10,000	10,000
Interest payable	-	5,000	-
Total payment	1,91,000	2,14,000	2,65,000
Closing balance [TR – TP]	60,750	1,04,250	85,500

Workings :

	July Rs.	August Rs.	Sep Rs.
Collection of credit sales			
(i) 50% in the month of sales are made	40,000	70,000	60,000
Less : Discount 5%	2,000	3,500	3,000
	38,000	66,500	57,000
(ii) 50% in the month following months Sales	50,000	40,000	70,000
Less : Discount 2½%	1,250	1,000	1,750
	48,750	39,000	68,250

July = 38,000 + 48,750 = 86,750
August = 66,500 + 39,000 = 1,05,500
Sep = 57,000 + 68,250 = 1,25,250.

Problem 3. *Sarathi & Co wishes to arrange overdraft facilities with its bankers during period April to June, when it will be manufacturing mostly for stock. Prepare cash budget for the above period from the following data. Including the extent of bank facilities the company will require at the end of each month.*

(a)
Months	Sales Rs.	Purchases Rs.	Wages Rs.
Feb.	1,80,000	1,24,800	12,000
March	1,92,000	1,44,000	14,000
April	1,08,000	2,43,000	11,000
May	1,74,000	2,46,000	10,000
June	1,26,000	2,68,000	5,000

(b) 50% of credit sales is realised in the month following the sale and the remaining 50% in the second month following. Creditors are paid in the month following the month of purchase.

(c) Cash at Bank on 1st April (estimated) Rs. 25000.

[M.Com., Madras] [B.Com Nov 95 Bharathiar]

Solution : Cash budget

Particulars	July	August	September
Opening Cash balance	25,000	56,000	3,000
Receipts			
Amount collected from credit sales	1,86,000	1,50,000	1,41,000
Total Receipts	2,11,000	2,06,000	1,44,000
Payments			
Amount paid to creditors	1,44,000	2,43,000	2,46,000

Wages paid	11,000	10,000	5,000
Total Payments	1,55,000	2,53,000	2,51,000
Balance	56,000	–47,000	–1,07,000
Bank Overdraft	–	OD + 50,000	1,20,000
Closing balance	56,000	3,000	13,000

Workings :

Credit sales Collection :

April = 50% of March + 50% of Feb
96,000 + 90,000 = 1,80,000

May = 50% April + 50% March
54,000 + 96,000 = 1,50,000

June = 50% of May + 50% April
87,000 + 54,000 = 1,41,000

NOTE :
(i) Wages are assumed to be paid in the same month.
(ii) Overdraft facilities are arranged to meet out the cash deficiency in the month of May and June.

Problem 4. *Prepare cash Budget for the month of May, June and July 1989 on the basis of the following information.*

I.

Months	Credit Sales Rs.	Credit Purchases Rs.	Wages Rs.	Manufacturing Expenses Rs.	Office Expenses Rs.	Selling Expenses Rs.
March	60,000	36,000	9,000	4,000	2,000	4,000
April	62,000	38,000	8,000	3,000	1,500	5,000
May	64,000	33,000	10,000	4,500	2,500	4,500
June	58,000	35,000	8,500	3,500	2,000	3,500
July	56,000	39,000	9,500	4,000	1,000	4,500
August	60,000	34,000	8,000	3,000	1,500	4,500

II. Cash Balance on Ist May 1989 is Rs. 8,000.

III. Plant costing Rs. 16,000 is due for delivery in July. Payable 10% on delivery and the balance after 3 months.

IV. Advance Tax of Rs. 8,000 each is payable in March and June.

V. Period of credit allowed (I) by suppliers – 2 months and (II) to customers one month.

VI. Lag in payment of manufacturing expenses – 1/2 month

VII. Lag in payment of office and selling expenses – one month. [M.Com. Adapted]

BUDGET AND BUDGETARY CONTROL

Solution :

Cash budget

Particulars	May (Rs.)	June (Rs.)	July (Rs.)
Opening Cash balance	8,000	13,750	12,250
Receipts			
Amount received from credit sales	62,000	64,000	58,000
Total Receipts	70,000	77,750	70,250
Payments			
Wages paid	10,000	8,500	9,500
Amount paid to purchase of plant	–	–	1,600
Advance Tax	–	8,000	–
Amount paid to creditors	36,000	38,000	33,000
Manufacturing expenses paid	3,750	4,000	3,750
Office expenses	1,500	2,500	2,000
Selling expenses	5,000	4,500	3,500
Total Payments	56,250	65,500	53,350
Closing Balance	13,750	12,250	16,900

Workings :

Manufacturing expenses

(i) May = $\frac{1}{2}$ of May + $\frac{1}{2}$ of April

2250 + 1500 = **3750**

(ii) June = $\frac{1}{2}$ of June + $\frac{1}{2}$ of May

1750 + 2250 = **4000**

(iii) July = $\frac{1}{2}$ of July + $\frac{1}{2}$ of June

2000 + 1750 = **3750**

Problem 5. *Prepare cash Budget for the three months ending on 30.6.1998 from the information given below.*

I.

Month	Sales Rs.	Material Rs.	Wages Rs.	Overheads Rs.
Feb.	14,000	9,600	3,000	1,700
March	15,000	9,000	3,000	1,900
April	16,000	9,200	3,200	2,000
May	17,000	10,000	3,600	2,200
June	18,000	10,400	4,000	2,300

II. **Credit terms**

Sales / Debtors – 10% sales are on cash, 50 % of the credit sales are collected next month, and the balance in the following month.

Creditors : Materials   2 Months
          Wages   ¼ Month
          Overheads   ½ Month

III. Cash and Bank Balance on 1.4.1998 is expected to Rs. 6,000.
IV. Other relevant information are :
   (a) Plant and machinery will be installed in Feb. 1998 at a cost of Rs. 96,000. The monthly instalment of Rs. 2,000 is payable from April onwards.
   (b) Dividend @ 5% on preference share capital of Rs. 2,00,000 will be paid on Ist June.
   (c) Advance to be received for sale of vehicles Rs. 9,000 in June.
   (d) Dividend from investments amounting to Rs., 1,000 are expected to be in June.
   (e) Income Tax (advance) to be paid in June is Rs. 2,000.   [ICWA (Int)]

Solution :

Cash Budget for the period of three months ending on 30.6.1998

	April Rs.	May Rs.	June Rs.
Opening balance (Cash)	6,000	3,950	3,000
Receipts			
Amount received from cash sales	1,600	1,700	1,800
Credit sales	13,050	13,950	14,850
Dividend	—	—	1,000
Advance received for sale of vehicles	—	—	9,000
Total Receipts	20,650	19,600	29,650
Payments			
Dividend paid on preference shares	—	—	10,000
Income tax paid	—	—	2,000
Capital expenditure	2,000	2,000	2,000
Amount paid to creditors [previous 2 months purchase]	9,600	9,000	9,200
Wages	3,150	3,500	3,900
Overheads	1,950	2,100	2,250
Total payments	16,700	16,600	29,350
Closing Balance	3,950	3,000	300

Workings :
   (i) *Collection of credit sales*
       April = 50% of March + 50% of Feb
              6,750 + 6,300 = 13,050
       May = 50% of April + 50% of March
              7,200 + 6,750 = 13,950

BUDGET AND BUDGETARY CONTROL

$$\text{June} = 50\% \text{ of May} + 50\% \text{ April}$$
$$7,650 + 7,200 = 14,850$$

(ii) *Wages*

$$\text{April} = \frac{1}{4} \text{ of March} + \frac{3}{4} \text{ of April}$$
$$750 + 2,400 = 3,150$$

$$\text{May} = \frac{1}{4} \text{ of April} + \frac{3}{4} \text{ of May}$$

$$3,200 \times \frac{1}{4} + 3,600 \times \frac{3}{4}$$
$$800 + 2,700 = 3,500$$

$$\text{June} = \frac{1}{4} \text{ of May} + \frac{3}{4} \text{ of June}$$

$$3,600 \times \frac{1}{4} + 4,000 \times \frac{3}{4}$$
$$900 + 3,000 = 3,900$$

(iii) *Overheads*

$$\text{April} = \frac{1}{2} \text{ of April} + \frac{1}{2} \text{ of March}$$
$$1,000 + 950 = 1950$$

$$\text{May} = \frac{1}{2} \text{ of May} + \frac{1}{2} \text{ of April}$$
$$1,100 + 1,000 = 2,100$$

$$\text{June} = \frac{1}{2} \text{ of June} + \frac{1}{2} \text{ of May}$$
$$1,150 + 1,100 = 2,250$$

Problem 6. *From the following forecasts of income and expenditure prepare a cash budget for three months commencing Ist June when the bank balance was Rs. 1,00,000/-*

Months	Sales	Purchases	Wages	Factory Expenses	Ad. Sell Expenses
	Rs.	Rs.	Rs.	Rs.	Rs.
April	80,000	41,000	5,600	3,900	10,000
May	76,500	40,500	5,400	4,200	14,000
June	78,500	38,500	5,400	5,100	15,000
July	90,000	37,000	4,800	5,100	17,000
August	95,000	35,000	4,700	6,000	13,000

A sales commission of 5% on sales, due two months after sales, is payable in addition to selling expenses, plant valued at Rs. 65,000 will be purchased and paid for in August and the dividend for the last financial year of Rs. 15,000 will be paid in July. There is 2 months credit period allowed to customers and received from suppliers.   [ICWA] [M.Com Madras]

Solution : Cash Budget for the period of three months

	June Rs.	July Rs.	August Rs.
Opening balance	1,00,000	1,11,400	1,03,075
Receipts :			
Amount received from credit sales	80,000	76,500	78,500
Total Receipts	1,80,000	1,87,900	1,81,575
Payments :			
Amount paid to creditors	41,000	40,500	38,500
Wages paid	5,400	5,400	4,800
Factory expenses	4,200	5,100	5,100
Adms Selling expenses	14,000	15,000	17,000
Sales commission	4,000	3,825	3,925
Payment of dividend	-	15,000	-
Purchase of Plant	-	-	65,000
Total Payments	68,600	84,825	1,34,325
Closing Balance [TR – TP]	1,11,400	1,03,075	47,250

NOTE :
(1) Assumed that wages, factory, administration and selling expenses are payable in the following month.
(2) Sales Commission

June	July	Aug
80,000 × 5/100	76,500 × 5/100	78,500 × 5/100
= 4,000	= 3,825	= 3,925

Problem 7. *Reliance India Ltd., A newly started company wishes to prepare cash budget from January. Prepare a cash budget for the first six months from the following estimated revenue and expenses.*

Months	Total sales	Materials	Wages	Overheads Production	Selling & Distribution
	Rs.	Rs.	Rs.	Rs.	Rs.
January	20,000	20,000	4,000	3,200	800
February	22,000	14,000	4,400	3,300	900
March	28,000	14,000	4,600	3,400	900
April	36,000	22,000	4,600	3,500	1,000
May	30,000	20,000	4,000	3,200	900
June	40,000	25,000	5,000	3,600	1,200

Cash balance on 1st January was Rs. 10,000. A new machinery is to be installed for Rs. 20,000 on credit to be repaid by two equal installments in March and April.

BUDGET AND BUDGETARY CONTROL

Sales commission @ 5% on total sales is to be paid within a month following actual sales.

Rs. 10,000, being the amount of IInd call, may be received in March. Share premium amounting to Rs. 2000 is also obtainable with the IInd call.

Period of credit allowed by suppliers	2 months
Period of credit allowed to customers	1 month
Delay in payment of overheads	1 month
Delay in payment of wages	$\frac{1}{2}$ month

Assume cash sales to be 50% of total sales.

Solution :

Cash Budget

Particulars	Jan Rs.	Feb Rs.	March Rs.	Apr Rs.	May Rs.	June Rs.
Opening balance	10,000	18,000	29,800	27,000	24,700	33,100
Receipts						
Second call money received	-	-	10,000	-	-	-
Share Premium received			2,000			
Amount received from customers	-	10,000	11,000	14,000	18,000	15,000
Cash Sales	10,000	11,000	14,000	18,000	15,000	20,000
Total Receipts (A)	20,000	39,000	66,800	59,000	57,700	68,100
Payments						
Amount paid to Purchase of Machinery	-	-	10,000	10,000	-	-
Sales Commission paid	-	1,000	1,100	1,400	1,800	1,500
Amount Paid to creditors	-	-	20,000	14,000	14,000	22,000
Payment of overheads (production + selling and distri)	-	4,000	4,200	4,300	4,500	4,100
Payment of wages	2,000	4,200	4,500	4,600	4,300	4,500
Total Payments (B)	2,000	9,200	39,800	34,300	24,600	32,100
Closing Balance (A – B)	18,000	29,800	27,000	24,700	33,100	36,000

Workings :

(1) Sales Commission

Jan 20,000 × 5/100 = 1,000
Feb 22,000 × 5/100 = 1,100
March 28,000 × 5/100 = 1,400
April 36,000 × 5/100 = 1,800
May 30,000 × 5/100 = 1,500
June 40,000 × 5/100 = 2,000

(2) Material suppliers treated as creditors.
(3) Cash Sales is 50% of total sales.

	Cash Sales Rs.	Credit sales Rs.
Jan	10,000	10,000
February	11,000	11,000
March	14,000	14,000
April	18,000	18,000
May	15,000	15,000
June	20,000	20,000

(4) Payment of wages

Jan = 50% Jan + 50% Dec
2,000 + nil = 2,000

Feb = 50% Feb + 50% Jan
2,200 + 2,000 = 4,200

March = 50% March + 50% Feb
2,300 + 2,200 = 4,500

April = 50% April + 50% March
2,300 + 2,300 = 4,600

May = 50% May + 50% April
2,000 + 2,300 = 4,300

June = 50% of June + 50% of May
2,500 + 2,000 = 4,500

Problem 8. *From the following forecasts of income and expenditure of TPK & Co Ltd., prepare a cash budget for six months commencing from 1st June 2000 when the bank balance is estimated to be Rs. 1,10,000.*

Months	Sales Rs.	Selling overheads Rs.	Purchases Rs.	Wages Rs.	Factory Overheads Rs.	Administration Overheads Rs.	Research Expenditure Rs.
March	82,000	5,000	40,000	10,000	8,400	3,400	2,000
April	88,500	3,250	37,000	8,000	5,600	2,500	2,400
May	84,000	4,100	40,000	8,400	5,900	2,760	2,400
June	93,000	3,710	39,000	8,800	5,920	2,480	2,400
July	72,000	3,210	39,900	6,000	5,440	2,600	2,400
Aug	82,500	3,600	35,000	9,600	5,880	2,520	2,600
Sep	98,600	3,450	36,400	8,000	6,000	2,700	2,600
Oct	92,800	3,210	36,500	8,400	5,680	2,560	2,600
Nov.	1,04,400	3,200	32,000	7,600	5,360	2,620	2,400

Lag in payment of wages : $\frac{1}{4}$ month

Lag in payment of factory overhead : 1 month

Lag in payment of Administration overhead : $\frac{1}{2}$ month

BUDGET AND BUDGETARY CONTROL

Lag in payment of Selling overhead : 1 month
Lag in payment of Research Expenditure : 1 month
Period of credit allowed by the creditors : 3 months
Period of credit allowed by the customers : 2 months
Other Information :
   (i) A sales commission of 5% on sales, and due two months after sales, is payable in addition to selling overheads.
   (ii) Capital expenditure planned is (a) Machinery purchased in June 2003 for Rs. 1,00,000 payable on delivery and (b) Building purchased in June 2000 for Rs. 8,00,000 payable in four half yearly instalments, the first being payable in July 2000.
   (iii) Interest on Bombay Port Trust Bonds amounting to Rs. 50,000 is to be received in October 2000.
   (iv) Cash sales are estimated at Rs. 2000 per month.
   (v) A dividend of Rs. 10,000 is to be paid in September 2000.
   (vi) Tax amounting to Rs. 30,000 is to be paid on 1st August 2000.
   (vii) A call money of Rs. 2 per share on Equity share capital of Rs. 5,00,000 divided into 50,000 shares of Rs. 10 each is to be received on 1st July 2000.

Solution :   **Cash Budget of TPK Ltd.**

Particulars	*June* Rs.	*July* Rs.	*Aug.* Rs.	*Sep.* Rs.	*Oct.* Rs.	*Nov.* Rs.
Opening balance	1,10,000	30,335	4,345	1,490	10,000	75,815
Receipts						
Interest on Bombay Trust Bonds	-	-	-	-	50,000	-
Cash Sales	2,000	2,000	2,000	2,000	2,000	2,000
Equity capital received	-	1,00,000	-	-	-	-
Amount received from credit sales	86,500	82,000	91,000	70,000	80,500	96,600
Total Receipts (A)	1,98,500	2,14,335	97,345	73,490	1,42,500	1,74,415
Payments :						
Sales Commission paid	4,425	4,200	4,650	3,600	4,125	4,930
Selling overheads	4,100	3,710	3,210	3,600	3,450	3,210
Purchase of plant & machinery	1,00,000	-	-	-	-	-
Amount Paid for the purchase of building	-	2,00,000	-	-	-	-
Dividend paid	-	-	-	10,000	-	-
Tax paid	-	-	30,000	-	-	-
Wages paid	8,700	6,700	8,700	8,400	8,900	7,800
Factory overheads	5,920	5,440	5,880	6,000	5,680	5,360
Research Expenditure	2,400	2,400	2,400	2,600	2,600	2,600
Administration						

	April	May	June	July	August	Sep.	Oct.	Nov.
Overheads		2,620	2,540	2,560	2,610	2,630	2,590
Amount paid to Creditors		40,000	37,000	40000	39000	39900	35000
Total payments (B)		1,68,165	2,61,990	97,400	75,810	66,685	61,490
Balance (A–B) (Surplus or deficit)		30,335	– 47,665	– 55	– 2,320	75,815	1,12,925
Overdraft (assumed)		—	+ 52,000	+ 1,545	+ 12,320	—	—
Closing Balance		30,335	4,345	1,490	10,000	75,815	1,12,925

Workings :

1. *Sales commission*

	April Rs.	May Rs.	June Rs.	July Rs.	August Rs.	Sep. Rs.	Oct. Rs.	Nov. Rs.
	4,425	4,200	4,650	3,600	4,125	4,930	4,640	5,220

2. *Wages*

	April Rs.	May Rs.	June Rs.	July Rs.	August Rs.	Sep. Rs.	Oct. Rs.	Nov. Rs.
$\frac{1}{4}$ of previous month	2,500	2,000	2,100	2,200	1,500	2,400	2,600	2,100
$\frac{3}{4}$ of current month	6,000	6,300	6,600	4,500	7,200	6,000	6,300	5,700
	8,500	8,300	8,700	6,700	8,700	8,400	8,900	7,800

3. *Administration overhead*

	June Rs.	July Rs.	August Rs.	Sep. Rs.	Oct. Rs.	Nov. Rs.
½ of previous month	1,380	1,240	1,300	1,260	1,350	1,280
½ of current month	1,240	1,300	1,260	1,350	1,280	1,310
	2,620	2,540	2,560	2,610	2,630	2,590

Credit sales

	March Rs.	April Rs.	May Rs.	June Rs.	July Rs.	August Rs.	Sep. Rs.	Oct. Rs.	Nov. Rs.
Sales	82,000	88,500	84,000	93,000	72,000	82,500	98,600	92,800	1,04,400
Less : cash sales	2,000	2,000	2,000	2,000	2,000	2,000	2,000	2,000	2,000
	80,000	86,500	82,000	91,000	70,000	80,500	96,600	90,800	1,02,400

Problem 9. *From the following information and the assumptions that the balance in hand on 1.1.2002 is Rs. 75,000, prepare cash budget.*

BUDGET AND BUDGETARY CONTROL

Months	Sales	Materials	Wages	Selling and Distri.cost	Production cost	Administration cost
	Rs.	Rs.	Rs.	Rs.	Rs.	Rs.
January	72,000	25,000	10,000	4,000	6,000	1,500
February	97,000	31,000	12,100	5,000	6,300	1,700
March	86,000	25,500	10,600	5,500	6,000	2,000
April	88,600	30,600	25,000	6,700	6,500	2,200
May	1,02,500	37,000	22,000	8,500	8,000	2,500
June	1,08,700	38,800	23,000	9,000	8,200	2,500

Assume that 50% are cash sales. Assets are to be acquired in the month of February and April. Therefore, provision should be made for the payment of Rs. 8,000 and Rs. 25,000 for the same. An application has been made to the bank for the grant of a loan of Rs. 30,000 and it is hoped that it will be received in the month of May.

It is anticipated that a dividend of Rs. 35,000 will be paid in the month of June. Debtors are allowed one month's credit. Sales commission@3% on sales is to be paid.

Creditors (for goods or overheads) grant one month's credit.

Assume all expenses are paid in the following month.

Solution :

Cash Budget

Particulars	Jan Rs.	Feb Rs.	March Rs.	Apr Rs.	May Rs.	June Rs.
Opening balance	72,500	96,340	1,21,330	1,55,650	1,51,292	2,05,767
Receipts						
Cash Sales	36,000	48,500	43,000	44,300	51,250	54,350
Bank loan received	-	-	-	-	30,000	-
Amount received from Debtors	-	36,000	48,500	43,000	44,300	51,250
Total Receipts	1,08,500	1,80,840	2,12,830	2,42,950	2,76,842	3,11,367
Payments						
Provision of capital expenditure	-	8,000	-	25,000	-	-
Dividend paid	-	-	-	-	-	35,000
Wages	10,000	12,100	10,600	25,000	22,000	23,000
Selling and distribution cost	-	4,000	5,000	5,500	6,700	8,500
Production cost	-	6,000	6,300	6,000	6,500	8,000
Administration cost	-	1,500	1,700	2,000	2,200	2,500
Amount paid to creditors	-	25,000	31,000	25,500	30,600	37,000
Sales Commission	2,160	2,910	2,580	2,658	3,075	3,261
Total Payments	12,160	59,510	57,180	91,658	71,075	1,17,261
Closing Balance [TR − TP]	96,340	1,21,330	1,55,650	1,51,292	2,05,767	1,94,106

NOTE : Sales commission paid in the same month itself.

Working :

	Sales Commission		
Jan	72,000 × 3/100	=	2160
Feb	97,000 × 3/100	=	2910
March	86,000 × 3/100	=	2580
April	88,600 × 3/100	=	2658
May	10,2500 × 3/100	=	3075
June	1,08,700 × 3/100	=	3261

Problem 10. *From the following information relating to Blue Star Engineering Co. prepare a cash budget for the half year ending on 30th September 2001.*

(a) Anticipated sales, purchases and costs :

Months	Sales Rs.	Purchases Rs.	Wages Rs.	Overheads Rs.
March	1,50,000	90,000	18,000	31,000
April	1,40,000	1,20,000	28,000	35,400
May	1,54,000	84,000	20,800	36,500
June	1,68,000	1,36,000	22,200	36,500
July	1,82,000	1,28,000	30,000	37,000
August	2,04,000	1,51,000	28,000	37,500
September	2,40,000	1,62,000	25,000	38,000

(b) Other Information :

 (i) Bank Balance on 1.4.2001 was Rs. 60,000.

 (ii) The loan instalment of Rs. 20,000 per month was to be remitted from July to December 2001.

 (iii) Sales commission@5% on Sales was to be remitted to the distributors in the month following the sales.

 (iv) Rs. 65,000 was expected to be received as deposit from the distributors in the month of July.

 (v) 50% of the sales are on credit, the period of credit being 1 month.

 (vi) 50% of the materials purchased can be paid for after a month.

 (vii) 25% of the overheads could be settled in the month following their incidence.

 (viii) Wages are paid on the first working day of the following month.

Solution :

Blue Star Engineering
Cash Budget for the period of 6 months

Particulars	June Rs.	July Rs.	Aug. Rs.	Sep. Rs.	Oct. Rs.	Nov. Rs.
Opening Cash Balance	60,000	40,200	13,975	1,000	21,525	9,200
Receipts						
Cash Sales	70,000	77,000	84,000	91,000	1,02,000	1,20,000
Amount received from credit sales	75,000	70,000	77,000	84,000	91,000	1,02,000

BUDGET AND BUDGETARY CONTROL

Deposit from distributors	-	-	-	65,000	-	-
Total Receipts	2,05,000	1,87,200	1,74,975	2,41,000	2,14,525	2,31,200
Payments						
Repayment of loan	-	-	-	20,000	20,000	20,000
Sales commission paid	7,500	7,000	7,700	8,400	9,100	10,200
Amount paid to Creditors (50% cash)	60,000	42,000	68,000	64,000	75,500	81,000
Amount paid to Creditors (50% in the month following)	45,000	60,000	42,000	68,000	64,000	75,500
Wages paid	18,000	28,000	20,800	22,200	30,000	28,000
Overheads paid	34,300	36,225	36,500	36,875	37,375	37,875
Total payments	1,64,800	1,73,225	1,75,000	2,19,475	2,35,975	2,52,575
Balance	40,200	13,975	– 25	21,525	– 21,450	– 21,375
Bank OD	—	—	+ 1025	—	+ 30,650	40,000
Closing Balance	40,200	13,975	1,000	21,525	9,200	18,625

Working :

1. *Credit Sales*

	Rs.
March	75,000
April	70,000
May	77,000
June	84,000
July	91,000
Aug	1,02,000
Sep	1,20,000

2. *Sales Commission*

	Rs.
March	7,500
April	7,000
May	7,700
June	8,400
July	9,100
Aug	10,200
Sep	12,000

3. *Amount paid to creditors*

	April Rs.	May Rs.	June Rs.	July Rs.	August Rs.	Sep. Rs.
50% paid in the same month	60,000	42,000	68,000	64,000	75,500	81,000
50% in the month following	45,000	60,000	42,000	68,000	64,000	75,500
	1,05,000	1,02,000	1,10,000	1,32,000	1,39,500	1,56,500

4. *Overheads*

75% current	26,550	27,375	27,375	27,750	28,125	28,500
25% of previous month	7,750	8,850	9,125	9,125	9,250	9,375
	34,300	36,225	36,500	36,875	37,375	37,875

III. Flexible Budget

Problem 1. *For production of 10,000 Electrical Automatic Irons the following are the budgeted expenses.*

Cost element	Cost Per unit Rs.
Direct material	60
Direct labour	30
Variable overheads	25
Fixed overhead (Rs. 1,50,000)	15
Variable expenses (Direct)	5
Selling Expenses (10% fixed)	15
Administration Expenses	
(Rs. 50,000 rigid for all levels of Production)	5
Distribution Expenses (20% fixed)	5
Total cost of sale per unit	160

Prepare a Budget for production of 6000, 7000 and 8000 irons showing distinctly marginal cost and total cost. [M.Com (CA) May 2004 PU]

Solution :

Flexible Budget

Particulars	6,000 Units CPU Rs.	6,000 Units TC Rs.	7,000 Units CPU Rs.	7,000 Units TC Rs.	8,000 Units CPU Rs.	8,000 Units TC Rs.	1,000 Units CPU Rs.	1,000 Units TC Rs.
Fixed Cost overheads	25	1,50,000	21.43	1,50,000	18.75	1,50,000	15.00	1,50,000
Administration expenses	8.33	50,000	7.14	50,000	6.25	50,000	5.00	50,000
Distribution expenses	1.67	10,000	1.43	10,000	1.25	10,000	1.00	10,000
Selling expenses	2.5	15,000	2.14	15,000	1.88	15,000	1.50	15,000
Total fixed cost	37.5	2,25,000	32.14	2,25,000	28.13	2,25,000	22.50	2,25,000
Variable Cost								
Direct material	60	3,60,000	60	4,20,000	60	4,80,000	60	6,00,000
Direct labour	30	1,80,000	30	2,10,000	30	2,40,000	30	3,00,000
Variable overhead	25	1,50,000	25	1,75,000	25	2,00,000	25	2,50,000
Variable expenses	5	30,000	5	35,000	5	40,000	5	50,000
Selling expenses	13.50	81,000	13.50	94,500	13.50	1,08,000	13.50	1,35,000
Distribution expenses	4.00	24,000	4.00	28,000	4.00	32,000	4.00	40,000
Total variable cost	137.50	8,25,000	137.50	9,62,500	137.50	11,00,000	137.50	13,75,000
Total Cost (TFC + TVC)	175	10,50,000	169.64	11,87,500	165.63	13,25,000	160	16,00,000

BUDGET AND BUDGETARY CONTROL

Working Notes :

1. Distribution expenses   Rs. 5.00
   Less : fixed   1.00

   variable   4.00

   Fixed cost × budgeted production
   1 × 10000 = 10000

2. Selling expenses   Rs. 15.00
   Less fixed 10%   1.50

   Variable   13.50

   Fixed cost × Budgeted production
   1.50 × 10,000 = 15,000

Problem 2. *ABC Ltd has prepared the budget for the production of one lakh units of the only commodity manufactured by them for a costing period as under.*

Raw materials	Rs. 2.52 per unit
Direct material	Rs. 0.75 per unit
Direct expenses	Rs. 0.10 per unit
Works overhead (60% fixed)	Rs. 2.50 per unit
Administrative overhead (80% fixed)	Rs. 0.40 per unit
Selling overhead (50%fixed)	Rs. 0.20 per unit

The actual production during the period was only 60,000 units. Calculate the revised budgeted cost per unit.

[MBA Madras]

Solution :   **Flexible Budget**

Particulars	1,00,000 units		60,000 units	
	CPU Rs.	TC Rs.	CPU Rs.	TC Rs.
Fixed Cost				
Works overhead	1.50	1,50,000	2.50	1,50,000
Administration overhead	0.32	32,000	0.53	32,000
Selling overhead	0.10	10,000	0.17	10,000
Total Fixed cost	1.92	1,92,000	3.2	1,92,000
Variable Cost				
Raw material	2.52	2,52,000	2.52	1,51,200
Direct labour	0.75	75,000	0.75	45,000
Direct Expenses	0.10	10,000	0.10	6,000
Works overhead	1.00	1,00,000	1.00	60,000
Administration overhead	0.08	8,000	0.08	4,800
selling overhead	.10	10,000	.10	6,000
Total VC	4.55	4,55,000	4.55	2,73,000
Total cost [FC + VC]	6.47	6,47,000	7.75	4,65,000

Workings : [CPU = Cost Per Unit, TC = Total Cost]

Fixed cost

1. Works overhead	2.50	(100%)
Less : fixed	1.50	(60%)
Variable	1.00	(40%)

Fixed cost 1,00,000 × budgeted production
1.50 × 10,000 = 1,50,000

2. Administration overhead	0.40	(100%)
Less : fixed 80%	0.32	(80%)
Variable	0.08	(20%)

Fixed cost × Budgeted production
.32 × 1,00,000 = 32,000

3. Selling overhead	0.20	(100%)
Less : fixed	0.10	(50%)
Variable	0.10	(50%)

Fixed cost × Budgeted production
.10 × 1,00,000 = 10,000

Problem 3. *Draw up a flexible budget for overhead expenses on the basis of the following data and determine the overhead rate at 70%, 80% and 90% of plant capacity.*

	Capacity level		
	70%	**80%**	**90%**
Variable Overheads			
Indirect labour	-	12,000	-
Stores including spares	-	4,000	-
Semi-variable Overheads			
Power (30% fixed, 70% variable)	-	20,000	-
Repairs & Maintenance			
(60% fixed 40% variable)	-	2,000	-
Fixed Overheads			
Depreciation	-	11,000	-
Insurance	-	3,000	-
Salaries	-	10,000	-
Total Overheads	-	62,000	-
Estimated Direct Labour Hours	-	1,24,000 Hrs	-

[B.Com. PU 2002]

Solution :

Flexible Budget

Particulars	Capacity level		
	70% Rs.	80% Rs.	90% Rs.
Fixed Cost			
Depreciation	11,000	11,000	11,000
Insurance	3,000	3,000	3,000
Salaries	10,000	10,000	10,000
Power	6,000	6,000	6,000
Repairs and maintenance	1,200	1,200	1,200
Total Fixed cost	31,200	31,200	31,200
Variable Cost			
Indirect labour	10,500	12,000	13,500
Stores including spares	3,500	4,000	4,500
Power	12,250	14,000	15,750
Repairs and maintenance	700	800	900
Total Variable cost	26,950	30,800	34,650
Total cost (FC + VC)	58,150	62,000	65,850
Estimated direct labour hours	1,08,500	1,24,000	1,39,500
Cost per hour = [Total cost/Total hours × 1 hour]	0.536	0.500	0.472

Workings :

Fixed Cost from semi variable overheads :

1. Power (100%)   Rs. 20,000
   Less : 30% fixed   6,000   (1) (20,000 × 30/100)
                          ─────────
   70% variable   14,000
                          ═════════

2. Repairs and maintenance   Rs. 2,000
   Less : 60% fixed   1,200   (2000 × 60/100)
                             ─────────
   40% Variable   800
                             ═════════

Variable Cost :

(a) Indirect labour   = 12,000/80 × 70 = 10,500
                           12,000/80 × 90 = 13,500
(b) Stores including spare = 4,000/80 × 70 = 3,500
                             4,000/80 × 90 = 4,500
(c) Power   = 14,000/80 × 70 = 12,250
                           14,000/80 × 90 = 15,750
(d) Repairs and maintenance = 800/80 × 70 =   700
                              800/80 × 90 =   900

Hours cost per hour :
   124000/80 × 70 = 108500
   124000/80 × 90 = 139500
   At 70% Capacity 58150/108500 × 1 = Rs. 0.536
   At 80% Capacity 62000/124000 × 1 = Rs. 0.500
   At 90% Capacity 65850/139500 × 1 = Rs. 0.472

Problem 4. *Prepare a manufacturing overhead budget and ascertain the manufacturing overhead rates at 50% and 70% capacities. The following particulars are given at 60% capacity level.*

Variable Overheads	At 60% capacity level
	Rs.
Indirect Materials	6,000
Indirect Labour	18,000
Semi Variable Overheads	
Electricity (40% fixed)	30,000
Repairs & Maintenance (80% fixed)	3,000
Fixed Overhead	
Depreciation	16,500
Insurance	4,500
Salaries	15,000
Total Overheads	93,000
Estimated direct labour hrs.	1,86,000 Hrs

[B.Com Madurai] [M.Com Madras]

Solution : **Flexible Budget**

	Capacity level		
Particulars	50% Rs.	60% Rs.	70% Rs.
Fixed Cost :			
Deprecation	16,500	16,500	16,500
Insurance	4,500	4,500	4,500
Salaries	15,000	15,000	15,000
Electricity	12,000	12,000	12,000
Repairs & maintenance	2,400	2,400	2,400
Total fixed cost	50,400	50,400	50,400
Variable Cost :			
Indirect Labour	15,000	18,000	21,000
Indirect material	5,000	6,000	7,000
Electricity	15,000	18,000	21,000
Repairs and maintenance	500	600	700
Total Variable cost	35,500	42,600	49,700
Total Cost (FC & VC)	85,900	93,000	1,00,100
Estimated direct labour hours	1,55,000	1,86,000	2,17,000
Overhead rate [TC/T. Hrs]	0.55	0.50	0.46

BUDGET AND BUDGETARY CONTROL

Overhead rate
Total cost/Total direct labour hrs.

85,900/1,55,000	=	0.55
93,000/1,86,000	=	0.50
1,00,100/2,17,000	=	0.46

Workings :

(i) Indirect material
600/60 × 50 = 5,000
600/60 × 70 = 7,000

(iii) Electricity Rs. 30,000
Less : 40% Fixed 12,000
Variable 60% 18,000

18000/60 × 50 = 15,000
18000/60 × 70 = 21,000

(ii) Indirect labour
18,000/60 × 50 = 15,000
18,000/60 × 70 = 21,000

(iv) Repairs and maintenance 3,000
Less : Fixed 80% 2,400
Variable 20% 600

600/60 × 50 = 500
600/60 × 70 = 700

Problem 5. *The monthly budget for the manufacturing overhead of a concern for two levels of activity were as follows.*

Capacity level	60%	100%
Budgeted production(units)	600	1,000
	Rs.	Rs.
Indirect wages	1,200	2,000
consumable stores	900	1,500
Maintenance	1,100	1,500
Power and fuel	1,600	2,000
Depreciation	4,000	4,000
Insurance	1,000	1,000

(a) Indicate which of the items are fixed, variable and semi-variable.
(b) Prepare a flexible budget for 80% of the activity.

[MCA Madras] [B.Com Hons - Delhi]

Solution : **Flexible Budget**

Particulars	Capacity level		
Capacity level Units	60% 600	80% 800	100% 1000
	Rs.	Rs.	Rs.
Fixed Cost :			
Depreciation	4,000	4,000	4,000
Insurance	1,000	1,000	1,000
Maintenance	500	500	500
Power and fuel	1,000	1,000	1,000
Total Fixed cost	6,500	6,500	6,500

Variable Cost :			
Wages @ Rs. 2 per unit	1,200	1,600	2,000
Consumable @ Rs. 1.50 Per unit	900	1,200	1,500
Maintenance @ Re. 1 per unit	600	800	1,000
Power and Fuel @ Re. 1 per unit	600	800	1,000
Total variable cost	3,300	4,400	5,500
Total Cost [FC + VC]	9,800	10,900	12,000
Workings :			
Cost per unit = Total cost/output	16.33	13.62	12.00

(1)   (i) *Fixed* : Depreciation and Insurance
         (ii) *Variable* : Wages consumable stores
         (iii) *Semi-variable* : Maintenance Power and Fuel.

(2) Budget for 80% capacity (output 800 units)

Wages @ Rs. 2 per unit	1,600
Consumable stores (1.50 × 800)	1,200
Maintenance Rs. 500 + (800 ×1)	1,300
Power and Fuel Rs. 1000 + (800 × 1)	1,800
Depreciation	4,000
Insurance	1,000
Total Cost	10,900

(3)   9,800/600   10,900/800   12,000/1000
      = Rs. 16.33   = Rs. 13.62   = Rs. 12.00

(4) *Variable Cost*
     (a) Wages 1,200/600 = Rs. 2 or 2,000/1,000 = Rs. 2
     (b) Consumable stores = 900/600 = Rs. 1.50 or 1,500/1,000 = Rs. 1.50
     (c) Maintenance 1,100/600 = 1.83 1,500/1,000 = Rs. 1.50
         So it is treated as semi variable
         i.e., 1,500 − 1,100 / 1,000 - 600 = 400/400 = Re. 1 is variable and Rs. 500
         (*i.e.,* 1,100 - 600) is fixed
     (d) *Power and Fuel* :
         1,600/600 = 2.66 and 2,000/1,000 = Rs. 2
         So it is also treated as semi variable cost
         i.e., 2,000-1,600/1,000-600 = 400/400 = Rs. 1 is variable and Rs. 1,000
         (*i.e.,* 1,600 - 600) is fixed.

Problem 6. *The cost of an article at a capacity level of 5,000 units is given under A below. For a variation of 25% in capacity above or below this level, the individual expenses vary as indicated under B below.*

	A (Rs.)	B
Material cost	25,000	(100% Varying)
Labour cost	15,000	(100% Varying)

BUDGET AND BUDGETARY CONTROL

Power	1,250	(80% Varying)
Repairs and maintenance	2,000	(75% Varying)
Stores	1,000	(100% Varying)
Inspection	500	(20% Varying)
Depreciation	10,000	(100% Varying)
Administrative overheads	5,000	(25% Varying)
Selling overheads	3,000	(25% Varying)
	62,750	

Cost per unit Rs. 12.55
Find the unit cost of the product at a production level of 4000, 6000 and 8000 units.

[MCA Madras]

Solution :

Workings for flexible Budget

		Fixed Cost
1. Material	Variable cost	Power
2. Labour	Variable cost	Repairs and maintenance
3. Power	Variable cost	Administrative overhead
4. Repair maintenance	Variable cost	Inspection
5. Stores	Variable cost	Selling overheads
6. Inspection	Variable cost	
7. Depreciation	Variable cost	
8. Administrative overheads	Variable cost	
9. Selling overhead	Variable cost	

1. Material
   25,000/5000 × 4000 = 20,000
   25,000/5000 × 6000 = 30,000

2. Labour
   15000/15000 × 4000 = 12,000
   15000/5000 = 6000 = 18,000

3. Power cost   1,250
   Less : Fixed 20%   250
   ─────
   Variable   1,000
   ═════

   1000/5000 × 4000 =   800
   1000/5000 × 6000 =   1,200

4. Repairs and maintenance
   Cost   Rs. 2,000
   Less : 25% fixed   500
   ─────
   Variable   1,500
   ═════

   1500/5000 × 4000 =   1,200
   500/5000 × 6000 =   1,800

5. Stores (no fixed)   Rs. 1,000
   1000/5000 × 4000 =   800
   1000/5000 × 6000 =   1,200
6. Inspection   = Rs. 500
   Less : fixed 80%   400

   Variable 20%   100

   100/5000 × 4000 =   80
   100/5000 × 6000 =   120
7. Depreciation   Rs. 10,000
   10000/5000 × 4000 =   8,000
   10000/5000 × 6000 =   12,000
8. Ad. overhead   Rs. 5,000
   Less : Fixed 75%   3,750

   Variable 25%   1,250

   1250/5000 × 4000 =   1,000
   1250/5000 × 6000 =   1,500
9. Selling overhead   Rs. 3,000
   Less : Fixed (75%)   2,250

   Variable (25%)   750

   750/5000 × 4000 =   600
   750/5000 × 6000 =   900

Flexible Budget

Particulars	4000 units TC (Rs.)	5000 units TC (Rs.)	6000 units TC (Rs.)
Fixed Cost			
Power	250	250	250
Repairs and Maintenance	500	500	500
Ad. overhead	3,750	3,750	3,750
Selling overhead	2,250	2,250	2,250
Inspection	400	400	400
Total Fixed cost	7,150	7,150	7,150
Variable Cost			
Materials	20,000	25,000	30,000
Labour	12,000	15,000	18,000
Power	800	1,000	1,200
Repairs & Maintenance	1,200	1,500	1,800
Stores	800	1,000	1,200
Inspection	80	100	120

BUDGET AND BUDGETARY CONTROL

Depreciation	8,000	10,000	12,000
Administrative overhead	1,000	1250	1,500
Selling overhead	600	750	900
Total variable cost [VC]	44,480	55,600	66,720
Total cost (FC + VC)	51,630	62,750	73,870

$$\text{Cost per unit} = \frac{TC}{\text{No. of units}} = \frac{51,630}{4,000} = \text{Rs. } 12.90 \quad \frac{62,750}{5,000} = \text{Rs. } 12.55$$

$$= \frac{73,870}{6,000} = \text{Rs. } 12.31$$

Problem 7. *The following data are available in a manufacturing company for half yearly period.*

Fixed Expenses	Rs. (in lakhs)	Rs. (in lakhs)
Wages and salaries	8.4	
Rent rates and taxes	5.6	
Depreciation	7.0	
Sundry Administration expenses	8.9	
		29.9
Semi-variable Expenses (at 50% capacity)		
Maintenance and Repairs	2.5	
Indirect Labour	9.9	
Sales Department salaries etc	2.9	
Sundry Administration expenses	2.6	
		17.9
Variable expenses (at 50% capacity)		
Materials	24.0	
Labour	25.6	
Other expenses	3.8	
		53.4

Assume that the fixed expenses remain constant for all levels of production, semi variable expenses remain constant between 45% and 65% of capacity, increasing by 10% between 65% and 80% capacity, and by 20% between 80% and 100% capacity.

Sales at various levels are	(Rs. in Lakhs)
60% capacity	100.00
75% capacity	120.00
90% capacity	150.00
100% capacity	170.00

Prepare a flexible budget for the half year and forecast the profit at 60%, 75%, 90%, and 100% of capacity. [MBA Anna]

Solution :   Flexible Budget

Particulars	60% Capacity Rs.	75% Capacity Rs.	90% Capacity Rs.	100% Capacity Rs.
Fixed Expenses				
Wages and Salaries	8,40,000	8,40,000	8,40,000	8,40,000
Rent Rates and Taxes	5,60,000	5,60,000	5,60,000	5,60,000
Depreciation	7,00,000	7,00,000	7,00,000	7,00,000
Sundry Administration Expenses	8,90,000	8,90,000	8,90,000	8,90,000
Total Fixed cost (A)	29,90,000	29,90,000	29,90,000	29,90,000
Semi Variable Expenses				
Maintenance and Repairs	2,50,000	2,75,000	3,00,000	3,00,000
Indirect Labour	9,90,000	10,89,000	11,88,000	11,88,000
Sales Department Salaries etc.,	2,90,000	3,19,000	3,48,000	3,48,000
Sundry Administration Expenses	2,60,000	2,86,000	3,12,000	3,12,000
Total Semi Variable Cost (B)	17,90,000	19,69,000	21,48,000	21,48,000
Variable Expenses				
Material	28,80,000	36,00,000	43,20,000	48,00,000
Labour	30,72,000	38,40,000	46,08,000	51,20,000
Other Expenses	4,56,000	5,70,000	6,84,000	7,60,000
Total Variable Cost (C)	64,08,000	80,10,000	96,12,000	10,68,000
Total Cost [A+B+C]	1,11,88,000	1,29,69,000	1,47,50,000	1,58,18,000
Sales	1,00,00,000	1,20,00,000	1,50,00,000	1,70,00,000
Less : Total Cost	1,11,88,000	1,29,69,000	1,47,50,000	1,58,18,000
Profit or loss	− 11,88,000	− 9,69,000	+ 2,50,000	+ 11,82,000

Workings :

1. *Material*
   - 24,00,000/50 × 60 = 28,80,000
   - 24,00,000/50 × 75 = 36,00,000
   - 24,00,000/50 × 90 = 43,20,000
   - 24,00,000/50 × 100 = 48,00,000

2. *Labour*
   - 25,60,000/50 × 60 = 30,72,000
   - 25,60,000/50 × 75 = 38,40,000
   - 25,60,000/50 × 90 = 46,00,000
   - 25,60,000/50 × 100 = 51,20,000

3. *Other Expenses*
   - 3,80,000/50 × 60 = 4,56,000
   - 3,80,000/50 × 75 = 5,70,000
   - 3,80,000/50 × 90 = 6,84,000
   - 3,80,000/50 × 100 = 7,60,000

BUDGET AND BUDGETARY CONTROL

Problem 8. *A company, working at 50% capacity, is manufacturing 10,000 units of a product. At 50% capacity the product cost is Rs. 180 and sale price is Rs. 200. The break up of the cost is as follows.*

Particulars	Cost per unit Rs.	
Materials	100	
Wages	30	
Factory Overheads	30	(40% fixed)
Administration overheads	20	(50% fixed)

At 60% working capacity, raw material cost goes up by 2% and sales price falls by 2%. At 80% working capacity the raw material cost increases by 5% and sale price decreases by same percentage i.e., 5%.

Prepare a statement to show profitability at 60%, 80% and 90% capacity.

[BBM May 2005]

Solution :
Profitability Statement

Particulars	60% Capacity 12,000 Units		80% Capacity 16,000 Units		90% Capacity 18,000 Units	
	CPU Rs.	TC Rs.	CPU Rs.	TC Rs.	CPU Rs.	TC Rs.
Sales (1)	196	23,52,000	190	30,40,000	200	36,00,000
Less : variable cost :						
Material	102	12,24,000	105	16,80,000	100	18,00,000
Wages	30	3,60,000	30	4,80,000	30	5,40,000
Variable factory overheads	18	2,16,000	18	2,88,000	18	3,24,000
Administrative overheads	10	1,20,000	10	1,60,000	10	1,80,000
Total variable cost (i)	160	19,20,000	163	26,08,000	158	28,44,000
Contribution [S-Vc] (i-ii) (iii)	36	4,32,000	27	4,32,000	42	7,16,000
Less : Fixed Cost						
Administrative overheads	8.33	1,00,000	6.25	1,00,000	5.55	1,00,000
Factory overheads	10.00	1,20,000	7.50	1,20,000	6.66	1,20,000
Total fixed cost	18.33	2,20,000	13.75	2,20,000	12.21	2,20,000
Profit [contribution − TFC]	17.67	2,12,000	13.25	2,12,000	29.79	4,96,000

[CPU = Cost Per Unit, TC : Total Cost]

Workings :

1. Number of units
   10,000/50 × 60 = 12000
   10,000/50 × 80 = 16000
   10,000/50 × 90 = 18000

2. Selling pricle at 50% Rs. 200
   At 60%

3. *Material cost at 60%*
   Material cost at 50% : Rs. 100
   + 2%   2
   ———
                              102

Sales price	Rs. 200	At 80%		
Decrease 2%	4	Raw material cost		Rs. 100
	196	+ 5%		5
At 80%				105

4. Factory Overheads at 50%	Rs. 30.00	5. Admt. OH at 50% cap	20.00
Less : (fixed 40%)	12.00	Less : Fixed 50%	10.00
Variable cost	18.00	Variable (50%)	10.00

[12 × 10,000 = 1,20,000 FC]   [10 × 10,000 = 1,00,000 FC]

Problem 9. *The expenses for budgeted production of 10,000 units in a factory are furnished below.*

Particulars	Cost unit Rs.
Material	70
Labour	25
Variable overheads	20
Fixed overheads (Rs. 1,00,000)	10
Variable expenses (Direct)	5
Selling expenses 10% fixed	13
Distribution expenses 20% fixed	7
Administration expenses (Rs. 50,000)	5
Total cost per unit	155

Prepare a budget for production of (a) 8000 units (b) 6000 units (c) Compute cost per unit at both the levels.

Solution :   **Flexible Budget**

	6,000 Units		8,000 Units		18,000 Units	
Particulars	CPU Rs.	TC Rs.	CPU Rs.	TC Rs.	CPU Rs.	TC Rs.
Fixed Cost						
Fixed overheads	16.67	1,00,000	12.50	1,00,000	10.00	1,00,000
Administration expenses	8.33	50,000	6.25	50,000	5.00	50,000
Selling expenses	2.17	13,000	1.60	13,000	1.30	13,000
Distribution expenses	2.33	14,000	1.75	14,000	1.40	14,000
Total Fixed Cost (A)	29.50	1,77,000	22.10	1,77,000	17.70	1,77,000
Variable cost						
Material	70	4,20,000	70	5,60,000	70	7,00,000
Labour	25	1,50,000	25	2,00,000	25	2,50,000
Variable overheads	20	1,20,000	20	1,60,000	20	2,00,000
Variable expenses	5	30,000	5	40,000	5	50,000

Selling expenses	11.70	70,200	11.70	93,600	11.70	1,17,000
Distribution expenses	5.60	33,600	5.60	44,800	5.60	56,000
Total Variable Cost (B)	137.3	8,23,800	137.3	10,98,400	137.3	13,73,000
Total Cost [A+B]	166.8	10,00,800	159.4	12,75,400	155	15,50,000

[CPU Cost Per Unit TC = Total Cost]

Workings :

1. Distribution expenses   Rs.   7.00
 Less : Fixed 20%   1.40
 Variable Cost   5.60

 Fixed cost = 1.40 × Budgeted production
            = 1.40 × 10000 = **14,000**

2. Selling Expenses   Rs.   13.00
 Less : Fixed 10% (13 × 10/100)   1.30
 Variable Cost   11.70

 Fixed cost = 1.30 × 10000 units
            = **13,000**

□□□

19
Inflation Accounting

Generally, Trading account, Profit and Loss account and Balance Sheets are prepared for the purpose of presenting the financial position of the concern and displaying the operational results achieved during an accounting period. But these financial statements are prepared on the basis of traditional concept of cost and revenue. *i.e.*, it is expressed in monetary units or rupees. The recording of business transactions under this assumption that monetary unit is constant is known as historical accounting. But this assumption is not valid, because there have been inflationary as well as deflationary conditions. Purchasing power of rupee in India keeps changing from time to time on account of changes in the general price level.

LIMITATIONS OF HISTORICAL ACCOUNTING

The following are the important limitations of historical accounts.
   (*i*) In actual practice the financial statements are prepared on the basis of the historical cost. So the financial statements may be incorrectly interpreted unless appropriate adjustment are made on the current price level.
  (*ii*) Unrealistic profit due to the depreciation calculated under the historical cost method
 (*iii*) Insufficient provisions of depreciations
  (*iv*) According to Companies Act 1956 fixed assets are shown at their historical cost and not at current cost.
   (*v*) Return on capital employed is misleading because the profits are overstated and fixed assets are understated.
  (*vi*) Incorrect ascertainment of operating capacity
 (*vii*) Historical cost accounting mixes up the holding gains and its operating gains which does not help in taking effective managerial decisions.
(*viii*) Misleading inter-period and inter-firm comparison
  (*ix*) Difficulty in comparison of profitability of two plants

To overcome the limitations of conventional accounting, accounting for price level changes is developed or advocated.

Accounting for changing prices (or inflation accounting) is a system of accounting which regularly records all items in financial statements at their current values.

APPROACHES TO THE PRICE LEVEL ACCOUNTING

Generally there are four important approaches to the price level accounting:
(A) Current Purchasing Power Accounting [CPPA]
(B) Current Cost Accounting [CCA]
(C) Specific and General Price Level Accounting [SGPLA]
(D) Periodic revaluation of fixed assets along with the adoption of the LIFO method of inventory

(A) Current Purchasing Power Accounting (CPPA)

According to this method any approved general price index is used to convert the values of items in the financial statement at a particular period of time. This method considers the changes in the value of item as a result of the general price level but it does not consider the changes in the value of an individual item.

Steps in Current Purchasing Power Account:
(i) Conversion Factor

$$\text{Formula} = \frac{\text{Index you are converting to}}{\text{Index you are converting from}}$$

or

$$\text{Conversion Factor} = \frac{\text{Price index at the date of revaluation}}{\text{Price index at the date of existing figure}}$$

(ii) Mid Period Conversion
(iii) Distinction between monetary accounts and non monetary accounts
(iv) Determine gain or loss on monetary items
(v) Cost of sales and inventories
(vi) Ascertainment of profit
    (a) Conversion income method
    (b) Net change method

(B) Current Cost Accounting (CCA)

Current purchasing power method considers only changes in the money value, but it does not take into account the changes in the value of individual item. Under this method, the value of particular item may be increased on the basis of general price index. But the actual value of that item might have decreased. In order to overcome this limitation, the UK Government formed an Inflation Accounting Committee headed by Franis Sandilands. This committee published its report in 1975, to recommend the adoption of current cost accounting for dealing with the problem of Inflation Accounting.

In this method, historic values of items are not taken into account. Rather current values of individual items are taken on the basis of preparing profit and loss account and balance sheet. These items are not adjusted as a result of change in the general price level as they are adjusted in the current purchasing power method.

Under current cost accounting approach of inflation accounting, accounting profit is divided into three divisions.

(i) Current operating profit.
(ii) Realised holding gain.
(iii) Unrealised holding gain.

(i) Unrealised Holding Gain

Unrealised Holding Gain is the excess of the replacement cost of a non-monetary asset sold on the closing date over its historical cost.

(ii) Realised Holding Gain

Realised Holding Gain is the excess of the replacement cost of a non-monetary asset sold on the date of its sale over its historical cost.

(iii) Current Operating Profit

For the computation of current operating profit, the following adjustments are to be made in the current cost accounting method.

(a) Depreciation adjustment
(b) Cost of sales adjustment
(c) Monetary working capital adjustment
(d) Gearing adjustment.

(a) *Depreciation Adjustment.* The current year depreciation change under current cost accounting method is obtained by apportioning the average net replacement cost over the expected remaining useful life of the fixed assets at the beginning of the period.

(b) *Cost of Sales Adjustment (COSA)*

Formula :

$$COSA = (C - O) I_a \left(\frac{C}{I_c} - \frac{O}{I_o} \right)$$

Where, O = Historical cost of opening stock
C = Historical cost of closing stock
I_a = Average index number of the period
I_o = Index number appropriate to opening stock
I_c = Index number appropriate to closing stock.

(c) *Monetary Working Capital Adjustment (MWCA)*

$$MWCA = C - O - I_a \left(\frac{C}{I_c} - \frac{O}{I_o} \right)$$

O = Opening monetary working capital
C = Closing monetary working capital
I_a = Average index number for the period.
I_o = Index number appropriate to opening MWC
I_c = Index number appropriate to closing MWC.

(d) *Gearing Adjustment*

$$\text{Gearing adjustment} = \frac{L}{L + S}$$

L = Average net borrowing
S = Average shareholders funds
A = Total of current cost adjustments

(C) Specific and General Price Level Accounting (SGPLA)

This approach of accounting has not been popular because it has not been proposed so far by any institutional body as other approaches have been recommended by institutional bodies.

(D) Periodic Evaluation of fixed assets along with Adoption of LIFO method of Inventory

LIFO method of inventory valuation got the world wide general acceptance and is made use of during inflation. The advantage of this method are of the view that periodic revaluation of fixed assets along with the adoption of LIFO method can reasonably reduce the effect of increasing prices.

ADVANTAGES OF INFLATION ACCOUNTING

(i) It helps to maintain the physical capital because of changing depreciation on their current values.
(ii) It facilitates comparison of profitability of the two plants set up at different dates.
(iii) Balance sheet exhibits a true and fair view of the financial position of a firm.
(iv) For supplying more meaningful information through the Ratio analysis that can be adjusted to the current values.
(v) To protect the employees, shareholders, and public. They are not misled because inflation accounting shows current profit based on the current prices.
(vi) To help the owners, creditors and management in order to adjust the rate of return on capital employed to the current price index.
(vii) Profit and Loss Account will not overstate the business income.

DISADVANTAGES OF INFLATION ACCOUNTING

(i) So many calculations make more complications.
(ii) This system is not acceptable to the income tax authorities.
(iii) Accounting for price level changes is not free from prejudice.
(iv) During the periods of deflation only lower amount of depreciation will be changed.
(v) Computation of profit under this system may not be a realistic profit.

Problem 1. *Compute the net monetary result of RPMS & Co Ltd as on 31.12.2001. The relevant data are given below :*

	1.1.2001	31.12.2001
	Rs.	Rs.
Cash	5,000	10,000
Book Debts	20,000	25,000
Creditors	15,000	20,000
Loan	20,000	20,000
Retail price index numbers :		
1st January	200	
31st December	300	
Average for the year	240	[B.Com (Hons) Delhi]

Solution :

Statement Showing the net monetary result on account of price level changes

		Rs.	Rs.
(i)	Monetary liabilities as on 1.1.2001 should have gone up with increase in price indices (35000 × 1.5)		52,500
(ii)	Increase in monetary liabilities during 2001 which should have gone up with increase in price indices (5000 × 1.25)	6,250	—
	Monetary Liabilities on 31.12.2001 should have stood at	58,750	
	However, the liabilities on 31.12.2001 stood at	40,000	
	Gain on holding of monetary Liabilities		18,750
(iii)	Monetary assets as on 1.1.2201 should have gone up with increase in price indices [Rs. 25.000 × 1.25]		37,500
(iv)	Increase in monetary assets during 2001 should have gone up with increase in price indices [Rs. 10.000 × 1.25]		12,500
	Monetary assets on 31.12.2001 should stood at	50,000	
	However, the monetary assets on 31.12.2001 stoot at	35,000	
	Loss on holding monetary assets		15,000
	Net gain on monetary items		3,750

Problem 2. *Ascertain net monetary result as on 31.12.2001 from the data given below.*

	1.1.2001	31.12.2001
	Rs.	Rs.
Cash at bank	15,000	21,000
Debtors	45,000	54,000
Creditors	75,000	50,000
General Price Index		
1.1.2001		100
31.12.2000		125
Average for 2001		120

[M.Com Apr. 2003]

Solution : Statement showing the net monetary Result

Particulars	Historical Amount Rs.	Adjusted Factors	Price Level Adjusted Amount (Rs.)	Purchasing Power Gain or Loss (Rs.)
Monetary assets at the beginning of 2001				
Cash at Bank	15,000	125/100	18,750 (15,000 × 125/100)	
Accounts receivable	45,000	125/100	56,250 (45,000 × 125/100)	
Add : Increase in monetary Asset during the year				
Cash at Bank (21,000 − 15,000)	6,000	125/120	6,250 (6,000 × 125/120)	

INFLATION ACCOUNTING

Accounts receivable (54,000 − 45,000)	9,000	125/120	9,375 (9,000 × 125/120)
Total	75,000		90,625
Purchasing power loss (90,625 − 75,000)			15,625
Monetary liabilities at the beginning of 2001 Accounts Payable	75,000	125/100	93750 (75,000 × 125/100)
Less : Decrease in Accounts Payable	25,000	125/100	26,042 (25,000 × 125/100)
	50,000		67,708
Purchasing Power Gain (67,708 − 50,000)			17,708
Net Purchasing Power Gain			2,083

Problem 3. *From the information given below calculate the net monetary gain or loss for the accounting year ending on 30th June 2002 :*

Net monetary assets as on 1.7.2001	Rs. 1,000
Net monetary asset as on 30.6.2002	Rs. 7,000
Transaction for the year are as follows :	
(i) Cash sales	Rs. 8,000
(ii) Credit sales	Rs. 10,000
(iii) Credit purchase of goods	Rs. 7,000
(iv) Wages incurred and paid	Rs. 2,000
(v) Other operating expenses	Rs. 1,000
(vi) Interest paid on 30.6.2002	Rs. 2,000
Index as on 1.7.2001	100
Index as on 30.6.2002	150
Average index for the year	125

Solution :

Particulars	Historic Cost Accounting Rs.	CF	CPP Rs.
Net monetary asset on 01.07.2001	1,000	150/100	1,500
Add : Sales	18,000	150/125	21,600
	19,000		23,100
Less : Purchases	7,000	150/125	8,400
Wages	2,000	150/125	2,400

Operating expenses	1,000	150/125	1,200
Interest	2,000	150/150	2,000
	12,000		14,000
Net monetary asset as on 30.06.2002	7,000		9,100
Less : Monetary assets on HCA basis	—		7,000
Net Monetary Loss			2,100

Problem 4. *HR & Co has the following transaction on the given dates and price indices of the first Quarter of 2000 :*

		Price Index
Opening Balance (Jan. 1)	Rs. 6,000	100
Cash Sales (Feb.)	Rs. 17,500	105
Payment to creditors (Mar. 1)	Rs. 12,000	108
Cash Purchase (Mar. 1)	Rs. 2,000	108
Payment of expenses (Mar. 31)	Rs. 2,000	110
Closing Balance (Mar. 31)	Rs. 7500	110

Calculate monetary gain or loss

[B.Com Madras]

Solution :   **Conversion Table**

Particulars	Conventional Accounting Rs.	Conversion Factor	Converted Values Rs.
Receipts :			
Opening Balance	6,000	110/100	6,600
Cash sales	17,500	110/105	18,333
A	23,500		24,933
Less : Payments :			
Creditors	12,000	110/108	12,222
Purchases	2,000	110/108	2,037
Expenses	2,000	110/110	2,000
B	16,000		16,259
Closing Balance (A – B)	7,500		8,674

NOTE : If the Actual Balance is more than the Expected Balance, the difference is called monetary gain. If the Actual Balance is less than the Expected Balance, the difference is called monetary loss.

INFLATION ACCOUNTING

Statement of Gain or Loss

	Rs.
Expected Balance	8,674
Actual Balance	7,500
Monetary Loss	1,174

Problem 5. *ABC Ltd follows LIFO system. From the following particulars given below, ascertain the cost of sales and closing inventory under CPP method.*

		General price index
Inventory 31.12.2003	Rs. 5,000	150
Purchase for 2002	28,000	180 (Average for 2002)
Inventory on 31.12.2004	60,000	240

Solution :

Particulars	Historic Accounting Rs.	Conversion Factor	Conversion Value
(i) Cost of sales			
Opening inventory	5,000		
Add : Purchases	28,000		
Total available for sale	33,000		
Less : Closing inventory	6,000		
LIFO valuation of cost of Sales	27,000	240/180 = 1.33	36,000
(ii) Closing inventory			
(a) Current purchases	1,000	1.33	1,333
(b) Rest from opening stock	5,000	240/150 = 1.60	8,000
	6,000		9,333

Problem 6. *The Balance Sheet of CBC Ltd as on 1.2.2003 and the income statement for the year ending 31.12.2003 are set out below.*

Balance Sheet as on 1.1.2003

Liabilities	Rs.	Assets	Rs.
Share capital	10,000	New machine	15,000
10% Debentures	6,000	Stock	2,400
Creditors	3,600	Debtors	1,200
		Cash	1,000
	19,600		19,600

Income Statement for the year ended on 31.12.2003

		Rs.
Sales		10,000
Cost of goods sold :		
Opening stock (FIFO)	2,400	
Purchases (Net)	4,600	
Cost of goods available for sale	7,000	
Less : closing stock (FIFO)	2,000	
		5,000
Gross profit on sales		5,000
Less : Operating expenses	800	
Depreciation	1,500	
Interest on debentures paid on 31.12.2003	600	
		2,900
Retained earnings		2,100

Debtors and creditors balances remained constant throughout the year. General price indices were as given below.

on. 1.1.2003	200
Average for the year	240
on 31.12.2003	300

You are required to prepare the final accounts for the year 2003 after adjusting the price level changes under CPP method.

Solution : *(i)* **Computation of Conversion Factors**

(to represent current purchasing power of the rupee as on 31.12.2003)

$$1.1.2003 = \frac{300}{200} = 1.5 \qquad 31.12.2003 = \frac{300}{300} = 1.00$$

$$\text{Average for 2003} = \frac{300}{240} = 1.25$$

(ii) **Income statement as per CPP method for the year ending on 31.12.2003**

Particulars	HCA Rs.	CF Rs.	CPP Rs.
Sales	10,000	1.25	12,500
Opening stock (FIFO)	2,400	1.50	3,600
Purchases	4,600	1.25	5,750
Cost of Goods for sale	7,000		9,350
Less : closing stock (FIFO)	2,000	1.25	2,500
Cost of goods sold	5,000		6,850
Gross profit on sales [Sales – CGS]	5,000		5,650

INFLATION ACCOUNTING

Operating expenses	800	1.25	1,000
Depreciation	1,500	1.50	2,250
Interest on debentures	600	1.00	600
Total expenses	2,900		3,850
Income before general price level gain or loss (GP–TE)	2,100		1,800
General price gain	—		2,550
Retained Earnings	2,100		4,350

(iii) Computation of monetary Gain or Loss

Particulars	HCA (Unadjusted)	CF	CPP (Adjusted)
Net Monetary Liabilities as on 1.1.2003	7,400	1.50	11,100
Add : Purchases	4,600	1.25	5,750
Operating expenses	800	1.25	1,000
Interest on debentures	600	1.25	600
Total	13,400		18,450
Less : Sales	10,000	1.25	12,500
Net Monetary Liabilities as on 31.12.2003	3,400		5,950
Deduct : Monetary Liabilities on HCA basis			3,400
Monetary Gain			2,550

Workings :

Cash		
Opening Balance	Rs.	1,000
Sales Receipts		10,000
		11,000
Less : Payment on account of purchases and expenses		6,000
		5,000

(iv) Computation of Monetary Liabilities on HCA Basis
Balance Sheet

Liabilities		Assets	
Debentures	6000	Cash	5,000
Creditors	3600	Debtors	1,200
		Balancing figure	3,400
	9,600		9,600

Balancing figure treated as monetary liabilities = Rs. 3,400

Balance Sheet as on 31.12.2003

Liabilities	HCA Rs.	CF	CPP Rs.	Assets	HCA Rs.	CF	CPP Rs.
Share capital	10,000	1.5	15,000	Cash	5,000	1.0	5000
Debenture	6,000	1.0	6,000	Debtors	1,200	1.0	1200
Creditors	3,600	1.0	3,600	Stock	2,000	1.25	2500
Retained earnings	2,100	—	4,350	Machinery	15,000	1.5	22500
				Less : Depreciation	(1,500)	1.5	(2,250)
	21,700		28,950		21,700		28,950

Problem 7. *A summary of Balance Sheet of India Ltd is given below.*

Cash and Accounts Receivable	Rs. 13,00,000
Plant and Machinery (Net)	Rs. 14,00,000
Total Asset	**27,00,000**
Current Debts	Rs. 6,00,000
Long Term Debts	Rs. 10,00,000
Owners' Equities	Rs. 11,00,000
Total Liabilities	**27,00,000**

The Current price index is 280. The Plant and Machinery and long term debt were acquired when the price index was at 180.

You are required to revise the summary balance sheet to restate, assess equities in terms of current rupees. How will you treat the monetary gain or loss if any ? [M.Com Delhi]

Solution :

Balance Sheet

Liabilities	Historical Values Rs.	CF	Current Values Rs.	Assets	Historical Values Rs.	CF	Current Values Rs.
Current debts	6,00,000	280/280	6,00,000	Current Assets	13,00,000	280/280	13,00,000
Long term debts	10,00,000	280/280	10,00,000	Plant & Machinery	14,00,000	280/180	21,77,778
Owners' equity	11,00,000	280/180	17,11,111				
Gain balancing figure	—	—	1,66,667				
	27,00,000		34,77,778		27,00,000		34,77,778

Monetary Gain is to be added to the owners' equity
  i.e., 17,11,111 + 1,66,667 = 18,77,778

INFLATION ACCOUNTING

Problem 8. *Markam Ltd had the following monetary items on January 1 :*

		Rs.
Debtors		41,000
Bills Receivable		10,000
Cash		20,000
		71,000
Less : Bills payable	10,000	
Creditors	25,000	
		35,000
Net Monetary Assets		36,000

The transactions affecting monetary items during the year were :
  (i) Sales of Rs. 1,40,000 made evenly throughout the year.
  (ii) Purchases goods of Rs. 1,05,000 made evenly during the year.
  (iii) Operating expenses of Rs. 35,000 were incurred evenly throughout the year.
  (iv) One machine was sold for Rs. 18,000 on July 1.
  (v) One machine was purchased for Rs. 25,000 in December 31.

The general price index was as follows :

On January 1	300
Average for the year	350
On July 1	360
On December 31	400

You are required to compute the general purchasing power, gain or loss for the year stated in terms of the current year-end rupee.

Solution :

Statement of General Purchasing Power Gain or Loss

Particulars	Historical Amount Rs.	Adjusted Factors	Price Level Adjusted Amount (Rs.)	Purchasing Power Gain or Loss (Rs.)
Conversion of monetary assets :				
Assets at the beginning of the year	36,000	400/300	48,000	
Increase in net monetary assets				
During the year : Sales	1,40,000	400/350	1,60,000	
Sale of machine	18,000	400/360	20,000	
Total	1,94,000		2,28,000	
Purchasing Power Loss (2,28,000 − 1,94,000)	—	—	—	34,000

Decrease in net monetary assets :			
Purchases	1,05,000	400/350	1,20,000
Operating expenses	35,000	400/350	40,000
Purchase of machine	25,000	400/400	25,000
Total	1,65,000		1,85,000
Purchasing Power Gain (1,85,000 − 1,65,000)	—	—	—	20,000
Net Purchase Loss			14,000

Statement of Net monetary Assets

Price level adjusted amount of net assets (2,28,000 − 1,85,000)	43,000
Less : Purchasing Power Loss	14,000
Net monetary assets at the end of the year (1,94,000 − 1,65,000)	29,000

❑❑❑

20
Human Resources Accounting

ORIGIN OF HUMAN RESOURCE ACCOUNTING

Recognising human being as an asset is an old one. From the observation of Indian History, it is evident that Emperor Akbar gave importance to the nine jewels. Freedom fighters in India like Shri Motilal Nehru, Mahatma Gandhi, Sardar Vallabh Bhai Patel, Pandit Jawahar Lal Nehru cannot be removed from the historical pages of freedom movement of India. Inspite of the uncountable sacrifices forgone by the above individuals, no one made efforts to allocate any monetary value to such individuals in the Balance Sheet of India.

The suitable work was started to determine the cost and value of human being by behavioural scientists from 1960 onwards. The experts in this field were Shultz (1960), William Pyle (1967), Flam Holtz (1972), Morese (1973), Kenneth Sinclare (1978) and Dr Roa (1983) etc who contributed appropriate methodology and correct methods for finding out the value of the employee to the organisation.

IMPORTANCE OF HRA

In any organization, the most valuable input is the human element. The success or failure of the company depends on the quality, calibre, capability and character of the employees working in it. So in business enterprise, a well expertised and loyal employee may be much more valuable than a stock of merchandise. It is worth recalling what Alfred Marshall said long ago that "the most valuable of all capital is that invested in human beings".

Even though this much of values is possessed by the human resources, it is unfortunate that till now there is not even a single generally accepted system to value and record the human resources as an important assets. So the balance sheet does not exhibit the value of human resource as the most vital asset while capital invested in other assets are shown. This is one of the severe limitations of present day financial statements which prevents the user of those statements from making effective use of them.

In the face of communication and technological changes, if the management could succeed in preventing the educated, trained and efficient employees from leaving the company or increasing their professionalism, an immense benefit could be achieved by the organisation. With the help of recording and transmitting human resource capital, the management will have access to a valid and reliable measure of expenditure on equipping the personnel with requisite knowledge and operating skills.

The ultimate aim of the financial accounting is to provide detailed information about the financial aspect to the decision makers. And at the same time, the conventional system fails to generate relevant data about one important asset of the organisation *i.e.*, human asset. It is termed as intervening variables. It refers to the loyalties, attitude, motivation, high morale, performance goals, collective capacity of the effective interaction, health of the organisation and decision making. The decision makers and executors should know to what extent such assets are either appreciated or depleted during a particular period.

The outcome of this process fails to reflect the level of business performance. In the real sense, it is always a failure to measure the economic value of people by the management. For this reason, the value of human resources is not to be considered. In order to overcome this difficulty, measuring and reporting the human resources would protect the management from liquidating human resources or obtaining more profitable investment in human resources in a period of profit squeeze.

MEANING OF HUMAN RESOURCE ACCOUNTING

Human Resource Accounting is a new branch of accounting. It is an accounting for people as the organisational resources. It is the measurement of the cost and value of people to organisation.

Some important definitions of Human Resource Accounting is given below :

(i) *"Human resource accounting is an attempt to identify and report investments made in human resources of an organisation that are presently not accounted for in conventional accounting practice. Basically it is an information system that tells the management what changes over time are occurring to the human resources of the business".*
—**Woodruff**

(ii) *"Human resources accounting is the measurement and quantification of human organisational inputs such as recruiting, training, experience and communication".*
—**Stephen Knauf**

OBJECTIVES OF HUMAN RESOURCE ACCOUNTING

(i) To assist the management executives in monitoring effectively the use of human resources.
(ii) To help the management decision makers take suitable decisions regarding investment of capital resources.
(iii) To communicate the value and importance of human assets to the organisation and the society at large.
(iv) To evaluate the effectiveness and efficiency of human resources in obtaining productivity and profitability.
(v) To provide a determination of asset control.

METHODS OF VALUATION OF HUMAN RESOURCES

In order to measure the appropriate value of human resources, it is difficult to comply with the commonly accepted accounting principles. However, there are two important approaches for the valuation of human resources.

First one is based on the cost *i.e.,* cost incurred by the enterprise to recruit, hire, train and development of employees.

Second one is to measure the economic value of the human resource based on capitalisation of earnings.

The important methods for the valuation of human resources are given below :

(i) *Acquisition Cost.* Under this method, costs incurred for the purpose of recruitment, hiring and induction and training of employees are taken into account. Expenditure incurred regarding the above activities is recorded properly and a proportion of it is written off to the income of the future periods during which human resources will provide service. But if in any situation, the human assets are liquidated prematurely, the amount which is not written off is changed to the income of the year the liquidation takes place. The historical cost of human resources is similar to the book value of other physical assets. This method is simple to understand, easy to work out and easy to implement.

(ii) *Replacement Cost.* In the case of acquisition cost, past costs are taken into account. But under this approach, one takes into account how much it costs to replace a firm's existing resources and thus represents a current value approach. Under this method, historic cost is adjusted according to the current market conditions.

(iii) *Standard Cost.* It is the cost incurred for the purpose of recruiting, hiring, training and development of human resources in the organisation. In connection with the above activities the standard costing principles are to be applied. *i.e.,* target is set for various components of human resources which are helpful to compare the actual and find the variations from the targeted one.

(iv) *Opportunity Cost.* Opportunity cost is the maximum alternative earning that is earned if the productive capacity or asset is put to some alternative use. Human resource valuation under the method of opportunity cost is difficult. Because alternative use of human resource within the organisation is restricted. And at the same time, this type of alternative use may not be identifiable in the real industrial environment.

(v) *Present Value of Future Earnings Method.* This model is developed by Lev and Schwartz in 1971 and is popular in India. It is otherwise called as capitalisation of salary method. According to this method, future earnings of employees are estimated upto the age of retirement and are discounted at a rate appropriate to the person or the group to obtain the present value. They have given the following formula for calculating the value of an individual.

$$Vr = \frac{I(t)}{(I+R)^{t-r}}$$

Where, Vr = The value of an individual r years old
$I(t)$ = The individual's annual earnings upto the retirement
t = retirement age
R = a discount rate

(vi) *Rewards Valuation Model.* It has been suggested by Flamholtz. This method identifies the important variables that determines the value of each and every individual employee in an organisation *i.e.,* his expected realisable value.

(vii) *Net Benefit Model.* This model was suggested by Morse (1973). According to this method, the value of human resources is equivalent to the present value of net profit earned by the enterprise from the services of the employee.

(viii) *Certainty Equivalent Net Benefit Approach.* This model has been suggested by Pekin Ogan in 1976. It is an extension of net benefit approach of Morse. Under this method, the value of human resource is determined by considering the certainty with the net profit earned by the enterprise in future.

(ix) *Aggregate Payment Approach.* This approach has been developed by Prof. S.K. Chakraborty 1976, the first Indian to develop a model on human resources of an enterprise. According to this method, the value of human resources can be calculated on a consolidated basis and not the individual basis. But the managerial and non-managerial values are evaluated separately.

(x) *Total Cost Concept.* This approach has been developed by Prof. N. Dasgupta (1978). According to his opinion both employed and unemployed persons should be taken into account for the determination of value of human resources of the nation. In order to prepare the balance sheet of a nation, the system should be such which shows the human resources not only for a firm but also of the whole nation.

(xi) *Input Out Control Mechanism.* Dr. Rao (1983) has suggested this approach. The system of human resource accounting was developed and applied in a transport equipment manufacturing concern. The output factors of the system are described to be the indicators of human resource development and utilisation.

ADVANTAGES OF HRA

(i) It supplies quantitative information about the human capital.

(ii) It helps the management to make proper interpretation of return on capital employed.

(iii) It will help to increase the productivity of human resources through the monetary value attached to human resources.

(iv) It assists the management to evaluate management development programme.

(v) It will provide an invaluable contribution for accounting to humanity and it will lead to improved efficiency and performance of employee while preserving human dignity and honour.

(vi) When and where human element is the prime factor that places human resource accounting to a significant role.

Example : A drama company, a professional accounting firm.

(vii) The value of organisation's human resources is very much helpful for the real investors and the entrepreneurs in making long term investment decisions.

(viii) It helps the management to reorient their attitudes towards employees and improving their administrative and leadership styles.

PROBLEMS AND LIMITATIONS OF HRA

(i) There is no specific and proper guidelines for finding cost and value of resources of an enterprise.

(ii) It may lead to dehumanising and manipulation among employees.

(iii) Continuous fear of opposition from the trade unions.
(iv) The measurement of human capital bristles with many difficulties and requires huge expense.
(v) The human capital cannot be purchased or owned by the firm and it would not be recognised as asset.
(vi) Accountants express their objection because human asset cannot be objectively measured.

HUMAN RESOURCE ACCOUNTING IN INDIA

HRA can provide information for both management and outsiders. However, some models are developed for the valuation of human resources. Even though, these much of benefits are contributed by the HRA, yet its development and application in different industries has not been encouraging. Because Indian companies Act 1956, does not provide any scope for showing any information about human resources in financial statements. Due to the development of business and industries, some of the Indian companies, both public and private, value their human resources and report this information in their annual report.

(a) Public Sector Enterprises Include

(i) Bharat Heavy Electricals Ltd. (BHEL).
(ii) Steel Authority of India Ltd. (SAIL).
(iii) Minerals and Metals Trading Corporation of India.
(iv) Cement Corporation of India.
(v) ONGC
(vi) Oil India Ltd.

(b) Private Sector Enterprises

(i) Tata Engineering and Locomotive Works.
(ii) Southern Petrochemicals Industries Corporation Ltd.
(iii) Associated Cement Company Ltd.

PROSPECTS

Until this date, Human Resource Accounting is not popular in India. So Indian Accounting Standard and also the International Accounting Standard Committee frame the format, provisions and guidelines. Through this effort only an importance of Human Resource Accounting will be created at all levels in the industrial concerns. However, this effort will take some time to incorporate Human Resource Accounting in Indian industries.

❑❑❑

21
Responsibility Accounting

INTRODUCTION

One of the foremost uses of management accounting is the managerial control. Among the various control techniques, 'responsibility accounting' plays a significant role.

The remaining control techniques are applicable to the organisation as a whole. But responsibility accounting represents a method of measuring the performance of various divisions of an organisation. The main aim of this chapter is to describe the organisational structure in which the management controls processes through responsibility accounting. Responsibility accounting is similar to any other system of cost but with greater emphasis on fixing the responsibility of the person assigned and executed a specific job.

DEFINITION

Eric Kohler defines responsibility accounting as *"a method of accounting in which costs are identified with persons assumed to be capable of controlling them rather than with products or functions. It differs from activity accounting in that it does not in itself requires an organisational grouping by activities and sub activities or provide a systematic criterion of system design."*

Robert Anthony defines responsibility accounting as *"the type of management accounting that collects and reports both planned and actual accounting information in terms of responsibility centres".*

Principles of Responsibility Accounting

(i) To identify the responsibility centres within an organization.
(ii) To define the responsibility for each responsibility centre.
(iii) It lays greater emphasis on human factor.
(iv) To specify controllable and uncontrollable activities at various levels of responsibility.
(v) To provide information about the performance report.

Requirements of Effective Responsibility Accounting

(i) The entire organisation is divided into responsibility centres *i.e.*, various responsibility centres should be created.
(ii) To establish a sound organisation structure.

RESPONSIBILITY ACCOUNTING

(iii) To define the authority and responsibility in a clear-cut way.

(iv) To prepare a detailed budget with full involvement of concerned managers.

(v) To obtain sufficient top management support for implementing responsibility accounting.

(vi) The actual performance of the responsibility accounting is to be communicated to the concerned managers.

(vii) The performance reports for all the divisions should be prepared and if corrective measures are suggested or taken it is also communicated to the respective managers.

(viii) A healthy organisational environment should exist.

Advantages of Responsibility Accounting

The ultimate aim of the responsibility accounting is to help and guide the management to achieving organisational goals. The following are some important advantages of responsibility accounting.

(i) It provides a system of closer control.

(ii) It defines and communicates the corporate objectives and individual goals in an efficient manner.

(iii) It helps to improve the quality of decision making.

(iv) Each and every employee knows what is expected of him. And at the same time no one can escape from anything that goes wrong.

(v) It measures the performance of individual employee in an objective manner.

(vi) It fosters a sense of cost-consciousness among managers and their subordinates.

(vii) It acts as a suitable tool of cost control.

(viii) It is helpful in planning for future costs and revenues.

(ix) It guides the management to make an effective delegation of authority and responsibility.

(x) If necessary, corrective action can be taken and efficient control over the cost can be obtained.

RESPONSIBILITY CENTRES

A small organisation can effectively manage the business with an individual or few people of the organisation. But in the case of large scale organisation, it is difficult to supervise by an individual or few people. In order to have an effective control of the entire activities, the large scale organisation can be divided into some small divisions or departments. Each and every unit has a separate manager and it performs its activities properly. The small units or divisions of enterprise for the purpose of effective control of its activities are called responsibility centres.

According to **Richard D. Irwin**, *"A responsibility centre is a unit of an organization under the supervision of a manager who has the responsibility for the activities of that responsibility centre."*

Responsibility centres, for the planning and control purposes, are classified into the following classes :

(i) Cost centre or Expense centre
(ii) Revenue Centre
(iii) Profit centre
(iv) Investment centre.

(i) *Cost Centre.* A cost centre or expense centre is a division of an organisation in which the manager is held responsible for the costs incurred in that division. Simply, a responsibility centre is called a cost centre when the manager is solely responsible only for cost incurred in that centre.

(ii) *Revenue Centre.* A revenue centre is a unit of the organisation which is ultimately responsible for sales revenue. A manager, under this division, does not possess control over cost, but he has to control the expenses of marketing department.

(iii) *Profit Centre.* A responsibility centre is called a profit centre where the manager is held responsible for both costs and revenues. In the profit centre, input and output values are measured in monetary terms.

(iv) *Investment Centre.* A responsibility centre is called an investment centre. Its manager is responsible for costs and revenues as well as for the investment in assets used by his centre. It is defined as a responsibility centre in which inputs are measured in costs and outputs are measured in terms of revenue.

TRANSFER PRICE

A transfer price is a mechanism which is used to measure the value of goods or services furnished by a profit centre to other responsibility centres within an organisation. A correct determination of transfer price is more essential because it affects the other centres of the organisation.

Following factors taken into consideration while determining transfer price :

(i) The accurate measurement of divisional profitability.
(ii) To motivate the divisional managers.
(iii) To ensure that divisional autonomy and authority is preserved.

Problem 1. *XYZ Ltd operates a number of divisions located in different regions. Division X incurred losses in the first half of the current year. Relevant revenue and cost data pertaining to these divisions are as follows.*

	Rs.
Sales revenue	6,50,000
Controllable variable costs	3,50,000
Controllable fixed costs	2,00,000
Attributable segment costs	50,000
Common firm-wide cost allocated to division X	60,000
Loss	(10,000)

You are required (i) To prepare a performance evaluation report of division X in the proper format and (ii) Advice the management whether its operation should be continued or shut down.

Solution :

(i) Performance Evaluation Report of Division X

Particulars	Amount Rs.
Sales Revenue	6,50,000
Less : Controllable variable costs	3,50,000
Controllable contribution margin	3,00,000
Less : controllable fixed costs	2,00,000
Controllable segment margin	1,00,000
Less : Attributable segment costs	50,000
Segment profit contribution	50,000
Less : Common firm wide costs	60,000
	10,000

(ii) In the short run, division X justifies its existence as it generates a positive segment profit contribution i.e., 50,000 regardless of its share of firm-wide costs. Of course, in the long run division X must collectively generate sufficient total profit contribution to allow the recovery of all firm-wide costs and the achievement of corporate profit goals.

Problem 2. *Ragal Angles Ltd deals in three products, Ace, Nice, and Grace and these are sold directly through salesmen in three zones : Prime, Extension and Outreach. The responsibility for sales promotion rests with the headquarters and so does the overall control of distribution and sales. Cost of sales as percentage of sales are Ace 85, Nice 80, Grace 75. Details of sales, selling and distribution expenses for the year are as follows.*

Zones	Products	Sales (Rs.)	Selling and distribution expenses allocated direct (Rs.)
Prime Zone	Ace	9,00,000	63,990
	Nice	9,00,000	84,465
	Grace	4,50,000	47,160
		22,50,000	1,95,615
Extension Zone	Ace	6,75,000	46,710
	Nice	4,50,000	47,700
	Grace	2,25,000	23,940
		13,50,000	1,18,350
Outreach Zone	Ace	2,25,000	18,900
	Nice	1,80,000	15,165
	Grace	4,95,000	66,375
		9,00,000	1,00,440

Selling and distribution expenses at the headquarters are as follows :

	Rs.
Office expenses	94,500
Advertisement	1,35,000
Other expenses	1,21,500

Advertisement costs are allocated to zones and product on the basis of sales. Office expenses and other expenses are apportioned equally to the zones or products, while computing the profit or loss for the zones or the product as the case may be.

Prepare a comparative profit and loss statement, presenting zonal performance as distinct from product performance.

Solution :

Comparative Profit and Loss Statement
[Evaluating Zonal performance.]

Particulars	Prime Rs.	Zones Extension Rs.	Outreach Rs.	Total Rs.
Sales revenue	22,50,000	13,50,000	9,00,000	45,00,000
Less : Cost of sales				
Ace (.85)	7,65,000	5,73,750	1,91,250	15,30,000
Nice (.80)	7,20,000	3,60,000	1,44,000	12,24,000
Grace (.75)	3,37,500	1,68,750	3,71,250	8,77,500
Total costs	18,22,500	11,02,500	7,06,500	36,31,500
Gross Profit margin (Sales – Cost of sales)	4,27,500	2,47,500	1,93,500	8,68,500
Less : Selling and distribution expenses				
Direct costs [allocated]	1,95,615	1,18,350	1,00,440	4,14,405
Advertisement Expenses [Apportioned in sales ratio 225 : 135 : 90]	67,500	40,500	27,000	1,35,000
Office expenses (apportioned equally)	31,500	31,500	31,500	94,500
other expenses (equally)	40,500	40,500	40,500	1,21,500
Total selling and distribution Costs	3,35,115	2,30,850	1,99,440	7,65,405
Net profit or loss [Gross profit-Total selling, Distribution cost]	92,385	16,650	5,940	1,03,095

RESPONSIBILITY ACCOUNTING

Assignment Problem

Good Luck Ltd has the following total operating results for the current year :

	Rs.
Sales revenue	56,00,000
Less : Variable costs	37,20,000
Contribution	18,80,000
Less : Fixed cost	10,00,000
Profit	8,80,000

The following additional information concerning the performance of each of the firm's three operating departments has been provided.

	Department		
	K	L	M
	Rs.	Rs.	Rs.
Sales revenue	24,00,000	20,00,000	12,00,000
Variable costs	16,80,000	12,00,000	8,40,000
Direct fixed costs	3,20,000	2,80,000	2,00,000

(i) Rank the three departments on the basis of their proportionate measure of relative profitability.

(ii) A proposal to increase advertising expenses by Rs. 1,23,200 is expected to generate 10% increase in sales in all three departments. Analyse the effect of this proposal on the firm as a whole and on each department. Assume that the cost of advertising will be allocated to divisions according to each division's percentage to sales and is to be considered as an attributable fixed cost of each department.

◻◻◻

22
Financial Management

Financial Management refers to the total managerial effort for the management of sources and uses of the financial activities of the enterprises.

Financial Management is a specialised function of general management which is related to the procurement of finance and its effective utilisation for the fulfilment of common goal of the enterprises.

Some of the definitions are being reproduced below.

1. *"Financial management is the operational activity of a business that is responsible for obtaining and effectively utilising the funds necessary for efficient operations".*
—**Joseph and Massie**

2. *"Financial management is the application of the planning and control functions to the finance function".*
—**Howard and Apon**

From the above definition it is clear that financial management is rendering a specialised service to the business in the way of obtaining and effective utilisation of the funds. Apart from this it also concentrates on financial planning, financial administration and financial control.

CHARACTERISTICS OF FINANCIAL MANAGEMENT

1. Financial management is a branch of business management.
2. It is an authentic and analytical process.
3. Centralised administration
4. A measuring tool of performance
5. It is essential for the management decisions.
6. Determination of Borrowing Policy
7. Key position in the organisational structure
8. Determination of future cash requirements

IMPORTANCE OF FINANCIAL MANAGEMENT

Adequate finance is very much essential for the success of all the business concerns. A firm could not expand its business or at least for the survival purpose it should need sufficient amount of finance.

FINANCIAL MANAGEMENT

The following are the important areas which highlight the importance of financial management.
  (i) It provides an easy approach to capital budgeting.
  (ii) Promotional activities of the business organisation.
  (iii) Financial management for optimum use of firm.
  (iv) To obtain co-operation in business activities.
  (v) Guidance to shareholders and investors.
  (vi) Determinant of business success.
  (vii) It is useful for minimising risks.
  (viii) It has long period values and profit maximisation.
  (ix) Helps to estimate the total requirements of funds.
  (x) Profit Planning.
  (xi) Controlling inventories.

OBJECTIVES AND FUNCTIONS OF FINANCIAL MANAGEMENT

Objectives of the financial management are listed below.
  (i) Maintenance of liquid assets
  (ii) Maximisation of the profitability of the firm
  (iii) Internal resources for expansion
  (iv) Determining financial needs
  (v) Project planning evaluation
  (vi) Decision on capital budgeting
  (vii) Working capital management decisions
  (viii) Acquisition and mergers
  (ix) Ensuring fair return to the share holders
  (x) Establishment of reserves for growth and expansion

FUNCTIONS

Functions of the Financial management can be classified thus.
(a) Executive Functions
(b) Incidental Functions

A. Executive Functions

Executive Finance Functions are those functions which require specialised administrative skill. Some of the executive functions are given below.
  1. *Financial Forecasting.* This is the foremost function of financial management. It forecasts the total financial requirements of the firm during a particular period. To determine the total fund requirement, various budgets are prepared to support fund requirement decision.

2. *Financing Decision.* Supplying the required funds at an appropriate time is a primary objective of finance manager. In this regard, the financial manager should identify the sources of funds raised and the amount that can be raised from each source and the cost of funds and other aspects.
3. *Dividend Policy Decision.* Construction of the suitable dividend policy is the next important function of the financial management and managers. This decision involves the determination of the percentage of profits earned by the enterprise which is to be paid to its shareholders. In the practical sense the market price of the shares and trend of the earnings can play an important role in the construction of dividend policy of the company.
4. *Cash Flow Management.* An efficient finance manager should ensure that cash inflows and outflows must be continuous and uninterrupted. At the same time, he concentrates on the cash flow statement.
5. *Determination of Borrowing Policy.* Each and every organisation plans for the expansion and modernisation of their business. In this situation, it requires additional resources. The finance manager of a company takes correct decision about the funds received through outside sources, how long it is needed and when it is repaid.
6. *Capital Budgeting Decision.* Capital Budgeting Decisions are the most complicated one. Because it involves long term implications. It requires huge amount of capital also. In this aspect, the financial manager is to identify the various investment proposals. The decision of the capital budgeting proposals are ranked on the basis of the urgency, liquidity, profitability and risk sensitivity.
7. *Negotiation for Various New Outside Financing.* In an organisation, finance manager must assess short term, medium term and long term financial requirements. To obtain these financial needs, he should start the negotiations at different levels for raising these funds.
8. *Checking upon Financial Performance.* For the benefit of rapid development of communication and technology, the finance manager has to employ various new software for the evaluation of financial performance of the company. An unbiased assessment of financial performance shall be of great value to the business in improving the standards, techniques and procedures of financial control.
9. *Acquisitions and Mergers.* An existing organisation may expand either by acquiring other concerns or by entering into mergers. Acquisition refers to the purchase of new firms or lease of smaller firm by a bigger firm. Merger refers to the joining of two or more firms together to form a new firm. During the periods of merger or acquisition, the major problem is the valuation of securities. In this aspect, the financial manager should follow correct valuation method, and do this process very carefully.

❑❑❑

23
Dividend

Dividend is the part of profits of the company which is distributed among its shareholders on the basis of their shareholding. It should be distributed according to decisions taken and resolution passed in the shareholders' meeting as well as meeting of Board of Directors.

In other words, it is the amount of profits of a company made available for the distribution among its shareholders.

It may be defined as the return that a shareholder gets from the company out of its profits on their shareholdings.

According to the Institute of Chartered Accountants of India dividend is "a distribution to shareholders out of profits or reserves available for this purpose". Normally dividend may be paid as a fixed percentage on the share capital contributed by them or at a fixed amount per share.

Dividend should be declared only out of divisible profits. In any particular year, if there is no profit, dividend shall not be distributed in that year.

DIFFERENT TYPES OF DIVIDENDS

Dividend may be classified according to the mode of distribution as follows.

(i) *Cash Dividend.* Cash dividend means shareholders are paid dividend in the form of cash. If the company has sufficient cash balance, it would arrange funds for the payment of dividend.

If the company wants to have a stable dividend policy, it would prepare cash budget and meet out the regular dividend payments of the company. The cash dividend may have two classifications *i.e.*, regular dividend and interim dividend.

(ii) *Stock Dividend.* In any particular year, if the company does not have an adequate cash balance, it might decide to pay dividend in the form of shares. It is known as stock dividend. In this regard, the company issues its own shares to its existing shareholders in lieu of cash dividend.

(iii) *Scrip Dividend.* Scrip dividend means when earnings justify a dividend, but the cash position of the company is temporarily weak. During this period, shareholders are issued shares or debentures if other companies are held by the company as investment. Such payment of dividend is called scrip dividends.

(iv) *Bond Dividend.* If the company does not have sufficient funds to pay dividends in the form of cash, it may issue bonds to its shareholders for the purpose of dividend.

(v) *Property Dividend.* Property dividends are those dividends which are paid by the company to its shareholders in the form of property instead of payment of dividend in cash.

DIVIDEND POLICY

Dividend Policy of a company means it is the policy concerning the amount of profits to be distributed as dividend. The basic concept of the dividend policy is that the company takes future action regarding the payment of dividend with the help of the company law board.

According to Weston and Brighan, *"Dividend Policy determines the division of earnings between payments to shareholders and retained earnings".*

Factors Affecting Dividend Policy

Number of factors affect the dividend policy of a company. The major factors are :

1. *General Economic Conditions.* General Economic Conditions greatly affect the management decision to distribute its earnings as dividend. During the periods of economic depression, the firm holds large sums of money in reserve in order to meet the liquidity position of the company. But in the case of prosperity, the company may not be liberal in dividend payments because of large profitable investment opportunity.

2. *Age of a Company.* Age of a company must decide the dividend policy. A newly established company may require huge amount of its earnings for development purpose and may formulate rigid dividend policy. But in the case of older company it can frame a consistent policy regarding dividend.

3. *State of Capital Market.* If the capital market position of the country is more favourable to the company, the company may raise funds from different sources without any difficulty. So the management may declare a high rate of dividend to attract the investors. But in stock market, the shareholders are not interested in making investment so the management should follow a conservative dividend policy by maintaining the low rate of dividend.

4. *Government Policy.* Some of the policies are announced by the Government from time to time. It may affect the profit earning capacity of the organisation. Sometimes, Government restrict the distribution of dividend beyond a certain percentage in a particular industry. So the dividend policy has to be formulated accordingly.

5. *Taxation Policy.* The tax policy announced by the Government also affect the dividends policy. High taxation reduces the earnings of the company and consequently the rate of dividend is lowered down.

6. *Past Year Dividend Rate.* At the time of formulating the dividend policy of the company, the directors must consider the dividend paid in past years. The current dividend rate should be around the average of past rates.

7. *Liquidity of Funds.* Payment of dividend represents actually a cash outflow. Availability of huge amount of cash and liquidity of the firm says it has better ability to pay dividend.

DIVIDEND

8. *Ability to Borrow.* Well established and large scale companies have better access to the capital market than the new companies. And they may borrow funds from other external sources as and when necessity arises. This type of companies may have a better dividend pay out ratio. But smaller firms have to maintain adequate reserve and low dividend pay out ratio.

9. *Regularity and Stability in Dividend Payment.* Dividend should be paid regularly to the investors. Because all investors expect regular payment of dividend. Through this process only, company will retain the existing shareholders on a permanent basis, and if necessary, to mobilise resources in an efficient manner.

Types of Dividend Policies

Different types of dividend policies are as follows :

(*i*) *Stable Dividend Policy.* When the company maintains more or less the stable rate of dividend, it is known as stable dividend policy. If the company has to maintain and follow stable dividend policy, the market price of its share will be of permanently higher value.

(*ii*) *Policy of Regular Stock Dividend.* It is the policy followed by the company to pay dividend in the form of shares instead of cash. Some companies follow this as a regular practice. Whenever the stock dividends are declared by the company, it does not affect the liquidity but increases the shareholdings of the shareholder.

(*iii*) *Policy to Pay Irregular Dividend.* Generally, this policy of dividend is followed by the companies having irregular earnings or inadequate profits. Based on this policy, the company earn an higher amount of profit to pay higher dividend. If there is no profit in any particular year, the company does not declare the dividend to its shareholders.

(*iv*) *Policy of no Immediate Dividend.* It is the policy followed by the company which decides to pay no dividend even when it earns large amount of profits. Because, either it may be a new company or the firm's access to capital market is difficult.

CONFLICTING THEORIES

There are conflicting theories regarding the impact of dividend decision on the valuation of a firm.

1. Irrelevance Concept of Dividend,   2. Relevance Concept of Dividend.

1. Irrelevance Concept of Dividend

This concept was developed by Soloman, Modigliani and Miller. According to their approach dividend policy of a firm is irrelevant as it does not affect the wealth of the shareholders. In their opinion, investors do not differentiate dividend and capital gains. There is no impact on the dividend policy or the share price of the company and further consequence.

2. Relevance Concept of Dividend

Myron Gordon, John Linter, James Walter, Richardson and others are associated with the relevance concept of dividend. According to their approach dividend policy has a positive impact on the firm's position in the stock market. In other words there is a positive relationship between the Dividend Policy and price level of the company's shares in the stock market. Higher dividend rate increases the value of stock while low dividend decreases their value in the stock market.

WALTER'S APPROACH

He pointed out that dividend policy always affects the goodwill of the company. According to his approach, It is a relationship between the firm's return on investment or internal rate of return and cost of capital or required rate of return.

Problem. *Following are the details regarding three companies A Ltd, B Ltd and C Ltd.*

A Ltd	B Ltd	C Ltd
r = 15%	r = 5%	r = 10%
Ke = 10%	Ke = 10%	Ke = 10%
E = Rs. 8	E = Rs. 8	E = Rs. 8

Calculate the value of an equity share of each of these companies applying Walter's formula when dividend payment ratio (D/P ratio) is (a) 50%, (b) 75%, (c) 25%.

What conclusion do you draw? [M.Com Delhi-1991] [MBA Anna]

Solution :

Prof Walter has suggested the following formula for determining the market value of a share.

$$P = \frac{D + \frac{r}{Ke}(E-D)}{Ke}$$

P = Market price of an equity share
D = Dividend per share
r = Internal rate of return
E = Earning per share
Ke = Cost of equity capital or capitalisation rate.

Value of an equity share according to Walter's Formula :

	A Ltd.	B Ltd.	C Ltd.
(i)	When D/P Ratio is 50%		
	$P = \frac{D + \frac{r}{Ke}(E-D)}{Ke}$		
	$P = \frac{4 + \frac{.15}{.10}(8-4)}{.10}$	$P = \frac{4 + \frac{.05}{.10}(8-4)}{.10}$	$P = \frac{4 + \frac{.10}{.10}(8-4)}{.10}$
	Rs. 100	Rs. 60	Rs. 80

DIVIDEND 417

(ii)	When D/P Ratio is 75%		
	$P = \dfrac{6 + \dfrac{.15}{.10}(8-6)}{.10}$	$P = \dfrac{6 + \dfrac{.05}{.10}(8-6)}{.10}$	$P = \dfrac{6 + \dfrac{.10}{.10}(8-6)}{.10}$
	Rs. 90	Rs. 70	Rs. 80
(iii)	When D/P Ratio is 25%		
	$P = \dfrac{2 + \dfrac{.15}{.10}(8-2)}{.10}$	$P = \dfrac{2 + \dfrac{.05}{.10}(8-2)}{.10}$	$P = \dfrac{2 + \dfrac{.10}{.10}(8-2)}{.10}$
	Rs. 110	Rs. 50	Rs. 80

Conclusion :
Based upon the above calculation
    (i) A Ltd : This Company may be characterised as a growth firm.
    (ii) B Ltd : This Company may be characterised as a declining firm.
    (iii) C Ltd : This Company may be characterised as a normal firm.

❏❏❏

24
Cost of Capital

INTRODUCTION

Cost of capital is one of the corner stones of the theory of financial management but it is a controversial topic in finance. And at the same time it provides suitable guidance for the formulation of capital structure of the firm. In the present financial world, it is used as a sophisticated technique of evaluating the profitability of capital investment proposals and also to examine the alternative sources of capital. In order to meet out the modern financial decision making process, in this chapter, it is proposed to discuss the concept and implications of the firm's cost of capital, procedure for the measurement of different sources of capital and also to explain its uses.

CONCEPT OF COST OF CAPITAL

The term cost of capital is the rate of return a firm must earn on its investment for the market value of the firm to remain unchanged. From the company's point of view, cost of capital is the measurement of profitability of investments and a yardstick to decide whether to make investment in particular project or not.

DEFINITIONS OF COST OF CAPITAL

(i) "The cost of capital is the minimum required rate of earnings or the cut-off rate for capital expenditures".
—G.C. Philippatos

(ii) "The cost of capital represents a cut-off rate for the allocation of capital to investment of projects. It is the rate of return on a project that will leave unchanged the market price of the stock".
—James C. Van Horne

(iii) "In a general sense, the cost of capital is any discount rate used to value cash streams".
—Haley and Schall.

From the above definitions, it is clear that the cost of capital is otherwise called as cut off rate. Because it is the suitable test of validity of committing a capital expenditure.

IMPORTANCE OF COST OF CAPITAL IN DECISION MAKING

(i) *Capital Budgeting Decisions.* Cost of capital may be very much used as the measuring rod for adopting an investment proposal. Generally, the company has to choose project based upon the satisfactory return on investment. It measures

COST OF CAPITAL 419

the financial performance and also determines acceptability of the project by discounting cash flows under present value method. Commonly, it is the technique used to accept or reject the project.

(ii) *Designing the Optimal Capital Structure.* The cost of capital is very much helpful in formulating firm's sound and economic capital structure. An excellent financial expert keeps an eye on the capital market fluctuations and analyses the comparative interest rate, and trend of the capital movement. Based upon the analysis, finance manager comes to correct conclusion and forms a suitable capital structure of the firm.

(iii) *Deciding about the Method of Financing.* An efficient financial manager has a thorough knowledge of the capital market fluctuation. The ultimate aim of the financial management is the wealth maximisation. In order to achieve these objectives, the financial manager finds the financing sources. Apart from these, comparing the specific cost of different sources of finance, the finance manager can select the most economical source of finance in a particular situation.

(iv) *Helpful in the Evaluation of Expansion Projects.* With the help of the cost of capital the financial manager can easily examine the financial possibilities of a given expansion project. If marginal return on investment exceeds the cost of financing, the expansion project should be accepted, otherwise it should be rejected.

(v) *To Evaluate the Financial Performance of Top Management.* The cost of capital can be used to evaluate the financial performance of top management people. It involves a comparison of actual profitabilities of the project undertaken with the projected overall cost of capital and an appraisal of the actual cost incurred in raising the expected funds.

(vi) *Other Areas.* The concept of cost of capital is also important in some other areas of decision making of the firm such as dividend decision, working capital management policies etc. The value of the firm normally depends upon its cost of capital.

DIFFERENT TYPES OF COSTS RELATED TO THE COST OF CAPITAL

The following are the various relevant costs associated with the problem of measurement of firm's cost of capital.

(i) *Marginal Cost of Capital.* It is the current interest on long term debt. In other words, the marginal cost of capital is the weighted average cost of new or additional funds raised by the company.

(ii) *Specific Cost.* Specific cost is the cost which is associated with the particular component of a capital structure.

For example. Equity shares, debentures etc. It is also known as component cost.

(iii) *Combined Cost.* It is the cost of capital of all the sources taken together *i.e.,* debt, equity and preference share capital. The combined cost of capital can be otherwise called as average cost or weighted cost of capital.

(iv) *Spot Cost.* Spot cost represents costs prevailing in the market at certain point of time.

(v) *Future Cost.* It is the cost which is related to the cost of funds intended to finance the expected project.

(vi) *Historical Cost.* Historical costs are the costs which are calculated on the basis of existing capital structure of the firm.

(vii) *Explicit Cost.* Explicit cost of any source of fund may be expressed as the discount rate that equates the present value of cash inflows that are incremental to the taking of the financial opportunity with the present value of its incremental cash outflows.

(viii) *Implicit Cost.* Implicit cost is the opportunity cost. It is the rate of return associated with the best investment opportunity for the firm and its shareholders that will be forgone if the project presently under consideration by the firm were accepted.

(ix) *Normalised Cost.* It is the long term cost. It indicates an estimate of cost by some averaging process from which cyclical element is removed.

DETERMINATION OF COST OF CAPITAL

Cost of capital is not only most crucial but also it is a controversial area in the financial management decisions. Under this background, determination of cost of capital is not a simple task. The finance manager has to face a lot of problems both conceptual and practical while determining the cost of capital of the company. Major problems in this regard are as follows.

(i) *Conceptual Controversy.* There is a major controversy whether or not the cost of capital is dependent upon the method and level of financing by the company. The traditional theorists pointed out a firm can change its overall cost of capital by changing its debt-equity mix. But the modern theorists argued that the change in the debt-equity ratio does not affect the total cost of capital of the enterprise.

(ii) *Computation of Cost of Equity.* The determination of cost of equity capital is also a difficult task. In the actual theoretical point of view cost of equity capital may be defined as the minimum rate of return that a company must earn on its capital employed. So the market price of the equity shares remain unchanged. This implies that to find out the cost of equity capital one has to require quantification of the expectations of the equity share holders. It is a very difficult task because different authorities have tried different approaches to quantify the expectations of the equity shareholders.

(iii) *Problems in Computation of Cost of Retained Earnings and Depreciation Funds.* Cost of retained earnings and depreciation fund is determined according to the approach adopted for computing the cost of equity capital which is itself a controversial problem.

(iv) *Problems in Consideration of Historical Cost, Future Cost.* As per the decision making point of view, the historical cost is not relevant. But future costs should be taken into account. This brings another problem whether to consider marginal cost of capital *i.e.,* cost of additional funds or whether to consider the average cost of capital *i.e.,* the cost of total funds.

(v) *Problem of Weights.* In order to ascertain the average cost of capital, the financial manager of the company has to face the problems of weights. In this aspect, computation as well as assigning of weights to each type of fund is a complicated

COST OF CAPITAL

problem. Because, there are two options in this respect, *i.e.*, book value weights and market value weights. Both of them have their own strengths and weaknesses. It is natural but results based on the two aspects differ significantly.

COMPUTATION OF COST OF CAPITAL

Computation of cost of capital involves the following :
(A) Computation of cost of each specific source of finance
(B) Computation of weighted average cost of capital.

(A) Computation of Cost of each Specific Source of Finance

Costs of each specific source of finance are as follows :
(i) Debt
(ii) Preference shares
(iii) Equity capital
(iv) Retained earnings.

(i) Cost of Debt

(a) *Debt issued at per :* at premium or discount
$$Kd = (1 - T)R$$
where, Kd = Cost of debt
T = Marginal Tax Rate
R = Debenture interest rate.

(b) *Cost of redeemable debt*
$$Kd = \frac{1 + (P - NP)/n}{(P + NP)/2}$$
where, I = Annual interest payment
P = Par value of debentures
NP = Net proceeds of debentures
n = number of years to maturity

(ii) Cost of Preference Shares

(a) Cost of Preference Capital
$$Kp = \frac{DP}{NP}$$
where, Kp = cost of preference share capital
DP = Fixed preference dividend
NP = Net proceeds of preference shares.

(b) *Cost of Redeemable Preference Shares*
$$Kp = \frac{DP + (P - NP)/n}{(P + NP)/2}$$
where, Kp = cost of preference share capital
DP = Fixed preference dividend
NP = Net proceeds of preference shares
n = Number of preference shares

(iii) Cost of Equity Capital

(a) *Dividend Price (D/P) Approach*

$$Ke = \frac{D}{NP}$$

where,
- Ke = Cost of equity capital
- D = Dividend per Equity share
- NP = Net proceeds of an equity share

(b) *Dividend Price Plus Growth (D/P + g) Approach*

$$Ke = \frac{D}{NP} + g$$

where,
- Ke = cost of equity capital
- D = Expected dividend per share
- NP = Net proceeds per share
- g = growth in expected dividend

(c) *Earning Price Approach*

$$Ke = \frac{E}{NP}$$

where,
- Ke = cost of equity capital
- E = Earning per share
- NP = Net proceeds of an equity share.

(d) *Realised Yield Approach*

In order to calculate the cost of capital under this approach, it is essential to determine the internal rate of return. This internal rate of return can be calculated by the trial and error method.

(iv) Cost of Retained Earnings

Generally retained earnings are undistributed profits represented by uncommitted reserves and surpluses. Computation of cost of retained earnings in the following formula.

$$Kr = Ke(1-T)(1-B)$$

where,
- Kr = Required rate of return on retained earnings.
- Ke = Shareholder's required rate of return
- T = Shareholders marginal tax rate
- B = Brokerage cost

(B) Computation of Weighted Average Cost of Capital

Weighted average as the name implies is an average of the cost of specific source of capital employed in a business properly weighted by the proportion they hold in firm's capital structure.

Following are the Steps involved in computation of weighted average of cost of capital :

(i) Calculation of the cost of each specific source of finance

(ii) Assigning weights to specific costs

(iii) Weighted cost of all the sources of finance taken together to arrive at an overall weighted average cost of capital

COST OF CAPITAL

Computation of Weights

Assigning weights to specific source of finance is a difficult task. Various approaches are followed in this regard, but, two of them are commonly used (a) Book value approach and (b) Market value approach.

Problem 1. *From the following capital structure of a company calculate the overall cost of capital using (a) Book value weights and (b) Market value weights*

Source	Book value (Rs.)	Market value (Rs.)
Equity share capital (Rs. 10 shares)	45,000	90,000
Retained earnings	15,000	—
Preference share capital	10,000	10,000
Debentures	30,000	30,000

The after-tax cost of different sources of finance is as follows :

Equity Share Capital : 14%, Retained Earnings : 13%, Preference Share Capital 10%, Debentures : 5%.

Solution :

(a) Computation of Weighted Average Cost of Capital
(Book value weights)

Source (1)	Amount (2) Rs.	After tax cost (3)	Total after tax Rs. Cost (4) = (2) × (3)
Equity share capital	45,000	14%	6,300
Retained earnings	15,000	13%	1,950
Preference share capital	10,000	10%	1,000
Debentures	30,000	5%	1,500
	1,00,000		10,750

$$\text{Weighted Average cost of capital} = \frac{10,750}{1,00,000} \times 100$$

$$= 10.75\%$$

(b) Computation of Weighted Average Cost of Capital
[Market value weights]

Source (1)	Amount (2) Rs.	After tax cost (3)	Total after tax Rs. Cost (4) = (2) × (3)
Equity share capital	90,000	14%	12,600
Preference share capital	10,000	10%	1,000
Debentures	30,000	5%	1,500
	1,30,000		15,100

$$\text{Weighted average cost of capital} = \frac{15,100}{1,30,000} \times 100$$

$$= 11.61\%$$

Problem 2. *A firm has the following capital structure after tax costs for the different sources of funds used.*

Source of funds	Amount (Rs.)	Proportion	After tax cost %
Debt	15,00,000	25	5
Preference shares	12,00,000	20	10
Equity shares	18,00,000	30	12
Retained earnings	15,00,000	25	11
	60,00,000	100	

You are required to compute the weighted average cost of capital. [M.Sc Dec 2001 PU]

Solution :

Computation of Weighted Average Cost of Capital

Source (1)	Amount (2) Rs.	After tax cost (3)	Total after tax Rs. Cost (4) = (2) × (3)
Debt	15,00,000	15%	75,000
Preference shares	12,00,000	10%	1,20,000
Equity shares	18,00,000	12%	2,16,000
Retained earnings	15,00,000	11%	1,65,000
	60,00,000		5,76,000

$$\text{Weighted average cost of capital} = \frac{5,76,000}{60,00,000} \times 100$$

$$= 9.6\%$$

Problem 3. *The Servex company has the following capital structure on 30-6-2004.*

	Rs.
Ordinary shares (2,00,000 Shares)	40,00,000
6% Preference shares	10,00,000
8% Debentures	30,00,000
	80,00,000

The share of the company sells for Rs. 20. It is expected that company will pay a current dividend of Rs. 2 per share which will grow at 7% for ever. Assume the tax rate may be 50%.

(i) *Compute the weighted average cost of capital based on existing capital structure.*

(ii) *Compute the new weighted average cost of capital if the company raises an additional Rs. 20,00,000 debt by issuing 10% debenture. This would result in increasing the expected dividend to Rs. 3 and leave the growth rate unchanged, but the price of share will fall to Rs. 15 per share.*

(iii) *Compute the cost of capital if in (ii) above growth rate increases to 10%*

[MBA Madras Nov 1997]

COST OF CAPITAL

Solution :

(i) Statement showing Weighted Average Cost of Capital

Source (1)	Amount (2) Rs.	After tax cost (3)	Total after tax Rs. Cost (4) = (2) × (3)
Equity share capital	40,00,000	17%	6,80,000
Preference share capital	10,00,000	6%	60,000
Debentures	30,00,000	4%	1,20,000
	80,00,000		8,60,000

Weighted average cost of capital = $\frac{8,60,000}{80,00,000} \times 100$

K_e = 10.75

NOTE : Computation cost of equity share is

$$K_e = \frac{D}{MP} + g = \frac{Rs. 2}{Rs. 50} + 0.7 = .17 \times 100$$

$$= 17\%$$

(ii) Statement showing Weighted Average Cost of Capital

Source (1)	Amount (2) Rs.	After tax cost (3)	Total after tax Rs. Cost (4) = (2) × (3)
Equity share capital	40,00,000	27%	10,80,000
6% Preference capital	10,00,000	6%	60,000
8% Debentures	30,00,000	(8-4) 4%	1,20,000
10% Debentures	20,00,000	(10-5) 5%	1,00,000
	1,00,000,00		13,60,000

Weighted average cost of capital $Ke = \frac{13,60,000}{1,00,00,000} \times 100$

= 13.6%

NOTE : Computation of cost of equity share is

$$Ke = \frac{D}{MP} + g$$

$$= \frac{3}{15} + 0.7$$

$$= .20 + .07 = 27 \times 100$$

$$= 27\%$$

(iii) Statement showing Weighted Average Cost of Capital

Source (1)	Amount (2) Rs.	After tax cost (3)	Total after tax Rs. Cost (4) = (2) × (3)
Equity share capital	40,00,000	30%	12,00,000
6% Preference capital	10,00,000	6%	60,000
8% Debentures	30,00,000	(8-4) 4%	1,20,000
10% Debentures	20,00,000	(10-5) 5%	1,00,000
	1,00,000,00		14,80,000

Weighted average cost of capital $Ke = \dfrac{14,80,000}{1,00,00,000} \times 100$

$= \mathbf{14.80\%}$

NOTE : Computation of cost of equity share is :

$$Ke = \dfrac{D}{MP} = g$$

$$= \dfrac{3}{15} + .10$$

$$= .30 \ i.e., 30\% \ (.30 \times 100)$$

NOTE : Tax Rate i.e., 50% to adjust only on Debenture after tax cost.
  (i) Table = 10% : 50% of 10% = 5% – 5% = 5%
  (ii) Table = 10% : 50% of 10% = 5% – 5% = 5%
  (iii) Table = 8% : 50% of 8% = 4% – 4% = 4%

Problem 4. *Following are the details regarding the capital structure of Sridhar & Co Ltd.*

Type of Capital	Book value Rs.	Market value Rs.	Specific cost
Debentures	40,000	38,000	5%
Preference capital	10,000	11,000	8%
Equity capital	60,000	1,20,000	13%
Retained earnings	20,000	-	9%
	1,30,000	1,69,000	

You are requested to determine the weighted average cost of capital using (i) Book value as weights (ii) Market value as weights. Do you think there can be a situation where weighted average cost of capital would be the same irrespective of the weights used.

[MBA Madras; M.Com.]

COST OF CAPITAL

Solution :

(i) Statement showing Weighted Average Cost of Capital
(Book value)

Sources (1)	Amount (2) Rs.	After tax cost (3)	Total after tax Rs. Cost (4) = (2) × (3)
Debentures	40,000	5%	2,000
Preference capital	10,000	8%	800
Equity capital	60,000	13%	7,800
Retained earnings	20,000	9%	1,800
	1,30,000		12,400

Weighted average cost of capital = $\dfrac{12,400}{1,30,000} \times 100$

= 9.53%

(ii) Statement showing the Weighted Average Cost Capital
(Market value)

Sources (1)	Amount (2) Rs.	After tax cost (3)	Total after tax Rs. Cost (4) = (2) × (3)
Debentures	38,000	5%	1,900
Preference capital	11,000	8%	880
Equity capital	1,20,000	13%	15,600
	1,69,000		18,380

Weight average cost of capital = $\dfrac{18,380}{1,69,000} \times 100$

= 10.87%

Result and Comments :

Cost of capital would be the same irrespective of the weights in case the Book value and the Market value of the securities are the same.

Problem 5. *Your company's share is quoted in the market at Rs. 20 currently. The company pays a dividend of Re. 1 per share and the investor expects a growth rate of 5% per year. Compute :*

(a) The company's cost of equity capital.

(b) If the anticipated growth rate is 6% p.a. calculate the indicated market price per share.

(c) If the company's cost of capital is 8% and the anticipated growth rate is 5% p.a., calculate the indicated market price if the dividend of Re 1 per share is to be maintained.

Solution :

(a) Cost of equity capital = $\dfrac{\text{Dividend}}{\text{Price}} \times 100 +$ Growth rate

$= \dfrac{1}{20} \times 100 + 5\%$

$= 5\% + 5\%$

$= 10\%$

(b) Market price = $\dfrac{\text{Dividend}}{\text{Cost of equity capital} - \text{Growth rate \%}}$

$= \dfrac{1}{10\% - 6\%}$

$= \dfrac{1}{4\%}$

$= .25 \times 100 =$ Rs. 25

(c) Market price = $\dfrac{\text{Re. } 1}{8\% - 5\%} =$ Rs. 33.33

Problem 6. *The capital structure of Reliance Ltd is as follows :*

3000 12% Debentures of Rs. 100 each	3,00,000
2000 10% Preference shares of Rs. 100 each	2,00,000
4000 Equity shares of Rs. 100 each	4,00,000
Retained Earnings	1,00,000

The earnings per share of the company for the past years have been Rs. 15. The shares of the company are sold in the market at Book value. The company's tax rate is 50%. The shareholder's tax liability may be assumed as 25%. Find out the weighted average cost of capital.

Solution :

(i) Cost of Debentures

$Kd = \dfrac{I}{NP}(I - T)$

$= \dfrac{36,000}{3,00,000} \times .50 =$ 6%

(ii) Cost of preference share capital   10%

(iii) Cost of equity share capital   12%

(iv) Cost of Retained Earnings   9%

Statement showing Weighted Average Cost of Capital

Source	Amt (Rs.)	Weights	Specific cost %	Weighted Average cost
Debentures	3,00,000	.3	6	1.8
Preference capital	2,00,000	.2	10	2.0
Equity capital	4,00,000	.4	12	4.8
Retained earnings	1,00,000	.1	9	0.9
	10,00,000			9.5

COST OF CAPITAL

Problem 7. *Calculate the cost of equity for a firm whose shares are quoted at Rs. 120. The dividend at the end of the year is expected to be Rs. 9.72 per share and the growth rate is 8%.*

Solution :

Cost of equity for a firm

$$Ke = \frac{DPS}{MP} + g$$

Ke = Cost of equity capital
DPS = Dividend per Equity share
MP = Market price of an equity' share
g = growth rate of dividend

$$Ke = \frac{9.72}{120} \times 100 + 8\%$$

$$= 8.1\% + 8.00\% = 16.1\%$$

Problem 8. *The current market price of an equity share of a company is Rs. 90. The current dividend per share is Rs. 4.50. In case the dividends are expected to grow at the rate of 8%, what is the shareholders' required rate of return ?* [MBA Anna May 2003]

Solution :

Shareholders' required rate of return :

$$Ke = \frac{D}{MP} + g$$

$$Ke = \frac{4.50}{90} \times 8\%$$

$.05 + .08 = 0.13$

i.e., $.13 \times 100 = 13\%$

Shareholders' required rate of return is 13%.

Problem 9. *(a) A company plans to issue 1,000 new shares of Rs. 100 each at par. The floatation costs are expected to be 5% of the share price. The company pays a dividend of Rs. 10 per share initially and the growth in dividends is expected to be 5%. Compute the cost of new issue of equity shares. (b) If the current market price of an equity share is Rs. 150. Calculate the cost of existing equity share capital.* [MBA Anna Dec 2003]

Solution :

(a) $$Ke = \frac{D}{MP} + g$$

$$= \frac{10}{100-5} + 5\% = 15.53\%$$

(b) $$Ke = \frac{D}{MP} + G$$

$$= \frac{10}{150-5} + 5\% = \frac{10}{145} + 5\%$$

$$= 11.89\%$$

25
Capital Structure

A company, in order to have successful operation, needs adequate amount of capital. The capital requirement starts right from the incorporation of the company. The foremost function of the finance manager is to make correct forecasting of financial requirements not only in present but future also. The required funds can be raised through various sources or forms.

CAPITALISATION : MEANING

The term capitalisation is the sum total of all long term securities issued by a company and the surpluses not meant for distribution.

A.S Dewing defines *"The term capitalisation is the valuation of the capital, which includes the capital stock and debt."*

According to **Gerrtenbeg**, *"For all practical purposes, capitalisation means the total accounting value of all the capital regularly employed in the business."*

CAPITAL STRUCTURE

Capital structure of a company refers to the mix of its capitalisation. A company obtains funds by issuing different types of securities *i.e.*, ordinary shares, preference shares, bonds and debentures. The combination, in which the various kinds of securities are issued is known as capital structure.

According to **Gerrtenbeg**, *"Capital structure of a company (or financial structure) refers to the make-up of its capitalisation."*

According to **Weston and Brighan**, *"Capital structure is the permanent financing of the firm, represented by long term debt, preferred stock and net worth"*.

Basic Patterns of Capital Structure

(i) Issuing only equity shares
(ii) Issuing equity shares and preference shares
(iii) Issuing equity and debentures
(iv) Issuing equity shares, preference shares and debentures

CAPITAL STRUCTURE

Factors Affecting Capital Structure

The following factors govern the capital structure of a company.

(i) Trading on equity
(ii) Nature of enterprises
(iii) Legal restrictions
(iv) Purpose of financing
(v) Period of finance.
(vi) Market conditions
(vii) Size of the company
(viii) Need of investors
(ix) Government policy.
(x) Cost of capital and availability of Funds

(i) *Trading on Equity.* A company may mobilise capital either by issue of shares or by debentures. In any situation, the rate of return on total capital employed is more than the rate of interest on debentures or rate of dividend on preference shares. It is known as trading on equity. In a particular situation, a company can pay higher rate of dividend than the general rate of earnings on the total capital employed. It is the benefit of trading on equity.

(ii) *Nature of Enterprises.* Foremost determinant of capital structure of a company is the nature of the business enterprise. Businesses having more risks but varying income prefer equity shares. Firms, engaged in public utility services, may prefer issue of debentures and preference shares.

(iii) *Legal Restrictions.* Each and every company has to comply with provisions of the law regarding the issue of different kinds of securities. So the promoter of a company has to follow the legal provisions. Specially in India, banking companies are not allowed to issue any type of securities other than equity shares.

(iv) *Purpose of Financing.* The purpose of financing for raising the fund must be taken into account at the time of formulating capital structure of the company. If funds are required for direct productive purpose, the company can afford to issue debentures. But the funds are required for non-productive purposes, the company should raise funds through issue of equity shares.

(v) *Period of Finance.* Generally, the period of finance also determines the capital structure of companies. Short term commitment of companies are met out through borrowings. Some times, if the funds are required for 8 to 10 years, it will be met by issue of debentures. If funds are required for more than 10 years, it can be met out by issue of equity shares.

(vi) *Market Conditions.* Movement of the capital market also decides the capital structure of the company. During the periods of depression, the investors will look for their safety and they prefer to invest in debentures and not in equity shares. But during the boom period any type of securities can be sold very easily in the market, hence equities also get the better market.

(vii) *Size of the Company.* The small scale organisations fully depend upon the owner's fund to run their business. Such companies find it difficult to obtain long term debt. But, large scale organisations are generally considered to be less risky by the investors. So, they can issue different types of securities and mobilise resources from different sources.

(viii) *Need of Investors.* Some of the investors prefer to invest in debentures because they provide safety of investment and stable income. Preference shares will be preferred by those who want a higher and stable income with sufficient safety of investment. Those, who want to bear higher risk, higher return and capital appreciation prefer equity shares only. So capital structure of the company depends upon the financial status and psychological attitude of the investors.

(ix) *Government Policy.* Any of the monetary, fiscal, financial policies, which are time to time announced by the union government, may straight away affect the capital structure decision of the company. For example, change in the lending policy of financial institutions may mean a complete change in the financial pattern. New provisions of the SEBI also affect the capital issue policies of various companies.

(x) *Cost of Capital and Availability of Funds.* The appropriate term of financing is, at times, the result of the study of comparative cost of various types of financing in relation to the level of risk involved and the availability of various alternative forms of financing. But, sometimes, debentures may be issued because of their cheapness and availability, the danger of the financial position and so on.

Theories of Capital Structure

Different theories have been developed by different authors. The important theories are :

(i) Net income approach
(ii) Net operating income approach
(iii) Traditional approach
(iv) Modigliani and Miller approach.

(i) Net Income Approach

According to NI approach, a firm can minimize the weighted average cost of capital and it can increase the value of the firm as well as market price of the equity shares by using more debt content in the company.

This approach is based upon the following assumptions.
- The cost of debt is less than the cost of equity.
- There are no corporate taxes.
- The debt content of the firm does not change the risk perception of the investors.

(ii) Net Operating Income Approach

This theory was suggested by Durand. It is entirely opposite to the NI approach. According to this approach, change in the capital structure of the company does not affect the market value of the firm and the overall cost of capital remains constant irrespective of the method of financing. Its implication is that the overall cost of capital remains the same whether the debt equity mix is 50 : 50, or 30 :70 or 10 : 90. Under this approach, all the structures are optimum capital structures. It is based on the following assumptions like
- The market capitalises the value of the firm as a whole.
- The business risk remains constant at each and every level of debt-equity mix.

(iii) Traditional Approach

This approach is also known as Ezra Solomon's approach. It is the intermediate approach between the net income approach and net operating income approach. According to this

CAPITAL STRUCTURE

approach, the value of the firm can be increased initially. The cost of capital can be decreased by using more debt as the debt is a cheaper source of funds than equity. The optimum capital structure can be reached by an appropriate debt equity mix.

(iv) Modigliani and Miller Approach

The Modigliani–Miller approach is similar to the net operating income approach. Under this approach, the value of a firm is independent of its capital structure. Simply, MM approach maintains that the average cost of capital does not change with change in the debt weighted equity mix or capital structure of the firm. The argument is based on a simple switching mechanism which is closely called arbitrage.

In the expression of Modigliani and Miller, two firms, identical in all respects except their capital structure, cannot have different market values or cost of capital because of arbitrage process. In case they have different market values or cost of capital, arbitrage will take place and the investors will engage in personal leverage as against the corporate leverage and this will again render the two companies having the same value.

Modigliani and Miller Approach is based on the following assumptions :

(i) There are no transaction costs.
(ii) All the investors are free to buy and sell securities.
(iii) There are no corporate taxes (But this assumption has been removed later).
(iv) There are no retained earnings. However, the dividend pay out ratio is 100%
(v) Borrowings are riskless.

Balanced or Optimum Capital Structure

Optimum or balanced capital structure means an ideal combination of borrowed and owned capital that may achieve the maximisation of market value per share and decrease the cost of capital when the real cost of each source of funds is the same.

Characteristics of a Balanced Capital Structure

(i) Profitability
(ii) Solvency
(iii) Conservatism
(iv) Effective Control
(v) Economy
(vi) Attraction to the Investors
(vii) Ease and Simplicity
(viii) Minimum Remuneration.

FORMULAS—FOR VALUATION OF FIRMS

1. *Valuation of Firms : NI approach*

    $V = S + B$

    Where, V = Value of the firm
    S = Market value of the equity
    B = Market value of the debt

Market value of Equity (S) can be ascertained as follows :

$$S = \frac{NI}{Ke}$$

S = Market value of the equity
NI = Earnings available for equity shareholders
Ke = Equity Capitalisation Rate
K = Overall cost of capital   Formula for $K = \frac{EBIT}{V}$

Net Income : Amount available for Equity Shareholder

Earnings before interest and Tax	xx
Less : Interest	xx
PBT	xx
Less : Tax	xx
PAT	xx
Less : Pre-dividend (if any)	
Amount available for equity shareholders	xx

2. *Valuation of firms : NOI approach*

$$S = V - B \qquad V = \frac{EBIT}{Ke}$$

S = Value of equity
V = Value of firm
B = Value of debt
Ke = Equity Capitalisation Rate

$$Ke = \frac{EBIT - 1}{V - B} \times 100$$

K = Overall cost of capital

$$K = Kd\left[\frac{B}{V}\right] = Ke\left[\frac{S}{V}\right]$$

Kd = Cost of Debt
B = Total debt
V = Total value of the firm
Ke = Cost of Equity Capital
S = Market value of Equity

3. *Valuation of firm : MM approach*
   (i) Value of unlevered firm

$$Vu = \frac{\text{Profits available for equity shareholders}}{\text{Equity Capitalisation Rate}}$$

(or)

$$Vu = \frac{(I - t)EBT}{Ke} \qquad t = \text{tax rate}$$

(ii) $\dfrac{\text{Value of levered firm}}{Vi = Vu + Bt}$

> **NOTE :** The term levered firm means there is debt content in its capital structure. The term unlevered firm means there is no debt content in its capital structure.

4. *Valuation of firm : Traditional approach*

Traditional approach contains some features of NI approach and some features of NOI approach. So there is no need for a separate formula for the valuation of firms under this approach

Problem 1. *M/s Nagu Ltd., has a share capital of Rs. 1,00,000 divided into 10,000 equity shares of Rs. 10 each fully paid. It has a major expansion programme requiring an investment of another Rs. 50,000. The management is considering the following alternatives for raising this amount.*

(a) *Issue of 5,000 Equity shares of Rs. 10 each*
(b) *Issue of 5,000 12% Preference shares of Rs. 10 each*
(c) *Issue of 10% Debentures of Rs. 50,000*

The company's present earnings before interest and taxes (EBIT) are Rs. 40,000 p.a. You are required to calculate the effect of each of the above modes of financing of the EPS (Earnings Per Share) assuming (i) EBIT continues to be the same even after expansion.

(ii) *EBIT increases by Rs. 10,000. Assume tax rate at 50%.*

Solution :

(i) **Computation of Earnings Per Share when EBIT is Rs. 40,000 p.a**

Particulars	Present Capital structure All Equity Rs.	Proposed Capital structure		
		(i) All Equity Rs.	(ii) Equity + Pref Rs.	(iii) Equity + Debt Rs.
EBIT	40,000	40,000	40,000	40,000
Less : Interest	—	—	—	5,000
PBT	40,000	40,000	40,000	35,000
Less : Tax	20,000	20,000	20,000	17,500
PAT	20,000	20,000	20,000	17,500
Less : Pref. Dividend	—	—	6,000	—
Profit available for Equity Share holders	20,000	20,000	14,000	17,500
Amount Available for Equity share holders	20,000	20,000	14,000	22,500
No. of Equity shares	10,000	15,000	10,000	10,000
EPS	2	1.33	1.40	1.75
Dilution against Initial EPS of Rs. 2	—	.67	.60	.25

The above solution shows that dilution of earning per share has been the least when the funds have been raised by issue of debentures.

(ii) Computation of Present and Projected Earnings Per Share when EBIT is Rs. 50,000 p.a. [40,000 + 10,000]

	Present Capital structure All Equity Rs.	Proposed Capital structure (i) All Equity Rs.	(ii) Equity + Pref Rs.	(iii) Equity + Debt Rs.
EBIT	40,000	50,000	50,000	50,000
Less : Interest	—	—	—	5,000
PBT	40,000	50,000	50,000	45,000
Less : Tax	20,000	25,000	25,000	22,500
PAT	20,000	25,000	25,000	22,500
Less : Pref. Dividend	—	—	6,000	—
Profit available for Equity Share holders	20,000	25,000	19,000	22,500
No. of Equity shares	10,000	15,000	10,000	10,000
EPS	2	1.67	1.90	2.25
Changes in EPS as against initial of Rs. 2	—	– .33	– .10	+ .25

The above table indicates that EPS has gone up by Rs. 0.25 per share as against the present EPS when the funds are raised by issue of debentures. Hence, the use of debentures is the desirable capital structure for raising funds. Because, for the other two, the EPS goes down.

Problem 2. *In considering the most desirable capital structure for a company, the following estimates of the cost of debt and equity capital (after tax) have been made at various levels of debt- equity mix.*

Debt as percentage of total capital employed	Cost of Debt(%)	Cost of Equity (%)
0	5.0	12.0
10	5.0	12.0
20	5.0	12.5
30	5.5	13.0
40	6.0	14.0
50	6.5	14.6
60	7.0	20.0

You are required to determine the optimal debt-equity mix for the company by calculating composite cost of capital. [B.Com adapted]

CAPITAL STRUCTURE

Solution :

Statement showing the Company's Composite Cost of Capital (after tax)

Debt Percentage of total capital employed	Cost of Debt	Cost of Equity	Composite Cost of Capital
0	5.0	12.0	$5 \times 0 + 12 \times 1 = 12.00$
10	5.0	12.0	$5 \times .10 + 12 \times .90 = 11.30$
20	5.0	12.5	$5 \times .20 + 12.5 \times .80 = 11.00$
30	5.5	13.0	$5.5 \times .30 + 13 \times .70 = 10.75$
40	6.0	14.0	$6 \times .40 + 14 \times .60 = 10.80$
50	6.5	16.0	$6.5 \times .50 + 16 \times .50 = 11.25$
60	7.0	20.0	$7.0 \times .60 + 20 \times .40 = 12.20$

Problem 3. *A new project is under consideration by Ram Ltd. which requires a capital investment of Rs. 150 Lakhs. Interest on term loan is 12% and tax rate is 50%. If the debt-equity ratio insisted by the financing agencies is 2 :1, calculate the point of indifference for the project.* [ICWA Final, Dec 1979]

Solution :

In case of project under consideration, the debt equity ratio insisted by the financing agencies is 2 : 1.

Following are some possible alternatives :

(i) Raising the total capital by issue of equity shares.

(ii) Raising Rs. 100 lakhs by way of debt and Rs. 50 lakhs by way of issue of shares. Thus maintaining a debt-equity ratio of 2:1.

There are two possibilities available :

(i) Issuing the entire capital by way of issue of equity shares.

(ii) Mobilising Rs. 100 lakhs by way of debt and Rs. 50 lakhs by way of issue of shares. In this situation, they can maintain a debt-equity ratio of 2:1.

In the first case, the interest amount will be zero. But in the second case, it will be Rs. 12 lakhs.

Computation of Point Indifference

$$\frac{(x - I_1)(1 - T) - PD}{S_1} = \frac{(x - I_2)(1 - T) - PD}{S_2}$$

$$\frac{(x \times 0)(1 - .5) - 0}{15} = \frac{(x - 12) \times (1 - .5) - 0}{5}$$

$$\frac{(x \times 0.5)}{15} = \frac{(x - 12) \times .5}{5}$$

$$2.5x = 7.5x - 90$$

$$5x = 90$$

$$x = \frac{90}{5}$$

$$= \text{Rs. 18 lakhs}$$

> **NOTE :** EBIT at point of indifference is therefore Rs. 18 lakhs. If EBIT is Rs. 18 lakhs, the earning on equity after tax will be 6% p.a. notwithstanding whether the capital is financed fully by equity or by any other mix of equity and debt provided. The rate of interest on debt is 12%.

Where, x = Point of Indifference or Break Even EBIT level
I_1 = Interest under plan 1
I_2 = Interest under plan 2
T = Tax Rate
PD = Preference dividend
S_1 = Number of Equity shares of plan 1
S_2 = Number of Equity shares of plan 2.

Problem 4. *(i) Murugappa & Co expects a net income of Rs. 80,000. It has 8% Debentures worth Rs. 2,00,000. The equity capitalisation rate of the company is 10%. Calculate the value of the firm and overall capitalisation rate according to the Net Income approach. (Ignoring income tax)*

(ii) If Debenture debt is increased to Rs. 3,00,000 what shall be the value of firm and the overall capitalisation rate ?

Solution :

(i) Calculate the value of the firm :

V = S + B
V = Value of the firm
S = Market value of equity
$B = \dfrac{NI}{K_e} = \dfrac{64,000}{10/100}$ *i.e.*, 64,000 × 100/10 = 6,40,000

Note :

(i) Computation of NI (Net Income)   Rs.
Net Income   =   80,000
Less : Interest on 8% Debentures of Rs. 2,00,000 =   16,000
Amount available for Equity share holders   =   64,000

K_e : Equity capitalisation rate = 10%
Value the firm = Rs. 8,40,000 [6,40,000 + 2,00,000]
[Value of Debenture 6,40,000 + 2,00,000 = 8,40,000]

(ii) Computation of overall capitalisation Rate :
Overall cost of capital (K) = EBIT/V
EBIT = Earnings before Interest and Tax

V = Value of the firm = $\dfrac{80,000}{6,40,000} \times 100 = 9.52\%$

CAPITAL STRUCTURE

(iii) Computation of value of the firm when debentures raised to Rs. 3,00,000

Net income	80,000
Less : Interest on 8% Debentures of Rs. 3,00,000	24,000
	56,000

Equity Capitalisation Rate 10%

Market value of Equity $56,000 \times \dfrac{100}{10}$ = 5,60,000

Market value of Debentures = 3,00,000

Value of the firm = 8,60,000

Overall Capitalisation Rate = $\dfrac{EBIT}{V} \times 100$

    EBIT : Earnings before interest and taxes
    V : Value of the firm
i.e., EBIT : 80,000
    V : 8,60,000

Therefore, Overall Capitalisation Rate = $\dfrac{80,000}{8,60,000} \times 100 = 9.3\%$

Findings :

In the above computation there is increase in the debt financing and the value of the firm also increased so the overall cost of capital has decreased.

Problem 5. *(i) SLM Ltd expects a net operating income of Rs. 2,00,000. It has 6% Debentures worth Rs. 10,00,000. The overall capitalisation rate is 10%. Calculate the value of the firm and the equity capitalisation rate according to NOI approach.*

(ii) If the debenture debt is increased to Rs. 7,50,000 what will be effect on the value of the firm and the equity capitalisation rate ?

Solution :

(i) Value of the firm : NOI approach

    Here,   S = V – B
                 S = Value of Equity
                 V = Value of the Firm
                 B = Value of Debt.

First Step :

$$V = \dfrac{EBIT}{K_e} = \dfrac{2,00,000}{10/100} = 2,00,000 \times \dfrac{100}{10} = 20,00,000$$

    EBIT = Earning before interest and taxes 2,00,000
    K_e = Equity capitalisation Rate 10%
    B = Market value of Debenture : Rs. 10,00,000

Second Step :

    S = V – B = 20,00,000 – 10,00,000 = 10,00,000

After arriving at the value of V & B, we can easily find the value of S

K_e = Equity Capitalisation Rate

$$K_e = \frac{EBIT}{V - B} \times 100$$

$$= \frac{2,00,000 - 60,000}{20,00,000 - 10,00,000} \times 100$$

$$= \frac{1,40,000}{10,00,000} \times 100 = 14\%$$

(ii) If the debenture debt is increased to Rs. 7,50,000, the value of the firm remains unchanged at Rs. 10,00,000. The equity capitalisation rate will be as follows.

$$\text{Equity Capitalisation Rate } (K_e) = \frac{EBIT - I}{V - B}$$

$$= \frac{2,00,000 - 45,00,000}{10,00,000 - 5,50,000} \times 100 = 22\%$$

Problem 6. *Two firms B and S are identical in all respects except the degree of leverage. Firm B has 6% of debt of Rs. 3.00 lakhs while firm S has no debt. Both the firms are earning an EBT of Rs. 1,20,000 each. The equity capitalisation rate is 10% and the corporate tax is 60%.*

You are required to compute the market value of the two firms.

Solution :

Value of unlevered firm :   *(No debt content)*

Formula :

$$Vu = \frac{\text{Profit available for equity shareholders}}{\text{Equity Capitalisation Rate}}$$

$$= \frac{1,20,000 - 72,000}{10/100}$$

$$= 48,000 \times 100/10$$

$$Vu = Rs. 4,80,000$$

NOTE :
Profit available for equity shareholders

Earnings before tax	1,20,000
Less : Tax Rate (1,20,000 × 60/100)	72,000
Profit available for equity shareholders	48,000

Value of levered firm

$Vi = Vu + Bt$

Vi = Value of levered firm $Vi = 4,80,000 + 3,00,000 \times .6$

Vu = Value of unlevered firm $= 5,60,000$

B = Value of Debenture Vu = Rs. 4,80,000

t = Tax rate Vi = Rs. 5,60,000

26

Working Capital

The first and foremost objective of the financial management is to maximise the wealth of shareholders. It is possible only when the company earns sufficient profit. The profitability of the organisation fully depends upon the magnitude of sales. However, sales are not converted into cash immediately. Because there is a time gap between the sale of goods and receipt of cash. During the time gap a certain amount is required to sustain the sales volume on a regular basis. That amount is known as working capital. Suppose adequate working capital is not available, the company will not be in a position to maintain the sales volume at an expected level.

Simply, working capital means circulating capital or revolving capital. In other words, working capital means amount required for the day-to-day expenses of the business activities.

According to J.S.Mill, the sum of current assets is the working capital of a business.

"Working capital is the amount of funds necessary to cover the cost of operating the enterprise" says **Shubin**.

Gesterrberg defines, Working capital is the excess of current assets over current liabilities.

Simply, Net Working Capital = Current Assets – Current Liabilities.

CONCEPTS OF WORKING CAPITAL

(i) Gross Working Capital (ii) Net Working Capital

(i) Gross Working Capital

The Gross working capital refers to working capital which represents investment in current assets such as marketable securities, inventories and bills receivables.

(ii) Net Working Capital

Net working capital refers to working capital. It is the excess of current assets over current Liabilities. This is the most commonly accepted definition.

TYPES OF WORKING CAPITAL

Working capital can be divided into two categories on the basis of time.

(i) Permanent working capital or core current assets

(ii) Temporary or variable working capital

(i) Permanent Working Capital

Permanent working capital refers to that minimum amount of investment in all current assets which is required to carry out minimum level of business activities on a permanent basis. In other words, certain current assets which are retained by the organisation on a continuous basis is called permanent working capital or core current assets.

(ii) Temporary or Variable Working Capital

Temporary working capital is an investment in current assets which are fluctuating from time to time on the basis of the operations of the business. The capital, required to meet the seasonal needs of a firm, is called seasonal working capital or temporary working capital. In other words, the amount of working capital which will vary from time to time depending upon the level of business activities, is known as variable working capital.

OPERATING CYCLE

Modern business enterprises face severe competitions. They produce goods based upon the demand. In this respect, all manufactured goods are not sold immediately. And at the same time, cash for sales is also not realised immediately. From the purchase of raw material to the conversion of cash, certain time gap is taken. This time gap is technically known as operating cycle of the business.

Stages of Operating Cycle

(i) Conversion of cash into raw materials
(ii) Conversion of raw materials into work in progress
(iii) Conversion of work in progress into finished goods
(iv) Conversion of finished goods into debtors
(v) Conversion of debtors into cash

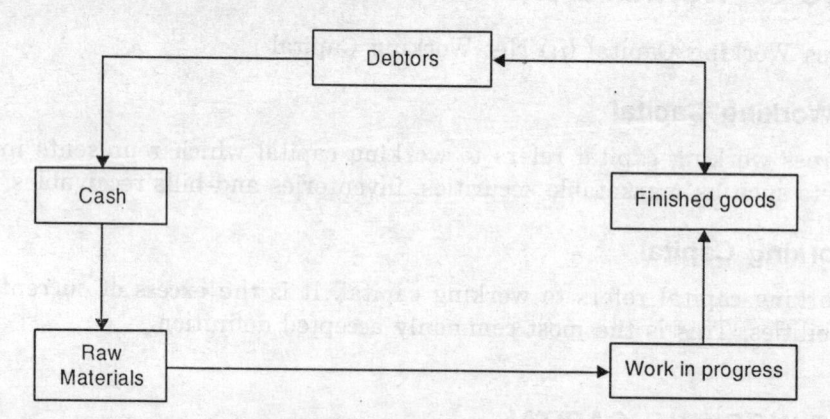

```
         ┌──────────── Debtors ◄────────────┐
         ▼                                  │
       Cash                           Finished goods
         │                                  ▲
         ▼                                  │
       Raw Materials ──────────────► Work in progress
```

Advantages or Importance of Working Capital

(i) Adequate working capital ensures the regular supply of raw materials and continued production.

(ii) Easy to get the loan from the banks and other financial institutions on easy and convenient terms

WORKING CAPITAL

(iii) It enables the firm to avail cash discount facilities on the purchases, thus it reduces the costs.
(iv) To follow as a prompt payment policy helps in establishment of goodwill.
(v) It helps the organisation to meet the financial crisis during the periods of depression or any emergencies.
(vi) The expansion programme of a concern is highly successful and obtains higher profitability.
(vii) It improves high morale among employees and executives in the organisation.
(viii) To encourage research programme
(ix) To obtain the higher level of productivity due to effective utilisation of assets
(x) Enables to pay higher return to its owner. So automatically the firm possesses a financial soundness. In this way it helps to generate additional funds in future.

Disadvantages or Danger of Inadequate Working Capital

(i) A concern cannot pay its short term liabilities because of inadequate working capital. This leads to borrowing funds at higher rates of interest.
(ii) It may not take advantage of cash discount because the concern may find it difficult to buy its requirement in bulk quantities.
(iii) Low level liquidity position of the concern may lead to winding up of the firm.
(iv) Fixed assets could not be fully utilised on account of lack in sufficient working capital. So the rate of return on investment falls.
(v) It is very difficult to obtain favourable market conditions and any of the profitable business opportunities.
(vi) Credit worthiness and reputation of the organisation may be damaged.
(vii) It leads to under-utilisation of production facilities.

Disadvantages of Excessive Working Capital

(i) Unnecessary purchases and accumulation of inventories lead to chances of more losses and waste.
(ii) Due to huge amount of idle funds the rate of return on its investment automatically goes down.
(iii) It leads to overtrade and chances of heavy losses.
(iv) Difficult to maintain the cordial relationship with the bank and other financial institutions.
(v) Large amount of bad debts arise.
(vi) It encourages mass production which may not have matching demand.

Determinants of Working Capital : (or) Factors Determining Working Capital

(i) Nature of Business
(ii) Production Policies
(iii) Length of the Manufacturing Cycle
(iv) Terms of Purchases and Sales
(v) Seasonal Variation

(vi) Fluctuations in Supply
(vii) Dividend Policy
(viii) Requirements of Cash.
(ix) Other Factors.

(i) *Nature of Business.* Working capital of the organisation basically depends upon the nature of business. Public utility concerns like Railways, Electricity etc would need only very little amount of working capital. On the other hand, manufacturing and trading concerns need huge amount of working capital in their operations.

(ii) *Production Policies.* Production policy of the organisation is also an important factor for determining working capital. In case of labour intensive industry the quantum of working capital is required only in smaller amount. But highly automatic plants require huge amount of working capital.

(iii) *Length of the Manufacturing Cycle.* The amount of working capital needed is highly influenced by the length of manufacturing cycle. If the manufacturing process is long, huge amount of working capital will be required and vice versa. So utmost care should be taken to shorten the period of cycle in order to minimise the working capital requirements.

(iv) *Terms of Purchase and Sales.* If an organisation provides liberal credit facilities to its customers, large amount of working capital gets locked up in sundry debtors and bills receivable. And at the same time if continuous credit is allowed by the suppliers, it tends to cause not only postponement of payment but also payment out of sale proceeds of the goods produced. The period of credit allowed and received also determines the working capital requirements of the company.

(v) *Seasonal Variations.* Seasonal changes in the economy also affect the quantum of working capital. Huge amount of working capital is required during the periods of inflation and depression and the requirement declines during the other periods of economic cycle.

(vi) *Fluctuations in Supply.* Certain industries purchase raw material at huge level due to their irregular supply throughout the year. It is specifically applicable to the manufacturing organisation which requires an unusual type of raw material that can be purchased only with limited sources.

(vii) *Dividend Policy.* According to the new provisions of the SEBI, all the companies are compulsorily to declare the dividend to the shareholders. So the dividend policy has a dominant influence on the working capital position of the organisation. As per the new provisions, need for the working capital is met with retained earnings. Once dividend is declared and the same has to be paid in cash requires large amounts from the pool of working capital.

(viii) *Requirements of Cash.* Need for the working capital depends upon the amount of cash required by the company for its various purposes. If greater the requirements of cash, the higher will be the working capital needs of the company and vice versa.

(ix) *Other Factors.* Apart from the above points, some other factors also affect the working capital requirements. For example, lack of transport and communication facilities, tariff policies of government etc. also influence the requirements of working capital.

WORKING CAPITAL

SOURCES OF WORKING CAPITAL

An efficient finance manager is always interested in maintaining the correct amount of working capital at the right time, at a reasonable cost and at the best possible favourable terms. The following are the important sources of working capital.

To obtain the working capital in the following two major divisions.

(A) Long term sources

(B) Short term sources

(A) Long-term Sources

(i) Share capital

(ii) Sale of debentures

(iii) Ploughing back of profits

(iv) Sale of fixed assets

(v) Term loans.

(B) Short-term Sources

I. *Internal Sources :*

(i) Depreciation Funds

(ii) Provision for Taxation

(iii) Accrued Expenses.

II. *External Sources :*

(i) Trade credit

(ii) Bank credit

(iii) Credit papers

(iv) Public deposits

(v) Government's assistance

(vi) Loans from directors etc.

(vii) Factoring.

FORECASTING TECHNIQUES OF WORKING CAPITAL

There are so many popular methods for forecasting the working capital requirements which are as follows.

(i) Cash Forecasting Method

(ii) Balance Sheet Method

(iii) Profit and Loss Adjustment Method

(iv) Percentage of Sales Method

(v) Operational Cycle Method

(vi) Regression Analysis Method.

(i) *Cash Forecasting Method.* Under this method, the working capital is to be determined on the basis of the closing balance of the cash, after considering the receipts and payments made during that period.

(ii) *Balance Sheet Method.* According to this method, a forecast is made of the various assets and liabilities of the concern. The difference between two is taken which will indicate either cash surplus or cash deficiency.

(iii) *Profit and Loss Adjustment Method.* Under this method, the forecasted Profits or Losses are to be adjusted on cash basis.

(iv) *Percentage of Sales Method.* Under this method, working capital is determined as a percentage of forecasted sales. It must be decided on the basis of past observations. This method is simple and easy to understand.

(v) *Operational Cycle Method.* Under this method, working capital is determined according to the operating cycle concept. In a manufacturing organisation the working capital cycle starts from the purchase of raw material and ends with the conversion of cash. It involves purchase of raw materials, work in progress, finished goods, sales, debtors and conversion of cash. This cycle will continue again and again. Each of the cycle stage is expressed in terms of number of days of relevant activity and requires a level of investment. The amount required for these stage-wise investments will be the total amount of the working capital of the organisation.

Following formula is used to express the framework of the operating cycle :

$T = (r - c) + w + f + b$

T = Stands for the total period of operating cycle in number of days.

r = Stands for the number of days of raw material and stores consumption requirements held in raw materials and stores

c = Number of days of credit allowed by creditors

W = Stands for the number of days of cost of production held in work in progress.

f = Finished stock storage period

or

T = Duration of operating cycle in number of days

r = Raw materials and storage period

c = Creditors payment period

w = Work in process period

f = Finished stock storage period

b = Debtors collection period

(vi) *Regression Analysis Method.* According to this method, statistical formula is used to determine the working capital requirement. Projection of working capital is made after establishing the average relationship in the past years between sales and working capital *i.e.,* current assets.

Procedure for Computation of Working Capital

Current Assets	
Raw Material	xx
Work in Progress	xx
Finished Goods	xx
Debtors	xx
Cash	xx
Total Current Assets	xx
Less : Current Liabilities	

Creditors	xx	
Wages	xx	
Any Other Expenses	xx	
Total Current Liabilities [TCA – TCL]		xx
Working Capital		xx
Add : Contingencies		xx
Amount of Working Capital required		xx

Workings :
  (i) First of all uniformly we have to find out the number of units. It is the basis for computation of cost of all the elements.
  (ii) Computation of finished goods

Raw material cost	xx
Labour cost	xx
Overhead cost	xx
Finished goods	xx

  (iii) Work in progress and finished goods value will be the same. But the production occurring evenly throughout the year given in the problem means we have to find out the work-in-progress value separately.
  i.e., Raw Material Cost Labour cost   xx
        (It is reduced to half)
        Overhead cost (It is reduced to half)   xx
        Work in progress   xx

Value of Debtors should be calculated either including profit element or excluding profit element.

Problem 1. *From the following information, prepare a statement in column form showing the working capital requirements. (i) In total and (ii) As regards each constituent part of working capital.*

Budgeted sales (Rs 10 per unit) Rs 2,60,000 p.a.

Analysis of Costs	Rs.
Raw Materials	3.00
Direct Labour	4.00
Overheads	2.00
Total Cost	9.00
Profit	1.00
Sales	10.00

It is estimated that
  (i) Raw materials are carried in stock for three weeks and finished goods for two weeks.
  (ii) Factory processing will take three weeks.

(iii) Suppliers will give full five weeks credit.
(iv) Customers will require eight weeks credit.
It may be assumed that production and overheads accrue evenly throughout the year.

[M.Com Madurai] [MCA Madras]

Solution : **Statement of Working Capital Requirement**

Current Assets   Rs.
    Raw Materials 78,000 × 3/52   = 4,500
    Work in Progress (Note)   = 9,000
    Finished Goods 2,34,000 × 2/52   = 9,000
    Debtors 2,60,000 × 8/52   = 40,000
                                                62,500

Less : Current Liabilities
    Trade Creditors (5 weeks) 5/52 × 78,000 = 7,500

    Working Capital Required   55,000

Working Notes :
(i) Number of Units   = 26,000
(ii) Finished Goods
    Raw Materials 26,000 × 3   = 78,000
    Direct Labour 26,000 × 4   = 1,04,000
    Overheads 26,000 × 2   = 52,000
    Finished Goods   2,34,000

(iii) Work in Progress
    Raw Material 78,000 × 3/52   = 4,500
    Labour 1,04,000 × 3/52 × 1/2   = 3,000
    Overhead 52,000 × 3/52 × 1/2   = 1,500
    Work in Progress   9,000

> **NOTE :** (i) Normally finished goods and work in progress are taken as same value. Suppose wages and overheads accrue evenly throughout the year given in the problem, we have to find out the work in progress value separately. At that time of computing work in progress labour, overhead value is reduced to half.
>
> (ii) At the time of calculating working capital, debtor value will be taken as either including profit element or excluding profit element.

Problem 2. *Prepare a working capital forecast from the following information :*

                                              Rs.
    Issued share capital   4,00,000
    12% Debentures   1,50,000

The fixed assets are valued at Rs 3.00 lakhs. Production during the previous year is 1.00 lakh units. The same level of activity is intended to be maintained during the current year.

WORKING CAPITAL

The expected ratios of cost to selling price are

Raw materials	50%
Direct Wages	10%
Overheads	25%

The raw materials ordinarily remain in stores for 2 months before production. Every unit of production remains in process for 2 months. Finished goods remain in the warehouse for 4 months. Credit allowed by creditors is 3 months from the date of delivery of raw materials and credit given to debtors is 3 months from the date of despatch.

Selling price is Rs 6 per unit. Both the production and sales are in a regular cycle.

[CAIIB May 1983]

Solution :

Working Capital Statement

	Rs.
Raw Materials	50,000
Work in Progress	67,500
Finished Goods	1,70,000
Debtors	1,27,500
	4,15,000
Less : Creditors	75,000
Working capital required	3,40,000

Working Notes :

$$\text{Number of units} = 1,00,000$$

$$\text{Sales Value} = 1,00,000 \times 6 = 6,00,000$$

$$\text{Material} = 6,00,000 \times \frac{50}{100} = 3,00,000$$

$$\text{Labour} = 6,00,000 \times \frac{10}{100} = 60,000$$

$$\text{Overheads} = 6,00,000 \times \frac{25}{100} = 1,50,000$$

(i) Finished Goods

Raw Materials	=	3,00,000
Direct Labour	=	60,000
Overheads	=	1,50,000
		5,10,000

$$\text{i.e., } 5,10,000 \times 4/12 = 1,70,000$$

(ii) Work in Progress

$$\text{Raw Materials} = 3,00,000 \times \frac{2}{12} = 50,000$$

$$\text{Direct Labour} = 60,000 \times \frac{2}{12} \times \frac{1}{2} = 5,000$$

$$\text{Overheads} = 1{,}50{,}000 \times \frac{2}{12} \times \frac{1}{2} = \underline{12{,}500}$$
$$\underline{\underline{67{,}500}}$$

(iii) Debtors = 5,10,000 × 3/12 = 1,27,500
(iv) Creditors = 3,00,000 × 3/12 = 75,000

Problem 3. *The management of G Ltd has called for a statement showing the working capital needed to finance a level of 3,00,000 units of output for the year. The cost structure for the company's product, for the above mentioned activity level is detailed below.*

Cost Element	Cost per unit (Rs)
Raw Materials	20
Direct Labour	5
Overheads	15
Total Cost	40
Profit	10
Selling Price	50

Past trends indicate that raw materials are held in stock on an average for two months.
Work in progress will approximate to half a month's production.
Finished goods remain in warehouse on an average for a month.
Suppliers of materials extend a month's credit.
Two months' credit is normally allowed to debtors.
A minimum cash balance of Rs 25,000 is expected to be maintained.
The production pattern is assumed to be even during the year. Prepare the statement of working capital determination. [MCA Madras]

Solution : **Working Capital Statement (or)**
Statement of Working Capital Requirement

Current Assets

	Raw Materials	$60{,}00{,}000 \times \frac{2}{12}$	=	10,00,000
	Work in Progress		=	3,75,000
	Finished goods	$1{,}20{,}00{,}000 \times \frac{1}{12}$	=	10,00,000
	Debtors	$1{,}50{,}00{,}000 \times \frac{2}{12}$	=	25,00,000
				48,75,000
Less :	Current Liabilities			
	Sundry Creditors	$60{,}00{,}000 \times \frac{1}{2}$	=	5,00,000
				43,75,000
Add :	Minimum Cash Balance			25,000
	Working Capital			44,00,000

Workings :

(i) Finished Goods

Raw Materials	3,00,000 × 20	=	60,00,000
Direct Labour	3,00,000 × 5	=	15,00,000
Overheads	3,00,000 × 15	=	45,00,000
Finished Goods			1,20,00,000

(ii) Work in Progress

Raw Materials	$60,00,000 \times \frac{.5}{12}$	=	2,50,000
Labour	$15,00,000 \times \frac{.5}{12} \times \frac{1}{2}$	=	31,250
Overheads	$45,00,000 \times \frac{.5}{12} \times \frac{1}{2}$	=	93,750
Work in progress			3,75,000

Problem 4. *The Board of KRN Ltd Pune wishes to know the amount of working capital which will be required to meet the programme they have planned for the year.*

You are required to prepare working capital estimate from the following information

		Rs.
(i) Issued Share Capital	=	4,00,000
5% Debentures	=	1,00,000
Fixed assets at cost	=	2,50,000
(ii) The expected ratio of cost to selling price are :		
Raw materials	=	60%
Labour	=	10%
Overheads	=	20%
Profit	=	10%

(iii) Raw materials are in stores for an average of two months. Finished goods are kept in warehouse for approximately three months.

(iv) Production during the previous year was 1,20,000 units and it is planned to maintain this level of activity in the current year also.

(v) Each unit of production is expected to be in process for one month.

(vi) Credit given by the suppliers is two months and allowed to customers is three months.

(vii) Selling price is Rs 5 per unit.

(viii) There is a regular production and sales cycle. [M.Com Pune 1983]

Solution : Statement of Working Capital Requirement

Current Assets   Rs.

Raw Materials	$3,60,000 \times \frac{2}{12}$	=	60,000
Finished goods	$5,40,000 \times \frac{3}{12}$	=	1,35,000

Work in Progress		=	37,500
Debtors	$5{,}40{,}000 \times \dfrac{3}{12}$	=	1,35,000
			3,67,500
Less : Current Liabilities			
Creditors	$3{,}60{,}000 \times \dfrac{2}{12}$	=	60,000
Working Capital Required		=	3,07,500

Working :

Number of units = 1,20,000
Sales value 1,20,000 × 5 = 6,00,000

(i) Finished Goods

Raw Materials	$6{,}00{,}000 \times \dfrac{60}{100}$	=	3,60,000
Labour	$6{,}00{,}000 \times \dfrac{10}{100}$	=	60,000
Overheads	$6{,}00{,}000 \times \dfrac{20}{100}$	=	1,20,000
Finished Goods			5,40,000

(ii) Work in Progress

Raw Materials	$3{,}60{,}000 \times \dfrac{1}{12}$	=	30,000
Labour	$60{,}000 \times \dfrac{1}{12} \times \dfrac{1}{2}$	=	2,500
Overheads	$1{,}20{,}000 \times \dfrac{1}{12} \times \dfrac{1}{2}$	=	5,000
Work in Progress		=	37,500

> **NOTE :** Amount of debtors should be calculated only on cost of sales *i.e.*, excluding profit elements.

Problem 5. *Raj and Kumar who want to buy a business, seek your advice about the average working capital requirements in the first year trading. The following estimates are available and you are asked to add 10% to allow for contingencies.*

(i) Average Amount Locked up in stocks   *Per Annum Rs.*
    Stock of Finished Products = 5,000
    Stock of Stores Materials etc. = 8,000
(ii) Average Credit given
    Local sales–2 weeks credit = 78,000
    Outside the state–6 weeks credit = 3,12,000

WORKING CAPITAL

(iii) Time available for payment
   For Purchases—4 weeks = 96,000
   For Wages—2 weeks = 2,60,000

Calculate the average amount of working capital required. Give details of your working.

Solution : **Statement of Working Capital Requirement**

Current Assets		Rs.
Finished products and work in progress	=	5,000
Stores, Material etc.	=	8,000
		13,000

Account Receivable

Local Sales	$78,000 \times \frac{2}{52}$		=	3,000
Outside the state	$3,12,000 \times \frac{6}{52} = 36,000$		=	36,000
Total Current Assets			=	52,000

Less : Current Liabilities

Account Payable	$96,000 \times \frac{4}{52}$	=	7,385
Outstanding wages	$2,60,000 \times \frac{2}{52}$	=	10,000
Total Current Liabilities			17,385
Working Capital			34,615
Add : 10% Contingencies (34,615 x 10/100)			3,462
Working Capital required			38,077

Assignment Problem

Problem 6. *Ram Ltd decided to purchase a business and has consulted you and one point on which you are asked to advice them is the average amount of working capital which will be required in the first year workings.*

You are given the following estimates and are instructed to add 10% to your computed figure to allow for contingencies.

(i) Average amount locked up for the stocks   Rs.
   Stock of finished products   5,000
   Stock of stores materials etc.   8,000
(ii) Average credit given
   Inland sales—6 weeks credit   3,12,000
   Export sales—1½ weeks credit   78,000
(iii) Lag in payment of wages and other outgoing
   Wages—1½ weeks   2,60,000
   Stores, Materials etc. 1½ months   48,000
   Rent Royalties etc. 6 months   10,000

Clerical Staff—½ month 62,400
Manager—½ month 4,800
Miscellaneous Expenses—½ month 48,000

(iv) Payment in advance
Sundry Expenses (Paid Quarterly in advance) 8,000
(v) Undrawn profits on the average throughout the year 11,000

Set up your calculations for the average amount of working capital required.

[M.Com Madurai]

Answer : Working Capital Rs. 25,950, Current Assets = Rs 53,250, Current Liabilities = Rs. 23,700.

Problem 7. *From the following estimates of Sethal Ltd you are required to prepare a forecast of working capital requirements.*

(i) Expected level of production for the year 15,600 units
(ii) Cost per unit : Raw Materials Rs. 90, Direct labour Rs. 40, overheads Rs. 75.
(iii) Selling Price per unit Rs. 265
(iv) Raw Materials in stock on an average for 1 month
(v) Materials are in process on an average for 2 weeks.
(vi) Finished goods in stock on an average for 1 month.
(vii) Credit allowed by suppliers is one month.
(viii) Time lag in payment from debtors is 2 months.
(ix) Lag in payment of wages 1½ weeks.
(x) Lag in payment of overheads is one month. All sales are on credit.
(xi) Cash in hand and at Bank is expected to be Rs. 60,000.

It is assumed that production is carried on evenly throughout the year. Wages and overheads accrued evenly and a period of 4 weeks is equivalent to a month.

Solution : Statement of working capital Requirement

Current Assets

Raw materials	1,08,000 × 1	=	1,08,000
Finished goods	2,46,000 × 1	=	2,46,000
Debtors 2 months	2,46,000 × 2	=	4,92,000
Work in progress		=	88,500
Cash in hand and at Bank		=	60,000
			9,94,500

Less : Current Liabilities

Creditors 1,08,000 × 1 = 1,08,000

Lag in payment of wages 1½ weeks

$48,000 \times \dfrac{3}{2} \times \dfrac{1}{4}$ = 18,000

Lag in payment of overheads (90,000 × 1) = 90,000

2,16,000

Working capital required 7,78,500
[9,94,500 – 2,16,000]

WORKING CAPITAL

Working Notes :

Estimated sales = 15,600 units

A period of 4 weeks is taken as equivalent to one month.

Therefore, sales per month = $15{,}600 \times \dfrac{4}{52}$ = 1200 units

Estimated sales per month = $265 \times 1{,}200$ = 3,18,000

Raw Materials p.m.	$1{,}200 \times 90$ =	1,08,000
Direct Labour p.m.	$1{,}200 \times 40$ =	48,000
Overheads p.m.	$1{,}200 \times 75$ =	90,000
Cost of Sales/Finished Goods	=	2,46,000

Work in progress

Raw materials (2 weeks)	$1{,}08{,}000 \times \dfrac{1}{2}$ =	54,000
Labour (2 weeks)	$48{,}000 \times \dfrac{1}{2} \times \dfrac{1}{2}$ =	12,000
Overhead (2 weeks)	$90{,}000 \times \dfrac{1}{2} \times \dfrac{1}{2}$ =	22,500
		88,500

NOTE : Labour and overheads are reduced to one half as they accrue evenly during the year.

Problem 8. *Prepare an estimate of working capital and projected Balance Sheet for the year ended on 31.12.2002 from the following information.*

(i) *Share capital Rs. 5,00,000, 15% Debentures of Rs. 2,00,000, Fixed assets at cost of Rs. 3,00,000.*

(ii) *The expected ratios of cost to selling price are Raw materials 60%, Labour 10%, Overheads 20%.*

(iii) *Raw materials are in stores for an average of 2 months.*

(iv) *Finished goods are kept in warehouse for 3 months.*

(v) *Expected level of production 1,20,000 units per year.*

(vi) *Each unit of production is expected to be in process for 1 month.*

(vii) *Credit given by suppliers is 2 months.*

(viii) *20% of the output is sold against cash. Time lag in payment from debtors is 3 months.*

(ix) *Selling price is Rs 5 per unit*

(x) *Labour and overheads will accrue evenly during the year.*

Solution : Statement of Working Capital requirement

Current Assets

Raw Materials (2 months)	60,000
Work in progress	37,500
Stock of finished goods (3 months)	1,35,000

Debtors 3 months		1,08,000
Total Current Assets		3,40,500
Less : Current Liability		
Creditors 2 months		60,000
Working Capital required [3,40,500 – 60,000]		2,80,500

Working Notes :

Estimated production units $\dfrac{1,20,000}{12}$ = 10,000 units

Sales p.m. 10,000 units × Rs. 5 = 50,000

(i) Finished goods :

Raw Materials 60%	= 50,000 × 60/100 =	30,000
Direct Labour 10%	= 50,000 × 10/100 =	5,000
Overheads 20%	= 50,000 × 20/100 =	10,000
Finished goods/Cost of sales	=	45,000

(ii) Work in progress (1 month)

Raw materials	=	30,000
Labour	5000 × 1/2 =	2,500
Overheads	10,000 × 1/2 =	5,000
W.I.P		37,500

(iii) Debtors (3months) at cost equivalent

Cost of sales pm	45,000
Less : Cash sales 20%	9,000
Cost of sales (credit) pm	36,000

Debtors (3 months) at cost equivalent
= 36,000 × 3 = 1,08,000

Projected Balance Sheet as on 31.12.2002

Liabilities	Rs.	Assets	Rs.
Share Capital	5,00,000	Fixed Assets at cost	3,00,000
15% Debentures	2,00,000	Current Assets :	
		Raw Materials	60,000
Creditors	60,000	Work in progress	37,500
		Stock of Finished Goods	1,35,000
		Debtors	1,20,000
		Cash (BF)	1,07,500
	7,60,000		7,60,000

WORKING CAPITAL

Problem 9. *On the basis of programme formulated to be part into operation with effect from 1.1.2003, the management of PV Ltd desires to know the quantum of working capital required to finance the production programme.*

The following percentages which the various elements of cost bear to the selling price have been extracted from the proforma cost sheet.

Materials 50%, labour 20%, Overheads 10%.

Production in 2002 was 1,00,000 units and it is proposed to maintain the same during 2003. Following particulars are available.

(i) *Raw materials are expected to remain in the stores for an average period of one month before being issued to production.*

(ii) *Finished goods are to stay in the warehouse for 2 months on the average before being sold and send to customer.*

(iii) *Each unit of production will be in process for 1 month on an average.*

(iv) *Credit allowed by suppliers from the date of delivery of materials is 1 month.*

(v) *Debtors are allowed 2 months' credit.*

(vi) *Selling price is Rs 9 per unit.*

(vii) *Sales and production follow a constant pattern.*

The relevant items of the Balance Sheet are	Rs.
Paid up share capital	10,00,000
6% Debentures	1,00,000
Fixed assets as on 1.1.2003	7,50,000

Prepare an estimate of Working Capital requirements as well as Forecast Profit and Loss Account and Balance Sheet of PV Ltd.

Solution :

Working Notes :

Number of units 1,00,000

Sales value   1,00,000 × 9 = 9,00,000

(i) Finished Goods

Raw materials	$9,00,000 \times \dfrac{50}{100}$	=	4,50,000
Labour	$9,00,000 \times \dfrac{50}{100}$	=	1,80,000
Overheads	$9,00,000 \times \dfrac{10}{100}$	=	90,000
Cost of sales/finished goods			7,20,000

(ii) Work in Progress

Raw Materials	$4,50,000 \times \dfrac{1}{12}$	=	37,500
Labour	$1,80,000 \times \dfrac{1}{12} \times \dfrac{1}{2}$	=	7,500
Overheads	$90,000 \times \dfrac{1}{12} \times \dfrac{1}{2}$	=	3,750
			48,750

Working Capital Statement

Current Assets

Raw Materials	4,50,000 × $\frac{1}{12}$	=	37,500
Finished Goods	7,20,000 × $\frac{2}{12}$	=	1,20,000
Work in Progress			48,750
Debtors	7,20,000 × $\frac{2}{12}$	=	1,20,000
			3,26,250

Less : Current Liabilities

Creditors	4,50,000 × $\frac{1}{12}$	=	37,500
Working Capital requirement			2,88,750

Projected Trading Account

	Rs.		Rs.
To Raw materials	4,50,000	By Sales	9,00,000
To Labour	1,80,000		
To Overheads	90,000		
To Gross profit	1,80,000		
	9,00,000		9,00,000
To interest on Debenture	6,000	By Gross profit	1,80,000
To Net profit	1,74,000		
	1,80,000		1,80,000

Balance Sheet

Liabilities	Rs.	Assets	Rs.
Share capital	10,00,000	Fixed assets	7,50,000
6% Debentures	1,00,000	Current assets	
Interest on Debenture	6,000	Raw materials	37,500
Profit & Loss A/c (Net profit)	1,74,000	Work in progress	48,750
Creditors	37,500	Finished goods	1,20,000
		Debtors	1,20,000
		Cash (B/F)	2,41,250
	13,17,500		13,17,500

Problem 10. *Maruthi Ltd is a newly set up enterprise. With the help of the following particulars, determine the magnitude of Working Capital.*

(i) *Various elements of cost bear the following relationship to the selling price. The cost is Rs. 200 per unit.*

Materials 40%, Labour 30%, Overheads 10%.

WORKING CAPITAL

(ii) Production in 1995 is estimated to be 5,000 units.
(iii) Materials are expected to remain in stores for an average period of 1 month.
(iv) Finished goods are likely to stay in warehouse for two month on average.
(v) Each unit of production will be in process for half a month on average.
(vi) 50% of the sales will be on credit. Customers are allowed two months' credit.
(vii) Credit period allowed by the suppliers is 1 month.
(viii) The lag in payment to labour is one month. 50% of the overheads consists of salaries of non-production staff.
(ix) Allow 20% to your computed figures for contingencies.
(x) Assume that sales and production follow a constant pattern. [M.Com Bombay]

Solution :
Workings :

Number of units   5,000
Sales value   5,000 × 200 = Rs.10,00,000

1. *Finished goods*   Rs.

   Raw materials $10,00,000 \times \frac{40}{100}$ = 4,00,000

   Labour $10,00,000 \times \frac{30}{100}$ = 3,00,000

   Overheads $10,00,000 \times \frac{10}{100}$ = 1,00,000

   Cost of sales/Finished goods   8,00,000

2. *Work in progress*   Rs.

   Raw materials $4,00,000 \times \frac{.5}{12}$ = 16,667

   Labour $3,00,000 \times \frac{.5}{12} \times \frac{1}{2}$ = 6,250

   Overheads $1,00,000 \times \frac{.5}{12} \times \frac{1}{2}$ = 2,083

   Work in progress   25,000

3. *Debtors*

   Cost of sales = 8,00,000

   Cost of credit sales = $8,00,000 \times \frac{50}{100}$ = Rs. 4,00,000

   Two months' credit sales = $4,00,000 \times \frac{2}{12}$ = Rs. 66,667

Statement of Working Capital requirement

Current Assets   Rs.

Raw materials $4,00,000 \times \frac{1}{12}$ = 33,334

Finished goods $8,00,000 \times \frac{2}{12}$ = 1,33,334

Work in progress	=	25,000
Debtors	=	66,667
Total Current Assets		2,58,335

Less : Current Liabilities

Creditors [4,00,000 × 1/12]	33,334
Outstanding wages [3,00,000 × 1/12]	25,000
Outstanding salary [1,00,000 × 50/100 × 1/12]	4,167
Total Current Liabilities	62,501

Working capital (2,58,335 – 62,501)	1,95,834
Add : 20% for contingencies	39,166
Working capital requirement	2,35,000

Problem 11. *XYZ Cements Ltd sells its products on a gross profit of 20% on sales. The following information is extracted from its annual accounts for the current year ended on 31st December.*

	Rs.
Sales at 3 months' credit	40,00,000
Raw material	12,00,000
Finished goods : 2 months credit	32,00,000
Wages paid—average time lags 15 days	9,60,000
Manufacturing expenses paid one month in arrears	12,00,000
Administrative expenses paid one month in arrears	4,80,000
Sales promotion expenses payable Half-month in advance	2,00,000
Cash in hand	1,00,000

[MCA Madras]

Solution :

Sales	Rs. 40,00,000	
Less : Gross Profit 20% [40,00,000 × 20/100]		8,00,000
Cost of sales		32,00,000

Statement of Working Capital requirements

Current Assets

Raw materials	12,00,000 × 1/12	=	1,00,000
Debtors	(32,00,000 × 3/12)		8,00,000

Finished goods	32,00,000 × 2/12	53,334
Prepaid expenses	[2,00,000 × .5/12]	8,334
Cash in hand		1,00,000
	Total Current Assets	10,61,668

Less : Current Liabilities :

Creditors (12,00,000 × 1/12)	1,00,000
Manufacturing expenses (12,00,000 × 1/12)	1,00,000
Wages [9,60,000 × .5/12]	40,000
Administrative expenses (4,80,000 × 1/12)	40,000
Total current liabilities	2,80,000

Working capital [TCA – TCL]	[10,61,668 – 2,80,000]	7,81,668
Add : 10% Contingency	[7,81,668 × 10/100]	78,167
Working capital required		8,59,835

❏❏❏

27
Capital Budgeting

INTRODUCTION

In the industrial and business world, all the business organisations and industries cannot have surplus money at all the times. And at the same time, they retain a certain sum of money to meet out the day to day operations. It is known as working capital. During the business period, at any time, the company has to face the problem of either replacement of fixed assets or purchase of fixed assets. In this respect, the company needs heavy capital outlay for the purpose of meeting out the capital investment in the fixed assets or development of new project. So, the capital budgeting plays a significant role in the management.

CONCEPT OF CAPITAL EXPENDITURE

Capital expenditure is one which is intended for future periods and generally includes investment in fixed assets and other developmental projects. In other words, capital expenditure is that which has to be incurred for the purpose of obtaining benefit not only for the current year but also for the specific future periods.

CAPITAL BUDGETING—MEANING

Capital budgeting refers to long term planning for the proposed capital outlay and their financing. In other words, it is the process of making investment decisions regarding the capital expenditures. Capital budgeting is also known as investment decision making, capital expenditure decision, planning capital expenditure, etc.

Charles T Horngreen has defined capital budgeting as "Capital budgeting is long term planning for making and financing proposed capital outlays".

According to Lynch "Capital budgeting consists in planning development of available capital for the purpose of maximising the long term profitability of the concern."

Need and Importance of Capital Budgeting

(i) Capital budgeting decision normally involves huge capital. If wrong decision is taken by the firm, it may affect the survival of the firm. So, it is very important for the firm to plan and control capital expenditure.

(ii) Funds involved in capital expenditure are not only huge but more or less permanently blocked in the organisation. In this respect, it involves longer time and greater risk. So careful planning is essential.

CAPITAL BUDGETING

(iii) Long term effect on profitability
(iv) National importance—generation of employment, economic activities and economic growth.
(v) Complications of investment decisions

Advantages of Capital Budgeting

(i) It is very useful to the concern for taking correct decision.
(ii) To determine the required quantum and the right source of funds for investment.
(iii) It influences the firm's growth in the future periods.
(iv) It informs about the right timings for the purchase of fixed assets.
(v) It guides the management for the effective utilisation of investment.
(vi) It minimises the risk of over-investment or under-investment of fund in fixed assets.
(vii) It acts as a tool for controlling capital expenditure.
(viii) It contributes a sound policy for depreciation and replacement of fixed assets.

Limitations of Capital Budgeting

(i) There may be controversial results among the application of various techniques.
(ii) There may be substantial loss in an investment of fund in the capital assets which are irreversible or reversible.
(iii) The application of capital budgeting techniques is normally a difficult task.
(iv) None of the various methods for evaluating profitability of the fixed assets or projects is free from drawbacks.

METHODS OF CAPITAL INVESTMENT PROPOSALS

Investment decisions of organisation may be classified in the following way :

(i) Independent investment proposals
(ii) Mutually exclusive proposals
(iii) Contingent or dependant proposals
(iv) Replacement and modernization schemes
(v) Cost reduction projects

The above said investment proposals are mostly profit-oriented and therefore they may be evaluated based on their cost and benefits.

Even though the investments are made wisely, the return would be difficult to measure on the following projects.

(i) Educational projects
(ii) Service projects
(iii) Research and Development
(iv) Welfare projects.

RELEVANT COST FOR CAPITAL BUDGETING DECISIONS

Normally costs and benefits, in the form of cash inflows, are associated with the capital budgeting. The following costs are generally essential for different types of investment decisions.
- (i) Future costs
- (ii) Opportunity costs
- (iii) Interest cost
- (iv) Incremental or differential cost
- (v) Depreciation and income tax.

CAPITAL BUDGETING PROCESS

The following steps are involved in capital budgeting process.
- (i) The capital budgeting process starts with identification of suitable investment proposals and also estimates the total cash outlay.
- (ii) To establish capital expenditure planning committee for the purpose of screening the various proposals received from various departments.
- (iii) Evaluation of the different investment proposals on the basis of costs and expected returns.
- (iv) To rank the various proposals and to establish the priorities after considering their risk and profitability.
- (v) The proposals recommended by the budget committee are sent to the top management along with a detailed report for final approval.
- (vi) Execution of the selected proposals with sufficient allocation of funds
- (vii) Final stage of the capital budgeting process is an evaluation of the performance of the project after it has been fully implemented.

CAPITAL BUDGETING EVALUATION TECHNIQUES

An organisation may face a situation where various investment proposals are identified but it has to select one or some of the proposals either for shortage of funds or for some other reason. A number of project evaluation techniques are available. The most important and normally used methods are.

(a) *Traditional Methods :*
- (i) Pay-back period or pay-out or pay off method
- (ii) Post pay back profitability methods
- (iii) Accounting rate of return method.

(b) *Time Adjusted Methods or Accounting Methods :*
- (i) Net present value method
- (ii) Internal rate of return method
- (iii) Profitability index or cost benefit ratio method
- (iv) Discounted pay back method.

(a) Traditional Methods

(i) Pay-back Period Method

It is a traditional method for evaluating the profitability of investment proposals. Pay back period is the period in which the project will generate necessary cash to recover

CAPITAL BUDGETING

original investment of the project. Normally, shorter pay back period of the project should be recommended.

Procedure for the calculation of pay back period :

(a) *In the case of even cash inflows*

$$\text{Pay back period} = \frac{\text{Original Cost}}{\text{Annual Cash inflow}}$$

Annual cash inflow = Net savings or net profit + Depreciations

> **NOTE :** Suppose cash inflow is given in the problem, then there is no need to find out cash inflow. If cash inflows are not given in the problem, we have to find out cash inflow.

(b) *In the case of uneven cash inflows*

If cash inflows are not uniform, the calculation of pay back period takes a cumulative way *i.e.,* arriving at net cash inflow until the total is equal to original cost of the project.

(ii) Post Pay Back Profitability Method

Calculation :

Total cash inflow from the Proposal during its economic life	x x
Less : original cost	x x
Post pay back profitability	x x

(iii) Accounting Rate of Return Method [Accounting Method]

This method is otherwise known as accounting rate return method or return on investment or average rate of return method. It can be expressed in the following ways.

(i) Average rate of return $= \dfrac{\text{Average annual profit}}{\text{Original investment}}$

(ii) Return Per unit of investment method

$$\text{Return per unit of investment} = \frac{\text{Total Profit}}{\text{Net Investment}} \times 100$$

(iii) Rate of Return on average investment method

$$\text{Return on average investment} = \frac{\text{Profit after depreciation tax}}{\text{Average investment}}$$

$$\text{Average investment} = \frac{\text{Original Investment}}{2}$$

(iv) Average return on average investment method

$$\text{Average return on average investment} = \frac{\text{Average annual profit}}{\text{Average investment}} \times 100$$

(v) Rate of return on original investment method

$$\text{Return on original investment} = \frac{\text{Profit}}{\text{Original investment}}$$

(b) Time Adjusted Method or Accounting Methods

(i) Net Present Value Method

This method is otherwise known as excess present value or net gain method or time adjusted method

Sum of Discounted cash inflows	xx
Less : original cost	xx
Net present value	xx

If the present value of cash inflows is more than (or equal to) the present value of cash outflows, the project would be accepted. If it is less, the project will be rejected.

(ii) Internal Rate of Return Method

The internal rate of return for an investment proposal is the discount rate that equates the present value of initial cost of the investment with the present value of the expected net cash flows. In other words, it is the rate which discounts the cash flows to zero. Normally, the internal rate of return is found by trial and error method. It can be stated in the following way.

$$\frac{\text{Cash inflows}}{\text{Cash outflows}} = 1$$

Procedure for Calculation

(a) *Where cash inflows are uniform.* In any project, the cash inflows are uniform. The IRR can be calculated by locating the factor in annuity table. The factor is calculated as follows.

$$F = \frac{I}{C}$$

Where, F = Factor to be located
I = Initial Investment
C = Cash inflow per year

The factor, thus calculated, will be located in table II on the line, representing number of years corresponding to estimated useful life of the asset.

(b) *Where cash inflows are not uniform.* The internal rate of return is calculated by making trial and error method.

Procedure

(i) *First trial rate may be calculated in the following way.*

In order to have an approximate idea about the rate, it will be better to find out the factor to be calculated in the following formula.

$$F = \frac{I}{C}$$

The above factor is treated as first trial rate.

(ii) *The second trial rate and third trial rate are determined.*

(iii) *After applying the second and third trial rates, we have to apply the following formula for the purpose of arriving at exact IRR.*

CAPITAL BUDGETING

$$\text{IRR} = \text{Lower trial rate} + \frac{\text{NPV at lower rate}}{\text{NPV at lower rate} - \text{NPV at higher rate}} \times \text{Difference between higher and lower trial rate}$$

(iii) Profitability Index Method

It is a time adjusted method of evaluating profitability of the investment proposals. By calculating the profitability indices for various projects the financial manager can rank the projects according to their profitability.

$$\text{Profitability index} = \frac{\text{Present value of cash inflows}}{\text{Initial cash outlay}}$$

(Or)

$$= \frac{\text{Present value of future cash inflows}}{\text{Present value of future cash outflows}} \times 100$$

Decision Rule

Present value index of the project is equal to or more than 1 or 100% is to be selected.

(iv) Discounted Pay Back Method

Under this method, the present values of all cash inflows and outflows are calculated at an appropriate discount factor. The present values of all inflows are cumulated in order of time. The cumulative present value of cash inflows equals the present value of cash outflows. It is known as discounted pay back period.

For example,

Project cost is xxx

Year	Cash inflow	P/V	DCF
1			
2			
3			
4			
5			

Sum of discounted cash flows equals the cash outflow. It is referred as discounted pay back period. Normally, the project which gives a shorter pay back period under the discounted cash flow is accepted.

CAPITAL RATIONING

Capital rationing situation thus arises when numerous projects may compete for limited resources. It may be defined as "A situation where a constraint is placed on the total size of capital investment during a particular period".

Factors Influencing the Capital Budgeting Decisions

The following factors influence the capital budgeting decisions of the organisation.

(i) Amount of investment

(ii) Cost of capital projects

(iii) Degree of certainty
(iv) Product demand
(v) Future earnings
(vi) Relative importance of the profit
(vii) Opportunity cost
(viii) Cost of production.

RISK ANALYSIS IN CAPITAL BUDGETING

Some of the important techniques of risk analysis in capital budgeting are :
(a) *General techniques* :
   (i) Risk adjusted discount rate
   (ii) Certainty equivalent.
(b) *Quantitative techniques* :
   (i) Sensitivity analysis
   (ii) Probability assignment
   (iii) Standard deviation
   (iv) Co-efficient of variation
   (v) Decision tree.

Problem 1. *Each of the following projects requires a cash outlay of Rs. 10,000. You are required to suggest which project should be accepted if the standard pay back period is 5 years.*

Year	Project X Rs.	Project Y Rs.	Project Z Rs.
1	2500	4000	1000
2	2500	3000	2000
3	2500	2000	3000
4	2500	1000	4000
5	2500	—	—

Solution :

All the three projects recovered their original capital Rs. 10,000 within the period of 4 years. Here project X has constant cash inflow. Project Y initially has higher cash inflows but gradually decreased.

Project Z initially has low cash inflows but it has gradually increased.

As per the constant return point of view, project X is recommended.

Problem 2. *A Company has to choose one of the following two mutually exclusive projects. Both the projects have to be depreciated on straight line basis. The tax rate is 50%.*

CAPITAL BUDGETING

Cash inflows (Profit before Depreciation and tax)

Year	Project A Rs.	Project B Rs.
0	15,000	15,000
1	4,200	4,200
2	4,800	4,500
3	7,000	4,000
4	8,000	5,000
5	2,000	10,000

You have to use pay-back period as the criterion.   [M.SC ITM May 2000 PU]

Solution : Project—A

Year	Profit Rs.	(–) Depreciation Rs.	Profit After Depreciation Rs.	Tax Rs.	PAT Rs.	Add Depreciation Rs.	Cash Inflows Rs.	Cumulative Cash Inflows Rs.
1	4200	3000	1200	600	600	3000	3600	3600
2	4800	3000	1800	900	900	3000	3900	7500
3	7000	3000	4000	2000	2000	3000	5000	12500
4	8000	3000	4000	2000	2000	3000	5000	17500
5	2000	3000	– 1000	—	1000	3000	2000	19500

[PAT = Profit After Tax]

Pay back period = 3 years and 6 months

Working :

Investment is Rs. 15,000

Upto three years i.e., first three years

Capital recovered is Rs. 12,500

Balance of Rs. 2500 recovered during the 4th year

I year	3,600
II year	3,900
III year	5,000
	12,500
Balance	2,500
	15,000

$$= \frac{12 \text{ months}}{5,000} \times 2,500 = \text{How many months ?}$$

Time taken for recovery of this amount of Rs. 2,500 = 6 months. Pay back period
= 3 years 6 months.

Project—B

Year	Profit Rs.	(−) Depreciation Rs.	Profit After Depreciation Rs.	Tax Rs.	PAT Rs.	Add Depreciation Rs.	Cash Inflows Rs.	Cumulative Cash Inflows Rs.
1	4200	3000	1200	600	600	3000	3600	3600
2	4500	3000	1500	750	750	3000	3750	7350
3	4000	3000	1000	500	500	3000	3500	10850
4	5000	3000	2000	1000	1000	3000	4000	14850
5	10000	3000	7000	3500	3500	3000	6500	21350

(PAT = Profit After Tax)

> **NOTE :** If necessary only prepare cumulative cash inflows, otherwise there is no need.
> Pay back period = 4 years and 8 days

Result and decision : Project A is preferable, because it has a shorter pay back period as compared to project A.

Workings　　　　　Initial investment is Rs. 15,000
Its recovered :
　　I year　　　-　　3,600
　　II year　　 -　　3,750
　　III year　　-　　3,500
　　IV year　　-　　4,000
　　　　　　　　　　14,850
　　　　Balance　　　 150
　　　　　　　　　　15,000

Time taken for recovery of this amount Rs. 150/- = 8 days.
For recovery of Rs. 6,500 in the 5th year.
Time required = 365 days.
For recovery of Rs. 150 in the 5th year.

Time required being $\frac{365}{6,500} \times 150 = 8$ days

Depreciation :

　　　　Project A　　　　　　　　　　　　　Project B

$\frac{\text{Cost}}{\text{Life}} = \frac{15,000}{5 \text{ years}} = $ Rs. 3,000　　　　$\frac{15,000}{5 \text{ years}} = $ Rs. 3,000

Problem 3. *Using the information given below, compute the pay-back period under (a) Traditional pay-back method and (b) Discounted pay-back method*

　　Initial outlay　　　　　　　　　　　　Rs. 80,000
　　Estimated life　　　　　5 years

CAPITAL BUDGETING

Profit after tax
End of the years   year 1   Rs. 6,000
                              2   Rs. 14,000
                              3   Rs. 24,000
                              4   Rs. 16,000
                              5   Nil

Depreciation has been calculated under straight line method. The cost of capital may be taken 20% p.a. and the PV of Re. 1 at 20% p.a. is given below.

Year	1	2	3	4	5
P/V factor	83	.69	.58	.48	.40

[MBA Nov.98 Madras] [M.Com Calcutta]

Solution :

Year	PAT (A) Rs.	Add Depreciation Rs.	Profit before Depreciation but after Tax Rs.	P/V factor at 20%	Present Value
1	6,000	+ 16,000	= 22,000	.83	18,260
2	14,000	+ 16,000	= 30,000	.69	20,700
3	24,000	+ 16,000	= 40,000	.58	23,200
4	6,000	+ 16,000	= 22,000	.48	15,360
5	Nil	+ 16,000	= 16,000	.40	6,400
	(PAT = Profit After Tax)			Total present value	83,920
				Less : Initial investment	80,000
				Net Present Value	3,920

(a) *Traditional payback method*

                     I year Rs.   22,000
                     II year Rs.   30,000
     Amount recovered for 2 years   52,000
                   Balance Rs.   28,000
                                               80,000

III year profit is Rs. 40,000. But we require only Rs. 28,000 to meet the original investment of Rs. 80,000.

$$= \frac{12 \text{ months}}{40,000} \times 28,000 = \text{How many months ?}$$

i.e., 2 years 8 months

(b) *Discounted pay back method*

                    I year   18,260
                   II year   20,700

	III year	23,200
	IV year	15,360
		77,520
	Balance Rs.	2,480
	Project cost	80,000

In the V year cash inflow is Rs. 6400. But actually we require only Rs. 2480 to meet the original investment of Rs. 80,000

$$\therefore \frac{12 \text{ months}}{6,400} \times 2,480 = \text{How many months ?}$$

i.e., 4 years 4 months

Pay back period = 4 year 4 months

NOTE : Depreciation :

$$\frac{\text{Cost}}{\text{Life}} = \frac{80,000}{5} = 16,000$$

Problem 4. *A choice is to be made between two competing proposals which require an equal investment of Rs. 50,000 and are expected to generate net cash flows as under.*

Year	Project I Rs.	Project II Rs.	P/V at 10% P.a.
1	25,000	10,000	.909
2	15,000	12,000	.826
3	10,000	18,000	.751
4	Nil	25,000	.683
5	12,000	8,000	.621
6	6,000	4,000	.564

Which project proposal should be chosen and why ? Evaluate the project proposals under discounted cash flow methods. [M.Sc ITM May 2000 Periyar]

Solution :

Net Cash Inflows

Year	Project I Rs.	Project II Rs.
1	25,000	10,000
2	15,000	12,000
3	10,000	18,000
4	Nil	25,000
5	12,000	8,000
6	6,000	4,000

CAPITAL BUDGETING

Pay back period under Traditional method

Project I

I year	25,000
II year	15,000
III year	10,000
	50,000

Pay back period is 3 years.

Project II

I year	10,000
II year	12,000
III year	18,000
	40,000
Balance	10,000
	50,000

∴ 3 years 4 months

$$\frac{2}{25,000} \times 10,000 = 4.8 \ i.e., \ 4$$

As per Traditional pay back period Project I is recommended because it has shorter pay back period.

Discounted cash flow method

	Project I				Project II		
Year	Cash Inflows Rs.	Discount Factor at 10% p.a.	Present Value Rs.	Year	Cash Inflows Rs.	Discount Factor at 10% p.a.	Present Value Rs.
1	25,000	.909	22,725	1	10,000	.909	9,090
2	15,000	.826	12,390	2	12,000	.826	9,912
3	10,000	.751	7,510	3	18,000	.751	13,518
4	Nil	.683	—	4	25,000	.683	17,075
5	12,000	.621	7,452	5	8,000	.621	4,968
6	6,000	.564	3,384	6	4,000	.564	2,256
	Total present value		53,461		Total present value		56,819
	Less : Original Cost		50,000		Less : Original Cost		50,000
	Net Present Value		3,461		Net Present Value		6,819

Criteria	Project X	Project Y
Pay back period	3 years	3 years 4 months
NPV	Rs. 3,491	Rs. 6,819

As per the pay back period point of view, Project X is recommended. But by NPV point of view, Project Y is recommended because it has surplus of Rs. 6,819.

Problem 5. *A project costs Rs. 5,00,000 and yields annually a profit of Rs. 80,000 after depreciation at 12% p.a. but before tax of 50%. Calculate pay back period.*

[M.Sc ITM May 2000 Periyar]

Solution :

$$\text{Pay back period} = \frac{\text{Original Cost}}{\text{Annual Cash Inflows}}$$

Initial investment = Rs. 5,00,000
Cash inflows = Profit after tax plus Depreciation.

	Rs.
Profit before Tax =	80,000
Less : Tax 50% =	40,000
profit after Tax =	40,000
Add : Depreciation =	60,000
Annual cash inflows =	1,00,000

∴ Pay back period = $\frac{5,00,000}{1,00,000}$ = 5 years

NOTE : Depreciation = $5,00,000 \times \frac{12}{100}$ = 60,000.

Problem 6. *ABC Ltd is proposing to take up a project which will need an investment of Rs. 40,000. The net income before depreciation and tax is estimated as follows.*

Year	Rs.
1	10,000
2	12,000
3	14,000
4	16,000
5	20,000

Solution :

Year	Net Income before Depreciation and Tax Rs.	Less Depreciation Rs.	Profit after Depreciation before Tax Rs.	Less Tax 50% Rs.	Profit after Tax and Depreciation Rs.
1	10,000	8,000	2,000	1,000	1,000
2	12,000	8,000	4,000	2,000	2,000
3	14,000	8,000	6,000	3,000	3,000
4	16,000	8,000	8,000	4,000	4,000
5	20,000	8,000	12,000	6,000	6,000

Accounting Rate of Return

(i) *Return on Average Investment Method*

Return = Average profit

= *i.e.,* $\frac{\text{Total Profit}}{\text{No. of Years}}$

CAPITAL BUDGETING

$$= \frac{16,000}{5} = 3,200$$

$$\text{Average investment} = \frac{\text{Original investment}}{2} = \frac{40,000}{2}$$

$$= 20,000$$

$$\text{Return on Average investment} = \frac{3,200}{20,000} \times 100$$

$$= 16\%$$

Problem 7. *Swamy Industries Ltd purchased a machine five years ago. A proposal is under consideration to replace it by a new machine. The life of the machine is estimated to be 10 years. The existing machine can be sold at its written down value. As the cost accountant of the company you are required to submit your recommendations based on the following information.*

Particulars	Existing Machine	New Machine
Initial cost (Rs.)	25,000	50,000
Machine hours P.a.	2,000	2,000
Wages per running hour Rs.	1.25	1.25
Power per hour Rs.	.50	2.00
Indirect material P.a. Rs.	3,000	5,000
Other expenses P.a. Rs.	12,000	15,000
Cost of materials per unit	1	1
Number of units produced Per hour	12	18
Selling price per unit	2	2

Interest to be paid at 10% on fresh capital invested.

Solution :   **Statement of profit and cost**

	Existing Machine Rs.	New machine Rs.
Production p.a. (units)	24,000	36,000
Selling price per unit Rs.	2.00	2.50
Sales value Rs.	48,000	72,000
Expenses :		
(i) Materials	24,000	36,000
(ii) Wages	2,500	2,500
(iii) Power	1,000	4,000
(iv) Indirect material	3,000	5,000
(v) Other expenses p.a.	12,000	15,000
(vi) Depreciation	2,500	5,000
(vii) Interest	—	3,750
	45,000	71,250

	Sales	48,000	72,000
	Less : Total cost	45,000	71,250
	Total profit	3,000	750
(viii)	Cost per unit	1.87	1.98
	Profit per unit	0.13	0.02

Workings :

	Existing Machine	*New Machine*
(i) Cost of material (24,000 × 1)	24,000	36,000 (36,000 × 1)
(ii) Wages (2,000 × 1.25)	2,500	2,500 (2,000 × 1.25)
(iii) Power (2,000 × .50)	1,000	4,000 (2,000 × .2)
	$\frac{45,000}{24,000} = 1.87$	$\frac{71,250}{36,000} = 1.98$
(iv) Cost per unit = $\frac{\text{Total Cost}}{\text{Number of Units}}$		
(v) Interest calculation	Investment in new machine Less : Sale value of the old machine (Rs. 25,000 − Depreciation Rs. 12,500 on fixed instalment system) i.e., $\left(\frac{25,000}{10} = 2,500 \times 5 = 12,500\right)$ Fresh Investment	50,000 12,500 37,500

∴ Interest @ 10% on fresh investment is as follows.

$$37500 \times \frac{10}{100} = 3,750$$

(vi) Depreciation = $\frac{\text{Cost}}{\text{Life}}$ Old machine   New machine

$$\frac{25,000}{10} = 2,500 \qquad \frac{50,000}{10} = 5,000$$

Problem 8. *Rank the following projects on the basis of*
(a) Pay back
(b) Accounting rate of return method
(c) Net present value

Particulars	*Year*	*Project A* *Rs.*	*Project B* *Rs.*	*Project C* *Rs.*
Investment	0	*30,000*	*30,000*	*30,000*
Annual savings	I	*13,800*	*36,150*	—
	II	*13,800*	—	—
	III	*13,800*	—	*46,827*

Discount factor for the year I, II, III, are 0.909, 0.826, 0.751 respectively.

[MBA Madras]

CAPITAL BUDGETING

Solution :

(a) Pay Back

Year	Project A Cash Inflows	Cumulative Cash Inflows	Project B Cash Inflows	Project C Cash Inflows
1	13,800	13,800	36,150	—
2	13,800	27,600	—	—
3	13,800	41,400	—	46,827

A. I year 13,800 + II year 13,800 = 27,600

$$\text{Balance} = 2,400$$
$$\overline{30,000}$$

$\dfrac{12}{13,800} \times 2,400 = 2$ months 8 days *i.e.,* 2 years 2 months 8 days.

B. $\dfrac{12}{36,150} \times 30,000 = 10$ months

C. $\dfrac{12}{46,827} \times 30,000 = 7$ months 23 days

(b) Accounting Rate of Return Method

$$\dfrac{\text{Return}}{\text{Original cost investment}} \times 100$$

Project : A = $\dfrac{13,800}{30,000} \times 100 = 46\%$

Project : B = $\dfrac{12,050}{30,000} \times 100 = 40.16\%$

Project : C = $\dfrac{15,609}{30,000} \times 100 = 52.03\%$

(c) Net Present value

If cost of capital detail is not given in the problem, we have to assume 10% as cut off rate.

Year	Project A Cash Inflows Rs.	P.V. Factor at 10%	Discounted Cash Inflows Rs.	Project B Cash inflows Rs.	Discounted Cash Inflows Rs.	Project C Cash Inflows Rs.	Discounted Cash Inflows Rs.
1	13,800	0.909	12,544.20	36,150	32,860	—	—
2	13,800	0.826	11,398.80	—	—	—	—
3	13,800	0.751	10,363.80	—	—	46,827	35,167
Total present value			34,306.80		32,860		35,167
Less : Initial cost			30,000.00		30,000		30,000
Net Present value			4,306.80		2,860		5,167

Ranking Table

Project	Pay back	Accounting Rate of Return	NPV.
A	III	II	II
B	II	III	III
C	I	I	I

As per the above Ranking table project C is preferable. It gets I rank in the application of all the three techniques. So it is recommended.

Problem 9. *Lal Ltd is considering the purchase of a new machine which will carry out operations performed by labour. A and B are alternative models. Prepare profitability statement and work out pay back period in respect of each machine based upon the following information.*

Particulars	Machine A	Machine B
Estimated life of machine (yrs.)	5	6
Cost of machine (Rs.)	1,50,000	2,50,000
Cost of indirect materials (Rs.)	6,000	8,000
Estimated savings in scrap (Rs.)	10,000	15,000
Additional cost of maintenance (Rs.)	19,000	27,000
Estimated savings in direct wages		
Employees not required (numbers)	150	200
Wages per employee (Rs.)	600	600

Taxation is to be regarded as 50% of profit(ignore depreciation for calculation of tax). Which model would you recommend ? State your reasons. [M.Com May 2000 PU]

Solution :

Profitability Statement

		Machine A Rs.	Machine B Rs.
	Cost of the machine	1,50,000	2,50,000
Savings			
	Estimated saving in scrap	10,000	15,000
	Estimated saving in Direct wages [150 × 600]	90,000	1,20,000
	Total Savings	1,00,000	1,35,000
Expenses			
	Cost of indirect materials	6,000	8,000
	Additional cost of maintenance	19,000	27,000
	Total Expenses	25,000	35,000
	Savings [Savings − Expenses]	75,000	1,00,000
	Less : Tax 50%	37,500	50,000
	Net saving [after tax]	37,500	50,000

CAPITAL BUDGETING

Pay back period

$$\frac{\text{Original Cost}}{\text{Cash Inflow}} = \frac{1,50,000}{37,500} = \frac{2,50,000}{50,000}$$

$$= 4 \text{ years} \quad = 5 \text{ years}$$

Pay back period in case of machine A is 4 years; machine B is 5 years. A has the shorter pay back period so it should be recommended.

> **NOTE :** Here Depreciation is not taken into account.

Problem 10. *A Ltd company is considering to invest in a project requiring a capital outlay of Rs. 2,00,000. Forecast for annual income after depreciation but before tax is as follows.*

Year	Rs.
1	1,00,000
2	1,00,000
3	80,000
4	80,000
5	40,000

Depreciation may be taken as 20% on original cost and taxation at 50% of net income. You are required to evaluate the project according to each of the following methods.

(a) Pay-back method
(b) Rate of return on original investment method
(c) Rate of return on average investment method
(d) Discounted cash flow method taking cost of capital as 10%
(e) Net present value index method
(f) Internal rate of return method

[M.Com Madurai] [MCA Madras]

Solution :

Profitability Statement

Year	Profit after Depreciation Rs.	Less Tax Rs.	PAT Rs.	Add Depreciation Rs.	Profit before Depreciation but after tax Rs.
1	1,00,000	50,000	50,000	40,000	90,000
2	1,00,000	50,000	50,000	40,000	90,000
3	80,000	40,000	40,000	40,000	80,000
4	80,000	40,000	40,000	40,000	80,000
5	40,000	20,000	20,000	40,000	60,000

(a) Pay Back Period

I year		90,000
II year		90,000
		1,80,000
Balance		20,000
		2,00,000

Balance amount recovered from IIIrd year

i.e., $\dfrac{12 \text{ months}}{80{,}000} \times 20{,}000 = 3$ months

∴ Pay back period = 2 years 3 months.

(b) *Rate of Return Original Investment Method*

Year	Net Profit after Tax and depreciation (Rs.)
1	50,000
2	50,000
3	40,000
4	40,000
5	20,000
Total Return	2,00,000

$$\text{Rate of Return on original investment} = \dfrac{\text{Return}}{\text{Original investment}}$$

Return represents the Average Return
Average Return should calculate in the following

$$= \dfrac{\text{Total return}}{\text{Number of years}}$$

$$= \dfrac{2{,}00{,}000}{5}$$

Average Return = Rs. 40,000

Rate of return on original investment = $\dfrac{40{,}000}{2{,}00{,}000} \times 100$

= 20%

(c) *Rate of Return on Average investment method*

$$= \dfrac{\text{Return}}{\text{Average investment}} \times 100$$

Return = Rs. 40,000

Average Investment = $\dfrac{\text{Original investment}}{2}$

$$= \dfrac{2{,}00{,}000}{2} = 1{,}00{,}000$$

Rate of Return on Average investment = $\dfrac{40{,}000}{1{,}00{,}000} \times 100 = 40\%$

CAPITAL BUDGETING

(d) *Discounted cash flow method [Cost of capital @ 10%]*

Year	Cash Inflows	Discount Factor At 10% p.a.	Present Value Rs.
1	90,000	0.909	81,810
2	90,000	0.826	74,340
3	80,000	0.751	60,080
4	80,000	0.683	54,670
5	60,000	0.621	37,260
		Total present value	3,08,130
		Initial Investment	2,00,000
		Net Present value	1,08,130

(e) *Net present value index*

$$\frac{\text{Total present value of cash inflows}}{\text{Total present value of cash outflows}} = \frac{3,08,130}{2,00,000} = 1.541$$

$$1.541 \times 100 = 154.1\%$$

(f) *Internal Rate of Return method.* The annual cash inflows are not uniform. We have to apply the following formula to determine the approximate rate of return.

$$F = \frac{I}{C}$$

F = Factor to be located
I = Initial investment
C = Average annual Cash inflow

$$F = \frac{2,00,000}{80,000}$$

$$= 2.5$$

Showed Table No II at this factor rate of return in the column for 5 years is 28%.

Discounted cash flow [cost of capital @ 28%]

Year	Cash Inflows Rs.	Discount Factor At 28%	Discounted Cash Inflows Rs.
1	90,000	.781	70,290
2	90,000	.610	54,900
3	80,000	.477	38,160
4	80,000	.373	29,840
5	60,000	.291	17,460
		Total Present values	2,10,650
		Less : Initial investment	2,00,000
		Excess Present Value	10,650

NOTE : The present value is higher on the level of Rs. 10,650. Now we apply higher discount rate *i.e.*, taking 30% as cost of capital.

Discounted cash flow at cost of capital is 30%

Year	Cash Inflows Rs.	Discount Factor At 28%	Discounted Cash Inflows Rs.
1	90,000	0.769	69,210
2	90,000	0.592	53,280
3	80,000	0.455	36,400
4	80,000	0.350	28,000
5	60,000	0.269	16,140
		Total present value	2,03,030
		Less : Initial investment	2,00,000
		Excess Present value	3,030

The excess present value at 30% is Rs. 3,030. So the internal rate of return be slightly higher than 30%. Small amount will not affect huge level in the organisation. Hence, internal rate of return is more or less 30%.

Results and Decision :

Investigation of project with the help of all the techniques show that the new project seems to be fairly attractive.

Problem 11. *The directors of Madura limited are contemplating the purchase of new machine to replace a machine which has been in operation in the factory for the last 5 years.*

Ignoring interest but considering tax at 50% of net earnings, suggest which of the two alternatives should be preferred. The following are the details.

Particulars	Old Machine	New Machine
Purchase price (Rs.)	40,000	60,000
Estimated life of machine	10 years	10 years
Machine running hours p.a.	2,000	2,000
Units per hour	24	36
Wages per running hour (Rs.)	3	5.25
Power p.a.	2,000	4,500
Consumable stores p.a.	6,000	7,500
All other charges p.a.	8,000	9,000
Material cost per unit	.50	.50
Selling price per unit	1.25	1.25

You may assume that the above information regarding sales and cost of sales will be held throughout the economic life of each machine. Depreciation has to be charged according to straight line method.

[M.Com Madras]

Solution :
Profitability statement

Particulars		Old Machine		New Machine
Cost of the machine (Rs.)		40,000		60,000
Life of the machine (yrs)		10		10
Output units.		48,000		72,000
Sales value (48,000 × 1.25)		60,000	(72,000×1.25)	90,000
Less : Expenses				
Material 48,000 × .50	24,000		(72,000 × .50) 36,000	
Wages	6,000		10,500	
Power	2,000		4,500	
Consumable stores	6,000		7,500	
Other Charges	8,000		9,000	
Depreciation	4,000	50,000	6,000	73,500
Profit before tax		10,000		16,500
Less : Tax 50%		5,000		8,250
Profit after tax		5,000		8,250

Workings :
Accounting Rate of Return

	Old Machine	New Machine

(i) Return on original investment

$$\frac{\text{Average net earnings}}{\text{Original investment}} \qquad \frac{5,000}{40,000} \times 100 = 12.3\% \qquad \frac{8,250}{60,000} \times 100 = 13.75\%$$

(ii) Return on Average Investment Method

$$\frac{\text{Return}}{\text{Average investment}} \times 100 \qquad \frac{5,000}{20,000} \times 100 = 25\% \qquad \frac{8,250}{30,000} \times 100 = 27.5\%$$

(iii) Return on incremental investment

$$\frac{\text{Incremental earnings}}{\text{Incremental investment}} \times 100$$

$$= \frac{3,250}{20,000} \times 100 = 16.25\% \text{ or } \frac{3,250}{40,000} \times 100 = 8\%$$

> **NOTE :**
> Incremental earning = 6250 − 5000 = 1250
> Incremental investment = 60,000 − 40,000 = 20,000

Result : Recommended to replace an old machinery.

Problem 12. *A project costs Rs. 1,00,000 and yields an annual cash inflow of Rs. 20,000 for 7 years. Calculate pay back period.*

Solution :

$$\text{Pay back period} = \frac{\text{Initial investment}}{\text{Annual cash inflow}}$$

Initial investment is = Rs. 1,00,000

Annual cash inflow Rs. = Rs. 20,000

$$\text{Pay back period} = \frac{1,00,000}{20,000} = 5 \text{ years}$$

Problem 13. *Himalaya Construction Ltd is considering the purchase of a new machine for its immediate expansion programme. There are three possible machines suitable for the purpose. Their details are as follows :*

	Machines		
	1 Rs.	2 Rs.	3 Rs.
Capital cost	3,00,000	3,00,000	3,00,000
Sales at standard price	5,00,000	4,00,000	4,00,000
Net cost of production :			
Direct material	40,000	50,000	48,000
Direct labour	50,000	30,000	36,000
Factory overheads	60,000	50,000	58,000
Administration costs	20,000	10,000	15,000
Selling and distribution costs	10,000	10,000	10,000

The economic life of machine No.1 is 2 years while it is 3 years for the other two. The scrap values are Rs. 40,000, Rs. 25,000 and Rs. 30,000 respectively.

Sales are expected to be at the rates shown for each year during the full economic life of expenditure resulting from each machine.

Tax to be paid is expected at 50% of the net earnings of each year. It may be assumed that all payables and receivables will be settled promptly, strictly on cash basis with no outstanding from one accounting year to another. Interest on capital has to be paid at 8% p.a.

You are requested to show which machine would be the most profitable investment on the principle of "Pay-back method".

[B.Com. PU]

Solution :   **Profitability Statement**

Particulars	Machine I Rs.	Machine II Rs.	Machine III Rs.
Capital Cost	3,00,000	3,00,000	3,00,000
Sales (i)	5,00,000	4,00,000	4,50,000
Less : Expenses			
Cost of production	1,50,000	1,30,000	1,42,000
Administration cost	20,000	10,000	15,000
Selling and distribution cost	10,000	10,000	10,000
Total Cost II	1,80,000	1,50,000	1,67,000
Profit before depreciation and interest [S − TC] [i − ii] (iii)	3,20,000	2,50,000	2,83,000
Less : Depreciation	1,30,000	91,667	90,000
Interest on borrowings	24,000	24,000	24,000

CAPITAL BUDGETING

Depreciation and interest (iv)	1,54,000	1,15,667	1,14,000
Profit before tax (iii – iv = v)	1,66,000	1,34,333	1,69,000
Less : Tax 50%	83,000	67,167	84,500
Profit after tax	83,000	67,167	84,500
Add : Depreciation	1,30,000	91,667	90,000
Net cash inflows	2,13,000	1,58,834	1,74,500
(a) Pay back period	1.41 years	1.89 years	1.72 years

Result : Machine I is preferable because it has shorter payback period as compared to the other machine.

Working :
(a) *Pay back Period*
Machine I

		Rs.
	I year	2,13,000
	Balance	87,000
		3,00,000

$$= \frac{12 \text{ month}}{2,13,000} \times 87,000$$

= How many months ? = 4 months

= 1 year 4 months

Machine II

	I year	1,58,834
	Balance	1,41,166
		3,00,000

$$= \frac{12 \text{ month}}{1,58,834} \times 1,41,166 = 10 \text{ months}$$

Pay back period 1 year 10 months

Machine III

	I year	1,74,500
	Balance	1,25,500
		3,00,000

$$= \frac{12}{1,74,500} \times 1,25,500 = 8.62 \text{ i.e., } 9 \text{ months}$$

= 1 year 9 months

	Machine I	Machine II	Machine III
Payback period	1 year 4 months	1 year 10 months	1 year 9 months

Result : As per the pay back period point of view, machine I is preferable because it has a shorter pay back.

(b) Depreciation

	Machine I	Machine II	Machine III
Cost − Scrap / Life	$\dfrac{3{,}00{,}000 - 40{,}000}{2}$ 1,30,000	$\dfrac{3{,}00{,}000 - 25{,}000}{3}$ 91,667	$\dfrac{3{,}00{,}000 - 30{,}000}{3}$ 90,000

Problem 14. *The ABTS Co Ltd is considering the purchase of a new machine. Two alternative machines (A and B) have been suggested each having an initial cost of Rs. 4,00,000 and requiring Rs. 20,000 as additional working capital at the end of the 1st year. Earnings after taxation are expected to be as follows.*

Year	Cash Inflows	
	A Rs.	B Rs.
1	40,000	1,20,000
2	1,20,000	1,60,000
3	1,60,000	2,00,000
4	2,40,000	1,20,000
5	1,60,000	80,000

The company has target return on capital of 10% and on this basis, you are required to compare the profitability of the machines and state which alternatives you consider financially preferable.

Note : *The following table gives the present value of Re. 1 due in 'n' number of years.*

Year	1	2	3	4	5
P/V at 10%	.91	.83	.75	.68	.62

[M.Com Madras]

Solution :

Present Value Statement
Machine A

Year	Cash Inflows Rs.	Discount Factor At 10%	Present Value Rs.
1	40,000	.91	36,400
2	1,20,000	.83	99,600
3	1,60,000	.75	1,20,000
4	2,40,000	.68	1,63,200
5	1,60,000	.62	99,200
Total Present value of cash inflows			5,18,400
Less : Total Present value of cash outflows (4,00,000 + 20,000 × .91)			4,18,200
		Net present value	1,00,200

CAPITAL BUDGETING

Machine B

Year	Cash Inflows Rs.	Discount Factor At 10%	Present Value Rs.
1	1,20,000	.91	1,09,200
2	1,60,000	.83	1,32,800
3	2,00,000	.75	1,50,000
4	1,20,000	.68	81,600
5	80,000	.62	49,600
Total Present value of cash inflows			5,23,200
Less : Total Present value of cash outflows (4,00,000 + 20,000 × .91)			4,18,200
		Net present value	1,05,000

Result : Machine B is preferable because it has a higher net present value as compared to Machine A. So machine B is recommended for purchase.

Problem 15. *A Company is considering two mutually exclusive projects. Both require an initial cash outlay of Rs. 10,000 each and have a life of 5 years. The company's required rate of return is 10% and pays tax at 50%. The project will be depreciated on a straight line basis. The before tax cash flows expected to be generated by the project are as follows.*

	Before Tax	Cash Flows			
Year	1	2	3	4	5
Project A	4,000	4,000	4,000	4,000	4,000
Project B	5,000	5,000	2,000	5,000	5,000

Calculate for each project :
  (i) *The payback*   (iii) *NPV*
  (ii) *The accounting rate of return*   (iv) *PI*
Which project should be accepted and why ?   [MBA Anna Dec 2003]

Solution :

Profitability Statement
Project A

Year	Cash Flows Rs.	Less Depreciation Rs.	PBT Rs.	Less Tax Rs.	PAT Rs.	Add Depreciation Rs.	Cash Inflow (profit after tax but before depreciation)
1	4000	2000	2000	1000	1000	+ 2000	3000
2	4000	2000	2000	1000	1000	+ 2000	3000
3	4000	2000	2000	1000	1000	+ 2000	3000
4	4000	2000	2000	1000	1000	+ 2000	3000
5	4000	2000	2000	1000	1000	+ 2000	3000

(i)   Pay back period = 3 years 4 months

I year	3,000
II year	3,000
III year	3,000
	9,000
Balance	1,000
	10,000

To recover balance amount of Rs. 1000 for how many months

$$\therefore \frac{12}{3,000} \times 1,000 = 4$$

i.e., = 3 years 4 months

(ii) Accounting Rate of Return = $\dfrac{\text{Return}}{\text{Original investment}} \times 100$

Return = Average Profit

Average profit = $\dfrac{\text{Total Profit}}{\text{Number of Years}} = \dfrac{15,000}{5} = 3,000$

= $\dfrac{3,000}{10,000} \times 100 = 30\%$

Project B

Year	PBT Rs.	Less Depreciation Rs.	PBT Rs.	Less Tax 50% Rs.	PAT Rs.	Add Depreciation Rs.	Profit after tax but before depreciation
1	5000	2000	3000	1500	1500	2000	3500
2	5000	2000	3000	1500	1500	2000	3500
3	2000	2000	0	0	0	2000	2000
4	5000	2000	3000	1500	1500	2000	3500
5	5000	2000	3000	1500	1500	2000	3500

(i)   Pay back period = 3 years 3 months

I year	3,500
II year	3,500
III year	2,000
	9,000
Balance	1,000
	10,000

To recover balance amount of Rs. 1000 in how many months

$$\frac{12}{3,500} \times 1,000 = 3 \text{ months}$$

CAPITAL BUDGETING

(ii) ARP : $\dfrac{\text{Return}}{\text{Original cost}} \times 100$, i.e., Return = Average Profit

$$\text{Average profit} = \dfrac{\text{Total Profit}}{\text{No. of Years}} = \dfrac{16{,}000}{5} = \dfrac{3{,}200}{10{,}000} \times 100 = 32\%$$

Statement showing net present value

	Project I			Project II		
Year	Cash Inflows Rs.	P/V fact at at 10% Rs.	Disounted Cash Inflows Rs.	Cash Inflows Rs.	P/V Factor at 10% Rs.	Discounted Cash Inflows Rs.
1	3,000	.090	2727	3,500	.909	3181.50
2	3,000	.826	2478	3,500	.826	2891.00
3	3,000	.751	2253	2,000	.751	1502.00
4	3,000	.683	2049	3,500	.683	2390.00
5	3,000	.621	1863	3,500	.621	2173.50
Total present value of cash inflows Less : Initial cost			11,370 10,000			12,138.00 10,000.00
Net Present value			1,370			2,138.00

$$\text{Profitability index} = \dfrac{\text{Sum of discounted cash inflows}}{\text{Cash outflow}} \times 100$$

Project A

$$\text{Profitability index} = \dfrac{11{,}370}{10{,}000} \times 100 = 113.7\%$$

Project B

$$\text{Profitability index} = \dfrac{12{,}138}{10{,}000} \times 100 = 121.38\%$$

Result :

Project	Pay back	ARR	NPV	PI
A	II	II	II	II
B	I	I	I	I

Result :

In all the four techniques project B is preferable. Because in all the four aspects project B should get I Rank. So it should be recommended.

Problem 16. *Calculate the net present value for a small sized project requiring an initial investment of Rs. 20,000 and which provides a net cash inflow of Rs. 6000 each year for six years. Assume the cost of funds to be 8% p.a. and that there is no scrap value.*

[M.Com adapted]

Solution :

The present value of an annuity of Re. 1 for 6 years at 8% p.a., as per the annuity table is Rs. 4,623.

Hence, the present value of Rs. 6,000 is

$$6,000 \times 4.623 = 27,738$$
$$\text{Less : original cost} = 20,000$$
$$\text{Net present value} = 7,738$$

Problem 17. *The initial cost of an equipment is Rs. 3,00,000. Cash inflows for 5 years are estimated to be Rs. 2,00,000 per year. Desired rate of return is 15%. Calculate the net present value and excess present value index.* [Dec 2004] [MBA Anna]

Solution : Present value of Re. 1 received annually for 5 years at 15% as per annuity Table = 3.352. Present value of Rs. 2,00,000 received annually for 5 years

Rs.

$$2,00,000 \times 3.352 = 6,70,400$$
$$\text{Less : original cost of the equipment} = 3,00,000$$
$$\text{Net present value} = 3,70,400$$

$$\text{Excess present value index} = \frac{\text{Total present value of cash inflows}}{\text{Total present value of cash outflows}}$$

$$= \frac{6,70,000}{3,00,000} \times 100 = \mathbf{223.4}$$

Problem 18. *KVP Ltd is considering the purchase of a new machine for Rs. 1,20,000. It has a life of 4 years and an estimated scrap value of Rs. 20,000. The machine will generate an extra revenue of Rs. 4,00,000 p.a. and has an additional operating cost of Rs. 3,20,000 p.a. The company's cost of capital is 20% and tax rate 50%. Should the machine be purchased or not ?* [MBA Madras]

Solution :   **Profitability Statement**

	Rs.
Annual revenue	4,00,000
Less : Operational costs	3,20,000
Net income before depreciation and tax	80,000
Initial investment	1,20,000
Less : Scrap	20,000
	1,00,000

Life of the machinery = 4 years

$$\text{Depreciation} = \frac{1,00,000}{4} = 25,000$$

Tax Rate = 50%

CAPITAL BUDGETING

Net income before Depreciation and tax is Rs.	80,000
Less : Depreciation	25,000
	55,000
Less : Tax 50%	27,500
Net income after Tax and Depreciation	27,500
Add : Depreciation	25,000
Cash inflows	52,500

Present value of Re. 1 for 4 years at 20%
52,500 × 2.588 = 1,29,400
Less : initial investment
[1,00,000 + 10,000 × .482] = 1,09,640
Net present value = 19,760

Result : As per the calculation there could be a positive NPV, so the machine may be purchased.

Problem 19. *Sumanth & Co Ltd is considering building an assembly plant. The decision has been narrowed down to two possibilities. The company desires to choose the best plant at a level of operations of 10,000 gadgets a month. Both plants have expected life of 10 years and are expected not to have any salvage value at the time of their retirement. The cost of capital is 10%. Suggest what should be the desirable choice.*

Cost of monthly output of 10,000 units.

	Large Plant Rs.	Small Plant Rs.
Initial cost	30,00,000	22,93,500
Direct labours : First half	18,00,000 (p.a.)	7,80,000 (p.a.)
Second half	—	9,00,000 (p.a.)
Overheads :	2,40,000 (p.a.)	2,10,000 (p.a.)

The present value of an ordinary annuity of Re. 1 for 10 years at 10% is 6.1446.

Solution :   **Profitability Statement**

		Rs.
Direct labour for small plant for both shifts (7,80,000 + 9,00,000)		16,80,000
Direct labour for large plant		15,00,000
Savings in indirect labour (using large plant)		1,80,000
Overhead costs for small plant =	2,10,000	
Less : overhead costs for large plant =	2,40,000	– 30,000
Net savings p.a. by using large plant		1,50,000

Present value of Re 1 saved annually for 10 years   6.1446

$$\begin{aligned}\text{Present value of Rs. 1,50,000 saved annually for 10 years} &= 1,50,000 \times 6.1446 \\ &= 9,21,690\end{aligned}$$

Cost of the large plant = 30,00,000
Cost of the small plant = 22,93,500

7,06,500

Present value of savings from large plant   9,21,690
Less : Additional cost of large plant   7,06,500

Net present value   2,15,190

Result : In the above computation the net present value is positive. So it is advisable to go in for the installation of large plant.

Problem 20. *PRP Ltd is evaluating two mutually exclusive proposals for new capital investment. The following information about the proposals are available.*

Particulars	Proposal A	Proposal B
Investment cost (Rs.)	80,000	1,00,000
Economic life (yrs)	4	5
Earnings before depreciation and tax	Rs.	Rs.
1	24,000	28,000
2	28,000	32,000
3	32,000	36,000
4	44,000	44,000
5	—	4,000

The company's cost of capital is 10% and tax rate is 50%. Advise the company as to which proposal would be profitable, using NPV technique.   [MCA Madras]

Solution :   **Statement Showing Profitability**

Proposal A

Year	Cash Inflows Rs.	Less Depreciation Rs.	PBT Rs.	Less Tax 50% Rs.	PAT Rs.	Add Depreciation Rs.	Cash Inflows (profit after tax but before Depreciation)
1	24,000	20,000	4,000	2,000	2,000	20,000	22,000
2	28,000	20,000	8,000	4,000	4,000	20,000	24,000
3	32,000	20,000	12,000	6,000	6,000	20,000	26,000
4	44,000	20,000	24,000	12,000	12,000	20,000	32,000
5	—	20,000	—	—	—	20,000	20,000

CAPITAL BUDGETING

Proposal B

Year	Cash Inflows Rs.	Less Depreciation Rs.	PBT Rs.	Less Tax 50% Rs.	PAT Rs.	Add Depreciation Rs.	Cash Inflows (profit after tax but before Depreciation)
1	28,000	20,000	8,000	4,000	4,000	20,000	24,000
2	32,000	20,000	12,000	6,000	6,000	20,000	26,000
3	36,000	20,000	16,000	8,000	8,000	20,000	28,000
4	44,000	20,000	24,000	12,000	12,000	20,000	32,000
5	4,000	20,000	16,000	—	—	20,000	20,000

NOTE : Calculation of Depreciation

Proposal A: $\dfrac{\text{Cost}}{\text{Life}} = \dfrac{80,000}{4} = 20,000$

Proposal B: $\dfrac{\text{Cost}}{\text{Life}} = \dfrac{1,00,000}{5} = 20,000$

Statement Showing Net Present Values

		Proposal A		Proposal B	
Year	Discount Factor	Cash Inflows Rs.	Present Value (Cash inflows × P/V factor) Rs.	Cash Inflows Rs.	Present Value (Cash inflows × P/V factor) Rs.
1	.909	22,000	22,000 × .909 = 19,998	24,000	24,000 × .909 = 21,816
2	.826	24,000	24,000 × .826 = 19,824	26,000	26,000 × .826 = 21,476
3	.751	26,000	26,000 × .751 = 19,526	28,000	28,000 × .751 = 21,028
4	.683	32,000	32,000 × .683 = 21,856	32,000	32,000 × .683 = 21,856
5	.621	20,000	20,000 × .621 = 12,420	20,000	20,000 × .621 = 12,420
		Total Present Value	93,624		98,596
		Less : Initial investment	80,000		1,00,000
		Net Present value	13,624		– 1,404

Result : Proposal A is recommended. Because it has the positive NPV.

Problem 21.

Initial outlay — Rs. 50,000
Life of the asset — 5 years
Estimated cash flows — Rs. 12,500

Calculate internal rate of Return.
(Cash inflows are uniform).

Solution :

$$\text{Present value factor} = \dfrac{\text{Initial investment}}{\text{Annual cash inflow}} = \dfrac{50,000}{12,500} = 4$$

To refer the Annuity Table II, the present value factor of 4 is located in the column of 5 years. The figure 3.9927 (nearer to 4) is found in the row of 8% so the internal rate of return is 8%.

Problem 22.

Initial Investment : Rs. 60,000
Life of the asset : 4 years
Estimated net annual Cash flows
    I yr   Rs. 15,000
    II yr   Rs. 20,000
    III yr   Rs. 30,000
    IV yr   Rs. 20,000

Calculate internal rate of return.   [MBA Anna May 2005]

Solution :

Present value of Re. 1 due in 'n' number of years.

Year	P/V factor at 10%	P/V factor at 12%	P/V factor at 14%	P/V factor at 15%
1	.909	.892	.877	.869
2	.826	.797	.769	.756
3	.751	.711	.674	.657
4	.683	.635	.592	.571

Statement Showing Cash Inflows at Various Discount rates of 10%, 12%, 14%, and 15%

Year	Annual Cash Inflows Rs.	Discount Factor at 10%	Present Value Rs.	Discount Factor at 12%	Present Value Rs.	Discount Factor at 14%	Present Value Rs.	Discount Factor at 15%	Present Value Rs.
1	15,000	.909	13,635	.892	13,380	.877	13,155	.869	13,035
2	20,000	.856	16,520	.797	15,940	.769	15,380	.756	15,120
3	30,000	.751	22,530	.711	21,330	.674	20,220	.657	19,710
4	20,000	.683	13,660	.635	12,700	.592	11,840	.571	11,420
			66,345		63,350		60,595		59,285

At the time of applying 14% of Discount rate, the present value of cash inflows is more or less equal to the outflows. So 14% is taken as the Internal Rate of Return. If we want the exact IRR the following techniques will be applicable.

At 14% total present value = 60,595
At 15% total present value = 59,285
                                 1,310

For the difference of 1,310, the difference in rate = 1%

For a difference of 595, what will be the difference in rate ?

$$= \frac{1}{1,310} \times 595 = .45$$

$$\therefore \quad \text{IRR} = 14\% + 0.45\% = 14.45\%$$

Problem 23. *Balimer Ltd has a machine having an additional life of 5 years which costs Rs. 50,000 and which has a book value of Rs. 20,000. If it is sold, it will fetch Rs. 5,000. A new machine costing Rs. 1,00,000 is available. Though, its capacity is the same as that of the old machine. It will mean a saving in variable cost to the extent of Rs. 40,000 p.a. The life of machine will be 5 years at the end of which it will have a scrap value of Rs. 10,000. The rate of income tax is 50% and the company does not make an investment unless it must if it yields less than 12%. Advise the company whether the old machine should be replaced or not.* [MBA Anna 2004]

Solution : Cash inflow if the new machine is installed

	Rs.
Gross savings in variable costs	40,000
Less : Depreciation (1,00,000 – 10,000) ÷ 5	18,000
Profit after depreciation	22,000
Less : tax 50%	11,000
Profit after Tax	11,000
Add : Depreciation	18,000
Total cash inflows	29,000
Present value of Re. 1 receivable annually for 5 years @ 12%	3.605
Present value of cash inflow for 5 years at 12% (29,000 × 3.605)	1,04,545
Present value of scrap value of Rs. 10,000 at the end of 5 years @ 12% (10,000 × 0.567)	5,670
Cash received from sale of old plant	5,000

Tax saving : Book value of old plant	20,000	
Sale price of old plant	5,000	
Loss	15,000	
Tax saved 50% (due to loss of Rs. 15,000) Rs. 7,500 available at the end of one year (0.893 × 7,500)		6,698
Total cash inflows		1,21,913
Cash outflows		1,00,000
Net present value		21,913

Result : The net present value is positive. So the replacement proposal is accepted.

Problem 24. *A company is considering to expand its production. It can go either for an automatic machine costing Rs. 2,24,000 with an estimated life of 5½ years or an ordinary machine costing Rs. 60,000 having an estimated the life of 8 years. The annual sales and costs are estimated as follows.*

	Automatic Machine Rs.	Ordinary Machine Rs.
Sales	1,50,000	1,50,000
Cost :		
Material	50,000	50,000
Labour	12,000	60,000
Variable OHS	24,000	12,000

Compute the comparative profitability of the proposals under pay back period and return on investment method. Explain the difference in the results obtained under the two methods.

[B.Com. PU, M.Com Madurai]

Solution :   **Profitability Statement**

	Automatic Machine Rs.	Ordinary Machine Rs.
Cost of the machine	2,24,000	60,000
Sales	1,50,000	1,50,000
Less : Variable Cost	86,000	1,30,000
Contribution or Annual cash inflow	64,000	20,000
Pay back period = $\dfrac{\text{Original cost}}{\text{Cash inflow}}$	$\dfrac{2,24,000}{64,000}$ = 3½ years	$\dfrac{60,000}{20,000}$ = 3 years

Profit after the pay back period

Automatic machine = 64,000 × 2 (5½ years – 3 ½ years) = Rs. 1,28,000

Ordinary machine = 20,000 × 5 (8 years – 3 years) = Rs. 1,00,000

On the basis of the payback period only, ordinary machine should be recommended. Because it has shorter payback period. But in the case of full life of the asset, the automatic machine is preferable, because it gives a surplus amount of Rs. 1,28,000. But ordinary machine gives only Rs. 1,00,000 for the 8 years.

Problem 25. *A project cost of Rs. 20,00,000 yielded annually a profit of Rs. 3,00,000 after depreciation @ 12½% and is subject to income tax @ 50%. Calculate pay back period.*

[MCA Dec 2001]

Solution :

Pay back period = $\dfrac{\text{Initial investment}}{\text{Annual cash inflow}}$

Initial investment = Rs. 20,00,000

Annual cash inflows = Profit after Tax + Depreciation

Profit before Tax   3,00,000
Less : Tax 50%   1,50,000

Profit after tax   1,50,000
Add : Depreciation
$(20,00,000 \times \frac{12.5}{100})$ 2,50,000

Annual Cash inflow   4,00,000

$$\text{Pay back period} = \frac{20,00,000}{4,00,000} = 5 \text{ years}$$

Problem 26. *Rank the projects according to their desirability under the pay back method and accounting rate of returns method assuming the cost of capital is 10%.*

Project	Initial Investment Rs.	Annual cash flows Rs.	Life in years
A	60,000	12,000	15
B	88,000	22,500	22
C	2150	1500	03
D	20,500	4500	10
E	4,25,000	2,25,000	20

[B.E. Anna June 2005]

Solution :

I. Ranking of the project according to pay back

Project	Initial Investment Rs.	Annual Cash Inflows (Rs.)	Payback Period in Years	Rank
A	60,000	12,000	$\frac{60,000}{12,000} = 5$	V
B	88,000	22,500	$\frac{88,000}{22,500} = 3.91$	III
C	2150	1500	$\frac{2,150}{1,500} = 1.43$	I
D	20,500	4,500	$\frac{20,500}{4,500} = 4.55$	IV
E	4,25,000	2,25,000	$\frac{4,25,000}{2,25,000} = 1.88$	II

II. Ranking of project according to accounting rate of return method

$$\text{Formula} = \frac{\text{Return}}{\text{Original investment}} \times 100$$

Project	Annual Cash Inflow Rs.	Less Depreciation Rs.	Profit Rs.	Accounting Rate of Retrun Rs.	Rank
A	12,000	– 4,000	8,000	$\frac{8,000}{60,000} \times 100 = 13.33\%$	IV
B	22,500	– 4000	18,500	$\frac{18,500}{88,000} \times 100 = 21.02\%$	III
C	1,500	– 717	783	$\frac{783}{2,150} \times 100 = 36.41\%$	II
D	4,500	– 2050	2,450	$\frac{2,450}{20,500} \times 100 = 11.95\%$	V
E	2,25,000	– 21,250	2,03,750	$\frac{2,03,750}{4,25,000} \times 100 = 47.94\%$	I

Ranking of project

Project	Pay back	Accounting Rate
A	5	4
B	3	3
C	1	2
D	4	5
E	2	1

Result : As the pay back period point of view, project C has 1st Rank, so it should be recommended. But in the case of Accounting Rate of Return point of view, project E gets 1st Rank. So it should be recommended.

Problem 27. *If expected rate of return is 30% do you recommend the following projects.*

	Project A Rs.	Project B Rs.
Capital cost	1,00,000	1,50,000
Annual Savings	30,000	50,000
Annual Savings	30,000	70,000
Annual Savings	40,000	80,000
Annual Savings	50,000	50,000

[MBA Madras Nov 1998]

CAPITAL BUDGETING

Solution :

	Project A		Project B	
Year	Cash Inflows Rs.	Cumulative Cash Inflows Rs.	Cash Inflows Rs.	Cumulative Cash Inflows Rs.
1	30,000	30,000	50,000	50,000
2	30,000	60,000	70,000	1,20,000
3	40,000	1,00,000	80,000	2,00,000
4	50,000	1,50,000	50,000	2,50,000

I.   Pay back period A = 3 years

         Pay back period B = 2 years 4 months

B :   I year   Rs.   50,000

         II year   Rs.   70,000

                           1,20,000

         Balance   30,000

                           1,50,000

$$\frac{12}{80,000} \times 30,000 = 4$$

i.e., 2 years 4 months

II. Return on Investment

         Return = Average Return

         i.e., = $\frac{\text{Total Profit}}{\text{Number of Years}}$

         Project A = $\frac{1,50,000}{4}$ = 37,500

         Investment = Average investment

         Average investment = $\frac{\text{Original investment}}{2}$

         = **50,000**

Project A :   = $\frac{37,500}{50,000} \times 100$ = **75%**

Project B :   Return = $\frac{2,50,000}{4}$ = 62,500

         Average Investment = $\frac{1,50,000}{2}$ = 75,000

∴ $\frac{62,500}{75,000} \times 100$ = **83.3%**

The expected return is only 30%, but actual return in both the projects is more than the expected rate. So both the projects are recommended.

◻◻◻

Solution :

	Project A		Project B	
Year	Cash Inflows Rs.	Cumulative Cash Inflows Rs.	Cash Inflows Rs.	Cumulative Cash Inflows Rs.
1	30,000	30,000	50,000	50,000
2	50,000	80,000	70,000	1,20,000
3	40,000	1,20,000	80,000	2,00,000
4	30,000	1,50,000	80,000	2,80,000

Pay back period A = 3 years

Pay back period B = 2 years 4 months

  I year   Rs. 50,000
  II year   Rs. 70,000
        1,20,000
  Balance   30,000
        1,50,000

$$\frac{12}{80,000} \times 30,000 = 4$$

i.e., 2 years 4 months

II. Return on Investment

$$\text{Return} = \text{Average Return}$$

$$= \frac{\text{Total Profit}}{\text{Number of Years}}$$

Project A = $\frac{1,50,000}{4}$ = 37,500

$$\text{Investment} = \text{Average Investment}$$

$$\text{Average investment} = \frac{\text{Original Investment}}{2}$$

$$= \frac{50,000}{2}$$

Project A : $= \frac{37,500}{50,000} \times 100 = 75\%$

Project B : Return $= \frac{2,80,000}{4} = 62,500$

Average Investment $= \frac{1,50,000}{2} = 75,000$

$$\frac{62,500}{75,000} \times 100 = 83.3\%$$

The expected return is only 30%, but actual return in both the projects is more than the expected rate. So both the projects are remunerative.

APPENDIX

Appendix 1

TABLE I
Present Value of Re. 1

Years	5%	6%	8%	10%	12%	14%	15%	16%	18%	20%	22%	24%	25%	28%	30%
1	0.952	0.943	0.926	0.909	0.893	0.877	0.870	0.862	0.847	0.833	0.820	0.806	0.800	0.781	0.769
2	0.907	0.890	0.857	0.826	0.797	0.769	0.756	0.743	0.718	0.694	0.672	0.650	0.640	0.610	0.592
3	0.864	0.840	0.794	0.751	0.712	0.675	0.658	0.641	0.609	0.579	0.551	0.524	0.512	0.477	0.455
4	0.823	0.792	0.735	0.683	0.636	0.592	0.572	0.552	0.516	0.482	0.451	0.423	0.410	0.373	0.350
5	0.784	0.747	0.681	0.621	0.567	0.519	0.497	0.476	0.437	0.402	0.370	0.341	0.328	0.291	0.269
6	0.746	0.705	0.630	0.564	0.507	0.456	0.432	0.410	0.370	0.335	0.303	0.275	0.262	0.227	0.207
7	0.711	0.665	0.583	0.513	0.452	0.400	0.376	0.354	0.314	0.279	0.249	0.222	0.210	0.178	0.159
8	0.647	0.627	0.570	0.467	0.404	0.351	0.327	0.305	0.266	0.233	0.204	0.179	0.168	0.139	0.123
9	0.645	0.592	0.500	0.424	0.361	0.308	0.284	0.263	0.225	0.193	0.167	0.144	0.134	0.108	0.094
10	0.614	0.558	0.463	0.386	0.322	0.270	0.247	0.227	0.191	0.162	0.137	0.116	0.107	0.085	0.073
11	0.585	0.527	0.429	0.350	0.287	0.237	0.215	0.195	0.162	0.135	0.112	0.094	0.087	0.066	0.056
12	0.557	0.497	0.397	0.319	0.257	0.208	0.187	0.168	0.137	0.112	0.092	0.076	0.069	0.052	0.043
13	0.530	0.469	0.368	0.290	0.229	0.182	0.163	0.145	0.116	0.093	0.075	0.061	0.055	0.040	0.033
14	0.505	0.442	0.340	0.263	0.205	0.160	0.141	0.125	0.099	0.078	0.062	0.049	0.044	0.032	0.025
15	0.481	0.417	0.315	0.239	0.183	0.140	0.123	0.108	0.084	0.065	0.051	0.040	0.035	0.025	0.020
16	0.458	0.394	0.292	0.218	0.163	0.123	0.107	0.093	0.071	0.054	0.042	0.032	0.028	0.019	0.015
17	0.436	0.371	0.270	0.198	0.147	0.108	0.093	0.080	0.060	0.045	0.034	0.026	0.023	0.015	0.012
18	0.416	0.350	0.250	0.180	0.130	0.095	0.081	0.069	0.051	0.038	0.028	0.021	0.018	0.012	0.009
19	0.396	0.331	0.232	0.164	0.116	0.083	0.070	0.060	0.043	0.031	0.023	0.017	0.014	0.009	0.007
20	0.377	0.312	0.215	0.149	0.104	0.073	0.061	0.051	0.037	0.026	0.019	0.014	0.012	0.007	0.005

Appendix 2

TABLE II
Present Value of Re. 1 Received Annually for N Years

Years	5%	6%	8%	10%	12%	14%	15%	16%	18%	20%	22%	24%	25%	28%	30%
1	0.952	0.943	0.926	0.909	0.893	0.877	0.870	0.862	0.847	0.833	0.820	0.806	0.800	0.781	0.769
2	1.859	1.883	1.783	1.736	1.690	1.647	1.626	1.605	1.566	1.528	1.492	1.457	1.440	1.392	1.361
3	2.773	2.676	2.577	2.847	2.402	2.322	2.283	2.246	2.174	2.016	2.042	1.981	1.952	1.868	1.816
4	3.546	3.465	3.312	3.170	3.037	2.914	2.855	2.798	2.690	2.589	2.494	2.404	2.362	2.241	2.166
5	4.330	4.212	3.993	3.791	3.605	3.433	3.352	3.274	3.127	2.991	2.864	2.745	2.689	2.532	2.346
6	5.076	4.917	4.623	4.335	4.111	3.889	3.784	3.685	3.498	3.326	3.167	3.020	2.951	2.759	2.643
7	5.786	5.582	5.206	4.868	4.564	4.288	4.160	4.039	3.812	3.605	3.416	3.242	3.161	2.937	2.802
8	6.463	6.210	5.747	5.335	4.968	4.639	4.487	4.344	4.078	3.837	3.619	3.421	3.329	3.076	2.925
9	7.109	6.802	6.247	5.759	5.328	4.946	4.772	4.607	4.303	4.031	3.786	3.566	3.463	3.184	3.019
10	7.722	7.360	6.710	6.145	5.650	5.216	5.019	4.833	4.494	4.192	3.923	3.682	3.571	3.269	3.092
11	8.306	7.787	7.139	6.495	5.937	5.453	5.234	5.029	4.656	4.327	4.035	3.776	3.656	3.335	3.147
12	8.863	8.384	7.536	6.814	6.194	5.660	5.421	5.197	4.793	4.439	4.127	3.851	3.725	3.387	3.190
13	9.394	8.853	7.904	7.103	6.424	5.842	5.583	4.342	4.910	4.533	4.203	3.912	3.780	3.427	3.223
14	9.899	9.295	8.244	7.367	6.628	6.002	5.724	5.468	5.008	4.611	4.265	3.926	3.824	3.459	3.249
15	10.380	9.712	8.559	7.606	6.811	6.142	5.847	5.575	5.092	4.675	4.315	4.001	3.859	3.483	3.268
16	10.383	10.106	8.851	7.824	6.974	6.265	5.954	5.669	5.162	4.730	4.357	4.033	3.887	3.503	3.283
17	11.274	10.477	9.122	8.022	7.120	6.373	6.047	5.749	5.222	4.775	4.391	4.059	3.910	3.518	3.295
18	11.690	10.828	9.372	8.201	7.250	6.467	6.128	5.818	5.273	4.812	4.419	4.080	3.928	3.529	3.304
19	12.082	11.158	9.614	8.365	7.366	6.550	6.188	5.877	5.316	4.844	4.442	4.097	3.942	3.539	3.311
20	12.462	11.470	9.818	8.514	7.469	6.623	6.259	5.929	5.355	4.870	4.460	4.110	3.954	3.546	3.316

Appendix 3

TABLE III : Compound value of Re. 1

Period	1%	2%	3%	4%	5%	6%	7%	8%	9%	10%	12%	14%	15%
1	1.010	1.020	1.030	1.040	1.050	1.060	1.070	1.080	1.090	1.100	1.120	1.140	1.150
2	1.020	1.040	1.062	1.082	1.102	1.124	1.145	1.166	1.188	1.210	1.254	1.300	1.322
3	1.030	1.061	1.093	1.125	1.158	1.121	1.225	1.263	1.295	1.331	1.404	1.482	1.521
4	1.041	1.082	1.126	1.170	1.216	1.262	1.311	1.360	1.412	1.464	1.574	1.689	1.749
5	1.051	1.104	1.159	1.217	1.276	1.338	1.403	1.469	1.539	1.611	1.762	1.925	2.011
6	1.062	1.126	1.194	1.265	1.340	1.419	1.501	1.587	1.677	1.772	1.974	2.195	2.313
7	1.072	1.149	1.230	1.316	1.407	1.504	1.606	1.714	1.828	1.949	2.211	2.502	2.660
8	1.183	1.172	1.267	1.369	1.477	1.594	1.718	1.851	1.993	2.144	2.476	2.853	3.518
9	1.094	1.125	1.305	1.423	1.551	1.689	1.838	1.999	2.172	2.358	2.773	3.252	3.518
10	1.105	1.219	1.334	1.480	1.629	1.791	1.967	2.159	2.367	2.594	3.106	3.707	4.046
11	1.116	1.243	1.384	1.539	1.710	1.898	2.105	2.332	2.580	2.853	3.479	4.226	4.652
12	1.127	1.268	1.426	1.601	1.796	2.012	2.252	2.518	2.813	3.138	3.896	4.818	5.350
13	1.138	1.294	1.469	1.665	1.886	2.133	2.410	2.720	3.066	3.452	4.363	5.492	6.153
14	1.149	1.319	1.513	1.732	1.980	2.261	2.579	2.937	3.342	3.797	4.887	6.261	7.076
15	1.161	1.346	1.558	1.801	2.079	2.397	2.759	3.172	3.642	4.177	5.474	7.138	8.137
16	1.173	1.373	1.605	1.873	2.183	2.540	2.952	3.426	3.970	4.595	6.130	8.137	9.358
17	1.184	1.400	1.653	1.948	2.292	2.693	3.159	3.700	4.328	5.054	6.866	9.276	10.761
18	1.196	1.428	1.702	2.026	2.407	2.854	3.380	3.896	4.717	5.560	7.690	10.575	12.375
19	1.208	1.457	1.754	2.107	2.527	3.026	3.617	4.316	5.142	6.116	8.613	12.056	14.232
20	1.220	1.486	1.806	2.191	2.653	3.207	3.870	4.661	5.604	6.728	9.646	13.743	16.637
25	1.282	1.641	2.094	2.666	3.386	4.292	5.247	6.848	8.623	10.835	17.000	26.426	32.919
30	1.348	1.811	2.427	3.243	4.322	5.743	7.612	10.063	13.268	17.449	29.960	50.950	66.212

Appendix 4

TABLE IV : The Compound value of an Annuity of Re.1

Period	1%	2%	3%	4%	5%	6%	7%	8%	9%	10%
1	1.000	1.000	1.000	1.000	1.000	1.000	1.000	1.000	1.000	1.000
2	2.010	2.020	2.030	2.040	2.050	2.060	2.070	2.080	2.090	2.100
3	3.030	3.060	3.091	3.122	3.152	3.184	3.215	3.246	3.278	3.310
4	4.060	4.122	4.184	4.246	4.310	4.375	4.440	4.506	4.573	4.641
5	5.101	5.204	5.309	5.416	5.526	5.637	5.751	5.867	5.985	6.105
6	6.152	6.308	6.468	6.633	6.802	6.975	7.153	7.336	7.523	7.716
7	7.214	7.434	7.662	7.898	8.142	8.394	8.654	8.923	9.200	9.487
8	8.286	8.583	8.892	9.214	9.549	9.897	10.260	10.637	11.028	11.436
9	9.368	9.755	10.159	10.583	11.027	11.491	11.978	12.488	13.021	13.579
10	10.462	10.950	11.464	12.006	12.578	13.181	13.816	14.487	15.193	15.937
11	11.567	12.169	12.808	13.486	14.207	14.972	15.784	16.645	17.560	18.531
12	12.682	13.412	14.192	15.026	15.917	16.870	17.888	18.977	20.141	21.384
13	13.809	14.680	15.618	16.627	17.713	18.882	20.141	21.495	22.953	24.523
14	14.947	15.974	17.086	18.292	19.598	21.015	22.550	24.215	26.019	27.975
15	16.097	17.293	18.599	20.023	21.578	23.276	25.129	27.152	29.361	31.772
16	17.258	18.639	20.157	21.824	23.657	25.672	27.888	30.324	33.003	35.949
17	18.430	20.012	21.761	23.697	25.840	28.213	30.840	33.750	36.973	40.544
18	19.614	21.412	23.414	25.645	28.132	30.905	33.999	37.540	41.301	45.599
19	20.811	22.840	25.117	27.671	30.539	33.760	37.379	41.446	46.018	51.158
20	22.019	24.267	26.870	29.778	33.066	36.785	40.995	45.762	51.169	57.274
21	23.239	25.783	28.676	31.969	35.719	39.992	44.865	50.422	56.764	64.002
22	24.471	27.299	30.536	34.248	38.505	43.392	49.005	55.456	62.872	71.402
23	25.716	28.845	32.452	36.618	41.430	46.995	53.435	60.893	69.531	79.542
24	26.973	30.421	34.426	39.082	44.501	50.815	58.176	66.764	76.789	88.496
25	28.243	32.030	36.459	41.645	47.726	54.864	63.248	73.105	84.699	98.346
30	34.784	40.567	47.575	56.084	66.438	79.057	94.459	113.282	136.305	164.491